Y0-CUN-062

EMILY DAVIES

VICTORIAN LITERATURE AND CULTURE SERIES
Jerome J. McGann and Herbert F. Tucker, Editors

EMILY DAVIES
Collected Letters,
1861–1875

Edited by
Ann B. Murphy and
Deirdre Raftery

University of Virginia Press

Charlottesville and London

University of Virginia Press
© 2004 by the Rector and Visitors of the University of Virginia
All rights reserved
Printed in the United States of America on acid-free paper
First published 2004

9 8 7 6 5 4 3 2 1

Library of Congress Cataloging-in-Publication Data

Davies, Emily, 1830–1921.
  [Correspondence. Selections]
  Emily Davies : collected letters, 1861–1875 / edited by Ann B. Murphy and Deirdre Raftery.
    p. cm. — (Victorian literature and culture series)
Includes bibliographical references and index.
  ISBN 0-8139-2232-1 (cloth : alk. paper)
  1. Davies, Emily, 1830–1921—Correspondence. 2. Girton College (University of Cambridge)—Presidents—Correspondence. 3. Women authors, English—Correspondence. 4. Women—Education (Higher)—England—History—19th century. I. Murphy, Ann B., 1948- II. Raftery, Deirdre. III. Title. IV. Series.
LF797.G54 D36 2004
370′.92—dc21

2004009136

COMMITTEE ON
SCHOLARLY EDITIONS
AN APPROVED EDITION
MODERN LANGUAGE
ASSOCIATION OF AMERICA

Contents

Acknowledgments	vii
Chronology	ix
Editorial Methods	xiii
Abbreviations	xvii
Introduction	xix
Letters	1
Biographical Register	481
Published Writings of Emily Davies	521
Appendices	525
Index	547

For Peter Caprani, whose belief in the importance of this project made all the difference, and for Leonard Raftery Caprani, for being a constant reminder of what really matters.

Acknowledgments

Work on this book took place in three countries over nine successive summers, and many friends and family members contributed to making it a pleasure and a labor of love. We want to thank all of them for their support, interest, and affection. Special thanks to Sydney, Ciara, Bernard, Belle, Claire, James, Becky, Susan, Lucia, Tom, Annie and Nicole, and our mothers: Lila and Val.

In the course of researching this book we wrote to dozens of libraries and archives searching for papers relating to Emily Davies. Our sincere thanks to the librarians and archivists who took the time to look through uncatalogued materials for us. Thank you also to fellow researchers who wrote letters with suggestions and words of encouragement.

We gratefully acknowledge the cooperation and assistance of the following institutions, libraries, and individuals:

The Mistress and Fellows of Girton College, Cambridge; Girton College Archives, Cambridge; Assumption College, Worcester, Massachusetts; University College, Dublin; Library of Trinity College, Dublin; the National Register of Archives; the British Library, London; the Syndics of Cambridge University Library; Duke University, Special Collections Library; the Friends' House Library, London; the Boston Athenaeum; Johns Hopkins University, Milton S. Eisenhower Library, Special Collections; London Guildhall University, the Fawcett Library (now The Women's Library); London School of Economics, British Library of Political and Economic Science; the Governors of Manchester High School for Girls; Newnham College Archives, Cambridge; North London Collegiate School; St. Andrews University Library, Scotland; St. John's College Archives, Cambridge; University College, London, Manuscripts and Rare Books Library; University of Manchester, John Rylands University Library; Harvard University, Widener Library.

Throughout this project, Kate Perry at Girton College Archives was informative and enthusiastic; we are most grateful for her support. Our sincere thanks also to Frances Gandy, Girton College; Vivien Allen and her associates at the *New DNB*; Sophie Badham, Royal Holloway University of London; David Blake, British Library; Elizabeth Crawford; Ann Dingsdale; Mary Ann Elston, Royal Holloway College; Judith Harford, University College, Dublin; Pam Hirsch, Homerton College, Cambridge; Robert Hirst, MLA; Felicity Hunt, *New DNB*; Ellen Jordan; Colin Matthew; John McManus; Susan Parkes, Trinity College, Dublin; Rita Russell, Manchester High School for Girls; Janet Sondheimer, *New DNB*; Norman Vance, University of Sussex at Brighton; Malcolm Underwood,

St. John's College, Cambridge; Maryann Valiulis, Trinity College, Dublin, and P. H. Waddington, professor emeritus, Victoria University of Wellington.

We also gratefully acknowledge the support of University College, Dublin (Publications Support Scheme, 2003).

At the start of the project in 1992, Nancy Essig of the University of Virginia Press offered support and guidance for which we are grateful. In the final stages—after a decade during which technology greatly changed the way in which scholars work—we relied on the computing skills of Carmella Murphy at Assumption College to speed us through the preparation of the manuscript; we are indebted to her for her patience and expertise.

We want to extend our special thanks to Dan Wajnowski for his research help and to Mary Brunelle for her invaluable assistance in copyediting.

Our warm thanks also go to those who made our successive summers living at Girton College all the more comfortable and pleasant: the gyps, the attendants, the staff at Hall, Tom in the college bar, and the actors whose performances of Shakespeare's comedies were carried on the warm evening breezes from the gardens of Girton to our desks.

Finally, we would like to acknowledge the support of the University of Virginia Press, and particularly that of Cathie Brettschneider and Ellen Satrom.

Chronology

1830	Sarah Emily Davies (ED) born 22 April, Southampton
1839	Davies family moves to rectory at Gateshead
1843	Governesses' Benevolent Institution founded
1848	ED develops friendship with Jane Crow
	Queen's College, London, founded
1849	Elizabeth Blackwell awarded M.D. in the United States
	Bedford College for Women founded
1853	Cheltenham Ladies' College founded
1854	ED meets Elizabeth Garrett
	Bodichon's Portman Hall School founded
1857	National Association for the Promotion of Social Science (NAPSS) founded
	First agitation about women's suffrage and married women's property
1858	ED travels to Algiers, meets Annie and Barbara Leigh Smith
	Jane and William Davies, ED's siblings, die
1859	Henry Davies, ED's brother, dies
	ED visits brother Llewelyn in London and meets the Langham Place Circle
	Elizabeth Garrett and ED hear Elizabeth Blackwell speak in London
	Society for Promoting the Employment of Women (SPEW), and Victoria Press founded
1860	Elizabeth Garrett admitted to Middlesex Hospital for medical training
1861	ED's father dies
1862	ED and her mother move to London, 17 Cunningham Place
	Elizabeth Garrett's application to matriculation exams at University of London rejected by one vote
	ED writes "Medicine as a Profession for Women," read for her by Russell Gurney at NAPSS
	Frances Power Cobbe reads paper on university degrees for women at NAPSS
	ED begins campaign to open Cambridge and Oxford Local Examinations to girls
	ED takes over as editor of the *English Woman's Journal* for six months
1863	First issue of *Victoria* published by ED and Emily Faithfull
	Cambridge Local Syndicate agrees to allow girls to be examined as experiment

	First examination of girls for Cambridge Local Exams on 12 December
1864	Special meeting of NAPSS discusses the Local Exams for girls
	Schools Inquiry Commission (SIC) is appointed under Lord Taunton
	ED's paper "On Secondary Instruction, as Relating to Girls" read by Joshua Fitch at NAPSS
1865	ED and Eliza Bostock convince SIC to include investigation of girls' schools. Nine women, including ED, are called to give evidence
	Cambridge Senate votes to open Local Examinations to girls permanently
	Elizabeth Garrett qualifies to practice medicine through the Society of Apothecaries
	First meeting of the Kensington Society
	John Stuart Mill is elected to Parliament
1866	ED forms London Association of Schoolmistresses
	Gladstone introduces Reform Bill. Women in the Kensington Society and Langham Place Circle circulate suffrage petition
	ED applies unsuccessfully for position as assistant secretary of Queen's College
	Mill presents suffrage petition in Parliament
	ED publishes *The Higher Education of Women*
	ED develops idea for College for Women, circulates it among friends
1867	ED drafts programme for College for Women
	New set of women's suffrage petitions presented in Parliament
	Meeting of London Association of Schoolmistresses formalizes rules, elects officers
	Mill moves to extend suffrage to women, defeated by 123 votes
	Anne Jemima Clough and James Stuart begin Lectures for Women
	ED and allies formally establish a committee to found College for Women
	North of England Council for the Higher Education of Women is formed
1868	Society of Apothecaries amends its rules to exclude women
	University of London adopts special examination for women
	Public meeting is held in London to discuss the College for Women
	Kensington Society is dissolved
	ED and committee investigate sites in Hitchin for College for Women

Subcommittee of College Committee is authorized to draft constitution for College for Women

College Committee draws up curriculum, decides students will be prepared for Poll (Ordinary) Degree

ED writes "Some Account of a Proposed College for Women," read at NAPSS

North of England Council asks Cambridge for special examinations for women, approved 23 October

1869 Entrance examination for College for Women is held

Cambridge Local Examination Committee is dissolved

College for Women, Benslow House, Hitchin, opens with five students

Mill publishes *The Subjection of Women*

1870 Elementary Education Act is passed, permitting women to elect school board members and be elected to school boards

Elizabeth Garrett is awarded M.D. degree at Sorbonne

College Committee establishes a building committee to coordinate residence for College for Women

London School Board elections: ED elected for Greenwich; Garrett for Marylebone

Four Hitchin students pass the Little-go Examination

1871 Elizabeth Garrett marries J.G.S. Anderson

Henry Sidgwick opens residence for women in Cambridge

1872 Girton College is registered as a company with the Board of Trade

Building begins at Girton, three miles outside Cambridge

ED is appointed Mistress of the College for Women at Hitchin

1873 Llewelyn Davies becomes principal of Queen's College

First women students unofficially sit the university Tripos Exams (March)

First building phase completed, Girton College opens (October)

ED resigns position on London School Board

1875 Newnham Hall, Cambridge, opens

ED resigns as Mistress of Girton College

1876 Russell Gurney passes parliamentary act allowing medical corporations to examine women

ED resigns as secretary of Girton College

1877 St. Leonard's School for Girls, St. Andrews, opens

Maria Grey Training College opens

1878 London University opens exams to women

1881 University of Cambridge admits women to Tripos Exams for titular degrees

1886	Girton College buys land, begins the next phase of building, which is completed in 1900
	ED renews involvement with suffrage campaign
1897	Cambridge University rejects move to admit women to degrees
1901	ED awarded honorary L.L.D. by University of Glasgow
1918	Partial suffrage for women is passed
1919	ED votes in the general election
1921	ED dies 13 July, in her ninety-second year

Editorial Methods

This collection of letters, written by Emily Davies between 1861 and 1875, represents the years of her greatest involvement in a number of public issues. These were the years in which she was most prolific, corresponding with many of the most prominent English men and women of her time. The broad categories into which her correspondence falls chart her involvement in the activities of the Langham Place Circle: the editing of the *English Woman's Journal* (*EWJ*); the opening of Cambridge Local Examinations to girls; the campaigns of the female suffrage movement and the London School Board; and the founding of the first college for women at Cambridge. By 1875, Davies had achieved her great ambition of building the first residential college for women in England, Girton College. In that year she resigned from the position of Mistress, and in 1876 she resigned from her position as secretary to the college. Davies's correspondence lessened considerably once she withdrew from the administration and governing of the college.

Few of these letters have been published before now, and this book represents the first attempt to gather together her correspondence. Emily Davies did not write an autobiography. However, between 1904 and 1907 she compiled a record of her achievements for her nephews in a six hundred-page manuscript that she titled the "Family Chronicle." This manuscript includes many extracts from letters and articles, and Davies clearly compiled it with reference to the letters that were subsequently given to Girton College. Though the Chronicle is a very valuable source, it has not been published. Where scholars have heretofore cited letters by Davies, they have invariably transcribed extracts included in Barbara Stephen's *Emily Davies and Girton College* (1927). Stephen's biography was completed with the cooperation of Girton College and charts Davies's efforts to found and build the college. Stephen relied on papers held at Girton, papers that reflect only Davies's public life. The Stephen biography does not attempt to recreate events from her childhood and youth; rather, it is a straightforward reconstruction of her professional concerns.

Our comparison of extracts from the Davies letters cited in the Stephen biography with our completed collection of letters made apparent that Stephen had quoted from letters written by Davies between 1861 and 1875 that are no longer extant. Our inquiries revealed that these letters—together with one hundred additional pages of the Family Chronicle—have been missing from the Girton College Archives since the biography was completed in 1927. It was therefore necessary for us to decide whether or not to include nonextant extracts from the Stephen biography. We created a census of all extracts in the Stephen book (see appendices A, B, and C). The census indicates that Stephen included 101 extracts from letters that no longer exist. Some of these are fragments (a line or two), and some comprise several sentences. It is probable that they were taken from about eighty letters in all. Thirty-five extracts were to the Mannings, and twenty-three were to Anna Richardson, close personal friends of Davies. We considered that the loss of these letters would greatly impoverish the reader's sense of Davies's personal voice, and we made a thorough search for the missing papers.

When our attempts to trace these letters were unsuccessful, we considered the relative merits of including the extracts printed in the Stephen biography. We decided that, as our edition of Davies's letters comprises only autograph letters that we have transcribed, Stephen's extracts from the missing letters could not be included in the main body of this book (though all the extant letters used by Stephen are contained within this volume). On a total of seventy-nine pages of the Stephen biography, there are citations from the missing letters within this time period (1861–75).[1] Had the Stephen biography been scrupulously accurate in its use of Davies's papers, there might have been some argument for the inclusion of the extracts from what was, after all, a sizable cache of papers. However, inaccuracies within the Stephen biography called its reliability into question. The errors in the Stephen biography are often small, but they are misleading for scholars (see appendix C). For example, Stephen ascribes to Davies an article titled "Female Physicians" (*EWJ*, May 1862). There was no such article: Davies had merely published together in the journal a number of letters on the theme. Stephen ascribes to Davies an article titled "On the Influence upon Girls' Schools of External Examinations" (*London Student*, May 1868). This article is in fact by Elizabeth Wolstenholme. Stephen also makes reference to an article by Davies published in *Victoria* (November 1863): we have found no such article.

However, while it is impossible to verify the accuracy of Stephen's transcriptions of the nonextant papers, we considered that a sample of these papers might be of some use to scholars. We have therefore included an appendix comprising one-third of the extracts, selected because they were dated and of a reasonable length (i.e., not fragments). These extracts have been electronically reproduced directly from the Stephen book; they have not been edited, and no guarantee is made as to their accuracy (see appendix D).

The work of locating, transcribing, editing, and proofreading the Davies letters was a lengthy process that comprised two main tasks: examining all collections of the Emily Davies Papers at archives and examining the papers of everyone with whom she might have carried on a correspondence between 1861 and 1875. We began by examining the Davies Papers held at Girton College, Cambridge. The Girton College Archive holds the most sizable single collection of her articles and letters and also holds the manuscript of the Family Chronicle. At Girton College, we located 421 letters written between 1861 and 1875. While most of these letters were returned to Davies by families of deceased correspondees, as was the custom of the time, some are Davies's drafts of original letters that are no longer extant. The original letters and the draft letters form the most significant part of this collection. In addition to these, we have included any letters no longer extant that were transcribed by Davies into the Family Chronicle.

The Davies Papers at Girton College—and the Family Chronicle in particular—provided a good indication of the range of people with whom Emily Davies regularly communicated. We examined the archives of all Cambridge colleges holding papers of those men and women with whom she might have corresponded; the archives of other universities, colleges, schools, institutions, and associations with related holdings were also searched.

A total of seventy-six letters were located in sources other than Girton College. They were located at the London School of Economics (20); the Fawcett Library (now The Women's Library) (12); Manchester University (17); Manchester High School (1); University College, London (3); St. Andrew's University (1); the North London Collegiate School (6); Newnham College (3); Cambridge University Library (9); the British Library (1); Johns Hopkins University (1); St. John's College, Cambridge (1); and Duke University (1).

Editing Principles

The letters have been transcribed exactly, without alterations to abbreviations, and Davies's spelling, punctuation and slips of the pen have been reproduced exactly. Where Davies made corrections to text, this remains unaltered. There are instances where information (usually dates) was later added to the letters. Some are in Davies's hand, and others were probably added by archivists. As these additional comments and dates were placed in square [ ] brackets, it was decided to reproduce them exactly. Any additions or corrections made by the editors are within angle ⟨ ⟩ brackets.

The recipient is indicated at the top of the first page of each letter. In a few instances, Davies did not indicate the name of the person to whom she was writing, and we have attempted to identify the recipients. Where the recipient's name appears with ⟨?⟩, this indicates that we have identified that person as the probable recipient. At the end of each letter, the provenance is indicated, and the type of letter is indicated using the customary abbreviations.

Many of the letters were written on headed notepaper. Davies was meticulous in having notepaper printed for each cause with which she was associated. Addresses that were printed on notepaper are indicated by the use of uppercase letters only, and handwritten addresses are indicated by the use of upper- and lowercase letters. Most of the manuscript letters were dated clearly by Davies, usually using the format of month, day, and year (for example, June 2, 1666). Where details were missing, we have identified them as accurately as possible and inserted them within brackets (for example, June ⟨2⟩ 1866). Some attempt was made by the archivists at Girton College to date the undated and partially dated letters within their collection. The archivists indicated these dates by inserting them within square brackets (for example, June [2] 1866). Where we are not in agreement with the dates ascribed by archivists, we have inserted both dates (for example, June [2] ⟨7⟩ 1866). The details of address and date on each manuscript letter often took up several lines. For clarity we run these details together but indicate where each line began with the use of a vertical line (for example, PROPOSED ADMISSION OF GIRLS TO UNIVERSITY LOCAL EXAMINATIONS. | 17, Cunningham Place, | London, N.W. | July 5, 1865).

Davies used some abbreviations in her letters. Frequently she abbreviated names of friends and colleagues to their initials. Where this is the case, we indicated the full name the first time it is abbreviated, by placing the rest of the name within brackets (for example, A⟨nnie⟩ C⟨row⟩). We then reverted to the abbreviated form used by Davies, unless a significant number of years elapse before that abbreviation is again used. In such a case, we again used brackets to include the expanded name.

Davies made liberal use of common abbreviations of her time such as &c (etcetera); & (and); thro' (through); tho' (though); yrs (yours); and affecn. (affectionately). We have reproduced all abbreviations exactly as she used them. She signed her letters in a number of ways. Letters to friends were usually signed with the initials E. D., while business letters were often signed Emily Davies. Some official letters were signed S. E. Davies.

Words and sentences underlined by Davies for emphasis appear in italic. We have reproduced faithfully all text through which Davies drew lines, and all of her insertions are included as superscript. There are some instances of illegible, damaged, or incomplete text, and these are clearly indicated. Her spelling of words has been reproduced (for example, "connexion"), and no attempt has been made to modernize spellings or correct misspellings.

Following a series of proofreadings and checks, the manuscript was submitted to the MLA for approval by the Committee for Scholarly Editions. It has been awarded recognition as an Approved Edition, MLA.

Abbreviations

AL	Autograph Letter
ALS	Autograph Letter Signed
AMs	Autograph Manuscript
AMsS	Autograph Manuscript Signed
AR	Administrative Records
BL	British Library, London, India Office Private Papers
C	Family Chronicle (Emily Davies)
CUL	Cambridge University Library
DAL	Draft Autograph Letter
DALS	Draft Autograph Letter Signed
DM	Draft Manuscript
Duke	Duke University Library
Faw	Fawcett Library, London
GC	Girton College, Cambridge
JCC	St. John's College, Cambridge
JH	Johns Hopkins University
LSE	London School of Economics
Man	John Rylands University Library of Manchester
MHS	Manchester High School
Newn	Newnham College, Cambridge
NLCS	North London Collegiate School
UCL	University College, London
St. A	St. Andrew's University

Introduction

Sarah Emily Davies (1830–1921) was at the heart of critical political, educational, journalistic, and social reform movements of mid-nineteenth-century England. Between 1861, when she arrived in London, and 1875, when she retired as Mistress of Girton College, Davies was an active member of the Langham Place Circle; edited both the *English Woman's Journal* and the *Victoria*; launched campaigns to open the Cambridge Local Examinations to girls and to request that the Taunton Commission (SIC) include girls' schools in its investigations; helped form the London Association of Schoolmistresses and the Kensington Society; organized the first campaign for women's suffrage in 1866; served on the London School Board; and founded Girton College, Cambridge University, the first residential college of higher education for women. She was an essential part of a movement that transformed her society: at her birth in 1830, England held only four universities, and none was open to women. At her death in 1921, the twelve universities in the country were all open to women. At her birth in 1830, women's suffrage was a barely discussed and entirely marginal possibility; before she died, however, Davies cast a vote in one of the first elections open—albeit still only in partial and incomplete form—to women.

The impressive scope and range of her activities make it all the more puzzling that, in the seventy-five years since Barbara Stephen published her biography of Davies, *Emily Davies and Girton College*, only one book-length study of Davies has been written, in contrast to numerous works on Davies's colleague and friend Barbara Leigh Smith Bodichon.[2] Furthermore, much scholarly recognition of Emily Davies locates her implicitly beneath Bodichon in significance or depicts her simply as one of the less colorful and charismatic members of the larger Victorian feminist world known as the Langham Place Circle.[3]

Even the recent generation of feminist scholarship and history, in seeking to identify "lost" Victorian feminists, has been misleadingly campaign specific in depicting Emily Davies, concentrating quite narrowly on particular efforts in which Davies was involved—to open the Cambridge Local Examinations to girls, for example, or to launch the women's suffrage struggle, or to found Girton College.[4] While these studies have been valuable in locating Davies in the context of Victorian feminism, their issue-specific focus has not fostered a fuller exploration of the important relationships among these reform campaigns and has at times obscured our understanding both of the shaping power of Davies's strategizing in an array of closely connected feminist efforts and of the extraordinary range and scope of her work.

This striking lack of full recognition for her achievements may be due, ironically, at least in part to Davies's remarkable success in destroying all of her personal documents and correspondence. For example, Davies met Elizabeth Garrett in 1854, when Davies was only twenty-four, and the two remained close friends and allies for all of their lives, yet not one letter from Davies to Garrett Anderson remains.[5] Thus, while occasional references in her published writings suggest that Davies thought long and hard—indeed angrily and rebelliously—about the role of women in her society, we have no extant letters written before 1861, when she was thirty-one, and no early letters directly expressing those rebellious feelings or depicting the evolution of her early feminist thought.[6]

Finally, we know that in 1905, at the age of seventy-five, Davies wrote what she called a Family Chronicle, a manuscript that begins by recording some family history and then turns to a depiction of her own political activities from 1861 to 1868. This document is essentially a compilation of family genealogies and a transcription of correspondence on political and reform issues with a thread of connective narrative explanation that erases as much as it describes and that does not illuminate our knowledge of the younger Davies or of the world that shaped her. The loss of some one hundred pages of the Family Chronicle that recorded her life between 1849 and 1861 further reduces the contribution of this work to our knowledge of Davies.[7]

Barbara Stephen opens her 1927 biography of Emily Davies with the explanation that Davies, at her death, had left among her papers a memorandum expressing her hope that no memoir "of an intimate personal nature" would be written of her, and adding her conviction that "there are not materials for [such a memoir]" (1). However, Davies apparently added, she *did* think it would be "reasonable that some information ... be [made] available as to the founders of Girton College.... It might be well to combine in such a sketch some account of Madame Bodichon, of whom there is not, so far as I know, any permanent record in existence" (1).

The memorandum Stephen cites is no longer extant.[8] However, the sentiments that her first biographer attributes to Davies here are characteristic of this single-minded nineteenth-century feminist and reformer.[9] The evidence suggests that Davies's objection to any biographical intrusion into her "intimate" and "personal" life led her to destroy all personally revealing letters she had in her possession, although she saved some professional passages by transcribing them into the Chronicle. The objection she expresses in this missing memorandum to potential violations of her privacy is thus consistent not only with the absence of any extant personal correspondence but also with the impersonal tone and content of the letters we do still have.

Perhaps most characteristic of Davies is her insistence that her own formidable achievements—as journalist, suffragist, educational reformer, and founder of Girton College—were not her own individual accomplishments but were rather part of a larger political and cultural context, and further that they owed much to the contributions of her admired long-time friend and ally, Barbara Leigh Smith Bodichon. Davies's recognition of the collaborative nature of feminist gains in the nineteenth century is not simply a gesture of false modesty; rather, it conveys her understanding that her own many achievements, as well as those of her allies, indeed had been possible only because these men and women were all part of a network of reform activity whose successes built on and reinforced one another. At the same time, the memorandum Stephen cites suggests that although Davies regarded her own achievements as important enough to merit a biography, she wished to define the limits of such a biography.

When Emily Davies is discussed by contemporary scholars, she is often critiqued for qualities that seem ironically disparate, indeed, antithetical: her apparent intransigence and unwillingness to compromise; her conventionality and conservatism on all issues other than feminist; and her pragmatism. Lee Holcombe describes her as "a small, sweet-faced woman of modest manner and unimpeachable respectability ... [whose] background and ... personal demeanor belied her iron will and dogged perseverance and her revolutionary convictions" (21–22). Pam Hirsch, in her study of Barbara Leigh Smith Bodichon, repeatedly criticizes what she sees as "Davies's tendency to cast herself at the centre of all feminist action ... underplaying Barbara [Bodichon]'s significance at key moments" (135) and claims that Davies "overpowered people by sheer force of purpose and wore them down until they acceded" (246). At the same time, Davies is also criticized—especially in studies of the suffrage movement of 1866–67—for her "gradualist approach" and pragmatism, her unwillingness to move more quickly in demanding change (Crawford 209).

Most scholars agree, however, that Davies was a consummate committeewoman, an indefatigable worker whose energy, dedication, and attention to detail contributed significantly to each campaign. Nor was her contribution merely a function of her capacity for hard work. She was also capable of articulating the goals of each campaign in the way calculated to appeal most to politically essential conservative supporters, and she possessed an astute understanding of contemporary journalism, acting as a kind of public relations expert in placing articles on feminist causes in strategically selected journals. Davies was the person who got the letters written, the meetings organized, the reports printed, and the journals and conference papers edited. But she was also the person who found new and imaginative ways to build on each success and to turn even liabilities into assets.

Davies was, finally, a paradoxical mixture of self-effacement and determination, flexibility and stubbornness, long-range vision and shortsighted obtuseness. She was the behind-the-scenes force in myriad feminist campaigns, the honorary secretary whose implacable will ensured that work actually got done. She was the obscure but lifelong friend of more charismatic and notorious feminists such as Barbara Leigh Smith Bodichon and Elizabeth Garrett Anderson. The trajectory of her career, from the Langham Place Circle to the colleges of Cambridge and Oxford, helped to establish connections between Anglicans and Dissenters, between London journalists and reformers and Oxbridge scholars and academics, and between—through more tenuously—feminists and Tories.

The contradictory qualities that scholars have noted in Davies are abundantly evident in her correspondence: she was unrelentingly radical, innovative, and single-minded in her desire to expand educational possibilities for women; on most other issues, including suffrage, she was profoundly conservative, ruthless in her determination to adhere to what she saw as the proper approach to achieving change, and frequently unwilling to compromise. As M. C. Bradbrook writes:

> The distinguishing quality of Emily Davies, as of Florence Nightingale, was to combine her vision of the New Jerusalem with gifts for organisation, administration and practical detail; she would have shone as Secretary of State, or the Governor of a Colony. In spite of her tireless energy, her work was impersonal.... She could be utterly intransigent and disastrously mistaken. Yet the driving force which she alone commanded was that which brought the New Jerusalem down to Hitchin Hill. (6)

The Early Years: Gateshead 1839–61

Sarah Emily Davies was born in Southampton in 1830, the fourth child and second daughter in a family that would eventually include five children. Her father, the Reverend John Davies, had recently moved his boarding school for boys from Chichester to Southampton, and at around the time of Emily Davies's birth he was also a candidate for the professorship of moral and political philosophy at the University of London. When Reverend Davies declined that offer, the family returned to the school in Chichester, and Reverend Davies resumed his religious writings. The family moved several more times during Davies's early childhood due to her father's poor health. In November 1839, however, the family finally settled when Reverend Davies accepted the living of a parish in Gateshead, in the north of England. Emily Davies was to live at the Gateshead rectory until her father's death in 1861, in a household that—although far removed from the dramatic tribulations Jane Eyre suffered at her fictional Gateshead—is strikingly reminiscent of the Brontë family in its narrowness, evangelicalism, isolation, and sibling deaths. The Reverend John Davies was an erudite and strictly evangelical Anglican minister of uncertain physical and emotional health whose best-known work, *Splendid Sins*, attacked people of rank for violating the Sabbath, and whose idea of appropriate reading matter for his children included Rollin's *History* and Milton's *Paradise Lost* (Chronicle 45).

Her mother, Mary Hopkinson Davies, was to be a staunch and loyal supporter of her daughter's later feminist activities, but the Chronicle offers few insights into her personality and depicts her as an essentially conventional Victorian parent. Davies does, however, cite one potentially revealing entry from her mother's diary. Describing Reverend Davies's decision to withdraw his candidacy for the position as professor of moral and political philosophy at the University of London, Mrs. Davies admitted that her "carnal heart would certainly have preferred London and the honour & fame which [she] anticipated" (Chronicle 16–17). This comment suggests affinities with her younger daughter's love of London almost twenty-five years later. ("How London spoils one! I feel quite injured now, if I don't see everything that's going on, the moment it comes out," Davies wrote in January 1864).

John and Mary Davies had five children: Mary Jane (1824), John Llewelyn (1826), William Stephen (1828), Sarah Emily (1830), and Henry Barton (1832). In the rectory at Gateshead, the children lived an essentially simple life.[10] Davies mentions that her father's curate kept a school in the vestry, adding without comment that "[t]here were girls in it, till my father restricted it to boys, under the impression I believe that the presence of girls lowered the status of the school" (Chronicle 64). Davies herself went for a few months to a day school for girls and did lessons with her sister in French, Italian, and music. "Our education answered to the description of that of clergymen's daughters generally, given by Mark Pattison in his evidence before one of the Education Commissions. 'Do they go to school? No. Do they have governesses at home? No. They have lessons & get on as they can'" (Chronicle 65). Davies's education also included writing "[t]hemes. i.e. bits of English composition, once a week" (Chronicle 65) that her father reviewed. This practice in writing may well have helped form her lucid and cogent prose style, though Reverend Davies could scarcely have expected his younger daughter to produce such essays as "Thoughts on Some Questions Relating to Women," "Medicine as a Profession for Women," or "Some Account of a Proposed New College for Women."

By contrast, of course, Davies's brothers were far more exhaustively and expensively educated: Llewelyn attended Repton in 1842, and then Trinity College, Cambridge, two years later. William too attended Repton and then Cambridge, while Henry went to Rugby, after which he was articled to a solicitor. Davies, however, experienced the common practice described by Virginia Woolf in *Three Guineas*: "Ever since the thirteenth century English families have been paying money into . . . [the sons' education fund]. . . . It is a voracious receptacle.... And to this your sisters... made their contribution. Not only did their own education, save for such small sums as paid the German teacher, go into it; but many of those luxuries and trimmings which are, after all, an essential part of education—travel, society, solitude, a lodging apart from the family house—they were paid into it too.... And the result is that though [women] look at the same things, we see them differently."[11]

Much of Davies's early life we can only infer obliquely, reading her minimal descriptions in the Chronicle backward against what we know of her later life. Thus, for example, we recognize the sharp contrast between the education Davies and her sister received and that offered to their brothers, but Davies herself does not explicitly draw attention to this distinction. Similarly, when she describes the family gardener, George Lister, as the children's "constant companion... [and a] Conservative in politics" who taught her "that the way to succeed was to 'have civil & religious liberty always on your tongue,'" we recognize the lasting effect of this teaching on her political sensibility. Yet perhaps the most telling fact in this anecdote is that Lister offered his advice to Davies when, as a little girl, she "was playing at being a candidate for Parliament" (Chronicle 83–84).

While the Brontë children invented literary fantasy worlds, Davies and her brother William each wrote small newspapers, his called the *Chronicle* and hers the *Herald*. "They contain[ed] advertisements, Parliamentary & Foreign Intelligence, Reviews, & Correspondence" (Chronicle 83) as well as "denunciations & warnings against Popery & Tractarianism" (Chronicle 84). These sentiments are scarcely surprising for children of an evangelical minister; nor do the remaining pages of the Chronicle provide an explanation of how a child of such conventional upbringing grew into a shrewd and radical feminist activist. Indeed, almost the only image we have of Davies as a child comes from a secondary source describing an advertisement she wrote for one of the childhood newspapers: "Wanted, a Governess in a gentleman's family. The lady who is to fill this situation must be a person of great firmness and determination, as the young lady who is to be the object of her care is rather inclined to be self-willed. Phrenologically speaking she has the organ of self-esteem rather largely developed and it will require the utmost care on the part of her governess to prevent this organ from being unduly developed" (Stephen 24).[12]

Like countless thousands of women in Victorian England, then—those whom Woolf describes as the "daughters of educated men"—Davies lived a life of at least outward decorum and protocol, of social visits and charitable works, as well as of unimaginable boredom, until 1848, when she was eighteen. In that year, the Crow (or Crowe) family moved to Gateshead with four daughters by Mr. Crow's first marriage: Elizabeth, Jane, Sophy, and Annie. Jane and Emily Davies were to become lifelong friends and allies in feminist activities, while Annie Crow—later Annie Austin—would also become active in feminist reform efforts and serve briefly as Mistress of Girton College. The arrival of the Crow family brought into Davies's world kindred spirits, a community of women with whom she could eventually share her ideas and aspirations. Small wonder, then, that Davies later emphasized that her own achievements had been made possible only by her friendships and by the support she received from and gave to other feminists.

Through the Crows, who had been educated at the Blackheath School, Davies six years later met Elizabeth Garrett, another Blackheath student, when Garrett, Davies, and Jane were bridesmaids at the wedding of Annie Crow in 1854. Because the pages of the Chronicle that cover these years are missing, we do not know how Davies herself assessed the impact of her friendship with Elizabeth Garrett. We have from these adolescent and young adult years only one brief and undocumented story that is cited frequently by several biographers, but without attribution. While it is probably apocryphal, this anecdote certainly fits the characters of the people involved:

> Emily, the story runs, went to stay with the Garretts at Aldburgh, and at night the two friends sat talking together by Elizabeth's bedroom fire. Millicent Garrett, then quite a small girl, sat nearby on a stool, listening, but saying nothing. After going over all the great causes they saw about them, and in particular the women's cause, to which they were burning to devote their lives, Emily summed the matter up. 'Well, Elizabeth,' she said, 'it's quite clear what has to be done. I must devote myself to securing higher education, while you open the medical profession to women. After these things are done,' she added, 'we must see about getting the vote.' And then she turned to the little girl who was still sitting quietly on her stool and said, 'You are younger than we are, Millie, so you must attend to that.' (Strachey 101)[13]

Another avenue toward the larger world opened up for Davies when her brother, Llewelyn, moved to London as a curate in 1851. In 1856, he was appointed rector of Christ Church, Marylebone, where he met and became involved with Frederick Denison Maurice and his circle of Christian Socialists. Davies may well have found this new vision of religious activism and social change more palatable than her father's evangelical Christianity. Certainly she was exposed, through her brother, to Maurice's innovative work with women's education at Queen's College and with the Working Men's College. "Through him," Stephen notes, Davies "was for the first time brought into contact with people whose plans for social reform included some effort to improve the position and education of women" (28).

During the mid-1850s, Davies's older sister, Jane, developed lung disease, and then their brother Henry also fell ill. Henry was sent to Algiers to recuperate, while Davies took her sister Jane to the seaside at Torquay, where she died in January 1858. When Henry too grew worse later that year, Davies and Jane Crow were sent to join him in Algiers and to bring him home, where he died the following summer. To compound family grief, Davies's brother William, who had gone to China as a naval chaplain, died there in October 1858 (Rosen 102 n. 3).

It was on this sad trip to Algiers that Davies first met Nannie Leigh Smith and, through her, Barbara Leigh Smith Bodichon, thus expanding her contact with the London world of Unitarians, feminists, and radicals that came to be referred to as the Langham Place Circle. These were women who were already challenging the laws that regulated married women's property rights, establishing a feminist magazine, the *English Woman's Journal*, and advocating employment for middle-class women.[14] These encounters, and the friendships with Jane Crow, Elizabeth Garrett, and Nannie and Barbara Leigh Smith, changed Davies's life dramatically. Writing of this change in a Chronicle passage that is cited by Stephen but now missing from the manuscript, Davies explains:

> On my return to Gateshead I went back to parish work, but tried to combine with it some effort in another direction. After making acquaintance in Algiers with Annie Leigh Smith (Madame Bodichon's sister)—the first person I had ever met who sympathized with my feeling of resentment at the subjection of women—I corresponded with her and she introduced me to others of the same circle and kept me up to what was going on. In 1858 the first organized movement on behalf of women was set on foot. The first number of the *Englishwoman's Journal* appeared in March. (Stephen 29)

By 1861, Davies was actively attempting to bring Langham Place reform activity to Gateshead. She reports making "some investigations into the conditions of women's work in the factories &c. in Gateshead & the neighbourhood, in some cases receiving polite answers from manufacturers who had taken [her] letters as being from [her] father. The results, which did not come to much, were published in a short paper in the Englishwoman's Journal" (Chronicle 201). She also describes launching "a Branch of the Society for Promoting the employment of women" in the Gateshead area (Chronicle 210).[15] Through this effort, she met an educated Quaker woman, Anna Richardson, who was to become another close and lifelong friend and supporter of Davies's feminist efforts.[16]

These new political and organizational efforts dominate her Chronicle's account of 1861. When she wasn't attempting to initiate reforms in Gateshead, Davies was visiting London and meeting a widening circle of often inspirational educators and reformers or being kept informed of events in London by Elizabeth Garrett, who had gone to the city in September 1861 to attend lectures as part of her effort to prepare for a medical degree. Thus even before she moved to the city, Davies had expanding connections with a wide range of feminist, Dissenter, and Christian Socialist reformers.

The London Reform Years: 1862–66

In October 1861, Reverend Davies—who had long suffered from poor health—died after suffering a bronchitis attack while visiting Ilkley Wells. After his death, of course, Davies and her mother had to leave the Gateshead rectory. In January 1862, they moved to a house in London on Cunningham Place in St. John's Woods, close to both Llewelyn Davies and Barbara Bodichon. Davies's depiction of herself in these early months in London is uncharacteristically tentative: "During this time I was considering what to do for the future in the changed circumstances, & came to the conclusion that to follow E[lizabeth]. Garrett was the only course to which I could see my way. The practice of Medicine had no attraction for me & I had no aptitude for the necessary study, for which I was very far from being prepared, but there seemed to be no other opening to any sort of career" (Chronicle 244). Perhaps because the practice of medicine "had no attraction" for her, however, Davies soon decided that she could not leave her mother in order to follow Garrett, who was going to Scotland to study. Instead, Davies began devoting herself to the kind of political activism for which she proved to be much more personally suited. According to one biographer, she learned two things about herself after her move to London: "She . . . discovered that she enjoyed committee work. . . . She was a natural committee woman, rejoicing in the meticulous preparation of agenda and circulars, of reports and resolutions. . . . She [also] discovered that quiet and serious though she might be she could more than hold her own in discussion, quite losing her habitual reserve in the cut-and-thrust of intellectual debate" (Forster 141, 143).

Langham Place/*English Woman's Journal*/NAPSS

Davies immediately found a focus for these skills at Langham Place, where, early in 1862, she took over the work of editing the *English Woman's Journal* (*EWJ*), which had been founded by Barbara Bodichon and Bessie Rayner Parkes in 1858. Facilities at Langham Place included "the office of *The English Woman's Journal*, a reading room, a luncheon room, a cloakroom for shoppers' parcels, a registry for job openings, and a committee room" (van Wingerden 3).

Langham Place was also the headquarters for Jessie Boucherett's Society for Promoting the Employment of Women (SPEW), "which sought to open careers for women in telegraph offices, printing, lithography, law-copying, and bookkeeping," as well as for Maria Rye's "Female Middle-Class Emigration Society, which helped women to find employment overseas" (van Wingerden 4). It was thus the center for coordinated middle-class feminist reform activities in London, and it became the training ground where Davies would develop the networks and launch the campaigns that led to the opening of the Cambridge Local

Exams to girls, the 1866 women's suffrage petition, and the 1869 foundation of the College for Women.

Langham Place was also, as Davies's letters reveal, fraught with the kind of personality disputes and ideological differences that seem inevitably to beset reform movements. Parkes was moving toward conversion to Catholicism, and she and Davies often disagreed on religious and editorial policies. Furthermore, money problems with the *EWJ* as well as the passionate friendships sought by some of the women, most notably Matilda Hays, complicated the work and personal relationships of the group. And Emily Faithfull's attempt to train women compositors in her Victoria Press brought additional personal and professional difficulties.[17]

Editing the *EWJ*, however, both honed Davies's prose style and introduced her to the world of mid-nineteenth-century London journalism, bringing her into contact with writers and publishers to whom she would turn in seeking press coverage for her later reform work. Working with and among these complicated personalities at Langham Place may also have sharpened her tendency to discount the personal and to focus almost exclusively on the professional.

The efforts of the women of Langham Place were encouraged and reinforced by their allies in an overlapping and related network of men and women who were members of the National Association for the Promotion of Social Science (NAPSS), an influential reform organization. "Founded in 1856 to provide 'a point of union for social reformers,' . . . [NAPSS] sought to unite in one body the plethora of individuals and groups involved in social reform. . . . [It] held a national congress every year from 1857 to 1884 to discuss the reform of every conceivable institution from prisons to international law" (Worzala 179). Perhaps most significantly, NAPSS offered a forum for women to speak and write, and even to work. In a groundbreaking move, NAPSS general secretary George Hastings had hired a woman, Isa Craig, as his secretary, and it was at NAPSS annual meetings that many ideas for feminist reform were tested, including the paper on university degrees for women that Frances Power Cobbe presented in 1862.

In the spring of 1862, while preparing for the NAPSS meeting to be held in London, Davies worked with Isa Craig, encountering more "people who afterwards became friends & allies, e.g. Mr. [John] Westlake . . . Mr. Ernest Noel & Mr. [Joshua] Fitch" (Chronicle 257). Davies too wrote a paper for that meeting, "Medicine as a Profession for Women," which was read for her by Russell Gurney.[18] Assessing the role of NAPSS, Davies wrote that it "was of immense use to the Women's Movement in giving . . . a platform from which we could bring our views before the sort of people who were likely to be disposed to help in carrying them out" (Chronicle 259). At the 1862 meeting, for example,

NAPSS unanimously passed a resolution supporting higher education for women, and in July, supporters (including Clementia Taylor, Lady Goldsmid, James Heywood, and Sophia Jex-Blake) began raising funds for "the effort to obtain for women admission to University Examinations in Arts & Medicine" (Chronicle 261).

The University of London and Medicine as a Profession for Women

While she was working as editor of the *EWJ* and writing papers for NAPSS, Davies continued to concentrate on the struggles of her friend Elizabeth Garrett to gain access to a medical education. The immediate problem Garrett faced was that she could not enter medical school without first matriculating from a university. In many ways, Davies's political career in London began in this fusion of personal and professional concerns, when "it came to [their] knowledge that the University of London was about to apply for a new Charter, & it was considered that this gave an occasion for an effort to obtain the admission of women to its Degrees. [They] therefore set to work, at first informally, without any Committee" (Chronicle 245). Working with the Langham Place and NAPSS network of reformers, Davies drafted a memorial to be signed by London University members and other prominent people. She and her supporters then wrote letters to each influential person they knew or with whom they could find connections, asking them for support and reminding them of the university's Dissenter origins and its commitment to provide education to all. "The women followed up these letters with personal visits to each senator and sent statements outlining their case to influential London newspapers" (Worzala 252).

This initial effort to open the Dissenter university to women brought Davies into contact with influential Nonconformists, radicals, and reformers such as George Grote and William Shaen. More significantly, it provided her with invaluable early experience in committee work, petition drives, letter-writing campaigns, and press contacts—allowing her to develop skills she was to employ with growing sophistication in subsequent education and suffrage battles. In April 1862, Garrett formally applied to the University of London Senate for permission to matriculate. In May, the memorial came before the University Senate and was defeated by one vote.

University Local Examinations

William Shaen, whom Davies met in these early days in London, was a prominent Dissenter, a member of the University of London Senate, and a NAPSS member. He was also to become a lifelong supporter of Davies's efforts and a member of Girton College. Shaen suggested to Davies "that the University of London did not like being treated as a *corpus vile*, on which all experiments were to be tried, & advised that [the reformers] should try to get something from the old Universities" (Chronicle 263). Davies immediately recognized the value of this suggestion and "cast about as to what [they] could reasonably ask for, & the Local Examinations, as involving nothing in the way of residence, seemed to suit the case" (Chronicle 263).

The Local, or Middle-Class, Examinations were themselves a recent reform instituted by the older universities in 1854 in response to political pressures and complaints from newer, middle-class schools that their candidates frequently failed to gain admission to Oxford and Cambridge. "Administered by special university syndicates, and offered nationwide every year to students under eighteen, . . . [the Local Examinations] were essentially a service offered by the universities to secondary schools. These examinations constituted a standard to measure the effectiveness of secondary schools and thereby provided a stimulus for educational improvement" (Worzala 255).

Shaen's suggestion resulted in Davies's first educational campaign not directly related to Garrett's medical career: opening the university Local Examinations to girls. To explore this new possibility, Davies began writing to Oxford and Cambridge men, including John Griffiths, the Oxford Local Examinations secretary, and George Liveing, the Cambridge Local Examinations secretary. Interpreting even the most ambivalent responses from the Oxbridge world as positive, Davies moved quickly to repeat the procedure she and her allies had used in dealing with the University of London. In October 1862, they formed a committee to obtain admission for women to the University Local Examinations that included Barbara Bodichon, Eliza Bostock, Isa Craig, Lady Goldsmid, Russell Gurney, G. W. Hastings, James Heywood, and Davies herself as honorary secretary, and set to work gathering support.

Her correspondence with Oxbridge men moved Davies beyond the Dissenter and reformer worlds of London and pushed her to sharpen her political arguments in order to respond both courteously and cogently to their resistance (including their persistent fears about "the terrible evils of overworking young women in intellectual pursuits" [Chronicle 281]).[19] The reactions of the university men, however, were not entirely negative, and after a long and arduous struggle, the campaign to open the Local Examinations to girls was ultimately successful. Oxford proved resistant, but Cambridge University unexpectedly granted Davies's committee permission to conduct an experimental Local Examination for girls in December 1863.

Following the success of this exam, Davies and her allies prepared a memorial to the University of Cambridge asking that it open the examinations to girls permanently. They then gathered over one thousand signatures and in October 1864 submitted the memorial to the university. During this time, the NAPSS/Langham Place reformers also wrote a report describing and analyzing the girls' performance in the Local Exams, using their failings as evidence of the need to improve girls' schools.[20] In February 1865, the university senate issued its report, recommending that girls be admitted to the examinations.

The Local Examinations campaign helped Davies establish connections between feminist and Nonconformist reformers from London and university dons from Oxford and Cambridge in the years before the older universities ended their practice of denying degrees to Dissenters.[21] More significantly, however, Davies and her committee ensured that in this first step in opening university education to women, the girls' exam would be exactly the same as that of the boys, and they successfully resisted the persistent efforts of the university to offer the girls a "separate," or special, examination ostensibly more suited to their presumed capacities.

For Davies, another important personal result of this campaign was that it introduced her to Henry Tomkinson, secretary of the Cambridge Local Exams Committee in London. Tomkinson was to become another of Davies's lifelong friends and allies, a person to whom she wrote with a degree of honesty and intimacy matched (in those letters still extant) only in her correspondence with Anna Richardson and Jane Crow. Indeed, despite her often strong-willed ideological intransigence, Davies demonstrated a remarkable ability to inspire loyalty among her friends and allies—including Bodichon, Crow, Garrett Anderson, the Gurneys, Charlotte and Adelaide Manning, Richardson, and Tomkinson.

Davies's writing skills and journalism contacts were further strengthened during these years by yet another responsibility. In March 1863, she left her post as editor of the *English Woman's Journal* and joined with Emily Faithfull in launching a new feminist periodical, the *Victoria*. Despite their high hopes for the venture, however, the journal did not go well initially, although Faithfull continued to edit it until June 1880. Davies left in less than a year, perhaps because educational reform activities had conclusively become the focus of her life.

Schools Inquiry Commission/London Association of Schoolmistresses

Work on the Local Examinations campaign brought Davies into contact with many of the progressive governesses, teachers, and headmistresses of girls' schools in England. However, the difficulty she experienced in trying to locate these educators also convinced her that teachers of girls needed the kind of organizational connection provided by NAPSS and Langham Place in order to share and develop their ideas and to push for reforms more effectively. At the same time, the initial results of the girls' participation in the Local Examinations suggested once again that the deplorable condition of girls' schools demanded immediate and drastic improvement. Davies responded to the first realization by organizing, in March 1866, the London Association of Schoolmistresses, of which she served as honorary secretary (Stephen 140).[22]

Even before this, however, she responded to the second issue—the disgraceful nature of girls' education in England—by initiating yet another campaign. In 1864, a Royal Commission to Inquire into Education in Schools in England and Wales (SIC), chaired by Lord Taunton, was appointed to report on the measures necessary to improve secondary education for the middle classes. Davies and her allies at NAPSS believed that the SIC should include girls' schools in its investigations, so Davies wrote to influential men whom she had met through NAPSS and the *Victoria*—such as Lord Lyttelton, George Grote, and Matthew Arnold—urging them to ensure that girls' schools be investigated. When the official response proved tepid, Davies and Eliza Bostock—a schoolmistress and member of the Local Examinations Committee—organized yet another memorial, signed by teachers including those at Queen's and Bedford Colleges. This memorial too was ultimately successful. The SIC agreed to include in its terms an examination of educational provision for middle-class girls, and in her ensuing correspondence with the commission, Davies met another friend and ally who would become a supporter of Girton College, SIC secretary Henry Roby. During the early months of the commission's work, Davies wrote frequently to Roby and the commissioners and strategized on the commission's collection of evidence from girls' schools. On 30 November 1865, she, Buss, and several other women educators were called to give evidence before the commission.[23]

To reinforce publicity about and discussion of this issue, Davies wrote another paper, "The Application of Funds to the Education of Girls," for the May 1865 annual meeting of NAPSS in Sheffield. Both in her Schools Inquiry Commission testimony and in her NAPSS paper, Davies raised the important question of school endowments. Her NAPSS paper noted that although few existing endowments had been left with the specification that they were to be used only for boys' education, girls had received virtually nothing from such endowments. Grammar schools for boys were well supported and, not surprisingly, were successful in preparing boys for further studies. Davies daringly called for the SIC to "throw open to girls at least half of the existing grammar schools."[24]

The Kensington Society

Davies's recognition of the need for a community of reformers and the importance of a place they could meet and work with one another as they did at Langham Place and NAPSS led her, in March 1865, to join in establishing yet another organization, the Kensington Society. Named for the home of its president, Charlotte Manning, the Kensington Society was a discussion group that had thirty-three initial members and met four times a year.[25] Davies served, once again, as the secretary. Other founding members included Dorothea Beale, Frances Buss, Frances Power Cobbe, Isa Craig, Elizabeth Garrett, Sophia Jex-Blake, Anna Swanwick, Helen Taylor, and Elizabeth Wolstenholme. An additional twenty-five women joined during the first year.

At each meeting of the Kensington Society, women read papers they had written on subjects they had previously determined and then discussed the ideas involved. "The first meeting, which took place in May 1865, considered a question proposed by Elizabeth Garrett: 'What is the true basis and what are the limits of parental authority?' Subsequent discussions included earnest inquiries into the nature of liberty, the right choice of amusements, the uses of fiction, and the meaning of success" (Worzala 284). Significantly, the Kensington Society was the location of the 1866 discussion of women's suffrage that led to the formation of an organized women's suffrage campaign.

During these early years in London, Davies was involved in a wide array of activities, ranging from personality disputes and ideological conflicts within the *EWJ* to editing two periodicals and participating in the development of expertise and professionalism among the women at Langham Place and NAPSS. Davies also worked and wrote for NAPSS, and helped form both the Kensington Society—where women's suffrage was first debated—and the London Association of Schoolmistresses, which grew directly out of the campaign to open the Local Exams to girls. She attended meetings of the Council of the Working Men's Clubs and SPEW, and she launched a letter-writing campaign that eventually ensured that the SIC would include girls' schools in its investigations. And in the Dissenter community, among London journalists, and within the feminist movement, she made friends and contacts that would prove essential in the forthcoming suffrage and women's college campaigns.

The Suffrage Movement and the College for Women: 1866–69

The movement to open educational opportunities to women was spreading throughout the country in the 1860s, and schoolmistresses' organizations similar to the one Davies had founded in London began forming in the north of England. "In 1867 these societies formed a regional association, the North of England Council for Promoting the Higher Education of Women ... [which] proposed to stimulate and coordinate educational activities for women throughout the region by organizing lecture series and promoting examinations for adult women" (Worzala 266). Anne Jemima Clough—later the first Mistress of Newnham College, Cambridge—and Josephine Butler, better known as the leader of the fight against the Contagious Diseases Acts, were the original organizers of this group, and they moved immediately to establish Lectures for Women in Leeds, Manchester, and Sheffield. These lectures "eventually furnished both the impetus and the model for the university-extension system.... [Furthermore,] by drawing ... large numbers of students, the council clearly demonstrated a widespread demand for advanced female education" (Worzala 268).

However, the North of England Council was moving in a very different direction, philosophically and politically, from the one being defined by Davies and her allies in London. Davies in particular insisted, as she had in the Local Examinations campaign, on maintaining "identity of standards"—scrupulously identical academic requirements for girls and boys, women and men—even if that insistence meant a slower, more laborious process of change and an acceptance of educational practices and standards that many of the young reformers at Oxford and Cambridge were questioning. By contrast, reformers in the North were interested in opening opportunities for women and didn't particularly care if those opportunities were defined as separate or different from existing male education. Indeed, many of the men in the North of England Council were convinced that the existing academic standards for men were antiquated and in need of change and saw the women's education movement as a way to effect such changes. These deep philosophical differences between the two groups were to grow and intensify as the women's education movement gained momentum.

For Davies, the first flush of reform excitement may have begun to subside by 1866. Or perhaps she was moving inevitably toward a greater specialization and focus on educational issues. Wide-ranging new reform initiatives were slowly giving way to ongoing daily responsibilities, as the Examinations Committee, for example, moved from the challenge of opening the Local Examinations to girls to the obligation of supervising those exams in a growing number of cities and towns. At the same time, the crucial network of NAPSS and Langham Place reformers began to formalize, as family friendships, religious connections, and loose social associations gave way to organizations such as the London Association of Schoolmistresses and the Kensington Society.

Davies herself was clearly ready for new challenges. She was beginning to define her field as specifically educational and to focus her efforts on women and higher education, rather than contributing to a range of campaigns and movements. In 1866, she published a book, *The Higher Education of Women*, which made a strong and cogent case for female education.[26] And in April of that year, she applied to Queen's College for the position of assistant secretary. "My idea," she wrote, "was that if I were inside the place, I might be able to help forward some plan for the affiliation of the College to the University of Cambridge, which at that time, was our modest aspiration. It was fortunate that I was rejected, as I could have done no good there, & should have been diverted from more useful effort" (Chronicle 456).

Women's Suffrage

Davies's growing concentration on education reform was interrupted by the first women's suffrage campaign of 1866. This suffrage movement grew in part out of national changes in England's political climate, and in part out of very local conditions created within the feminist reform circle by papers written for the Kensington Society. Politically, time began to seem ripe for a campaign when, in 1865, John Stuart Mill ran successfully for Parliament, in part on a women's suffrage plank. After Mill's election, the Liberal government in March 1866 introduced a bill to reform the franchise, which "provided an opportunity for practical action" (van Wingerden 9).

Meanwhile, the Kensington Society held a meeting in November 1865 to consider the question, "Is the extension of the parliamentary franchise to women desirable, and if so, under what conditions?" After the society debated the question seriously, "an informal vote revealed that the majority of women present favored some sort of female suffrage" (Worzala 285).[27] After this meeting, Bodichon wanted immediately to initiate a suffrage campaign, but Davies was reluctant to do so, concerned that such a movement would damage the credibility of their educational reform efforts; she was only overruled by the excitement resulting from the debate over the new Reform Bill the following spring.

In May 1866, Bodichon returned from Algeria and wrote to Helen Taylor about launching a women's suffrage campaign. Taylor, "though warning against unrealistic hopes of immediate success ... promised that John Stuart Mill would present the petition to parliament if the Langham Place women could secure at least 100 signatures" (Worzala 286). Helen Taylor then drafted a suffrage petition, which Davies edited to eliminate mention of married women, who were at that time legally disqualified from owning property. The revised petition sought simply to consider "the expediency of providing for the representation of all householders, without distinction of sex, who possess such property or rental qualification as your Honourable House may determine" (Blackburn 54). Davies, Barbara Bodichon, Jessie Boucherett, Jane Crow, Rosamond Hill, Bessie Parkes, and Clementia Taylor then worked to collect signatures for the petition. Surprisingly, the women quickly succeeded in gathering 1,499 names on this first suffrage petition.[28]

Davies does not describe this petition drive in any detail in her Chronicle, an omission perhaps reflecting her consistent ambivalence toward the suffrage movement, its more radical organizers, and the harm she feared it might cause to the movement to open education to women.

Davies and Elizabeth Garrett (Bodichon was ill) then took this petition to Mill in Parliament. There they met Henry Fawcett at Westminster, who sent an aide to find Mill. Davies wrote:

> we walked up & down the Hall, E. Garrett carrying the Petition, amid a crowd of people. The large roll was somewhat conspicuous, & not easy to conceal, so we asked an old applewoman to put it behind her stall. Almost immediately after, Mr. Mill suddenly appeared, finding us empty-handed. It was an embarrassing moment. E. Garrett, almost choking with suppressed laughter, said in broken accents, 'We've, put it, down.' It was of course at once recovered, & Mr. Mill, taking it up & waving it in the air, said 'I can brandish this with effect.' (Chronicle 486–87)

On 7 June 1866, John Stuart Mill and Henry Fawcett presented this petition for women's suffrage to Parliament. Debate on the issue resumed in July, "after the resignation of Lord John Russell over the defeat of his reform bill, and the appointment of Lord Derby as Prime Minister. On the 17th [of July], Mill . . . made his motion for a tally of women who were eligible to vote, appealing to both parties to support a proposal which was, 'like many of the most valuable Reforms, as truly Conservative, as I am sure it is truly Liberal,' and the motion was agreed to" (McCrimmon 104–5).[29]

Inspired by the success of their suffrage petition, Davies, Bodichon, and Clementia Taylor began to discuss forming an official committee for women's suffrage in London during the summer of 1866. Similar organizations were soon established in Manchester and Edinburgh, and Bodichon read a revised version of her Kensington Society paper on suffrage at the NAPSS annual meeting in October 1866. Despite internal factions and disagreement, the London group— not yet officially a committee—moved on to a second round of petition drives.[30] As was the case with so many reform movements, however, the suffrage effort was also trapped by its own initial success into moving too quickly. Organizers had some difficulty adapting to the shift in geographical focus, as Londoners now needed to work with women from the northern industrial cities. More important was the shift in political perspective, as the Local Examinations group was joined by new people bringing new ideas and approaches to the new campaign.

Disagreement became concentrated on two key issues: whether to pursue votes for married women, and whether to allow men to join the women's suffrage committee. Most of those involved had agreed that the second round of petitions should avoid the legally complicated problem of votes for married women, but during the summer Helen Taylor began to insist that they include married women in the new petitions (Crawford 355; Rosen 110–11): "The petition which Mill had presented ... in June had been ambiguous and could have been interpreted either to exclude or to include married women. But by the end of the summer the Langham Place members had decided that they could obtain more support if they asked for a limited franchise including only single women and widows" (Worzala 290). In her educational campaigns, Davies had insisted firmly on absolute identity of standards, and she had been—and remained throughout her life—unswerving in her demand for such identity of standards on both political and educational grounds. By contrast, she took a more conservative and pragmatic approach in the suffrage movement, siding with those who affirmed that to demand the vote for married women "would be self-defeating, since it would entail a complete revision of the existing property laws that decreed that a married woman could not own property unless her family had procured for her the prenuptial settlement of a separate estate—a legal stratagem available only to the wealthy" (Rosen 111).

Disagreements within the suffrage group in London thus grew out of political and ideological issues and were exacerbated by personality differences between Helen Taylor and Davies, as well as by personal and class differences between the "radicals," (Helen Taylor, Jessie Boucherett, and Clementia Taylor) and more pragmatic reformers including Davies, Elizabeth Garrett, Bessie Parkes, and (to a certain extent) Barbara Bodichon.

Finally, despite Helen Taylor's reluctance to formalize their arrangements as a society—especially one involving men—the London group decided to form a committee, and the first official meeting of the Enfranchisement of Women Committee was held on 20 October 1866.[31] Among those present were Barbara Bodichon, Jessie Boucherett, Frances Power Cobbe, Elizabeth Garrett, Isa Craig Knox, Lloyd, Bessie Parkes, Clementia Taylor, and Davies (Crawford 356).[32] Davies and Elizabeth Garrett's sister, Louisa Garrett Smith, were to act as cosecretaries, and Harriet Cook was to provide secretarial help and receive a salary. Isa Craig Knox was made honorary secretary.[33] Davies—who had been reluctant to be publicly involved in the suffrage movement for fear of damaging the image of her work on education—was urged to remain active; she consented but worked primarily behind the scenes in the subsequent suffrage campaign, strategizing the placement of sympathetic essays in periodicals and newspapers.

For the moment, then, the Langham Place contingent won both points of debate. The new committee included both men and women, and the petitions asked only for the limited franchise.[34] However, it proved to be a costly victory, for neither Mill nor Helen Taylor would join the committee, "despite Mentia Taylor's and Emily Davies's assurances that they would fight for married women's rights after the limited franchise was won" (Worzala 291), and the tensions were merely glossed over, not resolved.

Suffrage, however, had not completely diverted Davies's focus from education. In September 1866, she went to Leeds to attend a meeting on middle-class education for girls, which led to the establishment of a committee of women to supervise the next Local Examinations for girls. During this time, Davies also wrote to Edward Plumptre at Queen's College about the possibility of establishing an informal connection between Queen's and Cambridge—a possibility Plumptre eventually rejected.

In October, Davies attended both the NAPSS meeting in Manchester—at which Bodichon delivered her suffrage paper—and a schoolmistresses' meeting in Manchester, at which several people expressed a need for an institution of higher education for their better students. Davies explains in her Chronicle that "[a]s [she] drove back from the meeting . . . it was borne in upon [her] that the only way to meet the situation w[oul]d. be to found a new College, fulfilling the desired conditions. . . . On reaching home [she] spoke of the idea to friends, & in process of time, drafted a Programme" (Chronicle 500).

During much of 1867, then, Davies pursued two distinctly different and potentially conflicting goals: coordinating press coverage and public discussion of the women's suffrage campaign, and conceiving and drafting a program for a new college for women. In February 1867, Davies sent a printed copy of this college program to potential supporters including Dorothea Beale, Eliza Bostock, Lady Brodie, James Bryce, Joshua Fitch, Lady Goldsmid, Isa Craig Knox, Lord Lyttelton, Adelaide Manning, Anna Richardson, Henry Roby, Helen Taylor, John Westlake, and Elizabeth Wolstenholme.

On 28 March 1867, the London committee's suffrage petition with 3,559 signatures was presented to the House of Commons by Henry Bruce, M.P. "Though the signers included five professors, six Queen's counsels, eleven doctors, and twenty-six fellows of Oxford and Cambridge colleges, the petition attracted almost no notice. One week later a separate petition bearing 3,161 signatures collected by the recently formed Manchester society was presented to the Commons by Mill himself" (Rosen 118).[35] On 20 May 1867, Mill proposed amending the 1867 Reform Bill to enfranchise women by replacing the word *man* with *person*. The amendment was defeated by a vote of 196 to 73, or by a majority of 123.[36]

By July 1867, internal divisions within the London suffrage committee had become insurmountable, and the committee was dissolved, to be succeeded by the London National Society for Women's Suffrage.[37] Davies's role in the split remains controversial. Certainly she was uncomfortable working with people such as Clementia Taylor, whom she regarded as "radicals," although she had worked with women of equally radical families and sympathies at Langham Place without such evident acrimony.[38] Helen Taylor's role is equally complicated, and her apparent desire to manipulate the committee's actions from afar (she spent much time during these years in Avignon) could scarcely have helped the committee to resolve complex policy and personality issues. In any case, the verdict of Andrew Rosen appears convincing:

> dissolution of the first London committee and consequent removal of most of its members from suffrage affairs proved to have a lasting and detrimental effect on the shape of the women's suffrage movement. In the absence of strong London leadership, that movement remained for the next thirty years a shifting, loosely coordinated, and sporadically quarrelsome alliance of separate societies, led until 1890 by the methodical but hardly charismatic Lydia Becker of Manchester. (Rosen 120)

The College for Women

Davies's efforts were moving inexorably away from women's suffrage and toward a more single-minded focus on founding a women's college. During the winter, after her meeting with the schoolmistresses in Manchester, Davies began thinking concretely about designing a college for women and developing a draft program for such a college. Early that spring, on 3 April 1867, a new committee met and discussed the college idea: "A proposal to found a College for women, with a view to preparing candidates for the examns. of the University of Cambridge, having been laid before the Committee, it was resolved that the project be now undertaken by this Committee" (Chronicle 519).

In describing the people she considered for the committee, Davies revealed the paradoxical combination of radical purpose and conservative method—reinforced perhaps by her memories of the difficult work with the suffrage committee—that characterized all of her work on the college: "the list include[d] no one specially known as advocating the Rights of women. It was felt to be important to put forward only such names as w[oul]d. be likely to win the confidence of ordinary people" (Chronicle 519).[39]

The newly constituted College Committee endorsed four resolutions: "that the College shall be, if possible, connected with the University of Cambridge ... that efforts shall be made to obtain the admission of the Students, under suitable regulations, to the Examns. for Degrees of that University ... [t]hat the religious services & instruction shall be in accordance with the principles of the Church of England, but that where conscientious objections are entertained, attendance at such services & instruction shall not be obligatory," and that the resident authorities be women (Chronicle 539).

By January 1868, Davies was actively devoting herself to the daunting organizational task of founding the college and exploring potential sites in Hitchin, a town roughly equidistant between London and Cambridge. The desire for a Hitchin site reflected her hope that the University of London might yet provide an eventual home for the college.

On 28 March 1868, the committee held a public meeting at the Architectural Union on Conduit Street to discuss the proposed college for women. Over two hundred educators, reformers, and activists attended. Reporting on the meeting to Anna Richardson, Annie Austin noted that "all spoke as if their minds were made up, & of 'our College' & as if it certainly is to be done, which was very good to hear" (Chronicle 604). By September 1868, Davies had written another paper, "Some Account of a Proposed New College for Women," which was read at the annual NAPSS meeting in Birmingham.

Interpreting Davies's activities during these crucial years is complicated, once again, by the absence of any personal correspondence and any intimate reflections in her Chronicle. Indeed, the Chronicle itself breaks off before the end of 1868, well before the college opened. Many interpretations of her behavior are possible: that she was simply more motivated by opening higher education to women than she was by gaining the vote for women; that she preferred to work with old and trusted allies in a campaign over which she could wield greater personal control than she could in the suffrage campaign; that she had attained both the age and the professional expertise that made her want to concentrate on achieving concrete and significant change in a field she knew and cared about rather than to continue moving from one campaign to the next. In any case, by the spring of 1869, she had left behind much of her other work and devoted herself to the foundation of a college for women.

Hitchin and Girton: 1869–75

Reformers with the North of England Council were increasingly active, and many of their efforts ran directly counter to Davies's campaign to open higher education to women on the basis of identical standards with men. During the time that Davies and her committee were planning the College for Women, the North of England Council sent a memorial to Cambridge asking the university for a separate examination for women. This proposal proved popular for a number of reasons: it offered a way to improve educational standards for governesses, and it appeared simultaneously to expand educational opportunities for women and to foster educational reform. Yet it also assuaged the concerns of those committed to separate spheres for women, who believed "that since women's duties differed from men's, their education should be different too" (Worzala 273).

In March 1868, Davies's committee voted against participation in the North of England Council's memorial, but the Cambridge authorities were clearly interested, and they voted to sponsor a "special" examination for women over eighteen. These examinations, known as the Cambridge Higher Local Examinations, began in Leeds and London in 1869, and were eventually made available to both men and women through the University Extension Lectures. Many of the same educational reformers at Cambridge who had supported the North of England Council met in December 1869 under the leadership of Henry Sidgwick and Henry and Millicent Fawcett to plan for another approach to opening the university to women. At that meeting, "Sidgwick undertook to rent a house for them and persuaded Anne Jemima Clough to take charge of it. In the autumn of 1871 Clough welcomed her first five pupils" to Merton Hall (Worzala 274).

This effort, which led eventually to the formation of Newnham College, the second women's college in England, was initiated by educational reformers rather than women's rights advocates, and the two colleges moved in distinctly different directions during the early years at Cambridge. In most accounts, the Sidgwick/North of England position seems reasonable, indeed substantive, a matter of legitimate educational concerns about outmoded examinations, rigid university policy, "the low standard of the Ordinary Degree, the excessive emphasis placed on the study of Latin and Greek to the detriment of modern languages, science and social science, and the exclusiveness entailed by association with the Established Church (McWilliams–Tullberg 41). In essence, the Clough-Sidgwick faction is described both as "willing to compromise" (McDermid 111) and as "educationalists proper, who valued learning for its own sake, and who did not subordinate it to any other cause" (Strachey 144).

However, as Barbara Caine has noted, "it was a rather cruel irony that this very university education of which . . . [Davies and other women] had been deprived . . . should be deemed worthless by the men who had benefited from it at the very moment when she was seeking to make it available to other women!" (Caine 89–90). Furthermore, Caine suggests that it was

> understandable, although perhaps a little unfair, that Sidgwick's interest in educational reform and his efforts on behalf of women at Cambridge should have received so sympathetic a treatment from historians, while Davies is usually shown as the intransigent, destructive, and abrasive one. But the question which, at least by implication, she asked has only recently been posed by others. This is the question as to why he and his supporters should have been so

timid about trying to force through their desired changes in the ordinary Cambridge curriculum for men, choosing instead to try to get the women students to bring these about. (90)

The College for Women at Hitchin 1869–72

In the early stages of planning, Davies had imagined raising £30,000 to build a grand structure for the college. By the end of June 1869, however, the College Committee decided to begin more practically by renting a small house. They selected Benslow House at Hitchin for the new College for Women and offered an entrance examination for prospective students; the examiners included George Liveing, Henry Roby, Robert Seeley, and Sedley Taylor. Of the eighteen students who sat the entrance examination in July 1869, thirteen passed. Davies was preoccupied at this time with a vast array of organizational details, from renting and furnishing the house to petitioning the Schools Inquiry Commission for funding for the college; from writing to prominent people seeking their endorsement to finding a Mistress for the college. Above all, she was concerned with shaping public response to the idea of a college for women, which meant negotiating with Cambridge supporters resistant to the traditional curriculum and examinations while putting together a credible committee of supporters and placating some of those supporters, including Bodichon, who were almost obsessively concerned about the impact of higher education on women's health.

The college opened in October 1869 with five students. From this point on, Davies's life was defined largely by the myriad administrative details of running this new institution and by the endless political, educational, and procedural disputes arising at each step. Davies was on hand to greet the first students—Emily Gibson, Anna Lloyd, Louisa Lumsden, Isabella Townshend, and Sarah Woodhead—at Benslow House, which she had arranged to be, as far as possible, exactly like the traditional men's colleges, including an arrangement in the dining room with a students' table and a High table, despite the fact that there were only five students. "[S]he wanted everything to be done from the very beginning with due regard to dignity and decorum" (Stephen 221).

Four lecturers, three of them from Cambridge, came to work with the students.[40] According to Louisa Lumsden, they "had one lecture every day which everybody attended, the length of this lecture being fixed neither by [their] capacities of taking in knowledge, nor by the convenience of the lecturer, but by the hours of railway trains" (Stephen 229).[41] Eventually the strain of this situation grew too much for some of the lecturers, and Stuart left due to illness, while Seeley resigned in protest over Davies's insistence that the students follow the same schedule laid out for male students, taking the Little-go Examination—much despised by reformers—before they prepared for the Tripos, or Honors, Examinations.[42]

The first terms at Hitchin were further troubled by inevitable student complaints about food and by the equally inevitable difficulties women students faced meeting the academic demands of the college after their poor preparation in secondary schools. Differences also arose between Davies and the Mistress during the second term, Emily Shirreff.[43] Three new students arrived for the second year, and in 1871 a new Mistress, Annie Austin, was appointed. In October of that second year, the first students were due to take the problematic Little-go. Davies wrote to the university authorities asking permission for the students to take the examination unofficially. The council of the senate responded that it was not within their power to give such permission and suggested that Davies make private arrangements with the individual examiners. So she wrote to the senior examiner, James Cartmell, and laboriously pieced together the individual consent of each examiner. At the end of the Michaelmas term, Davies took the students up to Cambridge, and the first women students sat the Cambridge University exams. All five passed.[44]

Although Davies was not Mistress of the college during its first three years, she and many others visited Benslow House frequently. Stephen notes that Bodichon, Adelaide Manning, Lady Rich, and Lady Stanley all visited, as did Frances Power Cobbe, Elizabeth Garrett, Maria Shirreff Grey, and Anna Richardson. The college must have been hard-pressed to house these visitors, for it was already growing crowded with new students. In 1870, the committee erected an iron building—which the students named the "Tin Tabernacle"—to provide space for the overflow.

By 1871, however, such emergency measures clearly could not continue. Furthermore, Davies and the committee were feeling external pressures to move the college as well. The Lectures for Women in Cambridge had begun in 1870, attracting almost eighty women from the Cambridge area and beyond (Stephen 246). Sponsored by Henry Sidgwick and Henry Fawcett, these lectures seemed to Davies to constitute a profound threat to her vision of the college, so when Sidgwick proposed that Davies move the college closer to Cambridge and that the two groups merge, she urged the committee to reject his suggestion. Between July and November 1870, they debated the subject, and eventually the committee voted to look for a house or for land within three miles of Cambridge, but not within the town itself.[45] The Cambridge committee headed by Sidgwick strongly opposed this move, so the two efforts to open the university to women continued on separate paths.[46]

The committee proceeded with its plans to raise funds for a new building, launching its campaign with a meeting at St. James's Hall, Piccadilly, on 15 May 1871. Money began to come in, far less than they had hoped, but an impressive amount nonetheless: £600 was pledged as a result of the London meeting alone.[47] The committee also held meetings, at which Davies spoke, in Leeds, Birmingham, St. Leonard's, and Nottingham. But the amount of money they needed was far greater than the amount they were bringing in, so finally—following the advice of Sir Francis Goldsmid—the committee "decided to borrow on the security of a number of friends, who would each undertake to guarantee a share of the money, to be repaid when the funds were forthcoming" (Stephen 263).

In March 1872, the newly constituted committee purchased land near the village of Girton, three miles from the center of Cambridge, and hired a prominent architect, Alfred Waterhouse, to design a new college building. After formalizing its aims and methods by incorporating as an association under the Board of Trade, the College for Women (now Girton College) moved to Girton in October 1873.[48] With this move, Davies and the women's educational movement conclusively left the world of London reformers, politicians, and Dissenters and entered the more narrow, conservative, and Anglican world of Cambridge academics.

The London School Board

Davies continued working during these years on a host of other issues and organizations, including the London Association of Schoolmistresses. More significantly, she was drawn into new commitments arising from the Elementary Education Act of 1870. That law gave women the right both to vote for members of newly formed school boards and to be elected as members of those boards. Elizabeth Garrett—now a practicing physician and a soon-to-be-married woman, Mrs. James Anderson—was invited by the Working Men's Association in the Marylebone division of London to run for the London School Board (Stephen 120). Shortly thereafter, Davies was invited by Paul Frederick Tidman, a friend of John Stuart Mill's, to run for school board in the city. When the city committee did not adopt her as a candidate, Tidman suggested that she stand for his district in Greenwich. After some hesitation and reluctance—including, apparently, concern about the criticism of her contemplated move made by Tomkinson—Davies accepted the invitation.

Thus, while she was writing to university officials and individual examiners for permission to permit the Hitchin students to take the Little-go, Davies also found time to learn the electoral process, attend public meetings, and write and deliver election speeches. School board elections were held on 30 November 1870; both Davies and Garrett were elected in London, as were Flora Stevenson in Edinburgh and Lydia Becker in Manchester. Following her election, Davies attended school board meetings for three years and participated in the laborious process of extending to the children of London greater access to schooling.

According to the educational census of 1871, London had about 680,000 school-age children and was lacking places for about 100,000 children. The newly formed London School Board faced severe problems: finding or creating new spaces and schools; enforcing newly mandated school attendance and fees; and locating and training new teachers. Davies joined the Statistical Committee and the By Laws Committee of the London School Board. The former committee assessed the school accommodation necessary in different areas, work that required exhaustive investigation of each locality—during Davies's term, the London School Board approved plans to build over one hundred new schools. The By Laws Committee supervised enforcement of school attendance. Between June 1872 and June 1873, attendance in schools of the Greenwich division increased by about 5,500 (Stephen, 125–26).

Girton College 1873–75

The Cambridge world into which the college was now moving was profoundly conservative; it had changed only slowly and with great reluctance during the previous twenty years. "In the sixties, Oxford and Cambridge, though the Royal Commission of 1850 brought about many improvements, were still semi-reformed institutions, where standards of teaching were in process of being raised by vigorous movements from within. They had strict requirements of residence and very little else; less than half the young men who went up took a degree in honours" (Bradbrook 21).

Success in this new world required a very different set of skills from those Davies had previously developed. In London, she had been organizing and arguing to open or reform existing institutions; in Hitchin and in Girton, she was inventing, building, and administering an entirely new institution, simultaneously adapting to and challenging an ancient university rooted in traditions of celibacy, Anglicanism, and masculine power.

In the spring of 1872, in the midst of planning the move from Hitchin to Girton (and in the middle of Davies's term on the school board), Annie Austin, the college Mistress, fell ill. For the balance of that term, Bodichon and Lady Stanley shared the Mistress's responsibilities with Davies. Since they could not find a suitable person permanently, however, Davies was forced to assume the role of Mistress on her own for the May 1872 term.[49] In August 1872, the committee officially appointed Davies Mistress of the college for one year—she would ultimately serve for three—and she moved to Hitchin with the thirteen students. Again she wrote letters asking permission for the students to take the Little-go; the examiners were initially reluctant, but eventually enough of them agreed, allowing the students to comply with the university policy in taking this examination.[50]

The strain of studying for the Little-go and then having to prepare immediately for the Tripos was beginning to tell on the women at the college. In this they were no doubt reinforced by the enormous antipathy most progressive Cambridge lecturers felt toward the Little-go. In February 1873, "all the thirteen students in residence sent a memorial to the Committee, setting forth [their] considerations, and asking that students should be allowed to become candidates for any Tripos without passing the Previous, or Little-go, Examination. Some of the College lecturers sent in a statement of their views" as well (Stephen 277). Davies was enormously upset by what she saw as a rebellion within the college, a rebellion that, for her, struck at the heart of the principle of identity of standards that she had so stringently maintained against consistent prejudice and resistance for ten years. The rebellion was soon put down and the students and lecturers convinced or placated, but the incident seems to have convinced Davies that she was contending with enemies within as well as without, and her attitude toward the students grew more distrustful and distant.

When the College for Women moved to Girton in October 1873, the building was not yet complete, and they encountered the usual problems arising in new construction—including a chronically smoking chimney that figures prominently in the letters of these years. For the next three years, Davies lived at Girton and served as its Mistress, supervising the construction and decoration, cataloguing gifts, entertaining visitors, writing every year to university examiners to arrange for the women students to sit the examinations unofficially, and supervising the lives of the students. Not all of these activities drew on her strengths, and many seemed to exhaust her both emotionally and physically. Every development at the college, it seemed, demanded discussion, and almost every step encountered resistance.[51]

Indeed, as the movement to open university education to women grew more successful, it elicited more vehement criticism and resistance. Most notable was Henry Maudsley's article in the April 1874 *Fortnightly Review*. Maudsley argued that the strain of education would disrupt women's menstrual cycles, potentially threatening their reproductive capacities, and that education for women should be designed to suit their "special" needs. Garrett Anderson wrote a cogent and effective response to this article in the *Fortnightly* the following month, but the controversy suggests something of the fear and anger university education for women was provoking—resistance that even some of its supporters, such as Barbara Bodichon, found convincing.

New Debates and Continuing Controversies

In addition to concerns about female students' health and hygiene, three issues dominated discussion in the early years of the college: academic standards, the college location, and religion. Of these, perhaps the most consistent and most divisive involved the struggle over standards—between maintaining the dubious, outmoded practices of men's university education and accepting the separate exams and curricula for women that the university itself and many sympathetic reformers offered in one form or another as compromise measures. Davies and her closest supporters advocated that women students follow exactly the procedures and courses followed by men at Cambridge, while many of the university reformers associated with Newnham College hoped to challenge what they saw as absurd curricula and examinations by offering a reformed course of study to the women students.[52]

Davies, however, remained unshakably convinced that accepting separate standards would subvert the entire movement for women's higher education. In retrospect it is clear that by insisting that Girton students comply to the letter with the standards of men's curricula and examinations—no matter how clearly inadequate those standards were—Davies also ensured that when women students *did* succeed, their accomplishments could not be dismissed as meaningless or inferior. On the other hand, in accepting the existing procedures and practices of Cambridge, Davies and her allies lost all opportunity to challenge antiquated and patriarchal curricula, to invent a women's college genuinely "free of unreal loyalties" (Woolf 80). And unfortunately, this struggle between feminism and educational reform, Davies and Sidgwick, Girton and Newnham, seriously divided the women's campaign for higher education.

Davies and the committee also struggled, in the first years of the College for Women, with the question of its location. A site such as Hitchin, relatively far from Cambridge, clearly proved inconvenient for tutors who had to travel daily from the university to the college; a site too close to Cambridge, however, raised fears about the "safety" (meaning, by implication, the sexuality and chastity) of female students living in a traditionally male university town. Nor was this concern entirely misplaced. Women in the vicinity of Cambridge University who were even suspected of being prostitutes could be arrested without due process by university proctors and incarcerated in an institution called the Spinning House. This university power was well known and much debated; both the prison itself and the cultural values it reflected indirectly shaped the debate over the location of the women's college.

Finally, Davies and the committee also encountered serious debate and disagreement over religion. While religious tests at Cambridge had been significantly weakened by 1869, such tests still existed, and, according to Bradbrook, "[r]eligious affiliations and practice were a burning question at Cambridge in the sixties. Dissenters were first admitted to degrees in 1856, but senior offices were not open. From 1862 to 1871 a series of Parliamentary Bills attempted to abolish religious tests. In the university the warfare was almost incessant; the *status quo* was sustained, though supported only by a minority" (48). The new College for Women, in its effort to adhere to existing Cambridge policies and practices, imposed a modified allegiance to the Church of England, despite the fact that many of its early supporters and founders were Unitarians and Jews.[53]

Davies was intimately involved in the College for Women during its first six years: she served as Mistress of Girton College from 1872 to 1875, as well as secretary of the College Committee. Her tasks included arranging and overseeing construction, supervising students, writing letters to university officials seeking permission for women students to take the Little-go and Tripos examinations, raising money, welcoming visitors, helping to decorate the new buildings, responding to the growing public opposition to higher education for women, and developing the day-to-day administrative procedures and practices that would govern the institution for many years.

By 1875, clearly exhausted, she resigned her position as Mistress of Girton. Her supervision of the college's early years had left a pronounced mark on the new institution, particularly in her insistence on providing sitting rooms as well as bedrooms for the students, and on building more and more rooms to house more and more students rather than funding scholarships or research, and she remained intimately associated with Girton College after her retirement, helping in the unsuccessful campaigns to win official recognition of women's place at Cambridge that took place in 1881, 1887, and 1897.

"On Saturday, December 14, 1918, some seven million women made their way to the polls to cast their first votes ever in a parliamentary election. Among them was 88-year-old Emily Davies, one of two women who in 1866 had presented a women's suffrage petition to Parliament, marking the beginning of the organized women's suffrage movement.... Indeed, of the group of women who first organized for women's suffrage in 1866, Davies was the only one who lived long enough to cast her vote" (van Wingerden 1).

The Letters

The campaigns and reforms to which Davies contributed are not simply depicted in her letters; they are the dominating motivation for and content of that correspondence. For much of the time between her arrival in London and her retirement from Girton, Davies was writing letters: to friends reporting on the progress of the *EWJ*; to friends and associates soliciting papers for NAPSS and the Kensington Society; to acquaintances and potential political supporters seeking support for her campaigns to open the Local Exams to girls and to convince the SIC investigation to include girls' schools; to friends, allies, and associates arranging journalistic coverage of, and soliciting essays in support of, the women's suffrage movement; and to friends and allies asking for help with, and detailing the arduous struggle to found, the College for Women.

Those letters, collected here for the first time, vividly illustrate the way one reform activity either grew out of another or inspired the next, how strategies learned in the course of one effort were put to use in another, and how the people and organizations lending support to one reform were recruited for subsequent efforts. They also suggest ways in which the network of mid-Victorian reformers, friends, and allies operated and contributed to the changing construction of femininity in late Victorian England.

The letters of the London years (1862-69) offer an intimate perspective on the energy and enthusiasm of the mid-century reform movement, the belief in the possibilities for genuine social change.[54] Those of the college years (1869-75) offer insight into the debates that shaped the college and suggest—in the narrowing of their focus and hardening of their tone—the toll taken by these activities. This change in tone in Davies's later letters was undoubtedly reinforced by the deaths of two close friends—Charlotte Manning and Anna Richardson—whom Davies trusted completely and to whom she would have been likely to write intimate, personal letters.[55]

The letters that remain suggest the subtle political and personal costs as well as the obvious educational, feminist, and reform gains of the shift from London to Cambridge, from nonconformism to Anglicanism, and from women's rights to higher education. Once they moved to Cambridge, Davies and the College Committee were outsiders, both physically and politically, and her letters of these years betray a subtle loss of confidence and a corresponding need for scrupulous conformity to university standards.

As the past generation of scholars of women's history sought to find and interpret "lost" women of the nineteenth century, they focused initially on powerful individuals and on specific reform campaigns. While this research proved invaluable in challenging the old vision of the Victorians, scholars have now moved beyond such interpretations and have brought some of the sophistication of feminist, structuralist, and New Historical theory to bear on the reading of the nineteenth-century women's movement and its evolving and complicated political ideologies.[56] It is to just such an understanding of ideological struggles, and of the way feminists and reformers defined their own motives and goals, that Davies's letters can make a significant contribution. They clearly illustrate her attempts to think through and articulate an escape from the entrapping binary opposition between, on the one hand, essentialism and separate spheres for women (represented by the cult of domesticity as well as separate journals, examinations, and institutions) and, on the other, what she regarded as the equally dangerous position of radicalism with its dangerous claim of gender equality.

These letters also offer a valuable corrective to some of the misleading, erroneous, or unsubstantiated anecdotal information about Davies, resulting in part from the fact that most work about her has relied on one valuable but also unreliable book, the biography by Barbara Stephen. Many of the letters Stephen cites—letters that have been cited in turn by later historians—no longer exist, and several that do still exist have been misquoted by Stephen (see the editorial methods section). The result is that many scholars of feminist and educational history have been relying on a secondary source that, however well intentioned, is often seriously flawed. The letters in this collection are, whenever possible, edited with reference only to primary source material (published and unpublished).

The letters offer Davies's own views, her own voice, and her own interpretation of her life. However, these are only a small and potentially unrepresentative fraction of the letters she wrote during her life and can thus be distorting in their own way. There are, for example, numerous letters between Davies and Robert Potts on the Cambridge Local Examinations campaign, offering a vivid sense of the day-to-day operation of that effort. Yet there remain none of the letters Davies wrote to Henry Sidgwick before 1875 and no final versions of her letters to Richard Hutton. Indeed, from references in the extant letters, it can reasonably be assumed that Davies wrote to the following men: Henry Alford, Matthew Arnold, Walter Bagehot, Sir Benjamin Brodie, James Bryce, Henry Cookson, John Griffiths, George Grote, Tom Hughes, Richard Hutton, Henry Jackson, George Liveing, Lord Lyttelton, Thomas Markby, John Norris, Mark Pattison, Henry Roby, John Robert Seeley, William Shaen, Henry Sidgwick, Thomas Trollope, and Alfred Waterhouse. Yet none of the archives at which the papers of these men are located has any record of correspondence from Davies. As a result, the picture drawn by this collection of letters is incomplete, offering extensive views of some campaigns and truncated or unsatisfactory glimpses of others.

Finally, due to the effective censorship Davies imposed on her own life by destroying her personal papers, these letters do not discuss personal conflicts or emotional struggles; they do not offer revelations of intimate relationships, and they do not constitute what she so clearly wanted to avoid—a memoir "of an intimate personal nature." And because of the inadvertent censorship imposed by many of the men with whom she corresponded, few of whom saved her letters, this collection does not provide a comprehensive account of her work as a journalist, feminist, and educator. However, these letters do offer a "sketch" of her formidable contributions, and taken together they constitute a striking view of the changing world of middle-class women in nineteenth century England, seen through the eyes of a woman who was instrumental in bringing about some of that change.

Notes

1. See appendices for an accounting of the letters Stephens cites that are no longer extant.

2. Barbara Stephen, *Emily Davies and Girton College* (London, 1927). Daphne Bennett's *Emily Davies and the Liberation of Women* (London, 1990) is the only recent book-length study of Davies. By contrast, Sheila Herstein (*A Mid-Victorian Feminist: Barbara Bodichon* [New Haven, 1985]), Pam Hirsch (*Barbara Leigh Smith Bodichon: Feminist, Artist and Rebel* [London, 1998]), and Candida Ann Lacey (*Barbara Leigh Smith Bodichon and the Langham Place Group* [London, 1987]), all have written about Bodichon.

3. Margaret Forster, for example, describes Davies as "exactly the kind of young lady who in Victorian times was particularly trapped by her very common situation [with] neither the means nor the opportunity nor the daring to break out of the mould into which her circumstances were pushing her ... the dutiful daughter upon whom Fortune had not smiled in the way of beauty or wealth, destined to stay at home and serve" (*Significant Sisters: The Grassroots of Active Feminism 1839–1939* [London, 1984], 139).

4. Barbara Caine, for example, notes that "while most of Davies's campaigns have been studied, no attention has yet been paid to her ideas" (*Victorian Feminists* [Oxford, 1992], 54–55). See also Theodora Bostick, "The Press and the Launching of the Women's Suffrage Movement, 1866–1867," *Victorian Periodicals Review* 13, no. 4 (1980): 125–31; Caine, *Victorian Feminists*; Forster, *Significant Sisters*; A.P.W. Robson, "The Founding of the National Society for Women's Suffrage 1866–1867," *Canadian Journal of History* 8 (March 1973): 1–22; and Andrew Rosen, "Emily Davies and the Women's Movement," *Journal of British Studies* 19, no. 1 (1979): 101–21.

5. By contrast, Davies recorded numerous letters *from* Garrett Anderson in her Family Chronicle. These and other letters from Garrett Anderson convey a fully nuanced, complicated personal and professional picture of her character and contributions.

6. "Probably only women who have laboured under it can understand the weight of discouragement produced by being perpetually told that, as women, nothing much is ever to be expected of them, and it is not worth their while to exert themselves," Davies wrote in her 1868 article "Special Systems of Education for Women" (*London Student*, no. 3 [June 1868]: 138–39).

7. The Family Chronicle is held at the Girton College Archives in Cambridge. According to the explanatory note attached to the photocopy of the Chronicle, "Pp. 101–200, covering the period 1849–61, was used by Barbara Stephen when she was writing *Emily Davies and Girton College* (1927), and appears to have been lost at that time." Hereafter this manuscript will be cited as Chronicle.

8. No such memorandum is listed at the Girton College Archives, which contain the majority of the Davies papers, and which were the source of the materials Stephen used for the Davies biography. See the editorial methods section for a fuller discussion of the problems arising from missing materials.

9. The term *feminist* here means "a political movement that seeks to eradicate the in-

justices that women experience because of their sex," as explicated by June Purvis, *Women's History Britain, 1850–1945* (London, 1995), 17, n. 40. The term refers to Davies and her colleagues working in what she herself termed the *women's movement*, although it is not a word she would have used.

10. "The *menus* were very simple. At breakfast, coffee, bread & butter & cold meat; at dinner at one o'clock ... a joint & two vegetables & some simple pudding.... Tea at 6 p.m. consisted of tea, bread & butter, and dry toast. & after Prayers at 9 P.M., there was a slight supper in the Library, of milk porridge or bread & milk" (Chronicle 62–63).

11. Virginia Woolf, *Three Guineas* (New York, 1966), 4–5. Davies herself commented on this situation: "Parents are ready to make sacrifices to secure a tolerably good and complete education for their sons; they do not consider it necessary to do the same for their daughters. Or perhaps it would be putting it more fairly to say, that a very brief and attenuated course of instruction, beginning late and ending early, is believed to constitute a good and complete education for a woman" (*The Higher Education of Women* 33).

12. This newspaper is no longer extant, so we have only Barbara Stephen's account of it.

13. All three women did exactly as described: Garrett Anderson became the first woman doctor on the medical rolls in England; Davies founded Girton College; and Millicent Garrett Fawcett became a leading suffragist. Strachey's story is not documented, but her preface thanks both Millicent Garrett Fawcett and Barbara Stephen for their assistance, and she may have had access to the now-missing pages of Davies's Chronicle. A variant of this story, attributed to Louisa Garrett, is also cited by Bradbrook (10–11) and van Wingderden (11).

14. According to Stephen, Davies first visited Langham Place in 1859, on a trip to her brother's in London (55).

15. According to Worzala, SPEW branches also opened in Aberdeen, Brighton, Dublin, Edinburgh, Leicester, Manchester, Newcastle, and Nottingham (205).

16. See *Memoir of Anna Deborah Richardson* (Newcastle-on-Tyne, 1877) for a description of Richardson and discussion of her contribution to Davies's ideas about women's education.

17. "In 1866 [Emily Faithfull] defended herself against the charge of being an atheist in the letter columns of the *Times*. By that time the women of Langham Place were trying to dissociate themselves from her because of her involvement in the notorious Codrington divorce case" (Worzala 201).

18. "NAPSS provided the first major public forum for British women to present papers publicly on their work.... Even though NAPSS encouraged women to address its meetings, this innovation was greeted with a 'howl of abuse' in the press.... Not all women took full advantage of the opportunity to address NAPSS. Some submitted papers describing their work, but refused to read them" (Martel 33–35).

19. Davies most often alleviated the Oxbridge men's fears by assuring them that she sought no "neck-and-neck" competition between girls and boys, and that their only goal was education and the improvement of girls' schools, untainted by any desire for access to careers. By claiming they were inspired purely by a love of learning and desire to improve girls' education, she sought to assuage their fears about the economic consequences of opening education to women, although she had clearly become involved in the Local Examinations movement through efforts to open London University to Elizabeth Garrett in pursuit of a medical profession.

20. *Report of an Examination of Girls* (London, 1864) provided an extensive statistical analysis of the girls' performance and concluded that "[t]he want of an external standard could scarcely have been more conclusively shown than by this experiment.... There is no reason to suppose that the girls who failed in this examination came below the ordinary standard;

on the contrary, it is likely that they were rather above the average level of attainment" (5). Thus, rather than accepting that the girls' poor performance, especially in arithmetic, might suggest an inherent intellectual inability, Davies and her allies recognized that the problem lay in poor academic preparation and used the evidence of that poor performance to argue for improvements in girls' schools.

21. "The question of religious tests refused to lie down quietly. The settlement of 1856 had removed the requirement of a declaration of faith from those proceeding to all degrees except those in divinity, but membership of the Senate was still restricted to those prepared to declare themselves *bona fide* members of the Church of England, and the same bar, though withdrawn from scholars and exhibitioners of colleges, still applied to fellows [and heads of houses]" (Leedham-Green 159).

22. "Members met every two or three months to hear and discuss 'a paper on some subject interesting to teachers.' The society also established a professional library and registry, both of which were housed at the SPEW office" (Worzala 265).

23. The other women invited to give evidence were Dorothea Beale, Gertrude King, Susan Kyberd, [?] Martin, Mary Eliza Porter, Eleanor Smith, and Elizabeth Wolstenholme.

24. "The Application of Funds to the Education of Girls" (London, 1865). Unfortunately, "Section 12 of the Endowed Schools Act (which followed the Taunton Commission) left the position of girls open. It said they should share in the endowment of new schools 'so far as conveniently may be.' [This] hopelessly ambiguous phrase . . . [left] the way open for people to claim that while the boys needed new laboratories or playing fields it was not 'convenient' to let girls have a share of whatever money was available" (Forster 148).

25. Similar organizations had been formed by others in this circle, such as the Portfolio Club, formed by Barbara Bodichon in 1859.

26. Davies, *The Higher Education of Women*.

27. According to van Wingerden, "[t]he pro-suffrage vote scored a decided victory in the debate . . . carrying nearly all 50 members" (9).

28. According to van Wingerden, they collected these almost 1,500 signatures in two weeks (10). If true, this is a staggering accomplishment, given that it took the Local Examinations Committee almost a year to collect the signatures for the memorial to the University of Cambridge. And one wonders that they couldn't find one additional signature, to bring the total to an even 1,500.

29. Specifically, Mill motioned for "a return showing the number of freeholders and householders in England and Wales who, fulfilling the conditions of property or rental prescribed by law as the qualifications for the electoral franchise, are excluded from the franchise by reason of their sex" (Blackburn 57).

30. According to Worzala, "[d]ifficulties of communication accounted for part of the problem. Many of the women left London for long periods during the summer. . . . More important than inadequate communication, however, was the clash of personalities between Davies and Taylor" (289). Taylor, in Avignon for the summer, stayed in contact and sought to shape the direction of the movement through her correspondence.

31. Rosen, 114. At an earlier meeting in June 1866, Davies, Helen Taylor, Bodichon, and Isa Craig (now Knox) had met at Clementia Taylor's house and decided "not, in fact, to form a society but merely to press ahead with the gathering and presentation of further petitions" (Crawford 354). The official title of the committee they eventually did form was "The Enfranchisement of Unmarried Women and Widows, Possessing the Due Property Qualification" (Crawford 206).

32. Lloyd is probably Mary Lloyd, Frances Power Cobbe's companion.

33. The growing committee later included Henry Alford, John Cairns, Walter Clay, Lady Goldsmid, George Hastings, James Heywood, Adelaide Manning, and Mrs. Hensleigh Wedgwood (Blackburn 58–59).

34. The proposed permanent committee included Henry Alford, John Cairns, Walter Clay, Russell Gurney, George Hastings, James Heywood, and John Westlake, as well as Lady Goldsmid and Adelaide Manning (Crawford 356).

35. Some uncertainty exists about the timing of these two petitions. According to Crawford, Boucherett complained bitterly about the poor strategy implicit in this divided presentation. Davies's letters, however, suggest that she too assumed that the petitions would be presented simultaneously, leaving open the question of how they came to be presented separately. See ED to Lydia Becker, 30 March 1867.

36. This tally of the vote is taken from Helen Blackburn (252). Other scholars cite a prosuffrage vote of 79. See Rosen (119); most agree on the 123-vote margin.

37. The first executive committee of the new London National Society was composed only of women. Its members were: Frances Power Cobbe, Millicent Garrett Fawcett, Miss Hampson (a friend of Frances Power Cobbe), Mary Lloyd, Margaret Bright Lucas, Caroline Stansfeld, and Mentia Taylor (Crawford 351).

38. Describing the end of the suffrage committee in her Chronicle, Davies wrote, "It had been working thro' great difficulties, owing to the incompatibility of its chief elements . . . it was finally agreed to be best to leave the Women's Suffrage part of the women's movement to be worked for the time under the direction of the Radical section of the party" (Chronicle 509–10).

39. The names she listed included Dean Alford, James Bryce, Lady Goldsmid, Mrs. Gurney, George Hastings, James Heywood, Lady Hobart, Mrs. Manning, Henry Roby, Lady Stanley of Alderley, Sedley Taylor, Reverend Temple [later deleted], Tomkinson, and Davies herself (Chronicle 518).

40. The first lecturers were E. C. Clark in Latin and Greek, Fenton Hort and John Robert Seeley in English, and James Stuart in mathematics.

41. Stephen takes this account from Lumsden's article in the *Girton Review* (Michaelmas term, 1907).

42. The Little-go, or Previous, Examination tested knowledge of classics, mathematics, and the tenets of the Established Church, determining suitability to embark on study for a Cambridge degree. According to Leedham-Green, "[t]he 'Previous' [or Little-go] examination, taken in the fifth term, had been introduced in 1822 as an obstacle to the sort of academic idleness so elegantly enjoyed by Lord Byron in the early years of the century. . . . the standard was extremely elementary. Its enemies . . . maintained that it distracted serious students from their mathematical studies besides requiring college tutors 'to do the work of an under Master in a Grammar School'" (150). The Poll, or Ordinary, Degree was a Pass Degree course. The Tripos was an Honors Degree course (e.g., Mathematical Tripos).

43. According to Barbara Stephen, "[t]his was the first appearance of a perpetually recurring difference of opinion between Miss Davies and successive Mistresses" (233).

44. Five passed the Classics Examination, and two, Gibson and Woodhead, passed the Additional Mathematical Examination as well (Stephen 239). The other three students took that Additional Examination in 1871, and once again Davies ran into opposition to their sitting for it. The senior examiner for that year rejected her request, but Cartmell agreed to review the students' papers. Cook and Lumsden passed, but Townshend did not (Stephen 240).

45. None of the extant correspondence from Davies directly addresses the reasons she was so adamant about not locating the college within Cambridge itself. However, the dis-

cussion of location for the College for Women is fraught with unspoken fears about proximity and sexuality (see below).

46. Stephen cites extensive correspondence on this issue, including a long letter from Davies to Sidgwick, dated 31 December 1870, in which she explains her reasons for objecting to locating the college *in* Cambridge (251). This letter, unfortunately, is no longer extant in the Girton Archives, nor does it appear in Sidgwick's papers at Newnham or Trinity Colleges. We have included it in appendix D.

47. According to Stephen, "[d]uring the year 1871 the Committee succeeded in raising about £3,000, making a total of £7,200 since the College had been set on foot. Of this nearly £2,000 had been spent at Hitchin on furniture, iron rooms, and current expenses. The site at Girton had still to be paid for, and the new building there would cost about £7,800" (262).

48. Incorporating required that the college formally define its policies, and the declared intention eventually to affiliate with Cambridge University led one member, Joseph Lightfoot, to withdraw from the committee (Stephen 263).

49. According to Stephen, "[s]he tried to think that it might be possible to get through the year during which they must remain at Hitchin with the help of members of the Committee in turn. Lady Stanley, Madame Bodichon, and Lady Rich were all approached, but in vain" (270).

50. The University of Cambridge did not officially recognize the right of women students to take these examinations until 1881.

51. Simply ensuring that women students could attend lectures in the sciences, for example, was an ordeal, and Davies had to attend these lectures along with them as a chaperone.

52. In addition to disputing the value of the Little-go, reformers sought to replace Greek and Latin with more modern languages, or at least to challenge the unthinking primacy of the classics and to add French and German to the curricula.

53. Attendance at Church of England services was not mandatory; however, the college did not actively foster religious freedom to the degree that some of its supporters would have preferred. Clause 4 of the memorandum in the newly incorporated college specified religious instruction and services "in accordance with the principles of the Church of England as by law established" but did not require attendance from those with conscientious objections (Stephen 263).

54. When, for example, Llewelyn Davies first saw the list of names his sister and her friends had gathered for the petition to open the University of London to women, he said: "'Oh, you'll get it. These men are all advanced Liberals'" (Chronicle 247). Davies's enthusiasm, however, was seldom this naive. Commenting on her brother's optimism, she wrote dryly: "As to a good many of them, it turned out that their Liberality did not include women in its scope" (Chronicle 247).

55. Charlotte Manning died in 1871, and Richardson died in 1872. The loss of these two close friends within eighteen months of one another left Davies emotionally isolated during the years of the decision to resist Sidgwick's overture and to build at Girton.

56. See, for example, Mary Maynard, "Privilege and Patriarchy: Feminist Thought in the Nineteenth Century," in *Sexuality and Subordination: Interdisciplinary Studies of Gender in the Nineteenth Century,* edited by Susan Mendus and Jane Rendell (London, 1989).

Works Cited

Bennett, Daphne. *Emily Davies and the Liberation of Women.* London, 1990.
Blackburn, Helen. *Women's Suffrage.* London, 1902.
Bostick, Theodora. "The Press and the Launching of the Women's Suffrage Movement, 1866–1867." *Victorian Periodicals Review* 13, no. 4 (1980).
Boyd, Nancy. *Three Victorian Women Who Changed Their World.* Oxford, 1982.
Bradbrook, M. C. *'That Infidel Place': A Short History of Girton College 1869–1969.* Cambridge, 1984.
Caine, Barbara. *Victorian Feminists.* Oxford, 1992.
Crawford, Elizabeth. *The Women's Suffrage Movement: A Reference Guide 1866–1928.* London, 1999.
Davies, Emily. *The Higher Education of Women.* 1866. Reprint, London, 1988.
Forster, Margaret. *Significant Sisters: The Grassroots of Active Feminism 1839–1939.* London, 1986.
Herstein, Sheila. *A Mid-Victorian Feminist: Barbara Bodichon.* New Haven, 1985.
Hirsch, Pam. *Barbara Leigh Smith Bodichon: Feminist, Artist, and Rebel.* London, 1998.
Holcombe, Lee. *Victorian Ladies at Work: Middle-Class Working Women in England and Wales 1850–1914.* Newton Abbot, 1973.
Hollis, Patricia. *Ladies Elect: Women in English Local Government 1865–1914.* Oxford, 1987.
Lacey, Candida Ann, ed. *Barbara Leigh Smith Bodichon and the Langham Place Group.* London, 1986.
Leedham-Green, Elisabeth. *A Concise History of the University of Cambridge.* Cambridge, 1996.
Martel, Carol F. "British Women in the National Association for the Promotion of Social Science, 1857–1886." Ph.D. diss., Arizona State University, 1986.
Maynard, Mary. "Privilege and Patriarchy: Feminist Thought in the Nineteenth Century." In *Sexuality and Subordination: Interdisciplinary Studies of Gender in the Nineteenth Century,* edited by Susan Mendus and Jane Rendell. London, 1989.
McCrimmon, Barbara. "Helen Taylor, Suffragist." *Manuscripts* 30, no. 2 (1978).
McDermid, Jane. "Women and Education." In *Women's History: Britain, 1850–1945,* edited by June Purvis. London, 1995.
McWilliams-Tullberg, Rita. *Women at Cambridge: A Men's University—Though of a Mixed Type.* London, 1975.
Purvis, June. *Women's History Britain, 1850–1945.* London, 1995.

Report of an Examination of Girls, held (by Permission of the Syndicate) in Connexion with the Local Examinations of the University of Cambridge in 1863. London, 1864.

Richardson, Anna. *Memoir of Anna Deborah Richardson.* Newcastle-on-Tyne, 1877.

Robson, A.P.W. "The Founding of the National Society for Women's Suffrage 1866–1867." *Canadian Journal of History* 8, no.1 (March 1973).

Rosen, Andrew. "Emily Davies and the Women's Movement." *Journal of British Studies* 19, no. 1 (1979).

Stephen, Barbara. *Emily Davies and Girton College.* London, 1927.

Strachey, Ray. *The Cause: A Short History of the Women's Movement in Great Britain.* London, 1978.

van Wingerden, Sophia A. *The Women's Suffrage Movement in Britain, 1866–1928.* New York, 1999.

Woolf, Virginia. *Three Guineas.* New York, 1966.

Worzala, Diane Mary Chase. "The Langham Place Circle: The Beginning of the Organized Women's Movement in England, 1854–1870." Ph.D. diss., University of Wisconsin-Madison, 1982.

EMILY DAVIES

April 1861

To Anna Richardson

Gateshead Rectory | Tuesday, April 30th ⟨1861⟩

... It is difficult to make out how my father really is, the accounts are so contradictory. He writes of himself in the gloomiest tone, while on the other hand, Mary ⟨Crompton Davies⟩ says *they* could not see anything the matter, & gives reports of what he was able to do &c., which certainly did not look like extreme illness. He has been to two doctors in London, who concur in saying that there is nothing serious in the complaint & in recommending good food, & wine &c. ... I have great hopes that the warm weather, which we may now look forward to, will soon set him to rights.

I have read Silas Marner & am glad to find that we agree so well upon it. I think it is a more healthy & helpful book than the Mill on the Floss, tho' that is perhaps more wonderful as a work of art. In all that Mrs. Lewes writes, she shows the same marvellous power of dividing asunder, to the joints & marrow. I am afraid you will not understand this. I don't know how to express the merciless, yet merciful, way in which she cuts thro' plausible self-delusions. It *reminds* me of Thackeray, but he only exposes superficial meannesses, while she cuts deep down, & more than any writer I know, makes one thoroughly ashamed of oneself ... I have "considered" about taking you off the Committee,[1] & certainly will not do it. ...

I am rather sanguine about the examinations.[2] There are Local Boards in connection with both the Church Institute & the Mechanics' Institute,[3] & there seems to be no obstacle at all to the admission of women. They cannot go in *this* year, as the examination is going on this week, but I hope we may have six or eight candidates ready for the next. We shall be obliged to work it privately. It does not properly belong to the *Society* ⟨for Promoting the Employment of Women⟩ work, & it is questionable whether our Committee would even approve of it. I don't think they half believe in their own work. ...

There are a good many things that I should like to consult you about, if you would leave conscience out of the question for a little while. I fancy lay people see things from a point of view other than the clerical, & might give good advice if they would. The Garretts have bestowed a great deal of admonition upon me, mingled with wholesale abuse of the clerical order, which does not hurt my feelings at all, but when it comes to a definite question of what ought to be done, they pull up.[4] I rather suspect that you would be inclined to take the more clerical side of the question, your sympathies being in the High Church direction.[5]

E. D.

GC: AMsS C211

1. The Committee of the Society for Promoting the Employment of Women (SPEW).
2. Probably the examinations of the Society of Arts, for which the Society for Promoting the Employment of Women (SPEW) was preparing women in its bookkeeping class.
3. Mechanics' Institutes developed around the beginning of the nineteenth century. They were organized by Utilitarians, radicals and Unitarians, first in Edinburgh and later in the cities of the industrial North and in London. They grew out of the same reform movement that led to Chartism and were intended to teach science to artisans and mechanics of the working class. By 1851, there were over seven hundred such institutes in England, Scotland, and Ireland, with over 120,000 members.
4. Elizabeth Garrett's family, with whom Davies probably first became acquainted in 1854 through Jane Crow.
5. Anna Richardson was a Quaker and interested in spiritual issues. In 1866, she was baptized into the Church of England and came to believe in many of the forms and rituals of that church, although she maintained her membership in the Society of Friends. See J. W. Richardson *Memoir of Anna Deborah Richardson* (Newcastle-on-Tyne, 1877), 200.

To Barbara Bodichon

17. Cunningham Place | St. Johns Wood, N.W. | [1862]

Dear Mme. Bodichon

Lizzie Garrett has asked me to write to you about a matter in which I am sure you will be interested. We are going to try to get the London University open to women. Lizzie is advised that she had better make sure of getting admitted to the M.D. examination, before making any more attempts upon Medical Schools.[1] The Medical people make it an excuse for refusing her, that it would be of no use to admit her, as she would have no chance of being examined for an M.D. degree. Probably it is only an excuse, but it would be as well to take it out of their mouths, & the object is besides quite worth struggling for in itself. We intend to try the question entirely on general grounds, carefully keeping Medical schemes in the background, so as to avoid if possible, rousing the hostility of the doctors. There are a good many of them on the Senate & they seem to be the only people likely to resist the application. I will send you by Book-post some lists of the Senate, & a paper we are having printed, telling people in a few words, what we want.[2] Will you write to everybody you know, & get them to use their influence, either personally or thro' the press. It is important to get up some manifestation of public opinion, if possible, as the question will come before the general body of Graduates. They have a right to discuss & make recommendations, tho' the ultimate decision rests with the Senate. Lizzie will apply for admission to the Matriculation examination in a few days, & will be refused, on precedent. We shall then get up a Memorial, & signed by a *small* number of influential people, both men & ladies.[3] If the Senate are inclined to meet our views, the legal difficulties can very easily be got over, as they are just getting a new Charter, & it would be very easy to insert a clause, expressly providing for the admission of women. As soon as the Memorial is in course of signature, we can announce it in the papers, & that will be an occasion for them to take up the subject. There seems a very good prospect of success. My brother, who is generally discouraging, thinks we can scarcely fail.[4] He will bring a good deal of the ⟨Frederick⟩ Maurice interest to bear.

Adelaide Procter is at work, & the Drewrys will do all they can in their circle,[5] & I am going to stir up my Quaker friends. Don't you think it is a point worth making a good fight for? We are quite settled now, & I hope soon to get into some work. I should like to do something great, but am afraid home claims & want of nervous strength will keep me to an insignificant part. I am glad you are coming to England earlier this year. Yours affectionately

E. D.

GC: ALS ED B301

1. On 10 August 1861, Garrett wrote to ED describing a visit to Dr. Chapman, who advised her "to exhaust the question of the possibility of being examined anywhere in the United Kingdom before making any more attempts to enter a school" (Chronicle 226).

2. "Reasons for the Admission of Women to University Examinations," 1862.

3. The memorial requested that the Senate of the University of London "give the widest interpretation to the word of the Charter and . . . 'hold forth to all classes and denominations' of her Majesty's subjects, not excluding women, 'an encouragement for pursuing a regular and liberal course of education'" (Memorial to the University of London, 1862, GC ED3/24).

4. Davies noted that "after looking over the list, Ll.D. said 'Oh, you'll get it. These men are all advanced Liberals.' As to a good many of them, it turned out that their Liberality did not include women in its scope" (Chronicle 247).

5. Ellen and Louisa Drewry.

To Anna Richardson

17 Cunningham Place. N.W. | Saturday. July 12th 1862.

My dear Anna

I have several things to say to you, but first I must congratulate you on Lizzie's engagement, of which I heard from Jeanie.[1] I had thought of it as a likely & pleasant thing to happen, & I think you must all be pleased.

I liked Mr. Watson very much, so far as one could on so slight an acquaintance. Will you give Lizzie my love & hearty congratulations.

I have had a letter & papers from Mr. Furnivall, & I am fairly embarked in the work.[2] The amount of mechanical labour I see before me, is something stupendous, but I enjoy the kind of work. Are you inclined to give any help or advice in the matter of the Middle-Class, or as they are now called, *Local*

Examinations of the Universities?[3] We are going to make a try for them, & it has occurred to me that a Memorial from ladies actually engaged in tuition, would have considerable weight. If you think this a good plan, will you give me the names of any Heads of Schools, or governesses, whom you think likely to be interested. I have been looking at the subjects for Examination, & they seem to me as suitable for girls as for boys, & that the Examination would be worth having, tho' I do not care so *very* much for them in themselves, because I think the encouragement to learning is most wanted *after* the age of eighteen. It seems likely however that if we could get these Examinations, it would be a great lift towards getting the University of London. We are told that the real feeling of the opposition in the Senate, was the fear of lowering the dignity of the University, & that they would be very much influenced by any forward step on the part of the old Universities.

This agitation is hateful work, but it becomes clearer every day that incessant & unremitting talking & pushing is the *only* way of gaining our ends. I stop sometimes & ask whether the ends are worth such horridly disagreeable means, & if one had only a personal interest in the matter, I am sure it would be impossible to persevere. But we are fighting for people who cannot fight for themselves & as I believe, directly working towards preserving women from becoming masculine, in a bad sense.

I was very glad to see your cousins & that they should have such a pleasant time in London. When are you coming?

Do write & tell me what you are about.

Yours affectionately

S. E. Davies.

GC: ALS ED LOC-7

1. Anna Richardson's younger sister, Elizabeth, married Robert Watson. Jeanie was a cousin of Richardson who had been visiting London.

2. Probably Frederick James Furnivall (1825–1910), a founder of the Working Men's College who was associated with the University of London.

3. ED had been advised by William Shaen of the University of London that they should "try to get something from the old Universities.... & the Local Examinations, as involving nothing in the way of residence, seemed to meet the case" (Chronicle 263). In October 1862, a committee to obtain the admission of girls to the University Examinations was formed, including Bodichon, Bostock, Craig, Gurney, Hastings, Heywood, Goldsmid, and ED.

November 1862 5

To ⟨George Liveing⟩

17 Cunningham Place. N.W. | Nov. 11th 1862

Dear Sir

I am much obliged to you for your two letters & the papers relating to the University Local Examinations. We shall be very glad of any information you can give us as to the feeling of resident members of the University on the subject.

Our original plan was to send in a Memorial from persons actually engaged in the education of girls, accompanied by a list of influential supporters. It was suggested however that the Universities would be unwilling to appear to force an innovation upon the Local Committees, & that the application would come better from them.

I was therefore instructed to write to the Local Secretaries to ascertain as far as possible, the general feeling. The answers received are almost uniformly favourable.[1] They will be laid before our Committee at an early date, & some further steps will then be discussed.

I quite agree with you as to the practical difficulty in the way of sending up girls for examinations to centres some 30 or 40 miles from their homes. This does not however I think, much affect the general question. All we ask for is, that girls whose parents may think it worth while to incur the expense, should not be arbitrarily shut out from the examinations, merely on the ground of sex. Questions of detail might be open to consideration, but we are most anxious to make it understood that we do not wish to involve the Universities in extra trouble or expense. If there must be extra expense, it ought clearly to fall upon the parents, or teachers of the girls. I do not see however, why it might not be possible to make a girls' school a centre of examination, in case of necessity, if the schoolmistress agreed to abide by the rules & regulations for the year. If we can also obtain the inspection of schools, it will be an additional boon of very great value.

Thank you for mentioning your correspondence with Miss ⟨Anna⟩ Richardson of Newcastle.

I remain, dear Sir
Yours very sincerely
S. E. Davies

GC: ALS ED LOC-16

1. Griffiths wrote to ED "that the University would think the examination of young ladies a matter altogether beyond its sphere of duty" (Chronicle 266). Liveing offered to convey her communications to the university syndicate but expressed his doubt "whether the powers of the Syndicate extend so far as to make the necessary alterations without the con-

sent of the Senate." In a subsequent letter, he recommended they send a memorial to the Syndicate, adding that he was "not at all sanguine that they will like to undertake anything more than they have on hand already" (Chronicle 267–68).

To [Henry Tomkinson]

17 Cunningham Place. | Nov. 26th ⟨1862⟩

Dear Sir

I am so much obliged to you for your kind suggestions, which I have endeavoured to follow in altering the circular.[1] In its present form I hope it will answer its purpose better. I have not ventured to introduce what you say about the want of "character" in middle-class women, for I fancy some of your Committee would be more afraid of their having too much character than too little.

It may strike some people perhaps, that as we have got the Society of Arts examinations, we ought not to want anything more.[2] But they are intended for grown-up people of the artisan class, & do not answer the purpose of a standard in general education for teachers to work up to.

Perhaps if you have no objection, you would mention in your note, that you see no practical difficulty in conducting a mixed Examination. I send only 25 circulars, as we know my brother's opinion already. You may perhaps like to know the names of our Committee, of which I append a list.

I am, dear Sir
Yours sincerely
S. E. Davies.
T. O.
Committee.
Mrs. Bodichon   Russell Gurney, Esq.
Miss Bostock   G. W. Hastings, Esq.
Miss Isa Craig.   James Heywood, Esq.
Treasurer, Lady Goldsmid.

GC: ALS ED LOC-17

1. Henry Tomkinson was the London secretary of the Cambridge Local Examinations Committee. He had offered "to write individually to the members of his Committee . . . enclosing a circular giving information on the subject" (Chronicle 272). He was to become a stalwart supporter of efforts to open higher education to women.

2. The Society of Arts first began its examinations in 1856, covering a wide range of academic and vocational subjects. In 1858, the society opened the examinations to women. By 1862, twenty-two women candidates had been examined in eleven centers.

December 1862 7

To Barbara Bodichon

17 Cunningham Place, N.W. | Dec. 3d [1862]

Dear Mrs. Bodichon

I have had a letter to you on my mind for some time, but since I came home, I have had more to do than I have known how to get thro'. I suppose when I get *even* with my work I shall be able to manage it. It is the mass of arrears which almost overwhelms me at present. On the whole things are going on as well as one could expect. The number of subscribers to the ⟨English Woman's⟩ Journal is the same this month as last. I suppose some will go off at the end of the year. Kent has had an extra five & twenty, but till his account comes in, we don't know whether he has sold them.[1] Bessie ⟨Parkes⟩ has given up the working-printer scheme, & I am glad of it. Miss ⟨Sarah⟩ Lewin set her face against it steadily, & Isa ⟨Craig⟩ does not think it would have answered. It seems very doubtful whether the printer would have done it at the price *permanently*, & it would have been a great anxiety to me to have to look after him, knowing so little as I do about the matter. Bessie told me she did not feel up to managing the printing on the spot, when the Journal began, & if she did not then, certainly I don't now. I think Miss ⟨Emily⟩ Faithfull must be doing the work cheaply. Bessie says she took it to Adell & Ives, because Clowes was too dear, & Miss Faithfull's bills (as I find by a statement Miss Lewin has made out) are *considerably* less than Adell & Ives. You must have misunderstood what I said about her setting up another Magazine. What I meant was, that if we took away so much regular work, she would be driven, in self-defense to make it up in some other way, & as she has had overtures sometimes about starting Magazines, it would be not unlikely that she would choose *that* way. And if we considered only the Journal interests, I don't see exactly how we could blame her for considering *her* interests. However, I hope there will now be no further trouble. I don't think Bessie & Miss Faithfull will ever be friends again, but I hope they may be preserved from quarrelling.

I don't know whether you have heard from Bessie. She is in Ireland now. I will do what I can to persuade her to go to Algiers when she comes back. I find Miss ⟨A. E.⟩ Gimingham a very nice, straightforward person, & very ready to help. She has talked to me a great deal about the Journal. She thinks Miss ⟨Matilda⟩ Hays's connection with it did a great deal of harm to it, & I hear the same thing from people moving in the most widely different circles.[2] I don't think Bessie can be at all aware of the amount of mischief that was done. It will take a long time to outgrow it. I think too the Co-Editorship worked badly. Miss Gimingham says she sent in a paper of which she *heard nothing* for a year & a half, & she thinks that sort of thing discouraged people from sending good papers. Miss Smith (daughter of the Dictionaries) also sent a paper, of which she heard nothing, till after writing for it three times, she at last got it returned.³ These little disorders can of course be easily remedied, & I hope *some* good may be done by more careful & courteous management in little things, but I don't suppose it will make *much* difference. I get quite frightened sometimes, at the difficulty of carrying it on without money. Miss Lewin represents the receipts as £612., & the current expenses, £550, leaving £5 a month for contributors. Where Miss Hays's salary came from, does not appear. You see, there are 72 pages to provide for. Allowing 12 for Open Council & Passing Events,⁴ we have 50 left, which at 10/. a page (less than half what is paid by Macmillan & Good Words) costs £25 a month. I am offering some of the second-rate contributors three guineas a sheet (about 4/. a page) & that saves a little, but at the best I must provide from 30 to 40 pages monthly, gratuitously, & I don't find people at *all* willing to write for nothing. It is in fact tantamount to asking them to give so much money (if they could get it from other Magazines) & some of them have not much to spare. Isa has not been able to do anything as yet, & she is always so busy that one must not expect much from her. You must not think I am despairing. I don't think it follows that the Journal will *never* get on, if it does not prosper much this year. It has a great deal to out grow, & all help & sympathy are so powerfully attracted just now, in the direction of Lancashire, that other things must suffer.⁵ Miss Lewin says many people in that District have left off taking in the Journal. My brother says Propagandist things never pay. Macmillan is an instance in point.⁶ It has been made to pay, by diverting it from its original purpose, & making it instead, a Magazine to amuse & please the public. I don't know that this signifies, if we are all agreed that we are not working for money, but to spread our ideas. But it is as well to understand clearly what our object is, to save disappointment. Of course each individual must judge, whether the work is worth spending money & time & strength upon. I agree with you in not thinking the Nov. number good.⁷ ⟨I⟩ don't think much of December either. Caroline Pichler & the Campagna are both old stores. I am sorry to say some accepted MSS. of Miss ⟨Elizabeth⟩ Eiloart's, which look dreadful, are still on hand. The review of Rose & her mission was sent by Bessie's friend, Mr. Roscoe.⁸ It is very flat, I think. Do you like the Status of Jewish Women?⁹ That is the only thing I care for in this month, except Passing Events, which I think is this time, really interesting.¹⁰

Miss Dictionary Smith has made an abstract of Mrs. Mill's essay, which I am keeping for the present.¹¹ I don't like to come out with such a startling manifesto, till the Journal has a little recovered from the reputation Miss Hays has given it. It is very unfortunate that in spite of Bessie's extreme care to avoid everything startling in the *matter* of the Journal, by which it was made less interesting & genuinely respectable than it might have been, it has got the credit of Bloomerism &c. *for nothing*, so to speak. I dare say this applies principally to

London readers. I don't fancy people in the country know much about Miss Hays.

Mrs. ⟨Frances⟩ Notley sent a Christmas story, which I was obliged to return. It was too long, & had all the faults of Nabonassar in a much greater degree.[12] She is going to send another tale soon, which I hope may be better. She is very teachable in *spirit*, but I am very much afraid she is too old to improve much.

I have called on Miss Allen, & we hope to see her & Miss Sewall for an evening soon.[13] Miss Sewall has been very kindly received, & has got almost everything she wants, without any help from me. I like her, decidedly. She does not boast at all, & she seems inclined to go on very quietly & carefully. She has not the charm of an English *lady*, but it seems to me only absence of polish, not anything like vulgarity. Lizzie is staying on at St. Andrew's for the winter. She has a most valuable friend & teacher in Dr. ⟨George⟩ Day, the head of the Medical School there. He gives her private Anatomical lectures (which will count at Apothecaries' Hall) & a great deal of help in other ways. She has given up the idea of trying any more for the M.D. She can do excellent work as Licentiate of Apothecaries' Hall, & the next good fighting-woman we have, must go in & win, for the M.D.

Isa is in good spirits about the Lancashire book.[14] She has two beautiful poems by Christina Rossetti & G⟨eorge⟩. Macdonald, & a very fair sonnet by Emily Taylor. The paper & type &c. & the shape of the book are decided upon, & next Saturday we are to have a final hearing of all the poems, to arrange the order in which they should come. Mr Munro has promised two casts for the Exhibition—but I dare say you hear all this in other ways.[15]

I mean to write to you once a month, if possible, to keep you au courant of what is going on at Langham Place, & if you will tell me what you care most to hear, I will shape my letters accordingly. Will you sometimes send one on to Nannie ⟨Leigh Smith⟩? I dare say she will like to hear pretty much the same things, & I have such constant pen & ink work that I sometimes grudge writing the same thing twice over. I wish very much to hear how dear Nannie is, & how she likes Naples. Italy & Algiers must be a bright contrast to London just now, but I never swerve in my love of it. I am very fairly strong, & generally, hopeful.

Dec. 4th. L.P. Now for messages.

Miss Lewin wishes to know whether you want the additional copy of your collected writings from the Journal sent anywhere. She has got the vol. bound, as you wished, & waits for further orders.

I have sent on your letter.

I don't think I should be afraid to insert an anti-South article.[16] If we exist for anything, surely it is to fight against slavery, of Negro as well as other, women.

If you use any very tremendous language, I suppose I may cut it out. Bessie is splendid on the subject of editorial revision. She says the principle of despotism must be adhered to! I have heard from her to-day. From the *tone* of her letter, I gather that she is still far from strong, tho' she does not say anything. Mrs. Parkes has been here this afternoon. The last account of Adelaide is that she is no better.[17] The cough & breathing are still bad, & she is only able to be up for a short time in the day, wrapped in a blanket. Dr. Williams's opinion, as given by Edith to Mrs. Parkes, is that "it will be very slow."[18] I believe he has said something to the effect that it is bronchial, & what I hear sounds more like that than consumption. The appetite is very good. There is such a beautiful poem of Adelaide's in "Good Words" for this month.[19]

I hope you are enjoying Algiers. I dare say now you are there, you like it better than London. Miss ⟨Frances Power⟩ Cobbe is going to Lancashire, to see what she can do to help the girls there. Miss Hays is gone to Malvern, to see Dr. ⟨James⟩ Gully, who is said to be very seriously ill. She was very much cut up about it, quite in tears, Miss Lewin says. I have not seen her once, since we came to London in January.

Will you remember me very kindly to Dr. ⟨Eugene⟩ Bodichon. I suppose his patients are glad to have him back.

Yours affectionately, E. D.

GC: ALS ED B302

1. Probably William Charles Kent (1823–1902), who edited the *Sun* and the *Weekly Register*.
2. Matilda Hays was one of the seven founding shareholders of the *EWJ*. Hays coedited the *Journal* with Bessie Rayner Parkes until 1862, despite serious criticisms of her writing from George Eliot. Her personal life was the subject of controversy, as it entailed passionate friendships with women including Charlotte Cushman and Adelaide Procter. When Hays resigned in 1862, ED took over as editor.
3. Miss Smith was the daughter of William Smith (1814–93), a professor and antiquarian at the University of London whose lifework was the publication of dictionaries in Greek and Roman, biographies, antiquities, geography, and mythology.
4. These were regular features of the *EWJ*. Open Council was "intended for general discussion" and included letters from readers. Passing Events was a review of current events.
5. The American Civil War, especially the Northern blockade of Southern ports, had a profound and traumatic effect on the cotton mills of northern England, and Lancashire was especially hard-hit, facing unemployment and famine in the early 1860s.
6. *Macmillan's* (1859–1907) was one of the first "shilling monthlies." Intended originally to promote the Macmillan Publishing Company's new fiction, it was noted for serious articles on religion and politics and was one of the first Victorian periodicals to publish only signed articles.
7. The November issue contained articles on ideas for occupations for women; a discussion of German writer Caroline Pichler; a poem about St. Dorothea; a continuation of a fictional series, "A Dream of Nabonassar"; an article on infant mortality; the prospectus for the Society for the Professional Instruction of Women; an article (probably by Davies) on the

University Local Exam; and a mention, in Passing Events, of Elizabeth Garrett's passing the Preliminary Examination of the Apothecaries Hall. *EWJ* (1 November 1862), no. 57; and *EWJ* (1 December 1862), no. 58.

    8. Probably Thomas Roscoe (1791–1871), who wrote for local journals; translated literature from Italian, German, and Spanish novelists; and edited a series of English novelists, with illustrations by Cruikshank.

    9. "The Status of Jewish Women in Biblical Times," *EWJ* (December 1862).

    10. The December 1862 edition's Passing Events included a long discussion of the proposed admission of girls to University Local Examinations, with comments by members of NAPSS and a discussion of Garrett's application for permission to matriculate at the University of St. Andrew's.

    11. Probably Harriet Taylor Mill (1807–58), who wrote "The Enfranchisement of Women" for the *Westminster Review* (1851).

    12. Mrs. Frances Thomas (later Notley), "A Dream of Nabonassar," *EWJ* (October 1862).

    13. Probably Ellen Allen, a governess who taught at Bodichon's Portman Hall School in 1855, eventually serving as Chief Mistress. She married in 1863 and left teaching.

    14. Isa Craig, *Poems: An Offering to Lancashire* (London, 1873). Printed and published by Victoria Press for the Art Exhibition for the Relief of Distress in the Cotton Districts.

    15. Probably Alexander Munro (1825–71), sculptor. An "exhibition of works of art, chiefly by amateur artists, for the benefit of the Lancashire operatives" is noted in the *EWJ* (February 1863).

    16. Bodichon kept a diary of her visit to the United States in 1858, excerpts of which were published in the *EWJ* beginning in October and November 1858; and again in March 1860; October, November, and December 1861; and February 1863.

    17. Adelaide Procter was at this point seriously ill of tuberculosis. She died in 1864.

    18. Probably Charles James Blasius Williams, M.D. (1805–89), who helped establish the Consumption Hospital at Brompton; was Physician Extraordinary to Queen Victoria; and wrote on pulmonary illnesses.

    19. Adelaide Procter, "True or False," *Good Words* (December 1862): 721–22.

To Barbara Bodichon

Dec. 28th 1862. | 17 Cunningham Place. N.W.

My dear Mrs. Bodichon

If your paper on America comes in time, I shall be glad to have it for February. Am I to supply the Latin quotation out of my own head?[1] I don't see my way to that. I will correct the mistake about Mme. Luce's school in Answers to Correspondents.[2] There is a man called William Fleming Stevenson, who has written, I think, in Good Words, about the Rauhehaus. I dare say he could & would get the information about the girls' department if we offered to pay for it, but I don't like his style of writing at all.

I was very glad indeed to hear of Nannie & Isabella ⟨Blythe⟩. Tho' the accounts are not so good as one could *wish*, they are at least as good as we could expect, & it is a great thing that they like & can enjoy Palermo.

I wonder why Bessie does not write to you. Mrs. Parkes came into the office one day, & I think she said Bessie had not heard from you, & she supposed each was waiting for the other to write. About Algiers, she said she & Mr. Parkes would be very much afraid for Bessie to go alone, in case of her being ill on the way, & that Bessie herself said she was little inclined for such a long journey. She spoke quite with dread, of the journey from Liverpool to Willingham. She went from Ireland to Willingham, where Miss ⟨Jessie⟩ Boucherett says she won all hearts, "she was so good & kind," & from thence to "Aunt Julia ⟨Smith⟩." She talks of going back to Liverpool in a few days, & then I suppose she will come home. I don't know what she will do next. She seems very weak still, tho' she says she is well enough when she does not attempt to do anything. I don't think she gathers strength so quickly as might have been hoped. She may have been worrying herself about Adelaide's illness. I have not heard of her very lately. No doubt I *should* have heard, if there had been any decided change. Lady ⟨Theodora⟩ Monson has not yet appeared at Langham Place. Miss Lewin thinks she may come any day now. Miss Hays has entirely left, & taken away all her things.

Where is your Cherchelle article to be found?[3] Miss Lewin & Bessie deny all knowledge of it, & I have never seen it since I gave it up to you at Scalands.

A Newcastle friend of mine[4] wishes to know, if it is not a liberty to ask, who taught you water-colours, & how i.e. in what manner, you first began to sell your pictures.

Have you heard of poor Isa's trouble? Her grandmother, who had been her both father & mother, died at Edinburgh a week ago. Isa feels very much not having been able to get there in time to see her alive. I suppose the illness must have been very short. She was very old, past 80, & had never been ill before. I fancy Isa inherited a good deal from her. She was a very lively old lady, full of interest in everything. Isa herself was quite knocked up with overwork before she started. She was looking forward to coming back quite strong & well, after a few weeks rest, & she is so buoyant that I dare say she will soon be herself again, tho' her holiday will be saddened by this trouble.

Jane Crow has been better than usual lately. She is able to keep more steadily to her work than any one would have supposed possible, a few years ago. Emily Faithfull has revived in a most wonderful way, & has lately been able to take a share of sitting up all night at the Press. They have been excessively driven, with the Lancashire book, & other Christmas work, all coming on at once.

I wonder how you will like the Jan. Journal.[5] Lizzie finds it more interesting than the last. The review of Ragged Life in Egypt was written by Miss Gimingham, the other by a young man named Roscoe, a friend of Bessie's.[6] The Canter across the Campagana was by a Mrs. Montague Blackett, a friend of Miss Cobbe's, who spent last winter at Rome; the Coffee-party by Miss ⟨Sophia?⟩

Jex-Blake.[7] She is willing to contribute gratuitously any number of little sketches of that sort.

It would be very difficult to point out any definite conversion effected by the instrumentality of the Journal alone. I have never heard of any. If the Hairdressers' shop comes to anything, it may be remotely traced to Bessie's paper on Cooperation.[8] *Her* scheme would not work, as we found directly we began to try it at Newcastle,[9] but it put the idea into my head. As to Lancashire, I asked Bessie to write upon it, & she could not think of anything to say. I really don't see what there is to be said, beyond what is being said over & over again every day, in the papers. The article in Macmillan contained nothing but what was known before,[10] & there seems to be nothing done specially for the women, except the sewing schools, which have already been noticed in Open Council.[11] I have put a heading to your letter on ~~Fechter,~~ Hamlet, but it looked so horribly incongruous, I thought I had better let the tail alone.[12] It was to have appeared this month, but there was not room. Don't you think the letters would look better without Ladies or Madam at the top & the I am &c. at the bottom? In the Athenaeum they are inserted without anything of that kind, & I like it better.

I have so much to say to you about the EWJ that I quite tremble to begin. Your remark that we ought to have a serious consultation in 1863, as to whether it should go on or not, made me set to work to think more about it, & also to gather opinions. It is important to *me* to have the matter settled one way or the other soon, for you will understand how difficult it is to carry a thing on with spirit, under the impression that it may be decided any day to stop it altogether.

The people I have consulted are Isa, the Drewrys, Lizzie, Miss Gimingham, & two or three friends whom you don't know. I meant to have asked Isa to write to you herself, but of course I cannot trouble her now. The conclusion she comes to was, that the EWJ ought to have a fair trial for another year. that it could not possibly be carried on at all tolerably, with only £5 a month (or less) for contributors. & that the persons interested in it should be asked to come forward with a sufficient amount of capital to give it a *fair* chance, on the understanding that if in a year it did not seem to be getting on decidedly better, it should stop. She thought it ought not to drag on a miserable existence, as hitherto, but if it is proved that it cannot live, let it die right out.

Lizzie says "I will give you my opinion as you ask for it, but I hope you won't take it for more than it is worth. I feel extremely incapable of judging how far such an organ will really advance the principles we contend for, however good it may be, but I should think the experience of past reforms & how they have been gradually won by drumming facts & arguments (which must have seemed superfluous enough to the drummers) upon the public ear, may be taken as ᵗᵒˡᵉʳᵃᵇˡʸ conclusive that a well-worked organ *does* promote the advance of reforms in time. For my own part, I should be very sorry now to see the EWJ die, tho' I very rarely care much for anything in it. I like to know that anything of interest upon the question will appear there whenever it may turn up.... Perhaps it would be agreeable to Mrs. Bodichon to know that I believe some notice of Miss ⟨Elizabeth⟩ Blackwell[13] in the EWJ was the first thing which directed my mind towards medicine. Of course something else might have done so, as I was casting about for something to do, but I fancy girls are often just in the frame I was then: wishing to do something about everything in the world, but very much afraid that anything which would take me from home must be a temptation from beneath. I think most likely this longing for definite employment would have soon gone off, & that it does go off in other people, who end by driving away at schools & poor people.... I have wandered off from the EWJ, having only arrived at the conclusion that, in my opinion, it ought not to die. Now for its manner of life. I should most heartily approve of your bold policy, (that is, spending a *lot* of money on really good articles & a first-rate story, & advertising. E. D.) if I felt a little more clear that the EWJ has only to be good to increase the circulation sufficiently to make it pay. I have no doubt that *some* increase to the subscribers would follow, but I am greatly afraid it would not be a very large one.

I should fancy most of the people actively interested in the principle, are taking it in now, as I was, not so much for its own sake, as for the principle. If it gets decidedly better, every one will rejoice, & will at least lend it about & recommend it more heartily, so that perhaps in this way new people will be brought in thro' it. But as long as it is decidedly special in character, I fancy we must not look for a very large circulation. A good tale would take off its 'special' character, so perhaps it would be as well to compromise on this ground, by giving a novel to attract the public, & the solid matter of the mag. to be kept in some degree special. If you do go in for good articles at a high price, I think you should advertise the contents of each month much more than you do now. It is a good thing to accustom people's eyes to the fact that well known writers are contributing & also to remind them of your existence as an organ of special information. I would much rather vote for money to be spent in advertising than in getting a better cover. The financial questions are the hardest of all. I wish I could help at all in the money way, but I feel I am spending as much already as I have any right to do; a good deal more in fact, than the interest of the money I should have had, had I married. If you ever think I could do anything for you in the way of minor reviews, of course, I shall be only very glad to give you the best I can. I think surely all minor things might be unpaid, might they not? It would come to be an honour to be allowed to contribute to so dignified a Journal! Certainly six months' trial on a really good footing ought to bring forth some result in increased subscribers, & even if the outlay was not at once covered by the additions, they might be numerous enough to encourage you to go on. I think the division of matter would do very well. (i.e. 20 pages really good substantial matter on the special subject, in *one* article. 20 pages story. 10p. little things giving information on employments, &c &c. 12 pp. reviews. 10 Open Council & Passing Events. I don't mean that this division should be strictly adhered to, but taken as a general guide.) only I still hanker after a still smaller number of divisions. I am disposed to expect more from popular judgment than perhaps you & Isa are. (Isa said that if we put in only such things as Lizzie & I & two or three other people would like, the great mass of women, would never look at it, & we *must* have little things to lead people on to read the others.) I fancy it is safer to expect appreciation & good taste than not to do so. I am assuming now that to appreciate my plan of articles, few & ponderous, is a mark of good taste!

... I have kept this in case further consideration might bring me some new light or opinion about the EWJ. I feel only clear that it might be of considerable use, if it could be really good, but I am not at all sure that it will ever pay, so long as it is decidedly special. I think this is the result of all my cogitations."

I will now transcribe what Ellen Drewry says. "I have really endeavoured to consider the EWJ. case from the various points of view it admits of & I am more & more forced to the conclusion that the existence of the Journal is not at present either profitable or desirable, & not very likely ever to become so. There are two general ways of looking at the question. 1st. as profitable in a money point of view. 2d. as desirable in an intellectual point of view. As for the first, I gather from what you have already told me that the Journal is by no means profitable, & that any attempt to make it so would involve a considerable outlay of money, even then with uncertain results, because in any case it would have to compete with an immense number of serial publications, all first in the field, comparatively well established, & from whatever causes, rich enough to absorb for themselves the best of the talent which can be attracted to such work, talent often no doubt of the first order, but for that very reason, demanding high remuneration. The 2d. point of view is certainly in many respects the most important, but even there it seems that a preliminary question should be, whether the Journal can be made self-supporting; I do not think it can justify its existence under any other conditions. Considered with regard to its intellectual & literary merits, though it might under efficient management be much improved, it can never hope to supply anything which is not quite as well or better supplied in other ways. Suppose now, that it could be brought in quantity & quality, up to the mark of Fraser say, or Macmillan (& this is almost more than could be hoped for it) what would be gained? Nothing but an addition to an already over-stocked class of literature ... The only real ground which I can see for urging the continuance of the Journal (even in a greatly modified form) is, the scope which it would afford for the discussion of our especial social question, which it is supposed would not otherwise be sufficiently brought into public view; now this seems to me an altogether questionable advantage. I should be inclined to say, rather than afford scope for talk about women, we ought, where possible, put a check upon it. There is really nothing more to be said about it at present, & we only waste in talk the energy that should be spent in *doing*. Emily Faithfull with her Printing-press does more good than ᵃˡˡ the thousand & one things that are written & said on the subject; rather perhaps, does as much good as they do harm. Even when a great minded man like ⟨John Stuart⟩ Mill takes up the subject, it is not so much the masterly treatment that is useful, as the moral support that the question gains from such a name. As for any statistics or facts of real interest or value, surely they would always find their way to the public thro' other channels, even such as the best daily papers, & would carry infinitely more weight in public estimation in that case than when forced into notice in a publication the function of which is avowedly to collect in monotonous & wearisome profusion, all possible details, arguments, theories, speculations, concerning women & their wants. Vexatious as it seems that an enterprise which has dragged on a tedious & insipid existence for so long, should die as it were on the very eve of a promised improvement, I can conscientiously see no sufficient basis for a Journal, even could it realise one's best hopes & wishes, which however appears in the highest degree improbable."

Miss Gimingham says "Always bearing in mind the ideal to which we hope to see the Journal exalted, I do confess to viewing with deep regret its abandonment. What is there to take its place? And might it not, if properly conducted, supply that want which those who think & feel like us, have long wished for. No Journal now established will accept opinions & utter them as its own. Suppose an occasional paper appeared in some periodical, what good would it do, beyond directing attention to the subject for a moment? If all the trash now published under petticoat patronage (real or supposed) finds a market, it seems to me only reasonable that something of real & vital importance should command a respectable circulation. Social questions command attention, & it seems to me that *old-fashioned* folks would take in the Journal if they could identify it with some steady-going moderate party—say with a clergyman's daughter as Editor. Perhaps a good tale might float it. Papers upon art might be introduced. The correspondence carried on with spirit,—& a nucleus once formed, a thousand different channels would open & extend the circulation. But it must have a *business* & not a *charity* foundation. By this I mean, people must subscribe for it to please themselves, not for friendship; & the trade must be got to promote its circulation. Please take these suggestions for what they are worth, & no more."

Miss Gimingham has no money (only an allowance from her mother) but she is willing to do anything she can in the way of writing, & her practical hints are by no means to be despised. She has begun a set of papers on the status, manner of life &c. of women in England from the earliest times, the first of which, on the Britons, she has just finished.[14] She does not know how to write, but I think she will learn, & the subject matter is very interesting, to me at least. She has taken no end of trouble in hunting up the materials.

Two or three friends to whom I have written have not yet answered. One, an unliterary woman, assures me that people do want to know what is being done for & by women, & that the information they want can be got nowhere but in the Journal. Miss Lewin says it is read by people of her class, & that the things they care to hear about are employment & education. I have not written to Miss Jex-Blake, but I know she thinks the Journal *might* do very good work, & she means to do something (tho' I don't suppose it can be much) in the way of money. The Dictionary Smiths also think it quite worth while to have a Journal, if it can be made good. Probably what people say to *me* now, ought to be received with a grain of allowance, as they naturally think I should not like to be advised to drop it. I find they already begin to apologise for speaking their minds freely. It will be a great bore if they take to withholding the truth, under the impression that I cannot bear to hear it.

On the whole, I am in favour of keeping up the Journal, & of making an effort to put it on a decidedly better basis. I shall very willingly advance £200 towards it, as soon as matters are settled. I am afraid I cannot do more at present, tho' I feel that as Editor, I am *the* person who ought to take the risk. I don't think the Journal will pay in the trade sense. In that sense, to pay, means—to pay all the contributors, including an Editorial salary of say £150 a year, & a good per centage on the capital invested. We should be satisfied with paying in a much smaller sense than this. I cannot think of any other ^better^ way in which I could spend time & money & thought than this. Founding scholarship always seems to me a very good thing, but it is a very indirect way of helping on the general cause. Going into medicine is perhaps the most absolutely effective thing to do, but all are not doctors, any more than prophets, & I cannot help thinking that to work upon the public mind is a very important thing. An inspiring thought, once printed, may kindle somewhere & produce greater results than twenty printing presses. I think one must always expect that the work of the Journal will be unrecognised. To my mind, a great part of it consists in creating an atmosphere. I am quite sure that to young girls wondering, like Lizzie, whether their aspirations are temptations from beneath, must be exceedingly helped & sustained by finding that good & respectable people approve of them. Even if those girls have not strength to carry them out themselves, they will be more ready to support others with their sympathy. I know some now, who tho' by no means equal to the task of conquering their own rights, stand up for women generally, in conversation. And that is something.

I am told on all sides that if the Journal is to make its way & be extensively circulated, it *must* have a good story. With Bessie's concurrence, I have (thro' Jane) asked Miss ⟨Anne⟩ Thackeray to call at Langham Place. I shall ask her on what terms she would write a tale for us, & then we can judge whether we can afford it. Her "Story of Elizabeth" has excited very great & general interest.[15] I find the idea of getting her, if we can, approved by everybody that I have mentioned it to. I think it would be a great thing to get a *fresh* writer, not a half worn out hack.

My mother is very strong in favour of more advertising. She finds the people she talks to, have never heard of its existence. I think we ought to have a few more good names before we begin. I have been very well & strong lately. The Journal does not overdo me. It is very sufficient work, but not too much, & I enjoy it. But there are two things, I feel that I cannot do. I cannot put in things that I hate, & that I know will bring us all into contempt, & I cannot beg. In the meantime the hoard of MSS. is rapidly wearing away; a great deal of it, I am glad to get rid of, but at the same time, I am haunted with the fear of a dreadful deficit. My brother is going to contribute something, probably for next month.[16] You will be aghast at the length of this letter. It looks as if I had plenty of time on my hands. It is all along of your living in Africa when you are wanted in London. Please give my love to Nannie & Isabella. I am so glad to hear of them. My mother unites in cordial good wishes for the New Year.

Yours affectionately ED.

GC: ALS ED B303

1. Barbara Bodichon, "Of Those Who Are the Property of Others, and of the Great Power That Holds Others as Property," *EWJ* (February 1863). The article does not contain any Latin quotations.

2. Mme. Luce lived in Algiers and started a school for Algerian girls in 1845. The May, June, and July 1861 *EWJ* contained a description of her work.

3. Barbara Bodichon, "Six Weeks in La Chere Petite Bretagne," *EWJ* (May 1863).

4. Probably Anna Richardson.

5. This issue included a feature article on the Society of Arts Examinations; fiction by Caroline Oxenden; a poem by Isa Craig; an article by Annie Carey on schools of art for women; a discussion of "Work and Wages of Women in France"; and a letter, in French, from Elizabeth Garret; as well as an article describing two art exhibitions; a review of German literature; notices of books; and discussion in Passing Events on the Edinburgh Society for the Employment of Women.

6. *Ragged Life in Egypt*, by M. L. Whately, was reviewed by Gimingham in *EWJ* (December 1862). In the same edition appeared a review of *Rose and her Mission: A Tale of the West Indies*, by Mrs. Henry Lynch. Neither reviewer was identified.

7. "A Canter Over the Campagna" (unsigned); and "A German Coffee-Party in 1862" (unsigned) *EWJ* (December 1862).

8. SPEW had formed a class to train women hairdressers.

9. ED had helped open a branch of SPEW at Newcastle before she moved to London.

SPEW branches also opened in Aberdeen, Brighton, Dublin, Edinburgh, Leicester, Manchester, and Nottingham.

10. "The Distress in Lancashire and Present Modes of Relief," *Macmillan's*, no. 38 (December 1862): 153–60 (unsigned).

11. Sewing schools were being established with private funding to provide employment for "factory girls" who were unemployed due to the dislocations resulting from the American Civil War and the blockade of cotton.

12. Mrs. F. P. Fellows, "Notes on M. Fechter's Hamlet and Othello," *EWJ* (December 1862). An article signed "B" appeared in the February 1863 issue, disagreeing with Fellows's interpretation of the production.

13. Garrett had decided to pursue a career in medicine after hearing Elizabeth Blackwell, M.D., lecture in London.

14. A.E.G., "The Manner of Life of Women in England, from the Earliest Historical Period," *EWJ* (March and May 1863).

15. Anne Thackeray, *The Story of Elizabeth* (Leipzig, 1863).

16. Llewelyn Davies, "Christian Liberty and its Counterfeit" *EWJ* (February 1863).

To [Henry Tomkinson]

PROPOSED ADMISSION OF GIRLS TO UNIVERSITY LOCAL EXAMINATIONS.
17, CUNNINGHAM PLACE, LONDON, N.W.

Dec. 31st 1862.

Dear Sir

I certainly think the question of examining boys & girls in the same room, may be regarded as a matter of detail to be left to the direction of the Local Committee, either in conjunction with a Committee of ladies, or otherwise. I should have thought it might be very easily ˢᵉᵗᵗˡᵉᵈ by some such arrangement as that adopted at Bedford College, of requiring the presence of a Lady Visitor.[1]

But so long as the examination itself is the same, it is not at all essential that the candidates should be examined in the same room.

As to the publication of the names in the same class lists, I am not so clear, but if anybody thinks any possible advantage would be gained by separating the names, I should myself be inclined to give up the point.[2] In the Society of Arts it does not seem to have been found necessary to make any special arrangements, & I should think the experience of four years & twelve different localities, might be taken as a fair test. Tho' limited, it is more extensive than that of the University examinations would probably be for a good many years. The number of candidates would most likely be very small at first; quite insufficient seriously to affect the character of the examinations, either in the way of increasing the work, or lessening the value of the certificates in public estimation. I wish this was more generally understood, for I fancy the authorities are afraid that if the floodgates were opened, a great concourse of girls would rush in & overwhelm them.

Nothing of the kind has happened hitherto. Women have been very slow in taking advantage of any new openings, either educational or other, & perhaps it is all the better that there should not be too much haste & eagerness in running after novelties.

I am sorry this matter has involved you in so much troublesome correspondence. There must be, I should imagine, great variety & originality in the views expressed on the general subject of female education.

I remain, dear Sir
Yours sincerely
S. E. Davies.

GC: ALS ED LOC-18

1. Bedford College was founded in 1849 by Elizabeth Jesser Reid. It admitted females over the age of twelve, and Lady Visitors chaperoned the girls to all lectures. This practice was abolished in 1889.
2. Lists of examination candidates and their results were posted publicly.

To Nannie Leigh Smith

17 Cunningham Place, N.W. Jan. 2d 1863.

My dear Nannie

It was very pleasant to have your own letter with an authentic account of yourselves, tho' I had heard of you from Barbara since your arrival at Palermo. I am very glad you like the place & feel *better* than in England, tho' so little stronger. We must hope for that to come by & by, when the do-nothing plan has been tried a little longer. It has at any rate, I suppose the advantage of being a quite new remedy in your case. We are all well. The mildness of the season seems to keep down illness, tho' people have a way of calling it unhealthy. Thanks for your New Year's greeting & good wishes, which I return very heartily to you all.

I shall be very glad to have an account of Sicilian schools, which are a new & interesting subject, if the EWJ. lives as long![1] I am full of doubts & perplexities about it, & have written upon them to Barbara, at great length. I will not inflict such a preach upon you. In a letter from Barbara about a fortnight ago, she remarked that she was not sure, whether, if the Journal is always to cost money, it had not better stop. I was not sure either, so I set to work diligently to gather opinions. Of course they are confused & conflicting. The financial position of the EWJ. w is rather worse than I understood it to be from Bessie. I think the plan of getting subscriptions paid in advance, & getting deficiencies made up by friends, & so on, must have confused her & made the receipts appear more than they really were. The discrepancy is only of about £50 a year, but in the meantime matters have been getting worse. About 50 or 60 subscribers have left off during the last six months, & there have been I think only 10 or 12 new ones. Miss Lewin says many of those who have given up are old subscribers. She thinks they took the Journal in out of friendship, & have at last got tired of paying for a thing which they never read. Probably the Lancashire distress has had something to do with it, as some of the people live in that district. It is evident however that the circulation has been to a great extent artificial. At each ⟨National Association for the Promotion of⟩ Social Science meeting, Bessie got a certain number of people to subscribe, who dropped off at the end of the year, to be replaced by a new set. The ⟨NAPSS⟩ Meeting this year being held in London, nothing of that sort could be done, & in any case, it would be unsatisfactory to go on in that way. Bessie says she cannot do it any longer, & for me to ask people to take in a Magazine of which I am Editor, is quite impossible.

There is another consideration which affects the question. There is now a weekly Ladies' Journal, called the Queen, which takes our side.[2] It is a low kind of thing, & no educated person would think of looking at it, but it suits the taste of inferior readers better than the Journal could ever hope to do, & it would no doubt be glad to insert any articles we liked to offer, of a sufficiently popular cast. I argue from this that it is not worth while to continue the Journal, at considerable cost of money & strength, merely for the sake of existing, as it may have been at first, when there was absolutely no popular or unpopular Magazine open to us. If the Journal is to do any good now, I think it must be by lifting it to the level of Fraser & Macmillan, & appealing to the higher class of readers.

To do this involves a considerable outlay. Good articles must be well paid for. Even writers like Miss Cobbe, who are interested in our subject, require to be paid, & one does not see why they should be expected to work for nothing. Then again, to give the circulation a fair chance, we ought, as soon as we have anything good to speak of, to advertise a great deal more. My mother & Lizzie Garrett, whose circles of observation are not the same, agree in urging this point very strongly. I don't see any direction in which money can be saved. The whole thing seems to me to have been managed with a parsimony bordering on the penny-wise, pound-foolish. For the printing we pay *much* less than was charged by Adell & Ives, & they were cheaper than Clowes. The plan of employing a working printer on our own type seems to me quite out of the question. Isa & Miss Lewin both strongly condemn the idea, & I don't at all think we should save anything by it *permanently*. As to the Adves. Miss Faithfull pays us more than she gets for them, & they are not likely to increase while our circulation is so small. I could not honestly recommend it to anybody as a good medium.

The upshot of this is, that if the Journal is to go on & prosper, those who are interested in it must advance a considerable sum of money. I am not sure that it is worth while to do so. Isa suggests that the best plan would be to advance such a sum as would give the Journal a *fair* trial for one year more, with the distinct understanding that if we see little result, at the end of the year it should stop.

GC: AL ED B304

1. "Schools in Palermo", *EWJ* (October 1863) (unsigned).
2. The *Queen*, an illustrated journal and review, was inaugurated on 7 September 1861 and ran under that title through 27 June 1863. At that time it was incorporated in the *Ladies Newspaper* and published as *Queen, the Ladies Newspaper, etc.*

To ⟨Robert Potts⟩

PROPOSED ADMISSION OF GIRLS TO UNIVERSITY LOCAL EXAMINATIONS.
17, CUNNINGHAM PLACE, LONDON, N.W.

Jan. 3rd 1863.

Dear Sir

In your letter of Nov. 6th, you were good enough to say that you would make some inquiries at Cambridge as to what chance there may be of our obtaining from the Syndicate the admission of girls to the Local Examinations. We should be glad to hear, at your convenience, the result of your inquiries.[1]

A short statement of the views of our Committee, has been drawn up, for the information of the Local Committees. I enclose a copy, & also a list of our Committee. I should add however, that this is a small working body, intentionally limited in number, but representing a large number of persons interested in the object, especially those engaged in the education of girls.

I am, dear Sir
Yours sincerely
S. E. Davies
Committee.
Mrs. Bodichon.
Miss Bostock.
Miss Isa Craig.
G. W. Hastings, Esq.
Sec. of the Social Science Association.
James Heywood, Esq.
The Recorder of London.
(Russell Gurney, Esq.)

Treasurer, Lady Goldsmid.
Hon. Sec. Miss Davies.

GC: ALS ED LOC-20

1. Potts was secretary of the Local Examinations Centre at Cambridge. The committee had contacted him about opening the exams to girls. His response to Davies on 5 January 1863 explained that he had "brought the subject of [her] letter before several of the men . . . [at Cambridge]—and as might be expected, some laughed & others looked grave. & some considered that the subject was not unworthy of serious consideration" (Chronicle 276). Potts would become her chief contact with Cambridge in the subsequent campaign.

To Barbara Bodichon

Jan. 3d. 1863.

Dear Mrs. Bodichon

I have come to the conclusion that the Journal had better be wound up. Miss Lewin & I have had a confabulation upon it, & arrive at this result. There are several reasons; the one which weighs most with me is the conviction that a Magazine cannot be satisfactorily carried on by a company. Some time ago, Dr. Chapman said to me emphatically, that it was "*certain* to fail.", that there would be a subtle influence which would too much control an Editor to make it possible to work efficiently. I felt inclined to dispute it at the time, but I have learnt by experience that it is true, & I think it is nobody's fault, but in the nature of things unavoidable. Bessie has said a great deal to me about the trouble she has had in steering clear of "the religious difficulty." The result of her skillful steering is that Lizzie Garrett finds the tone of the Journal "atheistic." I think this is too strong an expression, but at the same time the careful elimination of all distinctive religion must I think lower the tone, & destroy the heartiness of even the best writers. At the same time, I don't see how a Company, composed of persons of very different opinions, can leave its Editor & other contributors free.

I will give you an instance. In this Jan. No. there is a story, which was originally really rather interesting, but as it was evidently directed against Romanism, I felt it due to Bessie to take her opinion upon it.[1] Accordingly she made some "gentle excisions," the result of which is that it has no point at all. I see now that it was a stupid thing to insert it, but Bessie thought it very pretty, & in its maimed state, satisfactory. Then again, I feel that at this moment, the question of Sisterhoods ought to be treated in the Journal.[2] But how can I, or anybody else, write freely upon it, knowing Bessie's views? She has written to me very strongly about Miss Cobbe's papers in Fraser.[3] This is one side. But there is another. This next month, I have a paper of my brother's on "Christian Liberty & its Counterfeit."[4] Miss Lewin in her submissive way suggested a doubt whether such a subject was admissible, & I feel that I am taking a questionable step. Of course he cannot help writing like a Churchman, & any shareholder, Nannie for instance, has a right to complain if I make the Journal a vehicle for spreading Church views. Then again, Miss Dictionary Smith has written a review in which she attacks Evangelical religion. Of course that must come out. I don't think we shall get good writers to give us their best, or even to write for us at all, if it must be under such fettering conditions. You see my position is different from Bessie's. She had the principal hand in starting the Company; it was *her* Journal, & she no doubt felt that she had a right to do as she liked. But I don't feel this. I should think it, & you would all think it, very hard upon Bessie, if taking up her work, I paid no attention to her wishes. And in the nature of things she cannot wish me to take my own course, which would run directly counter to her most cherished feelings.

All this makes me feel very doubtful whether it would be possible to make the Journal genuinely lively (in the best sense) even under the most favourable circumstances as to money. And the more I think of it, the more I incline to think that it would be a pity to sink more money in it. I am sure it must be a very large sum to do much good. Nannie's £200 last year scarcely seemed to make any difference. If we decide on winding up the Journal, it will be open to Miss Faithfull to start something, which she ~~will~~ could do under more advantageous conditions than we could carry on the Journal. In her case, the expense of an office, Miss Lewin's salary, the publisher's profit, &c. would be saved. She would get the money to start from people who probably would not spend it otherwise in helping our cause. A long time ago, in the Spring, I understood from her that if the Journal ceased, she would like to start a first-class Magazine, on the Fraser & Macmillan type, with myself as Editor. In that case, of course I should be paid. We should get our work done, with other people's money, & we should have our own saved, to expend in some other profitable way. Of course Miss Faithfull would have to ascertain whether there appeared to be a reasonable chance of success, but the risk would be hers. Several advantages would be gained by going off upon a new footing. The name could be changed, which has been very much pressed upon me, as an essential thing if we mean to get a good, *general* circulation, & we should not have an old bad character dragging us down. Unfortunately the EWJ. has *two* bad characters, one for license, which Isa tells me extends even into such circles as G. Macdonald's, the other for dulness, which I am afraid extends everywhere. I am not favourably disposed towards the plan of spending a large sum on the EWJ. this year as an experiment because I am almost sure the result would be that it would be a good deal better than in past times, (tho' still wanting in *life*, for the *company* reasons,) but that the increase in circulation would be trifling, & that to keep up to the mark, we must again advance money, & so, on & on. It seems to me bad policy to spend our money in this way, if we can get the same work substantially, done at other people's expense. I could get on with Miss Faithfull. Her views, so far as she has any, are the same as mine, & I don't think there is any fear now, of her turning out badly. Miss Lewin spoke to me very strongly to-day about the great improvement she has seen in her. She thinks that the revulsion from Miss Hays produced a sort of reaction which has made her particularly unlikely to imitate her in future. She says Miss Parkes does not do Miss Faithfull justice yet, but she thinks she will by & by. She is quite clear that to give up the Journal is the best thing we can do, under the circumstances. She says it is the anxiety about money that has worn out Bessie. It seems to have been always going on; the Journal has never anything like paid its expenses. Miss Lewin thinks Bessie would not attempt to carry it on herself; it would be a blow to her at first, but she would get over it, & it would be the best thing for all parties in the end. My mother, on whose judgment I place great reliance in practical matters, is very clear & decided in favour of the change. She has been continually drumming into me that the Journal would never get on, especially if its name could not be changed. I know Lizzie Garrett would take the same view as myself, & I could speak with almost equal certainty of Isa, judging by her tone the last time we discussed the Journal. I am very sorry she cannot be consulted just now. I have not had any discussions of this change with Miss Faithfull, & when I speak of what she would most likely do, I am only giving my own conjectures. If she had not the Journal to print, she would want something else, to employ the girls,[5] & as people are very ready to lend her money, the most probable thing is that she would start a Magazine.

 I don't wish to act suddenly or to put any one to inconvenience. If you wish it, I will go on with the Journal a few month longer, & do my best not to leave it in a worse state than I found it. But I think for various reasons, it would be better to wind up at the end of the Journal year.[6] You know I have not been appointed Editor, so there would be no resigning to do, except Bessie's & Miss Hays's, & their failure in health is a very good excuse for giving up. There is clearly no one to be got who would do the editing gratuitously, & I don't see any one who would do it well, even for a salary.

 Miss Hays's departure will make changes in the house arrangements, & I should think it would be more convenient to Lady ⟨Theodora⟩ Monson to have the whole thing settled at once. Lady Monson has not yet arrived at L⟨angham⟩.P⟨lace⟩, & Miss Lewin knows nothing of her plans, except that she says she means to manage the Institute herself.[7]

 "The Queen", now published by ⟨John⟩ Crockford, the publisher of the Critic, is a very remarkable periodical. It is in the form of the Ill⟨ustrated⟩: News. It gives crochet & embroidery patterns, cookery receipts, the fashions, papers on dress, on sports, skating, riding, flower-making & all sorts of things, & with all that, recommends the study of politics to women as a duty, & sticks up for their rights unreservedly. It is very curious & significant, that so intensely vulgar a manufacture, appealing to what one would call the lowest popular taste, yet thinks it expedient to take our side.

I don't know how you will like the idea of giving up the Journal, after taking an interest in it so long. I dare say some of its old friends will lament its death. The old subscribers generally don't seem to care for it much. They are dropping off at a dreadful rate, & that is what has brought me up to the slaying outright plan. I was quite prepared not to see any great increase in the number of subscribers for some time, but I did expect that by taking pains & improving a little, we might have kept the old ones. And even now, we are spending at the rate of £100 a year more than we receive, without shewing much for it. I meant to have written to Nannie, but if you will kindly forward this, with your own views it will perhaps answer the purpose better.

We ought to decide as quickly as we can, so as to be able to give notice in Feb. It makes me sorry to think of poor Bessie's disappointment, but after all, one blow is better than constant worry, & I believe it is partly the anxiety about money that keeps her from getting better now.

Miss Thackeray writes a kind note, explaining that she cannot write for us.

If the Journal is wound up, I shall very gladly contribute towards paying off its debts.

Monday. Jan. 6th. I have *slept upon* this two nights, & see no reason to change. Our efforts to increase the circulation have completely failed. We wrote to about 80 mechanics & Literary Institutes, sending a specimen & offering the EWJ. at trade price. Only one responded. We also wrote to a great many schoolmistresses, offering it at half-price, & only one (except two friends of mine) have taken any notice.

Bessie has lately been asked to write for the St. James's Magazine.

Isa has been asked to write on our subject in "Good Words," with its circulation of 60,000, monthly (equal to five years of the EWJ!) & it wd. probably be open to Bessie also. It seems to me a pity to waste our efforts on so limited a circle of readers, when there are *now* (unlike 4 years ago) so many wider channels open to us.

Yrs. affectn. E. D.

Jan. 8th. I had written so far a few days ago. Since then I have had a consultation with Miss Lewin, which ended in my writing to Bessie, proposing to ~~give~~ wind up the EWJ. She is quite aghast at the idea, & is evidently in a state of delusion about it altogether. So I think the best plan will be to postpone the whole question till you & Barbara return to England. I am not much in favour of making a special effort for one year, of which I suspect the result would be that ~~that~~ at the end of it, all the old perplexities would come back. I doubt very much whether we have strength to sustain a really good periodical. I am not up to being its Editor, either in education or otherwise, & I don't see where the writers are to come from, especially as the strength of the Maurician party is now absorbed in a new periodical called the Reader, of which ⟨John Malcolm⟩ Ludlow is Editor.

However, I am going on for the present, on the old footing, under Bessie. My love to Isabella. I hope you will have a pleasant Spring. Ever yours affecn.
E. D.

GC: ALS ED B305

1. Caroline Oxenden, "A Monk's Story. A.D. 1434," *EWJ* (January 1863). Parkes was growing interested in Roman Catholicism and would convert the following year.

2. The religious revival of the mid-nineteenth century had resulted in an increased number of charitable women's religious orders, primarily caring for the sick and the poor. When ED took over editing the *Victoria*, she published an article on sisterhoods by Frederick Maurice in August 1863.

3. "Female Charity—Lay and Monastic," *Fraser's Magazine* (December 1862).

4. [Llewelyn Davies], "Christian Liberty and its Counterfeit," *EWJ* (February 1863).

5. The women who worked at Faithfull's Victoria Printing Press.

6. The *EWJ* was incorporated into the *Alexandra* in August 1864 under the editorship of Parkes. It ceased publication in August 1865. In October 1866 it was revived as the *Englishwoman's Review*.

7. Monson had joined the board of directors at Langham Place in 1860. The Ladies' Institute included a reading room, a luncheon room, and an office.

To Barbara Bodichon

Jan. 8th 1863.

Dear Mrs. Bodichon

Your Ms. came to hand yesterday, & I have just been sending it off to Press. It is not too long for one article I think, & it would spoil it to divide it. I suppose I may put your initials to it.[1]

Bessie is amazed that I am not "full of hope & strength," under such highly exhilarating circumstances. The situation is extremely perplexing. Bessie seems as much under the power of her old delusions as ever. I feel more & more doubtful about our power of sustaining a good organ. The Maurician set have just started a new weekly, called the Reader, which will absorb their strength. They are spending a great deal of money upon it, without much apparent result. Mr. Ludlow is Editor, at a salary of 10 guineas a week, & there is a sub. Editor besides. It seems to me that if first rate people, having all the advantages of University education &c. added to natural gifts, & with money at command, find it difficult to make a periodical good, we have not much chance. Of course it is easy to do *badly* & produce a thing which (as I am told on all sides,) "nobody reads", but is that worth while? I think it is Bessie's entire ignorance of the state of religious parties in England which makes her think it an end worth living for, to report upon the proceedings of needlewomen's societies &c. As far as I have ever seen, each religious sect is kept fully informed as to the doings, Charitable

& otherwise, of its own set, & does not want to know about other people's. We must, as you say, have a consultation when you come to England. In the meantime, I have promised to go on editing the Journal for Bessie. I find I misunderstood Miss Lewin about the funds. At our present rate of payments & receipts, we are not losing more than about £40 a year. But subscribers are still dropping off. Three went off yesterday.

Miss Sewall is doing good work. She is to take me next week to see a Dr. Edmonds who wants to talk about a Medical School for women.[2] I saw Mrs. Russell Gurney yesterday. She has not been at all well, but is somewhat better. Lizzie Garrett flourishes. Isa is much better, & getting to work again, but will remain at Edinb. some time longer. Yours affectionately

E. D.

GC: ALS ED B306

1. Barbara Bodichon, "Of Those Who Are the Property of Others, and of the Great Power That Holds Others as Property," *EWJ* (February 1863).
2. Probably Dr. James Edmunds, who founded the Female Medical Society in 1862. In October 1865, it became the Ladies' Medical College.

To Thomas Dyke Acland

PROPOSED ADMISSION OF GIRLS TO UNIVERSITY LOCAL EXAMINATIONS.
17, CUNNINGHAM PLACE, LONDON, N.W.

Jan. 12th 1863.

Sir

Towards the close of last year, a Committee in furtherance of the above object was formed in London, & I was desired to communicate with the Secretaries of the Local Committees at the various centres, with a view to obtain, if possible, their cooperation.

The Secretary of the Exeter Local Committee for Oxford, refers us to you, as one of the persons most able to advise and assist us. I venture therefore to send you a short statement of the views of the Committee, & to request your favourable consideration of the object proposed.

I enclose also a list of our Committee. I may mention however, that this is a small working body, designedly limited in number, but representing a considerable number of persons interested in female education, including heads of girls' schools, and others actually engaged in the work.

I am Sir,
Yours obediently
S. E. Davies.
Hon. Sec.

Faw: ALS Vol. 4A

To Barbara Bodichon

Jan. [1863]

Dear Mrs. Bodichon. I am in the last degree of perplexity about the Journal. Ever since I came into it, Miss Lewin has been constantly in distress & difficulty about money, & yesterday she told me she had not enough to pay the rent. Evidently things cannot go on in this way. I have asked Miss Lewin to send you a statement of the accounts, as it is of no use to worry Bessie. Mrs. Parkes says the least thing upsets her, & is anxious that she should not be worried about anything. The present difficulties I could very easily get over, by paying up what is deficient, but I don't see my way about the future. The highest number of subscribers at all, any month, was last Sept. year, when there were 697. That month, Kent had 226. The next month he had only 200, & now he has regularly 250, but the number of subscribers from the office has gone down to 624. They have been gradually dropping off, but especially in the months of Sept. & Dec. Generally Bessie has made an effort at the Social Science meeting. This year nothing was done. But of course we cannot live upon that sort of forced circulation. People won't take a thing for more than a year or so, only to lay on the shelf. There is a *new* weekly periodical, the Queen, which takes our views of things, in a vulgarised form. It is of very low literary standing, as bad as the EWJ. in its worst days, only much more amusing, & furnished with woodcuts & other attractions. It would no doubt insert articles of a popular sort, but no cultivated person would read it.

I feel sure that if the EWJ. is to do much good *now*, it must be by appealing to the higher class of readers. For that, we must be able to pay for good articles, which are very expensive, & to compete at all fairly with other Magazines, we must spend a great deal more in advertising. I am not sure that the money would ever come back, & I am not sure that the good done would be worth so large an outlay, but I am sure it is not wise to carry on a poor thing, which brings us into contempt, now that things like the Queen, which take up the lower class of readers, are in existence. The question is whether it is worth while to spend a considerable sum of money in trying to interest the upper class of readers.

Yours affectionately, E. D.

GC: ALS ED B308

To Barbara Bodichon

17 C.P. Jan. 14th [1863]

Dear Mrs. Bodichon.

Thanks for your kind letter & the cheque, which I have transferred to Miss Lewin. The rent is paid, & the real difficulties of the case are not the momentary want of ready money. I could advance enough to meet immediate expenses, but what perplexes me is the general question of the future of the EWJ. I think we ought each of us to make a Memorandum of what we want the Journal to be, our "idea" of it, & the means of attaining the idea, & then, in the summer, hold a solemn conclave, & decide either upon carrying out one of the ideas, or stopping altogether. Hitherto I cannot see that the Journal has had any idea, but that of getting along, somehow, & Bessie seems to think its mere existence, good or bad, worth making sacrifices for, which I do not. To create an atmosphere, we must be *read*, & the EWJ. is not. I think it is of very little use as a rallying point. Nobody has rallied to it since I have been there, except an Irishwoman who, poor thing, is a great bore, & Mrs. Parkes. Other people come to me, but it is either as representing Lizzie, or as Sec. of our Examinations' Committee, or in some private capacity, not as Editor. At the same time it is no doubt something to have somebody sitting in a certain chair in a certain room at fixed hours every day, & it might possibly be turned to some account by & by. The Journal has been of no use in the Medical movement. It was of no use in the London University matter, & is of none now, that I can see, in the Local Exams. question.

 I had a talk with Miss Cobbe about it. Her notions are, that to have a weak, poor, Journal, purporting to represent women, is decidedly worse than nothing. that we ought to put down in black & white, what we want to do. that a really vigorous & interesting advocate of women, which should be *read*, would be a capital thing. that to be interesting we must leave off balancing between parties & take up one decided line of religious thought. that as a matter of policy, the most effective line at this time would be what she calls Broad Church. that to get good writing, we must pay high. & that whether we have strength among us to sustain such a Magazine as would be worth having, she is not sure. She is very ready to help, but will not be able to write at present. She is in London now for advice, for a sprain, complicated with gout, & happily, is already somewhat better. We had a long & delightful talk, partly on theological points. She seems to me a thoroughly good woman. I like her much.

 Bessie is quite willing for me to take any line of thought I like, so long as Miss Cobbe, whom she considers most dangerous, is well looked after! She says she can always get money, so I hope she will produce some soon. She says that if the EWJ. were to die, it would be talked of "in America & Paris, to say nothing of our own towns" as one more failure in women's attempts at working together. In everything Bessie says, I am struck with her amazing ignorance of what other people think & feel about things in general. If she had been brought up among either Church people or orthodox Dissenters, who between them, constitute the great mass of English society, she would know that there is nothing at all new in women's working together. All over the Country, there are

Ladies' Associations, Ladies' Committees, Schools managed by ladies, Magazines conducted by ladies &c &c, which get on well enough. The new & difficult thing is, for men & women to work together on equal terms, & the existence of the EWJ. is no testimony with regard to that. Its most unfortunate name, which I think *must* be altered, as the first step towards getting a good *general* circulation, puts it on the same level, in the public estimation, with the Ladies' Treasury, E.W. Domestic Magazine &c &c.

Only last week, a Cornish ~~magazine~~ newspaper informed its readers that all the articles in the EWJ. are written by women, that it has none of the elements of a low popularity! that it will be read by educated & thoughtful women, & if the "lords" don't read it, they may at least give it a kind wish. —A friend of Lizzie's writes to her & complains that he does not find in it what he has always considered the special characteristics of women. Instead of listening to what we say, & accepting it for what it is worth, people wander off on to the Characteristics of women. I think the only way to avoid this, is to take the line of a good general Magazine, assuming throughout that men & women are interested in the same things, tho' taking care to give information as to anything new or special which is being done by or for women, & advocating the removal of grievances as injurious to society generally, tho' in their *direct* action, bearing upon women only. One of Bessie's notions is, that people read the Journal with so much more attention than other Magazines, that an article read by 1000 people in the EWJ ~~woul~~ *tells* more than one read by 60,000 in Good Words. This seems to me pure delusion. But I think there are some things we want to say, that we could not get said in Magazines over which we have no control, & that if we really knew what we were about & people knew where they had us, so to speak, we might exercise some influence over public opinion. Hitherto, the Journal has *not*, thank Heaven, been at all generally recognised as representing women, any more than the Lady's Companion, or the Queen &c.

I think it would be great presumption for a few women, up in London, much divided among themselves, to pretend to represent anybody but themselves. Let us adopt some distinct, unwavering line of policy, & then, if a good many people *feel* themselves represented by us, why so much the better. But I should like to represent good *men*, as well as women. I feel daily more & more that the evils we are struggling against hurt them even more than us, & I think we should try to avoid the least appearance of exclusiveness. *Some* are willing to help us, & knowing this, it is very painful to me to assume what may even *seem* like an antagonistic attitude. I know Bessie feels this too, perhaps even more strongly than I do, but when she begins to talk about centres, & rallying.points & so on, & shewing that women *can* work together (at L.P. of all places!) it seems as if she had forgotten it. You must not think we are not on perfectly good terms. We get on extremely well together, & Bessie puts her case so plausibly, that she *almost* makes me disbelieve the evidence of my senses, but it has not quite come to that yet. Other people keep my eyes open. When I quote Bessie's remarks, they smile compassionately. The plan I proposed, of transferring the EWJ. to E. Faithfull would not I believe, answer much purpose. I have not said anything to her about it, but I fancy she would have some difficulty in raising the money, & if the shareholders are willing, as Bessie thinks they would be, to leave the Editor quite free, it might be better to go on, on the old footing. I don't think much of the subscribers. The wretches are constantly dropping off. No doubt a few care for the EWJ. on principle, but the connexion with those few might I should think, be maintained in some other way. They really do not constitute such an organization as we can turn to any practical account.

I don't think we need distract our minds much more till you come to England.

We are gradually getting in answers from the Local Secs. about the Examinations. Mr. Tomkinson, the London Sec. for Cambridge, is very friendly & has taken a great deal of trouble in corresponding with his Committee.[1] They are mostly University men, about my brother's standing, & their opinions would be rather amusing to know. Mr. T. would not tell me much, he said it was not fair to expose them, but he told me of one man (warning me not to put it into an article) who said he would be in favour, if the girls could pass a Preliminary ⟨examination⟩ in needlework, cookery & the care of children.

Mr. Tomkinson expostulated, but in vain. Did I tell you before that Mr. T.'s mother takes in the EWJ. & sends it to her daughter in India, who is the wife of the B⟨isho⟩p. of Calcutta? On the whole the London Committee are rather favourable than otherwise. Mr. Tomkinson thinks we ought to allow a long time for the idea to soak into the minds of the people at the Universities, & I have had a letter from Cambridge, very much to the same effect.[2] We are working slowly, but I think we are gradually getting into communication with the right people. It is the old question, Mr. Tomkinson says, as to whether it would not be undignified for the Universities to examine girls. I wonder how men could be taught to respect women. *Not* by keeping up feeble Journals, that I am convinced of.

Your Algiers Ms. came the day after I received your letter, with a message from Ellen, that she was very sorry it had been forgotten before.[3] I think it will go in this month. My mother has been reading it & finds it very interesting. I am so delighted to hear of the improvement in dear Nannie. Perhaps I am exaggerating it, but it seems to me that if she can now walk without suffering, there must be some real, radical change for the better, worth rejoicing over.

I am going this evening with Miss Sewall to a Dr. Edmonds & his sisters, who want to have some talk about women doctors. I am sure *that* matter progresses steadily, but as Lizzie said to somebody who was calling it, "only a question of time"—*time goes so slowly*. You know I dare say that the Nat⟨ional⟩. Review has passed into the hands of Professor ⟨Charles Henry⟩ Pearson. I have reason to believe that he is friendly to women, in the matter of education, at any rate.

Miss Lewin asks me to thank you for your note. We are all jogging along very harmoniously, & if we could shut our eyes & ears, we might imagine that we were converting the world, or at least getting listened to. Do you see the Reader? I don't think it is very good. Yours affectionately

E. D.

GC: ALS ED B309

1. Writing to ED on 10 January 1863, Tomkinson explained that "those members of the Committee who have expressed disapproval of the proposal added one or more of the following reasons for so doing: That it would be injurious to the existing Examns. as held for boys only. That it would be injurious to the Girls who should compete. That the Examn. as at present constituted is not adapted for the requirements of female education. That the University is not the proper body to undertake the direction of female education" (Chronicle 278–79).

2. In his letter of 5 January 1863, Potts said that he did "not yet consider that the question is so far favourably regarded by the majority . . . as to bring it before the Senate" (Chronicle 276). He explained that "in general it is found desirable to defer new questions, until the minds of the resident members of the Senate have either become favourable or indifferent to the new question," and he recommended as a "previous step . . . bringing Schools under University inspection" before allowing girls to take the University Examinations (Chronicle 277).

3. Barbara Bodichon, "Cleopatra's Daughter, Ste. Marciana, Mama Marabout, and other Algerian Women," *EWJ* (February 1863).

To ⟨Robert Potts⟩

PROPOSED ADMISSION OF GIRLS TO UNIVERSITY LOCAL EXAMINATIONS.
17, CUNNINGHAM PLACE, LONDON, N.W.

Jan. 15th 1863.

Dear Sir

We are much obliged to you for the information you are good enough to give us as to the state of feeling at Cambridge in reference to our proposal. It is not at all surprising that so novel a suggestion should be received with at least a considerable degree of hesitation & suspicion, & we are anxious to allow time for full & careful deliberation, before calling upon the Senate to make a decision. In the meantime it seems desirable to take some means of bringing our wishes before individual members of the University. Would it be desirable to send the short statement of the Committee's views, of which I think I enclosed a copy in my last letter, to each member of the Delegacy, with a list of our Committee? I will mention to Mr. ⟨James⟩ Heywood your plan of making use of some College Fellowships to provide the funds for authorised University inspection of schools. It does not seem to me however that it would be within our province to ask the University to make so important an innovation. It might be questioned whether University men are in all respects the fittest persons to inspect & pronounce upon, the internal arrangements of ladies' schools. Our claim for the admission, under suitable regulations, of a few more candidates to already existing examinations, is a much less serious demand.

Mr. Mayor's opinion that it would never do to examine girls & boys "of that rank" together, implies, I presume, that in a lower rank it might be possible.[1] It appears to me that if there is nothing essentially wrong in the principle, consideration of rank might be left to parents. No girl could be examined without the consent of her parents, & they might surely be trusted to take all reasonable care of their daughters in these respects. Questions of detail would naturally be left to the Local Secs., who might cooperate with a Ladies' Committee, if it should appear desirable. It would probably be found expedient to give the girls a separate room & to require the presence of a "Lady-Visitor" during the Examination. This plan is adopted in the various classes at the Ladies' Colleges, & is found to work well.

I remain, dear Sir
Yours truly
S. E. Davies.

GC: ALS ED LOC-23

1. Either John Eyton Bickersteth Mayor or Joseph Bickersteth Mayor.

To Thomas Dyke Acland

PROPOSED ADMISSION OF GIRLS TO UNIVERSITY LOCAL EXAMINATIONS.
17, CUNNINGHAM PLACE, LONDON, N.W.

Jan. 19th 1863.

Dear Sir

We are much indebted to you for so fully entering into the objections which have occurred to you, respecting our proposal.[1]

The Committee are I believe, quite alive to the paramount importance of guarding against anything like undue publicity or exposure in the case of girls. After a considerable amount of careful inquiry, they have satisfied themselves that, the admission of girls to the University Local Examinations might be so provided for as to avoid any risks of this sort.

No scheme of public or mixed *instruction* is proposed. The attendance at the Examination would take place only once in the year, probably for most of the candidates only once in their lives, & the sanction of their parents would always be indispensable.

The difficulties attending the *inspection* of schools, on the plan recently adopted by Cambridge, would appear to be greater than those of simple examination.

A French exercise would be judged by the same rules, whether written by a girl or a boy, but it may be questioned whether University men would be in all respects the persons best fitted to examine into & pronounce upon the internal arrangements of a girls' school.

The Committee feel very strongly the danger of overworking girls. It appears however that in girls' schools, almost without an exception, a half-yearly examination takes place, & it is believed that an improvement in the *character* of the examination would not materially increase the stimulus, though it would greatly add to the value of the results. In many schools also, what is called a "concert" is given once a year, to which the parents & friends of the pupils are invited, & where the musical proficiency of the girls is displayed. Some of the best teachers would be inclined to welcome a scheme of examinations which might give them some support in resisting the disposition to give an excessive prominence & an unreasonable amount of time to the attainment by girls without musical gifts, of mere mechanical excellence. As the Universities already examine in French, German, Drawing, Botany & the other ordinary subjects of female education, it seems scarcely worth while to incur the great additional expense of a new system of examinations, provided always that such arrangements could be made at the various centres as would ensure perfect decorum. The number of female candidates would probably be comparatively small, & it would therefore be necessary to provide for the expenses of a separate scheme by making the fee higher. So high indeed, as virtually to exclude many of the candidates whom we are most anxious to reach.

If the Universities were willing to sanction the proposal as far as *they* are concerned, it might be left optional with the Local Committees, to accept or refuse female candidates according to the circumstances of the case. It would no doubt be generally found expedient to give the girls a separate room, & to require the attendance of a Lady-Visitor. This plan is adopted at the various classes in the Ladies' Colleges & is found to work well. The safe conduct of the girls to & from the place of examination, would naturally be provided for by their parents & teachers.

The Leeds Local Secretary believes that there would be no insuperable difficulty in making suitable arrangements there, & the London Secretary (for Cambridge)[2] is of the same opinion as regards London. The Brighton Local Committee have already passed a resolution expressing their willingness to receive female candidates, under the sanction of the Universities.

I have not received the compilation you kindly speak of sending.[3]

Pray excuse my troubling you with this long letter.

I am, dear Sir

Yours truly
S. E. Davies

Faw: ALS Vol. 4A

1. Acland had responded on 14 January 1863, expressing a belief "that if publicity & freedom be by the general consent of educated men necessary to the full development of boy nature, a certain degree of privacy & clinging for protection is equally indispensable for the full ripening of the precious qualities of womanhood" and an "indisposition to throw the girls of England into public competition with the boys" (Chronicle 280). His letter also expressed concern about the ability of university examiners ("who are as a general rule unmarried men") to question girls, which he felt "requires considerable experience of family life & of the actual working of a schoolroom to judge of a girl's knowledge & mental training" and raised logistical problems with the administration of the Musical Examination (Chronicle 281). He concluded by recommending "an experiment of a parallel examination specially adapted for female schools" (Chronicle 283).

2. H. R. Tomkinson.

3. In his letter of 14 January 1863, Acland told Davies, "I have just discovered that I have a very few copies of my compilation on the Oxford Examination—as there are some points of reference to the Arts which may possibly be of use to you, I beg your acceptance of a copy" (Chronicle 283).

To ⟨Robert Potts⟩

PROPOSED ADMISSION OF GIRLS TO UNIVERSITY LOCAL EXAMINATIONS.
17, CUNNINGHAM PLACE, LONDON, N.W.

Jan. 23d. 1863.

Dear Sir

I have forwarded the correspondence (which I have myself read with great interest) to Mr. Heywood, asking for his opinion, & will take care to let you know as soon as I hear from him on the subject. It seems to me very desirable to obtain an enactment for the general inspection of schools, but judging by our past experience in such cases, a *general* scheme would not be allowed to include girls. This might perhaps be secured while the Act was passing thro' Parliament. I am not quite sure that inspection by University men would be the very best thing for girls' schools, tho' it would no doubt be much better than nothing. I think it has been found that a similar inspection of National Schools, has not been entirely satisfactory, that is, I believe it has been felt that *if* equally well-educated ladies could be found, they would, on the whole, answer better.

An examination, conducted chiefly by means of written papers, seems to me to stand on a different footing. In that case, the examiner has merely to judge of the quality of the work done, & it cannot make any difference whether the work was done by a girl or a boy.

But when it comes to such questions as how a girl's powers can best be brought out, how much ought to be expected from them, how their time should be divided between study & recreation & exercise, &c. &c. it seems to me that a sensible woman is the most competent judge. And I doubt whether ladies would be willing to put their schools under a man's inspection, tho' they might be eager to obtain for their pupils the advantage of a first-rate examination.

I should like to thank the lady who has been good enough to copy the correspondence in such a delightfully clear, legible hand. I return Mr. Mayor's letter, which I forgot to do before.

Yours very truly
S. E. Davies.

GC: ALS ED LOC-24

To ⟨Robert Potts⟩

PROPOSED ADMISSION OF GIRLS TO UNIVERSITY LOCAL EXAMINATIONS.
17, CUNNINGHAM PLACE, LONDON, N.W.

Jan. 27th 1863.

Dear Sir

I send you a letter from Mr. Heywood, giving his opinion on University inspection. I suppose most of the *Endowed* Schools are on a Church of England foundation.[1] The religious difficulty would no doubt be a stumbling block in the case of middle-class schools under Dissenting masters. It would be difficult, I should think, to arrange a scheme of inspection in which the religions department should be optional, & I suppose Dissenters would feel aggrieved if they were excluded from an authorized system of inspection. At the same time I do not see how they could fairly object to the use of University funds in improving Church schools. It is not as if the Inspectors were to be paid out of the taxes, as in the Government Schools.

I remain, dear Sir
Yours truly
S. E. Davies.

GC: ALS ED LOC-25

1. At this time, a number of schools of private foundation were supported by money left by benefactors for educational purposes. By the middle of the nineteenth century, some forty thousand boys were receiving secondary education in 830 endowed schools, while only twelve girls' schools received endowments.

To Thomas Dyke Acland

PROPOSED ADMISSION OF GIRLS TO UNIVERSITY LOCAL EXAMINATIONS.
17, CUNNINGHAM PLACE, LONDON, N.W.

Jan. 30th 1863.

Dear Sir

    I have to acknowledge with many thanks, your account of the Oxford Examinations, in which I find much that is interesting & useful to know. I had proposed to myself to make extracts from it, but I find there would be so much to transcribe that I am tempted to avail myself of your kind permission to retain the book.[1]

    I am sure there is great force in what you say as to the importance of concentrating our efforts on a single point, & for that reason I believe the Committee will be disposed to try first for the individual diploma only. We should be very glad to get inspection after, if it could be properly managed.

    Your suggestion that in case our application is refused, we might attempt something thro' individual examiners, is an idea which I think the Committee will find it worth while to consider.

    Where the Local Committees & the Examiners are favourable, some subsequent examination for girls might be managed, in which the papers & the *standard* should be the same.

    These are the points on which we feel it most necessary to insist. Exclusively female tests have no well-known, recognised value. For some years, Certificates have been given at Queen's College, but (speaking generally) nobody knows how much scholarship they represent, & it is even asserted that they are given unfairly.[2]

    This may be a calumny, but the mere fact that such an imputation is current, makes them comparatively valueless. In the present state of women's education, it is in the nature of things that exclusively female Certificates can have very little value. All they can attest is that the holders of them are a little less superficially taught than other girls.

    We think it has been already shewn that our ideas will march, by the Society of Arts. The cases are almost precisely parallel. Women were not at first admitted to those Examinations. The Council made the concession on the application of a Local Board, & they have had no reason to regret it.

    I have been told that the real hindrance at the Universities is the question of dignity. I see you had the same obstacle to contend with. It is one which it is very difficult to deal with, as it cannot be met by argument.

    With many thanks for your kind & valuable advice,
I remain,
Yours truly
S. E. Davies.

Faw: ALS Vol. 4A

1. Acland had written in 1857 a pamphlet entitled *Middle-Class Education: Scheme of West of England Examination and Prizes*, and another in 1858 entitled *Some Account of the Origin and Objects of the New Oxford Examinations for the Title of "Associate in Arts."*

2. Queen's College, London, was established in 1846 by Frederick Maurice together with the Committee of the Governesses' Benevolent Institution. Examinations for Certificates of Proficiency began in December 1847.

To Robert Potts

PROPOSED ADMISSION OF GIRLS TO UNIVERSITY LOCAL EXAMINATIONS.
17, CUNNINGHAM PLACE, LONDON, N.W.

Feb. 11th 1863.

Dear Mr. Potts

I must thank you very cordially for your useful & instructive book, which I shall have great pleasure in reading.[1] The history of our Universities must, I should think be a subject of great interest to any one whose thoughts have been directed to the various questions connected with Education.

I am very glad to find that you think our object is likely to be attained in due time. I should think the insertion of an article in the Cambridge Chronicle would be a very good preliminary step. Had we better get something drawn up here, or would they be more willing to put in an article written by a University man? Perhaps also, some one on the spot would better understand how to bring forward the subject in the best way.

Mr. Acland says he owed much of his success to having shewn beforehand that the thing could be done, by holding an examination such as he wished to obtain from Oxford. I think we might possibly do something of the same sort in London. The Local Sec. Mr. Tomkinson is quite on our side, & if the Examiner were willing to cooperate with him, we might perhaps get a few girls passed at the examination in December. Of course they could not receive Certificates, but if they passed the examination, it would shew that the difficulties of detail, at any rate, are not insurmountable.

I should be very glad to pay a visit to Cambridge, as you suggest, at some future time, if you think it desirable. In that case, it would give me great pleasure to avail myself of the hospitality you so kindly offer.

I remain, dear Sir
Your most truly
S. E. Davies.

I see Mr. ⟨Leonard⟩ Courtney of St. John's College was the London Examiner last year. Do you happen to know whether he would be likely to help us? I think something might also be done at Leeds, if Mr. Field would cooperate with the Local Secretary there.[2]

GC: ALS ED LOC-26

1. Potts wrote *Liber Cantabrigiensis* (Cambridge, 1855), which describes prizes and scholarships available in various Cambridge colleges.

2. Probably Thomas Field (1822–96), Tutor, Fellow, and University Scholar at St. John's College, Cambridge.

To Barbara Bodichon

19 L.P. Feb. 26th [1863]

My dear Mrs. Bodichon

I can scarcely tell you how much this number of the EWJ is liked. Bessie says she has heard several people speak well of it. I have not heard much either way, but the praise & blame have been about equally divided. One or two people have called it flat, but on the other hand, Miss Lewin says the newspapers have noticed us more than usual. The Sunderland Times says, "There has been a marked improvement in this serial lately. It is womanly, motherly, simple & genial."! That it should have *become* all this under my Editorship, amuses me intensely. I have quite come to the conclusion that Bessie's ideas & mine are different, tho' not antagonistic, & that they cannot be worked together. Bessie calls hers the 'practical' & mine the 'intellectual.' I don't know that this is a very accurate definition, but I am sure the distinction is at least as *much* as is expressed by those terms. I have been coming to this opinion gradually all the winter, but I have felt it much more strongly since Bessie came home & has been able to take part in the work here. Somehow or other, we scarcely ever, spontaneously, like or wish for, the same thing. I suppose it is what Bessie would call an intellectual difference. It certainly does not arise from mutual animosity or contradictiousness, for we are the best friends in the world, & each quite ready to give in. Bessie offers all sorts of concessions, which however, I feel unwilling to accept. I don't think the Journal can be vigorously worked on a system of mutual concessions, & as *my* idea would have no chance, except under a variety of unattainable conditions, I believe it is best to adopt Bessie's, (which I fancy is much nearer yours than mine is) & make the best of it, so to speak. She is rather shocked at the notion of letting me spend myself over what I don't consider the *most* important work in the world. So we have come to an agreement that I go on working for & with Bessie for the present, but I hold myself free to give up whenever anything else turns up in which I think I could employ myself more usefully. You must not suppose that my idea has been tried. It could not be, without large funds, & even ᶦᶠ money was forthcoming, it would involve such a revolution altogether that I could not attempt it on my own responsibility.[1]

Your box is still at Newcastle. There had been no Algiers ship before my friend Mr. Fedden went to Copenhagen. On leaving home, he left directions with a broker to send it by the first opportunity. Either there was none, or the man neglected it, I don't know which, & there has been none since Mr. Fedden came home. I have had a message from him to-day, asking whether you still wish it to go. By Bessie's advice, I have written to tell him not to *lose* an opportunity, ~~but~~ & as soon as you can tell me what you wish, I will let him know. I am writing now in great haste, so as to get your answer as soon as possible. I meant to have written a longer letter, but have had hindrances.

I did not know E. F. had got credit out of the Lancashire book.[2] She did what Isa wished, I know, for I assisted at a long conference about it. I believe Isa came to the conclusion that if it was left entirely to the Committee, it would fall thro' altogether. They were much taken up in looking after the pictures, & did not care for the book. I am afraid Isa is not at all strong. She has had a feverish attack lately, which completely prostrated her, & she seems to be getting subject to them. She says it is physical over-work, not overtasking her brain, that does it, but I think she wants nursing & looking after altogether. She is still in Scotland, & will not be back for 3 weeks or a month. I wish you could see Bessie before she knocks herself up again. She is full of life & energy, quite a different creature from what she was last autumn. We had a successful little tea here last Saturday.

In haste, Yours affectionately, E. D.

GC: ALS ED B312

1. During this month, ED and Faithfull were conducting a correspondence about a prospective new journal, the *Victoria,* which ED was to edit.
2. Isa Craig's *Poems: An Offering to Lancashire* was published by Faithfull's Victoria Press.

To Robert Potts

PROPOSED ADMISSION OF GIRLS TO UNIVERSITY LOCAL EXAMINATIONS.
17, CUNNINGHAM PLACE, LONDON, N.W.

March 3d. 1863

Dear Mr. Potts

I am much obliged to you for your kind attention in sending the papers relating to the Local Examinations, which I have no doubt we shall find useful. I see a Mr. ⟨Charles⟩ Gray has succeeded Professor Liveing as Hon. Sec. to the Syndicate. I hope he will be favourable to our plans.

I have also to thank you for a copy of the Cambridge Chronicle, received on Saturday. I hope the "Correspondent's communication" will excite attention & call forth some discussion & consideration of the subject.

I remain, dear Sir
Yours very sincerely
S. E. Davies.

GC: ALS ED LOC-27

To Barbara Bodichon

17 Cunningham Place. N.W. | Thursday. March 12th [1863]
My dear Mrs. Bodichon

I have written to Mr. Fedden & asked him to keep the box, if he can, till November. He always says it is no trouble. But I am sorry you talk about Nov. for it looks as if you meant to go back to Algiers next winter, & I thought you had said this was to be your last of absenteeism.

I have written to Isa for the Ms. about wearing cotton, which I have never seen yet, & I will put your questions into the EWJ.[1] I have this evening received a notice to the effect that "A number of Englishwomen have undertaken to form a Woman's Committee to cooperate with the Emancipation Society already existing, by all means in their power: & especially by the circulation of tracts &c. explanatory of slavery as it now exists in the United States, & of its bearing on the present struggle between the North & South." Communications & subscriptions to be forwarded to Mrs. Peter ⟨Clementia⟩ Taylor. I mean to go & see her next week, & will mention your questions & suggestions.

I think the Brittany Ms. is worth inserting.[2] We are keeping it back till the present story is done. How do you like the March no.?

Lady Monson has not made any changes at Langham Place. I believe she is detained in Scotland by the illness of a friend. She & Miss Hays have had a great quarrel about the Reading-room. I don't know whether it is settled yet. Miss Hays has been in London, but not at L.P., for two or three weeks. Jane said she looked ol worn & aged, but not much altered otherwise. She is pretty well, I believe. Bessie has been extremely anxious about Adelaide, & as far as I can make out, not without reason, but it is very difficult to judge. She has been better the last few days. Mrs. Proctor & Edith think very badly of her, & the doctors' reports are not favourable, but Miss Hays insists that the cough is nervous, not consumptive. The anxiety has tried poor Bessie very much. It shews she must be pretty strong, or she would have been more knocked up by it.

Miss Lewin is away for a holiday. We expect her back at the end of next week. A little Miss ⟨Isabella⟩ Fyvie is taking her place, & does very nicely. Something like the sort of experiment you describe, of a Magazine jointly managed by men & women, is going to be tried. After much consideration & confabulation, Miss Faithfull has decided on starting one, & has asked me to edit it. I made out the following Programme, which we intend to use as a basis of operations—"In announcing a new periodical, it may be desirable to indicate briefly, its scope & purpose.

The Victoria Magazine will treat of Literature, Art & Science. Theology &

Politics will not be excluded. A serial tale will form part of the contents of each number. The names of the writers will sufficiently guarantee the quality of their contributions. The Victoria Magazine will afford an outlet for the expression of moderate & well-considered opinions on those questions, which while more directly bearing on the condition of women, are in their wider aspects, of the highest importance to society generally."

Do you approve? We intended to have printed this, but Mr. ⟨George⟩ Hastings protested vehemently against the last sentence, evidently misunderstanding it, & as *he* did, we thought other people would too, & that it had better be kept back. Mr. Dicey suggested that we need not have a Prospectus at all, which pleased me much, & we have decided not to *advertise* anything but the subjects & writers of the 1st No. I believe we must have something in the shape of a Prospectus for private circulation. Mr. Hastings is going to write on the Law of libel from a moral point of view, Mr. E⟨dward⟩. Dicey on America, R⟨ichard⟩. Hutton on Spiritualism, & Mr. Nassau Senior has given us (I don't mean for *nothing*) his journal in Egypt, which will go on thro' a good many numbers. The story is our great difficulty. First rate writers have not got long serials lying on their hands, & cannot strike them off at a month's notice.[3] Mrs. ⟨George Eliot⟩ Lewes wrote very kindly, but has nothing ready at present. A⟨nthony⟩. Trollope is fully taken up, & ⟨Charles⟩ Kingsley & ~~Macm~~ Tom Hughes was pledged to Macmillan. People have been wonderfully cordial & encouraging about it. We mean to employ chiefly men at first, & not to press our special subject till we have got a character. *Then*, when we have once gained a hearing, we shall give the public as much of it as they will swallow. Miss Cobbe is a very cordial friend, but I am afraid she will not be able to write much, she is in such bad health. Of course this takes me off from the Journal. I am very sorry to leave it, especially as Bessie was anxious for me to go on, but I believe my capabilities, such as they are, will be better employed on the Victoria. I am to edit April, & Bessie will do May herself. After that, some other arrangement must be made. Bessie has entered into negociations with Jarrold. I believe the Company have offered him half the property, if he will take the pecuniary responsibility & push it. Bessie makes it a sine qua non that the office at L.P. is retained, & that subscribers' copies are sent direct from there. These are the only conditions I believe, but Bessie would supply part of the matter, & probably have some voice in the appointment of Editor. She told me to-day that she is thinking of trying to combine, with Miss ⟨Ellen⟩ Barlee, & making her the responsible person. One cannot help feeling it a misfortune that the Journal should fall into the hands of such an ignorant person, but I don't see very well how Bessie can help herself. She says she does not feel at all equal to retaining the headship, even with a regular Sub.Editor.

She wants some one who will take the responsibility entirely off her hands, & Miss Barlee would do that, supposing she came into it. She has plenty of energy, & I don't think she is a *bad* woman. Her faults are those of an ignorant, & vulgar woman. I don't like calling her vulgar, it sounds so harsh, but I cannot think of any milder term to express the absence of the qualities of a lady. I am sure she does not mean to tell stories, tho' she manages to convey false impressions, from the habit of using words carelessly. If she & Jarrold can manage to come to an agreement, I think between them they would give the Journal a good push. Bessie says she cannot Missionarise for it any more, & it evidently cannot live upon its merits. Miss Barlee has great powers of pushing, & the line she takes is popular. There is all this to be said in favour of having her, & yet I cannot help feeling it as a calamity.

I had looked forward to continuing in "the work", as Bessie calls it, & backing it up as much as I could, & I don't know whether that will be possible under Miss Barlee's reign. She will be putting in articles on the Employment of women, setting Political Economy at defiance, & then if some horrid newspaper gets hold of it & shews it up, we shall all feel uncomfortable. However, this is all in the future, & perhaps may never come to pass. I wish you would make haste home & look after things. We want you.

I am very glad there were no women concerned in the management of the Reader. They have come to a hobble, & have been obliged to put themselves under the government of the printer. I don't understand that there has been any quarrel, & the circulation has steadily increased, from the beginning, but the Company sort of management does not answer. They began in a hurry, without a definite plan of action, & that kind of thing always comes to grief. Miss Faithfull & I are taking great pains to define our mutual relations as clearly as possible in a written agreement, so that there may be no misunderstandings by & by. I have no notion of friendly vagueness in matters of business, & I believe a great deal of the trouble at L.P. has been caused by the want of distinct, definite arrangements. You may be as friendly as you like, *after* you have got your business-like basis, but let that be well defined, first. You will see by the Prospectus, that we go in for rivalry with Fraser, Macmillan & Blackwood. Macmillan has been very unsatisfactory lately. ⟨David⟩ Masson, the Editor, has taken a central line, & has failed either to amuse the public, or to interest any particular set. A good many of the Maurician people are very well inclined to the Victoria. Richard Hutton & E. Dicey have been exceedingly kind & their advice has been very valuable. I am going to ask my brother to write an article on Robt. Browning's new book, when it comes out. We have half engaged Geo. Macdonald to write on Tennyson, but his book may be delayed for a long time yet. Mr. Macdonald has something in his head about Shakespere's *Art*, meaning to shew that Shakespere always wrote artfully, with a purpose. Do you think he will do it well? I went to one of his lectures yesterday & liked it very much, but I am such an ignorant dolt about Shakespere that any teaching about him is to me, better than none. I was very sorry to hear from Mr. Macdonald that Isabella Blythe had been so ill. I suppose it is all over now, but it must have been very alarming at the time.

Last Saturday was a grand day & taught one not to despair of one's country. The burst of loyalty & patriotism & the keen sense of common citizenship pervading the vast mass of people, was intensely exhilarating.[4] I never felt so grateful to the Queen for her goodness & worshipfulness before.

My kind regards to Dr. Bodichon, please.

Isa is still at Edinburgh, & I am afraid, far from strong. She looks forward to coming back to London, to *rest*, in two or three weeks. If any brilliant ideas occur to you, please let us have them for the Victoria.

Ever yours affectionately, E. D.

GC: ALS ED B313

1. Passing Events, in the April 1863 issue of *EWJ*, contained a notice of a new strand of cotton being grown in Jamaica: "Why should not the women of England, one and all, resolve, now cotton may be obtained, as good and as cheap, by means of free labour in our own colonies, as it has heretofore been obtained from America, cultivated by slaves, that they will give a decided preference to the former, and never more countenance slavery and the slave-breeders, by using thread made from slave-labour cotton?"

2. Barbara Bodichon, "Six Weeks in La Chere Petite Bretagne," *EWJ* (May 1863).

3. Eventually, T. A. Trollope, Anthony's brother, provided a piece of fiction, and the first issue of *Victoria* featured part 1 of his novel *Lindisfarn Chase*.

4. Princess Alexandra of Denmark had arrived in England to marry Prince Edward, the future King Edward VII of England. On Saturday, 7 March 1863, Princess Alexandra—together with members of the royal family—processed through the city of London. "For a distance of between five and six miles [Princess Alexandra passed] through a series of streets walled on each side up the roofs of the houses with hundreds of thousands of gazers" (*Times* [London], Saturday, 7 March 1863).

To Anna Richardson

Brighton. Friday. [April 10th] ⟨1863⟩

... Mrs. Browning's book [The Greek Christian Poets & the English Poets. By Elizabeth Barrett Browning. Chapman & Hale. 5/.] is to be sent to you to keep.[1] We wish for a notice of about a page long, (i.e. 550 words) & that I think will scarcely admit of quotations except perhaps a sentence or two ... My "idea" of the notices of books is this. People see a book advertised, & wonder whether it would be worth while to order it into their Book Society, or to send to Mudie for it.[2] They ask one, What is it about? Is it worth reading? Is it trustworthy as far as it goes? Is it beyond the comprehension of ordinary readers? In writing a notice, I should try to answer these questions. Of course this is not a thorough review, but I think it is useful information. If you have read the notices in the Westminster Review, under the heading Contemporary Literature, you can understand the sort of thing I mean, only that our notices must be shorter as we have not much space to spare. The little notices in the Reader are of the same kind, but ours may be a little longer than those. I give these hints for your guidance, but it may be best for you to follow your own bent, if you don't like our plan. The first no. will be a sort of experiment, & we shall know better afterwards how to manage our matter. I am very anxious to give the contributors *rope*, as far as possible. Our watchword is Liberty & our Motto Let every woman do that which is right in her own eyes.

I have been staying two days here with the Bartons & go home to-day. I don't love Brighton, but I enjoy very much being with old friends, with whom one's childish life was bound up. Mary & the children are down here. Arthur Llewelyn is exceedingly fat, & promises to be a Crompton.[3] Dear little Charley has been rather alarmingly ill, with pains in the stomach, which could not be traced to any cause.[4] He is sadly pulled down, but as the pains are now got rid of, we hope he will soon pick up. The anxiety & distress about him here kept my sister back. Charley is the sweetest little child I ever saw, so gentle & tenderhearted.

E. D.

GC: AMsS C289

No letters written by ED between 10 April and 9 May 1863 are extant. During this period, a number of significant developments occurred at the University of London. On 26 March 1863, the Convocation of the University of London passed by one vote a resolution supporting a "provision for the examination and certification of Women," to be discussed at the 12 May 1863 convocation. On 23 April, ED received a letter from Shaen, recommending that ED and her committee circulate fresh copies of Frances Power Cobbe's paper "The Education of Women and How It Would be Affected by University Examinations" (London, 1862). On 30 April, the committee met and voted to circulate one thousand copies of a new, printed statement, "Reasons for the Admission of Women to University Examinations" (Chronicle 292–93).

1. The first issue of the *Victoria* appeared in May 1863. It contained a feature, Literature of the Month, to which ED wished Richardson to contribute.
2. Mudie's Select Library was Victorian England's largest lending library.
3. Arthur Llewelyn Davies (1863–1907).
4. Charles Davies (1860–1928).

May 1863 47

To Thomas Dyke Acland

PROPOSED ADMISSION OF GIRLS TO UNIVERSITY LOCAL EXAMINATIONS.
17, CUNNINGHAM PLACE, LONDON, N.W.

May 9th 1863.

Dear Sir

Your kind letter received this morning, gives us some hope as regards Oxford.[1]

What you said to us in the beginning of the year as to the state of feeling there, was so discouraging that we decided to concentrate our efforts on Cambridge. An additional reason for doing so was that Mr. Tomkinson, the London Sec. for Cambridge, was ready to help us, while the Oxford London Sec. appeared unfavourable to our plans. Mr. Tomkinson is now on our Committee & has proposed a plan somewhat similar to the one you suggest. He proposes to obtain first, the consent of the Local Examiners to the presence of girls in the Examination room, & then, to ask for so many additional copies of the Examination papers, enclosing the fees, but without the usual forms of application. He thinks the papers would be sent without further inquiry, but that of course remains to be seen. The Committee are quite ready to guarantee all expenses, & it was arranged with Mr. Tomkinson that the girls should pay their full share, even if no *extra* expenses are incurred. We should find it in some respects easier to try the experiment in London than elsewhere, because the ladies on our Committee could themselves be present at the Examination, & because London is the largest Centre from which to draw our candidates. The Professors of Bedford College are, I believe without exception, favourable to the proposal & would be ready to send in candidates.

But in connexion with Oxford, I believe it might be more easily managed at Brighton or Leeds. The Local Sec. at Brighton has already received applications from candidates & he is looking forward to presenting his own daughter for examination at some future time. The Leeds Sec. Mr. Barnett Blake, was in London a few weeks ago, & he assured me that there would be no *local* difficulties at Leeds. He mentioned having had an application from a schoolmistress at Malton some time ago. The Birmingham Local Committee have passed a favourable Resolution, but we do not know how far they would be ready to cooperate in any informal plan. The Committee entirely agree with you as to the desirableness of proving that the thing is feasible before asking the sanction of the Universities. The difficulty appears to be to contrive a scheme in which everything shall be open & above board & fair towards the Universities, on our part, without committing the official persons connected with the Examinations.

I shall have the pleasure of bringing before the Committee the plan you have sketched out, & also your suggestion for circulating a "fly-sheet" at Oxford. In case the Committee should wish to have the actual letters printed, should you object to having your own printed also, & giving it the form of a correspondence?

I cannot remember whether I sent you before, the enclosed short statement of our views. The Committee are very clear & decided in wishing for the admission of girls to the Examns., *as they are*. To our thinking, modern languages & the Arts are fairly provided for by the existing scheme, looking upon them as *studies*, & as mere accomplishments, they really do not want encouragement.

May I ask you to be kind enough to let us hear from you again, with Dr. ⟨Frederick⟩ Temple's view of the subject & any further suggestions that may have occurred to you.

I remain
Yours sincerely
S. E. Davies.

Faw: ALS Vol. 4A

1. Acland had written to ED on 8 May saying that her letters had "produced a considerable impression on minds at first indisposed to listen to . . . [her] plan on account of its previously assumed impracticability" and recommending a fly sheet to be distributed to college common rooms (Chronicle 293–94).

To Robert Potts

PROPOSED ADMISSION OF GIRLS TO UNIVERSITY LOCAL EXAMINATIONS.
17, CUNNINGHAM PLACE, LONDON, N.W.

May 18th 1863.

Dear Mr. Potts

I am sure you will be glad to hear that we are receiving some encouragement in our designs upon the Univ. Local Examinations. As the shortest way of showing you how matters stand at Oxford, I enclose a copy of a letter from Mr. Acland. He has since seen Dr. Temple, who gives it as his opinion, that we are "sure to succeed." We propose printing such a statement as Mr. Acland suggests, on the part of our Committee, & I should be glad to know whether you think it possible & desirable to circulate it at Cambridge also.

We are seriously thinking of trying a plan of an informal examn. such as Mr. Acland sketches out, in connexion with *Cambridge*. Mr. Tomkinson, the London Local Sec. is now on our Committee, & will do all he can to help us.

We shall of course not give up any chances we may have from Oxford, but it would answer our purpose better to try our plans in London, rather than anywhere else, & the London Committee for Oxford does not seem friendly. In the Cambridge London Committee we have a large majority on our side.

Will you kindly give us your opinion on these plans?
I am, dear Mr. Potts
Yours very sincerely
S. E. Davies.

GC: ALS ED LOC-28

On 12 May 1863, the Convocation of the University of London voted against opening examinations to women.

To Henry Tomkinson

PROPOSED ADMISSION OF GIRLS TO UNIVERSITY LOCAL EXAMINATIONS.
17, CUNNINGHAM PLACE, LONDON, N.W.

May 18th 1863.

Dear Mr. Tomkinson

Miss ⟨Eliza⟩ Bostock thinks you ought to know what is going on at Oxford. As the shortest way of explaining the whole story, I send you a copy of a letter from Mr. Acland. He has since seen Dr. Temple, who gives his opinion that we are "sure to succeed."

As there seems some prospect of our getting at least the informal examination, we are beginning to look about for candidates. Could you supply us with the "Regulations"?[1] We are likely to want a good many copies, as each member of the Committee will no doubt want some. The Examn. papers, I suppose we can only get by buying them.

We shall probably hold a Committee some day next week, which I hope you may be able to attend.

Yours sincerely
S. E. Davies.

I have written to Mr. Potts, to ask whether he thinks it would be desirable to circulate such a paper as Mr. Acland suggests, at Cambridge also. Of course the "statement" will be in the name of the Committee, & submitted to them before it is circulated.

I have drawn up a little paper, which is in fact the same that you made use of for your Committee, somewhat amplified, which may perhaps answer the purpose. We find we want some sort of printed statement, for general circulation.[2]

GC: ALS ED LOC-212

1. Cambridge printed "Local Examinations: Examination Papers with Lists of Syndics and Examiners, and the Regulations &c" each year.

2. On 29 May, the Examinations Committee "met & resolved—That Mr. Tomkinson be requested to write to the Secretary of the Syndicate for the Cambridge Local Examn. applying for leave to print some additional examn. papers & to make a private arrangement with the examiners to look over the answers & receive their report" (Chronicle 298).

To Henry Tomkinson

PROPOSED ADMISSION OF GIRLS TO UNIVERSITY LOCAL EXAMINATIONS.
17, CUNNINGHAM PLACE, LONDON, N.W.

June 10th 1863.

Dear Mr. Tomkinson

I suppose you have not yet received an answer to your application to Cambridge.

The secretary will of course have to bring it before the Syndicate, & it has occurred to me that, if there is time, it might be worth while to get some of the members written or spoken to, beforehand. The answer I *expect* is, that it is "beyond their powers" to do what we want. But it will probably depend very much on their wishes, whether they consider it within their powers, or not.

If Mr. Gray has told you when this matter will be discussed, would you kindly let me know?

I have been asked to go down to Brighton next week, & I propose making use of the opportunity to see some of the Local Committee there.[1] Sir Benjamin Brodie strongly advised us to try to get up Memorials from the local centres, asking for leave to examine girls in that particular place, & there seems to be a pretty good chance at Brighton, as they have already passed a friendly Resolution. Do you happen to know anybody there whom it would be useful to see on the subject?

Yours sincerely
S. E. Davies

GC: ALS ED LOC-33

1. Davies "went to Brighton, on a visit to Mrs. Jex-Blake, an interesting old lady, & her daughter Sophia." During this trip she "saw the Sec. of the Local Examns. Committee [Rev. James Porter.], & Mr. Elliott, of the Clergy Daughters' School, St. Mary's Hall" (Chronicle 299).

To Robert Potts

PROPOSED ADMISSION OF GIRLS TO UNIVERSITY LOCAL EXAMINATIONS.
17, CUNNINGHAM PLACE, LONDON, N.W.

June 10th 1863.

Dear Mr. Potts

Since I last wrote to you, I have, with another member of our Committee paid a visit to Oxford.[1] We saw Mr. ⟨John⟩ Griffiths, the Sec. to the Delegacy,

& he gave us a good deal of encouragement. It appears however that the Delegates are quite clear that it is not within their powers, to admit girls to the Local Examn. They could only recommend a modification of the Statute. It appears that the Oxford Statute is about to expire, & we are advised to send in at the proper time, a Memorial praying that the new Statute may be so worded as to admit girls. We shall be obliged to make this application before next June, so that Mr. Acland's advice to try for a preliminary Examination of an information character, as a sort of experiment, cannot be carried out in connexion with Oxford.

We are anxious however to make the attempt in connexion with the Cambridge Examn. in December, & at a recent meeting of our Committee, Mr. Tomkinson, the London Local Secretary, was requested to apply to the Syndicate for leave to print a few extra Examination papers, & to make a private arrangement with Examiners for looking over the papers done by girls. We have not yet heard the result of this application. I write to inform you of it, in the hope that you may be able to do something towards securing for it a favourable reception. If it is refused, we shall still be able to apply by & by, for a modification of the Statute. We are very anxious however to obtain permission to try this experiment, as a fair & reasonable preliminary step. We were advised at Oxford, to get up Memorials from various local centres, asking for the extension of the examinations in those particular places. I suppose this would also be a useful step to take as regards Cambridge, when the proper time comes. We were surprised to hear from Mr. Griffiths that our proposal had been brought before the Delegacy at Oxford, & no one objected. We are constantly receiving the most contradictory reports as to *which* of the two Universities is most likely to help us.

I remain, dear Mr. Potts
Yours very truly
S. E. Davies.

GC: ALS ED LOC-30

1. ED and Eliza Bostock visited Oxford on 28 May 1863 and visited John Griffiths and the Benjamin Brodies.

To Anna Richardson

17 Cunningham Place. N.W. | Saturday- [1863] | [June 13]

My dear Anna

I have just received a letter from Mr. Potts, which amuses me so much, I must write & tell you about it. He talks of sending you my letter! I must really stop him. I cannot possibly have you overlooking my private correspondence & laughing at it. I am getting quite nervous about letters. One never knows where they will get to. Mr. Acland sent mine ~~round~~ to Oxford, to be read to the Delegates & they ordered them to be sent round to the absent members. We have been doing a good deal lately & are much encouraged. A lady at Oxford,[1] the sister of one of the Professors, asked Miss Bostock (a member of our Committee) & me, to go down to Oxford, to be examined on the subject.

We saw the Secretary of the Delegacy, & some other people, who were all very friendly & nice. ~~I was charmed with Oxford, & made up my mind that if I could not live in London, I should like Oxford next best.~~ We are agitating now about a sort of experimental examination to be held, if they will let us, in connexion with Cambridge, here in London, in December. Mr. Potts says, "If you have no objection, I will write to Miss Richardson of South Ashfield. In fact, I think if I send her your letters, she will learn better what is now in agitation on the subject. I think if from the North & from the South, an attack can be brought to bear on us—notwithstanding opposition—I think it will give way & all you desire be accomplished."[2] On consideration, I think I had better let him write to you, & mind you send him a very nice letter back. You ought to get up a Memorial from the North. Sir B. Brodie, at Oxford, strongly advised us to get up Memorials from a variety of places, Brighton, Birmingham, &c. I am going down to Brighton soon, to see about it.

I am so glad you are pleased with the Victoria & especially flattered by your brother's approval, as he may be considered to represent the gay world. Does "Johnnie" like it?[3] I can scarcely believe that Jeanie has written a good novel, tho' I *am* of a credulous disposition.

I am all alone by myself now. I went down to Monmouthshire ⟨incomplete⟩

GC: DAL ED LOC-35

1. Eleanor Elizabeth Smith, sister of Henry Smith.
2. On 13 June, Potts had written to ED saying "that a private sort of examination next December such as you propose may be practicable . . . you might *compel* (I was going to say) us to do something, if you could show a large number of Ladies' Schools favourable to your scheme. . . . I think if from the North & from the South, an attack can be brought to bear on us . . . opposition . . . will give way & all you desire [will be] accomplished" (Chronicle 300).
3. One of Anna Richardson's brothers was named John.

To Robert Potts

PROPOSED ADMISSION OF GIRLS TO UNIVERSITY LOCAL EXAMINATIONS.
17, CUNNINGHAM PLACE, LONDON, N.W.

June 17th 1863.

Dear Mr. Potts

I am very glad to hear that you are coming to Town, as I should very much like to have a little talk with you. If you will kindly let me know a few days beforehand, I will try & arrange for you to meet also Mr. Tomkinson, who as Local Secretary, knows more about the management of the Examinations than I do. Perhaps you will kindly tell me whereabouts you will be staying, so as to arrange for the most convenient meeting place.

Cunningham Place (Maida Hill) is unfortunately rather out of the way for most people.

I enclose a printed statement just issued by our Committee.[1] We look forward to sending in a Memorial from teachers, eventually, but have thought it best to reserve it for our final effort, when we make a regular application for the formal Examinations under the sanction of the Universities. We intend to canvass for candidates as soon as we can hold out any prospect of an examination to go in for, & are already doing so privately to some extent. It is difficult to take any public general steps while the whole matter is so uncertain.

I think it would be worth while to re-open communications with Miss Richardson, tho' I am afraid she would scarcely be able to get up a Memorial from Newcastle, as no Examination is held there. Leeds might be a more likely place.

I am very glad to hear that the Secretary to the Syndics thinks our proposed plan feasible.

I remain, dear Mr. Potts
Yours very truly
S. E. Davies.

GC: ALS ED LOC-36

1. Probably the "Proposed Admission of Girls to University Local Examinations" authorized by the committee on 29 May 1863.

To Robert Potts

PROPOSED ADMISSION OF GIRLS TO UNIVERSITY LOCAL EXAMINATIONS.
17, CUNNINGHAM PLACE, LONDON, N.W.

June 20th 1863.

Dear Mr. Potts

Since I wrote to you last I have seen Mr. Tomkinson. I mentioned to him your intention of coming to Town shortly, & he said he thought it would be very useful if you could see some of the members of the London Local Committee. He has heard from Mr. Liveing & he thinks the amount of encouragement we have received at Cambridge is sufficient to justify our taking some farther steps with regard to the experimental examination. We should feel much more clear however, after consulting with you. Could you give us as much notice as ten days or a fortnight? In London it is so difficult to get hold of anybody, unless you give very long notice.

Mr. Tomkinson is himself going out of Town, but would come up to meet you.

I am so glad it seems likely that Cambridge will have the honour of being the *first* University which will do anything to help us! The others will no doubt follow.

Yours very sincerely
S. E. Davies.

GC: ALS ED LOC-39

To Henry Tomkinson

PROPOSED ADMISSION OF GIRLS TO UNIVERSITY LOCAL EXAMINATIONS.
17, CUNNINGHAM PLACE, LONDON, N.W.

June 20th ⟨1863⟩

Dear Mr. Tomkinson

Thank you for Professor Liveing's letter. It seems to me very encouraging; as he raises no objection except that about the increase of work, for the Examiners, which can be so easily met.[1] I have written to Mr. Potts to-day, & told him that you thought it would be useful for him to see some of the members of the Cambridge (London) Committee. I was obliged to give some reason for writing again & asking him to give us longer notice. You will see by his letter that he is very ready to help us.

I suppose you will at any rate call your meeting within the next fortnight. I saw Mr. Hastings this morning & he said he should be very glad to attend the meeting, if he had not left Town, but he will be going on Circuit, & I think he said that it begins on the 10th of July. As soon as you have fixed the day, Mr. Hastings will, if you approve, ask Lord ⟨George⟩ Lyttelton to join your Committee & attend the meeting. Lord Lyttelton is very friendly, & Mr. Hastings thinks he would have considerable weight with the people at Cambridge.

The "statement", as finally passed by the Committee is now ready. We have copies at Prince's St., if you can make use of any.[2] I ought to tell you that I do not often get to the office by three o'clock. Between four & five, I am almost sure of being there.

Yours sincerely
S. E. Davies

GC: ALS ED LOC-38

1. Liveing's letter to Tomkinson was less encouraging than ED here suggests: "It would be no use to the ladies to have the papers after our examn. was over & I do not see that the papers could be issued before that without leave from the Syndicate. . . . I do not think it so unlikely that the Senate would agree to have a special examn. for the girls as that the exam-

iners of the boys would undertake the girls also.... I think that most would decline to do anything extra.... I am quite willing that the girls should be examined & shall be glad to do all I can to extend the scheme to them but I think they ought to have an examn. to themselves or else a much larger staff of examiners be appointed" (Chronicle 301–2).

2. Prince's Street was the location of Faithfull's printing office, as well as the office of the *Victoria*.

To Anna Richardson

PROPOSED ADMISSION OF GIRLS TO UNIVERSITY LOCAL EXAMINATIONS.
17, CUNNINGHAM PLACE, LONDON, N.W.

June 20 1863

My dear Anna

Will you please give me a note of introduction to Miss Saunders.[1] I should like very much to see her if I go to Brighton, & I cannot call on her quite ~~promiscuous.~~ If you write to Mr. Potts, you can enlarge upon the badness of girls' schools, which you feel as strongly as anybody, & of which there are plenty of examples in & around Newcastle. If girls were at all commonly up to passing, the want of the examns. would not be half so great. Hundreds of boys have failed, especially in spelling, & the failures are considered the most conclusive evidence in favour of the scheme. The Bedford College people are doing what they can. They complain bitterly of the deplorable ignorance of the girls who come to them at fifteen & upwards. Their previous years seem to have been almost thrown away. Do you really think ⟨the Society of⟩ Friends would object to University Examns.?

GC: DAL ED LOC-40

1. Probably Emily M. Saunders, principal of a school in Brighton, who signed the Local Examinations memorial in 1864.

To Robert Potts

PROPOSED ADMISSION OF GIRLS TO UNIVERSITY LOCAL EXAMINATIONS.
17, CUNNINGHAM PLACE, LONDON, N.W.

July 23d. 1863.

Dear Mr. Potts

I have been hoping either to see or to hear from you, for the last two or three weeks. Since I wrote to you last the London Local Committee for Cambridge have met & passed a Resolution unanimously, promising to help us to carry out our views with regard to the informal Examination in December.[1] I believe we ought now to apply to the Syndicate for permission, but I should like to hear from you whether you think it advisable to send in our application to the Secretary at once, or to defer it still longer. We should be glad to have the matter settled as soon as we can, because the girls will want the ensuing half-year for preparation. Of course the refusal of the Syndicate to this private & irregular examination, if they *should* refuse, will not commit them either way upon the general question, which we do not propose bringing on as yet.

I remain,
Yours very truly
S. E. Davies

GC: ALS ED LOC-43

1. On 3 July, Tomkinson's Local Examinations Committee resolved to "give every facility in their power for carrying out the wishes of the Ladies' Committee with regard to their proposed private Examn. of girls" but advised that girls be examined in a separate room (Chronicle 305a). Tomkinson wrote to Davies saying that "the tone of the Committee was … 'We don't *mind* the girls being about at the time of Examns. but we don't feel bound or anxious to take active measures for bringing them in'" (Chronicle 306).

To Robert Potts

N⟨ewson⟩. Garrett Esq. | Aldeburgh. Suffolk. | Sunday | 31 Aug. ⟨1863⟩
My dear Mr. Potts

I am so very sorry to miss seeing you, & also that I cannot let you know in time to save you the trouble of calling at Cunningham Place. I came down here on Friday, for a week, & only received your note this morning. It is very unfortunate, as I so much wished for some talk with you about our prospects at Cambridge. I suppose we ought to send in our application to the Syndicate some time next month. At the best, I am afraid it will not be possible to get *many* candidates together for the Christmas examination.

I remain, dear Mr. Potts
Yours very truly
S. E. Davies.

GC: ALS ED LOC-44

To Robert Potts

17 Cunningham Place. N.W. | Sept. 23d. ⟨1863⟩
My dear Mr. Potts

I was very sorry that I could not manage to see you at Yarmouth, as you kindly suggested. I found it was so much out of the way that it would have involved quite a separate journey, & I had not the time to spare just then.

We propose sending in our application to the Syndicate before the end of this month, to secure having it considered as early as possible in October.[1] We shall ask leave to print a few additional copies of the Examination papers, for our use, & for leave to make an arrangement with the Cambridge Examiners to look over the girls' papers, of course guaranteeing all expenses. If, as I suppose is very likely, the Syndics consider it "beyond their powers", to do what we wish, they will not be in any degree committed against the general measure.

I remain, dear Mr. Potts
Yours very sincerely
S. E. Davies.

GC: ALS ED LOC-45

1. The application for permission to conduct an unofficial, private examination for girls.

To ⟨Charles Gray⟩

⟨September 26⟩ [1863]

Sir

On behalf of a Committee of ladies & gentlemen interested in the education of girls, I am desired to make application to the Syndicate appointed by the University of Cambridge to provide for the examination of students who are not members of the University, for permission to print a few additional copies of the examination papers for 1863, to be used in a private examn. of girls which it is proposed to hold simultaneously with the Cambridge Local Examination in London. I am also desired to ask leave to make a private arrangement with the examiners to look over the answers & report upon them. We should of course be responsible for the safe custody of the papers, & for all expenses.

I beg to enclose a Resolution passed unanimously by the London Local Committee in reference to the proposed private examn.

I am Sir,

GC: DAL ED LOC-31

To Henry Tomkinson

PROPOSED ADMISSION OF GIRLS TO UNIVERSITY LOCAL EXAMINATIONS.
17, CUNNINGHAM PLACE, LONDON, N.W.

Oct. 24th 1863.

Dear Mr. Tomkinson

I suppose you have heard from Mr. Gray.[1] The friendly answer from the Syndicate took me quite by surprise, as I had carefully prepared myself for a polite refusal. We must now look out for candidates, & make the necessary arrangements. We propose holding a meeting of the Committee at 3 Waterloo Place, on Tuesday at three o'clock. I hope that day & hour will be convenient to you. We shall want to know from you where the Examinations are to be held, & some particulars about the hours, & the latest date at which candidates' names can be received, &c. Of course we cannot make Nov. 2nd *our* latest date.[2] I am afraid the shortness of the notice will be against us in getting candidates, but a very small number will be sufficient for trying the experiment. I hope we shall not give you a great deal of extra trouble.

I remain
Yours very truly
S. E. Davies.

GC: ALS ED LOC-46

1. On 23 October, Gray, secretary of the Cambridge Local Examinations Syndicate, responded to the committee's request, saying that the syndicate "have agreed, to have printed the extra copies, of the Exam. papers, and to direct their Examiner in London to give these out to some responsible person . . . after he shall have given them out to the boys. The Syndicate decline to *order the* Examiners in the various subjects, to look over the answers of the girls, but leave it to your Committee to make what arrangements you please with the Examiners" (Chronicle 318a).

2. According to the Cambridge Local Examinations regulations for 1863, "The names of . . . Students must be sent to the Local Secretary on or before November 2, 1863" (University of Cambridge, Local Examinations, 1863).

To Charlotte Manning

PROPOSED ADMISSION OF GIRLS TO UNIVERSITY LOCAL EXAMINATIONS.
17, CUNNINGHAM PLACE, LONDON, N.W.

October 24th 1863.

My dear Mrs. ⟨Charlotte⟩ Manning

Rather to our surprise, we have received a favourable answer from the Cambridge Syndicate, & we must now exert ourselves to get candidates together. The notice is much too short, but that we must make the best of, as it cannot be helped.

Our Committee meets at 3 Waterloo Place, on Tuesday at three o'clock. I do hope you will be able to attend. I send you the draft of a circular which I propose submitting to the Committee for their approval.[1] I dare say you will be able to suggest some improvements in it.

We rely upon you for making the matter known in Queens College. They ought to send us some good candidates.

I write in some fear that you may be from home, but will hope the best. With love to Miss ⟨E. Adelaide⟩ Manning, I remain

Yours most truly

S. E. Davies.

GC: ALS ED LOC-47

1. In the circular, ED advised interested parties that the committee had "obtained permission from the [Cambridge University] Syndicate to make use of the examination papers prepared for the Local Examinations, and to submit the answers to the University Examiners." The examinations were to be held "from Monday, Dec. 14th, to Saturday, Dec. 19th inclusive" (circular detailing information on the Cambridge Local Examinations, 1863, GC ED VII/LOC-52a).

To Anna Richardson

17 C.P. Monday evening. | [October 26th 1863]

My dear Anna

I sent you the Scotsman regularly, & you ought to have had them every day. I suppose the Edinburgh Post-office broke down under the unusual pressure. Many thanks for your suggestions about articles. I was to have met Mr. ⟨Henry⟩ Fawcett at Mrs. Maclaren's, but he was obliged to leave by an early train, & I just missed him.[1] I wrote to him on getting home & send you his answer. The criticism on the Social Science dinner was called forth by some remarks of mine in a similar strain. It was the worst feature of the whole meeting.

Our breath was taken away on Saturday by receiving quite unexpectedly a favourable answer from the Camb. Syndicate to our application. I fully expected they would politely get rid of us by saying it was "beyond their powers." It has thrown us into dreadful agitation. We have only six weeks to work up our candidates, & who can expect them to come up on so short a notice? Do come to the rescue. We shall look unspeakably foolish if we have no candidates, after all, & people won't understand the reason. I send you the rough draft of a circular which I propose submitting to our Committee to-morrow.[2] It is sure to be altered somewhat (& will not appear in this form at any rate) but I send it as the shortest way of explaining our general policy. I will send you a packet of circulars as soon as they are ready, & please send them about. If any country girls like to come up, we will arrange to receive them & take good care of them during the Examn. week.

You might send us some *junior* candidates.[3] Girls at a good school ought to be able to go in for that without much special coaching.

Why should not your youngest sister come? She might be *here*, if you would let her come to us. And she would be almost sure to get a good prize. I am afraid no girls will come who are not certain to pass, whereas *hundreds* of boys failed the first year. You will see a notice of Wordsworth's Italy in the V⟨ictoria magazine).[4] If you like, you shall have it for 9/. It is perfectly new, with no Publisher's brand upon it, & only part of the leaves cut—a bargain not often to be met with!

My love to Mr. Richardson. I think you will like Marcus Aurelius.[5] Yrs. ever
ED.

GC: ALS ED LOC-48

1. Probably Priscilla Bright McLaren (1812–1905), who was married to Duncan McLaren. She raised money for the Anti-Corn Law League and worked to reform prisons, insane asylums and hospitals, and for the Rational Dress Society, medical education for women, and repeal of the C.D. Acts. She was a leader in the women's suffrage movement and a president of the National Society for Women's Suffrage.

2. The circular, together with a handwritten letter, was sent out to schoolmistresses, asking them to send students to the University Local Examinations.

3. The University Local Examinations were offered to Junior students (those who had not yet reached age sixteen) and to Senior students (those over age sixteen but not yet eighteen).

4. "Literature of the Month," review of *Journal of a Tour in Italy, with Reflections on the Present Condition and Prospects of Religion in that Country,* by Chr. Wordsworth, *Victoria* (November 1863): 94.

5. Matthew Arnold, "Marcus Aurelius," *Victoria* (November 1863): 1–19.

To Henry Tomkinson

PROPOSED ADMISSION OF GIRLS TO UNIVERSITY LOCAL EXAMINATIONS.
17, CUNNINGHAM PLACE, LONDON, N.W.

Oct. 28th 1863.

Dear Mr. Tomkinson

I send you a copy of the letter I have concocted for the Schoolmistresses. Miss Bostock sanctions it, & I am just about to send it to be lithographed, but if you can kindly suggest any improvements, there will be time to make alterations.

Yours very truly
S. E. Davies.

GC: ALS ED LOC-50

To Thomas Dyke Acland

PROPOSED ADMISSION OF GIRLS TO UNIVERSITY LOCAL EXAMINATIONS.
17, CUNNINGHAM PLACE, LONDON, N.W.

Oct. 28th 1863.

My dear Sir

I think you will be glad to hear that the Cambridge Syndics have sent a most friendly reply to our application. We followed your suggestions, to the letter, in the terms of our application, & they have granted all we asked.

They will print extra copies of the Examination papers & direct their Examiner to give them out to some one appointed by us, each day, after they have been given out to the boys. The Syndicate will not *order* the Examiners to look over the answers, but we are allowed to make a private arrangement with them, & the Secretary has no doubt that they will be quite willing to undertake it.

Our great fear now is that owing to the shortness of the notice, we shall have difficulty in getting the candidates together. A very small number however will be sufficient for the purpose of trying the experiment.

If you should happen to be in London during the Examination week, perhaps you will look in upon us, & see for yourself, how the *idea marches*!

I remain, dear Sir
Yours very truly
Emily Davies.

Faw: ALS Vol. 4A

To Henry Tomkinson

PROPOSED ADMISSION OF GIRLS TO UNIVERSITY LOCAL EXAMINATIONS.
17, CUNNINGHAM PLACE, LONDON, N.W.

Oct. 30th ⟨1863⟩

Dear Mr. Tomkinson

I am very much obliged to you for taking the trouble to criticise the circular.[1] There is nothing so provoking as being told vaguely that things will *do*. I would much rather be told that they *won't* do. I think there must be some discrepancy between the beginning & the end, for Miss Bostock approved of all *except* "the bit of humility at the end." As to the first phrase you have marked, I thought I was paying the people rather a compliment in assuming that they were interested in the subject. The other sentence was more deferentially worded at first, but it struck me that it had a kind of pleading air about it which would have a bad effect on the schoolmistress mind. I don't think it would do for them to think we are begging them to send in candidates as a favour to us. But I had a feeling that it *was*, as you say, a little dictatorial in tone, & tried to make up by growing polite at the end. As you don't press your objections & yours & Miss Bostock's rather balance each other, perhaps the note may as well stand as it is.

I have had a letter of inquiry from a lady at Cambridge this morning, & yesterday I heard from a lady who is willing to present candidates whether they are likely to pass or not. I did not think anybody would have been public spirited enough to send in pupils to *fail* for the common good.

I have asked Mr. Maurice to bring the matter before the authorities of Queen's College. *He* is friendly, but the other Professors seem to be doubtful.

Yours very truly
S. E. Davies

GC: ALS ED LOC-53

1. The letter circulated to schoolmistresses, inviting them to enter their students for the Local Exams.

To Charlotte Manning

PROPOSED ADMISSION OF GIRLS TO UNIVERSITY LOCAL EXAMINATIONS.
17, CUNNINGHAM PLACE, LONDON, N.W.

Oct. 31st ⟨1863⟩

My dear Mrs. Manning

I am very glad you & Miss Manning are not forgetting London & public interests, tho' you are *en retraite* for the present. Writing to Mr. ⟨Edward⟩ Plumptre is a most useful thing to do. I have asked Mr. Maurice to bring the matter forward, knowing him to be friendly, but I fancy the decision will be chiefly in Mr. Plumptre's hands. Unfortunately we cannot take candidates over 18, as we go by the University Regulations & that is their rule. I don't think it would do for us to make exceptions. Do you know any girls likely to go in? Miss Bishop, for instance?[1]

We are beginning to hear of candidates, which is a great comfort, for we were very much afraid the shortness of the notice would be fatal to our success. It suddenly occurred to me last night that by a very stupid oversight, we had told people to send in names on *Sunday*! Would you kindly alter the date in the circulars I sent you, to the 16th. We are having more copies struck off, in which the correction will be made, & are altering those we have on hand. I am sending the circular & a lithographed letter calling attention to it, to about 250 schoolmistresses, & a friend of mine at Brighton has undertaken to send to all the schools there, (about 100.) I have been offering all over the Kingdom to receive candidates & take good care of them during the Examination week, feeling pretty confident that the demand on our hospitality will not be more than we can meet.[2]

I am glad you will be at home by Dec. at any rate. You will be much wanted during the Examination. I attended the W.R.C. Union Council yesterday, & just got notice given of a motion to make the Council meetings monthly, & to appoint an Executive Committee. I think this would be a great improvement. The difficulty will be to get an *executive* Committee, who will work.

With love to Miss Manning
Yours affectionately
Emily Davies.

GC: ALS ED LOC-54

1. Probably Matilda Bishop (1844–1913). Educated at Queen's College, London, she was the Assistant Headmistress of the Oxford High School, and the first principal of the Royal Holloway College for Women.

2. In the end, the Russell Gurneys took in two students, and the Westlakes took two or three.

To Thomas Dyke Acland

PROPOSED ADMISSION OF GIRLS TO UNIVERSITY LOCAL EXAMINATIONS.
17, CUNNINGHAM PLACE, LONDON, N.W.

Nov. 2d 1863.

My dear Sir

Thank you very much for your kind offer of help in arranging for our examination, & for the suggestions you have made.

In our circular we offer prizes, tho' without giving any particulars about them. I am afraid we should scarcely have time, first to see about getting prizes offered & then to make them known. There is a little difference of opinion in our Committee about prizes. The London Committee for Cambridge does not offer them at all & there is some unwillingness to offer inducements to girls which are not held out to the boys. I do not think this applies in the present case, because the boys will have the *University* certificate, which we shall not be able to give.[1] But we do not say much about prizes, partly because we are anxious to avoid doing anything which may seem in the least like courting publicity. For this reason we do not advertise, & that will probably secure us from being overrun with incapable candidates. We are sending out a large number of circulars & have met with a much more hearty response than we at all expected, but it is from the better sort of teachers. The inferior ones would rather *not* have their work tested & are besides, excessively afraid of doing anything unusual. We have thought of holding such a preliminary examination as you suggest, to prepare the girls for the coming ordeal, but I do not know whether we shall be able to manage it.

Our examination will certainly be on a very small scale. The shortness of the notice gives the girls scarcely a fair chance, considering that there are definite subjects set which must be specially got up, but we do not like to pass by the opportunity of trying the experiment, however humbly. The place is not yet fixed upon, as it depends on the number of the boys. Last year it was Willis's Rooms, & we hope it will be the same again, as in that case we shall be able to have a convenient little room to ourselves, adjoining that of the boys.

Can you give us any hints as to what course it will be best for us to pursue with regard to Oxford? We should like very much to do a little good to Oxford, as you say we shall to Cambridge! Sir Benjamin Brodie advised us to get Petitions sent from all parts, but this is not very easy to do. Ladies are not used to getting up Petitions & don't know very well how to set about it, & the Local Committees do not *care* enough to take any active steps. Two or three have passed friendly Resolutions, but as a rule, they wait for instructions from the Universities. There would be no great difficulty in getting up *one* general Memorial, if that would be sufficient.

Of course we should like it much better if we could get what we want quite quietly, without making any fuss at all, but I suppose the University would scarcely alter the Statute (which at Oxford they say would be necessary) without some formal appeal. In any case I suppose we had better wait for the result of the informal Examinations before taking any fresh steps. We shall be much indebted to you if you will take the trouble to ascertain what the feeling is at Oxford & counsel us as to what we had better do next.

I saw in the Daily News that you had spoken very kindly of our doings, but we were a little disappointed that you did not express any opinion of your own, which would carry much more weight than anything that we can say.

I remain, dear Sir
Yours very truly
Emily Davies.

I send you a few of our circulars, in case you may find any use for them at Oxford.

Faw: ALS Vol. 4A

1. The University Grace of 11 February 1858 specified "That the Students who pass the Examinations to the satisfaction of the Examiners, be entitled to receive Certificates to that effect."

To Henry Tomkinson

17 C.P. Nov. 10th | ⟨1863⟩

Dear Mr. Tomkinson

I have one more question to ask. A Queen's College girl of fifteen wishes to know whether she may go in for a Senior Certificate. It does not seem a wise thing to do, but I cannot make out that there is any rule against it.

I suppose I must write to Mr. Gray for the Forms of Application, when we know the exact number of candidates.

Mr. Thornton has sent the names of two Candover girls.[1] They take up Divinity, Latin & perhaps Mathematics. I hope they will not break down ignominiously in the Preliminary.[2] Some of the schoolmistresses' letters are almost illegible & very funny. One is afraid the Examinations will foster the spirit of confidence & independence which is too common amongst girls of the present day. I fancy girls must be excessively insubordinate by nature, or they never would have a grain of spirit left, after going thro' school training.

Do you know whether Mr. ⟨Leonard⟩ Courtney means to recognise us?[3] As we shall give him, I suppose, more trouble than any of the other Examiners, I think we ought to communicate with him soon, but perhaps it will be best to wait till we know how many candidates there will be.

Miss Bostock is very strong on the cupidity of girls. I hope the Committee will not support you & Miss Craig in restricting us to olive wreaths as prizes.

Yours very sincerely
Emily Davies

GC: ALS ED LOC-55

1. Reverend F. V. Thornton, who ran an innovative coeducational school in Hampshire.
2. The Preliminary Examination included reading aloud, writing from dictation, English grammar, arithmetic, and geography.
3. Leonard Courtney of St. John's College had conducted the London Examinations in 1862, and Davies expected him to be supervising the examinations for 1863. However, A. B. Chalker was the examinations conductor in 1863.

To Robert Potts

17 Cunningham Place, | St. John's Wood Road, | Maida Hill.
Nov. 10th | [1863?] ⟨1863⟩

Dear Mr. Potts

It will give me great pleasure to make Miss Fison's acquaintance, if she will kindly take the trouble to call here, at any time that may be convenient to her.[1]

I am almost certain to be in any morning up till one o'clock. In the afternoon I am generally at the Victoria Press Prince's St. Hanover Square, & could arrange to meet Miss Fison there, if that would suit her better than coming here.

We are very much encouraged about our candidates. It seems likely that we shall have at least as many as forty, if they don't take fright at last.

A great many teachers who cannot send in on so short a notice, hope to do so next year.

I have heard from Mrs. Cooper.[2] She thinks she cannot manage to send candidates up to London. We scarcely expected any from the country, but it seems likely that we shall have a few.

I remain, dear Mr. Potts
Yours very sincerely
S. E. Davies.

GC: ALS ED LOC-56

1. Probably Anna Fison (1839–1920), a linguist.
2. Probably Lydia Cooper, principal of Wanstead House School, Cambridge.

To Henry Tomkinson

Nov. 11th ⟨1863⟩

Dear Mr. Tomkinson

I was under the impression that Mr. Gray had *offered*, in his letter to you, to let us have Forms of Application. If this is not so, or indeed in any case, of course we must treat it as a favour. Perhaps when you are writing to him, you will be kind enough to ask him about it. I think we are likely to want about 50. Mr. Plumptre speaks generally of wanting about 30 for Queen's, but I don't suppose more than half that number will actually come to the point.

I hope Mr. Courtney will be goodnatured. We shall be in an awkward position if he declines having anything to do with the girls, for I am afraid there is no lady on the Committee in the least fit to conduct an examination.

You are very wrong about the prizes. We are not going to have a public distribution at all, & if we had, we should not want the Bishop of Oxford. No one supposes that the girls would choose earrings or anything foolish, but the privilege of free choice is very dear to them, perhaps because they so seldom have the chance of exercising it.

Mr. Acland suggested our getting "noble ladies" like the Duchess of Sutherland, to offer prizes in their own name, but I knew you & Miss Craig would not let us have anything to do with such a vulgar proposition.

In fact I was afraid even to mention it.

Do you let anybody that likes come in to look on during the Examination? I invited Mr. Acland to come & see how we get on, & it occurred to me afterwards that I ought not to have done it.

Yours very sincerely
Emily Davies.

GC: ALS ED LOC-58

To Henry Tomkinson

17 Cunningham Place | Saturday. Nov. ⟨14⟩ 1863

Dear Mr. Tomkinson

I think perhaps it will be best for me to write to Mr. Gray about the Forms of Application, on the part of the Committee, as he did not offer them, & I can then explain to him that *we* have not been spreading false reports about the examns. I suppose you have seen his letter to the Times. I cannot understand how the matter got into the papers at all. I have only seen it in the Record, but I suppose they must have got it from somewhere else, with their singular knack of picking up inaccurate information. The list of candidates already amounts to 78, & I expect a few more on Monday. Will the room hold them all? Two or three schoolmistresses have asked leave to come with their pupils, & to that I think we can scarcely object. The want of room will be a quite sufficient reason for excluding mere idle spectators.

I hope you will always express your views with the most entire freedom, either about prizes or anything else. It is of no use to have a Committee if they won't say what they think. Mr. Acland's suggestion about the "noble ladies" did not come till after our Committee. I certainly should not have refrained from mentioning it if I had in the least wished to adopt it. As to its being "*convenient*" to have your help on the Committee, it is certainly *very* convenient, for we could not get on at all without it. It seems to me that you are the one member of the Committee who *has* a right to speak with authority. If we get these Examinations at last, it will be mainly due to your having so kindly advised & helped us all thro'—

I remain
Yours very truly
Emily Davies.

GC: ALS ED LOC-59

To Thomas Dyke Acland

PROPOSED ADMISSION OF GIRLS TO UNIVERSITY LOCAL EXAMINATIONS.
17, CUNNINGHAM PLACE, LONDON, N.W.

Nov. 14th 1863

Dear Sir

I am afraid we cannot now arrange for the examination of girls anywhere but in London. It would complicate matters very much if it were done *thro' us*, & we should be obliged to ask permission from the Syndics, who may not be disposed to give us anything more at present. The addition of a paper on teaching would involve somewhat similar objections. It would be a divergence from the University Regulations, in *exact* accordance with which (except in the matter of fees) this experimental examn. is to be conducted. The proposed arrangements are extremely simple. The whole thing is in the hands of the Local Secretary. He engages an extra room, which he would have been obliged to do if it had so happened that he had sixty more boys than usual to provide for.

The Examination papers will come thro' him, & he will return the girls' answers, with the boys', to the Secretary at Cambridge. We make the matter known, & the girls' names are sent in thro' me. Beyond that, our Committee does nothing except the superintendence, which I suppose is done by the Local Committees for the boys.

Besides the inconvenience of introducing a new subject into the examination, there is another objection to making the *teaching* question too prominent. It would be likely to convey the impression that the main purpose of the test is to certify *governesses*. Such an impression would tend to discourage girls who are not intending to teach from going in, & so would operate against our great object, that of raising the standard of education *generally*. Among the students whose names have been sent in, are ~~some~~ many who have no prospect of working for their bread in any way. They simply want to have their scholarship tested, to know, on good authority, where they stand, & we should be sorry to discourage this sort of disinterested competition, by treating the certificates primarily as passports to the profession of teaching. The special object which Miss ⟨Mary Eliza⟩ Porter has in view might I should think, be attained in some way thro' the College of Preceptors.[1]

Thank you very much for your suggestions about Oxford. I will write to Mr. Griffith & let him know how we have been getting on. The number of candidates has quite astonished us. Already more than 70 names have been sent in, & a few others are still to come. The candidates are from Queen's College, Bedford College, some large schools calling themselves collegiate, & from various private schools in London & the neighborhood. Candidates are also coming up from Hampshire, Somersetshire & Rugby. The letters from schoolmistresses show an appreciation of the advantages offered, which we did not in the least expect from them. A great many who cannot arrange to send up pupils on so short a notice, are eager to do so at a future opportunity. It does not appear that we shall have any difficulty in getting up a good Memorial. We shall not however I think take any steps about it till we have got thro' this experiment.

I was much obliged to you for kindly sending the Exeter paper, containing a fuller report of your speech than I had before seen. I am very glad it has now appeared in the Guardian.

I remain
Yours very sincerely
S. E. Davies

Faw: ALS Vol. 4A

1. The College of Preceptors was founded in 1846 to train teachers. The Ladies' Department of the College was established in 1847.

To Henry Tomkinson

PROPOSED ADMISSION OF GIRLS TO UNIVERSITY LOCAL EXAMINATIONS.
17, CUNNINGHAM PLACE, LONDON, N.W.

[? 18] Nov. 1863 | Wednesday

Dear Mr. Tomkinson

I think we shall be able to find our way out of the difficulty about the room. The Reformatory Union people have just taken a new office at 26 Suffolk St., Pall Mall, where they have a large room which they wish to let occasionally.[1] Miss Craig & I went to see it this morning. It is 42 ft. long (I believe) & wide enough to hold four *narrow* tables down the middle. We should have to provide the fittings but that I suppose could be done without much difficulty. We saw the Secretary Mr. ⟨Albert⟩ Charles, & he is to ask his Committee which meets tomorrow, whether, supposing we want it, we can have it, paying £20 for the week. He has no doubt they will be glad to let us have it, & he would arrange to let us have also a small room which they use as an office, for the Examiner's use. It is within five minutes' walk of Willis's Rooms, & there is the further advantage that Mr. Charles is rather a friend of Miss Craig's & mine, & would take pains to make convenient arrangements for us. I fancy a larger room would be better, if we could get it, but that this might do. On that & other points however, you would be much better able to judge than we are, & if you can manage to spare time to look at it some day when you are in that neighborhood, we can then decide. How would it do to let the boys go to Suffolk St., if they are the smaller number, & let us have the rooms you have taken for them? I am not much afraid of the expenses, but we should not like to have the boys put to inconvenience, as they are lords & we are only *beggars*! Thank you for the Forms. I am so sorry to take up your time, when you have none to spare. I should think the conducting Examiners must have a Fee, as they are not called Honorary.[2] If they do, I suppose we could not go wrong in offering the same for the girls that is usually paid for the boys, as the trouble will be at least doubled.

Yours very sincerely
Emily Davies.

GC: ALS ED LOC-67

1. The Reformatory Union was established by Lord Brougham, George Hastings, and Matthew Davenport Hill to promote juvenile reformatories and reform laws on delinquency. It held its first conference in Bristol in 1856.

2. The candidates were not asked to pay fees; therefore committee members contributed to cover the expenses associated with the examinations.

To Robert Potts

PROPOSED ADMISSION OF GIRLS TO UNIVERSITY LOCAL EXAMINATIONS.
17, CUNNINGHAM PLACE, LONDON, N.W.

Nov. 19th 1863.

Dear Mr. Potts

I dare say you have heard from Miss Fison, that we are likely to have plenty of candidates, 100, or 101. The fear now seems to be whether we may not have got together too many. I have had a rather alarming letter from Mr. Gray. He seems doubtful as to how the Examiners will like being asked to undertake so much extra work, as they have more than they like already.[1] Unfortunately all our candidates take up English, so that the bulk of the demand comes upon one department. Can you help us? If it were a question of fees, we should be quite ready to pay *more* than our proportion, as we are asking a special favour, but I fancy it is simply that the examiners do not want more of this sort of drudgery, on any terms. It must be extremely tiresome work. Of course if the examn. of girls was an admitted thing, it could be provided for by the appointment of more examiners. There seems to be no discouragement given to increasing the number of *boys*, to any extent. But I am afraid nothing can be done in that way this year.

If you should happen to know any of the Examiners, perhaps you may be able to do something for us. When we only expected a small number of girls, Mr. Gray seemed to have no doubt that the Examiners would be quite willing to look over the papers, & it will put us into a most awkward position if they decline. Of course we can give them as much time as they like to take. I was very glad to see Miss Fison the other day, & to hear from her some Cambridge news. I hope she has got rid of the bad cold from which she was then suffering.

I remain, dear Mr. Potts
Yours most truly
Emily Davies.

GC: ALS ED LOC-61

1. Gray had written to ED on 18 November, saying: "Your numbers are so large that I really cannot undertake to answer for the Examiners, & although I have already told them that your application would be made, yet I think you must apply to each one of them separately. The English Examiners are already overtaxed, how they will manage 20 per cent more work, I do not quite know" (Chronicle 325).

To Thomas Dyke Acland

PROPOSED ADMISSION OF GIRLS TO UNIVERSITY LOCAL EXAMINATIONS.
17, CUNNINGHAM PLACE, LONDON, N.W.

Nov. 20th 1863.

Dear Mr. Acland

I wrote to Mr. Griffiths, according to your suggestion, & he advises us to make our application to Oxford at once. He says the Vice-Chancellor will move the renewal of the Statute in the Hebdomadal Council almost immediately, so there seems to be no time to lose. Our notion is to have a Memorial signed by teachers, & supported by Members of Parliament & noble ladies, &c. Mr. Griffiths thinks this would do. But I do not see how we can get up a Memorial in less than three or four weeks at least.[1] Do you think the Vice-Chancellor could be induced to delay his motion for the presentation of the Memorial, so as to give the subject the chance of a hearing? I enclose a copy of a Memorial which was drawn up about a year ago, & which with modifications, may perhaps answer our purpose now. Do you think it necessary to mention the subject of expense in the Memorial? I do not quite see how a Committee like ours can make itself responsible for carrying out the details of a measure which is to be permanent & extending all over the country; & if, as we intend, the girls pay the same fees as the boys, I suppose their fees would cover ~~any~~ the extra expense. This might be mentioned in a "fly leaf", which Mr. Griffiths kindly offers to circulate for us. I believe the whole matter might be quite safely left to the Local Committees. Except for being present at the Examination, we find our ladies' Committee quite superfluous here. The simple plan would be to add a few ladies to the Local Committees, but if that was objected to, the Local Sec. could, I should suppose, easily invite two or three ladies to take part in the superintendence of the examination. I suppose it might be as well to wind up the Memorial to Oxford by some allusion to the approaching renewal of the Statute. We should wish to make the same Memorial serve as nearly as possible for both Universities, as we shall, I think, ask people to sign the two together. I am afraid we could not ᵍᵉᵗ two separate Memorials signed & supported, within a few weeks of each other. But that, the Committee will decide. We shall meet some day next week, & if in the meantime you can kindly give me any advice about the Memorial, I shall be glad to lay it before the Committee.

The Cambridge Sec. seems rather frightened at the amount of extra work we have provided for the Examiners. The girls, numbering a hundred, all want to be examined in English, which makes it come very heavy upon *some* of the Examiners.

I remain, dear Sir
Yours very truly
Emily Davies.

Faw: ALS Vol. 4A

1. The memorial they finally presented to Cambridge, which they began working on early in 1864, was not complete until October of that year.

To Robert Potts

PROPOSED ADMISSION OF GIRLS TO UNIVERSITY LOCAL EXAMINATIONS.
17, CUNNINGHAM PLACE, LONDON, N.W.

Saturday. Nov. 21st. ⟨1863⟩

My dear Mr. Potts

Thank you very much for your most kind & reassuring letter. If the Examiners object to looking over the girls' papers, we shall be most glad to have your assistance to fall back upon. But they have not yet been asked, & we still hope, notwithstanding Mr. Gray's doubts, that they will be willing to do it. As we are trying to make the Examn. as *regular* as possible, we should prefer having the papers looked over by the regular Examiners, & in Mr. Gray's first letter to Mr. Tomkinson he offered to take charge of the girls' papers with the boys'. It is the number that has frightened him, but he does not say that any of the Examiners have objected. I have put off sending our application, which Mr. Gray says must be made to each individually, till I could tell them exactly how many papers there would be. We have not yet got all the Forms of Application filled up, & so are not quite sure about the subjects taken up, except of course the Preliminary, which all must take. It appears to me that if you could see those of the Examiners whom you know, & pave the way for our application, it would be a very great help. But of course you are the best judge as to how far this course would be right & expedient. We shall make our application early next week.

 With many thanks for your kind assistance, I remain
 Yours very sincerely
 Emily Davies.

GC: ALS ED LOC-63

To Robert Potts

PROPOSED ADMISSION OF GIRLS TO UNIVERSITY LOCAL EXAMINATIONS.
17, CUNNINGHAM PLACE, LONDON, N.W.

Nov. 23d. 1863.

Dear Mr. Potts

 My letter of Saturday will have shown you that we were prepared to apply to the Examiners ourselves. I have written to-day to the Examiners in the Preliminary Subjects, English, French & Religious Knowledge.[1] Four of them my brother happens to know, & he has written to them, supporting my letter.

 I mentioned to those whose names you marked, your very kind offer of help. I have not yet written to the Examiner in Mathematics, because I am not sure whether we shall have any candidates in that subject. It will be only two or three at the most. We have not yet asked anybody to superintend the Examination, but I believe there will be no great difficulty about it. We should have preferred an Examiner appointed by the University, but Mr. Tomkinson says it would be impossible for one man to undertake the girls as well as the boys, even if he were willing. I am afraid we shall be obliged to divide the girls, as we cannot get a room large enough to hold them all. Four or five have taken fright, but there seems no prospect of our having less than about ninety.

 Can you tell me whether the Cambridge Statute is likely to be meddled with before long? The Oxford Statute is to be renewed next year, & we had thought of Memorializing for a modification which would permit the admission of girls. But it seems questionable whether such a step would not be premature.[2] We would much rather wait a year or two longer than risk defeat by hasty action.

 I remain, dear Mr. Potts
 Yours most truly
 Emily Davies.

GC: ALS ED LOC-64

1. Davies wrote, on behalf of the committee, to the examiners of subjects for which there were female candidates, offering them unlimited time to review the exams and fees "at their discretion." All agreed to read the exams, "for the most part very cordially" (Chronicle 326).

2. The Oxford Local Examinations were not opened to girls until 1870.

To Henry Tomkinson

PROPOSED ADMISSION OF GIRLS TO UNIVERSITY LOCAL EXAMINATIONS.
17, CUNNINGHAM PLACE, LONDON, N.W.

Nov. 23d. 1863.

Dear Mr. Tomkinson

How would it do to divide the girls into two parties, taking the Suffolk St. room for one set, & the small Willis's room for the rest?[1] Miss Craig & I have come to the conclusion that that would be the best plan under the circumstances, if the small room at Willis's is still to be had. We can easily manage as far as the superintendence goes, & it is a great point to keep within an easy distance of head quarters. The expense is an objection. The Suffolk St. room would be £15 for the week, & I suppose we should have to pay as much or more, for the other room.

But I think that can be managed. We shall have to ask some kind Christian to hear the girls read, & is not there also writing from dictation? Miss Craig is thinking of asking Mr. ⟨John⟩ Norris, the Inspector of Schools, partly for his own good, as he is in a state of semi-conversion & wants to be helped forward. If he declines, my brother thinks there will be no great difficulty in getting some London clergyman to undertake it.

We are to have a Committee on Friday, chiefly to settle what is to be done about Oxford. Mr. Acland & Mr. Griffiths write the most perplexing letters. The Oxford Statute is to be renewed next year, & if we mean to do anything about it, we must get up a Memorial at once. They think we had much better *not* memorialize, unless we are sure of success, & nobody can tell how much chance we have.

The Committee is to be at 3 P.M. on Friday, at Waterloo Place. I am afraid you will not be able to attend at that time. If you can kindly let me know what you think of the plan of having two rooms, & whether the small room at Willis's is still to be had, & on what terms, the Committee can decide. Have you received any Time Tables yet?[2]

Yours very sincerely
Emily Davies.

GC: ALS ED LOC-68

1. They had reserved a large room at the Society of British Artists, on Suffolk Street.
2. These were the daily schedules of subjects to be examined and the time of the examination.

To John Griffiths

Nov. 24th. 1863

Dear Mr. Griffiths

We are exceedingly indebted to you for the information you are kind enough to give us about our prospects at Oxford. I heard from Mr. Acland also yesterday, and he seems confident that our application would not be granted.[1] If he has good grounds for this belief, of course it would be better not to make it. We shall have a meeting of our Committee on Friday, at which the question must be decided.

Would you have the goodness to let me know, in the mean time, what we should lose by deferring our application, i.e., supposing we let this opportunity of asking for a modification of the Statute pass by, how long should we have to wait before we could make a similar application?

Could what we want be given to us in any other way, as for instance, by what I think is called at Cambridge a Grace of the Senate?

Whenever we make our formal application, it *must* be for full admission. The University Certificate is precisely *the* thing that is wanted for girls, and we would rather wait patiently for it, than expend labour in trying to get from Oxford a sort of examination which can already be obtained elsewhere. The arrangement we have made with Cambridge is essentially temporary and local, and would not work as a permanent scheme.

But if the Oxford Delegacy were willing to make a similar arrangement with us, we should gladly accept it for a year or two, in the hope that thro' the gradual working of public opinion, we might eventually obtain the more complete measure.

Should you advise the circulation at Oxford of a fly leaf such as you describe, supposing we decide *not* to memorialize at present?[2]

I am quite ashamed of troubling you with so many questions, but I hope you will kindly excuse it.

Yours very truly
Emily Davies

GC: ALS ED LOC-219

1. On 22 November 1863, Davies had received a letter from Griffiths recommending that she circulate at Oxford "a paper entitled 'Reasons for desiring that girls may be admitted to the benefit of the University Local Examinations' or bearing some such title" (Chronicle 332). Acland had written to her on 23 November, saying that the only examination she was "likely to set on foot in conjunction with Oxford [was] one equivalent to but not identical with that of the boys." He concluded: "I believe myself you would do wisely to deal with circumstances as you find them" (Chronicle 330–31).

2. On 25 November 1863, Griffiths responded to Davies's letter, providing details on the procedure for amending the university statute and recommending that the flyleaf be circulated at Oxford whenever they had "made or [were] on the point of making application *either* to the University for full admission *or* only to the Delegates for copies of the papers" (Chronicle 334).

To Robert Potts

PROPOSED ADMISSION OF GIRLS TO UNIVERSITY LOCAL EXAMINATIONS.
17, CUNNINGHAM PLACE, LONDON, N.W.

Thursday. Nov. 26th | ⟨1863⟩

Dear Mr. Potts

You will be glad to hear that Mr. ⟨A. B.⟩ Chalker, Mr. ⟨Thomas⟩ Markby, & Mr. ⟨Samuel⟩ Cheetham, consent very cordially to taking their part in looking over our papers.[1]

The other examiners have not yet sent answers, except Mr. ⟨William⟩ Pike, who will consult with his colleagues.[2] I hope they will not make any difficulty, as we shall have a great many candidates in French.

We are in communication with people at Oxford. They seem very much afraid, & not at all prepared to take a step in advance of Cambridge. They are going to try to have the Statute made permanent on its renewal, but do not feel sure that they will get it. If not, it will be renewed for three years, & we could not ask for any modification within that time. But from all we hear, I am inclined not to memorialize at present. A little delay is of no great consequence, whereas a refusal might be extremely damaging. Mr. Griffiths thinks the Delegacy would give us what Cambridge has already granted, which is quite worth having, as an instalment.

I do not see much force in Mr. Romilly's remark about monks & nuns, considering that in the present case they need never meet.[3] It could scarcely do the monks much harm to look over the nuns' papers, so long as they keep well out of sight. I wonder whether it is considered dangerous for monks & nuns to read each other's books. It would rather limit one's range, to be allowed to read nothing but what is written by married people. Your plan of taking people out for walks seems a very effective means of conversion. I hope none of our Committee will mar your work by writing foolish pamphlets!

Yours most truly
Emily Davies.

GC: ALS ED LOC-71

1. Reverend A. B. Chalker of Emmanuel College was the conducting examiner in London; Reverend Thomas Markby of Trinity Hall was the examiner in English, and Reverend S. Cheetham of Christ's College was the examiner in religious knowledge.

2. Reverend W. B. Pike of Downing College was the examiner in French.

3. Probably Edward Romilly (1838–86), who was educated at Caius College, Cambridge, and called to the bar at Gray's Inn. He was secretary to William James and clerk of records; he married Edith Cowie in 1871.

To Henry Tomkinson

PROPOSED ADMISSION OF GIRLS TO UNIVERSITY LOCAL EXAMINATIONS.
17, CUNNINGHAM PLACE, LONDON, N.W.

Nov. 28th 1863.

Dear Mr. Tomkinson

The room question was discussed at the Committee yesterday, & it was decided to try for a picture place in Pall Mall, which is to let, & which it is thought, would hold all the girls quite easily. If that fails, we propose taking the *two* rooms at 26, Suffolk St. & the card-room at Willis's. They now offer the room adjoining the one you inspected at Suffolk St., which I suppose would hold about 20, so that we *might* manage to make these three rooms do, if we cannot do better. Mr. Hastings has promised to find out about the Picture gallery to-day, & I will let you know directly I hear from him. We sent yesterday, but it was all shut up, & nobody could be made to hear, tho' there was a board up telling you to apply on the premises. It is the place where the Lancashire Exhibition was held.

I have had very pleasant answers from eight out of the eleven Examiners to whom I have written, & I think we are safe now about the looking over of the papers. Mr. Chalker seems very friendly, so I hope he will work pleasantly with whoever we get to conduct our part of the Examination.

I see the candidates do not bring their own stationary. Do *you* provide it? If so, would you kindly order a double quantity, & let us have our share? I make out 93 candidates now, but it is possible that two or three may drop off before the time comes.

There was a little discussion about prizes yesterday, & it was agreed that the prize fund should be kept distinct, in deference to the conscientious objections of some of the Committee to *all* prizes of any sort.

Yours very sincerely
Emily Davies.

GC: ALS ED LOC-69

To Thomas Dyke Acland

PROPOSED ADMISSION OF GIRLS TO UNIVERSITY LOCAL EXAMINATIONS.
17, CUNNINGHAM PLACE, LONDON, N.W.

Nov. 30th 1863.

My Dear Sir

It is really most kind of you to take so much trouble on our behalf, both in making investigations at Oxford, & in enlightening us as to our chances there. I laid your views before our Committee on Friday, & it was agreed not to memorialize at present. From what you say, it does not seem very likely that our application would be granted, & an unfavourable answer would be very damaging. If our experimental Examn. goes off well, we may probably ask the Delegacy for something of the same sort, which Mr. Griffiths thinks would not be refused.[1] Even if it were, I suppose it would be on the ground that it was beyond their powers, & such a refusal would not hurt us much. The Examiners at Cambridge are very friendly, & we are now advised to send in a Memorial in the beginning of next Term, but I am not sure that our Committee will think it wise to push on quite so fast.

I am afraid you must think us very obstinate in pressing for the full admission. What we are afraid of is that the something else which might be granted would not be genuinely equivalent. I am amused to find that our girls quite appreciate the difference between the real University certificate & the imitation we have to offer. They have been making anxious enquiries as to who will sign ours, & evidently only accept it as a pis aller.

Is there any chance of your being able to look in upon us while our examn. is going on?

I remain, dear Sir
Yours very truly
Emily Davies

Faw: ALS Vol. 4A

1. In his letter of 25 November, Griffiths suggested two possibilities: applying to Oxford University for full admission for women or applying only to the delegates for copies of the papers in an experimental scheme similar to the one being undertaken with Cambridge. He continued, "I am not able to say what answer the Delegates would give to the smaller request, but I cannot think they would refuse it" (Chronicle 335).

To Henry Tomkinson

PROPOSED ADMISSION OF GIRLS TO UNIVERSITY LOCAL EXAMINATIONS.
17, CUNNINGHAM PLACE, LONDON, N.W.

Monday evening. | [Nov. 30th 1863]

Dear Mr. Tomkinson

We can have the large room of the Society of British Artists, 6 1/2, Suffolk Street, & four small rooms if we want them, for £10 for the week. I have stupidly forgotten the number of feet. It is 70 by *something*, but there seems no doubt of there being abundance of room for us.

If you will kindly give the order to the carpenter for the desks, I suppose that is all that need be done just at present. A Mr. *Stych* has the charge of the place, & we shall have to pay him something for cleaning & putting it in order. The £10 will include all the rest.

Will the Oxford Committee have enough chairs for both girls & boys, supposing they are willing to lend them? I don't think they like us at all, but perhaps they will not carry their enmity so far as to refuse the chairs.

Several of the girls take up Drawing. I think ten or twelve, but not quite all the Forms have been returned yet.

I am so much obliged to you for setting my mind at rest about the practical details, which were the only thing I was frightened about.

Lady ⟨Louisa⟩ Goldsmid has sent a cheque for £30, & Mr. Heywood, who has heaps of money, is quite ready to give it, so I am not anxious about the expenses.

The Cambridge Examiners are sending delightfully kind letters, & Mr. Potts now advises us to memorialize at the beginning of next Term. I am not sure that it will be wise to push on quite so fast. We are to have a Committee next Tuesday ⁺ᵗᵒ⁻ᵐᵒʳʳᵒʷ ʷᵉᵉᵏ at 3 o'clock.

Yours very sincerely
Emily Davies.

GC: ALS ED LOC-70

To Robert Potts

PROPOSED ADMISSION OF GIRLS TO UNIVERSITY LOCAL EXAMINATIONS.
17, CUNNINGHAM PLACE, LONDON, N.W.

Dec. 2d. 1863. | 5 pm.

Dear Mr. Potts

Your scraps of good news are very welcome, & the favourable impression you give is confirmed by the friendly letters of the Examiners.

I must confess however that I am startled by your proposal that we should send in a Memorial at the beginning of next Term. Do you really think it safe to push on so fast?

Of course, being on the spot, you can judge much better than we can, but it seems to me that it would be more prudent, considering that it is our *last* card that we are going to play, to allow a little more time for the idea to become familiar. Should we lose much by waiting till Easter? By that time, the experiment will have been made, & we should be able to say something about it. In any Memorial that could be drawn up now, we could not do so, & if we were to send in at the beginning of next Term, we should be obliged to set to work almost immediately. Collecting the signatures will take up a good deal of time, especially if we back up the Memorial, as we have thought of doing, with a list of names of supporters.

Of course if we are likely to lose anything by waiting, it would be better to push forward at once, but if we shall only lose time, I think it would be better to incur that loss than to take the last step just now. I think we might get the Memorial better signed, & a better list of supporters, by allowing more time to work it.

Will you kindly let me hear what you think, after taking into consideration these reasons for delay.

I remain, dear Mr. Potts
Yours very sincerely
Emily Davies.

GC: ALS ED LOC-76

To Henry Tomkinson

PROPOSED ADMISSION OF GIRLS TO UNIVERSITY LOCAL EXAMINATIONS.
17, CUNNINGHAM PLACE, LONDON, N.W.

[Dec. ⟨5th⟩ 1863] | Saturday evening.

Dear Mr. Tomkinson

Will you kindly tell me what to say in answer to this letter? It seems a pity not to have Mr. Norris, as he is willing, & his being used to the work would be an advantage, but I don't know whether we could get on with so little *conducting*, especially when our inexperience is taken into consideration.

I suppose the only part which the conducting Examiner *must* do himself, is the Reading Aloud & Writing from Dictation, which I see, only takes half an hour on Thursday afternoon.

How do you do about giving notice of the time of examn. in German, &c.? We have one candidate in Geology, ten in Music, 12 Junior & 11 Senior in German, 14 Senior & 14 Junior in Drawing. I suppose you choose the time for examn. in Drawing, for instance, when the rooms at is comparatively empty. If that is the plan, it would not be wise for us to take the same time, because we shall have fewest students just when you are at the fullest, that is, when the Mathematical subjects are going on.

I have sent Mr. Gray our list & he has kindly given us some advice about the Examiners' Fees, & directions about numbering our candidates, a mysterious process which I hope somebody will understand. Do you think Mr. Gray will send you Drawing papers for us, with the papers?

All the Examiners are propitious, & Mr. Potts's letters are growing very sanguine.

Yours very sincerely
Emily Davies.

GC: ALS ED LOC-74

To Robert Potts

PROPOSED ADMISSION OF GIRLS TO UNIVERSITY LOCAL EXAMINATIONS.
17, CUNNINGHAM PLACE, LONDON, N.W.

Dec. 12th 1863.

Dear Mr. Potts

I am amused at your so keenly resenting *my* rashness in accusing *you* of it. Pray consider the charge as entirely withdrawn. I think we agree thoroughly as to the best plan of action, but I was not prepared to go on quite so fast as you seemed to propose, simply because I know the getting up of a Memorial will take a great deal of time, & labour, & till after Christmas I shall have none to spare.

We communicated with all the Local Secretaries at the outset of our operation, asking them to ^get ~~Pass~~ Resolutions ^passed in our favour.

At Brighton & Birmingham, it was done, & in several other places the Committees took a neutral course, leaving the matter in the hands of the Universities.

At a good many of the local centres the Committee never meets, & takes no part at all, so we could only get the opinion of the Secretaries, of whom the majority were inclined to be favourable. As soon as our experimental Examn. was arranged for, I wrote again to all the Local Secretaries, telling them what we were doing. From three or four, I received very friendly replies, & I have no doubt they will do something for us in communicating with schoolmistresses in their respective localities.

We shall be very glad to submit our Memorial to your supervision. I thought of making it rather short, & circulating with it, a statement of our views, with answers to objections. Do you think this would be a good plan?

Thank you very much for your most kind offer of gifts to our girls. I am sure they will be very acceptable, & we shall be pleased to have them to give.

We have *ninety* candidates. Would you kindly address the parcel to me, care of Mr. Stych, Gallery of Society of British Artists, Suffolk St. Pall Mall. Our arrangements for next week are now complete, & seem likely to go well. Mr. Norris, the Inspector of Schools, kindly undertakes the Reading Aloud & the Dictation. All the Cambridge Examiners have sent us friendly replies. Mr ⟨Francis James⟩. Jameson is the only one who shows any signs of hesitation & fear.

I hope you will bring him quite round before long.

I remain, dear Mr. Potts

Yours very sincerely,

Emily Davies.

GC: ALS ED LOC-79

To Anna Richardson

17 Cunningham Place. London, N.W. | Wednesday. Dec. 23d. | [Dec. 1863]
My dear Anna

It was a great satisfaction to me to get your letter & to hear from yourself how you all were. Mrs. ⟨Annie⟩ Austin often tells me about you, but that is not the same thing as hearing directly. I am so glad that you are able to feel so calm & happy at least sometimes. It will be a long time before that feeling becomes habitual, & I don't think it is any use to struggle to put away grief in a hurry.[1] So long as it is not weakly & sinfully nursed, God Himself will soften it, in due time. I think it is so good of you to go out & to take an interest in what is going on. Of course it is the wisest thing to do, but then so many people are neither good nor wise, especially when they are broken down by trouble. You will tell me soon again I hope, how you all go on. Thank you for your kind inquiries about our examination. It came to an end last Saturday, having been all thro' as completely successful as could possibly be desired. Every one connected with the University was most kind & friendly, & there seems little doubt now that it will be made permanent. Eighty-three candidates finally went thro'. A good many were kept away by illness & other causes. Those who came seemed quite to enjoy it, & went away hoping to be allowed to come up again next year. The schoolmistresses also spoke very strongly of the help that such an examination would be to them in making their work more thorough. We hope to get the list, knowing how the girls stand, in February. Of course we are prepared for a great many failures. If half our number pass, it will be about as much as I expect.

I suppose your little school girl will be at home by this time. Christmas is a sad season when it brings into prominence the blanks in a circle. I wonder sometimes how long the little circle at Blandford Square will remain intact.[2] It is a superstitious fancy, but I cannot help being frightened sometimes about Charley. He really does seem to me "too good to live", tho' I dare say he is not so much sweeter & more loveable than other people's nephews, if one knew them as well. As a simple fact I never see any little child to be compared to him, but I believe Lizzie Garrett has had just the same sort of fears about her little nephew.

Sometimes when my brother is preaching & looking a great deal *too* saintly, the same panic seizes me about him. There is no real cause for anxiety about any of them now. They are all quite well & we are looking forward to spending Christmas Day with them.

Wordsworth's book was not kept for you, but I want you to let me give it you, with my love, as a little Christmas token.

Please give my kind love to dear Mrs. Richardson. And do write to me soon. I want to hear about you *all*. I remain, dear Anna

Your loving friend
ED.

GC: ALS ED LOC-80

1. Richardson's father had recently died.
2. The household of Llewelyn and Mary Davies.

To Jane Crow

Sat. evening, N̶o̶ Jan. 2d 1864

Dear Dux[1]

I have told Isa I would send on her wild effusion, with an intimation that she is not quite 'left to herself,' tho' appearances are against her. I don't think the Edinb. row signifies much. It has not got into the London papers, & the Waterloo Place habitués seem to stick to Mr. Hastings.[2]

I have asked Fido[3] whether I might send you the Spectator, but she has not answered. You may expect it however, ere long. *I* can feel for you. I don't know how I should live without weekly & monthly stimulants. They do me a world of good. I had a great pleasure at the Enfield's party.[4] The dregs of society included the R. Huttons, & I had a lot of delightful talk with both. He was very kind & nice & amusing. He asked a good deal about 'that thing,' as he called the V⟨ictoria⟩., & expressed an emphatic opinion that 'Thomas Adolphus' ⟨Trollope⟩ had murdered us, & that it was a great pity. He said if he were Miss Faithfull, he would pay off Thomas Adolphus, get a first-rate story, & go on. But that simply cannot be done. I have heard nothing more of the negociations with Mr. Ward.[5] I was introduced to Mrs. Hutton & liked her very much indeed. She was so delightfully cordial, in five minutes I felt as if I had known her five years. She talked very freely about 'Richard' & all their home ways, & how he & Mr. ⟨Meredith⟩ Townsend divide the work of the Spectator between them, &c. &c. Richard's great ambition is to have time to write a book. It will be on Theology. She asked me if I had seen him, & when he came our way, called to him, 'Richard. I've been introduced to Miss Davies, & we've been talking about the Spec. (We call it the Spec.)' & so on. Richard told me he was quite on our side about the Local Examns, & he did not know why he should have been so attacked by us, when he had only said that in the present state of female education, the London Univ. examns. would do more harm than good. I am sure he is a friend at the bottom of his heart, & it is such a comfort to me to know that he has a nice wife. I thought she pulled him down, & it made me unhappy. They have no time for society, & scarcely ever go anywhere, so I am afraid there is not much chance of my being able to prosecute the acquaintance. It was a nice party altogether. The ladies were well dressed & looked pretty & ladylike. Mary looked particularly nice & was in great spirit. Her innocent gaiety was quite infectious, & I came home too full of enjoyment to sleep. What a pity it is there are not a few more nice people in the world, to make society as delightful as it *can* be.

I went to call on the ⟨James⟩ Wilsons yesterday, & saw Julia & Zoë ⟨Wilson⟩. Julia's cough is much better. She attributes the improvement to cotton-wool, which I recommended. The Portfolio is to be held at Mrs. Bostock's next time.[6] There is an invitation for you. I saw that the hand was Miss Bostock's, & knew what it must be, so opened it, to save waste of postage in forwarding it. Mamma sends her love & best wishes, & is glad to hear you are a little better. I thought I had a great deal to say, but it seems to have thinned down. The Enfield's party takes less space than I expected. I believe one thing that made it pleasant was the absence of chaff, that dreary subterfuge vainly used to hide the dulness of vacant minds. Mr. Hutton has rather taken to writing about women in the Spec. lately, which makes me wish all the more that I could talk to him a little sometimes. Did I say anything to you about Sir. Charles Lyell's wanting an amanuensis, &c? He is going to try Miss Patre. I went to read at Langham Place to-day, but saw only Mary. I suppose Jessie B. will be coming up soon. Mama & I dined with the Aldridges yesterday, & they made particular inquiries after you.[7] Mrs. A. hopes you will stay away a long time. Whereupon I suppose you will announce your intention of returning instanter. It's no use coming before you are well. It is rather interesting to be in Germany now, with excitement going on.[8]

I hope Miss Ashley has sent the V[ictoria].'s.[9] I told her, but she has been looking more demented than usual lately. It may be Fido's absence that is affecting her mind. I suppose Fido writes to you. I have been writing diverting letters to her, & recommending the Stoical philosophy.

I copy for you from to-day's Illustrated Times, the following choice piece of criticism.

'The Victoria Magazine has sterling qualities & a character of its own; it is a sort of milder Macmillan. The literary summary is so good that I cannot but suspect it is the hand of the one man of positive genius whose name I have seen in this serial. I hope the Victoria will be able to persevere; if so, it will make a footing for itself.'

I should like to know who our one genius may be. The Magazines are not noticed this week in the papers I have seen.

Wednesday. I kept this, to add to it, as it did not seem worth paying six-pences for. In the meantime I hope you will have received two Spectators, both infinitely more interesting than a letter. I have asked Fido to send you last ~~artic~~ Saturday's, containing an amusing article of Mr. Hutton's.[10] I suppose he must have gone home & written down his impressions of ladies in society, straight off. He had not seen any for a year or two before. I am afraid they are more mercenary than he thinks. People whose pleasures are all of the kind that can only be bought with money, *must* care for money & look out for it. Do *you* think girls & young women generally are indifferent about it?

I saw Miss Boucherett at Langham Place on Monday. She is disgusted with you for not answering her letter. She intends to stay two or three weeks, or perhaps longer, according as things turn out. Her immediate business is to set up Mrs. Burke & she is going to have a Committee very shortly.[11] They have left off taking the Cornhill, ~~wh~~ in the Reading room, which grieves me sore, for I always went there to read the Small House at Allington.[12]

How London spoils one! I feel quite injured now, if I don't see everything that's going, the moment it comes out. The National Review shows signs of decay. It contains an article of Mat. Arnold's on 'Joubert, the French Coleridge', which is quite below his standard.[13] Do you know anything of Joubert? I dare say Miss Masson does. Mary & I thought we had heard of him, but after racking our brains for some time it appeared that it was the photographer we were thinking of! The little Davies's have all got colds & Llewelyn's voice sounds hollow. They won't *listen* to codliver oil, much less take it, which is tiresome. The cold is now very severe, & we are not so well protected as you seem to be. (But you should not burn your gloves & shoes, it's extravagant.) I am glad winter is come. The sooner it's over, the sooner to sleep. & goodbye to the frost & our groaning. Speaking of very poor puns reminds me to tell you that your friend Miss Victoria Hamilton is going to be married to a Mr. ⟨James G.⟩ Goodenough , & the Boucheretts don't think it possible that anybody can be Goodenough for her.

You don't know how virtuous it is of me to sit on a chair writing to you. The alternative is that of sitting in the fire reading Vincenzo, which is worth reading, in its *whole* form.[14] I am going to write a notice of it, contradicting Mr.

Dicey & the Spectator.[15] They despise Vincenzo for not being master in his own house, as they call it, & I am going to show how foolish they are. I have been reading Hard Cash, & my opinion of Charles Reade has risen immensely.[16] There is a very beautiful & clever girl in it, such as a common man could not have imagined. Her characteristic is transparency, & it strikes me as singularly beautiful. It would be more so still, if she was the highest type of woman, but such as she is, the mere idea of perfect transparency is I think very beautiful & original. The opaqueness of the people one meets in society is very distressing. It is not reserve, which one respects, any more than Charles Reade's transparency is silly openness.

Here is Ellen come bothering about the hearth, & the next thing will be 'Will you ring when you're ready?' for that bothering dinner which is always pursuing one about. And I meant to have told you a great deal about a treat I had last night, hearing Jenny Lind & Mme. ⟨Charlotte⟩ Sainton in the Messiah. It was first rate in every way. Lady Crompton took us, with Llewelyn & Mary & Carrie & Emily. My enjoyment of such things always depends very much on the people I go with, & our party was a very pleasant one. Robert Browning was there, looking very nice & genial, but not in the least suggesting to my dull mind anything that he has ever written. He is not so astoundingly ugly as literary men generally. I had the pleasure of watching Mr. Russell Gurney who was sitting near us, taking great care of his nieces. His face is the most beautiful I have ever seen I think, except Mr. Maurice's. He was there too, but I did not see him. There were some very pretty people, & some ugly & inane looking.

I suppose the Masson's take no interest in contemporary history. By the by, you will be struck with the review in the Spectator of Mr. ⟨Richard⟩ Doyle's cartoons.[17] It is very clever. I cannot of anything more to say except Ohh how cold it is, & that grows monotonous. Mamma sends her love & good wishes & is glad to hear you are a little better. And now no more for the present from your servant to command, ED. Love to Jeannie.[18] I am glad to hear that you have not fallen out yet. Oh dear it's so cold.

GC: ALS C337a and b

1. Contemporary term for a school head girl, given to Jane Crow as a nickname.
2. Waterloo Place was the headquarters of the NAPSS.
3. Emily Faithfull.
4. Probably Edward Enfield (1811–80), a philanthropist who attended Manchester College and was a member of the Council of University College, London; treasurer of University College Hospital; and president of the Senate of University College. He married (first) Honora Taylor, and (second) Harriet Roscoe of Liverpool. Thanks to R. K. Webb, University of Maryland, Baltimore County, for information from the *New DNB*.
5. Ward and Lock published the *Victoria* between 1863 and 1868.

6. The Portfolio was a club started by Barbara Bodichon in 1859.

7. Probably Walter William Aldridge (1818–97), solicitor at Gray's Inn and partner in Aldridge, Thorn and Bromley, official solicitor to the Court of Bankruptcy.

8. One of the first stages in the unification of Germany was a war waged by Austria and Prussia against Denmark in 1864. The Danes were quickly defeated; Prussia took over Schleswig, and Austria took Holstein.

9. Probably Florence Emily Ashley (?), a poet and writer.

10. "The 'Club' View of Women," *Spectator* (2 January 1864).

11. The Society for Promoting the Employment of Women (SPEW), which Boucherett founded, and for which Crow worked as secretary. Mrs. Burke, a photographic printer, applied to the Society for a loan of £25 to equip her premises. (See Minutes of the General Committee for the Society for Promoting the Employment of Women, 1860–1901, GCA).

12. Anthony Trollope's novel, *The Small House at Allington* (London: Smith & Elder) was serialized in the *Cornhill* between September 1862 and April 1864.

13. "Joubert; or, a French Coleridge," *National Review*, no. 35 (January 1864): 168–90 [unsigned].

14. John Ruffini's "Vincenzo, or Sunken Rocks" ran in *Macmillan's* starting in May 1862.

15. John Ruffini, *Vincenzo; or Sunken Rocks* (London, 1863), was reviewed in the *Spectator* (26 December 1863).

16. Charles Reade, *Hard Cash* (London, 1863). The novel was reviewed in the *Spectator* (26 December 1863).

17. "Mr. Doyle's Cartoons," *Spectator* (supplement) (2 January 1864).

18. Jeannie Oswald, Crow's cousin, with whom she was traveling.

To Robert Potts

PROPOSED ADMISSION OF GIRLS TO UNIVERSITY LOCAL EXAMINATIONS.
17, CUNNINGHAM PLACE, LONDON, N.W.

Jan. 2d. 1864.

Dear Mr. Potts

I hope Miss Fison gave you some report of our experimental examn. I was very glad that she was able to come, & to speak as an eye-witness. It was perfectly successful, to the end, & our only anxiety now is, as to whether any of our poor candidates will pass.

I suppose it is now time to think seriously about our Memorial.[1] In accordance with your kind permission, I enclose the draft of one, wh on which I should like very much to hear your opinion, before submitting it to our Committee. Our plan would be to get it signed first by as many as are willing of the Professors at Queen's College & Bedford College, & then, by schoolmistresses & governesses all over the Kingdom. I think we should at the same time try to get up a list of distinguished ladies, & M.P.'s &c, as supporting the Memorial.

I suppose there is not much for *us* to do at Cambridge. We shall have to reprint the accompanying circular, with modifications. Do you think it would be worth while to make any arrangement for circulating it, or some similar document among Cambridge men? Any hints you can give us will be thankfully received.

I fear your ~~bookseller~~ publisher must have made some mistake & so frustrated, your kind intentions. The parcel of books did not arrive in Suffolk St. Perhaps next year, or rather *this* year, we may be more fortunate.

If it is not too late for the good wishes of the season, pray accept mine for you & yours, & Believe me,
    Dear Mr. Potts
    Yours very sincerely
    Emily Davies

GC: ALS ED LOC-81

    1. The memorial to Cambridge University requesting that the Cambridge Local Examinations be permanently open to girls.

To Robert Potts

PROPOSED ADMISSION OF GIRLS TO UNIVERSITY LOCAL EXAMINATIONS.
17, CUNNINGHAM PLACE, LONDON, N.W.

Jan. 9th 1864.

Dear Mr. Potts

On inquiry I find that the books were sent to Suffolk St., but not till after the examn. was over & we were all dispersed. They are in safe custody, & if you will kindly allow us, we should like to keep them till an opportunity comes for distributing them according to your wishes.

Thank you very much for the full consideration you have given to our Memorial & its subject. As to the circular, I think we shall probably require two, one for circulation among schoolmistresses & another of a somewhat different character, for Cambridge, if you think it desirable. I scarcely think we can modify our views so far as to ask for a separate scheme.

We should not care about having the *time* of the Examn. altered, because we expect that if Cambridge grants our application, Oxford will soon follow, & it would be more convenient to give schools the choice of Christmas or Midsummer, than to hold both examinations at the same time. In London I believe Christmas is the most convenient time. So I gathered, at least, from one schoolmistress, who brought up 25 candidates, & I had no complaints from any. We should be very unwilling to have any alteration made in the subjects of examn. As the scheme now stands, it includes everything that girls learn, except needlework & the *practice* of music, in which examn. is not required, & they are not obliged to take up any subjects in which they are not prepared. And supposing Greek & Higher Mathematics were left out, in a scheme for girls, don't you think it would be rather a pity to have to *refuse* examn. in those subjects to any girls who might happen to have a special predilection for them? I am afraid that if we began with alteration in the scheme, we should be in a sea of difficulties. Almost every individual that I meet, has a different theory about what is "apposite to the female mind," & to reconcile them all would be quite impossible. Mr. Norris, for instance, who undertook the Reading Aloud for us, expressed great regret that we did not include Needlework, & took to putting questions on Shirtmaking, thereby exciting the indignation of the schoolmistresses present. It seems to me that the ready acceptance of the scheme, *just as it is*, by the higher Class of teachers, proves its suitableness. I feel pretty confident on this point, having had much conversation both with the ladies who sent in candidates & others who hope to do so on a future occasion. My strongest objection to a separate scheme is that the girls' Certificates would not,—in the present state of opinion,—*could not*, have the same value. Even if the Examiners really made the standard quite as high, the public would not believe it. I will give you an instance of what I mean. A lady whom I know, wants to give lessons in Greek & Latin. She is a pupil of Professor ⟨Francis⟩ Newman's, & has taken the highest Certificates that Queen's College can give. But it all goes for nothing. Ladies won't go to her. Their notion is that when they are about it, they had better be taught by a man, who really knows the subjects. It is not enough to be told that the lady I speak of knows more than other ladies. *That* may be much less than the learning of an ordinary University man. It *may* be more, but she has no means of proving her relative competency. I don't quite understand what you say about the growth of the scheme beyond the management of the Examiners. I suppose if the number of boys was to be largely increased, say doubled, the extra work would be provided for, not by dividing the candidates, but by increasing the staff of Examiners? And this would appear to be the natural course, supposing the additional candidates were girls. Of course I speak in ignorance of the actual circumstances of the case & the University arrangements, as to which you are in a much better position to judge. Looking at the question from a distance, I do not understand how two different schemes could give less trouble than one.

 The addition of girls would in some degree balance the work of the Examiners, as they would probably preponderate in French, while the mass of the boys take up Mathematics. I do not think myself that the number of female candidates would be very large. I believe our success this time was greatly owing to our giving up the Fees, which of course could not be done again. Parents are singularly unwilling to pay any more than they are obliged for the education of their daughters, & even as small [a] sum as £1, would I believe be a stumbling block to a great many. The tangible value of the certificate would not be nearly so apparent as in the case of boys, & the idea that it is of some consequence whether girls are properly taught or not, has not yet penetrated the middle-class mind. Probably the admission of girls would increase the number of local Centres. Where say twenty boys only are forthcoming, the addition of a dozen girls would just turn the scale. But I suppose the University *wishes* the scheme to extend & would scarcely look upon a probable increase in the number of candidates as a valid objection to an extension of the scheme. There may however be other difficulties at headquarters, which I know nothing about.

As to the *local* arrangements, our experience has convinced me that the more closely the two Examns. could be connected together, the better for both parties. The infinitesimally small element of separateness which there was in ours, gave a little more trouble without doing anybody any good. I am not speaking of the separate *rooms*. That I think would generally be desirable, but if we had been in the same *building*, it would have been more convenient. Where the number of candidates is large, two conducting Examiners would be required, but that is already done at Liverpool. I suppose they have a very large number of boys there.

You will be quite tired of this long letter. I am anxious to make it as clear as I can to you why, unless there are reasons & obstacles which we know nothing about, we should be unwilling to accept a separate scheme.

Hoping to hear from you again,
I remain, dear Mr. Potts
Yours very sincerely
Emily Davies.

GC: ALS ED LOC-82

To Jane Crow

Tuesday evening. Jan. 12th 1864

Dear Dux

Receiving a letter always stirs me up to answer it, unless it is a very flat one indeed. As one is just come from you, I yield to the impulse & start off, tho' it is quite too soon to be writing again. Do you mind this pink paper? The green is all used up. You are a stupid thing not to tell me how you are, but fortunately Isa gave me her report yesterday. I am glad you are giving up Rome. To go travelling about with Nannie would be the height of imprudence. If Isabella Blythe had only you to take care of, it would be a different thing, but she will be absorbed in looking after Nannie, & somehow or other, their ways of doing things always seem to me to have a great deal of "roughing it," about them. Kind as they are, I should not like to be a patient in their hands. Not much seems to have happened since I last wrote. Fido comes down to-day, at last. I get very despairing about her. Isa & Miss Boucherett were using strong language about her idleness yesterday, & I did not know what to say. She *does* neglect her business scandalously. But it's no use bothering either you or myself about it. It is odd to feel that in a fortnight I shall have cut the V⟨ictoria⟩. I don't think it can live many months in Fido's hands. Your cheerfulness on the subject is difficult to understand. I don't see any other work to do, of a more useful kind. But I am not fretting. I did all that three months ago, ~~but~~ when I was tortured by *le doute*. *La mort* is very easy, comparatively. It bores me very much that people at parties will ask questions about it. I suppose that will go on for several months. As to its stopping being injurious to Fido's business, there are different opinions. Mr. ⟨Walter⟩ Bagehot & I say it would not be. Mr. Aird & Fido say it would.[1] Of course it would be a help to her business if it prospered, but that is not the question. She does not herself expect to do more than just pay expenses, cutting down everything to the lowest point. There is a new man at Coram St.[2] in Gibon's place, who seems likely to do well. I like him very much. I also like Miss Green, who is at Prince's St. now.[3]

Lizzie came over yesterday, & we went together to the F⟨rank⟩. Mallesons. We both enjoyed the party, which we did not expect to do. I talked to Mr. W. Malleson, Mr. Conway, a Bedford College girl, Mr. Neill & Mr. Litchfield, & an odd Scotch doctor, named Drysdale.[4] The latter is most enthusiastic about women-doctors, thinks we shall never be civilised till we have them, & I don't know what all. He remembered my paper, which he said strengthened him in his previous convictions.[5] He seemed very much surprised that I had any belief in a future state. He thought that believing in medical women was going such a very long way that I could not be far from disbelief in immortality. He argued about it in a most extraordinary way, starting off by saying that belief in immortality was destructive of all poetry. It is curious to find how little one has to say in support of even such a fundamental belief as that. I was not in the least prepared to meet his arguments. I had a few words with Mr. McCallum. They came back from Switzerland only last Saturday. I had been rather wondering that I had not met them anywhere lately.

I shall be very glad if you can make anything of Nina Wilson on the side of art. It may be that that is the one thing apart from mere personalities which she is capable of taking an interest in. I believe she is going to give up Bedford College, having only begun it apparently to please Fido. Of course I know Art is not a little thing to you. It is almost everything. But to me it is just about as much of a meeting point figuratively as a pin's head might be literally. I dislike ugliness as I dislike pain, but it no more interests me to be descanting upon the laws of beauty than upon the laws of health. Of course it is all right that there should be some people to study Art, as it is necessary that some should study Medicine. Probably one may be as useful as the other, but by Jove, I have quarrelled with them all. And I do get desperately tired of people like the Wilsons, who look at everything from a personal point of view. It is like the Greatorex's. She likes them for their good nature, but it is very little to go upon. The Wilsons have something more, but the small things come uppermost, & I feel constantly as if I ought to be showing sympathy about things which are not of the slightest consequences, or they will call me severe or *exalté*. I can partly understand their being liked by people like Richard Hutton. His mind is constantly at work on serious subjects & it may be a relief to him to come down now & then to their prattle, especially as they have a certain liveliness & smartness in their way. But I have enough of childishness always about me, & I go to friends for a change from it. You must take the foregoing remarks as explanatory, not accusatory.

I never heard of little Parminter before. Is he son of the chaplain? I am not asked to the Portfolio, so I shall only be able to report upon it secondhand. Mrs. P. Taylor has started a rival society, called the Pen & Pencil.

Monday. I am in the midst of work, & must only add a few lines. We are to have a ⟨Local Examinations⟩ Committee next Friday, to decide upon a Memorial to Cambridge, & after that, I shall have to work it, which will be a considerable undertaking. I hope I shall be clear of the V. by that time, but I feel by no means sure.[6] I don't in the least think Ward & Lock will take it, tho' Fido thinks they will, & if they decline, I don't see very well how I can leave her in the lurch. I am sure the longer she goes on the worse it will be, but unfortunately, Mr. Aird, whose opinion on *this* point, is not worth much, rather encourages her to go on. I suppose it will be settled before very long.[7]

Nina ⟨Wilson⟩ gives up Bedford Coll: because she & her family consider it both improper & dangerous for her to go in a cab by herself, & she cannot always have the footman to sit on the box! Their code of morals is founded on the experience gained by associating with officers, & is the most *im*moral I have ever come in contact with. It is very sad. Conventual stiffness, & carelessness, to say the very least, as to refinement in conversation. There could scarcely be a worse combination.

I send you Anna Richardson's letter, which I think is worth reading, if only as a work of art. You can burn it.

I am delighted to find that the schoolmistresses are quite excited about the examns. It is the most hopeful sign we have. But still I don't feel in the least confident that we shall get what we want. I have had a nice letter from one of the examiners this morning. He says the papers he has looked over are very fairly done.[8] The spelling is remarkably good, the writing scrawly, tho' not illegible. I thought it frightful. I am afraid the Sec. of the Syndicate is not very friendly, but Mr. Potts says he has not much influence.

The Portfolio does not seem to have been very brilliant. I spent Saturday evening very pleasantly with Lizzie (& Louie ⟨Garrett Smith⟩) at Whitechapel. As regards parties, business is dull just now. Lizzie & I remarked with a sigh, that we had no engagements in view. The love of dissipation grows upon me, as I get more at home in society. But it is always a risk, & a really dull party is a dreadful sell.

I don't think I have told you that Anna is obliged to leave us. She is wanted at home, & with much reluctance has decided to go. She can scarcely speak of it without tears. We have nearly engaged a sister of Mary's nurse, Jane. They are an intensely respectable family, & it will be pleasant to have a person that we know something about. Another sister is lady's maid at Hyde Park Square.

I don't think there is much astir at L.P.. They are all having colds & getting better of them. I saw Mrs. Parkes on Saturday, & she gave rather a better account of Adelaide. She sits up for five or six hours a day, & has begun to *wish* to get better. But she is still very weak, & the enormous quantity of food that she takes does not seem to nourish her much. It strikes one as a good sign that she should be at all better, at this time of the year. She still has severe fits of coughing.

I have not heard from Annie for some time. My love to Jeannie. I shall feel quite ignorant & untravelled beside you, when you come home. I wonder how you will get on at Grosvenor St.[9] It is a dreadfully long way off. Ever your E.

GC: ALS C337c

    1. Probably David Mitchell Aird (?–1876), a Scotsman who lived in London and began the *London Daily Telegraph*, the first London penny daily newspaper. He edited the *Mirror* and wrote plays and poems.
    2. Faithfull's Victoria Press was located at Great Coram Street.
    3. The headquarters of the *Victoria* were at Princes Street.
    4. Probably Moncure Daniel Conway (1832–?), American lecturer, man of letters, and abolitionist who visited England to lecture on slavery and became the minister of the South Place Religious Society in Finsbury. He wrote memoirs of his friendships with Emerson, Carlyle, and Mill. Probably Charles Neill (?), a writer. Probably Richard Buckley Litchfield (1832–1903), educated at Trinity College, Cambridge, and married to Henrietta Darwin, the eldest daughter of Charles Darwin. Probably Charles Robert Drysdale (1829–1907), a supporter of women's education and of opening the medical profession to women. He was born in Edinburgh and educated at Trinity College, Cambridge, and founded the Malthusian League to advocate contraception. He published "Medicine as a Profession for Women" in 1870 and lectured to women medical students.
    5. Davies had written "Medicine as a Profession for Women" for the NAPSS in June 1862 and edited a collection of letters on female physicians for the *English Woman's Journal* (May 1862).
    6. As work on the memorial for the Local Examinations became more demanding, ED devoted less time to her editorial responsibilities. She ceased editing the *Victoria* in March 1864, although the journal continued publication until 1880.

7. The scandal of the Codrington divorce case was covered extensively by the press, and this affected not only Faithfull's reputation but also that of the magazine.

8. Those who were reading the girls' examination papers began writing to Davies in January with their reports. The printed report, containing all of their comments, was published in the spring of 1864.

9. Crow was living with Faithfull, and they planned to move to Grosvenor Street upon Crow's return.

To Robert Potts

17 Cunningham Place. | N.W. | Jan. 12th 1864.

Dear Mr. Potts

I feel sure that you are right in insisting that the Memorial be as simple & direct as possible, & that all mention of details be avoided. I send you a fresh copy in which I have omitted, besides the passage you marked, a sentence near the beginning which seemed superfluous. Very likely the Committee may make some alteration in the wording, but we should be particularly glad to have the opinion of Cambridge men as to the substance. Fortunately we are not tied to any fixed time, so that we are not obliged to hurry on at a dangerous pace. From what you say, I understand that the decision will rest with the Senate. I should like to know where we can get a list, as it is probable that a good many of the members may be personally known to one or another of our Committee. There are a good many Cambridge men in London who might be induced to go up & vote, in case of necessity. Of course there will be opposition, & I should think we ought to make sure of a clear majority before we venture upon the final push. Mr. ⟨John⟩ Westlake is unfortunately a bad speaker. Mr. Fawcett, the new Professor of Political Economy speaks very well, & is sure to be willing to do all he can for us. Do you know whether Mr. Gray is in our favour? As Sec. of the Syndicate, I suppose he will have great influence.

We shall be quite willing to leave details to be arranged by the Senate. I don't think any members of our Committee would care in the least about having the Examn. in the same building as the boys. That is a mere matter of convenience. All that we are really anxious about is that the standard & the classification should be the same. That is what would constitute the special value of these examns. to us. We think also that the subjects are very suitable. Of course no scheme is absolutely perfect, but we are satisfied with this, & should be rather afraid of alterations.

I fancy Mr. Norris, when he began to examine in needlework, mistook the class of girls he was dealing with. them. I heard some of them laughing among themselves afterwards & remarking that he talked to them as if they were National School girls.[1] They seemed to think it a very good joke. Young ladies now don't make shirts. It would be very silly to spend their time & eyesight in doing by hand what can be done just as well & a great deal more expeditiously by a machine. Of course they ought to be able to sew on buttons, but any baby can do that. My little niece could sew pretty *well* before she was two! But I think perhaps we have a special gift for plain needlework.

I do not quite understand what sort of paper you would approve for circulation among members of the Senate. The circular I sent you was originally drawn up with a view to Oxford, & our friends there told us it was the right sort of thing. But perhaps Cambridge men have different tastes. Can you give us any hints?

I remain, dear Mr. Potts
Yours very sincerely
Emily Davies.

GC: ALS ED LOC-83

1. National Schools were state primary schools for children under age 14.

To Charlotte Manning

17 Cunningham Place. N.W. | Jan. 20th. [1864]

My dear Mrs. Manning

We are to have a meeting of our Committee on Friday, at which I propose submitting the enclosed draft of Memorial & circular for approval. Will you kindly take the trouble to look over both & suggest any amendments that may occur to you? I think we must also send in a list of distinguished ladies, M.P.'s, &c, as supporters of the Memorial, & in that case I hope you may be able to help us in getting some good names. I believe the names of *ladylike* ladies have great influence in a matter of this sort, & our success at Cambridge seems to depend entirely upon the amount of pressure we can bring to bear. It is not very easy to get at the schoolmistresses. A lady called here a day or two ago who would have liked very much to prepare candidates for the experimental, but she only heard of it by accident, when it was too late. Unfortunately there is no complete list of girls' schools published anywhere. The only resource seems to be to ask all our friends to supply us with lists of those they know. I think we shall ask the Professors at Queen's College to sign first, then Bedford, & after that, all teachers of girls indiscriminately. I suppose you could not do anything more than you have done already with Mr. Plumptre? A great deal will depend on how he takes it up. I wrote & asked him to come & look at the experiment, but I suppose he was too busy, as their own examn. was going on that week. Some of the girls told me he had been very kind in advising them about it.

Mrs. Taylor has kindly asked me to join the Pen & Pencil Society, of which I see Miss Manning is a member. What does she contribute? I have offered grateful appreciation of other people's performances, but they do not seem quite satisfied with that sort of ~~app~~ contribution.

I remain, dear Mrs. Manning
Yours affectionately
Emily Davies.

GC: ALS ED LOC-84

To Robert Potts

17 Cunningham Place. Jan. 21st | ⟨1864⟩

Dear Mr. Potts

I am very glad to hear that Mr. & Mrs. ⟨Edward⟩ Selwyn are inclined to ~~place~~ help us. At Blackheath they are quite surrounded by schools. People who cannot do *more*, may be of service by simply giving us lists of schools in their respective neighborhoods. Unfortunately there is no complete list of girls' schools published anywhere, so that we run an unavoidable risk of missing some schoolmistresses who might be friendly. One called on me the other day, who had been passed over in this way, when we sent out our circular. She would have liked very much to prepare candidates for the experimental examn., but only heard of it by accident, when it was too late.

Our Committee meets to-morrow, so we shall now be able to set to work. Would you kindly tell me whether the Memorial ought to be addressed to the Vice-Chancellor only, or to the Vice-Chancellor & members of the Senate. This matter of form will have to be decided before we can circulate the Memorial.

Yours very sincerely
Emily Davies.

GC: ALS ED LOC-87

To Jane Crow

Saturday evening. Jan. 23d ⟨1864⟩

I like your discursive letters on general subjects, what you call flippant, much better than the descriptive ones, & I feel much more inclined to answer them. I always skip descriptions in books. When you put them into your letters, I think they are very good & they do you credit & I ought to like them, but I wish you would write about something else. Several points in your last letter require comment. But first I may as well observe that descriptions provoke no comment or reply. There is nothing to say but, oh! Of course the oh may be said with various intonations, but that is all. Disquisitions on other subjects are something like Hutton's articles, which always excite me. I am either vehemently agreeing, or contradicting or questioning, and wishing I could get hold of him to ask exactly what he means, & to tell him he is quite right about this, but altogether in the wrong about that, & that when he said so & so he was talking of something he did not know anything about. But if you make an assertion about art, it may be wonderfully right or flagrantly wrong. Either way, my appreciation of it is something like Harriet Baxter's of Mr. Alford's love. You remember the anecdote. I am very idle this evening. There is work which might be done, but I cannot get myself up to it. I dare say it was not wise to begin the Cornhill directly after tea, & go straight thro' with it, but I do so love a novel, & after all there is no such great hurry about the Memorial, & the V. is done for this month. I am all at sea about it for the future, but I foresee that I cannot drop it just yet. Fido has not come to any arrangement with Ward & Lock. I think & hope they won't take it, for I find their name is not to appear, & for such a thing as they would make of it to be still accepted as representative, would be horrid. The other alternative, Fido's carrying it on herself, seems to me impossible. In the meantime, I see that it will be less trouble for me to manage it myself than to help her, so I shall probably go on for two or three months. It is not very pleasant, for I cannot ask people to write for nothing & Fido seems inclined to take it easily, tho' she says she is in low spirits, & I believe *is*, now & then. Her carelessness is mixed up in a remarkable way with grief & self-pity.

I believe my last letter was dispatched on Monday, so I will try to journalize from that time. Unfortunately the pens are bad, & that always affects the flow of my ideas. I like to see my writing look pretty, or "picturesque" as Anna sweetly calls it, as I go along. The principal events of the week have been, dining at the ⟨William⟩ Hodgsons, & a Committee yesterday. For the Committee, I had to prepare a Memorial to Cambridge, & to modify an old circular, to be circulated with it. I sent copies to all the Committee & received criticism from most. (oh dear dear, what a smudge!) I will quote some of the most interesting. Mr. Gurney advised leaving out one sentence, & Mrs. ⟨Emelia⟩ G⟨urney⟩. puts "a query to the word 'simultaneously' because it rather suggests the idea, to superficial readers, of boys & girls being examined together. Cd. you say 'tho' separately'—or preclude the shocking possibility of their being in the same room by any other word." In a postscript she says, in reference to the Messiah, "A very bad cold kept me from hearing that blessed woman, who is always inspired when she has such words to interpret to us. I longed to go to have my lamp fed with fresh oil." Mrs. Manning submitted the MSS. to the Serjeant,[1] who made a great many small emendations, which did not signify either way. Mr. Heywood wanted to leave out a paragraph. Dr. Hodgson approved of all but two words. Miss Bostock wrote out a whole new Memorial or rather a new edition of mine, spun out & weakened. She sent it with the remark that people who don't like our principles fall upon our style. It is very funny. She always attacks my style, & offers her own, which I think unusually *poor*, instead. Happily Isa does not like her, & the Committee rejected her improvement with very little hesitation. Mr. Tomkinson says, "There is only one passage in the MSS. at which I felt at all disposed to stop. viz. in the Memorial 'there appears to be no valid reason for their exclusion.'[2]

May not this seem like saying all who advocate exclusion are geese? You are I know, less hesitating than I. & I envy you. & perhaps you meant this. [1] But in reading a plea for a cause one always tries to read it like an opponent: & in that temporary character, I felt a little taken by storm & consequently still more inclined to oppose." I agree to this, & with infinite labour & difficulty we managed to alter the clause into something civiler & feebler.

⟨incomplete⟩

GC: AL C337e

1. James Manning, her husband. Serjeant at Law is a title for a barrister of the highest rank.
2. The letter sent to the university contained the sentence, "it appears to us that no valid objection can be urged against the admission of girls to similar benefits."

To Robert Potts

PROPOSED ADMISSION OF GIRLS TO UNIVERSITY LOCAL EXAMINATIONS.
17, CUNNINGHAM PLACE, LONDON, N.W.

Jan. 26th. 1864.

Dear Mr. Potts

I am very glad to hear that the late Vice-Chancellor is inclined to be friendly From what you say, it seems to me that our fate will depend very much on the character of the Syndicate appointed to report upon us. If it is composed of enemies, they are not likely to make a favourable report.

Our Committee have ~~appointed~~ adopted the Memorial of which I sent you the draft, with a few verbal alterations. It was decided that unless there is some strong reason to the contrary, it should be addressed to the Vice-Chancellor & the Senate.

It is now in the hands of Mr. Plumptre of Queen's College. When we have got the signatures of the Professors & teachers there, we shall begin to circulate it far & wide. Your suggestion to get Local Secretaries to act for their respective neighborhoods is very good, & we shall act upon it as far as we can.

I had a visit yesterday from a lady who is at the head of a Training-school for governesses, near Tiverton.[1] She said she thought she could get at least 50 or 60 names from among her old pupils. I have Crockford's book, but as a list of first-class schools, it is very incomplete. A lady the other day sent me a list of nine, of which only three appear in Crockford. At this rate, we shall be missing two-thirds. But I think we shall be able to do a great deal thro' private friends. Do you think it would *now* be desirable to get anything said in the newspapers? Mr. Hutton would I think, put a little notice in the Spectator, & the Telegraph & the Record, would probably do the same. We could get at some of the educational periodicals too. What I mean is simply a short paragraph, notifying that a Memorial is in course of signature, & has received the names (if we get them) of the Professors at Queen's College & Bedford College.

How many copies of the Memorial shall I send you? We mean to print some of the best signatures, but perhaps for Cambridge, you would rather have it without any names attached.

Yours very sincerely
Emily Davies.

GC: ALS ED LOC-88

1. Probably Mary Eliza Porter, superintendent of Educational Home for Training Governesses, Bolham, Tiverton.

To Jane Crow

Wednesday morning. ⟨Jan. 27th,⟩ 1864

Dear Dux.

I suppose in a few days I shall be getting another rampagious letter, full of your dreadful sufferings from letter *wehr.!*, so I may as well be prepared with a dose while I have time to get it ready. The Memorial is being printed, & I cannot do much till I get it. The Magazine also being in a state of uncertainty does not give me much work. Mr. Gunning[1] is making a hitch, which hinders Fido from making a proposal to Ward & Lock, & I cannot get her to think about what she will do, if they decline it. I want her to put in two parts of Lindisfarn for the next three months, so as to get thro' with it & stop without beginning a third vol. She says A. Trollope would think it dishonourable, but that seems to me rather straining a point, considering how much she must lose per month by carrying it on. She does not like me to tell people that I am not responsible for it, but I must do so, if she won't stop. If she would promise to stop in three months I would go on with it for that time, but she won't promise anything till the matter is settled with Ward & Lock. So we are all in a muddle, & cannot give people answers about their MSS., nor nothing. The printing business is much more satisfactory. Mr. ⟨William Wilfred⟩ Head has come into the partnership & has begun to work at Coram St. This is what has been wanted all along, a responsible manager who knows the business. Mr. Head seems a very nice person. He fully believes in women-printers but not in indulging them. He talks of having them all down, & telling them that he knows they can do the work, but they must *do* it, that there has been enough of philanthropy, & now the business is to begin. All the people, both men & women seem to have been cheating tremendously. No doubt the disorganised state of the whole concern has been very demoralising to the York people.[2] Mr. Head is quite a man of business & says Ma'am, which rather surprises one from an elegant young man with a moustache. I feel very hopeful about the business now. *The* thing wanted seems to have been got at last.

Llewelyn's Irish curate is such a take-in. He preaches nonsense. It is another lesson. Llewelyn had always hated Irishmen, & determined to get over it in this case, & this is the result. He is not *bad*, but silly. Stanley, who sent him to Llewelyn, must have been taken in too.

Fido was to take up her quarters at Grosvenor St. last night. I suppose I must go & see them soon. She says it is very near Belgrave St., which is I think about two miles from here. Fido is in good spirits, poor thing, having closed with Mr. Head, & pretty nearly accomplished the sale of Farringdon St. I saw Isa yesterday. She had not anything remarkable to say. Llewelyn had been calling on Mrs. Hughes, & she told him she & Tom could not think what the young men were about, not to get hold of Caroline Crompton.[3] Mary said she did not think she would ever marry, she is so particular, hates everybody. "Ice is nothing, to Carrie when a gentleman approaches her."

Thursday. I saw Fido for a few minutes yesterday. She has lost the Spectator, so I can neither see it myself, nor send it to you. I don't think it had anything very particular in it.

I saw Bessie at Langham Place. She told me of an amusing letter from Miss ⟨Maria⟩ Rye, which she said she was going to read to Adelaide in the evening. Adelaide has been suffering temporarily from indigestion, but they had found out the cause & she is better again. The night before last Miss Annie Thackeray was with her, & the other one was at the Procters, but could not bring herself up to seeing Adelaide. She, Minnie ⟨Thackeray⟩, has broken down much more than Annie. They are going to sell their house, pictures & books. Annie wants to take a house & settle. Minnie inclines to spend some time first in going about among friends. Bessie says Annie is extremely like her father, & Minnie, she fancies, takes after the mother. The Parkes's have been very much concerned by a report of Nannie thro' some relations of the Blythes. It is nothing worse than what Isabella said in that letter to you, but Nannie seems to insist on keeping it concealed from her own family. Of course I simulated ignorance. It is a very trying position for the Blythes to be in.

Isa has heard from Mrs. Herman Bicknell. She is going to have a baby, & they are both in the most exuberant state of happiness.

By the by Jessie reports that you are sleighing six hours a day. Is not that too much?

I have had a very nice note from Mr. Plumptre, last night. He undertakes to bring the Memorial before the Queen's Coll. Professors. He says those to whom he has mentioned it look on it very favourably. It will be a great point to get them, especially if they all sign, without an exception. Miss Bostock undertakes Bedford. I should not wonder if some of them pull up. Being Radicals, they are sure to be illiberal. The clergy are on the whole, the most liberal body of men in the Kingdom, let Richard Hutton say what he likes. I find Llewelyn was struck as I was, by the ignorance shown in that article on the widening chasm between the clergy & laity.[4] He talks as if the laity cared for truth!

⟨incomplete⟩

GC: AL C337f

    1. Mr. Gunning was "a partner with Miss Faithfull in the proprietorship of the Magazine" (Chronicle 289).

    2. The NAPSS conference was to be held in York in September 1864. Faithfull's printing shop usually did the work for the NAPSS.

    3. Probably Thomas Hughes (1823–96), who was active in Christian socialism; one of founders, with Kingsley and Maurice, of the Working Men's College in London; and author of *Tom Brown's School Days*.

    4. "The Widening Chasm between the Clergy and Laity," *Spectator* (16 January 1864).

To Robert Potts

PROPOSED ADMISSION OF GIRLS TO UNIVERSITY LOCAL EXAMINATIONS.
17, CUNNINGHAM PLACE, LONDON, N.W.

Jan. 28th. 1864.

Dear Mr. Potts

I think we shall have no difficulty in getting our work done at Brighton. A friend of mine who sent round to all the schools before our experimental examn., will I expect, undertake the working of the Memorial.[1] Mr. ⟨Barclay⟩ Phillips will do what he can with the Local Committee, but I should not like to put the matter into his hands. I saw him in the Spring, & gathered that he was not on good terms with the Brighton schoolmistresses generally. His position is very much the reverse of influential, in every way.

Miss Richardson is a friend of mine. She has lately lost her father & had other domestic trouble, & in any case she would not have been able to do much for us. There are two other friends of mine, clergymen's wives, who will I expect, work Newcastle & Gateshead very thoroughly.

Generally, I think it will be better to get independent people rather than schoolmistresses. There is often a little jealousy among rival schools, & one schoolmistress would be apt to hesitate in coming forward prominently as leader in the movement. I fancy, from what Mrs. Cooper says, that she feels some delicacy of this sort, but I will write to her & see what she is disposed to do. I have no doubt that employing Local Secs. is the most effective way of working, where we can get people who are heartily interested, but we ought to be able to rely upon them. If half & half people undertake it & only half do it, it will be worse than leaving it to us. Of course I should be disposed to take advantage of of all the help we can get everywhere, only not to rely upon it *exclusively*, except where we are quite sure of the people. I intend to write to all the Local Secretaries for the Examn. Some of them have already promised to give what help they can. The different members of our Committee will also be able to do a good deal in their several circles. Mr. Plumptre, who is very influential at Queen's College, undertakes to bring the matter forward there. He says those of the Professors to whom he has already mentioned the Memorial, look upon it very favourably. I hope to send you copies in a day or two. We shall not print any names at present, at any rate.

With thanks for all your kind suggestions,
I remain, yours very sincerely
Emily Davies.

GC: ALS ED LOC-89

1. Possibly a member of the Barton family from Brighton, to whom she refers in other letters and in the Chronicle.

To Robert Potts

PROPOSED ADMISSION OF GIRLS TO UNIVERSITY LOCAL EXAMINATIONS.
17, CUNNINGHAM PLACE, LONDON, N.W.

Feb. 4th 1864.

Dear Mr. Potts

I am very glad to hear that you like the Memorial, & also that the plan of working you suggest is precisely what the Committee had decided upon. Wherever we cannot get a local agent who can be relied upon for working the matter efficiently, we intend to send a copy of the Memorial, with an explanatory circular, to the heads of schools, ⟨& a letter⟩ asking for the signature of the recipient & for any aid that can be given in making the matter known.

I do not think we differ about the schoolmistresses. I am quite disposed to take advantage of all the help they can give, but I think some who would gladly do all they can privately among their own acquaintances, would shrink from giving their names as Local Secretaries, simply from the fear of being charged with a desire to "put themselves forward." Perhaps I may be mistaken in this impression, but the schoolmistresses I have known have generally been very sensitive in matters of this sort.

I expect to get our circulars in a day or two. In the meantime I have had encouraging answers from persons to whom I have sent the Memorial.

Yours very sincerely
Emily Davies.

GC: ALS ED LOC-90

To Charlotte Manning

PROPOSED ADMISSION OF GIRLS TO UNIVERSITY LOCAL EXAMINATIONS.
17, CUNNINGHAM PLACE, LONDON, N.W.

Feb. 12th

[1864 | Memorial presented to Camb. Senate in Mich⟨aelmas⟩. Term.]
Dear Mrs. Manning

I have not been asleep all this time, as you must have suspected. First, I ran short of Memorials, & since, have put off writing, from various reasons.

You will see that several of the corrections Mr. Serjeant Manning was good enough to suggest, were adopted by the Committee. I sent the Memorial to Mr. Plumptre, & received a very kind note from him in reply, promising to bring it before the Queen's Professors, who he said were generally friendly. I suppose he is now collecting the names.

At Bedford College, 11 out of the 13 Professors have signed. The two who decline are Mr. ⟨Edward⟩ Beesly & Mr. ⟨John⟩ Hullah. On the whole, we are getting on very well. For *numbers* we must depend on the schools scattered all over the country, & gathering in the names will be a work of time. It seems very essential, by what we hear from Cambridge, that the signatures should be numerous. You will see that *any* teacher of girls, master or governess, may sign. Nothing was settled at the Committee about a list of supporters,[1] & I am a little doubtful whether it may not be safer to drop it. The selection of names would be very difficult, & if we got the wrong people, they might do us more harm than good. What do you think? I believe I am growing morbidly cautious, it is so strenuously urged upon ~~us~~ us that we must mind what we are about & take care that we don't do anything rash, which might give offense.

We are promised the Class-list, with full particulars as to the subjects in which the girls have done well or ill, next week. The Seniors' Arithmetic seems to have been a weak point. The Sec. writes in a very friendly tone about it.

I could not go to the first Pen & Pencil meeting. At the next, I hope I may have the pleasure of meeting Miss Manning. In obedience to your orders, I have been trying to think of subjects. "Promise" occurred to me. Either Promise & failure, or Promise & fulfillment, or, which I should like better, simply "Promise." But I think probably "Cradle" was treated partly as Promise. I have also thought of "Town." I don't mean London, but a sort of idea of town, as distinguished from the country. It seems to me that there must be a sort of *essence* of town, which is the thing some people delight in & others so utterly hate, & I fancy something might be said & painted in illustration of this *thing*—which I don't know how to define less vaguely.

I hope you are all better than when you last wrote, & are beginning to think of coming home. The last accounts of you have not been quite so cheerful as could be wished.

With love to Miss Manning,
I remain
Yours affectionately
Emily Davies.

GC: ALS ED LOC-101

1. Eventually the memorial included names from Queen's and Bedford Colleges and the University of London, followed by an alphabetical list of teachers, schoolmistresses, governesses, tutors, etc., and a list of supporters that included titled ladies and others of influence.

To Robert Potts

PROPOSED ADMISSION OF GIRLS TO UNIVERSITY LOCAL EXAMINATIONS.
17, CUNNINGHAM PLACE, LONDON, N.W.

Feb. 25th 1864.

Dear Mr. Potts

I send you some more papers. We have been obliged to get some printed with signatures, so many people asked for them, but I suppose you prefer having them without.

I have written to the friends whose names you sent me. We are getting on very well, but the gathering in of signatures is a slow process.

Teachers generally are such busy people, it is very difficult for them to find time for any extra work.

Is there any particular time by which we ought to send in the Memorial?
Yours very truly
Emily Davies.
T.O.
Could you oblige me with a few copies of the Regulations for 1864? My stock is exhausted, & I have already made such a heavy demand upon the London Local Sec. that I am really ashamed to ask him for more. People are constantly writing to me for them.

GC: ALS ED LOC-102

To Charlotte Manning

PROPOSED ADMISSION OF GIRLS TO UNIVERSITY LOCAL EXAMINATIONS.
17, CUNNINGHAM PLACE, LONDON, N.W.

March 4th [1864]

Dear Mrs. Manning

I was so much obliged to you for your delightful letter.

I have only time to-day to tell you that we are to have a Committee at 3 Waterloo Place, on Tuesday next, at 3 P.M. to receive the Examiners' Report, & transact some other business.[1]

Much hoping to see you soon,
I remain
Yours affectionately
ED.

GC: ALS ED LOC-103

1. On 4 March 1864, ED received a letter from Chalker in which he reported concerning the girls' performance in arithmetic: "The opinion I have formed from the examn. goes no further than this—that the Senior girls had been very deficiently instructed in Arithmetic & that in consequence of this they were not at present competent. . . . I shd. wish you distinctly to understand that I make no comparison of their relative abilities. . . . Should . . . proper instruction be forthcoming I see no reason why they shd. not come up to the University Standard" (Chronicle 341).

To Robert Potts

PROPOSED ADMISSION OF GIRLS TO UNIVERSITY LOCAL EXAMINATIONS.
17, CUNNINGHAM PLACE, LONDON, N.W.

March 12th 1864.

Dear Mr. Potts

I was very much obliged to you for the copies of Regulations, which are already disposed of. I suppose you have heard that only 33 of our candidates passed, the bulk of the failures having been in elementary Arithmetic! We are going to print a Report, founded on the remarks of the Examiners. I shall have the pleasure of sending you a copy as soon as it is ready.

We are very much afraid of that there will be a proposal to lower the standard for the girls. I am charged to impress upon "the Cambridge people," that we do not want this. I suppose the Cambridge people will decide as *they* think best, but we should like them at any rate to know what we wish. The girls must be brought up to the mark, not the standard brought down to them. We have no doubt that it *can* be done, when the scheme has had a little time to work, & teachers know what is expected of them.

Names are coming in. I have received seven, with a friendly letter, from Mr. ⟨John⟩ Raven of Bungay. Some of the schoolmistresses are timid about signing. One, who had sent her name, wrote in a great fright to withdraw it. She had discovered that the examns. were for the middle-class, & her pupils were of the upper-class, & their parents she was sure would not approve of the examns.

What do you think of Mr. ⟨Joshua⟩ Fitch's article?[1] It is generally liked.

It seems a long time since we have had any *bulletin* or hints from you.

No doubt you have been very busy.

I remain,

Yours very truly

Emily Davies.

GC: ALS ED LOC-107

1. Joshua Fitch, "The Education of Women," *Victoria* (March 1864): 432–53.

To Anna Richardson

March 15th [1864]

My dear Anna

I have not heard much of you lately, & I am afraid you are not getting on very fast, but if your progress is slow, I hope it is steady. One must not expect very much till the clear soft summer days come, when you can get out and drink strength from the sunny air. I don't much believe in air that is not sunny.

Miss Green has given me this list of prices. I think she would like to go to Newcastle if by any means a certain amount of work weekly could be guaranteed, at least for a time. Is there any chance of this? Of course, she ought to be tried first. I mean the quality of her work. She is helping in Miss Faithfull's stationer's shop pro tem. & they speak very well of her. They don't intend to keep her permanently, because they want some one who understands the business, which she of course does not. If Mr. ⟨Robert Spence⟩ Watson thinks it worth while to send her any work, as a trial, it will find her at ¹⁴ Prince's St., (see back of card) & she will do it at once. The prices she has put down are what customers pay, not what the Clerks receive.

I believe I have not told you that I have given up the Editorship of the Victoria & am now responsible for the notices of books only. It has not paid, & Miss Faithfull is going to try if she can make it do so by new methods. It is to be of lighter quality & the expenses are to be reduced. I could not edit a light Magazine, nor can I edit one at all, unless I may go to the best writers & pay them properly. So there was no alternative but to give up. I am sorry, but I have been so thoroughly inured to what you call "the discipline of disappointments" that nothing of that sort takes much hold of me. The Victoria has done pretty well in London, but in the country it has been a dead failure. The provincial booksellers report that their customers won't look at it.

I enclose some papers which I think you will like to look at. A good many of your friends,—Miss Procter, Miss Taylor, Miss Sanders & Miss Richards have signed the Memorial.[1] There seems a good prospect of success. I have had some very nice letters from Cambridge about it. If only men would *think*, we should soon get all we want.

I must tell you about a party I went to at the Wilson's the other night. Matthew Arnold was there, and Bonamy Price, & Mr. ⟨Edward⟩ Forster of Bradford. I listened to a little discussion between Mr. Forster and Mr. Bagehot (of the Economist) about our duty to the Danes. Mr. Bagehot urged that tho' it is not our interest, it may be our duty to fight for them, if the Germans won't give up Schleswig. Mr. Forster said it was much more other people's duty than ours, & that we had never done such a thing before as to fight for a cause in which English interests are not even *supposed* to be involved. Afterwards I had a talk with Mr. Bagehot about Women and Scepticism. Have you seen an article with that title & another by the same writer (Fitzjames Stephen) on Parker's Works, in Fraser?[2] They are exciting a good deal of notice, & discussion among the people I know. Have you seen Miss Cobbe's new little book "Broken Lights"?[3] I dare say you avoid all these things, but I hope you are not so isolated from your fellow man as to do otherwise than rejoice at the Judgment.

I must not write more in this ramble-scramble. With much love,
Ever yours
ED.

GC: ALS ED II4/7

1. Jane and Elizabeth Procter both signed the memorial. They are identified as "Principal of School, Darlington." Several women named Taylor signed the memorial: Hannah Taylor, listed as a governess; Maria Taylor, from Newbury; Mary Taylor and Wilhelmina Taylor, principal of a school in York. Two women named Sanders signed the memorial: Anna Maria

Sanders, principal of school at Claremont House, Old Kent Road, Surrey; and Emily M. Sanders, principal of school, Brighton. Emma and Eliza Richards signed the memorial, listed as "conducting a School for the Daughters of 'Friends,' 10, Laura Place, Bath."

2. Fitzjames Stephen, "Women and Scepticism," *Fraser's* (December 1863).

3. Frances Power Cobbe, *Broken Lights* (London, 1864).

To Robert Potts

PROPOSED ADMISSION OF GIRLS TO UNIVERSITY LOCAL EXAMINATIONS.
17, CUNNINGHAM PLACE, LONDON, N.W.

March 23d 1864.

Dear Mr. Potts

I am always bothering you about something. I now want to ask your help in getting a supply of Regulations. The London Sec. sent me 30 copies the other day, but they are a mere drop in the ocean, not enough to supply the applications already waiting. It seems not quite fair to expect London to supply the whole country, & I don't like to ask Mr. Gray, because I suppose we have no right to anything, & we have already given him a great deal of trouble, one way & another. Could you manage it for us? A hundred copies would not be too many. Naturally the demand is immense, as every head of a school who signs the Memorial writes up for the Regulations. Of course we are quite ready to *pay*, if that is any use.

We are getting on very well with the Memorial. I think we must have got signatures from every county in England, & even now, I don't suppose half the teachers in England have heard of it. I forget whether I mentioned before, that we have now the names of all the Professors at Queen's College except two, Mr. Hullah & Sterndale Bennett. I dare say the Queen's names are not thought much of at Cambridge, but they have very great influence with the schoolmistresses, who are a timid race, dreadfully afraid of losing caste by doing anything not universally approved of.

I hope to be able to send you our Report before long.[1] Mr. Chalker's strictures on the Arithmetic were so frightfully severe, we are obliged to leave part of them out. It seemed rather too bad to prove our case at the expense of the few valiant ones who came forward & exposed themselves, & who are probably much better than their neighbours who kept their deficiencies safely out of sight.

Yours very sincerely
Emily Davies

GC: ALS ED LOC-108

1. "Report of an Examination of Girls, Held (by Permission of the Syndicate) in Connexion with the Local Examinations of the University of Cambridge in 1863" (London, 1864). Reprinted in *Victoria* (May 1864: 82–86).

To Robert Potts

PROPOSED ADMISSION OF GIRLS TO UNIVERSITY LOCAL EXAMINATIONS.
17, CUNNINGHAM PLACE, LONDON, N.W.

Sat. April 2d. ⟨1864⟩

Dear Mr. Potts

I was very much obliged to you for the timely supply of Regulations which you were so kind as to send. I hope we have not exhausted the printer's stock, for I find myself again reduced to two copies, & as there is a daily demand for them, I should be very glad to have some more.

I send you the Scotsman, with an account of the good deeds of the University of Edinburgh. I feel almost sorry that the Scotch have got before Cambridge, tho' certainly the Syndicate took the lead, & probably their liberality to us last year had great influence with the Edinburgh people.

Yours very sincerely
Emily Davies.

GC: ALS ED LOC-123

To Robert Potts

PROPOSED ADMISSION OF GIRLS TO UNIVERSITY LOCAL EXAMINATIONS.
17, CUNNINGHAM PLACE, LONDON, N.W.

April 12th 1864.

Dear Mr. Potts

I think your plan of having some copies of the Regulations printed for us, is very good, but we shall not want more than 500. Would you kindly see Mr. Gray & take the necessary steps about it? The Social Science people are going to have a discussion of our question on the 29th. Inst.[1]

Lord Lyttelton has promised to preside & our report will be read. We have some hope that Mr. J. S. Mill will be present & speak, but this is not settled yet. If you know any Cambridge men in London who it would be worth while to ask, perhaps you will kindly tell us.

I remain,
Yours very truly
Emily Davies.

GC: ALS ED LOC-124

1. On Friday, 29 April, the NAPSS held a special meeting at its headquarters, 3 Waterloo Place on Pall Mall, to discuss the "Proposed Admission of Girls to the University Local Examinations."

To Henry Tomkinson

⟨April 14th 1864⟩

...The Social Science people are going to have a discussion about the Local Examn. on Friday the 29th of this month, & we very much want you to come & testify (if you can, conscientiously?) that everybody behaved properly & nothing alarming or scandalous happened at the experimental examn. Somebody, you know, must speak about it & it wd. come better from you than from any one else.... Lord Lyttelton has promised to preside, & there is some hope that Mr. J. S. Mill will come. He takes an interest in the question & sometimes takes part in the Discussions at Waterloo Place. They are going to invite Cambridge men, especially enemies, to give them a chance of being converted....

GC: AMsS C357

To Robert Potts

PROPOSED ADMISSION OF GIRLS TO UNIVERSITY LOCAL EXAMINATIONS.
17, CUNNINGHAM PLACE, LONDON, N.W.

April 15th 1864.

Dear Mr. Potts

I have to thank you very sincerely for your kind thought of sending me your Euclid.[1] It seems to me very desirable that Mathematical studies should at least form a part of the education of girls, even if they do not go very far, as a means of training & disciplining the mind, which is of course just as necessary for girls as for boys.

We are getting on with the arrangements for the Discussion on the 29th, & are inviting friends & enemies quite impartially. It is only fair to the latter to give them a chance of being converted from their errors.

We have now in hand nearly 500 names & I know of about 100 more which are yet to come in. We do not think of presenting the Memorial, unless you decidedly advise it, before the Long Vacation.

During the next two or three months we may be able to get the number of signatures considerably increased, as the matter is not even yet, at all universally known. How many signatures do you think we ought to consider a minimum?

I remain,
Yours very sincerely
Emily Davies.

GC: ALS ED LOC-125

1. Robert Potts, *Euclid's Elements* (London, 1845).

April 1864 111

To Robert Potts

PROPOSED ADMISSION OF GIRLS TO UNIVERSITY LOCAL EXAMINATIONS.
17, CUNNINGHAM PLACE, LONDON, N.W.

April 18th 1864.

Dear Mr. Potts

I shall be very glad to write to Mrs. Heaton, if you will kindly give me her address. I suppose "Mrs. Heaton, Leeds," will scarcely be sufficient.[1]

Since I last wrote to you, we have had some more signatures sent in. Our number is now above 700.

I am afraid I have mislaid the letter in which you gave me the address of a gentleman you thought we had better invite to the Discussion. It has occurred to me that it might be the best plan for me to send you a few circulars, say half-a-dozen, for you to distribute according to your own discretion. We are obliged to be rather select in our invitations, as the space is limited, but Cambridge men of any influence, would of course be welcome.

Yours very sincerely
Emily Davies.

GC: ALS ED LOC-126

1. Probably either John Deakin Heaton (1817–80), who was a senior physician at Leeds General Infirmary and a member of the Leeds School Board, or John Aldham Heaton (1830–97), also from Leeds, who attended Repton and was later an architectural decorator in London.

To Henry Tomkinson

⟨April 18th 1864⟩

...We are very glad to find that you are able & willing to come on the 29th. If you will state facts, that is just what is wanted. I only hope the speakers on our side won't go off, as our enemies always do, into theories. It is dreadfully unsafe.

...Do you know that the University of Edinburgh has instituted a scheme of Local Examn. in which they are including girls at once, as a matter of course. If only people wd. always do things in that reasonable way, it wd. save a great deal of trouble & fuss ...

GC: AMsS C357a

To Anna Richardson

⟨April 19th 1864⟩

... I have been engaged in fine sports to-day, helping to present an address to Garry Baldy, as the Londoners call him.[1] It was as being on the Committee of the Ladies' Emancipation Society that I had the honour & happiness of going. I felt rather unworthy of it. The face is very fine in its calm composure, not at all foreign in the common sense of the word. We were a disreputable set of people (except myself & one other lady.) & our address was a most inflammatory production. I felt as if I had got among conspirators, & was relieved when I discovered two clergymen in the company. Mr. Forster was there & George MacDonald. Isa Craig was tearing her hair with disappointment at not being asked. She spent Sunday in writing a poem & thought it hard that she might not present it. There is great dissatisfaction about Garibaldi's sudden change of plans. It is said that his illness is all a make up, & that he is really leaving England in obedience to our Government, set on by Louis Napoleon.

I am glad Lizzie was able to be useful to your friend. She will not begin to practice regularly yet. She has another examn. to pass at Apothecaries Hall, which she will take at the end of her apprenticeship, i.e. about a year & a half hence. She has been applying to the Royal College of Physicians for permission to go in for their examn. They have decided to take the opinion of counsel as to whether 1st they can *admit*—2d they can *exclude*—a woman.[2]

... I am going to read the B⟨isho⟩p. of Calcutta's Charge.[3] His brother-in-law, Mr. Tomkinson, was a very valuable friend to us in our experimental examn., of which he took the whole charge. Can you get any signatures to our Memorial? I will send you some papers, in case you can do anything with them. There is to be a Discussion at Waterloo Place next week, in which we hope J. S. Mill will take part. Our cause seems to be looking up at Oxford. Lady Brodie reports that people seem more interested, & the old gentlemen are decidedly friendly. ...

GC: AMsS C350

1. In April 1864, Giuseppe Garibaldi visited London and received an enthusiastic welcome from the British public. His intention to liberate Venice and Rome placed the Foreign Office in a difficult position, as it did not want to endanger relations with the Hapsburg Empire and the Papal States.

2. Garrett's application to the Royal College of Physicians was rejected. She would not finish her clinical practice until March 1865, and she took the Apothecaries' Examination in September 1865.

3. Sophia Tomkinson, Henry Tomkinson's sister, was married to the Reverend G. E. Cotton, bishop of Calcutta.

To Henry Tomkinson

⟨April 20th 1864⟩

I think I told you that J. S. Mill was to be asked. Unfortunately he is gone off to Avignon. Sir James Kay Shuttleworth is coming, & Mr. ⟨Thomas⟩ Hare, the writer on Representation. . . . What is to be done with Mr. Norris if he comes? I am afraid he will insist on proclaiming that the girls were ignorant of elementary needlework, & people will think that much worse than not knowing the principles of Cube Book. . . .

GC: AMsS C358

To Robert Potts

April 22d 1864

Dear Mr. Potts

Thank you very much for your kind offices about the Regulations, which I have already received.

I have written to Mrs. Heaton & to Dr. Wilson. Mr. ⟨John⟩ Westlake is an active friend & will bring people to the Discussion as well as come himself. We mean to have some enemies to make a feeble opposition which will be at once annihilated by our supporters. Do you think we may be satisfied when we have got 1000 signatures?

Yours very sincerely
Emily Davies.

GC: ALS ED LOC-127

To Robert Potts

PROPOSED ADMISSION OF GIRLS TO UNIVERSITY LOCAL EXAMINATIONS.
17, CUNNINGHAM PLACE, LONDON, N.W.

April 25th 1864.

Dear Mr. Potts

We certainly cannot get all our signatures in by the 1st of May. It is probable that some little additional effort will be made after the Discussion on the 29th, & we ought to allow at least a fortnight after that. Would that make it too late to bring the matter on this Term? We should be glad to get forward if it could be done without risk of failure, but we would much rather wait than run any risks. There will be very little to organize if the decision is once given in our favour. A simple notification at each of the Local Centres would be sufficient.

As to the manner of presenting the Memorial, I think our Committee will be very much guided by your opinion. How would it do to send the Memorial to the Vice-Chancellor, holding ourselves ready for a summons, in case the Council of the Senate should wish to put any questions? Or would it do any good to get up a Deputation? I think we might get some men of influence to go up.

Thank you very much for all you are doing. Your advice is most useful. Is the Council of the Senate a large body? Perhaps you could oblige us a list. I am often asked for such things by members of our committee. I will let you hear how we get thro' the Discussion on the 29th.

Yours most truly
Emily Davies.

Do you know anything of a Mr. Samuel Sanders of St. John's? He wrote to me for papers.

GC: ALS ED LOC-128

To Henry Tomkinson

⟨April 28th 1864⟩

...Will you, if you can, come a little before 8 to-morrow & see Mr. Hastings before the Discussion begins. We are threatened with opposition from the lawyers. I only hope our friends will be civil to our enemies....

GC: AMsS C358a

To Robert Potts

PROPOSED ADMISSION OF GIRLS TO UNIVERSITY LOCAL EXAMINATIONS.
17, CUNNINGHAM PLACE, LONDON, N.W.

April 30th 1864.

Dear Mr. Potts

You will be glad to hear that we had on the whole, a very good discussion last night. I suppose there will be some notice of it in the papers, but I think we shall probably print a report of it ourselves.[1] If so, I will send you a copy.

It does not seem to me that we have any chance of getting our 1000 signatures made up for some weeks yet, & as the idea is still new at Cambridge, it might be as well on other grounds, to allow a little more time for people to get used to it. Supposing the decision cannot be given in time to be made use of this year, it is after all, no very great loss to miss *one* more examination.

I send you our report.² Could you oblige me with a list of the Syndics, as I suppose we ought to send a copy to each? When I asked for a list of the Council it was not with any idea of communicating with them as a Committee. Members of our Committee like to know the names, in case any of them may be personal friends. We quite understand that our Memorial must be sent to the Vice-Chancellor & there I suppose we must leave it, unless the Council chooses to open communications with us, in which case we shall of course be ready to answer questions. But if we do not present the Memorial till after the Long Vacation, all this is a matter for future consideration. We have a few more good names added to the Memorial. The Duchess of Argyll has signed as one of the Lady-Visitors at Queen's College. The Dean of Queen's Coll., Mr. Plumptre, made a very good speech last night.

Yours very sincerely
Emily Davies.

GC: ALS ED LOC-109

1. On 29 April 1864, the NAPSS held its special meeting to discuss the examiners' comments on the performance of the girls in the Cambridge Local Examinations. The proceedings of this meeting were subsequently published in "Report of a Discussion of The Proposed Admission of Girls to the University Local Examinations" (London, 1864). Hereafter cited as "Report."

2. The Local Examinations Committee had published "Report of an Examination of Girls, Held (by Permission of the Syndicate) in Connexion with the Local Examinations of the University of Cambridge in 1863" (London, 1863).

To Adelaide Manning

17 Cunningham Place. | Sat. evening. | [?1864] ⟨April 30 1864⟩

My dear—What am I to call you?

I will give you any name you like, if you will be fair & drop the Miss Davies. My name is Emily.

I have no engagement next Friday & shall very much like to join your early tea. I shall I suppose have to go to the W⟨orking⟩.M⟨en's⟩. Committee at half-past four & will find my way from thence to Phillimore Gardens.¹ I thought your party last night a particularly enjoyable one. You & Mrs. Manning seem to have a gift for making parties go pleasantly.

Yours affectionately
Emily Davies.

GC: ALS ED LOC-104

1. The Mannings lived at 44 Phillimore Gardens, London.

To Adelaide Manning

Sat. evening. | [April 1864]

Dear Adelaide

Your note confirms a remark I had already made two or three times, that Mr. ⟨Henry⟩ Roby's was the most mischievous speech of the evening![1] I did not think he would have converted *you*. My views on this subject are exceedingly strong, & I do not despair of bringing you round to them when I see you & can explain them fully. In the meantime I enclose a note, which shows how differently things strike people. (I don't want it returned.) On the whole I think the discussion went well. Mr. ⟨Samuel⟩ Solly was *capital*.[2] He is the sort of witness we very much wanted. Were not you delighted with the ladies?[3] I gazed at them with serene satisfaction, feeling that their presence was doing as much good as the other people's speeches.

Dr. Hodgson is an erratic sort of man, who never sticks to anything. Miss Craig calls him a genius & he is certainly very clever. I think we must print an abridged report of the speeches. Was not Mr. Maurice's characteristic? I liked Mr. Plumptre's very much.[4] I suppose you will read Matthew Arnold's Part III in this month's Macmillan. His writing *stirs* me more than almost anybody's.

I have a whole row of things to say, but they must be left till this day week.
Yrs. affectionately
ED.

GC: ALS ED LOC-119

1. Roby suggested that "the examinations might be modified so as to suit girls' schools rather better." He proposed more emphasis on modern languages, needlework and music, and less on the classics and higher mathematics ("Report" 17–18).

2. Solly argued, "It is one thing to overtax the brain and another to give it healthy action; and I do believe that these middle-class examinations, as applied to the female mind will be extremely useful" ("Report" 9–10).

3. ED had worried that the women at the meeting would look "strong minded." Hence her relief when Isa Craig "secured three lovely girls for the front row" (Chronicle 359).

4. Reverend E. H. Plumptre affirmed girls' "desire [for] knowledge and self-knowledge for their own sakes" ("Report" 11).

To Robert Potts

PROPOSED ADMISSION OF GIRLS TO UNIVERSITY LOCAL EXAMINATIONS.
17, CUNNINGHAM PLACE, LONDON, N.W.

May 4th 1864.

Dear Mr. Potts

We are anxious to present the Memorial whenever you think it is most likely to meet with favourable consideration. If you think Cambridge is ready for it, we are ready to send it in, but we *would much rather give up this year's examn. altogether, than run any risk* of damaging our chances for the future by premature action. On this point, you being on the spot, can judge much better than we can, & we shall be very glad to hear the result of your inquiries. The Duchess of Argyll & Lady ⟨Henrietta⟩ Stanley of Alderley have signed the Memorial as Lady-Visitors of Queen's College & we can get a few more good names in that capacity. I am afraid we could not get any considerable number of supporters unless we allowed *a long* time for collecting them, & a short list would I imagine be worse than none. Grand ladies know nothing at all about the Local Examns., & they are very shy of giving their names (naturally enough) to a new thing which they only half understand.

I am sorry you think the title of our Report likely to give offence.[1] It was difficult to find a suitable heading, & the following lines seemed to us a sufficient explanation. It would certainly have been better to say on the title-page where the examn. was held, tho' I think it is indicated by the address given at the foot of the Report that the Committee have their headquarters in London. I am afraid it would scarcely do to make any alterations *now*. I have already sent the Report to the Examiners, & to supply an amended version to the Syndics would seem scarcely straight forward.

At the same time it seems due to report to them the results of the examn. they gave us leave to hold. I will however defer sending them copies till I hear from you again.[2] Our Committee will have to decide whether we print any Report of the Discussion. The speeches were not very striking, but coming from people of experience, they may carry some weight. I suppose we must print the names appended to the Memorial, & send the vouchers in with them. I thought of putting the principal London Colleges & schools first, & letting the others follow promiscuously. Will that do?

Many thanks for all your kind help.
Yours very truly
Emily Davies.

GC: ALS ED LOC-132

1. Some of the Cambridge Syndics complained about the heading of the Local Examinations Committee Report, as they believed that the committee "had no right to put 'Cambridge Local Examn.' at the head of the Report" (Chronicle 360).

2. Potts had opposed her plan of sending copies of the Report to the Council, saying "I am disposed to think it wd. be best not to let it become public, but simply restricted to those who sent up pupils into that experimental Examn" (Chronicle 360).

To Henry Tomkinson

⟨May 9 1864⟩

I want to know whether any of the ladies struck you as strongminded looking. We were afraid Miss Craig wd. have ruined us by her recklessness in inviting anybody that liked to come. She insisted that they had a right to have 'Mission stamped on their brows', if they liked, but I don't think she did any serious mischief. Miss Garrett was sitting very near you, looking exactly like one of the girls whose instinct it is to do what you tell them.

GC: AMsS C359

To Robert Potts

17 Cunningham Place. N.W. | May 10th 1864.

Dear Mr. Potts

We are to have a Committee meeting on Friday. I hope you may be able to send us some further advice by that time. I feel very much inclined to defer presenting the Memorial, unless you see some good reason for pushing forward. A great part of our supporters have been gained gradually, one by one, & the more time we allow for these conversions to go on, the better our chance.

I am sorry Mr. Latham is so obdurate.[1] He is a friend of my brother's & has expressed himself rather fiercely against us to my sister-in-law. I am afraid if we had asked leave of the Syndics to print our report, they would have said (the *enemies* I mean) that we were trying to make them responsible for a thing they had nothing to do with.

I have not yet sent copies to the Syndics. I suppose I must do so. I have had a very friendly letter from the Sec. of the Oxford Delegacy to-day. They are fighting over the Religious Knowledge clause in their Statute.

We are going to print a report of the Discussion of the 29th, very much abridged. I think it will be useful for distribution. I will consult the Committee on Friday about getting ladies' names as supporters. If we can have *time*, I think we may get a good list.

Yours very sincerely
Emily Davies.

GC: ALS ED LOC-133

1. Probably Henry Latham (1821–1902), educated at Trinity College, Cambridge; Fellow, Vice Master, and Master, Trinity Hall, Cambridge. He was a mathematician and wrote books on geometry and university issues.

To Robert Potts

PROPOSED ADMISSION OF GIRLS TO UNIVERSITY LOCAL EXAMINATIONS.
17, CUNNINGHAM PLACE, LONDON, N.W.

May 16th 1864.

Dear Mr. Potts

At our Committee meeting on Friday, I brought forward your suggestion to make an alteration in the title-page of the Examiners' Report, before sending it to the Syndics. After some discussion, it was agreed that as the report had already been sent to Mr. Gray & to the Examiners, several of whom are members of the Syndicate, it would be inexpedient to issue an altered edition. A further reason for not doing so is that in the report of discussion, the Examiners' Report appears in full, without the obnoxious heading, & this will be available for circulation at Cambridge.

I will send you some copies as soon as it is ready. We have decided not to present the memorial before the October Term. In the meantime we shall endeavour to make up a list of influential ladies who support the proposal.

I remain
Yours very sincerely
Emily Davies.
I think you will be pleased with some of the speeches.

GC: ALS ED LOC-134

To Adelaide Manning

PROPOSED ADMISSION OF GIRLS TO UNIVERSITY LOCAL EXAMINATIONS.
17, CUNNINGHAM PLACE, LONDON, N.W.

Saturday. ⟨May⟩ [1864]

My dear Adelaide

I have no complete set of the examn. questions, only a few stray papers left over after our examn., which I think are scarcely worth sending. The whole set of papers can be bought at Rivington's for 2/.

I send the Examiners' Report, which I ought to have sent before. If you would like to have some to send about, I can let you have some more, but I think the Report of Discussion, which will soon be ready, will be more useful for general circulation.

I am amused at your talking of my "correspondence" with Mr. Arnold. It remains to be seen whether I shall be able to muster up courage to write to him at all. I have a great horror of inflicting letters upon busy people who may be annoyed or at least bothered, by them. I always feel as if they would be justified in looking upon it as impertinence.

Mr. Solly has returned his Proof with a very good sentence added. I think the Discussion will read well, on the whole. Did you hear the fight Miss Garrett & I were carrying on with Mr. Shaen the other night? It was about the workingmen. Those Radicals always make them out to be so excessively virtuous that Lizzie & I were tempted to have a go the other way & to point out their love of drinking, wife-beating &c. At the end, we came to an explanation, by which it appeared that we did *not* consider them worse than other people & that Mr. Shaen *did*! It shows how disputants may misunderstand each other, when they separate without a final explanation.

I was so much obliged to you for talking to my Quaker friend. She enjoyed the evening very much. Will you please give the enclosed to Mrs. Manning.

Yours affectionately
ED

GC: ALS ED LOC-105

To Henry Tomkinson

⟨May 1864⟩

... I send you the Report of the Discussions at last. We ought really now to do something in the Rank & Influence direction. There is no excuse for putting it off any longer. I think Mrs. Russell Gurney & Lady Goldsmid will give their help & Mrs. Manning is very good. Did you see Mr. Hutton's notice of our examns. in the Spectator?[1] It is all very fine to call it the *first*, as if we were quite sure of a second & third, but I don't feel at all confident that it will not be the first & 'only.' I wonder what Mr. Latham will say, if he sees it. My brother thinks it is the best policy to assume that it is all settled.

GC: AMsS C365

1. News of the Week, *Spectator* (28 May 1864).

To Robert Potts

PROPOSED ADMISSION OF GIRLS TO UNIVERSITY LOCAL EXAMINATIONS.
17, CUNNINGHAM PLACE, LONDON, N.W.

July 26th 1864.

Dear Mr. Potts

You will see by the enclosed copy of the Memorial that we are getting on pretty well with our list of supporters. We have about 920 signatures of *teachers*, & are still going on collecting names. We propose printing the Memorial with the names in pamphlet form, for circulation among members of the Senate. It must of course be presented at the *beginning* of the October Term.

The Dean of Canterbury (Alford) has accepted the office of Chairman of our Committee & promises to do all he can to help us.[1]

I send you some more copies of the Report. It is very good of you to take so much trouble in distributing them.

Yours very sincerely
Emily Davies.

GC: ALS ED LOC-135

1. On 8 July, the committee asked Henry Alford, dean of Canterbury, to act as chairman. Alford initially expressed reservations about the possibility that the committee might seek university degrees for women: "I should deprecate introducing anything like *competition* or personal ... *designation,* into the characteristic of female society in England" (Chronicle 367), but Davies reassured him.

To Lord Brougham

PROPOSED ADMISSION OF GIRLS TO UNIVERSITY LOCAL EXAMINATIONS.
17, CUNNINGHAM PLACE, LONDON, N.W.

July 30th. 1864.

My Lord

I am desired respectfully to call your attention to the accompanying Memorial & to request the favour of your name as supporting it.

The Memorial has been signed by upwards of 900 teachers, & it is now proposed to collect the names of influential ladies & gentlemen, not directly connected with education, who approve of the proposal. These names will be sent in on a separate list, when the Memorial is presented at the beginning of the October Term.

I do not know whether Mr. Hastings has had an opportunity of speaking to you of girls' schools in connexion with the proposed Commission of inquiry.[1] We are extremely anxious that girls' schools should be included in the investigation, and shall feel greatly obliged by your exerting your influence for this object, if you concur with us in thinking it desirable.

I am, My Lord
Yours obediently
Emily Davies
Hon. Sec.

UCL: ALS Brougham 4521

1. Royal Commission to Inquire into Education in Schools in England and Wales (Taunton) 1864–1868 (SIC). The government had appointed the SIC, under the chairman-

ship of Lord Taunton, to report on measures needed to improve secondary education in day and boarding schools. It examined those primarily middle-class schools that had not been examined in previous commissions.

To Lord Brougham

PROPOSED ADMISSION OF GIRLS TO UNIVERSITY LOCAL EXAMINATIONS.
17, CUNNINGHAM PLACE, LONDON, N.W.

Aug. 10th 1864.

My Lord

I regret that there has been some delay in the acknowledgment of your kind letter of the 31st ult. I understand from Mr. Hastings that he has sent you all the information we have at present. If anything fresh should occur before the York meeting which may seem worthy of notice, I shall have the pleasure of letting you know.[1] Mr. Hastings has probably told you that the Dean of Canterbury (Alford) is now Chairman of our Committee.

With many thanks for your kind cooperation.

I remain, My Lord,
Yours truly
Emily Davies.

UCL: ALS Brougham 4522

1. The NAPSS meeting was scheduled to be held in York, 22–29 September 1864.

To Robert Potts

PROPOSED ADMISSION OF GIRLS TO UNIVERSITY LOCAL EXAMINATIONS.
17, CUNNINGHAM PLACE, LONDON, N.W.

Aug. 19th 1864.

Dear Mr. Potts

I quite meant to have answered your former kind letter before this. I now send you another packet of Reports, & also enclose the latest Edition of the Memorial, that you may see how we are getting on with names. I am afraid it is impossible to omit Mrs. ⟨Frances⟩ Kingsley's, after having asked for it, & perhaps as it is only one, it may not do any great harm. What sort of names do you think we ought to get? Great ladies are not very easy to get at, & one can scarcely imagine that the mere fact of being a Marchioness will tell much at Cambridge.

I forget whether I told you that Dean Alford is now Chairman of our Committee, & the Memorial will therefore be sent out thro' him. We are putting the names of the Professors of three London Colleges at the head, & the rest of the names alphabetically. To arrange them in counties would be troublesome, & a good many signatures have no address. I am glad to hear that Mr. ⟨William⟩ Campion is friendly.[1]

Yours very truly
Emily Davies.

GC: ALS ED LOC-139

1. Campion was on the University Local Examinations Syndicate for 1863.

To Robert Potts

PROPOSED ADMISSION OF GIRLS TO UNIVERSITY LOCAL EXAMINATIONS.
17, CUNNINGHAM PLACE, LONDON, N.W.

Aug. 22d. 1864.

Dear Mr. Potts

I am afraid we shall not be able to have everything quite ready by the 1st of October, on account of the Social Science meeting, which will be going on from Sept. 22d. to the 29th. We hope to get some fresh support at this meeting.

Lord Brougham intends to bring the subject forward in his opening address, & Mr. Norris the Inspector of Schools, is I believe, writing a paper upon it, which will at any rate, lead to discussion, & after that we may expect some accession of names. So it seems worth while to incur a little delay, for the sake of the extra support that may be gained.

I do not quite understand the course to be pursued in presenting the Memorial. The Chairman will I suppose send it (a *printed* copy in the form of a pamphlet?) with a letter to the Vice-Chancellor.

Ought he to send at the same time a parcel of copies for the V. C. to distribute, & if so, how many? Will you tell me also how many copies we shall want *for distribution* among the resident members of the Senate, & how to get their addresses? (if we are to send them.) Does the Calendar indicate which of the members are resident? We are printing the Memorial as a pamphlet of the same size as the Report of Discussion.

The signatures of course follow immediately, & I suppose the supporters must be at the end, or would you have them on a separate sheet? We put the address whenever we know it. I am going to try to get it added, where it is absent. Mrs. Cooper & others are preparing pupils for examn. I hope they may not be disappointed.

Yours very truly
Emily Davies.

GC: ALS ED LOC-140

To Henry Tomkinson

Sept. 7th 1864

... I enclose the list of supporters of the Memorial. You will see that I have included your name (as a member of our Committee) along with the representatives of rank & fashion. It has occurred to me since that as you & Mr. Hastings are probably members of the Senate, perhaps as a question of etiquette your name ought not to appear in connexion with the Memorial addressed to yourselves.[1] I shd. like to keep your name, but of course we shd. care much *more* for having you in the Senate, to speak in *your* behalf.

As there are only two or three of our friends who in the least understand what we aim at, we shall really want those who do to be on the spot to explain for us....

Lord Brougham is going to bring the subject forward [at the Social Science meeting] & Mr. *Norris* is writing a paper, which is I believe quite in our favour.

GC: AMsS C371

1. The names of both Hastings and Tomkinson appeared in the final memorial.

To Henry Tomkinson

Sept. 16th 1864

I am afraid Mr. Norris may do us some harm at York.[1] ... Could not you come down & help Mr. Hastings to silence him? The proposal of a new scheme will look very reasonable to people who don't know anything about the matter.

... My brother is vegetating in Worcestershire. A third little boy is now come to add to our happiness.[2]

GC: AMsS C373

1. On 10 September 1864, Norris explained his unwillingness to open University Local examinations to girls, citing three reasons: that "even the remotest appearance of competition between men & women shd. be avoided"; that university men were "the last men likely to judge wisely as to such modifications of the girls' examns. as experience might suggest. The Examiners ought to be married men of older standing & more knowledge of society ... [and that] The Universities wd. be departing from all their traditions, purposes, & habits in undertaking such examns" (Chronicle 372–73).
2. Maurice Llewelyn Davies (1864–1939).

To Robert Potts

J. G. Fitch, Esq., York. | Sept. 22d.

Dear Mr. Potts

I send you by this post a Proof of our list of names. There are still a few names to be added & a few corrections to be made, but I think we may be able to have it ready for presentation in about ten days. There may possibly be a little delay caused by its having to go thro' the hands of the Dean of Canterbury as our Chairman.

I hope we may gain some support here. The Education Department is I am told, likely to be very well attended & the Meeting generally promises to be an interesting & successful one.[1]

I remain
Yours very truly
Emily Davies.

We have done our best to fill up the addresses but have not been able to get them in every case.

GC: ALS ED LOC-143

1. The Education Department of the NAPSS. The organization was divided into sections: Jurisprudence and Amendment of the Law; Education; Health; Economy and Trade.

To Robert Potts

"J. G. Fitch, Esq., York." | Monday. ⟨Sept. 26 1864⟩

Dear Mr. Potts

I am glad you are pretty well satisfied with our ~~Memorial~~ lists. I am adding some addresses & names & hope to have it quite ready for presentation in a few days. Will you kindly let me know how many copies will be wanted for Cambridge & in what way they can best be distributed. I shall be here till Thursday. I do not see what difficulty there need be in the arrangement of details. The University has only to let the Local Secs. know that they may receive female candidates, & they can then make arrangements, according to local circumstances. Yours very truly.
Emily Davies.

GC: ALS ED LOC-144

To Robert Potts

PROPOSED ADMISSION OF GIRLS TO UNIVERSITY LOCAL EXAMINATIONS.
17, CUNNINGHAM PLACE, LONDON, N.W.

Oct. 1st. 1864.

Dear Mr. Potts

Thank you very much for your kind offices. I am a little perplexed at finding that the Vice-Chancellor expects an official, by which I suppose is meant a *M.S.*, copy of the Memorial. I rather pressed in our Committee for having a written copy with all the signatures appended, but other people of more experience said it was quite in order to present a printed form with the signatures printed, & I do not think we can do anything else now. The vouchers could of course be sent up, if necessary, but the gentlemen of our Committee said it was more customary to send in only the printed list. I enclose a draft of the letter I propose sending with the Memorial.

~~Dean~~ We shall send at the same time a quasi-private letter from our Chairman, Dean Alford, of an explanatory & persuasive character. I think we may be able to get the 25 copies struck off & dispatched on Wednesday or Thursday. I am just now sending to the printer 23 additional names, & I do not mean to take any more. We have taken a great deal of pains to make sure that the signatures are all those of bonâ fide teachers of young ladies, but when so many people are concerned in collecting them, one cannot feel absolutely certain that a few names of National Schoolmistresses or ~~or~~ masters may not have slipped in. We had a good many signatures sent from Irish *schools*, all of which we have omitted, as far as we know. *Governesses* may be looked upon as cosmopolitan, & competent to sign, wherever they may be temporarily employed.

Yours most truly
Emily Davies.

I suppose some notice will be given of when the Discussion is to come on in the Senate. We should like to let our friends know in good time.

GC: ALS ED LOC-146

To Robert Potts

PROPOSED ADMISSION OF GIRLS TO UNIVERSITY LOCAL EXAMINATIONS.
17, CUNNINGHAM PLACE, LONDON, N.W.

Oct. 4th 1864.

Dear Mr. Potts

Many thanks for all your suggestions. I have arranged to meet one or two of our Committee who are in Town to-morrow, & I hope we may be able to get the official copy of Memorial in readiness by the end of the week. I am going to look over the names again. Miss Kyberd's is the head of a school which sent up candidates. May I ask your acceptance of the accompanying copy of the paper which was read for me at York.[1]

Yours most truly
Emily Davies.

Are you *sure* that ~~the~~ F. & S. A. Richardson live at Newcastle?[2] Do they keep a school?

GC: ALS ED LOC-147

    1. Emily Davies, "On Secondary Instruction, As Relating to Girls" (NAPSS, 1864).
    2. Probably Frances Richardson and Sarah S. Richardson, governesses at Pickering.

To Robert Potts

PROPOSED ADMISSION OF GIRLS TO UNIVERSITY LOCAL EXAMINATIONS.
17, CUNNINGHAM PLACE, LONDON, N.W.

Oct. 6th 1864.

Dear Mr. Potts

It is quite impossible to dispatch the Memorial to-day. I cannot get the Dean's signature to the formula guaranteeing the signatures before to-morrow at the earliest, & the Memorial itself is not ready. It is to be printed on foolscap in the usual form of Petitions & will I hope look tolerably imposing. I believe the number of names is just over 1000.

The Miss Richardsons are governesses at Pickering. Miss Richardson of Newcastle is a friend of mine & has never had anything to do with schools, except as a voluntary teacher. I have omitted all the names with Irish addresses, except those to which we are authorised to add governess. I have looked thro' the names again omitting any that look at all suspicious. If there is anything wrong now, it must be thro' some special interposition of Satan, impossible to provide against. The great majority of the signatures will have the address in full.

I am glad you approve of my little pamphlet. If you will kindly mention the names of any Cambridge men to whom it might be worth while to send copies, I shall be much obliged to you. I am sorry for the unavoidable delay in presenting the Memorial, but it may perhaps be as well to give people a little more time to think, before the Discussion comes on.

Yours very truly
Emily Davies.

GC: ALS ED LOC-148

To Robert Potts

17 Cunningham Place. | Sat. evening. ⟨Oct. 8? 1864⟩

Dear Mr. Potts

Thank you for the list of names. I shall be very glad to send my little pamphlet to any one who you think might be influenced at all by it. I wrote it chiefly in the hope of its being made of some use at Cambridge.

I will send you 300 unofficial copies of Memorial as soon as I get them. We shall be very much obliged to you if you will take the trouble to get them distributed in the regular way, & perhaps you will kindly let us send the fee thro' you, whatever it may be. Do you think it would be worth while to send to each Combination room with the Memorial, a copy of the enclosed circular? If so, I will send 20 copies with the Memorials. It seems desirable that there should be some explanation of our objects, accessible to any one who really wishes to know what we are aiming at. I find I cannot get the official copy from the printer before Tuesday. I could not in any case have sent it off to-day, as I have not yet got an answer from the Dean. I fancy he has been from home this week.

I have written to the Examiners who helped us in the experimental examn., asking for their support. I see only two of them are on the Council. I am very glad to hear that Mr. Campion is friendly. Yours truly
ED.

GC: ALS ED LOC-149

To Robert Potts

PROPOSED ADMISSION OF GIRLS TO UNIVERSITY LOCAL EXAMINATIONS.
17, CUNNINGHAM PLACE, LONDON, N.W.

Oct. 13th 1864.

Dear Mr. Potts

I am to-day sending the Official Copy of the Memorial to the Vice-Chancellor & the unofficial copies for distribution. I despatched yesterday 300 unofficial copies by train. I hope you will receive them to-day or to-morrow. You will kindly let me know what is paid for the carriage.

Have you any idea within what time we may expect an answer? I am constantly being asked by schoolmistresses & others.

I will send my pamphlet to Dr. Howson, tho' without much hope of doing good.[1] He told my sister-in-law that he had been disposed to be friendly, but in the Liverpool Committee an argument was brought forward which seemed to him to have great weight, namely, that "the admission of girls would give rise to so many jokes!" One fancies people must be rather hard up for reasonable objections, when they resort to *such* arguments. Liverpool is the only place at which we have heard of opposition on the part of the Local Committee.[2]

I had already sent my pamphlet to Professor Liveing. Thank you for mentioning Dr. ⟨James⟩ Challis. I am afraid I have inadvertently destroyed your note without taking down his address.

Yours very truly
Emily Davies.

GC: ALS ED LOC-150

1. Probably John Saul Howson (1816–85) who was the principal of the Liverpool Collegiate Institute; Hulsean Lecturer at Cambridge; and contributor to the *Quarterly Review* and other periodicals.

2. On 12 August, Davies had received a letter from N. Waterhouse, the Local Exams secretary for Liverpool, advising her of "a resolution which was unanimously adopted by the Liverpool Committee last autumn, & of which copies have been sent to the Universities [stating] 'That this Committee seriously doubts whether the proposed examination of girls by the Universities wd. be beneficial; whilst it is strongly of opinion that it wd. tend to lower the character of the University Local Examn. in the estimation of the public'" (Chronicle 368–69).

To Robert Potts

PROPOSED ADMISSION OF GIRLS TO UNIVERSITY LOCAL EXAMINATIONS.
17, CUNNINGHAM PLACE, LONDON, N.W.

Oct. 19th ⟨1864⟩

Dear Mr. Potts

Thank you very much for letting us know how our Memorial was received & for keeping so efficient a watch on the progress of our affairs.[1] I am beginning to feel much more hopeful of success, but not in the least *impatient*. From all you & others have said it seems to me that what we have to do now is to keep very quiet & not to seem to be hurrying the University by making demonstrations of any sort. I do not mean by this that we are unwilling to answer objections. I think your notion of seeing any hostile letters that may be likely to appear is very good, tho' I think perhaps it might be sufficient if the answer appears in the week following.

I do not know how much influence the local papers have on the University mind. I should have fancied it would be very little, but I have no means of judging. I feel a little doubtful about your own letter, on the ground that you are I presume a good deal identified with the "Married Fellows" question, & it might be running some slight risk of mixing the two things together in the minds of hasty people. We do not want, if we can help it to rouse the opposition of the people by whom Married Fellows are "regarded as an abomination."[2] I merely throw out this in case it may not have occurred to you. We have taken infinite pains to keep this movement entirely distinct from any others with which it might be supposed to be connected, & to have it judged on its own merits, & I think we have hitherto been pretty successful in so doing.

The Vice-Chancellor seems to be acting a very friendly part.

I remain, Dear Mr. Potts

Yours very truly

Emily Davies.

GC: ALS ED LOC-155

1. On 17 October 1864, Potts wrote to Davies describing the university's reception of the memorial: "This morning your Memorial was laid before the Council of the Senate by the Vice-Chancellor.... I am sure you will feel gratified to learn that the Memorial was respectfully received by the Council.... It is highly probable that a Special Syndicate will be appointed to consider the memorial & to Report upon it" (Chronicle 378–79).

2. Potts himself had raised this issue, explaining in his 17 October 1864 letter that he was "terribly assailed one day last week in the Corpus Combination room on the subject of married Fellows, who there & at other Colleges are regarded as an abomination" (Chronicle 380). The Oxford and Cambridge University Commissions of 1850–52 had aimed at making academic careers more feasible and desirable. As a consequence, they had suggested that the requirement of celibacy be relaxed, and that Tutors be permitted to marry without foregoing the possibility of becoming Fellows. At Cambridge, each college determined the requirement of celibacy for Fellows separately. It was not until the 1880s that all Cambridge Fellows were free to marry.

To Robert Potts

PROPOSED ADMISSION OF GIRLS TO UNIVERSITY LOCAL EXAMINATIONS.
17, CUNNINGHAM PLACE, LONDON, N.W.

Oct. 20 ⟨1864⟩

Dear Mr. Potts

Thank you for your kind offices in getting the Memorial distributed. I had 1000 copies struck off, & can at any time send you as many more as you are likely to require. We are receiving every day fresh assurances of support, which make us very hopeful of success.

Yours most truly

Emily Davies.

GC: ALS ED LOC-156

To Robert Potts

PROPOSED ADMISSION OF GIRLS TO UNIVERSITY LOCAL EXAMINATIONS.
17, CUNNINGHAM PLACE, LONDON, N.W.

Oct. 29th 1864.

Dear Mr. Potts

I was very much obliged to you for sending the Cambridge papers & also for letting us know the progress of affairs. On the whole we feel very much encouraged, but we shall be anxious to hear who are the members of the Syndicate appointed to report upon the Memorial. I suppose much will depend on whether the report is friendly or the reverse.[1]

I have consulted a friend who knows Liverpool about answering Dr. Howson's objections.[2] If she thinks it desirable & can give me the necessary information as to which of the Liverpool papers would be most likely to insert a letter on the subject, &c. I shall be glad to write. But have the Liverpool people much influence at Cambridge?

I suppose the preparation of the report will occupy two or three weeks at least, so that we may consider it pretty nearly settled that there will be no examn. of girls *this* year. We are quite content to wait.

Yours very truly
Emily Davies.

I believe Mrs. Cooper will have some candidates ready for you, if the answer is given in time.

GC: ALS ED LOC-159

1. A letter to Lyttelton from William Whewell said that "the proposal will be fairly considered here, but the University must be allowed time & quiet, & not be disturbed by external urgency," while William Thompson said he did "not anticipate any opposition in the council" and that he expected "that the matter will be viewed without disfavour. but naturally fellows of Colleges know less about young Ladies than a body of husbands & fathers would" (Chronicle 381–82).

2. See ED to Robert Potts, 13 October 1864.

To Robert Potts

PROPOSED ADMISSION OF GIRLS TO UNIVERSITY LOCAL EXAMINATIONS.
17, CUNNINGHAM PLACE, LONDON, N.W.

Monday ⟨Oct. 31 1864⟩

Dear Mr. Potts

I am very glad to hear of the favourable article in the Liverpool Mercury. Do you think articles in the local papers would do us much good? I believe we might get a good many inserted in different parts of the country, if you think they would have any weight with the University. I suppose if it is done at all, it ought to be at once.

I have sent to all the *crossed* names on the list. The others perhaps you would kindly supply, as I don't know their addresses.

Yours most truly
Emily Davies.

GC: ALS ED LOC-160

To Robert Potts

PROPOSED ADMISSION OF GIRLS TO UNIVERSITY LOCAL EXAMINATIONS.
17, CUNNINGHAM PLACE, LONDON, N.W.

Nov. 1st 1864.

Dear Mr. Potts

I will see what can be done about getting articles & letters into the newspapers.

It is like sowing bread on the waters, in the doubtfulness one feels as to whether many of the papers will ever find their way to Cambridge, but we must not neglect any chance.

In the meantime, we are not anxious to press the matter forward. I believe our only chance of success lies in giving the University ample time. We find people a great deal more ready to help us when they have thought a little about the matter.

The first impulse is to say no, & it must naturally take some time to leaven & bring round such a large number of men as will be concerned in this decision. We have adopted Patience as our Motto, & I believe we owe much to having always kept it in mind.

I saw to-day one of the most active members of our Committee, & she took this view very decidedly. I do not of course mean that we shall not be glad to see the affair moving. All I mean is that we do not at all wish for an examn. of girls before Christmas, 1865. The girls will be all the better for having another year to work up their Arithmetic, which I suspect is still sadly deficient.

I remain, Dear Mr. Potts
Yours very truly
Emily Davies.
Who is to be the new Vice-Chancellor?

GC: ALS ED LOC-161

To Henry Tomkinson

November 1864

The Liverpool people some months ago passed a strong Resolution against us, & sent it up to Cambridge. They are I believe the only local Committees hostile to us. The objection urged, which influenced at least one member of the Committee, Dr. Howson, was that the admission of girls 'wd. give rise to so many jokes.' Dr. Howson was inclined to be friendly before, but this difficulty was new to him & he did not see how it was to be got over.

GC: AMsS C384

To Robert Potts

PROPOSED ADMISSION OF GIRLS TO UNIVERSITY LOCAL EXAMINATIONS.
17, CUNNINGHAM PLACE, LONDON, N.W.

Monday. [Nov. 7] ⟨1864⟩

Dear Mr. Potts

Thank you for the Camb. paper. The Liverpool article is as you say, excellent, & Mr. ⟨Albert⟩ Wratislaw's letter very much to the purpose. I was glad to hear of Dr. ⟨Henry⟩ Cookson's re-election.[1]

Yours very truly

Emily Davies.

I suppose the question will scarcely be decided this Term. *We are in no hurry.*

GC: ALS ED LOC-164

1. As vice chancellor.

To Robert Potts

PROPOSED ADMISSION OF GIRLS TO UNIVERSITY LOCAL EXAMINATIONS.
17, CUNNINGHAM PLACE, LONDON, N.W.

Nov. 14th 1864.

Dear Mr. Potts

I am glad to hear that the Camb. Chronicle has inserted the Scotsman article, & that a Syndicate is shortly to be appointed. I should like to know what the difficulties are which are considered likely to interfere with the extension of the Scheme. There may be some which we have not thought of.

Yours very sincerely

Emily Davies.

I have heard to-day from a schoolmistress who talks of sending her girls to Edinburgh!

GC: ALS ED LOC-165

To Robert Potts

PROPOSED ADMISSION OF GIRLS TO UNIVERSITY LOCAL EXAMINATIONS.
17, CUNNINGHAM PLACE, LONDON, N.W.

Nov. 25th ⟨1864⟩

Dear Mr. Potts

I am very glad to hear that the Syndicate was appointed without opposition. Would you kindly send me a list of this year's *Examiners*? I enclose the sum due to you in postage stamps, with many thanks.

Our Committee intend to issue a short paper with a view to meeting the objections raised by the A⟨rch⟩b⟨isho⟩p. of York.[1] If you can let us know what are the difficulties most dwelt upon at Cambridge, it will be a help in drawing up the paper. Do you know at all which member of the special Syndicate is likely to be commissioned to prepare the draft report?

In haste,
Yours most truly
Emily Davies.

GC: ALS ED LOC-166

1. "The Education of Girls," *Spectator* (1 October 1864). The archbishop of York said, "A great mistake would be made if without any attempt at an independent treatment of female education we catch at some existing scheme of examination for boys, and assume that it will suit both purposes."

To Robert Potts

PROPOSED ADMISSION OF GIRLS TO UNIVERSITY LOCAL EXAMINATIONS.
17, CUNNINGHAM PLACE, LONDON, N.W.

Dec. 7th ⟨1864⟩

Dear Mr. Potts

I fancy I must have somehow expressed myself in such a way as to give you a wrong impression about the little paper I spoke of. It is merely a circular, very similar to the one we printed before, but brought down to the present moment

& meeting the present state of feeling. I think when you see it, you will approve of its being issued.[1]

I was very glad to hear of the insertion of the article from the Hull paper. I am afraid we could not get up a good discussion in a London paper, but I hope to be able to do something more in the way of articles. Some of the ~~country~~ papers have refused letters. I suppose next week will be a busy time with the examns.[2]

Ever yours very truly
Emily Davies.

GC: ALS ED LOC-167

1. Emily Davies, "Reasons for the Extension of the University Local Examinations to Girls," (London, 1864). Hereafter cited as "Reasons."
2. The Cambridge Local Examinations were held from Monday, 12 December to Saturday, 17 December 1864.

To Robert Potts

PROPOSED ADMISSION OF GIRLS TO UNIVERSITY LOCAL EXAMINATIONS.
17, CUNNINGHAM PLACE, LONDON, N.W.

Dec. 10th ⟨1864⟩

Dear Mr. Potts

I am going to make another claim upon your kind services. We want to get the enclosed circular distributed to all the resident members of the University before they leave Cambridge. Could you engage the Junior Marshall to undertake it as before? I suppose it ought to be done before the 16th.

We are anxious that all the people who will have to decide upon the question should have a brief statement of the case in their hands before Christmas, as they will probably be making up their minds one way or the other during the comparative leisure of the vacation.

May I venture to send you the parcel as before?

I don't know what we should do without your kind help in these matters.

Yours most truly
Emily Davies.

GC: ALS ED LOC-168

To Henry Tomkinson

Dec. 12th 1864

... I was rather surprised that you passed the sentence (inserted tentatively) about feminine grammars.[1] Miss Bostock objected to it as too sarcastic, but the Dean said it was only 'a gambol' & the others insisted on keeping it in. I thought myself that gambols were scarcely in place in a grave official paper, but if the Committee chooses to take the responsibility, I suppose it is all right. The Dean is very goodnatured & pleasant & makes a very improving Chairman. He gave us a valuable lesson in spelling & Composition.

GC: AMsS C386

1. Addressing the concern that the examiners would be Fellows at colleges, not "husbands and fathers," Davies pointed out that the "purely intellectual examination, conducted through the medium of written papers" could scarcely require different qualifications for girls than for boys. The circular then reads, "It has not yet been proposed to restrict girls to the use of feminine grammars and dictionaries, nor do we hear of manuals of arithmetic or geography specially adapted to the female mind, and if boys and girls are learning common lessons from common schoolbooks, a common examination seems to follow as a matter of course" ("Reasons" 3).

To Robert Potts

PROPOSED ADMISSION OF GIRLS TO UNIVERSITY LOCAL EXAMINATIONS.
17, CUNNINGHAM PLACE, LONDON, N.W.

Dec. 13 ⟨1864⟩

Dear Mr. Potts

I am very glad to hear that the Syndicate has got so far as to affirm the possibility of doing something. Did they take *three* meetings before arriving at that conclusion? I strongly sympathize with your feeling in favour of letting well alone, & perhaps it will be better to confine ourselves for the present to getting our "Reasons" into as many newspapers as possible. At the beginning of next Term, I think I should wish to have it distributed among members of the University. Our difficulty is to get at the dead mass who as a rule oppose everything new. Unless we can *partially* convert them beforehand, they will probably have made up their minds to vote against us before the matter is discussed at all. At our last meeting Dean Alford said that as far as he had heard, what opposition there is arises from ignorance & misconception, & he thought it very desirable therefore to diffuse as much information as possible in the interval before the discussion.

The newspapers are a valuable medium, but one can never be sure that they will happen to be read by the people who most need the information. I hope you approve of the ~~paper~~ ˢᶜⁱʳᶜᵘˡᵃʳ as it stands. We took great pains to avoid making any statement that might give offense, while meeting the objections which have been urged at York & elsewhere.

I suppose you are busy with the Examns. this week.
Ever yours sincerely
Emily Davies.

GC: ALS ED LOC-169

To Henry Tomkinson

Dec. 14th 1864

... Thank you for your note & 'permission to view' the Boys' Examn. I hope to look in on Friday afternoon. Perhaps you will tell me then, what you think it best to do about circulating the 'Reasons.' I wrote to Mr. Potts, asking him to distribute them thro' the Junior Marshalls, as he did with the Memorials. In reply, he advises us to let well alone, & at any rate, to do nothing at Cambridge till the beginning of next Term. He says the circular wd. have no chance of getting attention now. You are so crushing about Mr. Potts, I am afraid even to mention his name, but in this case (tho' quite admitting the fact of his lunacy, as a general proposition) I think he may be right. My notion was that University men wd. be making up their minds (with the help of their mothers & sisters) during the leisure of the Christmas Vacation, & that we had better give them something to guide them to a right conclusion. But I suppose it is useless to bother people with statements when they are too busy to look at them....

GC: AMsS C386a

To Matthew Arnold

Dec. 23d 1864

Dear Mr. Arnold

At the risk of wearying you, I ~~dare~~ venture to send you another little manifesto just issued by our Committee.[1] We seem to be prospering at Cambridge. ~~There We have a considerable majority in the~~ ᴬ Special Syndicate, has been appointed to ~~report upon~~ ᶜᵒⁿˢⁱᵈᵉʳ the Memorial, & we are told that their report will almost certainly be favourable. How it may be recd. ~~by the Senate~~ is another question. The Senate are a very numerous body, & are ᵃˢ ᵃ ʳᵘˡᵉ ~~more likely to~~ ᵗʰᵉʸ are ~~be guided by~~ ʳᵃᵗʰᵉʳ ᵒᵇᵉᵈⁱᵉⁿᵗ ᵗᵒ prejudice than ~~by~~ ᵗᵒ ᵃ the prescriptions of reason—wh. is of course on our side.

I am sorry to see that your name is not included, as we hoped it would have been, in the new Royal Commission.² I suppose Mr. Forster will to some extent, represent you. Do you happen to know with whom it rests, whether girls' schools are included in the inquiry? Lord Lyttelton ~~said~~ told us he thought they wd. be, as a matter or course. Mr. Norris has since ~~written to Miss~~ stated, on I do not know what authority, that "the Commission will not extend their inquiry to girls unless a strong effort is made to persuade them." If this is the case, I suppose we ought to do something, but we do not wish to torment ~~the Commissioners~~ ^people with appeals unless it is necessary. One does not see what objection ~~there~~ there can be to inquiry, except the ~~extra~~ work, which some of the Commissioners ~~might~~ ^would perhaps be glad to lessen.

We ~~seem to~~ have a very zealous advocate in the Nat⟨ional⟩. Rev⟨iew⟩.—¹ ^am afraid more zealous than wise. At least, it seems to me that he expects a great deal too much from education in the technical sense of the word. He scarcely takes into account at all the ~~immense~~ atmospheric ~~influence of~~ education of circumstances & responsibilities, which must I shd. think have more influence in the formation of character than any systems of instruction, however cunningly contrived & judiciously carried out.

GC: DAL ED SIC-4

1. "Reasons."
2. The Schools Inquiry Commission (SIC).

To Thomas Dyke Acland

PROPOSED ADMISSION OF GIRLS TO UNIVERSITY LOCAL EXAMINATIONS.
17, CUNNINGHAM PLACE, LONDON, N.W.

Dec. 28th 1864.

Dear Sir

It is very good of you to take my troublesome letters so kindly. I have written to Professor ⟨Montague⟩ Bernard, sending him the List of names & some other papers.¹

We have not been able to find out yet whether girls' schools are to be included in your inquiry.

Lord Lyttelton told us he thought they would be, as a matter of course, but it has since been reported that the Commission will not undertake them unless strongly persuaded to do so. We shall think it very hard if the Commissioners narrow their field by shirking half their duty.²

I don't know much about the Lady members of the College of Preceptors, but I fancy they don't stand very high. It does not seem to be quite the sort of place at which one would expect to find *ladies*, & people are naturally as anxious about that as anything else in choosing a governess or school. I think too that their standard must be rather low, as several girls who had passed their exams, failed in ours last year.

I hope you do not suspect our Committee of wishing for anything so repugnant to one's taste & feelings as "a neck and neck race between the sexes." As far as I know, we should all be very sorry to see boys & girls racing with each other as boys v. girls, on *any* course. Our idea is that women may learn & labour even in the same field as men, without a thought of rivalry. For instance, girls are taught to spell, because it is supposed to be a good thing in itself, not with any intention of encouraging them to outshine their brothers. Or, to take another example. When Mrs. Gaskell & Miss Yonge & Mrs. Oliphant write novels, I suppose they enter into competition, *as novelists*, with Kingsley & Trollope, but surely without a suspicion of rivalry between women as women & men as men. It seems to me that you may carry out the same principle all thro'. That is— that you may quite safely let women do anything they like, as well as they can.

Probably they will never do so well as men. I mean to say that very likely there will always be *some* men in every field who will do better than any woman. But that does not seem to be a reason for hindering women from doing their best, & choosing for themselves what they will try at. It is not likely that they will ever want to be soldiers or sailors or navvies. If they do attempt things for which they are unfit, they will be taught their folly by failure, but I fancy we scarcely know yet what occupations are really, & what only conventionally, appropriate. It seems odd that it should be considered quite endurable, if not entirely desirable, that young girls should be working barefooted on wet clay, helping to make bricks, (as I have often seen them doing) while men are cutting & dressing ladies' hair. We have not treated the Examinations question as connected with the employment of women, our object having been to claim a sound education for women, apart from considerations as to what mercantile use they may make of it, but as regards fitness, the cases are perhaps analogous. It is difficult to see why, apart from habit, it should be good for girls to learn German & not good for them to learn Greek. As far as use goes, one would fancy that modern languages must be *more* necessary to middle-class men than to women, as they travel more & are more likely to want French & German in their business transactions.

I shall be very glad to see you here at any time that may be most convenient to you. I am generally at home in the evening, but perhaps you will kindly let me know beforehand that I may make sure of not missing you.

I remain, Dear Sir,
Yours very truly
Emily Davies.

Faw: ALS Vol. 4A

1. Acland replied to ED on 31 December 1864:"On second thoughts I have thought I might help you with the Guardian by writing to Professor Bernard, All Souls College, Oxford. You might as well send him one of your lists. I have sent him your letter so if you write to him you will not be a stranger" (Chronicle 392).

2. In December 1864, Lyttelton wrote to ED saying:"I have no doubt girls are to be included in our Commission which is to enquire into the education of the middle class generally; but I will mention it to Ld. [George] Granville" (Chronicle 388). The same month, she received a less encouraging letter from Acland, in which he stated:"I do not see my way quite clearly except to this principle. If the men of England are not prepared to maintain all the women they are bound not to refuse them any means of maintaining themselves unless it can be shown to put them in a worse position." He also expressed his distaste for a "neck & neck race between the sexes *on the same course*" (Chronicle 391).

To George Grote

Dec. 30th 1864.

Dear Mr. Grote

I hope you will not think it unpardonably troublesome, when I again venture to ask your help in connexion with female education.[1]

We are very anxious that ~~girls'~~ ladies' schools shd. be included in the inquiry by the new Royal Commission. Hitherto we have not been able to discover what is intended, reports & opinions being contradictory, ~~but as far as we can learn~~ it appears that the decision rests with Lord Granville, & it occurred to me that you would perhaps be kind enough to ~~represent~~ speak to him on the subject. In the Commission for inquiry into the education of the poor, there was no thought of leaving out girls' schools, & it will be a great disappointment to those who are interested in middle-class female education, if a different course ~~is~~ shd. be adopted in the present case.

~~We~~ Our cause seems to be prospering at Cambridge. ~~A Special~~ The Memorial has been referred to a special Syndicate who we are told will certainly report favourably. It is by no means so certain however that their report will be favourably received by the Senate. The decision will be given some time during next Term.

Miss Garrett is still attending lectures & hospitals. ~~practise.~~ She hopes to pass her final examn. & receive her Diploma about next Sept. In the meantime patients are beginning to find her out & press themselves upon her. Mrs. Grote will I am sure be glad to hear this. I hope she has not been suffering lately from her old enemy, tic. The changes in the weather have been rather trying.

GC: DAL ED SIC-6

1. Davies had previously written to ask Grote to write in support of the memorial to the Cambridge Senate and had sought his assistance for Elizabeth Garrett in her pursuit of a

medical degree. Both George and Harriet Grote signed the April 1863 memorial requesting that the University of London open its examinations to women.

To Anna Richardson

Jan. 3rd 1865

... I believe 'Reasons' appeared in last week's Guardian & I want you to write a letter on the subject ... I am very anxious to have a good deal said in the Guardian, as it is a paper much read by the clergy & University men ... I want to make people see that the adoption of this scheme wd. not force a masculine education upon girls, but at the same time I don't want to give up too much. There is some reason to fear that the Syndicate will recommend a modified scheme for girls, giving a different value in marks to certain subjects, as for instance, exalting German into the place of Greek. The papers & the standard wd. be the same, but the classification wd. be different. I shd. be very sorry if this was done, as it wd. tend to *dis*courage Greek, & it seems to me more worth learning than German. Of course in writing to a newspaper, one cd. not refer to this private information, but you might point out that tho' we don't want the same classification for the sake of showing that girls can do as well as boys (which is nothing to the purpose) we *do* want the whole thing left open. We don't think anybody has a right to say that Greek & Latin are good for middle-class boys, whose education is expected to end at eighteen, & not good for girls, who may probably have leisure to go on studying for some years longer. Also you might say that some girls, tho' as yet not many, do learn & love Greek & Latin, & *their* favourite pursuits ought to have fair play....

I am glad you like Rabbi Ben Ezra, which I also like best in that volume. George MacDonald's favourite is Abe Vogler. I cannot understand the Epilogue.[1] Have you seen Isa Craig's new vol.?[2]

My dear mother is I am thankful to say, as well as usual, that is, well enough to go about & take part with pleasure in parochial work &c. There is to be a party to-morrow evening of the women who attend a sort of Mothers' Meeting. On festive occasions they bring their husbands, & we expect about 80.

GC: AMsS ᶦC398

1. Robert Browning, *Dramatis Personae* (London, 1864).
2. Isa Craig, *Duchess Agnes and Other Poems* (London, 1865).

To John Griffiths

Jan. 4th 1865.

Dear Mr. Griffiths

We have been thinking lately that it would be very useful to us if we could have next June an informal examn. of girls, in connexion with the Oxford Local Examns., similar to the experimental examn. we were allowed to hold in connexion with Cambridge, in '63.

~~The sch~~ Do you think it likely that the Delegacy wd. be willing to let us make use of the papers, &c.? I send you a pamphlet, containing the letter of Mr. Gray, the Sec. to the Camb. Syndicate, which will show you what it is that we want.[1] We should be glad to have the examn. held at any of the local centres where there are suitable persons ~~(e.g. the Local Sec.)~~ prepared ~~willing~~ to take the responsibility & the L⟨ocal⟩. S⟨ecretaries⟩. are willing to cooperate. Our Committee wd. be answerable for the whole expense, & wd. make arrangements with the Examiners &c., as in the case of Cambridge. It wd. however ~~entail~~ give you some additional Before making an application to the Delegacy, we shd. like to know ~~whether there is a reasonable prospect of its being granted~~. what you think about it. Wd. you kindly ~~take~~ let us have your opinion?

GC: DAL ED LOC-222

1. Probably the report of the NAPSS discussion, which contained a full description of the process followed in the Experimental Cambridge Local Examinations and included a copy of Gray's letter.

To John Griffiths

PROPOSED ADMISSION OF GIRLS TO UNIVERSITY LOCAL EXAMINATIONS.
17, CUNNINGHAM PLACE, LONDON, N.W.

Jan. 7th 1865.

Dear Mr. Griffiths

Many thanks for your kind letter. The little delay has not caused us any inconvenience. In fact my first letter scarcely required an answer, unless there had been some~~thing~~ step to be ~~done~~ taken & I understood from your silence that there was nothing to be done ~~just then~~ at that time.

~~With regard to~~ I scarcely know what view our Committee will take of your suggestion that we should make an ~~immediate~~ application to Oxford at once. We shall have a meeting I hope in a few days.[1] In the meantime, would you kindly let us have some particulars about the University procedure in such cases?

To whom shd. our application be ~~made~~ addressed. I think you told us before that ~~an~~ a Memorial would first be ~~come before~~ considered by the Delegacy, then by the Hebdomodal Board, & finally by Convocation. ~~To whom should it be addressed? You speak of a decision being given about your Statute as likely to be given on the 6th. Feb.~~

Could ~~our application~~ it be got thro' all these stages ~~& be decided at the same time?~~ by the 6th Feb.?

And should we have any chance in Convocation if the matter was brought before ~~th~~ it so suddenly. I am assuming ~~perhaps~~ that the question has not been much discussed *generally* at Oxford. If it is already familiar to members of the University, of course that alters the case. We have found all thro' that it is necessary to allow a great deal of time for discussion & deliberation. With most people the first impulse is to dismiss the idea at once as utterly absurd & impracticable. It is only when they have had time to look at it & get used to it, that they begin to think it may perhaps be not altogether unreasonable, & for this reason I think our Committee would be very much afraid of anything like hurry. We would rather wait another year or two than run ~~the~~ much risk of failure, especially as a refusal from Oxford would of course very seriously damage our chances at Cambridge. On the other hand, *success* at Oxford wd. probably turn the scale in our favour at Cambridge. If ~~the Comm~~ we decide on making an application at once, I suppose it must be from our Committee, as it would be impossible to get up a General Memorial in so short a time. Copies of the Memorial to C. with the list of names might be put in circulation, which wd. perhaps do as well as a separate Memorial to Oxford.

With regard to the informal examn., it seems scarcely worth while to say anything about it, if the application for the whole thing is to come on immediately as one of the chief objects of it wd. have been to accustom the Oxford imagination to the spectacle of girls undergoing Univ. examns.

I feel sorry to trouble you with ~~so many questions~~ these matters when you are already suffering from overwork, but there is no one else on whose advice we can place as much reliance. A very few lines will I hope suffice to answer my questions. With many thanks,

I remain

GC: DAL ED LOC-224

1. Griffiths had advised "that an application be made for the insertion of a clause authorising the admission of girls, in the New Statute which was about to be submitted to the University" (Chronicle 401). The committee met on 12 January 1865 and voted to make this application.

To John Griffiths

Jan. 13th 1865.

Dear Mr. Griffiths

I hope you will not be alarmed by the voluminous packet I am venturing to send you. A cursory glance will I hope, enable you to judge as to which of the documents will answer best for circulation at Oxford. The two pamphlets and the Edinb. Regulations, tho' not issued by our Committee are equally available for distribution.[1] I enclose a copy of the application we propose sending to the Vice Chancellor. Perhaps you will be kind enough to tell us whether it is in proper form. As to the statement about it, we are in some perplexity. At Cambridge the enclosed paper was circulated immediately after the presentation of our Memorial, but it was done by the Vice Chancellor. We had nothing to do with it. Would it do for us to print our letter to the Vice Chancellor, with the preface—"The following application has been addressed to the Vice Chancellor"? We want in some way to make known that we should have sent in a Memorial at least as numerously signed as that to Cambridge, (probably more so, for some signatures came in too late) if there had been time. Do you think the last sentence of our letter is sufficient, or would it be better to add "The following is the Memorial referred to" . . . and then "A similarly signed Memorial could have been presented to the University of Oxford, if there had been time to collect the signatures before the day on which the Statute is likely to come under discussion."[2]

Dean Alford is rather afraid that the Oxford authorities may think we are treating them disrespectfully in sending only an application from our Committee, after presenting a very numerously signed Memorial to Cambridge. I should scarcely have thought that this would occur to any one, but of this you can judge better than we can.

Thank you very much for the two lists. I am afraid Dr. Temple's personal influence will be very much against us, tho' ~~has~~ he has probably had less opportunity of forming a judgment than most people.

I remain Dear Mr. Griffiths
Very truly yours
Emily Davies

GC: ALS ED LOC-227

1. Probably these pamphlets included the NAPSS report and the reprint of Joshua Fitch's article.
2. On 20 January 1865, the committee sent the memorial to the Oxford vice chancellor. The final wording of the last paragraph was, "You will not fail to observe that the terms of this Memorial are not limited to Cambridge, but apply to both the Universities alike; and

we are desired to assure you that a similar Memorial would have been addressed separately to the University of Oxford, if there had been time to collect the signatures afresh before the day on which the statute is likely to come under discussion there" (GC, "Proposed Admission of Girls to University Local Examinations," 20 January 1865.)

To Robert Potts

PROPOSED ADMISSION OF GIRLS TO UNIVERSITY LOCAL EXAMINATIONS.
17, CUNNINGHAM PLACE, LONDON, N.W.

Jan. 24th ⟨1865⟩

Dear Mr. Potts

I suppose Cambridge men will be reappearing this week, & setting to work. I hope their minds may have received a wholesome bent during the holidays, & that they will come back prepared to discuss innovations in a candid spirit.

I send you a pamphlet written by one of the Inspectors of Schools,[1] in which our question is, I think, very judiciously treated. We have ordered a large supply for distribution & it has occurred to me that it might be a good plan to send them round at Cambridge by the Junior Marshall, as before. What do you think? It seems to me that we want to get the subject ventilated in every possible way, & above all, to reach, not the Special Syndicate, who seem to be well disposed already, but the "dead mass", who will need I fear a great deal of enlightening before they will be at all fit to deal with the question in the Senate. Perhaps the 'Reasons' might be inserted in the Cambridge Chronicle. I send you also a letter ~~to~~ [in] the Record, in case you may think it worth doing anything with. If not, will you kindly return it.

Two ladies from Leamington, the heads of a superior school there, have been with me to-day, making anxious inquiries about our chances of success.[2] I suppose we shall know our fate before Easter.

I remain
Dear Mr. Potts
Yours very truly
Emily Davies.

GC: ALS ED LOC-171

1. Joshua Fitch.
2. Probably E. A. Dean, 18 Wellington Street, Leamington; and/or Anne Keeley, principal of school, 44 Clarendon Street, Leamington.

To Robert Potts

PROPOSED ADMISSION OF GIRLS TO UNIVERSITY LOCAL EXAMINATIONS.
17, CUNNINGHAM PLACE, LONDON, N.W.

Jan. 27th ⟨1865⟩

Dear Mr. Potts

Many thanks for your two letters. I am very glad the Cambridge Chronicle will insert "Clericus Dunelmensis."[1] May I ask you to be kind enough to order for me six copies of the paper? I could not get an extra copy of the Record, & there are several people I wish to send it to.

On the whole, I think your news is encouraging. I will forward 300 pamphlets by rail as before, & we shall be greatly obliged if you will engage the Junior Marshall to distribute them.

Yours most truly
Emily Davies.

GC: ALS ED LOC-172

1. ED wrote a letter on girls' education to the *Record* that her father's curate, then the rector of Winston, sent under the signature "Clericus Dunelmensis" (Chronicle 407).

To Robert Potts

PROPOSED ADMISSION OF GIRLS TO UNIVERSITY LOCAL EXAMINATIONS.
17, CUNNINGHAM PLACE, LONDON, N.W.

Jan. 31st. 1865.

Dear Mr. Potts

I despatched the parcel of pamphlets yesterday. Will you kindly arrange about the Junior Marshall's fee, & let me know to what extent we are indebted to you. There will be the Cambridge Chronicles, received this morning, for which I am much obliged. I am sorry that anybody should mix up our movement with anything of a strongminded character, but I am afraid there is nothing we can do, to dissipate such an unfortunate impression.

Your old correspondent, Miss Richardson of Newcastle, is coming [here] today on a short visit. I am afraid she will have left us before the time at which you propose coming to town, or I am sure she would have been glad to make your personal acquaintance. She will be pleased to hear of all that you are & have been doing for us at Cambridge.

I remain
Dear Mr. Potts

Yours very truly
Emily Davies.

GC: ALS ED LOC-173

To Robert Potts

17 Cunningham Place. N.W. | Feb. 1st 1865.

Dear Mr. Potts

I enclose 7/. in postage stamps, which I hope you will not find troublesome. As you say nothing about it, I suppose no charge was made to you for the carriage of the parcel.

I hope the pamphlet may do some service in dissipating the impressions of those who are afraid of strongmindedness. If only they could have seen the meekness & gentleness & entirely feminine deportment of the girls who came up to one examn., I think they would have been satisfied on that score. I am afraid an examn. at Midsummer would scarcely answer our purpose.[1] We have already sent in an application to Oxford for the extension of their examns. (which are held in June) & the Secretary of the Delegacy tells us that among the members of the University who take any interest in the question at all, he thinks there is certainly a majority in our favour.

Yours very sincerely
Emily Davies.

GC: ALS ED LOC-174

1. See ED to Potts, 9 January 1864.

To Robert Potts

PROPOSED ADMISSION OF GIRLS TO UNIVERSITY LOCAL EXAMINATIONS.
17, CUNNINGHAM PLACE, LONDON, N.W.

Feb. 7th ⟨1865⟩

Dear Mr. Potts

The pamphlet reprinted from the Museum is by a Mr. Fitch, one of the Inspectors of Schools.

I am glad to find that it is liked at Cambridge.

We hear from Oxford that at a meeting of the Delegacy on Saturday a resolution in favour of our application was passed by a majority of twelve to two. The resolution was not very strong, being simply to the effect that the proposal was worthy of serious consideration. The two who declined voting did so on the ground that the University had enough to do already. I suppose we shall hear before long what view is taken by the Hebdomadal Council.

 Yours very truly
 Emily Davies.

GC: ALS ED LOC-175

To Robert Potts

PROPOSED ADMISSION OF GIRLS TO UNIVERSITY LOCAL EXAMINATIONS.
17, CUNNINGHAM PLACE, LONDON, N.W.

Feb. 20th 1865.

Dear Mr. Potts

 I have just received from the Dean of Canterbury, a copy of the report of the ⟨Cambridge University⟩ Special Syndicate.[1] It is in almost all respects, everything that we could desire, & much more favourable than I expected. I am afraid it is not very likely that the printer will have kept the type standing, but in case he should have done so, would you be kind enough to ask him to strike off 100 copies for us, & let us have them at once. If not, I suppose the report will appear in the Camb. Chron. for next Saturday, & they would perhaps print off 100 slips for us. May I ask you to be good enough to arrange this for us, as you may find best? We shall want a good many copies for circulation & the sooner we have them, the better.

 I suppose we must not calculate upon getting this report passed by the Senate. You will be sure to let us know when the day for the discussion in the Arts' School is fixed. Will the vote in the Senate follow closely upon it?

 I remain, Dear Mr. Potts
 Yours very truly
 Emily Davies.

Is this Report sent to all resident members of the Senate?

GC: ALS ED LOC-176

 1. On 16 February 1865, the Cambridge University Special Syndicate had issued its report, recommending that girls be allowed to take the Cambridge Local Examinations twice a year, simultaneously with the boys, with the same papers and subjects, but that the class lists and names of the girls should not be published. The syndicate recommended this arrangement be tried for three years. This report then had to be voted on by the university senate following a meeting at the Arts School on 2 March 1865.

To Robert Potts

PROPOSED ADMISSION OF GIRLS TO UNIVERSITY LOCAL EXAMINATIONS.
17, CUNNINGHAM PLACE, LONDON, N.W.

Feb. 22d. 1865.

Dear Mr. Potts

The arrangement you propose with respect to copies of the report seems to me quite the best, & we shall be very much obliged to you for undertaking it. It struck me afterwards that it would not be quite the thing to get them from the University printer.

I should be glad to know which of the clauses in the scheme of the Syndicate you would desire to amend. We are so glad to have a favourable report that we do not feel inclined to be hypercritical. A good deal is left to the Syndicate, which seems to me a sensible plan, as they will be able to guide their course as experience may suggest.

I think the schoolmistresses would be glad to have class lists printed for private circulation, but the point does not seem to me very important. I suppose we cannot know till after the 2d., what course things are likely to take, & perhaps not even then. I dare say a good many men will quietly vote against us who may not care enough to raise an opposition in the Senate.

I remain
Yours very truly
Emily Davies.

GC: ALS ED LOC-177

Although ED's correspondence from this period, relating to the SIC, is no longer extant, she was clearly active in the movement to ensure that the terms of the commission include girls' schools. On 23 January 1865, a memorial, organized by ED together with Eliza Bostock and a group of schoolmistresses and educational reformers, was sent to the SIC, urging that "the Education of Girls and the means of improving it [were] within the scope" of its inquiry.[1]

On 28 February 1865, ED received a response from Henry Roby, secretary to the SIC. Roby's letter advised that: "Subject . . . to . . . limitations, which arise from the nature of the case, the Commissioners will endeavour to embrace in their inquiry the education of both sexes alike. Accordingly, they will instruct the Assistant Commissioners . . . to report upon the state and prospects of girls' education as well as on that of boys" (Chronicle 418b).

1. GC, To the Royal Commissioners of 1864 on Education, 1864.

To Robert Potts

PROPOSED ADMISSION OF GIRLS TO UNIVERSITY LOCAL EXAMINATIONS.
17, CUNNINGHAM PLACE, LONDON, N.W.

March 4th 1865.

Dear Mr. Potts

Thank you for the Cambridge Chronicle & also for testifying to the genuineness & respectability of our signatures. I should scarcely have thought anybody would have accused us of forgery.[1]

Would you kindly let me know when the vote is to be taken?[2] I hope you will not be found on the postponing side. My own feeling is that the Scheme recommended is worth *trying* at any rate.

If after the three year experiment, it is found not to work well, we can then ask for modifications.

I am surprised to find no notice about the vote. We are anxious to know when the matter is likely to be settled.

Shall I send a Post-office order for the Cambridge Chronicle account, or may I send you postage stamps for the amount? I should prefer the latter, if it is not giving you too much trouble.

I remain
Yours very truly
Emily Davies.

GC: ALS ED LOC-180

1. The *Cambridge Chronicle* (4 March 1865) contained a discussion of the syndicate's report and a transcription of the debate.
2. On 2 March 1865, the Cambridge University Syndicate's positive report was discussed in the university senate. The voting took place on 8 March 1865.

To Robert Potts

PROPOSED ADMISSION OF GIRLS TO UNIVERSITY LOCAL EXAMINATIONS.
17, CUNNINGHAM PLACE, LONDON, N.W.

March 7th ⟨1865⟩

Dear Mr. Potts

I felt sure that you must have been unavoidably detained yesterday. As I was myself obliged to go out soon after three, I should have missed you if you had come later.

With regard to the Grace which will I suppose come under discussion on Thursday, I think our Committee are quite unanimous in favour of supporting it.

Whatever modifications it may be desirable to introduce could probably be better judged of after the three years' trial, & if the Scheme now suggested were to be thrown out, it is more than doubtful whether any other could be carried thro'.

By what I hear from schoolmistresses & others, there seems to be no objection to the Scheme strong enough to justify organising an opposition to it. We hope therefore that our friends will sink minor differences, as you are so kindly willing to do, & combine together to carry it thro'.

We hear from Oxford that they are only waiting for Cambridge to move first, to take a similar step. I enclose stamps for the Cambridge Chronicle account. The slips have been very useful for distribution. We shall not require any more copies.

I remain
Dear Mr. Potts
Yours very truly
Emily Davies.

GC: ALS ED LOC-182

To Henry Tomkinson

PROPOSED ADMISSION OF GIRLS TO UNIVERSITY LOCAL EXAMINATIONS.
17, CUNNINGHAM PLACE, LONDON, N.W.

Thursday evening. [March 9th] ⟨1865⟩

Dear Mr. Tomkinson
Many thanks for your kind note. I know you would have gone up if you could. But after all, we are safe.[1] The scheme has passed, by a majority of four. I had so thoroughly made up my mind to defeat, never having counted on success even when things looked most promising, that now it is come, I cannot half believe it. A telegram received by Miss Buss from Cambridge is the authority. I suppose I shall have a letter from Mr. Markby to-morrow.

I don't pity the Liverpool people in the offensive sense of the term, but I sympathize with them a little in their disappointment.[2] Probably however they care very little about it. I feel inclined to thank everybody very much who has helped us, & you especially, because I am quite sure that it is to the experimental examn., which we could not have done without you, & to the general co-operation of the London Committee, that our success is mainly due. I thought we were quite lost when Mr. Markby's telegram came yesterday.[3] I wonder what Miss Bostock will say. She announced about a month ago that she was going thro' the pangs of disappointment beforehand, that she might bear an heroic front when the time came.

She won't know how to behave under these unexpected circumstances.
Yours most truly
Emily Davies.

GC: ALS ED LOC-184

1. On 9 March 1865, by a vote of fifty-five to fifty-one, the Cambridge University Senate accepted the syndicate's report, and the Cambridge Local Examinations were opened to girls.
2. The Liverpool Local Committee had sent a memorial in opposition, while memorials in support were sent from London, York, Gateshead, Northampton, and Tiverton (Chronicle 405, 409).
3. On 8 March 1865, Markby telegraphed ED saying "Send up all you can to-morrow. Voting at 12. Opposition organized" (Chronicle 413).

To Robert Potts

~~PROPOSED~~ ADMISSION OF GIRLS TO UNIVERSITY LOCAL EXAMINATIONS.
17, CUNNINGHAM PLACE, LONDON, N.W.

March 10th ⟨1865⟩

Dear Mr. Potts

I must just send you one line to thank you for your note, & for the support you gave us yesterday. We should have looked upon you as a dreadful traitor if you had lifted up your finger against the Grace, after all you have done for us. Whatever may be its faults, it is well worth trying, at any rate. London men would not believe that there could be any serious opposition, & thought it a matter to be left to the decision of resident members.

Yours very sincerely
Emily Davies.

GC: ALS ED LOC-188

To Barbara Bodichon

UNIVERSITY EXAMINATIONS. 17, CUNNINGHAM PLACE. LONDON. N.W.

March 18th 1865

Dear Mrs. Bodichon

The Committee will meet at 9 *Conduit St.*, on Thursday the 26th at three o'clock.[1] There will be the Report of the Syndicate & some little matters about prizes to discuss, & the statement of accounts to be received, besides Mr. Myer's business. I find the Memorial he speaks of is to be done to order. He wrote to Miss ⟨Elizabeth⟩ Wolstenholme proposing ⁱᵗ to her, the same day that he wrote to me, to say that they were going to do it. He tells Miss W. what kind of Memorial it must be, and that "of *course* it must not attempt to dictate the *kind* of examn." Miss W. sends me a copy of his letter, so there can be no mistake about it. If it gets known at Cambridge that the Memorial is got up in this way, not spontaneously but ordered from Cambridge, it will be very damaging to it. It is just what University men dislike.

I don't think we need trouble ourselves any more about the Fawcett scheme. That it is "not worth discussing." "utterly untenable" &c. are the replies I get.

We shall have uphill work at Bristol, the Lecture schemes having got possession of the field, but I am sure it is worth while to go. I don't feel ⁽ᵃˡᵗᵒᵍᵉᵗʰᵉʳ⁾ discouraged by opposition. It rouses me, and when it gets *very* bad, it begins to assume a grotesque aspect & I feel inclined to laugh. I learned that from Friends in Council a long time ago. There is always something humorous in a very desperate state of affairs. On reflection, I do not think the party is so completely disorganised as it has appeared to you. The Fawcett business is an individual freak. And Miss ⟨Anne⟩ Clough has never really belonged to the party at all. I always hear of everything that is going on and as a rule I think I am as much consulted as I have any claim to be.

But I am very grateful to you for what you have done in the Fawcett business, on E. Garrett's account. She was being led astray by family affection & I am very glad you have opened her eyes.

Ever yours, ED.

GC: ALS ED B12

1. The Local Examinations Committee met at the Architectural Gallery at Conduit Street.

To Henry Tomkinson

PROPOSED ADMISSION OF GIRLS TO UNIVERSITY LOCAL EXAMINATIONS.
17, CUNNINGHAM PLACE, LONDON, N.W.

March 28th ⟨1865⟩

Dear Mr. Tomkinson

I send you the Cambridge Regulations & the circular agreed upon by our Committee. Our application has been rejected by the Oxford Council, & will therefore go no further.[1] Mr. Griffiths attributes the decision very much to the Liverpool opposition. There were 10 against, 8 for, & 3 who did not vote. Dr.

⟨Edward⟩ Pusey is reported to have said that at Cambridge, the minority only were in earnest. The majority who carried it, did it as a joke! Was that the case in the London Committee?

    Yours very truly

    Emily Davies.

P.S. Since writing the foregoing, I have received a letter from Mr.⟨Thomas⟩ Bodley,[2] which I enclose, I suppose we had better do as he advises, & print a little circular. Our Committee seemed to take for granted the other day that we should conduct the girls' examns. in London (if not all over the country!) so I suppose I may put my name as Local Sec. Do you think Mr. Bodley's circular, modified as the enclosed, will do? The only thing I am in doubt about is the local fee. I don't know how Mr. Bodley comes to spend 10/. on each candidate. Our experiment cost only £26.18, which divided between eighty-three comes to about 6/6 each. Supposing that on an average sixpence was spent on postage for each candidate, that would only bring it up to 7/. Our room was unusually cheap, I believe, but then you get Burlington House for nothing. Is it necessary, or very desirable, to announce the amount of the local fee so long beforehand? I have no idea how many candidates we shall have, & that may make some difference. Probably the amount of the fee will in some degree affect the number.

    I have had a letter from a schoolmistress, probably the first of a series, begging to have the limitation of age extended or removed.[3] I see that in 1863, the Syndicate allowed some candidates at West Buckland to go in for examn., over age, but not to receive certificates. Would it be a good plan to ask for this? I should be sorry to have the limitation taken away, partly because when we go to the London University it will be a good point in our case to say that the old Universities do not ~~examine~~ take candidates above eighteen.

    Is not it rather false in the London Committee to throw us upon our own resources after making such grand promises of cooperation? Perhaps they think it would be carrying the joke too far, actually to *do* anything. I hope the schoolmistresses will not be tormenting Mr. Bodley with letters. I am sending the Regulations to all who signed the Memorial.

GC: ALS ED LOC-190

In addition to her work on the Cambridge Local Examinations Committee and her involvement with the SIC, ED continued to pursue opening the examinations of the University of London to women. However, much of her correspondence on this issue is no longer extant. On 9 May, the Convocation of the University of London met, and Arthur Charles made a motion, seconded by Joshua Fitch, "that it be referred to the Annual Committee to consider & report whether any, & if any, what, steps should be taken to establish Examinations for women in this University" (Chronicle 425). Charles then wrote to ED, asking for further information.

1. On 20 March 1865, Griffiths wrote to Davies saying: "The Vice-Chancellor was able to bring the question on to-day, & I am extremely sorry to say that the decision of the Council was adverse to your wishes. I was not at all prepared for so resolute an opposition from those who did oppose it" (Chronicle 403). On 22 March 1865, Vice Chancellor Lightfoot wrote to Dean Alford that: "The application respecting the admission of females to the Oxford Local Examns. was formally considered by the Council.... [it was decided] not at present to make any proposal to the Congregation on the subject" (Chronicle 405).

2. London local secretary for 1864.

3. The syndicate's proposal had authorized exams for Junior girls, not over sixteen, and Senior girls, not over eighteen, in accord with the regulations for the boys. Because of the paucity of good academic education for girls, it was difficult to find girls under eighteen who were adequately prepared to take the examinations.

To Anna Richardson

May 10th 1865

...Did I tell you that I had seen Mr. Mill? He spoke a little while ago at a Social Science meeting. His outward shell does not to my mind express what he is—& in that respect he is very unlike Mr. Maurice, who sat near him at the same meeting. Miss Garrett says 'Mr. Mill's characteristic is clearness, & his face expresses it; Mr. Maurice's is reverence, & his face expresses it.' Miss Craig says Mr. Mill reminds her of a French philosopher, say Voltaire!

I do not agree with either of these views, but rather with Mr. Hare that they are à posteriori judgments, but I hope in the future state, Mr. Mill's outward form will be more expressive of the many-sided soul. It may be, that being very shy, he does *choose* to express anything but what he cannot help, namely, refinement. *That* cannot be concealed. It was very beautiful to see the varying expression of Mr. Maurice's face while Mill was speaking.

I wish you belonged to the Kensington.[1] We are getting a delightful set of members. Some of the papers already sent in are very good, & we are looking forward to an interesting discussion upon them on the 23rd.

GC: AMsS C421

1. According to ED, "the agitation for the opening of the Local Examn. had brought into communication with each other a good many people having more or less common interests & aims, & it seemed desirable that the cessation, for the moment, of the special occasion for cooperation shd. not result in our losing touch with each other. With a view to supplying some sort of link between us, a small society was started, for the discussion of questions of common interest" (Chronicle 423). The first meeting of the Kensington Society was held on 23 May 1865. The subject to be discussed, "What is the true basis, & what are the limits, of parental authority?" was proposed by Elizabeth Garrett (Chronicle 424).

To Anna Richardson

May 23rd 1865

I am not very anxious about this evening. The main responsibility rests with Mrs. Manning, & she always manages people beautifully. . . . The little Davies's grow in wisdom & stature & loveliness. . . . Do you think I ought to make Charley learn his catechism? He finds Mrs. Barbauld's Hymns in Prose, hard to understand, but 'the Peep of Day is still difficulter. It's a *very* difficult book, the Peep of Day is.' . . .

GC: AMsS C422

To Anna Richardson

May 30th 1865

We had a pleasant meeting of the Kensington. If you will let me propose you as a member, I will send you the selection of papers read. We have announced 10 vacancies, & intend to select from the members proposed, who may be 20 or 30, those we think most desirable. This is a strategem (borrowed from the Century Club) for sifting, without personal offence to anybody. . . .

GC: AMsS C422a

To Anna Richardson

~~PROPOSED~~ ADMISSION OF GIRLS TO UNIVERSITY LOCAL EXAMINATIONS.
17, CUNNINGHAM PLACE, LONDON, N.W.

July 5th ⟨1865⟩

My dear Anna

I send you the Cambridge ⟨Local Examinations⟩ Regulations, ~~but~~ (for which there is no charge.) but I should advise you also to get the Examination Papers for last year, as they will probably give you a better idea of what is required. It is necessary to bear in mind that examns. are never so hard as the questions would lead one to suppose. I don't think a few failures will do us any harm, but no doubt there will be plenty. We expect that girls will be examined at Manchester, Cambridge, Torquay, Brighton, Wolverhampton & probably Leeds, as well as London.[1] I suppose London would suit Nellie best, unless you prefer taking her to Cambridge. As far as we can tell so long beforehand, we should be very glad to have her here for the Examn. week. I am very anxious to have some candidates in Latin & Mathematics. In Greek I am afraid we have no chance. Mr. Maurice said some beautiful things on education the other day, & made me respect mathematics more than I had known how to do before.

Are the ⟨Thomas⟩ Hodgkins at home now? I want to send them the Bishop of Natal's autograph. I should like also to tell them about the Kensington, but I don't want to write it. Mrs. Manning thinks your reasons for keeping aloof are very poor. There are still two vacancies to fill up before November. Some of the new members are very nice.

I have not written anything in the Reader lately. I should think the Fortnightly is certainly taken in at the Lit. & Phil. & you might get it from there.[2] It is very dear, & I hate ⟨George Henry⟩ Lewes, but each number hitherto has contained something that I found worth reading. Have you seen Grote's Plato?[3] It is very a-great-deal-of-it. (Is there any adjectival form for that sentiment?) & one gets rather tired of the repetition, but the dialogues, given in an abridged form are always very interesting & instructive to me. I was going this evening to hear Mr. Mill address the Electors of Westminster at St. James Hall. A good many p

Some people, including Mrs. Lewes, don't care about his getting into Parliament, thinking that he will gain no more influence by it, but I cannot help wishing to have all the best men in the governing body, even tho' there seems to be not much for them to do at present.

Do tell me how you *all* are. Do you mean to stay at Newcastle till October? Ever yr. affecn. ED.

GC: ALS ED LOC-191

1. Examinations for girls were eventually held in Brighton, Bristol, Cambridge, London, Manchester, and Sheffield.
2. The Literary and Philosophical Society at Newcastle-on-Tyne.
3. George Grote, *Plato and the Other Companions of Socrates* (London, 1865).

To Annette Akroyd

17 Cunningham Place. N.W. | Oct. 3d 1865

My dear Miss Akroyd

I am glad to tell you that on Miss Bostock's proposal, you have been elected a member of the Kensington Society. I enclose the Rules & the questions for the current Term.

Will there be any candidates from your neighborhood for the Cambridge

Examn.? For this year only, girls over age may go in. They will not receive a formal certificate.

    Yours very truly
    Emily Davies.

BL: ALS MssEur C176/177, ptC, f24

To Anna Richardson

Oct. 25th 1865

    Mr. ⟨James⟩ Bryce is going into the Lake district & will be at Grasmere this week or the beginning of the next. Please be kind to him. He gets plenty of cold water thrown upon him by other people.... I forget whether I told you about Miss Colborne.[1] She was admitted as a regular student at Bartholomew's, & we hope she will be able to go thro' with it. 155 students have memorialised against her, asking the authorities to re-consider the matter, without giving any reason. The thing that pleased me most in the matter is the admirable manner Miss Colborne has managed matters so far. There is something quite touching in her anxiety not to disgrace us. She does not seem to think of herself at all. That is the characteristic of the present generation of "Women's Rights"-ers. The self-seeking people have dropped off. Of course by & by, when it has become common, the enthusiastic, self-sacrificing spirit will not come in here more than elsewhere. In the meantime it is a pleasant aspect of human nature to contemplate.

GC: AMsS C432

    1. Elizabeth Garrett had written to Davies on 27 June, telling her that "A Miss Colborne called on me on Saturday ... [she] wants to study Medicine.... I want you to see her. Could you have her to tea?" (Chronicle 425–26).

To Henry Roby

Nov. 8th [1865]

    Dear Mr. Roby. You may perhaps like to see the enclosed Manchester circular. They expect to have rather ~~more than~~ ^between^ 30 & 40 candidates. I suppose the Sub. Committee of teachers will help to keep them in order. We did without a C⟨onducting⟩ E⟨xaminer⟩ in the experimental, except for the R⟨eading⟩. A⟨loud⟩. Mr. Norris undertook that, & hurt the girls' feelings by making them stand up to read, & calling them by their Christian names. They reported that he treated them like N⟨ational⟩. S⟨chool⟩. girls. We have 56 candidates in

London. ~~The numbers are rather smaller than I expected, but I think it is very well for a beginning.~~ The schools which sent in before, send fewer candidates this time, being afraid I suppose of the Arithmetic. We have Senior candidates in every Section, & in every Sub. Section except Greek & Applied Math.

I am so much obliged to you for letting me see the ⟨SIC⟩ Evidence. The C.⟨ommissioners⟩ seem to ~~be much~~ better disposed than I had imagined. Dr. ⟨John⟩ Storrar has been here to-day, discoursing at great length on 'the subject in which we take a common interest.' I am rather perplexed by his friendly demonstrations, as Mr. Bryce had represented him to me as our bitterest foe.[1] Are you *all* enemies at the bottom of your hearts? Have you thought of examining Dr. ⟨Joseph⟩ Angus, of the Regent's Park College? He teaches in a girls' school up here, & his daughter is coming up for the Local Examn. My brother knows all about the Phil. School, & has examined other schools. With regard to girls he says his misfortune is that he thinks them so nicely educated already, but he could be primed with an answer to that fine comprehensive question which somebody seems to put to every witness—'What, in your opinion, would most conduce to the general improvement &c?' If they put questions that he could not answer, he could say 'That is for the statesman, not for the scholar.' (I have thought of several things since seeing you, that I should like the Commissioners to recommend, if they seem likely to do it.) I should like to have ⟨Thomas⟩ Huxley examined officially about the brain, because that physiological argument is constantly used and people believe it. It seems to me the most rational plan to examine schoolmistresses, who know ~~something about~~ the subject, but considering the Commissioners' native preferences, & also that the evidence of distinguished ~~men~~ people has ~~more~~ some chances of being read, it might answer our purposes best to get some men like Mark Pattison & Lord ⟨John⟩ Wrottesley to testify. I don't think they know anything but they might be primed. Would you mind telling me what witnesses are coming on for examn. during the next four weeks?

GC: DAL ED SIC-17

1. While he was on the University of London Senate in 1862, Storrar had voted against the petition initiated by Elizabeth Garrett to modify the university charter permitting female students to matriculate and receive a university degree.

To Henry Tomkinson

Nov. 10th 1865

... We have 56 candidates[1] ... I hope you will be able to come & talk to our girls before the examn. begins. I attribute the good behaviour last time entirely to the solemnising ~~effect of~~ influence of the opening discourse.... Would you kindly give me an opinion on the subject of the enclosed note? Some people are inclined to begin a subdued kind of agitation for the Franchise.[2] I have rather tried to stifle it, & they are willing to be stifled if there seemed to be any risk of their damaging other things by it.... I don't see much use in talking about the Franchise till first principles have made more way. The scoffers don't see how much is involved in improved education, but they are wide awake about the Franchise. You see I lean to compromise, tho' I should like also to keep clear of hypocrisy, & the line between the two is rather faint.

GC: AMsS C438

1. In all, 51 Junior and 77 Senior girls took the Cambridge Local Examinations in 1865, compared to 986 Junior and 231 Senior boys.
2. The topic for the Kensington Society's second meeting on 21 November 1865 was to be, "Is the extension of the Parliamentary suffrage to women desirable, and, if so, under what conditions?"

To Barbara Bodichon

17 C.P. Nov. 14th 1865.

Dear Mme. Bodichon

I find your paper capital. It is much the best that has come in, to my mind, as furnishing a basis for discussion. Miss ⟨Helen⟩ Taylor has sent one, but I am a little disappointed in it. There are three very strong against.[1]

In your paper there are two or three expressions I should like to have altered, e.g. I don't think it quite does to call the arguments on the other side 'foolish.' Of course they *are*, but it does not seem quite polite to say so. I should like to omit the paragraph about outlawry. You see, the enemy always maintains that the disabilities imposed upon women are not penal, but solely intended for their good, & I find nothing irritates men so much as to attribute tyranny to them. I believe many of them do really mean well, & at any rate as they say they do, it seems fair to admit it & to show them that their well-intended efforts are a *mistake*, not a crime. Men cannot stand indignation, & tho' of course I think it is just, it seems to me better to suppress the manifestation of it. I should not mind *saying* a few indignant things at the meeting, but these papers travel about the country & go into families, where they may be read by prejudiced men. So it is necessary to be careful.[2]

I don't see my way about the Committee.[3] I have taken further advice, & it is all against. If we could have a perfect Committee, it might do good, but I doubt whether the sort of people who can really help us would join, *yet*, & wild people might do great harm. I am inclined to think that the first thing to do is to stir up women, chiefly thro' private channels, to use the rights they already possess, of voting for ⟨Poor Law⟩ Guardians &c. So long as those rights remain unused, they are an almost incontrovertible argument against us. To get women to work on ~~Com~~ mixed Committees is also very useful. It accustoms men's imaginations to the spectacle of women taking part in public affairs. You will be glad to hear that the W⟨orking⟩.M⟨en's⟩.C⟨lubs⟩. Union's Sub.Committee have appointed a woman to the secretaryship & we hope to get the appointment confirmed to-day.[4] If she turns out as capable as I expect, it will have a very good moral effect. I hope to see you at Adam St. to-morrow. Yours affectionately, ED.

GC: ALS ED B1

1. Five women, including Bodichon and Helen Taylor, wrote papers on women's suffrage for the Kensington Society.

2. Bodichon's paper on suffrage, delivered at this November 1865 meeting of the Kensington Society, was later edited with ED's help (see ED to Bodichon, 6 September 1866) and presented at the NAPSS meeting in October 1866. This edited version contained no references to the foolishness of the opposition or the tyranny of men.

3. Bodichon had raised the possibility of starting a suffrage committee.

4. The Working Men's Clubs were begun by Henry Solly. At Davies's instigation, "a woman, Miss Horsbrugh, was appointed as Sec., under Mr. Solly" (Chronicle 307).

To Henry Tomkinson

Nov. 14th 1865

... Miss ⟨Gertrude⟩ King tells me she has asked you to let her call on you at your office on Wednesday. [to inquire as to whether women could be employed in Insurance offices.] That seems to be the best plan. I wonder how you found out that I had anything to do with her. She asked Mr. Hart for an introduction on purpose that you might think she was a quite separate interest.[1]

I have enough to answer for in the education line, without tormenting people about anything else.... Thanks for your opinion of Mrs. Bodichon's plans. What you suggest about putting Mr. Mill's views before girls is I think pretty much what she proposed, only that she means to put them before 'qualified women.' i.e. women who have the householder or property qualification. She thinks (& so do I) that more women care for the suffrage than is supposed, & that more still would care if they thought about it. Mrs. Bodichon would certainly wish her Committee to go very quietly to work. My doubt is whether a safe Committee could be formed, & if wild people got upon it, who would insist on jumping like kangaroos. (the simile is not flattering.) they would do harm. I don't think I agree with you that rights ought to be seized by force. Take the extreme case of Slavery. It would surely be better that the right of freedom should be restored by the people who have stolen it, than that it should be extorted by an insurrection of the slaves. As to the suffrage, my view is that, the object of representation being, not to confer privileges but to get the best possible government, women should be politely invited to contribute their share of intelligence in the selection of the legislative body. As to their 'asserting their rights successfully & irresistibly,' the idea is, if I may say so, rather revolting to my mind. It goes against me to think of it. But I remember you & Miss Craig always go in for hard hitting. I wonder what you mean by 'your body.'? I don't think I belong to any 'body', except the Church & two or three Committees.

GC: AMsS C440

1. Probably Ernest Abraham Hart (1835–98), who wrote and coedited the *Lancet*, the *British Medical Journal*, the *London Medical Record*, and the *Sanitary Record*.

To Henry Roby

17 Cunningham Place. N.W. | Nov. 18th 1865

Dear Mr. Roby

I have seen some of the Bedford College ladies, and we think Miss Buss will be the best person to summon for the 30th.[1] Her address is "North London Collegiate School for Ladies,

12 Camden St.

N.W."

What I have to say might I think be arranged under ~~three~~ four heads.
Local Examinations.
Education of girls after leaving school.
Uses of Endowments. &[2]
Government of Endowed Schools.
'Education' of course means the absence of it. I suppose that head will be understood as including the want of examinations for women.
If you think these ~~three~~ four points would make a very long story, the ~~last~~ Uses of Endowments might be left out.

I should be very sorry to take up too much time, so as to run Miss Buss short, as she can speak from ~~actual~~ long experience in ~~the working of a school, & my ideas are chiefly founded on what I have picked up from other people.~~ school work & knows the subject thoroughly. ~~It seems doubtful whether it is worth the Commissioners' while to take that secondhand sort of evidence, but I suppose it is better not to hold back if they like to hear it. One knows one's own class, of course, from personal intercourse & I have had something to do with middle-~~

~~class women generally in the clergyman's-daughter capacity. My father was Rector of Gateshead for a good many years & I had to teach the Sunday School teachers & came in contact with the young ladies of the parish in many ways. Are witnesses expected to give the sources of their information?~~

I suppose it is not worth while to exert oneself to invent schemes for Colleges or schools, as the Commissioners are not likely to make specific recommendations.

I have an extreme repugnance to thinking about details any more than is ~~absolutely~~ necessary.

I remain
Yours very truly
Emily Davies.

GC: DALS ED SIC-19

1. ED and Buss were to give evidence before the SIC on 30 November 1865. The other women involved in education who were invited to give evidence were Dorothea Beale, Gertrude King, Susan Kyberd, [?] Martin, Mary Eliza Porter, Eleanor Smith, and Elizabeth Wolstenholme. Beale collated and published the evidence given on the education of girls in *Reports Issues by the Schools Inquiry Commission on the Education of Girls* (1869).

2. ED had delivered a paper at the NAPSS Meeting on 3 May 1865 entitled "The Application of Funds to the Education of Girls," in which she argued that since most founders of endowed schools did not specifically exclude girls from the benefits of endowments, the best course of action would be "to throw open to girls at least half of the existing grammar schools." She explained how "money might be spent upon the education of girls of the upper and middle classes" (London, 1865).

To Henry Tomkinson

17 Cunningham Place. N.W. | Dec. 8th ⟨1865⟩

Dear Mr. Tomkinson

I shall of course be only too glad to give any help I can in executing Mrs. ⟨Sophia⟩ Cotton's commission. I know very little about schoolbooks at first hand, & I am afraid such information as I could give you by Monday would be too uncertain to be of any use. But I know people who are likely to be able to tell one which are the best books, & I think that in a few days I could let you have a tolerably complete list. I should be glad to have it for future use, as every now & then schoolmistresses write for advice about books.

Mr. Acland examined Miss Buss the other day in the Schools Inquiry Commission on this question. He seemed to have it on his mind that a good deal of the badness of school teaching was owing to the use of bad books, which agrees with Mrs. Cotton's view. I wonder whether it would be possible to begin teaching history at this end, instead of starting from Pharaoh or Cecrops, so as to bring out the interest which lies in its bearing on our own times. Was that Mr. Herbert Spencer's idea?

I hope the high patrons will let the girls learn Latin. Don't you think they ought? And ought not they to be advised to study Mr. Potts's Euclid. He sent me a copy, which I should be glad to give to somebody more able to appreciate it.

Perhaps I may see you on Monday, as Mr. Bodley said he should ask you to take compassion on our incompetence & see that the preparations are all right before the Examiner comes.

I rather quake at the prospect of the examn., having no one this time to depend upon for remembering & doing everything. Mr. Bodley has been very good, but he must have enough to do in looking after so many boys. Is it the admission of girls that has made the boys come pouring in as they never did before?[1] We can at any rate call attention to the coincidence.

Yours very truly
Emily Davies.

GC: ALS ED LOC-194

1. In December 1864, 665 Junior and 179 Senior male candidates had taken the University Examinations. In December 1865, the numbers rose to 986 for the Juniors and 231 for the Seniors.

To Anna Richardson

Examn. now going on.
Architectural Gallery. Conduit St. | Dec. 12th ~~12 P.~~ 11.45 A.M. ⟨1865⟩
My dear Anna

I have been wanting to write to you for a long time, partly to thank you for the letters about the Morayshire Railway. It is not very encouraging but I did not expect anything better. Thank you also for the answers to Mr. Bryce's questions.[1] There is a levity about yours which is scarcely becoming, but on the whole I like them very much. What did you mean by telling Mr. Bryce that I meant to keep back some of the papers? I don't think I ever said so, & he has been writing a threatening letter ~~about it~~.

We are enjoying ourselves here. The girls are very nice, & Mr. Chalker, the Conducting Examiner keeps testifying to their not looking jaded, & to their seeming to enjoy it &c. We have had some visits of inspection. Dr. Storrar, who is on the Commission & also is Chairman of Convocation came this morning to see how we were getting on. He was obliged to admit, which he did very goodnaturedly, that the girls were very nice looking & "wise-like" & did not look overdone. This afternoon we have had Mr. ⟨Daniel⟩ Fearon, the Asst. Commissioner for the London District. He wanted to know whether we had had any fainting or hysterics, as he said he had examined four years at the Durham Training College for schoolmistresses, & they never got thro' without something of that sort. There has been an extraordinary & quite unaccountable increase in the number of boys this year. Last year there were between eight & nine hundred, this time over 1200. It will be hard work for the Examiners. I am glad to find that Mr. Chalker thinks the girls' papers in Arithmetic, which they did this morning, look very much more promising than last time. So one may hope for fewer failures. What funny people Dissenters are. We have five candidates from a Dissenting school, all of whom choose to take the Prayerbook. One is a daughter of Dr. Angus, of the Regent's Park Baptist College. She says her Papa coached her up. He likes teaching on the Prayerbook & the Church Catechism. The Commissioners are examining a Quaker to-day, about Achworth. Their programme for this week embraces a Peer, an ex-M.P., a Wesleyan, an Independent, a Quaker & a Jesuit. You may have seen perhaps, tho' you despise the contemporary history to be found in newspapers, that Miss Buss & I have been had up.[2] If there had been any choice given, I might perhaps have represented your view, that I know nothing about the matter. But we were simply ordered to come, & we went. It was not so terrible as I expected. Seven people asking questions are not so bad as one alone, & they were goodnatured & encouraging to the last degree.

Papers are being handed in, so goodbye.

Ever yr. affecn. ED.

GC: ALS ED LOC-195

1. On 4 December 1865, Bryce had written Davies from Liverpool, saying in part, "I must not forget to thank you for introducing me to Miss Richardson, whom I saw two or three times at Grasmere, & whom it was delightful to hear upon any subject. What I shd. chiefly like, now that the end of this work begins to appear, is to have certain specific points suggested, with regard to which one might direct the examn. of a school, or of a schoolmistress as witness, so as to get at some 'Yes' or 'No' result" (Chronicle 447). The answers to the questions probably refers to the SIC questionnaire.

2. Before the Schools Inquiry Commission.

To Henry Tomkinson

17 Cunningham Place. N.W. | Dec. 21st ⟨1865⟩

Dear Mr. Tomkinson

I never heard of Miss Prescott, but I have seen a Miss Page, who kept a middle-class school near Bombay, & would I should think, be pretty sure to know Miss Prescott. The rise of prices obliged Miss Page to give up her school. She brought home a dazzling set of testimonials; from the Bishop & the Governor & a whole row of parents, & she looks rather a sensible person.

I suppose what you require to know about Miss Prescott is whether she is a sort of person who ought to be helped on in any plans she may have. If it would be of any use, I could very easily ask Miss Page what she thinks, & I should not be sorry to have an occasion for writing to her. I think her opinion would be worth something. Of course, I need not tell her what it is wanted for.

Why should not Bombay girls learn Latin? It is much more useful than Arithmetic (to women, who have no money to add up.) & quite as amusing.

The Examn. ended without any crash. Everything worked well, except the porter, who made it a principle to conceal himself whenever we wanted him. Dr. Storrar, my enemy on the Commission, came to look at the girls & went away seriously impressed. I thought it too bad of you, when Mr. Chalker asked if it would die, to make that sarcastic remark (in the face of 52 girls all as lively as they could be.) that it would have to live before it could die. Mr. Chalker will go & tell the Cambridge people that enthusiastic ladies expect it to go on, but experienced men, who know the world, see that it is only a flash which will go out as soon as the novelty is over.

Yours very truly
Emily Davies.

GC: ALS ED LOC-196

To Barbara Bodichon ⟨damaged⟩

My dear Mme. Bodichon

I am sending you the Evidence Miss Buss & I gave before the Commission. We got thro' very well. The Commissioners were excessively kind & encouraging, & they struck me as being favourably disposed towards women generally. I think you will be pleased with Miss Buss's evidence. She is thinking seriously about building, & wants to do it before she is past work. Her notion is to borrow about £5000, which is about what it would cost to do the thing completely, at moderate interest, the buildings themselves being the security.[1] She would wish the school to be made a public institute, under the control ⟨damaged⟩ money could be more usefully spent on education than in helping such a scheme as this.

I feel very hopeful about things in general. The schoolmistresses seem very ready to join in any effort at improvement, & of course that is an immense point. It is quite striking & almost pathetic to see the eagerness with which they respond to any encouragement or anything like a helping hand held out to them. We had a gathering last week to meet some of the Commission people. We put Dr. Hodgson in the Chair & he conducted very nicely. To my surprise, several of the schoolmistresses spoke, & did it very well. The best speech was from Mr. Roby, the Secretary to the Commission. He said he thought there was a great ferment going on about the education of women, & he hoped it would go further & be helped by the investigations of the Commission. This is exactly what I think is the fact. The Assn. Commissioners, with scarcely an exception, 'go in for the girls,' & it is most useful to have them going about, stirring up & encouraging the schoolmistresses. I send you some questions propounded by Mr. Fearon.

Will you kindly answer those that you have an opinion upon, & return them to me as soon as you can. I send two copies as I should think you & Nannie & Isabella Blythe might fill up two between you. The object is not merely to get information, but to gather together a respectable body of evidence, to back up conclusions already arrived at.

I hear from Cambridge that of our 128 girls, 91 have passed. This is very fair success & better than the boys were for the first two years. The girls break down is in *Scripture*. In Arithmetic they have done extremely well this time. It is very amusing to hear the Assn. Commissioners' theories about the female mind.[2] I am looking forward to their Reports with great curiosity. They are all drawing them up now.

The London University has appointed a Committee to consider the extension of their examns. to women. Mr. Charles, who has got the charge of the matter, is a very able man, & likely, I think to manage it as well as possible.[3]

I write about nothing but business, because I really have not time for anything else, & I hear of Nannie & your other concerns from Jane Crow. Please give my love to Nannie & Isabella.

Ever yours affectionately
Emily Davies.

GC: ALS ED B2

1. In 1871, Buss launched an effort to raise £6,000 and opened a second school, the Camden School.

2. The SIC acknowledged "long-established and inveterate prejudices . . . that girls are less capable of mental cultivation, and less in need of it, than boys . . . [and that this had] a very strong root in human nature." The commissioners stated that "the essential capacity is the same, or nearly the same, in the two sexes, . . . [but] the complete assimilation of the education of the sexes should not be attempted" (*Reports Issued by the Schools Inquiry Commission on the Education of Girls* [1869], 3–7). The reports and evidence of the commissioners were issued in twenty volumes between 1867 and 1868.

3. Charles wrote to ED on 14 February 1866, asking for results of the recent Local Examinations for girls "as to the comparative merit of the candidates, improvement in respect

of more difficult or substantial subjects" and requesting background information on women and education (Chronicle 453–54).

To Barbara Bodichon

17 Cunningham Place. N.W. | Feb. 19th 1866

My dear Mme. Bodichon

Many thanks for your answers, which I shall be very glad to convey to Mr. Fearon. I hope the other paper will come soon, as he is now doing his Report. Mr. Bridell's remarks are very interesting & instructive.

The girls have done very well in the Cambridge Examn. Only 6 have failed in the Preliminary, i.e. the elementary part. Rather less than one-third have failed on the whole. The per centage of failures is rather less than that of the boys. In our experimental, only 6 Seniors out of 40 passed the Preliminary. (they broke down in Arithmetic.) now, only 2 out of 77 have failed in it. Is not that impressive, as a sign of the progress that can be made in two years, when any inducement is held out. We are about to organise a Schoolmistress's meeting, a thing analogous to a clerical meeting, which I expect will be useful, partly as a propagandist institution, the more intelligent gradually enlightening the dark & ignorant, & partly as a body (if it ever grows strong enough) which can speak & act with some authority.[1] Mr. Charles is getting up our case for the London University in a most businesslike manner. He is a very able man, a barrister, & is likely I believe to take a high stand in his profession. What possesses him to take up our cause, nobody knows. His goodness is quite spontaneous & unaccounted for.

I don't suppose anything will be done in the London University at present. They are a very narrowminded body, & there is a terrible phalanx of doctors, who are dead against us. But the discussion may do good. We are scarcely ready yet to take advantage of their examns., if they throw them open at once. I have much more hope of the old Universities. They have more courage. But we cannot expect anything more from Cambridge at present. There is a move going on in the North to get the ⟨University of⟩ Durham Local Examns.[2] The adhesion of Durham, after Cambridge, is not of much consequence, but the agitation is likely to do a great deal of good. My friend Mrs. ⟨S. A.⟩ Herbert, the wife of an old curate of ours, is working it, & is quite delighted with the cordial help she is getting on all sides.

Miss Buss's building affair is in a very perplexing state. There are 4 ways of doing it. 1. It might be put into the hands of the local clergy. There is one who would I believe, get the money, but it would be on conditions which Miss Buss is not prepared to accept. i.e. he would insist on narrowing the basis of the school, as to exclude Jews, Turks, Infidels & Heretics, who are now made welcome. 2. Miss Buss might borrow the money, in which case it would be her private property. There are family difficulties about this, & it would be giving up the school as a public institution. At Miss Buss's death, it might be sold, or turned into something else, or in many possible ways, alienated from its original purpose. 3. It might be made a proprietary school. This might do, but the experience of the proprietary principle in other schools is not encouraging. They are very apt either to break up, or to be turned into private schools, or in some other way to go wrong, after about ten or twenty years. 4. A certain number of rich people might be got to put down £1000, or £500, or less, each, & they might make they school a public one (reserving of course Miss Buss's personal rights) under the control of a *mixed* Board of Trustees. This seems to be the best plan, but it is also the most difficult. Miss Buss could not very well go herself to people about it, & I don't see my way to doing it. My line seems to be to work at general measures, not at any specific schemes, & besides, I know so few rich people that I should have a bad chance of getting it done. Perhaps when you come to England, we may be able to settle upon something. If a few people like Lady Goldsmid, Mr. Heywood, &c. could be interested in it, it might so easily be done. The sum required is so small, as compared with what is bestowed on other objects.

My love to Nannie & Isabella. Who is Miss Edwards?[3]

Ever yours, ED.

GC: ALS ED B3

1. The first official meeting of the London Association of Schoolmistresses was held on 9 March 1866. ED was elected secretary.

2. At the 15 March 1866, meeting of the University Examinations Committee, "A Memorial to the University of Durham, praying for the extension of the Local Examns. to girls, was read, & it was agreed that an expression of the good wishes of this Committee be conveyed to the Sec. of the Durham Committee" [Mrs. S. A. Herbert]. Durham complied and opened its examinations to girls (Chronicle 457).

3. Both Matilda Betham-Edwards and Amelia Blandford Edwards were associated with ED's circle. Bodichon met Betham-Edwards in Algiers in 1865 and traveled with her the following year.

To Robert Potts

17 Cunningham Place, N.W. | March 21st 1866.

Dear Mr. Potts

It is indeed a long time since we have had any communication. I have heard of your kind gift of prizes to the Cambridge girls, but did not know who was the donor, as Mrs. Cooper said she was not at liberty to mention the name.

I think you must be pleased at the success of the scheme you helped to promote. I have no doubt that the movement will go on & prosper.

May I ask you once more to help us with the Cambridge paper, as you did before?

I enclose an article from the Scotsman, which I think it might be worth while to circulate farther. If you are of the same opinion, perhaps you would kindly take the trouble to see the Editor of the Cambridge Chronicle & ask him to insert it.

I have not heard of Miss Fison for a long time. I hope she is quite well.

I remain
Yours very truly
Emily Davies.

GC: ALS ED LOC-200

In April 1866, Davies applied to Queen's College for the position of assistant secretary, after being informed of its availability by Mr. Plumptre. "My idea," she wrote, "was that if I were inside the place, I might be able to help forward some plan for the affiliation of the College to the University of Cambridge, which at that time, was our modest aspiration. It was fortunate that I was rejected, as I could have done no good there, & should have been diverted from more useful effort" (Chronicle 456). On 25 April 1866, Davies met with John Stuart Mill and Helen Taylor to discuss the ongoing parliamentary debate on the Reform Bill, and the possibility of introducing the women's suffrage question.

On 8 May 1866, the University of London passed a resolution authorizing examinations for women. However, these "Special Examinations" were not the same as those taken by men. ED and her committee met on 15 May 1866, and voted "that in the opinion of this Committee, special examinations for women are not desirable" (Chronicle 460). This conflict provoked a correspondence between ED and R. H. Hutton, which ED cites in her Chronicle. The originals of these letters are not extant, and ED warned that "the letters sent to Mr. Hutton may not have been quite the same as the above drafts—there may have been omissions— but they seem on the whole to fit in with the replies" (Chronicle 477–78).

To R. H. Hutton

June 2d 1866

...I think you may perhaps like to see the enclosed notice of the admission of girls to the Durham Local Examn. You will see that what they give, they give ungrudgingly, & without reservations. I am afraid the people who are interested in improving the education of women are a thankless crew. Instead of accepting as a great boon, the admission of women to the London University Examns. '*in the manner proposed*', they have come to the conclusion that they do not consider a special examn. any boon at all, & will have nothing to do with it. Please do not publish this however, as we should not like to seem ungrateful. We are really obliged to Convocation for their kind intentions in offering us a serpent when we asked for a fish, tho' we cannot pretend to believe that serpents are better for us. I know you think it very stiffnecked & wrongheaded of us to stand out for the fish just as *we* think that if you could only spare the time to look more closely at the matter in all its bearings, you would be sure to come round to our view.[1]

GC: AMsS C461

    1. Hutton responded to ED on 4 June 1866: "I think you are thankless, & I think moreover that you will have no choice in the matter. What is proposed we did not propose for you enlightened ladies, but for girls, & if girls accept the boon how can you middlewomen come in & cut them off from what we propose? We did not, as far as I know, grant *you* anything. We offered something to girls in general & I shall be surprized if your influence proves so mischievously great as to prevent its being accepted.... When women in general are better educated it will be time enough to see whether the line of general education ought to be the same for them as for men, i.e. whether average women's faculties have not some strength which men's want, & some weaknesses which men's want. But you are so eager to be reckoned equal, that you will not hear of *difference* even tho' difference involves as much superiority as inferiority.... Why too if you repudiate it should you be ashamed of its being known that you do?" (Chronicle 462–63).

To R. H. Hutton

⟨Spring⟩ 1866

    I really must explain. Your Report says [omitted in draft.] It seemed to ⟨me⟩ that so comprehensive a phrase must include even the enlightened ladies (& gentlemen) who are trying to get something done. I submit also that the proposed examn. appeals to enlightened ladies, rather than to girls. The Report says they do not expect any candidates under 19 & makes an especial recommendation that no woman (not girl) be permitted to be ⟨incomplete.⟩

    And it has been represented to us all along that the London Examn. was to make the case of women, or if you like the word better, girls over eighteen, who are ineligible for the Local Examn. As there is no superior limitation of age recommended in your Report, the Examn. would be open to girls of 60 if they liked to go in for it. Girls under 18, having Cambridge, Edinburgh & Durham open to them, do not want an examn. from the University of London.

    I confess that 'we' is a vague & arrogant sounding expression, but I fancied you knew enough about us to understand what was meant. From what you say now, I think perhaps you do not know that there is a permanent Committee, having for its object to obtain the extension to women of University Examns. Whether our existence suggested this more in the London University, I do not know, but we have been in frequent communications with Mr. Charles

& have supplied him with facts & documents. When this Report came out, it seemed necessary to agree upon some course in reference to it, & the decision was what I told you. The reason we do not wish to blazon abroad our discontent is that we know that the people who carried this Report thro' thought they were doing us service, & that it was a great step to get even so much as this passed in Convocation. Of course we shall tell them privately that what they call a compromise we consider a capitulation, but we should not like them to think that we are ungrateful to them for undertaking what must have been a troublesome & disagreeable business, even tho' it did not end as we wished.

I think perhaps 'we' are a little more representative than you give us credit for. Thro' the Local Examns. we have got into communication with a very large number of schoolmistresses. There are Committees at the Local Centres as well as in London, & in one way or another I believe we have links with a very considerable proportion of the people who are interested in the improvement of the education of women.

Without pretending to influence girls in general very strongly, I think we may fairly claim to know something about their wishes. If you had to do with them, I am afraid you would find them terribly 'premature' worse than the middlewomen. (I wonder you can use such an impolite word.) Of course there is a vast mass whom we neither influence nor know much about, but then they are not the sort of women—or girls, to go in for a University Examn. at all. It requires some degree of enlightenment to wish even for a special examn. in Crochet & Deportment.

I don't think we object so much as you suppose to being called 'different.' What we cannot help doubting, is the competence of the London University to decide what the differences are, & to frame a curriculum to suit them. The immense number of failures in Arithmetic in our experimental examn. seemed to show that that was a subject in which the standard for girls ought, for a time at any rate, to be somewhat lower. That was the view taken at Cambridge, & they proposed lowering the standard. It was a case in which they might fairly have appealed from the middlewomen to the girls in general, who would no doubt have dutifully accommodated themselves to a lower standard, if it had been offered. However, tho' I dare say we were looked upon as ambitious & 'premature, we were listened to, & the result was that whereas in 1863, 90 per cent. of the Seniors were rejected in Arithmetic, in the very next examn, only one failed in it. I have questioned the schoolmistresses a great deal as to what girls are interested in, & the answer is that some are interested in everything & some in nothing. The discussions about equality always seem to me extremely barren & tiresome. I don't the least in the world mind being called inferior on behalf of women in general, except in so far as that continually telling people that they cannot do things is apt to make them incapable, & in the interest of the human race it is not desirable for women to believe e.g. that they *cannot* be reasonable.

There is one point in which I believe men & women are about equal, tho' it does not seem to be generally admitted, namely in numbers.

I find that in educational endowments, it is usually taken for granted that in families there are twelve boys to one girl, & the same principle is carried out all thro' in the distribution of charity money. One would like to see that altered.

I am sorry to write such a disagreeable, contradictious letter.

GC: AMsS C464

On 9 May 1866, Bodichon wrote to Helen Taylor about starting a petition on women's suffrage. Helen Taylor then drafted a suffrage petition, which ED edited to eliminate reference to married women, who were legally disqualified from owning property. The revised petition sought merely to consider "the expediency of providing for the representation of all householders, without distinction of sex, who possess . . . property or rental qualification." ED, Bodichon, Boucherett, and Rosamond Hill met at Garrett's to draft this petition, and during May and June they worked to collect signatures for it.

To Helen Taylor

17 Cunningham Place. | N.W. | June 5th ⟨1866⟩

My dear Miss Taylor

I hope Mr. Gurney has undertaken to perform his part on Thursday, if Mr. Mill still thinks he can present the Petition on that day.[1] I suppose we shall hear what day the Motion is to come on, & we can arrange for Members to have copies of the Petition with the list of names, by that time, if it is thought desirable. I think that at any rate it will be useful to have the list for newspaper writers &c., as we can mark the names that are most likely to influence them. I should like to see the faces of the Members when the question is brought forward for the first time in the House of Commons. After this, I should think Mr. C[harles]. Buxton will have to include it in his Ideas of the Day.

Mrs. Manning has been talking to Mr. Maurice about the Petition & reports that he is very much interested. Mrs. Knox (Miss Isa Craig) is at home now. I propose going down to see her on Friday, & hope to ascertain what part she is likely to be able to take in the approaching campaign. I think there must be truth in your theory as to the peculiar fitness of women for fighting. I cannot help enjoying it.

We very much hope that you will be able to come up to the Kensington Meeting at Mrs. Manning's on Monday.

Ever yours most truly
Emily Davies

LSE: ALS 174

1. On Thursday, 7 June 1866, John Stuart Mill presented the women's suffrage petition to Parliament. Mill had invited Russell Gurney to join him in presenting the petition, but Gurney declined.

To Helen Taylor

17 Cunningham Place. | N.W. | June 6th [1866]

My dear Miss Taylor

I think Mrs. Knox would scarcely be prepared to say anything decisive on Friday, & that it would therefore be scarcely worth while for you to have the trouble of calling.[1]

I think after I have seen her & given her some idea of what we wish, she will want a day or two to make up her mind. I think it is very desirable that three or four of us, not too many, should meet next week. I will talk to Mrs. Bodichon about it & see what she says. It occurred to me that we might have two Secretaries, one of whom should be unmarried, & that Miss Manning would make an admirable second to Mrs. Knox, being in many ways, *complimentary*. I will find out whether she is willing. If it is worth while to have a Treasurer, which would be a merely nominal office, I should be inclined to propose Lady Goldsmid, who has resources to fall back upon in case of deficit. If all our officers are women, do you not think we might then have men on the Committee? Some of those who are on our Examns. Committee would I am sure join us, if asked, & they have been of real use on that Committee.[2]

I hope to see Mrs. Bodichon & the others to-morrow morning, to settle the final arrangements about the Petition. I think I may venture to promise that it shall be in Mr. Mill's hands by two o'clock. I hope Mr. Gurney will not fail.

Yours most truly
Emily Davies.

LSE: ALS 175

1. On 5 June 1866, ED had suggested inviting Isa Craig Knox to join the proposed suffrage committee.
2. The Enfranchisement of Women Committee eventually included: Alford, Boucherett, Professor Cairnes, W. L. Clay, Harriet Cook, ED, Lady Goldsmid, Hastings, Heywood, Isa Craig Knox, Adelaide Manning, Louisa Smith, and Clementia Taylor.

To R. H. Hutton

⟨June⟩ 1866

I am not going to trouble you with another long letter, but I want just to tell you how heartily I agree with almost every word you say.[1] All I maintain is that neither the enlightened ladies nor the London University know what the intellectual differences between men & women may be, but what I argue from this is, that *therefore* existing examns., having already a recognised standing, had better be thrown open without reservation & let us see what comes of it. The moment you begin to offer special things, you claim to know what the special aptitudes are. The London examns. do not strike me as eminently suitable ~~for~~ either for men or women, but if girls like to go in for them, why should they be stopped? Unless we know that they were unsuitable, which indeed, your Report 'feels' them to be. Take the case of a girl coming up to examns. You say to her: 'Oh, so you want to be examined in Greek? But that is not a feminine subject; we cannot examine you in that, you must take German instead.' If she happens to delight in Greek, & does not care for German, she is discomfited, & more than that, so long as this arbitrary dictation of studies goes on, we have no chance of finding out what women would choose, if they had a free choice, say between Ancient & Modern languages. As it is, all the encouragement goes to the last, which makes it the more surprising that even now, so many women read & enjoy Homer & Virgil. I suppose it must be the same wilfulness which you discover in my holding on to my poor opinions.

What I said about not publishing our discontent was only half-serious. It so happens that the 'false delicacy' was suggested by a man. [it was Mr. Shaen.] but our Committee would have practised it anyhow. We do not in the least shrink from stating our views whenever there is occasion for it, but we do not want to go out of our way to attack the London University or anybody else when there is nothing to be gained by it. One gets a horror of those smart paragraphs in the Spec⟨tator⟩. There is no saying what you might not have distorted my innocent observations into, & therefore announced as the middlewoman's view. I was instructed to tell Mr. Grote that we don't want a special examn., & that was all that we felt called upon to do. If you like to exert yourselves to do in *your* way, what Cambridge, Durham, & Edinburgh are doing in *our* way, we have neither the right nor the inclination to interfere. We don't want another examn. for schoolgirls. We *do* want one for women, & we shall get it by & by from Cambridge. In the meantime we have a good deal to do in making use of what we have already gained. The most amazing thing in your letter is where you ask 'Is it not really that you distrust the soundness of your own decisions?' If only one could see as clearly & feel as confident about a few other things! I am sorry to say my stock of beliefs is but small, but on this point I have no doubt whatever. I mean as to the general principle. In practical measures, it may often be expedient to compromise & I did in fact propose a compromise to our Committee, to the effect that we should ask the Senate to give us (forgive the obnoxious expression) the Matriculation Examn. with an option between Greek & German. The suggestion was ⟨incomplete⟩

GC: AMsS C472

1. Hutton had written to Davies on 6 June 1866, saying: "You do not understand what we did. We expressly waived the question of degrees on the ground that it was—as it is—quite premature to say, what the *University* standard for women's education ought to be.... University education really determines the bent of the intellectual pursuits thro' *life*, which school education does not, & it would be a serious mischief to point it hastily in a wrong direction. If you know that you are not in danger of doing this by your present efforts, you know a great deal more than you have the means of knowing. But then you enlightened ladies *do* know so much" (Chronicle 468–70).

To Helen Taylor

17 Cunningham Place. | N.W. | June 9th ⟨1866⟩

My dear Miss Taylor

I saw Mrs. Knox yesterday, & told her what we wished about the Secretaryship. She said she had plenty of time to spare for it, & her only ground of hesitation seemed to be the doubt whether she was the best person for it. She intends to live for the next year at least, at New Cross in a very quiet retired way, & she would not be able to do much, she thinks, in the way of pushing the question, by going about in society. Anything in the way of correspondence, she could do perfectly well.

It seems to me that our work will have to be done, at present at any rate, almost entirely by correspondence, & that a person living quietly, & therefore with sufficient leisure to do the work *well*, is just what we want. Mrs. Knox would like Miss Manning as a coadjutor, if it is thought desirable to have two Secretaries. I have not yet had an opportunity of speaking to her on the subject. I feel anxious to secure Mrs. Knox, as after thinking a good deal about it, I cannot think of any one else who would do nearly so well. She has the great advantage of being known & cordially liked by all the people who are most active in the matter, which seems to me important. She said she should like to have a day or two to think about it, before deciding. If you think it worth while, perhaps you would write to her or see her. Her address is 14 Clyde Terrace, Brockley Road. As her doubt is as to her fitness, it may make just the difference to her, to know that most of us are agreed in wishing her to undertake it.

Mrs. Bodichon was called out of Town on Thursday, & I have not yet been able to see her. Supposing we cannot arrange for ^{meeting on} Thursday, would you kindly let me know what later day would suit you? I think that Mrs. Bodichon, Mrs. Knox, Miss Manning & our two selves would sufficiently represent the various parties concerned, & that for discussing confidentially the very first preliminary steps, we should do better than a larger number. Miss Boucherett is at Ambleside. I will write & tell her of the proposed meeting, so as to give her the opportunity of making suggestions.

The printer promises revised proofs of the Petition with the list of names, in slip, by Monday evening. These will do for sending to newspaper writers. Miss King, the Sec. of the Society for the Employment of Women, has written to the proprietor of the Standard, & will see the editor of the Athenaeum, whom she knows intimately. I have asked Miss Boucherett to call on Harriet Martineau & see what she will do about the Daily News, in which she writes pretty regularly. Miss Bostock will look after the Spectator, & Miss Garrett will I think try the Scotsman. I am going to write to Mr. Courtney, who is on the staff of the Times, tho' without much hope of his being able to do anything. If there is any one to whom you would like the list of names sent on Tuesday, perhaps you will kindly let me know. We shall not get copies in the pamphlet form till some days later, but the slips can be used in the meantime.

I remain
Yours most truly
Emily Davies.

LSE: ALS 177

To Helen Taylor

17 Cunningham Place. N.W. | June 16th 1866

My dear Miss Taylor

Thank you for the trouble you have taken about the lists. I hope we shall get them correct at last, but it takes longer & is more difficult when a good many people are concerned.

I dare say you have seen a paragraph which I suppose began in the Pall Mall Gazette, giving a resumé of the Petition & fifteen of the best names. It looks very well. The Record inserts bits of information & has not yet pronounced against us. On the whole I think the papers have behaved rather better than might have been expected. The article in to-day's Saturday looks as if it had been written by a man who like Mr. Leslie Stephen in the former case, thought he would rather write on that side than the other, but did not really care a bit either way.[1]

I am very glad that you agree with my little book so far as you had read.[2]

I have thought since that I might perhaps have ventured to go a little further, e.g. that I might have spoken of the Franchise as an educational influence. But perhaps it is as well not to have made the dose too bitter.

Yours most truly
Emily Davies.

The Petition must of course be at the head of the list, when it is made up into pamphlet the form. These are merely rough Proofs.

LSE: ALS 178

1. "Women's Rights," *Saturday Review* 21, no. 555 (16 June 1866): 715–16.
2. Davies, *The Higher Education of Women*.

To Helen Taylor

17 Cunningham Place. | Sunday. | ⟨June 17, 1866⟩

My dear Miss Taylor

I shall be very glad to join you at the time you propose on Wednesday.[1] You would see that our notes crossed.

I agree with you as to the two Secretaries. I think one is better unless there is some reason for having two, which there is not in this case, if Mrs. Knox will be the one. I had not spoken to Miss Manning about it.

Yours very sincerely
Emily Davies

LSE: ALS 176

1. ED, Bodichon, Helen Taylor, Clementia Taylor, and Isa Craig Knox met on 20 June 1866 at Aubrey House and decided not to form an official committee but rather to continue gathering signatures for additional suffrage petitions.

To Helen Taylor

17 Cunningham Place. | N.W. | June 19th | [1866?]

My dear Miss Taylor

Many thanks for your kind invitation for next Sunday, which I gladly accept. I hope to see you also on Thursday at Mrs. ⟨Clementia⟩ Taylor's. I think you are right about the Association.[1] From what I hear in various ways I am afraid we should not be able to get together a sufficient number of influential members *at present*, to answer your purpose of making the existence of the Association a protest. I mean that I fear the people we could get would not be important enough to make the protest effective.

I have not much hope of the Conservatives, tho' I think that a few here & there may be willing to help us, & that whatever they do will in this particular case have a greater proportionate value than its intrinsic worth. My hope is that we may eventually get some Liberals to think the extension of the Franchise a very good thing, & the rest of the world to think it not a very bad thing, & then I suppose we should carry it.

The terms in which you speak of my little book give me very great pleasure. I was very much afraid lest in trying to be conciliating, I might have seemed to be giving up some part of our essential principles. If I had fallen into this snare I think you would have been sure to find it out, & for this reason among others, your approval is specially gratifying to me.

With hearty thanks for your kind note, I remain
Yours most truly
Emily Davies.

LSE: ALS 179

1. Taylor had written to Davies, saying she was glad to hear that Bodichon was no longer intending to form a women's suffrage association.

To Helen Taylor

17 Cunningham Place. | N.W. | July 7th 1866

My dear Miss Taylor

Immediately upon receiving my note, Miss Cobbe wrote to Mr. Edward Dicey, who she says has been editing Macmillan lately, to ask if he would put in an article from her on the Franchise. She did this of course not knowing that Mr. Dicey was abroad, & there the matter stands. Miss Cobbe is afraid she could not get an article into Fraser till October or perhaps later, as one of hers on another subject is to appear in a month or two.

My impression is that Mr. ⟨David⟩ Masson[1] would be more likely to accept an article from you than from Miss Cobbe & that it would be better to get something written by a new person. Miss Cobbe is thoroughly identified with the rights of women, so that anything she says comes with an ex parte air, & she always writes with her name. It seems to me that it must have a bad effect for the same names to appear continually, as if we had only about half-a-dozen people capable of saying anything on our side. But if we can be pretty sure of getting your article into as good a Magazine as Macmillan, that of course alters the question. I should think the Cornhill would be best, its circulation is so wide

& so miscellaneous. Its having no party character is also an advantage, with a view to making extracts from the paper for insertion in newspapers.

I have ordered 400 additional copies of the extract from the Law Times, for the purpose of sending to some of the signers of the Petition.[2] We have not yet received copies of the Petition. Getting it out seems to be a very tedious business.

I ordered 100 copies of the extract from the Working Man,[3] thinking that it might be inserted in a good many local papers, & that on the principle of incessant hammering & saying the same thing over & over again by different mouths, it might do some good. I propose also to send some copies to Miss Horsburgh for her friends among working men.

If you will kindly return the Pall Mall Gazette, I will keep the Mysogynist among our Chronicles.

At the Social Science Meeting the other day, we had some talk about Mrs. Bodichon's paper & the best means of getting a good discussion upon it. Mr. Hastings thinks there will be plenty of people to speak on our side, & that the thing is to get up a good opposition. Mr. Hastings & Mr. ⟨Walter⟩ Clay are extremely anxious to have Mr. Mill at the meeting, even if it were for only one day. If he would undertake the Presidency of the Economy & Trade Department, they would put Mrs. Bodichon's paper into that & they say they should then be quite sure of a capital discussion upon it. It seems the Manchester people object to introducing the general question of lowering the Suffrage, but Mr. Clay thinks there will be no difficulty in bringing forward *our* question. Mr. Hastings proposes also to bring forward the Property of Married Women. A new Code lately introduced at New York is to be discussed. The man who is responsible for it (I forget his name) is to be at the meeting, & Mr. Hastings says he is sure to talk about what the Code does for women, 'he is so proud of it.' I hope we shall also get something said about girls' schools. Sir James Kay Shuttleworth is going to write a paper on the question. "What central & local bodies are best qualified to take charge of and administer existing Endowments for Education, & what powers and facilities should be given to such bodies?" Mr. Clay has promised to talk to him & to see if he will bring in girls. If not, Mr. Clay will let us know, & he says we could then have a supplementary paper specially about girls. What I want to get said is that such bodies ought to include women. If we could get that, I think everything else would follow.

I think you may perhaps like to see the enclosed letter. It was Mr. Fitch who in conjunction with Mr. Charles obtained the appointment of a Committee to report on Examns. for Women. I believe our best plan now will be to leave the University of London alone. The ladies at Bedford College think it will be quite possible & very desirable for their students to pass the Cambridge Examns., & if we can once point to a considerable number of women, who have passed, even informally, an examn. in the same papers with the same standard as those of men for ordinary Degrees, the question as to whether they can & will do it, without going out of their minds, will be settled.

I remain
Yours most truly
Emily Davies

LSE: ALS 180

1. Editor of *Macmillan's* from 1859 to 1868.
2. The *Law Times* had written that it was "unable to suggest a single sound objection to the claim of female householders to vote" (16 June 1866).
3. *Working Man* (23 June 1866).

To R.H. Hutton

⟨July⟩ 1866

... Many thanks for your kind note. I am glad to know that the notice in the Economist is yours.[1] I still do not quite understand why you think it right for women to try being Apothecaries with an L⟨icentiate of the⟩.S[chool of⟩.A⟨pothecaries⟩., & wrong for them to try being physicians with an M.D. Degree. But perhaps you do now know that the M.D. is the great bone of contention in the London University. I don't think we shall struggle for it any more. The course of instruction & the legal qualification are the essential things & they are secure now.[2] For the rest, we expect to get from Cambridge examns. for the Colleges (which will I think be more useful in some respects than the London.) The same papers with the same standard as those for the University examn. will be used. Only College students will be allowed to go in & the final Certificates will certify the having passed thro' a prescribed course of instruction & discipline, which seems to me a better thing than a mere certificate of knowledge. It will be equivalent to a Cambridge Degree, but at first, as in the case of the Local Examns., without the title or the formal sanction of the University. The arrangements have not yet been made, but we are told that there is not likely to be any difficulty at Cambridge. The Colleges must agree to send their Students to a common centre, & the University will then send down Examiners to conduct.[3]

I did not intend to convey the impression that I thought professions (or even political life, which seems to me infinitely more interesting) would fill up the blank in women's lives. I did not suppose that they satisfied men, or that anything ever satisfies anybody. It would be scarcely worth while going to Heaven, if satisfaction were attainable in this world. But there are degrees of dissatisfaction, & I think the women who have professions, or something equivalent, are happier than those who have not. It is very good of you to deny yourself the use of your favourite epithet. You did not even fasten it upon the unlucky people who signed the Franchise Petition.

I wish you had more opportunities of knowing average women. If you were a clergymen & had to work with commonplace men & women on Committees & in other ways, you could not possibly retain your present sentiments about their respective capacities.

GC: AMsS: C476

1. R. H. Hutton, "Masculine Monopolies," *Economist* (7 July 1866). On 12 July, Hutton wrote to Davies, saying: "I send you to-day an Economist in which I said something of your little book & expressed rather more of my ground of difference from you. However I thank you very heartily for it" (Chronicle 475).
2. In May 1868, the Society of Apothecaries would revise its constitution to exclude women.
3. Davies notes in the Chronicle that "[t]his scheme came to nothing" (477).

To Helen Taylor

17 Cunningham Place. | N.W. | July 18th 1866

My dear Miss Taylor

Ought we not all to congratulate each other on the respectful reception of Mr. Mill's speech last night? It is very encouraging. No doubt we owe it mainly to the admirable manner in which the case was stated. But still, some time ago it would have provoked laughter I suppose, however stated.

I have sent the Petition to-day to all the weekly papers of any consideration, that in case they take notice, they may know what they are commenting upon. The speech is very well reported in the Post, better than in the Globe. The enclosed is the only comment I have seen yet.

In speaking of the Examiner, you mentioned Mr. Chadwick's name. Would it be better to send anything we have for insertion, thro' him? I am making gradually a list of papers with the names of people who have access to them. A lady whom I met a day or two ago, writes for the 'Queen', a weekly paper with a circulation of 5000, chiefly among women. It is weak & timid, but they will admit now & then something in our interest. I wish we could do a little more in the way of reviewing books, from which extracts might be made such as the one you were kind enough to send me. It is very striking. I suppose the great thing now [however] will be to get up Petitions. I should like very much to have one from the borough of Marylebone & hope to be able to find some one to work it.

There are a great many well-known people living in the borough, who would, I think, sign it. It seems to me that Petitions either from a place, or from some definite body, are likely to be much more effective than those which come vaguely from the whole country. But I suppose we ought to have one general Petition to include stray people, such as the Deans of Durham & Canterbury, who would both be very likely to sign, I think, & whose boroughs are not likely to have Petitions of their own. Do you know whether it is usual for the inhabitants of *County* electoral districts to send up Petitions?

I have been thinking of the Lankesters who would be very good people to work a Petition, & who, as they live at Hampstead, must I should think be outside of any borough.

The case of married women complicates things very much. Ought we not to come to some decision about the line to take about it? Do you think it better to leave it open, as in Mr. Mill's Motion & in our own Petition, or in future, to ~~make~~ limit our demand definitely to unmarried women & widows?[1] The limitation seems to strengthen our position so very much with most people, that one feels tempted to adopt it, if it could be done honestly & without embarrassing future action. The position taken up by "One of the Petitioners" in the Spectator, (do you know who it is?) is so advantageous, that it seems a pity to be driven out of it by such a rejoinder as the note appended.[2] I was going to ask you whether you think it best that we should have Petitions from women only, or from men & women, but I am sure you will say "Both".

It has occurred to me that a Petition from the class defined in Mr. Mill's Motion might be *specially* effective. Do you think so?

I should like to know how soon, & in what shape, we may expect to have the Return. Is there any means of knowing with respect to married women of property, whether their property is freehold & set apart for their separate use? I trouble you with all these questions because I want to be thoroughly primed, for the sake of helping other people. I intend going to the Social Science Meeting ~~chiefly~~ partly for the Education matter, but also because if a discussion is got up on the Franchise, & people are stirred up to work, they will have all sorts of questions to ask, & I want to be able to answer them. I find that the people who have helped at Education are for the most part, quite ready to work at the Franchise also & much less afraid than I expected of doing it openly. The Enfranchisement of women is treated as *a whole*, more than I was aware of. Mrs. Knox is getting in the bills & the subscriptions & asks me to say that she will be glad if you will kindly let her have yours some time soon. I think you have her address (14 Clyde Terrace, New Cross.) She is going to write a notice of Serjeant Manning's pamphlet for the Scotsman, making use of the occasion to bring in our question. I wish somebody with Conservative sympathies would write an article for the Quarterly or Blackwood, pointing out that the exclusion of women is one of the "theoretical anomalies" which Lord Derby "cannot deny" & which a Conservative Government might very properly deal with.[3]

I have to thank you very much for sending me the notices of my book, & also for the Magazines. The latter especially, I really have no right to trouble you about when they contain nothing on our subject. It is very curious however to note how continually some sort of reference to it appears, e.g. those remarks of Kingsley's about what women owe to Physical Science, & parts of Miss Thackeray's story. I think she really helps us, tho' she does not profess to have any sympathy with our ideas, by the impressive way in which she shows the dreary side of women's lives.

I will bear in mind about the chances for women at Aberdeen. At present I do not know any girls who would be able to try the experiment. The remoteness of the locality would be a great additional difficulty in the way of English girls.

Does Mr. Mill know how deeply & warmly we all thank him for what he is doing? One feels an almost irrepressible impulse to try to tell him & then we are held back by feeling that it would be an impertinence. I think you [are] perhaps scarcely aware how much your steady sympathy & your prompting helps & sustains those who have to carry out the details. I speak now of the past, before you had begun to take part in the actual work. The advantage of making your personal acquaintance will count for still more in one's life's work. I must not return evil for good by inflicting long letters upon you. Pray forgive the prolixity of this & Believe me

Ever yours most truly
Emily Davies.

LSE: ALS 181

1. The argument for women's suffrage, growing out of debate over the Reform Act, was rooted in assumptions about the relationship between property ownership and citizenship. The petition sought franchise rights for "all householders, without distinction of sex, who possess ... property or rental qualification." At this time, married women could not own property; thus extending suffrage to them would have required considerable changes in property law. The first Married Women's Property Act was passed in 1870.

2. *Spectator* (14 July 1866), Letters to the Editor: "Your correspondent ... asserts that only exceptionally gifted or circumstanced women desire the franchise, and infers that as these do not represent the average of women, it would not be expedient to bestow upon all the power which only a few desire to use.... To say that because only a few desire it their wishes ought not to be taken into consideration, is an argument altogether unworthy of any one who believes in progressive civilization."

3. Edward Geoffrey Stanley, fourteenth earl of Derby (1799–1869), served in Parliament and was the chief secretary for Ireland. He helped pass the Reform Bill of 1867.

August 1866

To Helen Taylor

17 Cunningham Place. | N.W. | Aug. 4th 1866

My dear Miss Taylor

I send you twelve copies of the Petition. There are plenty more on hand if you should want them.

I am extremely glad to hear that your article has been accepted for Macmillan.[1] I hope it will lend itself to extracts, as that seems to me a very important propagandist agency. There is a great deal yet to do in bringing people to understand that our proposals are serious, & the name of Macmillan carries with it a certain amount of authority.

Mrs. Bodichon went the other day & took me with her, to see Mrs. ⟨George Murray⟩ Smith of the Cornhill. As Mr. Smith was not at home, nothing was said of the article, but we talked a little about the Petition for the Franchise & Mrs. Smith said that was an old hobby of hers. So far, that is promising.

I am not sure whether we quite understand each other about the Petition & the Social Science discussion. I did not mean to propose that the Petition should be brought forward or even mentioned in the discussion, but only that we should have it ready. I do not expect much good from the discussion *itself*. It is as likely as not that the paper will fall dead & provoke no discussion at all. The great difficulty in most of the Social Science meetings is that nobody will oppose. If only somebody would say something on the other side, it would be triumphantly answered at once, but it is excessively dispiriting to be arguing against nobody, & the consequence is that the best speakers won't say anything or cannot do their best, & then foolish people get up and put one to the torture by talking nonsense on *our* side. The real value of the meetings, so far as I have seen, is in gathering together the people who are interested. The question will be *raised* by the mere fact of having a paper read, & questions will naturally follow as to what we propose to do. This will furnish an occasion for introducing the Petition to a good many people, & I think it would be a pity to lose such an opportunity of getting it afloat. If a few good names had been already procured it would be an encouragement to the timid, & would help the thoroughgoing in starting it in their respective neighbourhoods.

The chief part of the work would be done in the early winter, that is, when people have settled down after their holidays. I have found November and December a good time for getting things done. People are lively and strong after their rest & are not yet distracted by the bustle of the London season. I don't care about hurrying the Petition forward, but I think we ought to allow a considerable time for working it. So much slips away in delays at all points & when we are attempting a demonstration it seems very desirable to make it as strong as possible, both as to the quality & the number of the names. For the first especially, time is required, as getting people of weight is done to a great extent thro' social intercourse & seizing favourable opportunities. I saw Lady Goldsmid last week & asked her opinion about limiting our claim to single women & widows. She was against it, chiefly on the ground that the phrase is ugly (on which I quite agree with her) & open to ridicule, & also because she thought it would not look well for women to ask for a thing for a section of themselves, as if they did not care for married women equally. She thought we ought to begin by asking for it broadly, on the legal qualification only, & that *when* the difficulty about wives was raised, that married women might withdraw their claim. Sir Francis said he thought we had better from the outset keep to what could be maintained in argument, & that with regard to wives, there *was* something to be said on the other side. Also he thought that a Petition on behalf of unmarried women & widows would not be more laughed at than any other. They were both very cordial on the subject, & I have no doubt Lady Goldsmid will help us in getting good names.

I hope we shall get a good many local Petitions. Miss Florence Hill thinks she can get one up at Bristol, & there is a Miss Kinglake, a sister of the M.P. ⟨Alexander William⟩, living at Brighton, who is very much interested in the subject.[2] The Westlakes will I believe get one from Marylebone. I should think these Petitions would be very telling, as they will at any rate force the question upon the consideration of local members. If we spend money freely, as I think we ought, on these Petitions & on the agitation generally, a considerable sum will be required. I half proposed to Mrs. Bodichon & Mrs. Knox a general subscription but they did not at all like the idea. In the Examns. agitation we got what money was wanted from the people immediately concerned, but in that case the expenses were very small. I think that in some way or other, we ought to put money into Mrs. Knox's hands before the agitation begins, so that she may not be called upon to advance it. I should say that not less that £200 will be required. The number of signatures, & even their quality, will greatly depend on the amount of money spent in getting them. To cover a wide field & bring the matter before everybody who may possibly be interested will necessarily involve a great waste of printing & postage. If we knew beforehand what sort of people would be likely to respond, we might confine our appeals to them, but we have not the materials even for a guess. Serjeant Manning was quite pleased to answer your questions. He is very much alive on the subject & likes having his legal knowledge turned to account.

I dare say you have seen a paragraph from the Lancet about "a fair young creature" who has been nursing at the London Hospital.[3] It is Miss ⟨Ellen⟩ Phillips, the Quaker girl whom you may remember seeing at one of Miss Garrett's lectures. She wanted to go in for Medicine, but as her parents were very much opposed she thought she had better begin by learning Nursing, which would at any rate be better than nothing. She had been a few weeks at the London Hospital when the Cholera broke out & her services then became most valuable.[4] She told Miss Garrett she had never been so happy in her life, & she was so glad the work had come in her way. A day or two ago, her father went down to the Hospital, & in spite of her protestations that she ate well, slept well, & felt perfectly well, he carried her off. She told Miss Garrett she meant to come back, & we hope she will have firmness enough to maintain her point, but it is dreadfully hard upon her.

I am so glad to know that you will soon be resting at Avignon. Mrs. Bodichon is in Sussex, & I shall be going North at the end of this month.

Ever yours sincerely
Emily Davies

LSE: ALS 182

1. H[elen].T[aylor], "Women and Criticism," *Macmillan's* (September 1866).
2. The Bristol and West of England Society for Women's Suffrage was formed in 1868, with Florence Davenport Hill serving on the first executive committee.
3. *Lancet* (28 July 1866).
4. A number of cholera epidemics broke out during the nineteenth century. The final epidemic, in 1866, killed almost four thousand people in the East End of London alone.

To Helen Taylor

17 Cunningham Place. | N.W. | Aug. 6th 1866

My dear Miss Taylor

I cannot answer your question about Miss Cobbe positively, but when I saw her a fortnight ago, she spoke a little doubtfully as to whether ⟨James Anthony⟩ Froude would accept an article on the Franchise & I am pretty sure that she would not begin to write without asking him first. I can easily find out, or if you would prefer communicating with Miss Cobbe directly, her address is 26 Hereford Square, S.W.

I am afraid I may have seemed more in a hurry for the Petition than I felt. I only want to have it by October & there is plenty of time before then. I entirely agree with you in not wishing to say anything, either in Petitions or elsewhere, which would involve the principle of excluding married women. It would be dishonest, as misrepresenting our real opinions. To avoid touching upon the position of married women and not in any way to mix up the marriage laws with the question of the Franchise, is exactly what I wish. The difficulty is how to do it.

I do not see how we can exclude wives from the discussion, unless we in some way limit our claim, because our opponents will, if they can, insist on discussing wives & nothing else. If the law is indefinite on the question whether husbands could give votes to their wives, it alters the question a little. But Serjeant Manning on this point quite agrees with Mr. Westlake, & I believe you are of the same opinion. If this is so, can we maintain the position taken up in your letter (if I remember it right) that the claim is made for a small class? In the last Petition, the word 'householder' was used, which seemed to limit it, but unfortunately that word is applicable only to boroughs, & does not include single women living with their parents, who as possessing the freehold qualification would have a county vote. This defect in our Petition was pointed out by Professor Huxley & some one else, when it was too late to alter it. My difficulty is simply a practical one. The promoters of the Petition will be constantly asked—"Does this include married women? If not I will sign. If it does, I cannot." After the legal opinions that have been given, I think we should be obliged to say—"In certain cases, Yes." This would not signify so much in private, but it seems to me that in a public controversy, it would be awkward. Even if it is only that the law is indefinite, it seems to me a pity to let people go off into discussion upon whether our claim includes wives, when we want to fix their attention upon the claim itself. I do not see that in *limiting* our claim, we necessarily pronounce any opinion upon the rights of other people, outside that claim. We ask on behalf of Englishwomen, but we do not imply that Frenchwomen ought not to have the Franchise also. It is to my mind, a practical question of policy. We ask for what there is some remote chance of getting. If we ask for married women also, we get it neither for them nor for the smaller class. When the wedge is inserted, we can go on for more, including liberty for married women in other directions. Mrs. Bodichon insists very much on having a Petition which shall embrace as many Petitioners as possible, i.e. the sort of Petition that a great many people can sign, & it appears to me that it is important not only as securing a large number of signatures, but as being what a great many people can advocate. Sir Francis Goldsmid evidently felt that it would be an ~~great~~ advantage in debate to be able to dismiss the question of wives as irrelevant—to be able to say to the other side—"Your jokes & your menaces about domestic happiness are beside the question. The Petitions don't ask for the Suffrage for wives." I feel sure that he *himself* would be in favour of giving that *and* other liberties, to married women, but as a matter of policy, he thought it better to make the smaller claim first.

Your letter to the Spectator is with our other Chronicles, which are at this moment in Mrs. Bodichon's hands. I will write to her for your letter & send it to you at Avignon.[1]

Mrs. Bodichon wrote a letter to the Spectator, dictated by Serjeant Manning, which they did not insert. I was sorry, but not surprised. They had given us more space than I expected. The expenses of the Petition are all paid, except those of distribution, which will I expect amount to about £5. When that is paid, I think Mrs. Knox will have about £12 or £15 in hand. She has all the accounts in order. We must certainly have accounts kept, however the money comes. The usual plan I believe in small institutions which do not publish annual reports, is to print an annual statement of accounts & issue it to the subscribers.

In the Univ. Examns. case, we did not think it worth while to *print* a statement last year, the number of subscribers being very small, but the accounts are carefully kept, & audited at the end of the financial year.

In the Franchise matter, the financial year will I suppose date from the day on which the first subscription was paid. When the time comes, Mrs. Knox will prepare a Statement of Accounts, & the Committee can decide whether it is worth while to print it. I should think there would be no serious difficulty in raising even a large sum (which two general Petitions on a large scale will certainly demand) if the right people know that money is wanted. They can scarcely be expected to offer it without knowing that anything is going to be done. I am to see Mrs. Taylor on Wednesday & will ask her what she thinks had better be done. I have been thinking lately that the time has come for those of us who met at Mrs. Taylor's to *call* ourselves a Committee. We are at present labouring under the disadvantage that there is no one person, & not even any definite body, to take the general direction of affairs, & we shall feel the inconvenience of this more & more as we go on. Mrs. Knox says she is made Secretary after all, by taking the direction of the Petitions, & so we have come in fact to a part of your original proposal ~~of~~ i.e. a Managing Committee of five ladies, with Mrs. Knox as Sec., with only this difference, that my taking the Press department relieves Mrs. Knox of the particular kind of responsibility that she shrank from. It seems likely to work fairly well. I can do my part almost entirely anonymously, & I find already that it works in with my other concerns. If we could have found one competent person, able and willing to take the *whole* direction, no doubt it would have been better, but under the circumstances, the present arrangement seems to me the best that is open to us. If you will kindly let me know your opinion, I will get those of Mrs. Taylor, Mrs. Bodichon & Mrs. Knox, & if we all agree in thinking it desirable to constitute ourselves a Committee, we can do so without meeting again. There need be no publication of names, but we shall be able to say that there *is* a Committee at the centre of affairs, & we can say who compose it, to any one that cares to know.

I send the enclosed, as a specimen, tho' I dare say you have seen the kind of thing often enough before. I don't want it back. Please do not hurry to answer this. There is nothing that requires immediate attention.

Yours very sincerely
Emily Davies

LSE: ALS 183

1. The 14 July 1866 *Spectator* contained the letter from "One of the Petitioners," which ED cited. (See ED to Helen Taylor, 18 July 1866). This may be the letter to which ED refers.

To Barbara Bodichon

17 Cunningham Place. N.W. | Aug. 10th 1866

My dear Mrs. Bodichon

I have written to Miss Taylor, in answer to the enclosed, & have promised to ask you for her letter to the Spectator, which is among the Chronicles. Will you please either let me have it, or send it to Miss Taylor. Her address is simply 'Avignon.'

She does not seem to understand the case as to limiting our claim. If there *is* a loophole for wives, as to which the law is *not* indefinite, (& that seems to be agreed.) the only way to keep them out of the discussion is to limit our claim, without expressing any opinion as to the rights of other Claimants. I have written to Miss Taylor to this effect.

The idea of our having no accounts *kept* is very odd. I think Miss T. must have used the word by mistake. I have told her that Mrs. Knox has the accounts all in order, & will prepare a statement at the end of the financial year, which we can 'do' as we like about printing. In the meantime, clearly somebody must be responsible for getting the money; whether it is easy to get it or not, is not the question, but who is to do it. Isa certainly won't.

I saw Mrs. Taylor on Wednesday, & she thinks that if Isa becomes Sec., we ought to have a distinct Treasurer. She offered to do it, & if she undertakes it, she will hold herself responsible for getting the money. I told her frankly the one objection to her (the Reform League &c.) & she said she would of course leave it to us. I promised to consult you & Isa about it, & I should like to hear what you think before I go to Isa, on Monday. I have talked to Mrs. & Miss Manning, & they think Mrs. Taylor is much the best person we are likely to get, as to doing the work, & that the objection is not very serious, as her name need not be prominent. We shall of course avoiding publishing names as much as possible, & the Treasurer appears much less than the Secretary. I do not think her name need appear in any document except the Statement of Accounts, which only need go to the subscribers. The Mannings think that if we are to have Mrs. Taylor on the Committee, which we cannot avoid, having her as Treasurer is very little worse. Personally, I feel sure that Mrs. Taylor will be good to work with. Mrs. Manning said the other day, that on a Committee, Mrs. Taylor would always "take" the reasonable side, & I believe that is quite true. I have proposed to Miss Taylor that the five who met at Mrs. T.'s should constitute ourselves a Committee. I don't think we can do without one any longer. There must be some organised body to decide such questions as that of the Petitions. Mrs. Taylor has written to Miss T. & has I believe proposed adding Miss Manning. I shall be glad if this is agreed to. Will you please send me a letter by Monday, saying whether you wish a Committee thus constituted. Mrs. Knox, Sec. Mrs. Taylor, Treasurer, Miss Taylor, Miss Manning, yourself & myself. If you say Yes, it may be considered "settled", as Mrs. Taylor & I agreed upon it, & I have ascertained that Miss Manning is willing to act. In any case I shall propose that Miss Manning (assisted by the Serjeant) be requested to prepare a draft of Petition from legally qualified women, for consideration by the Committee.

If the Cornhill or any other good Magazine (except the Fortnightly) will insert your present paper, I shall be inclined to suggest taking up a different ground, (for the S(ocial).S(cience).) & bringing forward all the arguments *for*. It is much more difficult & dangerous, but it would be more likely to provoke discussion, which is what we want at Manchester. Your present paper leaves one with the impression that it is simply unanswerable & there is nothing more to be said. At Manchester we shall have to deal with people who will be inclined to give a languid assent. And we want to stir them up to action. I think very much of the *local* petitions, & Manchester will be the great opportunity for stirring people up about them.

This week has brought me another little, or rather big, nephew, for he is reported to be of great weight.[1]

My mother is at Chichester.

The higher orders seem very ready to help in the Cholera. The Bishop of London seems to have an unlimited supply of ladies who are ready to go anywhere & nurse.

I hope the mischief of the riots is dying away. I fancy the Reform League has had a lesson.[2] But it clearly will not do to identify ourselves too closely with Mill. The Guardian (Liberal Church) remarks that the weight of his support has much diminished since he has shown that he can be as often & as vehemently wrong as other people.

Ever yours affectionately
ED.

GC: ALS ED B314

1. Harry Llewelyn Davies (1866–1923).
2. In July 1866, police and Reform League supporters clashed in Hyde Park. When the British government avoided confrontation with working-class franchise reformers, in part by passing the Reform Act of 1867, the Reform League became more associated with the Liberal Party.

To Helen Taylor

17 Cunningham Place. | N.W. | Aug. 16th 1866

My dear Miss Taylor

I saw Mrs. Taylor one day last week & we agreed that as Mrs. Knox is now going to act as Secretary we ought to have another Treasurer. Mrs. Taylor kindly offered to undertake it, & I feel sure that you will agree with Mrs. Bodichon & Mrs. Knox & myself in wishing that she should do so.

Mrs. Knox will send her the list of subscribers at once & will transfer the accounts as soon as Mrs. Taylor returns to Town. I saw Mrs. Knox yesterday & she showed me the accounts. When the outstanding bills are paid there will be about £10 or £12 in hand. Mrs. Taylor has I believe mentioned to you that she would like to add Miss Manning to our Committee. I think we should all be glad to have her help.

My immediate object in writing to you to-day is to ask if you could be kind enough to let me get an extract from your article in Macmillan *before* it appears.[1] It takes a few days to get extracts reprinted & dispatched, & I think *they* ought to reach the Editors simultaneously with the publication of the Magazine. A good many of the provincial papers insert extracts from the Magazines regularly every month. If our extract reached them at the right moment, they might insert it, if only to save themselves the trouble of selection. If it came to hand a week later, when an extract had already appeared, it would have a worse chance. The easiest plan I think would be if you have no objection to ask Mr. Masson to send you two Proofs for correction, one of which you would perhaps kindly send on to me. I find there are about 500 local papers to which it seems more or less worth while to send. This is a selection from about 900.

Some letters are appearing in the Pall Mall on Nuns, Sisterhoods & Nurses. As soon as the series is finished, I will send them to you, in case you should have time & inclination to answer them. You would have the advantage in doing so of being able to speak from knowledge of foreign Sisterhoods.

Mrs. Bodichon proposes writing another paper for the Social Science meeting, stating the arguments *for* the extension of the Franchise. I am glad of this as I think it will be more likely to promote discussion. The paper she wrote before was almost too unanswerable. Lord Shaftesbury is to be President this year. I am afraid this is rather against us as regards political rights, but it may be to our advantage in other parts of the question. People who have never shown any interest in education before, become suddenly alive on *that* point, when the Franchise question presents itself. They seem to look upon it as a choice of evils & accept the smaller of the two.

What do you think of some such formula as the following, for defining the class for whom the Franchise is asked. "All persons, without distinction, who fulfill the conditions of property or rental prescribed by law as the qualification of the electoral franchise, & who exercise in their own names, the other rights attaching to those conditions." I fancy most people would suppose that the words "who exercise, &c." were thrown in to add to the force of the argument, not with a view to exclude married women, tho' it would have that effect practically, as wives cannot manage property *in their own names*. So at least Serjeant Manning tells us.

I hope you & Mr. Mill are both enjoying the rest & pure air, after all the fatigues of the Session. Yours very truly

Emily Davies

LSE: ALS 184

1. See ED to Helen Taylor, 4 August 1866.

To Barbara Bodichon

17 Cunningham Place. N.W. | Aug. 16th ⟨1866⟩

My dear Mme. Bodichon

I am delighted at the success which seems to be coming to you as an artist.

I hope you will very soon make £1000 a year, & *not* give it all away, chiefly to Emigration.[1]

I saw Isa yesterday. She will send Mrs. Taylor the subscription list at once, & transfer the accounts as soon as Mrs. T. comes to Town. Isa has not much zeal in the matter, but I hope she will get more interested when she begins to work. She has never seen *into* the question yet, & I don't know whether she ever will.

Your paper containing the reasons *for*, is very much wanted for Isa & people like her.[2] I don't think I have any ideas for the Fortnightly, at present. Is not Mr. Harrison's letter a sufficient text?[3] The Social Science paper is the one I am anxious about just now. You will of course put in the low-form argument. It tells with benevolent & narrow people. But it does not with thinkers. What they want to be shown is that Reforms of this sort, tho' they look small, *tend* to benefit society very deeply & widely. I think it might be urged that the great work of Parliament now is to carry out social improvements, & that on these points women actually *know* more than many men. Also that it is good for women to feel that they have *direct* influence, as it increases the sense of responsibility. I will send you the report of our Kensington discussion, in which there are a good many reasons *for*, given.

I should like to see your paper when it is ready & to make an abstract of it beforehand, for the Times. If we have the same man again that we had last year, he will put in what I give him. I bribe him, by reporting the Education

Department for him. Lord Shaftesbury is to be President this year. He is not particularly good for us, as regards politics, but he is favourable to the employment of women, & may perhaps take a good turn as to education. At any rate he will be likely to bring people to the meeting, which is a good thing so far. I do hope you will be able to come.

I have suggested to Miss Taylor the following formula. "All persons, without distinction, who fulfill the conditions of property or rental prescribed by law as the qualification of the electoral franchise & who exercise in their own name, the other rights attaching to those conditions." This excludes wives, (Serjeant Manning says) practically, without sacrificing any principle.

Yours affectionately, ED.

GC: ALS ED B315

1. With funding from Bodichon, Maria Rye had set up the Female Middle Class Emigration Society in 1861.
2. Bodichon, "Reasons for the Enfranchisement of Women," NAPSS, October 1866.
3. Probably Frederic Harrison (1831–1923), who was active in the Working Men's College and Positive School, which he cofounded, and published in journals such as the *Fortnightly Review* and the *Westminster Review*.

To Barbara Bodichon

17 Cunningham Place. | N.W. | Aug. 21st ⟨1866⟩

Dear Mrs. Bodichon

The only magazines I can think of that are worth sending to are Fraser, Meliora & the Social Science Review. I think Froude might perhaps insert your article, with only your initials, & I think it would be to our advantage to have our subject brought forward by a new hand, rather than by Miss Cobbe.

If you incline to try it with Fraser, I suppose you would write to Miss Cobbe first. She is not at home now, but letters are forwarded. I am afraid Masson would not put another article into Macmillan, besides Miss Taylor's, but he might be tried. Miss T.'s is general I believe, not definitely on the Suffrage. As Mrs. Taylor knows Masson pretty well, she might be the best person to send it by. Meliora put in a strong article about the Marriage Laws, but I fancy the circulation is very small & it only appears quarterly.[1]

I may probably see Mrs. ⟨Phebe⟩ Lankester to-day, & will ask her generally if they would put anything on the Suffrage into the S⟨ocial⟩. S⟨cience⟩. Review.

If all these fail, I think our Committee might print the paper, without a name, for circulation with the Petitions. I am rather in favour of doing things without names at present. Isa advises sending to the newspapers without anybody's comps., on the ground that a thing coming in an unknown way suggests a greater force in the background. That is a reason for not sending anything to the Fortnightly. I wonder whether there would be any chance of getting a mystical article into the Quarterly or the Edinb. Miss Bostock I think knows the Editor of the Edinburgh. If we cannot get into tolerably respectable & orthodox organs, I think it is better to publish our things as pamphlets, anonymously. We can circulate them very widely in that way, & avoid identifying ourselves with Atheism & Democracy.

Miss Wolstenholme tells me that the Editor of a newspaper who inserted our extract from the Liverpool Mercury, at the request of a friend of hers, had before put it aside, under the impression that we were asking for womanhood suffrage.

There are some very good things in Mrs. Mill's article which you might perhaps incorporate into your Social Science paper. I should have liked to reprint the article, but the tone is too bitter. It gives offence to half & half people. In anything that we do now, I shall be inclined to omit Mr. Mill's name. The newspapers have got into a way of treating the question as an individual crotchet of Mr. Mill's. That secures to us all the support that his name can bring. What we must show is that it is not a personal crotchet of anybody's. If Mr. Mill had made it his *first* concern, it would have been a different case. As it is, we get mixed up in the public mind with Jamaica & the Reform League, which does us no good.[2]

Mr. Clay thinks we shall have a good Meeting at Manchester. Mr. ⟨Henry⟩ Bruce, who is to be President of the Education Department is friendly to us, & so is Sir. J. K. Shuttleworth, who is to be President of Economy & Trade. I believe your paper will have to go into that, or may, if we like. Mr. Clay finds his work heavy, & wonders how Mrs. Knox got thro' it, as he thinks she is "not the woman to scamp it."

Please give my love to Mrs. ⟨Isabella⟩ Ludlow. I hope she will soon get stronger & better in such a sweet resting place.

Yr. affecn. ED

I have cheerful letters about our Education prospects from Leeds & Manchester.

GC: ALS ED B316

1. "The Legal Position of Women and Its Moral Effects," *Meliora* 8, no. 30 (1865).
2. J. S. Mill was active in forming the Jamaica Committee to prosecute Governor Eyre. Darwin, Huxley, Shaen, Charles Buxton, Russell Gurney, and Peter Taylor were also involved. See also ED to Helen Taylor, 16 August 1866.

To Barbara Bodichon

17 Cunningham Place. N.W. | Aug. 22d. ⟨1866⟩

Dear Mrs. Bodichon

I saw Mrs. Lankester yesterday. They will be very glad of an article on Female Enfranchisement for the Social Science Review, if not for September, certainly for October. Would you like me to send yours? It might do good in preparing for the discussion, & the S.S. Review is an independent authority, which at any rate could not damage us. I have been reading it with a view to extracts & I cannot find any one paragraph which one could take out by itself. Would you mind my making little alterations which would obviate this? I should like also to leave out the quotation from Mill's speech, which seems to me to break the flow, without adding strength. Miss Boucherett has sent me a bit of information about women's fo having voted in the time of Henry IV., which I think might be added to your note about Austria & Sweden, but I should like to verify it first, if I can.

What do you think of the wisdom of circulating the enclosed in *Conservative papers only*? I feel a little doubtful, but on the whole it seems to me so important to get anything said that is not decidedly adverse, that I think it will do rather good than harm. There is a sensible article in yesterday's Pall Mall on Sisterhoods.[1] I am sending it to Miss Taylor.

Yr. affecn. ED

GC: ALS ED B317

1. "Sisterhoods," *Pall Mall* (21 August 1866).

To Helen Taylor

17 Cunningham Place, | London. N.W. | Aug. 28th 1866.

Dear Miss Taylor

There seems to be a little misunderstanding between us about "the Committee" which I hope to be able to clear up.

I think it was distinctly understood when we met at Mrs. Taylor's that all idea of forming a *Society* was abandoned. The new idea, which has been called up by new circumstances, is different except as to the object & the proposed personnel. Perhaps I can best explain it by describing how a similar organisation grew up in the education movement. That movement as regards examinations first assumed a definite shape in the Spring of 1862. It was discovered on Miss Garrett's proposing to apply for Matriculation at the London University, that they were just going to get a new Charter & that the best thing would be to get the admission of women authorised by it.

Mr. ⟨Newson⟩ Garrett took the matter up. He had a great many ideas & devices, but he wanted some one to carry them out & he asked me to act as Sec. I drew up statements &c. and conducted the correspondence, signing myself vaguely Hon. Sec. Mr. Garrett paid all the expenses. After this had been going on some time it occurred to some of the people who were interested, that agitation of some sort must go on, & that it was not quite fair that the whole responsibility should rest upon Mr. Garrett. It was agreed to open a "Fund for incidental expenses connected with the effort to obtain for women admission to University Examns. in Arts & Medicine." Lady Goldsmid was Treasurer & it was agreed that she & I took the responsibility of spending what money was put into our hands. Very soon it appeared that we wanted a little more organisation. Our friends in the London University told us they could do nothing till Oxford or Cambridge took some step, & that pointed to trying for the Local Examns. For this we wanted something in the shape of a body to authorise official communications with the Universities. So a few of us agreed to meet at Miss Craig's office on the 23 Oct., 1862. There were present, Mrs. Bodichon, Miss Bostock, Miss Craig, Mr. Heywood & myself. It was resolved "That a Committee be formed for obtaining the admission of women to University Examns. That the Committee consist of the following ladies and gentlemen. (viz. ourselves, with Mr. Gurney, Mr. Hastings & Lady Goldsmid as Treasurer.) with power to add to their number." We passed one more Resolution, suggested by Mr. Heywood, "That this Committee shall communicate with the Local Boards in connexion with the Local Examns. of the Universities of Oxford & Cambridge, with a view to obtaining their cooperation."

We have no rules & no fixed methods of working, only an object, a personnel, & the unwritten law of Committees for our guidance. If you had been in England, I should have liked to show you the Minute-book in which our doings are recorded. We have from time to time added to our Committee any one who seemed likely to be specially helpful in that capacity, but have always aimed at keeping it small. I think that our present number, is the highest we have had. Any suggestion, whether coming from a member or from friends outside, is laid before the Committee, discussed & decided upon. Nothing has ever gone to the vote. We have circulated a good many documents of various sorts, every one of which (except perhaps the first, which I am not quite sure about) has undergone revision & some alteration in Committee, before being issued. Some two or three of the members, e.g. Mrs. Bodichon & Mr. Gurney, are rarely present. They help with their advice & their names, & have enough confidence in the rest of the Committee to let them act for them. We do not consider ourselves responsible to anyone but ourselves. The money is either offered or privately asked for.

It seemed to me that we might work the Franchise for the present in a similarly semi-public, semi-private manner, i.e. with an object (the extension of the Suffrage to women) a personnel, & a fund collected privately, the manner of working being decided upon from time to time as occasions arise. If we could have met again, it would of course have been more satisfactory, but as that was impossible for many months, I thought we might arrange it by writing, & constitute ourselves, if it was agreed to be desirable, without a formal meeting. I saw Mrs. Taylor & consulted her, & then saw Mrs. Knox, tho' I knew before hand that she wished for this kind of organisation, as she said so some weeks ago. I also wrote about the same time to you & to Mrs. Bodichon. It was Mrs. Taylor's proposal to ask Miss Manning to join us. She thought that as Miss M. had been asked to the meeting at her home, she might be considered one of the party & that we rather wanted one more, as when you & Mrs. Bodichon are abroad, if one of the others happened to be prevented from attending, the Committee would be reduced to two.

I think that a permanent Committee for the general object would do better than one limited to the preparation of a single Petition. It has already been proposed to have two Petitions, one from 'qualified' women besides the general one, & we are pretty sure to be asked for help & guidance by the promoters of the local Petitions. We might, if it were thought desirable, in some case help by a grant toward the local expenses, & in other cases in other ways. Then again the money contributed never exactly tallies with the amount expended on a single object. e.g. we have at this moment a balance in hand which must be got rid of in some way. We shall also have to circulate propagandist documents with the Petitions. I don't know whether that would be considered as included in what I undertook. I only *meant* to undertake circulating things in newspapers & I would rather not be singly responsible for anything more. This not on my own account, but because I think my single judgment would not be so good as that of the Committee collectively.

As to the Secretaryship, it seems to me that on the whole, I had better not undertake it. It is not so much that I am afraid of injuring the Education but ⟨illegible⟩ as that I think it likely to be detrimental to the *whole* movement, for the same names to appear very often. We *must* employ the same *people*, because those who care most for the whole question have, naturally, set to work already at some branch of it. But we can keep names out of sight. Mrs. Knox is quite sure that women ought to have the Suffrage. It is only that from not having thought very much on the subject in all its hearings she does not feel its importance as strongly as we do.

I hope the Cornhill will accept your paper. If not, there is an education magazine which I think would be glad to have it. Or should you be inclined to send it to the Fortnightly? Mrs. Bodichon's article is going into the Social Science journal. She has written another, a capital thing in the form of a dialogue, which there is some faint hope of getting into Blackwood, thro' Dr. Tulloch.[1] Miss ⟨Harriet⟩ Cook of St. Andrew's is going to try.

Miss Phillips very soon got back to the London Hospital.[2] Miss Garrett has more than 400 Dispensary patients now. She had 71 yesterday, all spontaneous, i.e. not sent by letters. I leave home next week, but letters will be forwarded.

Ever yours truly,
Emily Davies

LSE: ALS 185

1. Probably John Tulloch (1823–86), the principal of St. Mary's College, St. Andrews, who contributed to the *British Quarterly* and the *Contemporary Review*.
2. See ED to Helen Taylor, 4 August 1866.

To Barbara Bodichon

17 Cunningham Place. (not St. John's Wood) | London N.W.
⟨late August/early September 1866⟩

Dear Mme. Bodichon

I almost hope Mr. Lewes will refuse your paper, as I particularly wanted *that* one for the Cornhill. It is suited to commonplace people & meets the illogical, sentimental objections which we are now at the stage of dealing with. We have plenty of converts among sceptics & ~~dis~~ theorists of all sorts. We want now to make it understood that we have got out of the region of theory & are asking seriously to have our proposal put in practice. I am very much inclined to believe that our victory is not so very far distant. We have only to get a few people to take it up as a *practical* matter, & we may expect the rest to follow, as there is no party interest of any sort, political, theological, academical or professional, which would suffer by it. *Please* don't waste anything upon the Westminster. I have an eye to my extracts, & the Westminster would do us no credit.

Miss Wolstenholme says the moderate Liberal paper at Manchester is going against us, she suspects for no reason but that the extreme Liberal has pronounced for us.

The Fortnightly is not so bad as the Westminster, but Miss Boucherett says it is disapproved of by the sort of people she knows, & I don't fancy it has much weight, in *itself*, with anybody. But of course I should be glad to have something in it. It is only that I would rather it was a paper of the mystical sort, to meet the Comtists & keep the popular ones for popular periodicals.

If you see Mrs. ⟨Alice⟩ Westlake will you tell her that there are 150,000 people in the parish of Marylebone, besides St. Pancras & Paddington, & that we expect her to get them all to sign. If she gets it re-engrossed, it can appear as from Marylebone, which would be better. I should like a copy of the Petition. I suppose she will get it printed? Is there any one at Hastings who will get up a Petition from the town?[1]

I am glad your interest in the subject increases. Mine is perennial. There is so much in the subject, looked at broadly that as matter for thought it is inexhaustible. I am delighted with Felix Holt.[2] It seems to me to present a view of women that we want to have looked at.

Yours affectionately
ED.

GC: ALS ED B319

1. The town near Bodichon's English home at Scalands Gate.
2. George Eliot, *Felix Holt* (1866).

To Barbara Bodichon

Sept. 6th ⟨1866⟩

My dear Mrs. Bodichon

I have received your paper this morning & some sheets, partly of extracts yesterday. I will take it with me, & mark the parts that seem to me most suitable for the S⟨ocial⟩.S⟨cience⟩. meeting. I suppose I may cut it up. I mean literally, not figuratively. It strikes me, on a cursory glance, that some re-arrangement will be required.

I don't like the farmers' widows argument, any more than you do.[1] It sounds to me very like saying that as votes are worth from £5 to £50 (in some places) it is unjust that women should not be in a position to claim a bribe. Exactly the same principle is involved.

Miss Cook has returned the Dialogue. She thinks it interesting, but that the facts are stated in such a way as to give the impression that *everything* has been said, which of course is not the case. I don't think this matters so much in a dialogue, because in talking, it is natural to mention any fact that comes into one's head, in a casual kind of way, but in a formal essay, it always seems to me that giving a few specific facts (& you can never give more than a few) rather weakens the argument.

~~On~~ Facts, if they are to be the argument, ought to be overwhelming, & on such an enormous subject as the condition of women, half a hundred facts appear as nothing. One has the impression that if you quote 20 facts (which would fill a great space) there may be 20,000 on the other side. Miss Cook—I had better send you her letter. Please return it.

I am almost as glad that Blackwood has come out against, as if it was for us.[2] It is such a great thing to have something to demolish.

Do you think the enclosed will ᵈᵒ· from the lonely & bereaved? If Bessie is with you, perhaps she will kindly give an opinion also. My brother thinks it 'unexceptionable.' which means simply that there is nothing to find fault with in it. The signatures will be the argument, so I wanted to secure chiefly that the Petition should be what anybody could sign. I will send the Dialogue to Miss Wolstenholme & ask her to try to get it into ~~Frazer~~ Chambers.

I shall not have an opportunity of working at your papers before Tuesday, & perhaps not till the end of the week. I suppose that will do. The Manchester people are delightful.

Yours ever, ED.

GC: ALS ED B4

1. In "Reasons" (NAPSS, 1866) Bodichon quotes a woman farmer from Suffolk as saying, "'I think you would find very few farmers who do not consider their wives or daughters quite as capable of voting as themselves, and would not show their faith in their business capacities by making them executrixes and administrators of their property.... Instances daily occur of the widow of a deserving tenant being ejected from her farm with a large young family unprovided for, simply because she cannot vote.'"
2. "The Late Elections," *Blackwood's Edinburgh Magazine* (August 1865), discussed the recent parliamentary elections, criticizing "the noble lords and wealthy gentlemen who went in at the late elections for the representation of such places as Westminster, Leeds, and Chester" (259). "Our Political Prospects," *Blackwood's Edinburgh Magazine* (September 1865), also condemned Radical parliamentary candidates, including J. S. Mill.

To Adelaide Manning

Leeds. Sept. 8th ⟨1866⟩

My dear Adelaide

I had not time to go up to Phillimore Gardens before leaving home, even if I had felt sure that you would be disposed for seeing any one, but I want very much to hear how you & Mrs. Manning both are.[1] I am hoping that you will both get away to some quiet place for a little change. There seems some prospect now of finer weather, & you must both want the sort of tonic that fresh air is to you. Will you write to me please soon. I go on Monday to "Winston Rectory, near Darlington" to stay till Thursday. After that my address will be "Mrs. Fedden, Harworth, near Darlington."[2]

I came here yesterday.[3] There is to be a meeting of schoolmistresses this afternoon, at which Mr. Fitch is to speak about the Cambridge Examns., & if information is wanted about the practical working, I shall be ready to give it. I am staying of course with Mrs. Heaton. She is extremely nice in her own house, very intelligent & interested in all that is going on, & efficient in practical matters also. It gives one a great idea of the good that one superior woman can do, to see the influence that Mrs. Heaton evidently has in her circle. She wields a kind of elevating & inspiring influence all round her. I think too from what I have seen of Leeds people that it must be better than most manufacturing towns. There seems to be a good deal more intelligence & refinement than either at Newcastle or Sheffield. I had a letter from Mrs. Bodichon a little while before I left home. She wished me to say to you how much she sympathised with you & Mrs. Manning in your sad loss. I shall write again soon, but I want to hear from you first. Please give my love to Mrs. Manning.

Ever yours affectionately
ED.

GC: ALS ED LOC-202

1. The Mannings lived at Phillimore Gardens. James Serjeant Manning had just died.

2. Isabella Fedden was a schoolmistress whom Davies had met doing parish work in Gateshead. She was involved in the North of England Society for Promoting the Employment of Women, which Davies had started, and she signed several of the petitions for opening educational opportunities to women.

3. ED went to Leeds to attend a meeting on middle-class education for girls, including the opening of the Cambridge Local Examinations. Fitch and Henry Sales also attended. The result of the meeting was the establishment of a committee in the West Riding to supervise the next girls' Local Examinations.

To Barbara Bodichon

Mrs. Fedden. Harworth, | near Darlington. | Sept. 17th ⟨1866⟩

My dear Mrs. Bodichon

If the Petition I sent you is adopted, I think we must circulate with it a short statement, explaining Par. 3., & also more definitely, the nature of the qualifications. Mrs. Taylor approves of it, except the first sentence which suggests ~~th~~ "other rights" instead of "the rights." Serjeant Manning expressly suggested "*the*" as the best form, & I think it is more exact & emphatic. I sent the draft to Miss Taylor last week, & told her there would be time to make alterations, ⟨before striking off⟩ if she would write soon. I have sent it to Isa to be set up in type, & I don't think we ought to wait long for Miss Taylor. I have heard nothing from her since those letters about the Committee. It is rather inconvenient to be kept waiting so long for the draft of the general Petition.

The article in Blackwood is the most foolish & insulting thing I have seen for a long time.[1] I enclose an extract in the Nonconformist. Don't you think the ~~false~~ inaccuracy about the number of signatures ought to be corrected? It struck me that as Sec. to the Petition, you might write a short letter, stating the number of signatures, & the time it took to collect them, winding up by quoting that sentence of Mr. Mill's about the signal unexpectedly answered &c. as a literal account of the facts. You might write to the Nonconformist first, but I should write also to Blackwood, as Magazines sometimes insert corrections of misstatements of facts. I should do it with the most intense politeness. That seems to be the most effective way of meeting insolence.

The Guardian (Liberal High Church) the Nonconformist (fierce Dissenting) & the Pall Mall, reviewed my book favourably last week.[2] The Guardian notice is a very pleasant one, & I am glad of it, as it is a paper read at the Universities.

I am seeing life & enjoying the variety. We had a successful Schoolmistresses meeting at Leeds, preparatory to forming an Association.[3]

I like the latter part of your paper, the *positions* part, very much. Miss Edwards's letter is very telling. I think I can work up your material into a very suitable paper for the S⟨ocial⟩.S⟨cience⟩. ⟨Journal⟩, but I will send it to *you*, in case there should be anything you don't like about it.

The 1st article has appeared in the S.S. Journal & Dr. Lankester has promised to send me some copies, but they have not come to hand yet. I suppose you are taking care of the newspaper extracts. I should like to have them back some time.

Yours ever, ED.

GC: ALS ED B318

1. "The Great Unrepresented," *Blackwood's Edinburgh Magazine* (September 1866). Written by a woman who rejects the demand for female suffrage, the article asserts that "women, in England, and in most other civilised countries, are by no means badly off" (367) and criticizes Mill and his followers.

2. "Woman's Work," *Guardian* (Supplement), no. 1084 (12 September 1866): 954; "The Higher Education of Women," *Pall Mall* (14 September 1866): 833–34; *Nonconformist* (12 September 1866): 746.

3. "University Examinations for Girls" (Leeds, 1866) cited in GC Chronicle, 487b.

To Edward Plumptre

September 1866

... I have been asked to attend a meeting of schoolmistresses at Manchester on the 6th [October], chiefly for the purpose of talking to them about the London College. I am going to write to ⟨Queen's College⟩ Harley Street for

Prospectuses, but I should be much obliged if you would kindly let me know if there is anything not to be found in the Prospectus which it wd. be desirable to say with respect to Queen's College. I find among the higher class of schoolmistresses in all parts of the country, a strong disposition to put themselves into friendly relations with the London Colleges. They wd. like their schools to be to the Colleges what the Public Schools are to the Universities, but with that view they want the Colleges to be *really* places of higher education than schools can be. Hitherto they have been more like rival schools. In fact I have heard of a case in which a girl was sent first to College & then to school to finish. I do not see how this can be got over excepting by raising the age of the College students & giving them some higher kind of examn. than any that is open to schools. I believe there wd. be no difficulty in getting there from Cambridge, if the Colleges are willing to accept what the University has to give, that is, the examns. for ordinary Degrees. Mr. Markby thinks there wd. be no objection to holding examns. in the same papers, to be judged by the same standard, simultaneously with the examn. at Cambridge. They wd. have to send down a Conducting Examiner, which cd. be done as easily as in the case of the Local Examn. It wd. have to be done informally at first, as an experiment. If it were to be made permanent on the part of the University, some guarantee wd. probably be required as to the discipline of the College. It seems to me that this kind of affiliation to Cambridge wd., in the case of Queen's College, be much more satisfactory than anything we are likely to get from the London University, & I am sure it wd. make the College much more popular with the schools & more looked up to in the country generally than it now is. I am afraid Bedford College will be shut out by its constitution, as the Cambridge Little-go Examn. includes some little Theology & at Bedford College they get over the religious difficulty by excluding it.[1] I suppose Greek is more likely to be the stumbling block at Queens.

I do not know whether you have an entrance examn., except for the purpose of classification. The schoolmistresses insist very much that they want something to work up to. They wd. gladly prepare for the Colleges if they knew in what direction to work. I do not know how far it may be possible to meet them in this & other respects. There are now means of mutual communication which might be made use of, if necessary. There are Associations of Schoolmistresses already in London & at Manchester, & one is in course of formation for the West Riding. I think there will probably be some similar organisation before long for Newcastle & the neighborhood. We have come to these thro' the Local Examns., but we are finding more & more that the Local Examns. are not enough. They are very useful so far as they go, but the higher class of schools are not satisfied to 'finish' their pupils at seventeen. In fact they distinctly prefer not finishing at all, but transferring them to a different kind of discipline & a somewhat different kind of teaching.[2]

I shall be here [at Grasmere, with Anna Richardson] till the end of this week. Next week I go to Manchester....

GC: AMsS C489

1. The "Little-go," or Previous, Examination at Cambridge University was introduced in 1822; it tested elementary knowledge in classics, mathematics, and the tenets of the Established Church. Success in the Little-go Examination was a prerequisite for entrance into both the Honors (Tripos) course and the Ordinary Degree course.

2. Plumptre responded on 29 September 1866: "I doubt whether it wd. be wise to raise the age limits of admission until public opinion has ripened on the matter of employment for women" (Chronicle 494). Davies comments, "The failure of this effort was a great disappointment to me at the time, but it was no doubt a blessing in disguise, as if the existing Colleges had responded to our overtures, it would probably have stood in the way of the better things which were in store" (Chronicle 494–95).

To Helen Taylor

Benwell Parsonage. | Sept. 28th. 1866

My dear Miss Taylor

I was much obliged to you for your criticisms on the draft of the Petition. I had felt some hesitation about the clause which you find indefensible, & put it in tentatively. As except yourself, no one has made any remark upon it, I suppose it is a case in which authorities differ, & it is perhaps as well to get that view expressed in one of the Petitions. Mrs. Bodichon also pointed out the vagueness of Clause 3, & I should have liked to alter it, but did not see how to get rid of the vagueness without going more into detail than is admissible in a Petition.[1] So I am afraid we must be satisfied with such explanation as can be given in a statement circulated with the Petition. In the draft you have been good enough to send, I see nothing that I should hesitate about signing, but I think perhaps the two last Clauses might be made more generally acceptable by some slight alteration.[2] With regard to the phrase "no possibility of dangerous consequences"—there are people (of the Angel in the House school) who think there is danger (tho' they do not say it ought not to be incurred) that this & similar measures might diminish the tenderness & reverence with which some men are disposed to treat women. And I suppose that might be considered a dangerous consequence, tho' not in the ordinary sense of danger to the State.

In the last paragraph, the words "on the same conditions as men"—seem to me a little too definite.[3] Commonplace people, women as well as men, have a horror of what they call "women ~~pushin~~ wanting to be on an equality with men." And I should be glad to avoid anything that might possibly suggest that unpleasant phrase. There is also to be said that some people think if women vote, it must be by polling-papers, & they might sign a Petition, with that reservation unexpressed. Also, it is one of Miss Boucherett's ideas that we might perhaps get at first, the extension to women, with a higher qualification. I mention these considerations in case you may think there is sufficient reason for leaving the conditions indefinite. I showed the Petition to a clergyman a day or two ago, & he suggested that it would be better if the last clause were less specific. I am sending the draft to Mrs. Gurney & have asked her to let me know if she or Mr. Gurney have any suggestions to make. I think you would wish them, tho' you do not mention it. In such an important Petition as this, it seems desirable to get as great a variety of observations as possible. I do not think we could have managed to get ~~get~~ it printed in time for collecting signatures at Manchester, & this does not seem to me of much consequence, as the names we should get there, we can get almost as easily afterwards. It will be more an occasion for mutual consultation than for actual work. I am glad to learn from what you say, that Members of Parliament may sign. I had been told that they could not. With regard to the Committee, nothing is fixed. We propose to meet as soon as we can after we get back to Town. The first thing will be to settle whether to have a Committee at all. If that is decided in the affirmative, we must then pass some formal Resolutions, constituting ourselves, and we can then transact what business there may be on hand. In the meantime I think we may consider Mrs. Knox as our Sec., as she undertook before the Committee was proposed at all, to act as Sec. to these two Petitions. I am very sorry to hear from Mrs. Taylor that she & Mr. Taylor are both somewhat out of health. Their holiday has not done so much for them as they hoped.

    I saw *a* Report of the Conservative Meeting at Greenwich, but from what you say, I fancy the Telegraph must have represented the meeting as more definitely in our favour than I had supposed. I have been consulting my clerical friends here as to their influence over women. They are not conscious of possessing it. Some young ladies run after curates, but Mr. Maugham does not think any lady of the voting class would ~~not~~ consult him about her vote. I cannot help thinking that we may get this extension in less than ten years. The people I talk to seem very favourably disposed. But perhaps those I come across are above the average of reasonableness.

    Thank you for the Magazines, which my mother has received. I shall be sure to hear if there is anything in the Spectator. The Nonconformist put in some extracts from Blackwood, containing false statements about the signatures to our Petition. Mrs. Bodichon has sent an official contradiction. If they insert her letter, I hope it may be copied into some other papers. The same number of the Nonconformist contained a friendly notice of my little book. During the last two or three weeks it has been favourably noticed in the Guardian, the Inquirer, the Pall Mall & the Press.[4] So much approval from doubtful sources makes one suspect that the purport of the book must be unintelligible. Lady Goldsmid has sent me a letter from Mr. Bruce, who is President of the Education Dept. of the S.S. Association this year, promising to bring forward the education of girls in his opening address. He writes a very sensible, friendly letter about it. I think I had better send Lady Goldsmid a copy of the Petition. Her opinion is often worth having, as representing what other people are likely to notice. I am afraid there may be a little delay in hearing from Mrs. Gurney, as I believe they are from home, & I do not know where. I will write as soon as I hear, but I mention the possibility of delay, that you may not wait, unless you think it worth while. I received your letter on Tuesday, & should have answered it at once, but I have been so taken up with going to see old friends & parishioners at Gateshead, that it has been difficult to attend to anything else.

   I remain
   Yours very truly
   Emily Davies
I go on Tuesday to H. Philips, Esq.
   Crumpsall Lodge
   Cheltham Hill, Manchester
I feel a little hesitation in showing the Petition about without being expressly desired to do so, but I feel almost sure that you will like to have a variety of observations upon it before it is finally offered for signatures.

LSE: ALS 186

   1. The final wording of the petition from women householders included, as Clause 3: "That the reasons alleged for withholding the franchise from certain classes of Her Majesty's subjects do not apply to your Petitioners."
   2. The final petition included four clauses and no mention of "dangerous consequences."
   3. The final paragraph read: "Your Petitioners therefore humbly pray your Honourable House to grant such persons as fulfil all the conditions which entitle to a vote in the election of all Members of Parliament, excepting only that of sex, the privilege of taking part in the choice of fit persons to represent the people in your Honourable House."
   4. See ED to Barbara Bodichon, 17 September 1866.

To Helen Taylor

   "the beneficial effects of which would not be attended by any risk of danger to the State." or

"Would be unattended by any risk of dangerous political consequences."

"Your Petitioners therefore humbly pray that any Act for the Reform of Parliament hereafter to be passed may contain provisions granting the suffrage to women on such conditions as your Honourable House may see fit to determine."
or
"that in any Act for the Reform of Parliament hereafter to be passed, the disability of sex, by which the ~~right~~ privilege of voting is withheld from women otherwise legally qualified, may be abolished."

---

17 Cunningham Place. | London. N.W. | Oct. 15th 1866

My dear Miss Taylor

I have put down above the alterations which it might perhaps be desirable to make in the Petition. I doubt however whether it is worth while to alter the last paragraph but one, as no one to whom I have shown the original draft has raised any question about this clause. As to the last paragraph, I should rather prefer the first of the two alterations I have suggested, as being likely to be more generally acceptable, but the second expresses better what we do actually want. I enclose the draft as returned to me by Mrs. Russell Gurney. She says "We cannot pick any holes in this Petition. It seems to me very good. We just suggest a slight verbal alteration." I have heard nothing from Lady Goldsmid, from which I conclude that she has no objection to make. Miss Manning says "We think the Petition cleverly written & in an *interesting* way." She suggests (with hesitation) one or two little verbal alterations, which do not seem to me to be needed. My impression is, that the Petition as originally drawn, would be accepted by the great mass of our supporters without hesitation, but that some such alteration as I have suggested in the last clause, would make it more entirely satisfactory. We are well pleased with the work done at Manchester, in spite of Dr. Mary Walker, who was a grievous marplot. Mrs. Bodichon's paper is reported almost in full in the Manchester Guardian (which I sent you on Saturday) & this report has been copied into the Morning Post. There has been an article since in the Post, rather sneering & urging that women have so much power already that they would rather lose by having votes, but on the whole, more respectful & *neutral* than might have been expected. The subject was wonderfully well treated by the Association. It was announced in the Notices as "the principal subject for discussion on Tuesday." and Canon Richson, who was specially asked to take the Chair, consented very cordially. There were some funny little episodes. In coming out of the room, Mrs. Bodichon heard it remarked that the Association had received its death blow. "That the two Secretaries (Mr. Hastings & Mr. Clay) should speak in support of such a paper as *that*!"—We have the names & addresses of a good many people who are ready to help with the Petitions. A Tory squire who was staying in the same house with me was quite with us, & his wife took copies of the "qualified women's" Petition to show to her friends.

Miss Boucherett is coming up to-morrow to talk about "the winter's campaign." I do not see my way very clearly yet as to the best mode of working. Miss Boucherett says it is a crisis & she is going to sell her diamonds. "Plenty of money means plenty of Petitions & plenty of petitions means the Suffrage. D'Israeli would be very glad to give us the Suffrage, I believe, if we can only give him a good excuse for so doing." I don't ^quite^ agree with this, but that a person who lives among Tories should take such a sanguine view is in itself significant. I quite agree with Miss Boucherett that Petitions are *the* thing. I scarcely meet with anybody who objects, & where that is the case, all you have to do is to show that a good many people want it. I believe also, that with organisation & money, we can get up almost any number of Petitions & any number of signatures. There seems to me to be numbers of people only waiting to be asked, & that every signature is in a manner reproductive, as it emboldens somebody else, who would otherwise be afraid to sign. The expense however will be considerable. I think we shall have to go to the country for money, & that as in the case of the ^signatures to the^ first Petition, it will come when the signal is given. I have not seen Mrs. Taylor yet, but hope to do so before long.

It was in the September no. of Blackwood that the article on "The Great Unrepresented" appeared.[1] I think we ought to beg some, if not all, of Mrs. Bodichon's papers printed for distribution as soon as we can. That is one of the things to decide about when those of us who are in Town can meet, which I hope will be in a few days. Miss Wolstenholme very much wants papers for distribution. Are you intending to publish or reprint your article in Macmillan? I believe that would be very useful, & that Miss Wolstenholme would be glad to have fifty or a hundred at least. Among other things, we succeeded in starting an Association for Promoting the Employment of Women at Manchester which seems likely to do well. The point they are going to press is the introduction of women of a superior class into the factories. To get women into a *governing* position anywhere, seems to me a good thing, & there are plenty of reasons for getting it done in factories where women are already employed in the servile departments. There are some thorough people on the Committee who will not, I hope, let the matter drop.

I attended an interesting meeting of the Manchester Schoolmistresses' Association.[2] I was asked to go expressly to talk to them about the Colleges, and two facts were distinctly brought up. 1. That the schools want a place of higher education for which to prepare their pupils, which should be to them what the Universities are to boys' schools. and 2. that the existing ladies' Colleges do not supply the want. The chief reason of this is that the Colleges have no higher examns., of an external & public character, which are not also open to schools, &

unfortunately there is no chance of their getting them. The University of London will do nothing, & the ^secular^ constitution of Bedford College precludes it from being affiliated to Cambridge. (or, at least its manager thinks so, which comes to the same thing. The Cambridge Examns. for Degrees include a little Theology, which is not taught at Bedford College.) Queen's, which ~~might~~ need have no difficulty of this sort, will not move. It is under the management of the Professors, & they carry it on so successfully as a school for girls from 14 to 18, that they do not care to go in for changes. The only resource seems to be to found a new College. If we could start a College on a broad Church basis, accepting the University examns. as they are, ~~but~~ and accepting as much control as the University might desire, but with a Conscience clause effectually securing that religion should not be forced upon anybody that did not want it, I believe we might get affiliated to Cambridge, & that by so doing we should not only get the direct advantages of having one College connected with one of the old Universities, but should also shame the University of London into opening its examns. There would be a Nonconformist "case." We should be able to say, "Here are Churchwomen able to get a University Examn., & Dissenters are excluded from what professes to be their own University." In case such a College were ^attempted to be^ started, should you be disposed to help? It cannot be set on foot yet. The Local Examns. scheme, which is nominally on its trial, must be confirmed, & there must be a great deal done in the way of preparation both at Cambridge & among the Schoolmistresses. But the idea will have to be presented to people some time before we can attempt to carry it out, & I should like to know what you think of it.

I am afraid I have been rather long in returning the Petition. I did not want to write in a hurry, & one way & another, the Manchester meeting has made rather a drive, tho' not an unpleasant one.

Yours very truly
Emily Davies

LSE: ALS 187

1. See ED to Barbara Bodichon, 17 September 1866.
2. On 6 October 1866, ED attended a meeting of schoolmistresses in Manchester at which people expressed the need for an institution of higher education for their better students. ED reflected: "As I drove back from the meeting . . . it was borne in upon me that the only way to meet the situation wd. be to found a new College, fulfilling the desired conditions. . . . On reaching home I spoke of the idea to friends, & in process of time, drafted a Programme" (Chronicle 500).

To Helen Taylor

17 Cunningham Place. | N.W. | Oct. 31st 1866.

My dear Miss Taylor

I believe Mrs. Bodichon has written to you about our meeting & told you of the decisions arrived at.[1] I dare say she explained that the somewhat complicated arrangement finally adopted was not chosen as absolutely the best, but only as the best open to us.

That the nominal & the acting Secretary could be the same person would clearly be better, & if as we go on any one appears who is able & willing to be both, we shall be at liberty to make a change at any time. Miss Cook gladly accepts the proposal to be my coadjutor. Miss Manning cannot at present take any part beyond being on the Committee. She says she could not be even nominal Secretary without taking a great interest in what was going on, & for the present she is strictly forbidden to take an active interest in anything. She hopes that by taking great care for a few months she will get quite strong again, & then she may be able, if no one else has been found in the meantime, both to be Hon. Sec. & to do some work at it. I believe Mrs. Knox will act *pro tem*. I think we shall most likely begin to work the qualified women's Petition first, as that is already in circulation & there is no necessity for waiting. We shall send copies of it very extensively I expect & with it, Mrs. Bodichon's two papers, the one answering objections, & the Manchester one, giving reasons. For the general Petition I should think it would be wiser to do a good deal of preliminary work in the way of getting eminent names, before beginning to circulate it promiscuously. If you have no objection, I will ask Mrs. Knox to lay it before the Committee as originally drawn. Of course those who work under this Committee will be obliged to accept their decision, whatever it may be, but my impression is that it will be accepted without alteration as I have not heard any one express a *strong* opinion ~~on~~ against the last clause, & the fact that Mr. Mill & yourself are strongly for it will have great weight with the Committee. You have quite understood the drift of my suggestions. It seems to be a question as to the meaning of terms. I thought that in asking for the abolition of the law which makes sex a disability, we should imply equality. And as to the ⟨illegible⟩ alternative suggestion, my notion was that in leaving it to the House to improve conditions, we were not expressing any opinion of our own as to what the conditions ought to be, but only showing a confiding disposition, & a readiness to take as much as we could get. It seems very unlikely that a different qualification would be proposed. (& the earlier part of the Petition seems to me decidedly to imply that we think it ought to be the same.) & if it were, it could scarcely be considered final. I think the inequality would be the sort of inequality that there is between the thin & the thick end of the wedge. If any one asked me what I meant by "such conditions &c." I should reply that *I* think the conditions ought to be the same as for men, but that if the House chose to make the qualifications higher for women, or to make a rule that they should vote by polling papers, I would take that rather than nothing. It seems to me that to get *any* women allowed to vote on *any* conditions would be such an immense step that it would certainly lead very quickly to a great deal more. However, as I said before, I have no idea that a different qualification would be proposed, & my hesitation about the phrase is merely the result of having heard a great deal of repugnance, expressed by women as well as men, to definite assertions of equality. I think so much will depend on the weight of names attached to our Petitions. so much more than on anything we can say in the Petitions themselves—that I am perhaps over anxious not to frighten away anybody.

With regard to the clause about "dangerous consequences"—no one has pulled up at it. So that I am inclined to think it would be better to leave it as it was. I enclose a letter from Lady Goldsmid, received since I wrote to you last. I need not trouble you to return it. We shall probably be having a meeting of our Committee in about ten days. Perhaps you will be kind enough to let me have a final copy of the Petition within that time.

I agree with you that only supporters ought to be asked for money, & that it ought to be very carefully managed. A great deal may be done with a little money, if care is taken that none is wasted. The cheapest agitation I have heard of is that which resulted in the opening of the Durham Examns. They agitated three counties, got up a Memorial signed by mayors & Magistrates, Bishops & clergy & all sorts of people—& got what they wanted. And the whole thing cost less than ten pounds. They have just had their first Examn. Out of nine girls who went in, eight passed, & two came out in Honours, with the title of Literatee. I am afraid however that Durham honours do not count for much. The standard must certainly be lower than that of Cambridge. We shall have a fair increase in the numbers of our candidates this year & two or three new Centres. One girl, a clergyman's daughter, takes up among other things, Latin, Greek, Mathematics & Political Economy. It is a good thing to have these subjects taken up, as it contradicts the assertion (which they are always making in the London University) that whether they ought to be or not, they *were not* taught to girls. The Manchester Board of Schoolmistresses are going to discuss our Kensington question about subjects of education at their next meeting, & have asked for your papers & Mr. Fitch's to read.

I am glad you liked Miss Garrett's paper.[2] It was not *very* well reported, even in the Manchester Guardian. It is a protest against the theory that women, *as such*, are to be expected to work for love & not for money, & very forcibly put.

I remain, Yours very truly,
Emily Davies

LSE: ALS 188

1. The first official meeting of the Suffrage Committee was held on 20 October 1866. Present were ED, Bodichon, Boucherett, Cobbe, Garrett, Parkes, and Clementia Taylor. Louisa Garrett Smith, Harriet Cook, and Isa Craig Knox also joined.

2. Elizabeth Garrett, "Hospital Nursing" (NAPSS, 1866).

To Sir Edwin Chadwick

17 Cunningham Place. N.W. | Nov. 16th 1866

Dear Sir

I send you by this post, a copy of the Morning Post for to-day, containing an article on the Female Suffrage question. The article is founded on a letter of mine, suggested by your paper in the October Fraser, on Workhouse Reform. My point was, that in the case of Workhouses, the "influence" of ladies had failed, & I supported the argument by quotations from your article, which however (owing to the fear of making my letter too long) seem to have been too short to make *your* point clear, namely that the fault lay with the higher powers.

If you would kindly take the trouble to address a letter to the Morning Post, clearing this up, I think it would be useful. I am sorry that I have not retained a copy of my letter. It was anonymous (signed One of the Disabled) & I should wish to remain so.

I must ask you to forgive me for venturing, without introduction, to trouble you on a matter in which we take a common interest.

I remain
Dear Sir
Yours truly
Emily Davies

UCL: ALS ChadwickMSS.590

To Helen Taylor

17 Cunningham Place. | N.W. | Nov. 26th 1866.

My dear Miss Taylor

I send you a copy of the Minutes of our first meeting, held last Friday, which will I hope explain what we are proposing to do.[1] I also enclose two notes from Lady Goldsmid, which I will not trouble you to return. The Committee adopted Lady G.'s suggestion, & the last clause of the Petition now runs thus, "Your Petitioners therefore humbly pray that your Honourable House will take such measures as to your wisdom may seem fit for granting the suffrage to unmarried women & widows on the same condition on which it is, or may be, granted to men."

Mr. Hastings agrees with Sir Francis Goldsmid & Mr. Westlake on the legal question, & the Committee felt that in the face of their opinions, whether right or wrong, we could not assert that the terms of the Petition as originally drawn up would *not* include married women. It was also felt that the only way to get a fair hearing & to secure a large number of signatures is to keep quite clear of the wives question, which unless we can distinctly exclude it, would be perpetually brought forward by the newspapers & made the basis of discussion. Perhaps I ought to add that those who are strongest in favour of limiting the present claim do not consider themselves as at all giving up the rights of married women. It seems to be a question as to what is implied by the terms used. If asking for the suffrage for unmarried women & widows implies that we do *not* also desire it for wives, the most earnest advocates of the measure would be debarred from signing, but those who have expressed an opinion on the subject do not attach that meaning to the terms.

I will send you copies of all our papers as soon as I get them from the printer. The reason we enclose a Form of Adhesion instead of sending the Petitions for signature at once to "qualified" women, is that the as the signature includes a rather long statement about the qualifications, it was necessary to print the Petition on a large sheet, & the whole packet would be over the 1/2 oz. The present plan will involve writing again with the Petition, or at least sending a copy of it, to those who are preferred to sign, but as that will probably be not more than about one in ten of those to whom we send, the expense will be worth saving. Have you any idea when the return of the number of female freeholders & householders is likely to be forthcoming?

I should like to send a copy of the Petition & Mrs. Bodichon's pamphlet to each. To what extent that will be possible depends on the amount of money at our disposal. It will be a costly mode of agitation, but I think very effective in proportion to its cost, being generally educational, as well as directly tending to advance the immediate object.

I am glad to say Miss Manning is improving in health, but she & Mrs. Manning are both keeping very quiet for the present, & Mrs. Knox also will not be to be relied upon for work of any sort for some months. We have therefore decided to let the Kensington Society go to sleep for a little while. We shall not hold any discussions at present, & the new set of questions will not be issued till after Christmas. By that time I hope we may be able to resume work, having simply skipped one term.

The Law Officers of the Crown have decided that the Charter of the London University does not enable them to grant special Certificates to women. So we have escaped the offer of the Special Examn., which might have been very troublesome.

    I remain Dear Miss Taylor
    Yours very truly
    Emily Davies

LSE: ALS 189

    1. The Suffrage Committee met again on 23 November 1866, at which time the provisional committee was made permanent. The committee included eight women and five men: Alford, Boucherett, Cairnes, Clay, Cook, ED, Lady Goldsmid, Hastings, Heywood, Knox, Adelaide Manning, Smith, and Clementia Taylor.

To Helen Taylor

    17 Cunningham Place. | London N.W. | Dec. 15th 1866

My dear Miss Taylor

    I dispatched yesterday a packet of our various papers, including the general Petition as finally adopted by the Committee. With regard to connecting your name with it, I quite understand your feeling & should have respected it, even if you had said nothing. The Petition is now issued by the Committee & no individual is responsible for it. We are to meet again next week, to decide upon some plan for a systematic canvass for signatures. It will also be considered whether we ought to ask Members of the House of Commons to sign. I am inclined to think it will be better to leave them out altogether, as I fancy many would refuse on the ground of its not being in accordance with usage, & it would perhaps be rather damaging than otherwise to have only a few, & those not very influential.

    I do not quite know yet what will be done about the Kensington, but I think we shall most likely issue two new questions next month. The papers on Sacrifice are in circulation & ought to reach you before long. Instead of returning them to me, will you kindly forward them to "Mrs. Horace Davey, 15 Norfolk Square, W."

    You may not have heard perhaps that Mr. Fawcett is going to marry a younger sister of Miss Garrett's.[1] So we may now rely upon his being kept in the path of duty. Miss M. Garrett is rather young. (only nineteen) In other respects they seem likely to suit very well.

    Dean Alford has asked me to find some one to write an article on the Enfranchisement of Women for the Contemporary ⟨Review⟩. If you think of any good person to ask, would you kindly let me know.

    I remain

Yours very sincerely
Emily Davies.

LSE: ALS 190

1. Millicent Garrett. She married Henry Fawcett on 23 April 1867.

To Lydia Becker

ENFRANCHISEMENT OF WOMEN.
17 Cunningham Place. N.W. | Jan. 3d 1867

Madam

We have received the signed Petitions & I send you by this post some more copies. If you require more of the other papers we shall be glad to supply you. For the present, it is perhaps best to communicate with Mrs. Smith. But a Committee is in process of formation at Manchester & as soon as they get into work it will probably be most effective to work with them.[1] They intend, I understand, to canvass all the female householders in Manchester, so you will be sure to hear of them. I suppose they will also announce themselves in some way in the newspapers.

If you can favour us with any hints as to what may be most useful, in the way of papers &c. to those who are working with us, we shall be very much obliged to you. I write for Mrs. Smith, who is at present I am sorry to say, incapacitated by illness.

I am, Madam
Yours truly
Emily Davies.

Man: ALS M50/1: 2/1

1. The Manchester Suffrage Society was formed on 11 January 1867. The first meeting included Jacob Bright, Mrs. Gloyne, Max Kyllman, Reverend S. A. Steinthal, and E. Wolstenholme.

To Lydia Becker

ENFRANCHISEMENT OF WOMEN.
17 Cunningham Place. N.W. | Jan. 7th 1867.

Dear Madam

I now send you a packet of Petitions, which I fear I must by some inadvertence have omitted to do before. I will at once let the Manchester Committee know that you are ready to assist them, & will consult with them as to the best use to make of your paper. I have read it with much interest. It seems to me that tho' of course many of the arguments have been used before, there is a freshness in your manner of putting them, & we very much want to have the same thing said over & over again in a variety of forms.

There are some points on which I think you lay yourself open to reply. They are not very important, but we ought if possible to publish only what is unassailable. I will make a few notes that have occurred to me & ~~return~~ send them to you with the paper, in a day or two. Have you seen an article in the Spectator for Dec. 29th on "Political Women"?[1] It is a statement of some arguments on the other side. What you say as to the desirableness of bringing out our opponents, I entirely agree with. The result of the debate you mention is very significant. Do you know any persons in other places, out of Lancashire, who would help us in canvassing? If so, I should be glad to supply them with papers.

The plan of sending indiscriminately to female householders is in some respects very effective, but it has the disadvantage of being very costly.

I remain
Yours very truly
Emily Davies.

Man: ALS M50/1: 2/2

1. "Political Women at Washington," *Spectator* (29 December 1866).

To Lydia Becker

ENFRANCHISEMENT OF WOMEN.

17 Cunningham Place. N.W. | Jan. 12th 1867

Dear Madam

I think I understood that in your paper you speak of the number of Petitioners absolutely, not relatively.[1] But I fancy that readers, especially hostile ones, will rejoin—"Yes—1500—but what are they among so many?" I think it is usually taken for granted that every woman might have signed, & that the overwhelming majority who did not, abstained deliberately. This consideration applies also I think to the question of indiscriminate canvassing. There can be no doubt that the more we canvass, the better chance we have of obtaining a larger number of signatures, & as nobody knows (speaking generally) how much or how little we have canvassed, the absolute number is of great importance. We have also to remember that this is our only way, or almost the only way, of getting at people. Men can hold public meetings, which get noticed in the papers,

& so attention is called to what they are doing. But this kind of agitation would probably do us more harm than good.

I think too that what you say about the want of preparation in people's mind tells in favour of general canvassing. In the great number of cases in which we get no response, we may have done good by preparing the way.

There is also to be considered that at present we are finding out our friends. We do not know yet how many people there may be all about the country who would be glad to help if they knew of an organisation to which they could attach themselves.

The people who wish to form a Manchester Committee were to meet yesterday. I dare say you will hear from them soon. Thank you for mentioning Miss Susan Davies. I have seen her & she will I know be glad to help. We have not done anything at Brighton yet.

The statement about qualifications was compiled from a book on the subject by a Parliamentary agent. It says "land" simply, & nothing about houses, so I think the latter cannot be included. I cannot find in this book a distinct answer to your other question, but I will make inquiry & let you know the result.

I remain
Yours very truly
Emily Davies.

Would you be kind enough to send me your paper when it is ready? I think may be able to make use of it *soon*.

Man: ALS M50/1: 2/3

1. Becker was working on a paper on women's suffrage.

To Lydia Becker

ENFRANCHISEMENT OF WOMEN.

17 Cunningham Place. N.W. | Jan. 14th. 1867

Dear Madam

The enclosed letter (from the wife of a lawyer) shows that you are right about the qualifications.[1] We must add the word "house" to any future edition of the explanatory statement. Many thanks for the circular, in which I am much interested.

Yours very truly
Emily Davies.

Man: ALS M50/1: 2/4

1. Alice Hare Westlake.

To Lydia Becker

ENFRANCHISEMENT OF WOMEN.
17 Cunningham Place. N.W. | Jan. 17th 1867

Dear Miss Becker

I have written to the Dean of Canterbury, who is the Editor of the Contemporary Review, about your paper.[1]

The Dean wrote to me some time ago about an article for the Contemporary, & I have great hopes that he will insert your paper.

If he asks to see it, I will take the liberty before sending it to him of making some slight alterations, which will I think make it more suitable for the Contemporary. e.g. I think it will be better to omit what you have said about Mr. Mill. I should like also to omit the sentence in which you say that we cannot tell without trying whether women would use their votes better tha or worse than men. That argument is often used with reference to opening professions, & the rejoinder is that we can judge by what we know already without having specific experience in every particular case. I think this argument, when not pressed too far, is sound. E.g. it might be said. "We cannot tell beforehand what would be the effect of giving votes to idiots, therefore let us try it." This is is putting it in an extreme way, but many people say, in effect—"We know what women are. We know that they have not the qualities which are essential to a good voter. So what is the use of trying?" There are a good many answers to this argument, such as that we do not know yet what women would be under altered conditions, &c. But I think it is better not to provoke the rejoinder, without at the same time answering it, & it is very difficult to answer effectively, because there are such endless differences of opinion about the nature of women &c.

I quite agree with what you say as to the Manchester Committee. It seems to me also that as the Petitions *are* in circulation, there can be no doubt as to the desirableness of working at them, whether this may be the very best time or not. I quite expect that Mr. Mill's advice will be to this effect.

You will certainly have a Proof of your paper, if it gets so far.

Yours very truly

Emily Davies.

Man: ALS M50/1: 2/5

1. Lydia Becker's paper, "Female Suffrage," was published in the *Contemporary Review* (March 1867). See ED to Lydia Becker, 12 January 1867.

To Lydia Becker

ENFRANCHISEMENT OF WOMEN.

17 Cunningham Place. N.W. | Jan. 19th [1867]

Dear Miss Becker

I think you are right about your paper, & that it will be best to make a fair copy for the Dean. Would you try to write as plainly as possible? I find your hand rather difficult to read, especially when an I or a t happens not to be dotted or crossed. I enclose Dean Alford's note. He was evidently interrupted in writing, & then sent off his note without remembering that it was unfinished.

If the article does not appear till April, it will probably require some modification, but that can be done in Proof.

What you say about the sentence on ownership in Mrs. Westlake's letter struck me also. I think it is a mistake. The real fact I believe is that ownership goes for nothing unless the person resides within seven miles, & that probably I will try & get a more definite answer to your question and let you know.

The Manchester Committee seem to be a little confused about the Petitions. They might help in a systematic way at the National Petitions without getting up a local one, & that I should think would be the best thing to do at present. At any rate it is not worth while for you to send us your paper till they have decided.

Do you ever write letters to newspapers? I believe there is to be an letter attack upon us in to-day's Spectator.[1] If you could get hold of it & answer it, I think it would be useful.

Ever yours truly
Emily Davies.

Man: ALS M50/1: 2/6

1. *Spectator* (2 February 1867). The letter, signed S.D.C., argued "that English women in general have not yet reached the stage of development at which [voting] would be useful, either to themselves or others."

To Barbara Bodichon

17 Cunningham Place. N.W. | Jan., 29th 1867.

My dear Mrs. Bodichon

I wonder whether you are still full of the earthquake.[1] I hope not *quite*, as I am full of the College & must discourse about it. Since I wrote to you last, I have been staying with the ⟨Sir Benjamin⟩ Brodies & learnt a great deal from them & in other ways, at Oxford. I saw Mr. Mark Pattison, & he entered warmly into the idea. It grieves him that we look to Cambridge instead of Oxford, but Lady Brodie says they are not ready for it yet, & if we can do it with Cambridge first, they will get up another by & by, perhaps at Reading. In the meantime, both Lady Brodie & Sir Benjamin take to ours in the friendliest way, & will I believe give us very valuable help. It raised my spirits still higher than they were before to find them so interested in the idea, because they can look at it from both sides, knowing both the College system, & the sort of young women whom we hope to get. Their approval seems like the sanction of practical people. I believe it is partly owing to their having found it answer so well to send their eldest girl from home. They did it with great hesitation & it has worked most satisfactorily.

Now that the Scheme is about to be brought down from the clouds, it seems necessary to make some sort of statement about it. I have drawn up the Programme of which I enclose a Proof. Several people have seen it & approve, but it is only a kind of preliminary statement, subject to modification. I believe the next step must be to get up a Committee. I propose bringing it before our Examn. Committee, at our next meeting, but not asking them to take it up *as* a Committee, as I think we want a larger & more influential body, to give weight. The best plan seems to be to have a rather large general Committee of distinguished people, to guarantee our *sanity*, & a small Executive, to do the work. Mr. Roby, the Sec. of the Schools Inquiry Commission, who has befriended us very much all thro', thinks Lord Lyttelton will very likely accept the office of Chairman, & that we could not have a better. If we can get Lord Lyttelton who has the reputation of being rather High Church, to be Chairman, & Lady Goldsmid to be Treasurer, I think the comprehensiveness of the Scheme will be pretty well guaranteed.

The next question will be how to set about raising the money.[2] We are told that we ought to ask for £30,000 at least, as besides the expense of building we ought to have something in hand, in case we do not at first get students enough to make the College pay. It is not a large sum, considering that there is to be but one College of this sort for Gt. Britain & Ireland & the Colonies, & considering how easy it is to raise immense sums for boys' schools. But considering how few people really wish women to be educated, it is a good deal. Everything will depend I believe, on how we start. If we begin with small subscriptions, a low scale will be fixed & everybody will give in proportion. I do not know yet what anybody is going to do, except myself. I mean to give £100, & I believe Lizzie Garrett will do something the same, but she cannot put down her name at present, as she is still partly dependent on supplies from home. Will you consider what you can do, & will you also talk to Nannie about it. The money need not of course be paid at present. What we want is a few promises of large sums, to lead other people on. I think that for one thing, it will make a good deal of difference as to getting support in other ways.

I don't think Lord Lyttelton would like to be Chairman of a beggarly concern that would be struggling with pecuniary difficulties all its days. And I am anxious to get him, as besides being a thoroughly *good* man personally, & very much respected, he has access to the Prince of Wales & Miss Burdett Coutts & all sorts of people. As soon as I hear from you, I shall go to Lady Goldsmid, Mr. Russell Gurney, Mr. James Heywood, the Westlakes & two or three other people who are likely to be interested, & we may then I hope make a beginning at looking out for a site &c. I hope we shall be able to get ⟨Alfred⟩ Waterhouse, the architect of the Manchester Assize Courts. He is going to restore Balliol College, which is as Lady Brodie says, is the very best training he could have for our purpose. I am anxious that the building should be as beautiful as we can make it. As we cannot have traditions & associations we shall have to get dignity in every other way that it open to us.

You will no doubt see somewhere that the three medical students, Misses ⟨Sarah⟩ Goff, ⟨Frances⟩ Morgan & Phillips passed their first examn. at Apothecaries Hall.[3] Miss Goff is married to-day to one of the London Hospital doctors.[4] She means to go on, & her husband is quite indignant if it is suggested that she is likely to stop. Miss Philips also is engaged. The two bridegrooms were waiting outside till the result of the examn. was known. Miss Morgan said she felt like the ugly duck, having to walk away unattended.

The Franchise affairs are going on fairly well, so far as we can tell, but all we know is that a good many people are at work in different parts of the country. The uncertainty about what may happen in Parliament makes it difficult to know what is best to do. Miss Cook is in London now. She works well & is a very pleasant companion. We talk a good deal about the College. She is anxious that it should be set on foot before all the girls she knows are too old to go to it. We have not received our Class-list from Cambridge yet, but I hear the girls have done very well in Shakespeare. Bessie has given me your message about the brooch.[5] I think we shall probably be glad to have it for the best Junior, to whom no prize has been offered otherwise.

I hope Algiers is suiting Nannie this winter. I hear of her & of you all pretty often from Jane Crow.

Please give my love to the party.
Ever yours affectionately
Emily Davies.

GC: ALS ED B5

1. On 2 January 1867, a severe earthquake occurred in Algiers, destroying hundreds of homes and killing at least seventy people.

2. Plumptre had advised ED that it would not be possible to "build . . . anything worth speaking of for less than £30,000" (Chronicle 512).
3. Probably Ellen Phillips. See ED to Helen Taylor, 4 August 1866.
4. Nathaniel Heckford.
5. Bodichon offered a brooch as a prize for the girls taking the Examinations.

To Edward Plumptre

February 1867

I send you a kind of Programme of a new College for women, which we hope to get affiliated to Cambridge. The project has grown out of the ⟨Schoolmistresses⟩ meetings ~~of~~ . . . about which I wrote to you in the autumn. After seeing the schoolmistresses & hearing what they had to say, I felt that what they wanted could not be supplied by either of the existing colleges. It wd. take them too far out of their track. The only resource seems to be to try what we can do with a fresh start. The Scheme is rather in the clouds as yet, but there seems to be a fair prospect of its being carried out. If it comes to anything, I hope you will kindly allow us to draw upon your experience for advice & & suggestions, as occasions arise.

GC: AMsS C511

To Lydia Becker

ENFRANCHISEMENT OF WOMEN.

17 Cunningham Place. N.W. | Feb. 4th 1867

Dear Miss Becker

I forwarded your MS at once to Dean Alford, & as I have not heard from him since, I hope it is accepted. I dare say it will want a little modification to bring it down to the date at which it will appear, but that can be done in Proof.

We are to have a meeting of our Committee on Friday. By that time I hope we may see our way a little more clearly as to what is best to be done. We are getting some very good names, but I think we shall have to make a vigorous effort towards the end, for *numbers*.

I remain
Yours very truly
Emily Davies.

Man: ALS M50/1: 2/7

To Anna Richardson

Feb. 4 1867

...I send you also a kind of Programme of the College, by which you will see that the vision is beginning to come down from the clouds.[1] This is merely a preliminary statement, submitted to criticism (which please give,) but there seems a fair prospect of getting to work. I forget how much I have told you already, but I know it is since I last wrote that I have been at Oxford, staying with the Brodies [Sir Benjamin & Lady B. who was a Miss Thompson, friends of Mme. Bodichon's.] & have got my ideas about College life made clearer than they were. The Brodies take up the idea of the College in the friendliest way, & I value their sanction very much, because they have 5 daughters of their own, from seventeen downwards, about whom they are constantly thinking & in an enlightened unselfish spirit. We are going to ask Lord Lyttelton to be our Chairman & to have a large general Committee of great people (to guarantee our sanity.) & a small Executive to do the actual work. Miss Wolstenholme has brought the Scheme before the Manchester Board of Schoolmistresses & they passed unanimously a vote of warm approval.... It seems to be agreed that we must not ask for less than £30,000. That sounds a large sum, but considering that we have Great Britain & Ireland & the Colonies to get it from, & an unlimited time, it does not seem to be hopelessly large. The great thing is to begin with considerable sums. I have written to Mme. Bodichon to ask her what she & Nannie Smith will do, & when I hear from her I must see about Lady Goldsmid & the Russell Gurneys & two or three other rich people who are likely to be interested, & who will I hope head the subscription list with considerable sums. I do so hope we shall be able to get a beautiful building. We shall want to get dignity in that way, as we cannot have traditions & associations, at least for some time. Waterhouse, the architect on whom we have set our affection, is going to restore Balliol College, which as Lady Brodie says, will be the very best training he could have for our purpose.

I enjoyed my little visit to Oxford extremely. It is a delightful place & there are delightful people in it. Mr. Mark Pattison, the Rector of Lincoln College, is much interested in our Scheme. He asks pathetically, 'But *why* Cambridge? Why not Oxford?' & says I think we have more hold at Cambridge because I have not talked to Oxford men. But Lady Brodie says we are quite right to begin with Cambridge & they will follow by & by. I saw Mr. ⟨Friedrich⟩ Max Müller & had a little talk with him about his method of teaching language. I have the French book on 'Grammaire comparée' & also the volume containing Mr. Müller's Evidence, which I want you to read. The volume is very large, much too big to send by post, so I think I had better keep it till you come for it. When will that be? Are you coming up to the Yearly Meeting? [Quaker.] Do come at any rate for something. I will take you to see Mrs. Russell Gurney, who grows more & more heavenly, & her beautiful house, & the picture of Mr. Gurney if he is not forthcoming.

I want you very much to talk about the College. There is so much to say about it, to talk over, I mean. & it must be with a kindred spirit. Miss Cook & I talk about it continually. She is very anxious that it shd. be begun before all her young friends are too old to go to it. We are composing a hymn in its praise, partly adapted from an ancient composition. It begins—

For thee, O dear dear college
Mine eyes their vigils keep
For very love, beholding
Thy happy name, they weep.
O sweet & beloved College
The home of the elect,
O sweet & beloved College
Which eager hearts expect.
&c. &c.

Will you finish it? (Remember I *have* a reverent soul at the bottom, tho' it is a little way down.)

I want to know how you are all getting on. We are all very well, the 5 children rosy & plump & improving in behavior. They are precious little gifts....

GC: AMsS C512

1. The first draft programme "proposed to establish a College, in which the instruction and discipline ... [would] be expressly adapted to advanced students, and the results tested by sufficiently stringent examinations." The Programme also proposed "to place the College ... equidistant between London and Cambridge ... [and specified that] the projected institution ... [was] designed to be, in relation to the higher class of girls' schools and home teaching, what the Universities are to the public schools for boys" (Programme for a College for Women, 1867, GC: ED VII-GC I/4).

To Lydia Becker

ENFRANCHISEMENT OF WOMEN.
17 Cunningham Place. N.W. | Feb. 9th 1867.

Dear Miss Becker

Since I wrote to you last, we have had a great trouble. The illness of our Secretary, Mrs. Smith, terminated fatally Wednesday last.[1] She had been getting worse for some time, but hopes were entertained of her recovery almost to the last. Of course this stops everything almost, for the moment. There is great difficulty in appointing a successor, as those who are engaged in other departments of our work do not feel it desirable to make themselves officially responsible for this also. In our dilemma, we have fallen back upon Mrs. Bodichon. I have her authority to use her name & address & we shall do so for the present, Miss Cook & I doing the actual work.

As soon as possible we shall have fresh letters &c. drawn up in Mrs. Bodichon's name. In the meantime, we can of course go on supplying people with Petitions &c. I am sorry to say I have mislaid your letter containing the address of a lady to whom you wished me to send papers. Will you kindly let me have it again? We have done a good deal at Cambridge, & are preparing a new list of names, containing those of Senior Wranglers, Fellows of Colleges, &c. Mrs. Liveing has been written to. Mr. Fawcett is strongly in our favour. He thinks Mr. Mill ought to bring the subject before the House in some way or other, & evoke an expression of opinion, which he thinks would very likely show that we had more adherents than we are aware of.

Mr. Darwin has been asked to sign & has declined. I think his wife signed. At any rate she has sent a subscription.

Mr. ⟨Samuel⟩ Steinthal was present at our Committee yesterday, for part of the time. He told me they hoped to have you as Sec. at Manchester, & if so, the pushing forward of the matter will be practically in your hands. It was agreed yesterday that we could not fix a time for presenting the Petitions. Miss Helen Taylor advises presenting both this Session, but to keep the lists open to the last moment. And I suppose that is Mr. Mill's opinion also. I shall write again, either to Miss Wolstenholme or yourself before your committee meets. Yours very truly E. D.

Man: ALS M50/1: 2/8

1. On 6 February 1867, Louisa Garrett Smith, who had been ill for a week, died suddenly. Her death left the suffrage committee without a secretary while they were gathering signatures for the petition.

To Lydia Becker

ENFRANCHISEMENT OF WOMEN. | 2, WARRINGTON CRESCENT, LONDON. W.
17 Cunningham Place. N.W. | Feb. 15th 1867.

My dear Miss Becker

I enclose Mr. Westlake's answer to your question about qualifications. When you have done with it, will you kindly return it. In any fresh edition of our explanatory statement, we must make some modifications.

I am anxious to hear what plan of action you have decided upon for Manchester. May I ask you to be kind enough to keep me informed occasionally of what is going on? I was very glad to hear that you had received your Proof, as it shows that the article is at at any rate accepted & will appear some time, even if it does not, as I hope it may, next month.

I believe Mr. Mill has quite decided to bring the question before the House very soon.

I fancy he cannot quite decide till the Liberal party have made up their minds what course to take upon the Govt. Resolutions. My idea is that the best plan will be to present one general Petition *soon*, then the Manchester one, if you make it separate (as I rather hope you may have decided to do) & perhaps a little later but still during the present Session, the Householders'. I think it very important that the last should be as numerously signed as possible, because *the* thing we have to persuade people of is that the women who would get it, want it.

I shall like very much to see any report that may be printed of your Literary Society.[1] I was very glad to hear that your first meeting had been successful.

I remain
Yours very truly
Emily Davies.

Man: ALS M50/1: 2/9

1. Becker founded the Manchester Ladies' Literary Society in 1868.

To Lydia Becker

ENFRANCHISEMENT OF WOMEN. | 2, WARRINGTON CRESCENT, LONDON. W.
17 Cunningham Place. N.W. | Feb. 16th. 1867

Dear Miss Becker

I am afraid it is now too late to answer S.D.C.[1]

I doubt very much whether the Spectator would put in an answer so long after, & I am not sure that it may not be as well to let the matter die. If it were taken up at all *now*, I think it must be in a manner on its own ground, with only an allusion to the letter of S.D.C.'s as containing some arguments on the other side.

In any case, I think it would be better to deal with her arguments only, without any reference to her manner of stating them. It is not a matter of much interest to the public whether S.D.C. writes good grammar or not, & tho' it is a temptation to criticise & *expose* one's enemies, it seems to me better not to do it.

I think people are more inclined to listen to any one who has manifestly tried to understand & make the very best of the arguments on the other side.

In women especially the slightest appearance of being angry or contemptuous, offends, & provokes opposition. Even tho' I am so strong on your side, the impression your letter gives me is that you have not quite understood S.D.C. E.g. with regard to the paragraph about obscurantism, I think what she means to say is this—"You, who have set your hearts on getting votes, fancy that we, who take the other side, want to keep women in darkness. It is not really so. We want to encourage thought & political life, only we do not think this is the way to do it." ~~When you come~~ It is for us to show that it *is* the way, & when you come to that, I think you do it very triumphantly, & in an *interesting* way. But I fancy it would be more telling without the preface which would strike many people as almost a personal attack. It is I suppose a general rule that in all controversy, a tone of even exaggerated courtesy to the other side, is best, but I am sure it is so as regards to women. People notice our manners more than our arguments, & the one thing they fear is that by descending into the arena, as they call it, women might get their polish rubbed off. Sarcasm, unless it be of the tenderest sort (like Melissa's "gentle satire, kin to charity, that harms not.") will not be endured from women. S.D.C. damages herself, not us, when she calls our arguments "childishly absurd." I venture to make these very free remarks, because I think those who have not had experience in this controversy scarcely know how much depends on scrupulous avoidance of the slightest tinge of bitterness. It was because your article contained so much good sense expressed in a somewhat playful form, & so little indignation, that I was anxious to have it published.

Our Committee have decided not to ask Members of Parliament to *sign* the Petition, as it would be unusual, but the question of sending it to them, has not been considered. I think it was sent last year, after it had been presented. The only reason for not sending it is that Members get such an enormous quantity of papers of all sorts sent to them, that they for the most part, simply consign the whole mass to the waste-paper basket. And it does not seem worth while to spend money & time with so small a prospect of any result. It is possible that our Committee may send round a little notice just before Mr. Mill brings the question up. But we do not know yet what he is going to do, & I don't suppose he will decide till after the meeting of the Liberal party next Thursday.

Are you going to have a separate Petition from Manchester? I suppose you know that you can have any of our papers, pamphlets &c. at cost price, which would probably be rather less expensive than getting them reprinted.

I hope this work will not be too much for you. There will be a great deal to do, & I am afraid you are not very strong.

Ever yours truly
Emily Davies.

Man: ALS M50/1: 2/10

1. *Spectator* (2 February 1867). See ED to Lydia Becker, 19 January 1867.

To Lydia Becker

ENFRANCHISEMENT OF WOMEN. | 2, WARRINGTON CRESCENT, LONDON. W.
17 Cunningham Place. N.W. | Feb. 22d 1867

Dear Miss Becker

I have to thank you for copies of the Manchester Petition & of your address, which I shall be very glad to read.

As I have not yet heard anything from Miss Taylor of what Mr. Mill intends to do, I have not much to report. Signatures have been collected at Nottingham by two ladies, Miss Turner & Miss Sunter. I do not know anything of them personally. If a Committee is formed at Liverpool, I should think they would arrange with the Manchester Committee for some division of labour. I do not think we in London can do anything about it, not knowing the locality, beyond forwarding to you any Lanchashire letters that come to us.

I have forwarded part of your letter to Miss Wolstenholme. It seems to me a very good rule to try to understand the meaning of what people definitely say—only it is not always sufficient, owing to the defectiveness of language & of our powers in using it. E.g. the meaning I attribute to S.D.C. seems quite obvious & certain, not conjecture at all, to me, while to you it is quite otherwise. Perhaps that is because the most important word, 'obscurantism,' is familiar to me, & conveys a definite meaning, which it does not to you.

Ever yours truly
Emily Davies

Man: ALS M50/1: 2/11

To Lydia Becker

ENFRANCHISEMENT OF WOMEN. | 2, WARRINGTON CRESCENT, LONDON. W.
17 Cunningham Place | Feb. 25th 1867

Dear Miss Becker

Miss Taylor wishes to supply her pamphlet gratuitously for distribution.[1] She does it thro' Mrs. Peter Taylor, who will send you 100 copies, & more if you want them. I suppose Miss Taylor prefers this mode of helping to direct contributions to our funds. She & Mr. Mill have not subscribed.

I wonder in what way it is that the Manchester independent organisation has already worked for good. One likes to know the particulars of anything encouraging that may be going on. I hear nothing from Miss Taylor & begin to fear that after all, Mr. Mill is not going to do so much for us in Parliament as we had hoped. Were not you rather disappointed to see that he had given notice of something àpropos of the Reform Resolutions, about voters in different constituencies joining together to return a member? If Mr. Mill postpones our claims, & cares more for the representation of minorities than for removing our disability, what can we expect from other people? However, I don't want you to share my feeling of discouragement.

Yours very sincerely,
Emily Davies.

Man: ALS M50/1: 2/12

1. Helen Taylor, "The Ladies' Petition," *Westminster Review* 31 (January 1867): 63–79. Reprinted as "The Claims of Englishwomen to the Suffrage Constitutionally Considered," London.

To Lydia Becker

ENFRANCHISEMENT OF WOMEN.

17 Cunningham Place. N.W. | Feb. 28th 1867

Dear Miss Becker

I have to-day received a letter from Miss Helen Taylor in which she says, "It would greatly increase the practical value of the Petition if they could be presented within a fortnight or three weeks, as if any move is made in the House of Commons on the subject, it is very likely to be made within that time, and it would be desirable that the Petitions should have been presented first."

We shall have a meeting of our Committee on Friday the 8th, & I suppose it will then be decided to call in the signatures at once, & to issue a notice to that effect to our supporters, so far as we know where to find them. I dare say the Manchester Committee will hear something from Mr. Mill before your next meeting, but as you are concerned in the Householders' Petition, it may be convenient to you to know at once, what (as far as I can guess) our Committee is likely to do.

I suppose you will very soon see your article in the Contemporary. I am so glad it appears just now, at the most opportune moment.

We have sent a copy of our general Petition with the list of names & *one* of Mrs. Bodichon's pamphlets. (Reasons.) to all the Members of Parliament.

It was not in deference to Mr. Kingsley that our headings has been altered. The limitation of the demand was decided upon after elaborate consideration & discussion, last autumn. The limitation was expressed in the qualification-statement, & at the head of the list of names. It was omitted, for brevity's sake, on the note-paper. But at the last meeting it was agreed that it would be better to put it in, everywhere, that there might be no mistake. It is a point on which the Committee & the great majority of the people who are working for us, are unanimous. I mean as to the *expediency* of the limitation. Of course if there was any chance of getting the whole loaf, we should like it better than the half. Ever yours sincerely

Emily Davies

Man: ALS M50/1: 2/13

To Lydia Becker

ENFRANCHISEMENT OF WOMEN. | 2, WARRINGTON CRESCENT, LONDON. W.
17 Cunningham Place. N.W. | March 9th 1867

Dear Miss Becker

At our meeting yesterday it was decided to close the lists of signatures on the 25th Inst. I suppose this will allow time enough to get the Petitions presented before Mr. Mill's motion comes on. We are to meet again next Friday, (the 15th.)

Thank you for the report of your correspondence. It seems to me likely to be extremely useful. Part of Mr. James's letter was copied into the yesterday's Pall Mall Gazette. I suppose you have seen your article in the Contemporary by this time. It is being read & talked about & people ask—"Who is Miss Becker?"

Miss Taylor's pamphlets were sent you by Mrs. P. A. Taylor of Aubrey House, Notting Hill. W. I have let her know that they arrived safely.

I remain

Yours very truly

Emily Davies.

We have had a letter from a gentleman who does not like our Petition, because Clause 4 is not logically consistent with Clause 2. I dare say he will sign yours if you think it worth while to ask him. His address is

Sir George Young
Temple
London
E.C.

Man: ALS M50/1: 2/14

To Barbara Bodichon

ENFRANCHISEMENT OF WOMEN. | 2, WARRINGTON CRESCENT, LONDON. W.
| 17 Cunningham Place. | March 9th 1867

My dear Mrs. Bodichon

We have been very grieved to hear of your illness & are glad now to think of your being better.[1] By the time this reaches you, I hope you will be almost well. But I am not going to trouble you with a long letter.

Bessie will explain to you that we have had some trouble in arranging the Franchise business. About a month ago, Mrs. Smith was unexpectedly taken from us. The old difficulty about a Sec. revived, & as before, we fell back upon you. We are venturing to use your name & address for the present, & we hope to hear from you that you do not object & that we may go on, at any rate till those Petitions are presented, which will, we hope, be in less than a month.

Mrs. Smith's death was a great blow to us. To Elizth. Garrett, the loss is quite irreparable, & she was one of my most intimate friends. But of course the loss to her little children is the worst. Hoping soon to hear of or from you, I remain

Your very affecn.
ED.

GC: ALS ED B6

1. Bodichon, who was in Algiers, was seriously ill with a fever.

To Lady Brodie

March 11th 1867

... I have been getting a good deal of criticism from schoolmistresses.[1] They are very cordial & more encouraging than anybody else. What they say is that they think the girls will want to come to the College & that if girls set their hearts upon a thing they can generally persuade their parents.... I suppose you have heard of Mrs. Bodichon's illness, a rather bad attack of fever. She seems much better now. I saw a letter from her yesterday which was quite like herself, but she is ordered to leave Algiers, & Miss Parkes is going off to-day to meet her at Marseilles.

GC: AMsS C517

1. ED had been sending out copies of the programme for the proposed College for Women to schoolmistresses and potential supporters. She received a good deal of encouragement from schoolmistresses. On 14 February 1867, Plumptre responded favorably to the

programme, saying "I shall be very glad to give any counsel or information in my power, if your scheme ripens into a fact. I am, I own, a little startled at the magnitude of your enterprise" (Chronicle 512). Roby's response on 27 February 1867 mentioned that he had received a letter from Dr. [Frederick] Temple, who felt that the "scheme deserves encouragement, but that it will fail, the Public not being yet in a right frame of mind to accept such schemes" (Chronicle 516). Roby concluded, "I am disappointed at Dr. Temple's not being more sanguine, but at the same time am not at all inclined to be deterred by it" (Chronicle 517).

To Lydia Becker

ENFRANCHISEMENT OF WOMEN. | 2, WARRINGTON CRESCENT, LONDON. W.
17 Cunningham Place. N.W. | March 16th 1867

Dear Miss Becker

No day has been fixed for the presentation of the Petitions. I suppose it will be left to the convenience of the members who present them, on the understanding that it is to be as soon as possible after the 25th Inst. We are sending a formal application to Mr. Russell Gurney & Mr. Bruce (late Vice-President of the Committee of Council) to present the Householders' & the general Petition, respectively. Mr. Bruce has already signified his willingness, & we are pretty sure of Mr. Gurney. We hope the local Petitions will be presented by the local members. You have a very good man in Mr. E. James.[1] They are doing well at Edinburgh, but the want of workers is felt everywhere. At Edinb. they employ a paid agent to canvass the poorer districts.

Miss Boucherett found her statement about Mr. Disraeli on a remark made by him in the House last Session, which a good many people understood as a reductio ad absurdum but which Miss Boucherett thinks was meant for advocacy.

Your article was not offered to the Contemporary as an unpaid contribution, & I have no doubt it will be paid for eventually tho' it may be some time hence. I do not see however why that should make any difference as to reprinting it, as it is a private matter with which no one but yourself has any concern.

It would be convenient to us to have the bulk of your householders' signatures on Saturday. Any that come in after might be sent by post on Monday. I am afraid the number of householders will not be very large, even when they are all collected together, but if we get 1000, as I think we shall, it will be enough to make an impression.[2]

Ever yours truly
Emily Davies.

Man: ALS M50/1: 2/15

1. See ED to Lydia Becker, 9 March 1867.

2. The London committee collected 3,559 signatures. The Manchester committee collected 3,161.

To Lydia Becker

ENFRANCHISEMENT OF WOMEN. | 2, WARRINGTON CRESCENT, LONDON. W.
17 Cunningham Place. N.W. | March 19th 1867

Dear Miss Becker

As the sum you have to send is so small, will you kindly send it in stamps. That is less trouble on both sides than a Post-office order. You will be glad to hear that Mr. Russell Gurney & Mr. Bruce have consented to present the Petitions. We consider it a great lift to have the support of two Members, so much respected with in & out of the House.

Mr. Myers wrote to me for Petitions, having I suppose obtained my address in some way thro' you. In any future case, will you be kind enough to give Mrs. Bodichon's name & address, not mine. I am only acting as deputy because there is no one else to do it & I do not wish to appear in the matter any more than is necessary.[1] As soon as an acting Sec. can be found, which I anxiously hope may be before long, I shall give up this work & confine myself to my special business, which has lately been rather inconveniently interfered with.

I remain
Yours very truly
Emily Davies.

Man: ALS M50/1: 2/16

1. ED explained: "My name was to be kept out of sight, to avoid the risk of damaging my work in the education field by its being associated with the agitation for the Franchise" (Chronicle 507).

To Barbara Bodichon

17 Cunningham Place. N.W. March 21st [1867]

My dear Mrs. Bodichon

It was a very great pleasure to receive your note to-day. I am so glad to think of your being pretty well again & on your way towards England. I am glad you do not mind our using your name. We won't do it again. And we *did not do* it, knowing that you were ill. It was not till it was all arranged, which had to be done very suddenly, that I heard you of your fever & that I must not write to you.

Very little has been done in your name, except sending formal notices & writing to Mr. Bruce & Mr. Gurney, who have both consented to present the Petitions. The lists of signatures are to be closed on Monday the 25th, & I suppose the Petitions will be presented in the course of the week. We have circulated about 10,000 of each of your pamphlets. They seem to be just what was wanted. Sir Thomas Erskine May thinks Reasons "unanswerable." There is a strong letter from Kingsley too, which I must show you when you come to England.

I will send the Report of the girls' examn., & some other things to Dr. Bodichon. Just after Bessie left, I received the prize locket & the one for myself, which I want to thank you very much for. It is exceedingly pretty, but I value it most as a *token*. The inscription makes it worth a great deal more to me, besides the pleasure of wearing it as a remembrance. I am longing for you to be at hand.

⟨MS damaged⟩

make room for you. He has been very much kept to the house by bad colds but on the whole they seem to jog along pretty comfortably. It has been pleasant to me to have them so near.

I have so much to say to you about the College, but perhaps I had better not enlarge upon it at present.

The remarks upon the Programme are very encouraging & I think we must certainly make a beginning this year. Miss Cook hopes to be one of the first Students & to bring with her a little band of old schoolfellows.

I will not weary you with a long letter. I hope it is nice & warm & reviving ⟨MS damaged⟩

your message. Thank you for your kind messages to Elizth. Garrett.

With love to Bessie.
Ever your affecn.
ED.

GC: ALS ED B7

To Robert Potts

March 25th 1867.

Dear Mr. Potts

Thank you for kindly sending me the Regulations for girls.

I shall want a good many copies & should be much obliged to you if you would make an arrangement with the printer, as you were good enough to do before, to strike off some copies for us. We shall want I think about 250 copies.

I am glad to see that the examinations for whole schools are thrown open to girls at the same time.

I remain
Yours very truly
Emily Davies.

GC: ALS ED LOC-203

To Lydia Becker

ENFRANCHISEMENT OF WOMEN.

17 Cunningham Place. N.W. | March 30th 1867

Dear Miss Becker

I am sorry I have not kept the Manchester names which came in too late to be attached to the Householders' Petition. They were however so few that the loss is not serious. I enclose a signature received yesterday & will send you any others that may drop in before the 8th.

Mr. James Heywood, who conveyed the general Petition to Mr. Bruce reports that he will probably consult with Mr. Gurney & arrange to present both Petitions the same day. I should think it will most likely be next Monday.[1] There are also to be Petitions from Edinb., Aldeburgh, Dumfries, & perhaps Hastings, presented during the next ten days. It is very odd about the wording of the Reform Bill.[2] I made a similar search to that of Mr. Steinthal & with the same result. The use of the phrase "male person" in the clause relating to the Local Examns. looks as if they wanted to exclude the women who have passed the Cambridge Examns. & no others.

I will send you our selected list of names as soon as it comes from the printer. We seem to have a good many duplicates. The large proportion of Cambridge names almost justifies the announcement in the Pall Mall that a Petition was being got up from the University of Cambridge. Do you know by what agency Dr. Temple's signature was obtained? You seem to have been more fortunate in getting good names out of Manchester than in it. I hope you have recovered from the painful ailment from which you were suffering a short time since. You will want a good rest when this work is over.

Ever yours truly
Emily Davies.

Man: ALS M50/1: 2/17

1. On 28 March 1867, the petitions for women's suffrage, with 3,559 signatures obtained by the London committee, were presented to Parliament by Henry Bruce. Signers included five professors, six Queen's counsels, eleven doctors, and sixteen Fellows of Oxford and Cambridge.

2. The Reform Bill of 1867 granted suffrage to certain qualified "men." Earlier legislation in 1850 had established that legislative language denoting masculine gender was to be taken as including women unless the contrary were specifically established. The switch from "male person," used in the 1832 Reform Act, to "man" in the 1867 Reform Act thus raised hopes that women were, by implication, being enfranchised.

To Emilia Gurney

March 30th 1867

... Of course before going to the public there must be a statement about the amount of money wanted & what is going to be done with it.[1] We have heard of a building in Hertfordshire which is being abandoned by the Literary Guild & it is to be sold for £2000. The situation, near a Station on the Great Northern line, seems to be just what we want, & there are 30 small rooms which might be convenient if there is vacant space to add what might be wanted. ... As there will be various kinds of business to do, I shd. like to have one or two members [of Committee] in each peculiar walk, who wd. not be expected to come when there was nothing going on in their line. On this principle, if you wd. be one, I cd. always let you know beforehand whether you wd. be specially wanted or not.

GC: AMsS C517a

1. ED was developing plans for fundraising and founding a college for women.

To Barbara Bodichon

17 Cunningham Place. London. N.W. | April 6th 1867

My dear Mrs. Bodichon

I was very glad to get your second note (from March) tho' I did not think the first at all unkind. This Franchise business has been a great trouble & very *thorny* in many ways, but as the Petitions are now out of hand the fire of letters has almost ceased & I hope soon to forget all about it.[1]

We had a meeting of the Examns. Committee on Wednesday & agreed to give your brooch to the best Junior candidate, a Miss D'Argent. Her family live in France, but she has been taught by an Aunt at Gloucester & was examined at Bristol. Miss West, a clergyman's daughter, has gained the Scholarship, & is going to hold it at Bedford College.

We had an exciting debate over *the* College project.[2] Lady Goldsmid, who could not come, wrote to say that she could not make up her mind to take any part at present. She thought we had better wait till the ferment about the Franchise is over. Mr. Gurney sent word that we could not give his adhesion till he knew more about the domestic arrangements & how the young ladies were to be looked after. Mr. Hastings said he would do anything he could for us & then went away. (He had an engagement.) Miss Bostock made a protest against mixing it up with the Examns. Committee. So we agreed to consider that the Chairman had left the Chair, and then went on. Miss Bostock opposed, Mrs. ⟨Hensleigh⟩ Wedgwood hesitated, Mr. Tomkinson & Mr. Clay were very strongly in favour. Mrs. Wedgwood asked whether we thought young women would like to go from home to College, & then our side had to admit that the weak point of our scheme was that the girls would ~~so~~ want to come & would hate to go home. Miss Bostock's point was that whatever there is a demand for, Bedford College is ready to give, & we were rather embarrassed in replying, as it was awkward to insist that the people we expect to get have either never heard of Bedford College or despise it & won't think of going near it. However as soon as Mrs. Wedgwood & Miss Bostock were gone, we relieved our feelings by enlarging upon these facts.

Mr. Clay & Mr. Tomkinson are almost too strong on our side & too determined to make the College a paradise. They insisted that the girls should have breakfast in their own rooms (instead of all together like a school) as if the whole thing depended upon it. Mr. Clay said if we could only open it, he was sure we should be overflowing with students, & that if it had been in existence ten years ago, his two sisters would certainly have come to it.

It was amusing to hear them talk about the examns. They evidently thought the ordinary Degree examns., which we are going for, rather beneath our notice. Mr. Tomkinson, who was a Wrangler himself, said he was sure girls could take Mathematical Honours with very little teaching. I see that we shall have to change our order of procedure, & instead of beginning with a large general Committee & then appointing a small one to carry out the project, we must first get together a small Committee & work out the Scheme in detail, & then get as many great people as we can to sanction it. I do not think we shall be ready to come to the public before the autumn or next spring, but the delay is perhaps rather an advantage. I am going on the 15th to the Lakes & shall see there my friend Anna Richardson, & Miss Wolstenholme, & I hope we shall be able to devise a plan of action. I don't think there will be any *work* for you to do. It is because it cheers one up to see you that I want you. I went to see Isa on Monday. She thinks she is going to have a baby & is advised to keep very quiet, which she finds a difficult task.

Will you thank Bessie for her letter. I should like very much to know when you are likely to be in England. With love to Bessie, Ever yours affecn.

ED.

I made a mistake in speaking of the Hastings's coming in June. There has been no change of plans that I know of.

GC: ALS ED B8

1. On 5 April 1867, John Stuart Mill presented the Manchester petition separately, with 3,161 signatures. Russell Gurney presented the householder's petition, with signatures of 1,605 women qualified as freeholders or leaseholders, on 8 April.

2. On 3 April 1867, the University Examinations Committee met and discussed the idea of a college for women; they "resolved that the project be now undertaken by this Committee" (Chronicle 519).

To Barbara Bodichon

17 Cunningham Place. N.W. | May 28th 1867

My dear Mrs. Bodichon

I must just send you a word of welcome on your coming back to England. It is hard to have you escaping away to Oxford & passing us coldly by, but perhaps it is best till you are stronger.

I am glad you thought the Division good. It was pretty much what I expected, & certainly, on the whole, encouraging.[1]

We are getting out a fuller Programme of the College, which I will send you as soon as it is ready.

I am longing to talk to you about it. We cannot do anything of a public sort before the autumn, but in the meantime there are endless things to talk about. It frightens me a little to see our castle coming down from the clouds and *substantiating* itself on the solid earth. For I really think it will be done.

You will tell me when you are within reach. I feel it already elated by the sense of having you in England.

Ever yours, ED.

Please give my kind remembrances to Lady Brodie & Sir Benjamin. They were very kind to me when I was at Oxford.

GC: ALS ED B9

1. On 20 May 1867, Mill moved to amend the Second Reform Bill by replacing the word *man* with *person*. Although the amendment was defeated by a majority of 123 votes, a total of 73 votes were cast in its favor. Both ED and Bodichon were encouraged by the fact that such a significant proportion of the votes had endorsed women's suffrage.

To Henry Tomkinson

17, Cunningham Place. N.W. | June 1st 1867

Dear Mr. Tomkinson

As it was settled that the College was not to be considered part of the business of the Examns. Committee, I am afraid it is scarcely fair to ask you for opinions. But perhaps you would be kind enough (as a work of supererogation) to read the enclosed & tell me what you think of the additions. Mr. Gurney is satisfied with what is said about the discipline.[1]

We do not propose actually setting to work before the Autumn, but in the meantime we hope to find out who will be ready to help us when the time comes, & also to hear everything that is to be said against the scheme. Please let me know the worst.

Yours very truly
Emily Davies

GC: ALS ED XII/4/1

1. See ED to Barbara Bodichon, 6 April 1867.

To Barbara Bodichon

UNIVERSITY EXAMINATIONS. 17, CUNNINGHAM PLACE, LONDON, N.W.

June 3d 1867

My dear Mrs. Bodichon

Thank you for the cheque. I am to see Mrs. Taylor to-morrow & will transfer the Franchise £5 to her. We have been considering what will be best to do about the Franchise & have come to the conclusion that the Committee must be dissolved. Mrs. Taylor proposes it, so there will be no opposition from her side, & Lady Goldsmid, Miss Manning & E. Garrett, who may be taken as representing the quiet section agree that it is the only thing we can do.

It is clearly impossible to go on as we are. No Secretary would with her eyes open, undertake the task of keeping Mrs. Taylor in check, who is, in fact, resolved not to be kept in check any longer. We *might* have two Committees, one moderate & the other under Mrs. & Miss Helen Taylor's leadership. But that would expose our divisions to the world & it would be said that "women never can work together" &c., which would be very damaging. So on the whole, I think with Lady Goldsmid that "We had better quietly withdraw & stick to our middle-class." (i.e. to education.)

The best course will perhaps be for you to write to me, resigning the Secretaryship. If you could at the same time suggest that the Committee might now be dissolved, we could call a meeting for the purpose of receiving your resignation & discussing whether to dissolve or not. So that all the Committee will know that it is going to be proposed. We should be obliged to have one more meeting to receive a statement of accounts & finally wind up our affairs, but I do not think it would be necessary for you to be present at either, & I should think it would be best for you to keep out of the mêlée altogether. Best for *yourself*, I mean of course. It is a great relief to me to look forward to dissolution. It is such a constant harass to be mixed up with uncongenial people.[1]

Ever yours
ED.

GC: ALS ED B10

1. The Suffrage Committee formally dissolved on 17 June 1867. For ED, "It had been working thro' great difficulties, owing to the incompatibility of its chief elements.... it was finally agreed to be best to leave the Women's Suffrage part of the women's movement to be worked for the time under the direction of the Radical section of the party.... From that time until many years after, I took no active part in the agitation for Women's Suffrage" (Chronicle 509–10).

To Henry Tomkinson

June 21st 1867

... Many thanks for your criticism of the College Programme & for your suggestions, which you will see, have been adopted in the final edition. It was simply a mistake about the ten Terms. I had been going upon old recollections of the time my brothers spent at Cambridge & had not noticed the alteration. The object of mentioning the time is to show how short it is. People bring up the objections to semi-conventual life as if the Students were to be shut up for twenty years at least.... We have been instigated by one of the Asst. Commissioners & encouraged by Mr. Roby, to get up a Memorial to the Schools Inquiry Commission.[1] The chief object of it is to give the schoolmistresses an opportunity of stating their views, as people are generally very much surprised to hear that *they* want anything beyond their own schools. If you know any nice orthodox people whose names are known, wd. you kindly ask them to 'support' the Memorial. We cd. get plenty of people with peculiar views of the most various sorts, but unfortunately two contradictory heretics do not make one reasonable person, which is want we want....

GC: AMsS C524

1. On 4 June 1867, ED received a letter from Bryce regarding the proposed college. He suggested that they "bring the matter officially before the [Schools Inquiry] Commission... [and] memorialize them to ask for a grant" (Chronicle 521). ED consulted with Roby and Anne Jemima Clough and brought a memorial before the London Schoolmistresses meeting on 14 June 1867. The memorialists wrote: "As managers of ladies' schools and as governesses in families we observe a deficiency in the education of women ... namely, the want of adequate means and inducements for continuing study beyond the school period.... There are in England no public institutions for women, analogous to the Universities for men ... and we venture to ask that ... special regard may be paid to the need for such an institution, and to other measures providing for the higher education of women" (Memorial from the London Association of Schoolmistresses to the Royal Schools Inquiry Commissioners of 1864).

To Helen Taylor

ENFRANCHISEMENT OF WOMEN.

5, Blandford Square, | London. N.W.
17 Cunningham Place. | N.W. | June 24th

Dear Miss Taylor

You may probably have heard that the Committee formed last autumn for the enfranchisement of women, has been dissolved. At the last meeting of the Committee it was agreed to place the "property," consisting chiefly of pamphlets and stationary, at Mrs. Bodichon's disposal. I intend transferring to her also, as soon as she is able to receive them, the letters and other papers which are at present in my hands, and as I shall no longer be in any special sense a depository of documents on this subject, I will ask you to discontinue sending me the Magazines which I have hitherto regularly received from you according to the agreement of last year.

I remain
Dear Miss Taylor
Yours truly
Emily Davies.

LSE: ALS 191

To Anna Richardson

July 18th 1867

I must try & catch you at Vesey, if only for the sake of telling you how glad I was to have your two letters. The last came at a very opportune time, just after an unusual rush of correspondence.

A little while after you left, Mr. Bryce made a suggestion that we shd.

memorialise the ^(Schools Inquiry) Commission about the College. As it was thought likely to be useful, it seemed a duty to do it, & it of course involved a good deal of negociation, besides the actual work. It has been I think a successful stroke.

The Memorial was signed by about 500 schoolmistresses, & 'supported' by a row of other people of the more singularly varied character. Tennyson, Browning, Ruskin, ⟨John⟩ Tyndall, Huxley, Sir Charles Lyell, Mr. ⟨James⟩ Martineau, Mr. Grote, Professor ⟨Alexander⟩ Bain, the proprietor of The Record, Dr. Angus, champion of orthodoxy of various sects, the Bishop of St. David's, five Deans, a good sprinkling of Archdeacons, Canons, Fellows & Tutors & Professors, M.P.'s, eminent lawyers & physicians, with Mr. Frederick Harrison & a few other Comtists to complete the medley. I have had some curious letters about it. Most of them are from people who cannot yet see their way, but there are a few for & against. Browning wrote saying that the proposed measure had been explained to him by the Dean of Ely (Harvey Goodwin) & he altogether approved & wished it well. Miss Anna Swanwick says it has her warmest sympathies. Ladies generally are very shy about it. I suppose they know that if they give their names, they must be prepared to fight, & unless they are very clear about it, the prospect is not pleasant . . .

I had almost forgotten to say that our Franchise Committee is dissolved. Mrs. P. Taylor has formed another, with herself as 'manager of the Executive.'[1] It is a great relief to me to get away from uncongenial companionship & to abandon the vain effort to work with Radicals. Heaven protect me from trying it again! The more I see of them, the worse they appear, quâ Radicals. No doubt some of them have the domestic virtues.

Mrs. Bodichon is come home, recovered, but easily overtired . . . Elizth. Garrett has had a touch of scarlatina, a troublesome interruption to her practice, but so slight as to be of no consequence otherwise. My mother has been very much pulled down by a kind of nervous prostration, affecting the digestion. It seems to have been brought on by taking too long a walk at Caerleon. I hope she is getting over it, but it is tedious work. Failure of strength is so very difficult to deal with, when the digestion & the appetite are at fault. Mary & the children are in Shropshire with Lady Crompton, exuberant with health & enjoyment. Llewelyn is very well. The Church is soon to be closed for a few weeks, for alterations in the Ritualistic direction.

GC: AMsS C529

1. The London committee was reconstituted as the London National Society for Women's Suffrage.

To Anna Richardson

Aug. 1st 1867

...The evening I missed you, I was spending with Mrs. & Miss Manning, talking over a design for a volume of essays on questions relating to women.[1] It was proposed by Mr. ⟨Albert⟩ Rutson (one of the writers on Reform) a friend of Mrs. G⟨eorge⟩. Butler's. I have been asked to edit it, & we are considering whether it can be done. I enclose a list of subjects & writers which have been thought of, but it is all in the speculation stage at present. If we decide on asking Mr. Bryce to write about Quakers, wd. you supply him with material or tell him where to get it? And do you think there is any one else more competent for the subject? Hints & suggestions with regard to the volume generally, will be welcome.

GC: AMsS C532

1. Josephine Butler, *Woman's Work and Woman's Culture* (1869). Contributors included Cobbe, Boucherett, Jex-Blake, and Wolstenholme.

To Anna Richardson

August 1867

...Many thanks for your kind inquiries & projects for my mother. She *was* a good deal better & I hoped the change to the bracing Northern air wd. finish setting her up, but a day or two before she was to have started, she broke down again.... She is better again, but far from strong.... The most hopeful thing is that last year she began to get better as soon as the cool autumnal weather set in. In the meantime she is keeping very quiet & taking tonics & trying in every way we can think of to get up strength. Annie Austin is with her & Elizth. Garrett has been looking after her very sedulously, or I cd. not have staid away....

This place reminds me of Heugh Folds, only that the rusticity here is less polished.[1] It is not a place for all the year round, but in the heat of summer it is delicious. I don't think I have ever been in such a perfectly reposeful retreat.... There are noises, but they are all rural, the murmuring of the wind in the trees, the buzzing of insects, barking dogs, lowing bullocks, birds twittering—nothing to remind one of mental labour & strain. I have been entering into the spirit of the place, & *almost* forgetting even the College. I send you however a list of the signatures to the Memorial. I have had some letters since it was sent in from people who were abroad &c. a very cordial note from Lady Hobart, & one from Professor ⟨John⟩ Seeley....

I suppose you know about Mrs. Butler's sister, Mrs. Smyttan, who lives with her father near Haydon Bridge. She is anxious to be of use at Newcastle & will of course do what she can to further Miss Clough's scheme.[2] I am glad there is a prospect of its being tried. Even if it only gives a little temporary stimulus, it is something, & it may be an encouragement to the mute inglorious blue girls of the district to find that there are people in the world who do not disapprove of their tastes. If James Stuart [of St. Andrew's] comes to Newcastle, please be kind to him for my sake & for Harriet Cook's. He is a raw Scotch youth, but I think of great promise.

Mrs. Bodichon is I am sorry to say, sadly broken down by her fever. It was a very bad attack & she has never had a fair chance of recovery, for people *won't* let her alone. It is quite a caution against forming the habit of beneficience, it is so difficult to break it off. . . . Llewelyn & family are at Aberystwith, all flourishing . . .

GC: AMsS C534

1. Heugh Folds was the home Richardson had built in Grasmere.
2. The Lectures for Women that Clough had begun with James Stuart.

To Henry Tomkinson

Nov. 9th 1867

. . . You will see by the enclosed draft that we are preparing to carry out the College scheme, & to claim your promised help.[1] The reason for moving just now is that the Local Examns. Committees are active about Christmas, & we hear that they are likely to form Local Committees in aid of the College, which of course they cannot do till there is some body in existence to authorise something.

People who join the Committee are supposed to agree to the four Resolutions.[2] There has been a question whether to mention Cambridge definitely from the beginning, but it seems not unreasonable as the whole thing has grown up out of the Cambridge Local Examns, & it saves trouble to have the matter settled. . . .

GC: AMsS C545

1. The College Committee met for the first time on 5 December 1867. Present were: ED, C. Manning, Sedley Taylor, and Tomkinson. They discussed and adopted four resolutions.
2. The resolutions were: that the college be connected with the University of Cambridge; that it try to obtain admission of students to degree examinations at the university; that it be in accord with the principles of the Church of England, while allowing latitude for Nonconformists; and that its resident authorities be women (Chronicle 539–40).

To Henry Tomkinson

Nov. 15th 1867

... I quite agree with you that it will be much better for the College to be carried thro' by a large number of people than by a few fanatics & there seems a fair prospect of very general support. We shall get Local Committees very soon in several of the large provincial towns & they will enlighten their respective neighbourhoods.

I suppose the Committee must be considered entirely new, as the old one is not extinguished. I am glad to say Miss Bostock has quite come round & says now that the new College will be a great help to Bedford College.

Your note was forwarded to me at Birmingham & I acted at once upon your suggestion about Cambridge, in so far as to ask Mr. Sedley Taylor, who happened to be staying in the same house, to be on the Committee, to which he very readily consented.[1] We had thought that Cambridge residents cd. not conveniently attend meetings in London, & that as we hope to get a Local Committee there, it might be better for them to be on that. There is another slight difficulty, that I suppose they are all young men, & our Committee is I am afraid rather deficient in the due proportion of age & experience. If we cd. get a few more old ladies like Lady Stanley of Alderley, who has six grown-up daughters & a multitude of grandchildren, they might counterbalance the levity of young Cambridge.

I hope we may get some good Oxford names on the general Committee. Mr. Griffiths reports that the Council has 'for the second time refused to sanction to the examination of girls.' ...

GC: AMsS C547

1. ED was visiting the C. E. Mathewses for the NAPSS annual congress.

To Barbara Bodichon

17 Cunningham Place. N.W. | Nov. 20th 1867

My dear Mrs. Bodichon

I went to see Mrs. Lewes yesterday, & we had a long & most interesting talk about the College.[1] The first thing she touched upon was the religious question, on which we very quickly came to an understanding. I told her my idea was that if we kept on the same platform as Cambridge, we should share any changes which might be made as public opinion changes, & that we could not have a better security for liberality. She quite agreed & reported it all afterwards to Mr. Lewes who also agreed. They thought it desirable however that a sentence should be inserted in the Programme about prayers, by way of showing that we do not intend to have a Chapel or Chaplain. She thought it most desirable that we should attach ourselves to Cambridge & get their Degrees if possible, but at the same time approved of the proviso that the Examns. should not be compulsory. She also strongly approves of having women only as resident authorities, & thought that people who recommended a man & his wife could not have much knowledge of life. It was delightful to find her taking such a warm interest in the whole thing. She said she thought the higher education of women was *the* thing about which there could be no doubt.

I told Mrs. Lewes what Emily Blackwell had proposed to you, about your £1000, namely to withdraw the condition about Miss Blackwell, & to substitute two, first that the £1000 should not be paid till the whole £30,000 had been raised, and second that a promise should be made to provide for teaching hygiene. The first condition we both thought very good. The second is more difficult. Miss E. Blackwell told me that she should think it a sufficient security if the Committee would pass the enclosed Resolution. I doubt very much however whether they would, & Mrs. Lewes thinks that they ought not. She says that the principles of Hygiene are so few & so simple that anybody could learn them from a book like Combe, without a teacher, & that the sanitary influence of the College must depend upon the resident authorities. Of course she holds as strongly as anybody the necessity of obedience to the laws of health, especially for women. The only question is about the means. She thinks that it is by the formation of habits in the College, not by direct teaching. After we had been talking about this for some time, she fetched Mr. Lewes, who took exactly the same view. He thought it desirable to have some teaching of the laws of life, but that, he said, would come under Zoology. ~~She~~ They both said we *could not* have a Professor of Hygiene, & that the reason people make themselves ill is that they wilfully do what they know to be unhealthy. Mr. Lewes thought the only thing we could do would be to insert a sentence in the Programme, to the effect that we do not mean to infringe the laws of health, & Mrs. Lewes suggested that it might be brought in among the duties of the resident authorities. I think I see my way to putting in a sentence of this sort, in the last paragraph but one.

I am anxious that it should be *possible* to accept your £1000 at the outset, because this is the only way, as you will not be on the Committee, that you can be counted among the founders of the College. If you wait to see whether we do things in a proper manner, we shall not be able to reckon you among the believing few, who walk by faith & not by sight. It is quite clear to me that if the thing is to be done at all, there must be, not only faith in the idea, but trust in the people who are to carry it out. I have no doubt at all now that we shall do it. It is only a question of a little sooner or later & a more or less beautiful building, & so on. But you know how much pleasure it would give me to feel to be doing it *with* you, who have believed in the idea from the very first.

Our visit to Birmingham was most encouraging. People *asked* for the College, before I had given a hint of its being in contemplation. We made a beginning of a Local Committee for the Cambridge Examns., and I have no doubt it will be carried on in a zealous & effective way.

Nearly all the College Committee have now agreed to serve. Mr. Bryce is doubtful. He objects to our connexion with Cambridge, & wants us to go off upon our own basis & do something better than either of the old Universities. Oxford has again "refused to sanction the examn. of girls."

Our candidates have increased this year from 202 to 230, which is satisfactory, especially as in the corresponding year (the third.) the boys fell off largely.[2]

Two little Miss Mathews's are promised for the College. Miss ⟨Dorothea⟩ Beale of Cheltenham College hopes to send us some pupils. You will be glad to hear that Miss Bostock has quite come round. She says now. "Nothing would help us more than that you should make a grand start." I think our first meeting will be about a fortnight hence.

I will not trouble you with a longer letter. Miss Blackwell gave a pretty good account of you.[3] It is something to be getting on, however slowly.

The bit of blue was a little darker than the Cambridge blue.

Ever yr. affecn. Emily Davies.

GC: ALS ED B320

1. Mrs. Lewes (Marianne Evans), hereafter George Eliot. ED received a letter from George Eliot on 16 November 1867, inviting her to visit three days later.
2. In 1867, 141 Junior girls and 91 Senior girls took the Cambridge Examinations in eleven cities.
3. Bodichon was still recovering from her illness.

To Charlotte Manning

Nov. 25th 1867

...The first meeting of the College Committee is fixed for Thursday, Dec. 5th, at three o'clock, at the Architectural Gallery, 9 Conduit St., Regent St..[1] Please come early. The Dean is terribly punctual, & will want you to talk to him. Since I saw you, Mrs. Gurney & Lady Goldsmid have agreed to be on the Committee. I am sure you will like your coadjutors.

Mrs. Gurney was extremely interested in hearing about Mrs. Lewes. She says it wd. be like a gin palace to her to have the temptation so close at hand & prophesies that now I have once crossed the threshold I shall be constantly going. She takes the same view that you do, that it is justifiable to go & see Mrs. Lewes herself, but not to meet people at her house. She also thinks that having once taken the false step, the only thing they can do now is to stick together to the end.

GC: AMsS C553

1. The first meeting of the College Committee took place in London on 5 December 1867. See ED to Barbara Bodichon, 9 December 1867.

To Barbara Bodichon

17 Cunningham Place. N.W. | Nov. 25th 1867

My dear Mrs. Bodichon

Thank you heartily for your good, trustful letter. The sentence I propose putting in is this. "In all the arrangements special care will be taken to guard against the infringement of the laws of health." If you take this in connection with the studied moderation of the language of the Programme generally, I think you will see that it is pretty strong. I do not expect any serious difficulty in getting all that you wish done about Miss Blackwell, if she is content to be known by that title. I find the Dr. Elizth. is strongly objected to, and not the least by those who value her most.

I should like very much to see you soon, but I could manage it better after the girls examn. is over. The first meeting of the College Committee is to be on the 5th, and there will be a good deal to do before & after it.

Then the Examn., for which there is also a good deal of preliminary work, begins on the 16th and goes on for a week. After that, there will be a lull, and I should much enjoy an opportunity for a little quiet talk with you. It rests me to be with you, which I cannot say of very many people.

Mrs. Gurney has been intensely interested in hearing about Mrs. Lewes. She had seen her several times at Ella's Concerts, & been quite captivated by her face alone. Mrs. Gurney says it will be like a gin palace to me, & certainly having once crossed the threshold it has become very difficult to keep away.

I have a great deal more to say, but fear tiring you. If ~~Miss~~ Aunt Julia is still with you, please remember me to her most kindly.

Ever your affecn. ED

GC: ALS ED B321

To Sedley Taylor

17 Cunningham Place, N.W. | Nov. 25th 1867

Dear Mr. Taylor

We propose to hold the first meeting of the College Committee on Thursday week, Dec. 5th, at three o'clock, at the Architectural Gallery, 9 Conduit St., Regent Street. I hope this will be a convenient time and place for you.

I enclose a draft of some Resolutions to be proposed at the meeting, as a sort of basis of action.

I remain
Dear Mr. Taylor
Yours very truly
Emily Davies.

CUL: ALS Add.MS.6258(E)12

To Anna Richardson

Nov. 27th 1867

... is there any chance of Miss Thöl's going to the College eventually, & ought not she & others to begin preparing themselves, like the young Americans, in Plato & Conic Sections, & also to work upon their parents' feelings, so that they may not have to spend a year melting them after the College is ready? I have been to see Mrs. Lewes, as Mrs. Bodichon wished me to hear what she had to say about the College. She is warmly in favour of it, on good grounds. ...

As to beginning on a small scale, as we mean to succeed, I do not see much use in laying ourselves out for failure & thereby probably getting it. But I do not think we need put off beginning till the building is completed. As our course is to be for three years, we may fairly open shop as soon as we have accommodation for one-third of our Students. I do not think the commercial analogies go far. There are some things which must be speculations, & take the chance of failure, & sometimes people supply a thing in the hope of thereby creating a demand. The last is partly our case, but I think the want has already been made one to a considerable extent. As to the other conditions, the only question is whether breakfast alone wd. not be greater happiness than the female character cd. bear, & it will take years of experience to find out how much felicity is safe for the weak natures we shall have to deal with. I have a strong impression that we shall have to devise some appropriate forms of torture as a counterpoise to the too exhilarating influences of the place. But that is surely a question for the future . . .

GC: AMsS C555

To Henry Tomkinson

Dec. 7th 1867

. . . Thank you very much for negotiating with the Bank. . . . I shd. think the best plan will be to pay in at once all the money I have received, amounting to £14.60. There is no need to draw the £20– authorised by the Committee till we have a respectable sum to draw upon, which will probably be pretty soon. . . . I am so much obliged to you for instructing me about business. I feel very ignorant about it, & it wd. be disastrous to be making mistakes.

GC: AMsS C559

To Barbara Bodichon

17 Cunningham Place. N.W. | Dec. 9th [1867?]

My dear Mrs. Bodichon

I must send you a line with the enclosed copy of the Minutes of our first College meeting.[1] It was very small, as you see, so many people being out of Town, but all the more efficient. We stuck to our work, without a moment's wandering, for nearly 3 hours. Miss F⟨anny⟩. Metcalfe is elected as representing the schoolmistresses. Lady Stanley of Alderley is prevented by her husband from joining us (dislikes publicity.) She is evidently disappointed, & will I am sure help us as much as she can privately. I believe we shall have Lady Augusta ⟨Stanley⟩. My brother & sister have been talking to her, & report that she thoroughly approves. They are going to arrange for me to go & see her about it.

I had a flying visit from Aunt Julia on Saturday. She wanted to know whether I was going to see you, & I explained. She seemed much relieved to hear that we were not going to imitate Cambridge in every particular, or to create a vast building all at once. The counsels of experience seem to be to *build*. (not to attempt adapting an old house.) ~~but~~ and with a *view* to large numbers, but not actually to provide rooms for more than say five & twenty students, to begin with. If we were to begin with 100, we should want rooms for another 100 the next year, & another the third, it being a three years' course.

I feel very hopeful. Your liberal promise is an *immense* help at starting. I hope to send you Programmes in a few days. The first thing to do is to ask people to be on the General Committee. This we are to do with great discretion, that it may be composed of persons of real weight.

I wish you a happy Christmas.

Ever your affecn.

ED.

GC: ALS ED B322

1. Present at the first meeting of the College Committee were ED, C. Manning, S. Taylor, and Tomkinson. Five resolutions were passed. The first resolution was that "a Committee for the purpose of founding a College for the higher education of women" would be established, with the following members: "Lady Hobart, Lady Goldsmid, the Very Rev. the Dean of Canterbury, Mrs. Russell Gurney, G. W. Hastings Esq., James Heywood Esq., Mrs. Manning, Miss F. Metcalfe, H. J. Roby Esq., Reverend Sedley Taylor, H. R. Tomkinson Esq., Hon. Sec. Miss Davies." The Committee also resolved that "the College shall be if possible connected with the University of Cambridge and that efforts shall be made to obtain . . . admission . . . to the Examinations for Degrees of that University." Finally, the Committee resolved that religious services be "in accordance with the principles of the Church of England," that the "resident authorities shall be women," and that the Secretary communicate with persons interested in the project and make reports and suggestions to the Committee (MS Minutes of the First Meeting of the College Committee, 1867, GC B323).

To Henry Tomkinson

Dec. 11th 1867

. . . There is to be a meeting on Saturday at the Soc. of Arts rooms at half-past-twelve, to discuss a scheme for the examn. of teachers by a Voluntary Board.[1] The meeting is called, I believe, by Mr. Bryce, Mr. Myers, Mrs. George Butler of Liverpool & Miss Wolstenholme, & they are anxious that the members of our University Examn. Committee shd. be present. If you are not specially busy at that time, wd. you look in?

GC: AMsS C560

1. In the winter of 1867, the North of England Council for the Higher Education of Women (NEC) had been formed by a committee that included James Bryce, Josephine Butler, Anne Jemima Clough, and Henry Sidgwick, and that organized the lectures for Women. By December 1867, the NEC proposed establishing a Voluntary Board of Examiners from Oxford and Cambridge to provide a test for the women attending the lectures. By implication, the NEC plans jeopardized the effort to secure identical tests for men and women. In addition, ED was concerned that such a Voluntary Board would place excessive demands on the time of Cambridge men whose support she wished to secure for the College for Women.

To Anna Richardson

Dec. 13th 1867

... To lose no time, I send you a Proof of the Programme finally agreed upon at the first meeting of the College Committee. ... We have come to no decisions as yet upon details. With regard to beginning on a small scale, the counsels of experience seem to be these. That to adapt an old house is apt to cost more in the long run than to build a new one, but that it wd. be unwise to put off opening till we have accommodation for the full number of students. We shall *probably* (but nothing is fixed) provide for only about twenty-five at first. We shd. like to be obliged to refuse some at first. That wd. be much better than having empty rooms. But there will be a great deal to consider about the staff of teachers, &c. &c. &c. & I do not see my way even to an opinion as yet.

I believe we shall have Lady Augusta Stanley as a warm ally. I am to go & see her after next week. (which will be completely occupied by the girls examn.) She sympathises '*deeply*' but wishes to be instructed farther, before giving her name. I shd. like to have her very much, she has such a good, honest face.

I have seen Mrs. G. Butler & we have come to an agreement about the Essays.[1] There are to be two vols. She promises not to use my subjects, & I promise not to draw upon her friends as writers. I give up however 'the Quaker system,' as she seemed to wish to have it, so I shall not have to trouble you any more about it.[2] Her contributors will be lively young Radicals, mine, grave ancient women & men. Do you remember Burke's sentiments? 'A disposition to preserve & an ability to improve.' That is what my vol. is to show. ...

GC: AMsS C560a

1. See ED to Anna Richardson, 1 August 1867.
2. Ibid.

To Sedley Taylor

17 Cunningham Place. N.W. | Dec. 13th 1867

Dear Mr. Taylor

There is some delay in getting the circular struck off, owing to the caution of the managers of the Bank, who wanted to see the Programme before letting their name be used. I send you a Proof and perhaps you will kindly let me know about how many copies you are likely to be able to make use of.

The vacant space on the first page, which the printer has made larger than

I intended, looks rather awkward, but I suppose we shall get it filled up before long. Do you think the Master of Trinity would give his name?
  Yours very truly
  Emily Davies

CUL: ALS Add.MS.6528(E)14

To Anna Richardson

Dec. 17th 1867

... Your suggestion that we shd. get High Church names on our committee is admirable. I made the same myself to Mrs. Gurney the other day. Please get us some at once. I shd. like Dr. Pusey.

I am afraid it is too early yet to do anything about authorities. They are always on my mind, but I do not see what can be done. I am not old enough or distinguished enough, apart from the fact that my mother hates the idea of living at the College in any capacity.

As to what you say about taking a house for five years, you have not perhaps considered that as our course is to be for three years, we expect to begin with say 25, to whom the next year will add 25, & the next 25 more. That is why we may as well add from year to year, instead of beginning with our full number.... It is curious to think of your having Professor Seeley with you tomorrow evening. I saw him on Saturday at a meeting got up by Mr. Bryce, Mr. Myers, & Mrs. Butler of Liverpool, about a scheme for a special examn. of women by a self-appointed Board composed of men belonging to various Universities. The project seemed to me very unthorough & likely to waste the energy we want so much for the machinery already at work, so I was very glad to hear Professor Seeley opposing it.

I am taken up this week with the girls' [local] examn.... Mr. ⟨Robert⟩ Romer, our Conducting Examiner, is very pleasant to do with & a most hearty ally. He represents the feeling at Cambridge as most favourable to all our designs....

GC: AMsS C562

To Anna Richardson

Dec. 28th 1867

... There are few names I shd. like better than that of Miss ⟨Charlotte⟩ Yonge, but I despair of getting it. I wrote to Miss ⟨Elizabeth⟩ Sewell about the

Memorial & she declined on the ground that the project reminded her of the Princess. Miss Rossetti declined joining anything that did not belong to the Catholic Church (*Anglo*-Catholic, I suppose.) ....[1] Miss ⟨Frances⟩ Longley (the Archbishop's daughter) says the idea of the College is quite contrary to her notions of women's sphere. You see I have some reason to be discouraged, but on the other hand your friend Miss ⟨Mary⟩ Taylor[2] seemed as much on our side as anybody, & I certainly shd. not wish to lose either Miss Yonge or Mrs. ⟨Margaret⟩ Gatty, for want of asking. ... I am going to write to Sir W⟨illiam⟩. Page Wood, & I have asked Mr. ⟨William⟩ Bullock, the Sec. of the S⟨ociety for the⟩.P⟨ropagation of the⟩.G⟨ospel⟩., who in that capacity is known & believed in by High Church people. ... I am glad you liked Professor Seeley & his Lectures. He can scarcely have thought he was opposing *me* at the meeting at the Adelphi, but all the other ladies I believe voted for the new scheme. Mrs. Butler, Miss Clough & Miss Wolstenholme certainly did. If I had been able to stay to the end, I shd. have felt bound to express my objection more distinctly & forcibly, but I was not altogether sorry to escape the necessity of doing so & thereby irritating the other side & perhaps creating a permanent division. It was a case in which a victory might have been more damaging than a defeat. Mr. Seeley's desire to know what 'the ladies' want, is natural but not quite reasonable. 'The gentlemen' don't all want the same thing, & there is no reason to expect greater unanimity among 'the ladies.'

I had a pleasant talk with Lady Augusta Stanley the other day. She said the idea of the College was of course received with shouts, but she did not seem to care much for them. She wishes to be present at our next meeting, after which she will be better able to judge whether she can be of use on the Committee. I fancy the Dean is the obstacle in her way. ...[3]

GC: AMsS C564

1. Probably Maria Francesca Rossetti (1827–76), the elder sister of Christina Rossetti. She taught language and history, and entered an Anglican sisterhood.
2. Mary Taylor, daughter of an M.P. and granddaughter of a Mrs. Fletcher, near Grasmere, was a lifelong friend of Richardson's.
3. Dean A. P. Stanley, Lady Augusta's husband.

To Anna Richardson

Dec. 30th 1867

... I enclose Miss Rossetti's letter, which I rather misquoted to you. It was as a teacher (of Language & History) that I asked her to sign. You are probably thinking of Christina. I doubt whether her mere name, & it wd. be only that— wd. be worth taking much trouble to get. ...

I have not a copy of the Report of the Syndicate on last year's Examns., & it does ⁿᵒᵗ say very much. A more effective thing wd. be to write to ~~the~~ Mr. Markby, the Sec., for his opinion. If you were to ask him whether what he has seen of the work of girls in the Local Examns. leads him to think that something more ought to be done for them, you wd. get a very emphatic Yes in reply. And the inquiry wd. come better from you than from me, as I am a known partisan. . . .

Many thanks for your kind offer of help in copying. Harriet Cook, who is at home now, has been very good in making similar offers, but there is really scarcely anything of that sort to do. When there is, Jane Crow comes & helps me. Nearly all the work that I have to do consists in seeing people, & in writing letters of a more or less personal nature, which cannot be delegated to any one else. I mean of course that *my* share cannot. The Committee & others do a good deal on their own account.

. . . I cannot help wishing that the introduction of the Lecture scheme into new places might be postponed for the present. It is working against the College at Liverpool & Manchester. At the meeting of the Northern Council the College was opposed on the ground that the Lectures wd. develop into what was wanted. At Edinburgh they have destroyed all chance of doing anything for what the Scotch call the 'English' College. One regrets it there less than elsewhere, as there is reason to hope that by & by, the local college will be connected with the University. At Sheffield, the Lectures have prospered & the Local Examns., which had been successful for two years before, have gone to the wall. They have had no candidates at all this year. At Liverpool, Miss Clough & Mrs. Butler have begged me not to do anything for either the Local Examns. or the College, lest the Lectures shd. suffer.

And we shall of course not think of interfering with their field. I do not mean by this that the different agencies are in the least really antagonistic. It is simply that we have not strength to work so much machinery. This was borne in upon me more than ever before, during our visit to Birmingham.[1] We found the people there quite ready, but completely ignorant, & in order not to bewilder them, we were obliged to confine ourselves closely to the one matter of the Local Examns.

We talked a *little* about the College, because it was *asked* for as nearly as a thing unknown cd. be, but I doubt whether anything effectual can be done till the Examn. Scheme has got into work. If we had had the ill luck to be forestalled by the Lectures, we cd. have done nothing. As to the comparative importance of the two things, opinions will of course differ. I have no doubt that Local Colleges, into which the Lectures, if they are to be permanently useful, must grow, are wanted. But in the nature of things they must always be second-rate. The essential weakness of the scheme has already begun to show itself in the difficulty of getting competent lecturers.

Mr. Stuart spent four days a week on the mere delivery of the Lectures, apart from preparation. Evidently, only a very young man, not yet embarked in any profession, or else a second-rate man, not succeeding in his profession, could afford, except in some casual & occasional way, to give up all that time. The wear & tear of so much travelling must alone be a great drawback to anybody with at all sensitive nerves. The resource will no doubt eventually be to employ lecturers living on the spot. And I shd. think there is no doubt that by & by all the largest towns will have institutions for both men & women, similar to Owens College.[2] That is clearly a thing much to be desired. But it seems to me that the want of the higher thing is the more pressing. When we get that, the rest will follow. The notion that the Lectures wd. prepare the way for *the* College, is showing itself to be a mistake. Wherever there is a Local Examn., the demand for the College naturally arises, because there are always young women too old for admission, who take to clamouring for a test, & wear out the lives of the Local Secs. & of Mr. Markby, with their letters. These tiresome creatures have been most useful to us, both at Cambridge & elsewhere. But it is not lectures that they want. The *knowledge* they think they cd. get, but hook or by crook. What they want is the test. . . .

GC: AMsS C566

1. See ED to Henry Tomkinson, 15 November 1867.
2. Owens College, Manchester, was founded by the philanthropist John Owens in 1851. It emphasized the sciences as well as more traditional disciplines and imposed no religious tests for admission.

To Helen Taylor

THE KENSINGTON SOCIETY. | 17, CUNNINGHAM PLACE, LONDON. N.W.

Jan. 22d. 1868

Dear Miss Taylor

I send you ^(by Book post) the Kensington question, for the last time. For several reasons, it has been decided to wind up the Society at the end of its third year, namely in March. I find it very difficult to spare the time for the Secretary's work, which owing to the universal forgetfulness & inaccuracy of mankind, is much more burdensome than might have been expected, and the Society does not seem now to be so much wanted as when we began. During the last three years, the Suffrage Committees, Schoolmistresses' Associations, and other organisations, have come into existence, which supply links between our members and also consume their time and energy, so that they have less to spare for writing papers.

We shall have one more meeting, at which I hope it may be possible for you to be present, as it will be in March.

I send you by Book post the final and authorised edition of the Programme of the College, to which we hope to join eventually a medical school. Miss Garrett thinks there is at least as good a chance of getting the Cambridge Medical Degree as any other legal qualification. At Hitchin, near which we hope to locate the College, there is already an Infirmary, which by enlargement might be made available for Hospital practice, and some of the regular College Lectures, as e.g. Chemistry, Botany & Zoology could be shared by the medical students. It is thought best not to bring the medical branch forward publicly till we see our way more clearly. We do not yet know the disposition of the doctors attached to the Hitchin Infirmary. If they should happen to be friendly, it would of course be a great assistance.

I hope you have got thro' the severe weather with tolerable comfort. The incessant changes here have been trying.

Ever yours truly
Emily Davies.

LSE: ALS ED 193

To Sedley Taylor

PROPOSED COLLEGE FOR WOMEN. | 17, CUNNINGHAM PLACE. N.W.

Jan. 31st 1868

Dear Mr. Taylor

I have received a letter from Dr. Cookson, which I think you ought to see. As he seems favourably disposed, I should think he might possibly be induced to join a *Local* Committee, especially if he can be convinced that the Executive is in the hands of safe and wise people. The Executive Committee have really been chosen for their trustworthiness in that respect. Except Mr Heywood, whose name is I dare say rather alarming to Dr Cookson, none of us are Reformers in the extreme, fanatical sense.

The next meeting of the Committee will probably be on the 20th of February.

By that time I hope you may be able to report some progress at Cambridge. With thanks for your kind note, I remain

Yours ever truly
Emily Davies.

CUL: ALS Add.MS.6258(E)28

To Anna Richardson

Jan. 31st 1868

... I sympathise entirely with Mr. [R. Spence] Watson's view about the desirableness of mixed education, & I admit that the foundation of a separate College seems to stereotype the idea of separation. I feel this so much that if there had seemed any ~~chance~~ reasonable chance of getting the whole, by waiting, I wd. not have grasped at the half. But all good things have to be worked up to, & the only way open to us of working toward common education seems to be to stand out for common subjects, common examns. & common standards. It is not a case in which you can begin at the top end. You cannot artificially separate boys & girls, & then suddenly throw young men & women together at eighteen.[1] And unhappily the working-up by mixed schools seems to be rather dying out than growing. I know of one experiment which has seemed to work well, but the idea does not seem to have taken root. The school was started in Hampshire, & when its founder, Mr. Thornton, migrated to Cornwall, he left the school in the hands of a clergyman, Mr. Gwynne, but gave up the girls. He transferred the mixed principle to Cornwall, where it seems to be working well, as almost anything will do, which is carefully managed by people who care for it. But it seems to me that as an experiment, it is discouraging experience. It is the first step that costs, but after that has been made, we ought not to fall back. I don't mean that I despair of final success, only that I do not think it wd. be true policy at present to throw our strength into fighting for common instruction.

By & by, when the Colleges at Oxford & Cambridge are open to women, we will open ours to men. It will not be a superfluous institution, if, as Mr. Seeley says, we want more Universities, besides developing the old ones....

My mother's cold is better. She can go backwards & forwards to Blandford Square.[2] Charley pays us visits, & the others are going on well, except the baby, who is sadly pulled down.

GC: AMsS C574

1. Coeducation was relatively common in Scotland and in working-class schools. Grammar and preparatory schools in England remained largely single-sex throughout the nineteenth century.
2. The Llewelyn Davies home.

To Anna Richardson

Feb. 4th 1868

... Since I wrote last, we have added the names of Mr. Maurice & Dr. ⟨William⟩ Gull to the General Committee. Mr. Maurice came to Blandford Square on Sunday & there was a long talk about the College & also about mixed education. As to the latter, we all seemed to agree that it was a thing to be desired, but not to be tried for in the present case. Llewelyn mentioned one objection, which I think is a real one & very strong, namely, that if the College were at Cambridge, the discipline must be much more strict. It wd. be impossible to give as much liberty as we may hope to do in the country.[1] The experience of the Local Examns. at Cambridge is evidence of this. Whether all the precautions they take are *necessary*, I very much doubt, but at any rate they think they are, & the result is to make the girls very uncomfortable.... I suspect that this timidity wd. tell especially in hindering the thing I sigh for most, that is, the society of cultivated men for the mistresses. There wd. be such an amount of gossip & scandal ready to cluster round the College, that its managers & their male friends wd. be obliged in self-defense to shun each other, & shd. perhaps be in the position of shutting ourselves out from Cambridge society even more than if we were 50 miles off. This may be a fancy, but I have been told that at Oxford, unmarried ladies are obliged to be excessively cautious in their demeanour....

Our children seem to be pulling thro' their coughs pretty well. They were in great force on Sunday, clinging & shouting & dancing round Mr. Maurice. Even the poor little baby, who is the most pulled down, cd. point to the picture on the wall when asked 'Where is Mr. Maurice?' They are taught to adore the image of the Prophet before they can speak....

GC: AMsS C576

1. ED's attitude toward locating a women's college in Cambridge was based on more than middle-class Victorian propriety. Cambridge was strictly regulated by university officials, who exercised enormous control. University proctors had the power to detain women suspected of prostitution and to incarcerate them in a reformatory and workhouse known as the Spinning House.

To Sedley Taylor

PROPOSED COLLEGE FOR WOMEN. | 17 CUNNINGHAM PLACE. N.W.

Feb. 6th 1868

Dear Mr. Taylor

I see no reason at all for waiting for another meeting of the Executive Committee before proceeding to form a Local Committee at Cambridge, and

I quite agree with you as to the desirableness of acting without delay. I enclose a copy of the Resolution under which the Local Committees are being constituted. It will be a great encouragement to us in London if you should be able to bring a good list of Cambridge names to our next meeting. It will be I think on the 20th, but I will send you a notice.

I saw Mr. Maurice on Sunday & we had a long talk about the College. He gave his name very cordially for the General Committee & will I am sure be ready to help in any way he can at Cambridge. I fancy the names of Professors would be rather specially useful, as people ask in a sceptical tone if they are likely to take part in the work of the College. The names of physicians also, seem to be taken as a guarantee that we are not going to kill the students with overwork. Dr. Gull has sent his name, since the list was printed.

I remain
Yours very truly
Emily Davies

CUL: ALS Add.MS.6258(E)29

To Anna Richardson

Feb. 18th 1868

...At our Committee meeting on Thursday I shall have to report what has been done toward carrying out the Resolution about Local Committees. Will you kindly tell me what I may say about Northumberland & Durham. that a Committee is in the course of formation. or that steps are being taken for the formation of a Committee? Could you also let me have a few words about probable students?

People are always asking in a skeptical tone—What sort of young women do you expect to get? or Where are the students to come from? Please help me to give an answer. Mrs. Gurney replies helpfully that she does not know but Miss Davies does. Obviously the testimony from some other quarters wd. be more convincing. Wealthy Londoners (like the Charles Buxtons, with whom my brother & sister have had a controversy) can give their daughters such great advantages, both in the way of teaching & of cultivated society that they don't easily see what more they can want. Even they, do really want something else, but the need is not so pressing nor so conspicuous.

...We have not been successful among High Church people, but shall go on trying.

GC: AMsS C578

To Anna Richardson

Feb. 21st 1868

...With the principle of all that you say about the Lecture system I heartily agree. In fact Mr. Bryce & I said it all to each other, the day before yesterday.

I think we ought not only to accept, but to *desire* the introduction of the Lectures into every large town, with a view to their growing into local Colleges, or as Mr. Bryce put it, institutions like the Scotch Universities.

But I do not agree with Miss Ogle that *the* College is 'the natural consequence of the system of Lectures', or that 'no one cd. wish to stop there'.[1] One might as well say that Oxford & Cambridge are the natural consequence of Owens College. They are not antagonistic, but occupy a different field. As to practical policy there is much to be said on both sides. We have not found hitherto that the Lectures are paving the way for the *Cambridge* College, but the contrary. You see one must take into account that when you give the choice of the difficult best, or the easy second best, the latter is most likely to be taken. It is what Mat. Arnold might call an appeal to our relaxed self, & such appeals are very likely to be successful. Then, when people have grown eagerly interested in the second best thing, instead of wanting to press on, they get afraid of damaging it, & cannot bear to confess that anything higher than the thing they love so much is still wanting. Miss Ogle seems to have arrived at this point already, when she speaks of local Colleges as 'better than all.' It seems to me that in the nature of things they can never reach a high pitch of excellence. There are not enough first rate people to supply all the towns in England with first rate teaching. The perambulating system cannot work permanently. Men of high standing cannot afford to spend their strength in knocking about on railways, to say nothing of the huge hole it makes in their time. But as you say, there is no reason why the large number of people who cannot reach the best thing, shd. not be helped in getting what is possible, & it is merely a question of policy, to be decided partly by local circumstances. At the Leeds meeting, Mrs. Butler objected to forming an auxiliary College Committee, lest it shd. injure the Lectures, & Mrs. Gloyn of Manchester also opposed the College in the interest of the Lectures. At Edinburgh, as you know, the local movement had destroyed all chance of doing anything for what they call the English College.[2] The amount of cold water Miss Clough has thrown upon me is such that I cannot *think* of her without a shudder. So that to my mind it comes to this. It is better frankly to acknowledge that at present the Lectures stand in the way of the College. Then one has to consider *how much* in each case, one will have to sacrifice of the College interest, & whether the immediate & prospective advantages to be gained from the Lectures, are worth the cost. I incline to think that where there is a strong local feeling in favour of the Lectures, it is better to take advantage of it, but without entirely abandoning the College. Let the thorough people form an auxiliary Committee & help as much as they can, & let them also join the unthorough in working for the less perfect measure. This is what I expect will be done at Bristol. I learnt the other day to my dismay that the Lecture idea had penetrated there also, & that the prospect of a College Committee had become clouded.

However I am to go down towards the end of March, & see what can be done, & I expect to get a tolerably strong propagandist body there, to do exactly what you propose, that is, to use the local press & in other ways to diffuse information. Would not Mr. Hodgkin join you & Mr. & Mrs. Maugham? I think you are on the right tack in looking out for county names. They are useful by way of sanction. But the really important people are the Secretaries. I think by & by we ought to give in our general circular, a list of the auxiliary Committees with the addresses of their Secretaries, simply in order to let people in all parts of the country know to whom they may apply for the most recent information & personal explanation. This last is the most useful & necessary part of our work, & it is impossible to do it all thro' an Executive Committee, even if we were twice as able as we are. And I want to have you & Miss Greenwell as Co, Secs. I will not now go into the question of the Voluntary Examining Committee. Mr. Bryce came on Wednesday & we had a long talk about it & other things. He sees the objections to it & the difficulties in its way. (especially the disadvantage of coming into direct competition with the London University scheme.)[3] & thought it might after all be best to withdraw it. I showed him the letter from Mr. Shaen of which I enclose a copy.

... Mr. Bryce definitely gives in his adhesion to the College. He said with a suppressed sigh that he supposed one must sacrifice something. So I asked what he was sacrificing, & it seemed to be the religious point. As to the connexion with Cambridge he said he had pretty nearly come round to our opinion, & he admitted that the religious difficulty was a merely sentimental one.

He is a very strong Voluntary, & cannot bear the faintest recognition of a National Church. It is rather important to have Mr. Bryce secured, as he is the governing mind of the Liverpool faction. He has been eager for the College *idea* all thro, only he *imagined* that we were carrying it out in an unwise way, & we had had no opportunity for a mutual *éclairissement*.

I am very glad Mr. Watson joins us.

Mr. Bryce thinks we might as well throw our Programme into the fire at once, as propose a College *in* Cambridge.

I have been interrupted & have not time to say all I meant, but I must just tell you that we had a full & satisfactory meeting yesterday. It was agreed to hold a little Conference or semi-public meeting some time in March, & a Sub-Committee (Mrs. R. Gurney, Mrs. Manning, Mr. Roby, Professor Seeley & myself) were appointed to make the necessary arrangements, & to prepare a sketch of proposed organisation, to bring before the meeting. Lady Augusta Stanley (who was present) & Professor Seeley, were added to the Executive Committee. Their names will not give confidence either to the extreme right or the extreme left, but we are not likely to get much help from either of those quarters, & the enlightened Moderates are strong enough to carry thro' a a little bit of a thing like this if they get heartily interested in it. I really care most for getting *wise* people on the Executive, who will do the work well in future times when it becomes more serious & complicated than it is now. . . .

Thank you for Miss Ogle's & Archdeacon Prest's notes. I am not surprised that the Archdeacon does not join. *I* shd. not have asked Mr. Trevelyan, but it is thought that he may be useful as representing the flippant interest, & it is perhaps better that he shd. talk *for* (tho' unworthily) than against us. . . .

I go on Monday for 3 days to 'Care of Professor Liveing, the Pightle, Cambridge.'

Mr. Hutton's note will perhaps amuse you, if you can read it. I ought to explain that I asked him very briefly to help in launching the scheme, & I suggested that it wd. be an opportunity for the exercise of 'the subtlety of equitable kindness' for which the Spec. is famous. It has been much lauded on this ground in the Contemporary. . . .[4]

GC: AMsS C579

1. Probably Annie Charlotte Ogle, author of *A Lost Love* (1858) and *The Story of Catherine* (1885).
2. The movement for Lectures for Women.
3. The recent move by the University of London to inaugurate a special examination for women. On 25 February 1868, the University of London voted "with exceptions and modifications hereafter to be introduced" to open the existing Matriculation Examination to women. The vote was formally adopted on 18 March 1868.
4. Probably a reference to Thomas Markby, "On the Education of Women," *Contemporary Review* 7 (February 1868).

To Anna Richardson

Feb. 22d 1868

Private . . . I do not know that there is much to add to what I said yesterday on the subjects of Mrs. Butler's letter. I do not like it, because I feel it is not quite true . . . I have found her not strictly truthful & it makes me shrink from having more to do with her than is necessary. I do not mean that she is not a genuinely good Christian woman. I am sure she is. And I believe her 'inaccuracies' are a good deal caused by a kind of looseness & slipperiness of mind. But all the same, by means of them she conveys false impressions, & the task of correcting her statements is very invidious & disagreeable. Her 'letter to Mr. Bryce' about the Voluntary Board requires *much* correction to bring it into harmony with facts, & it goes about among people who hear that side only. This is of course, a personal matter, & it does not affect the question as to whether the thing advocated is desirable, except in the general sense that I *now* feel that any statement made by Mrs. Butler must be confirmed by somebody else before I can rely upon it....

It is not true that University men are eager to take part in this scheme. It is true that there is a great deal of friendly feeling towards women, (chiefly owing to the Local Examns., which bring not two or three, but *dozens* of men into communication with women) but there has been very great difficulty in getting suitable Lecturers....

GC: AMsS C585

To Sedley Taylor

PROPOSED COLLEGE FOR WOMEN. | 17, CUNNINGHAM PLACE. N.W.
Saturday. ⟨February 1868⟩

Dear Mr. Taylor

As I propose coming home on Thursday morning I am afraid there is no chance of my seeing you at Cambridge, unless it could be on Monday afternoon. I go down by the mid-day train and shall I suppose be at The Pightle by two o'clock.

Since writing to you it has occurred to me that to print *all* your names on the circular, as the "Cambridge Committee" would have a very imposing effect, and make a great impression on the public mind. I should like to know what you think.

Yours very truly
Emily Davies.

CUL: ALS Add.MS.6258(E)39

To Anna Richardson

Cambridge. | Feb. 28th 1868

... I am going to-day & I have not time to tell you any particulars of the delightful visit I have had here, but I want to let you know without delay, that there is a prospect of getting all our differences arranged. I have been seeing, by their own wish, the promoters of the Voluntary Board & have succeeded in making them understand the objections to it. Mrs. Butler's friend, Mr. Myers now proposes, if others are willing, to adopt some University examn. as a standard, & so to get rid of the female stamp. It is scarcely worth while perhaps to go into details. The Examn. thought of is the Cambridge Little-go, with the modification, offered as a compromise from our side, of making Greek optional with German. The hatred to Greek among some of the extreme people here is so intense that they can scarcely make up their minds ^{even} to give it so humble a place as this. But I have hopes that they will. & as they now *take in* the objections to a female examn., they will at any rate be fairly considered.

It is a great consolation to me to have seen them & convinced them (indirectly) that the opposition to the Voluntary Scheme has nothing to do with jealousy on behalf of the College. There has been a great deal of misrepresentation, very trying to bear. But I felt that it was better not to volunteer corrections, especially in writing. To answer questions, when one is asked, is a different thing. The best men here really wish to know what women want, as Professor Seeley told you. If you shd. have any application for an opinion, shall you be able to give it in favour of a men's examn.—(or a *human*) modified as much as they like, so long as they do not give any sanction to the female principle? The sweetness & light here is in the highest degree refreshing. I am amazed, bewildered, almost stupefied by the reception of the College idea. It is far beyond anything I had hoped for. . . .

GC: AMsS C587

To Anna Richardson

March 6th 1868

(a) . . . I owe you many thanks for your exhilarating letter. It was delightful to me to find you so firm on the Special Examn. question. There has been so much defection that I did not know who might be giving in. I have not heard much of their proceedings since I came home, but I hope it may be possible to work with the promoters of the Voluntary Board in their particular case, tho' there are some of them one can never *trust* again. . . .

(b) thing, it being so strikingly the reverse.

I hope you will not get very tired of the arduous business of talking. I am going to write to Miss Taylor in a day or two, to solicit the honour of a visit. (I know all about Roswitha, &c. Mr. M. Dupauloup's "Femmes Savantes & femmes studiouses.")[1] I hope *they* will do the talking. Let me tell you my Programme for Monday. 1 Lunch with Lady Goldsmid, on purpose to talk about the College. 2 Afternoon tea at Mrs. Gurney's, to meet with Lady Colvill & Lady Rich.

ditto—[2] 3. Professor Seeley & Mrs. Bodichon coming to dinner, to talk over the College curriculum, a most important & difficult business.

I ought to begin the day with Bedford College, but Annie ⟨Austin⟩ is going to take it for me. This will not sound much to you country people, who pass your lives in the extraordinarily fatiguing process of "spending the day" with each other & talking from morning till night. but to a quiet, not to say stagnant, Londoner, so much working of the jaws is a considerable effort.

I do not know anything of Miss Hughes.

I am hoping to hear a good result of your talk with Miss Greenwell & Mr. Ashwell.[3]

Yours ever

ED.

You had better be *joint* Secs. It is awkward to be doing work in another person's name.

⟨incomplete⟩

(a) GC: AMsS C589

(b) GC: ALS ED XVII GC1/2

1. Richardson had cited Mary Taylor in offering as an argument that "'in the . . . middle ages, the great monasteries of women were true women's Colleges . . . where Roswitha, of the Latin plays, Hildegard and Gertrude were examples, not exceptions'" (*Memoirs* 221). *Femmes studiouses* referred to groups of women with intellectual interest. The term derived from a French seventeenth-century movement, the *querrelle des femmes*.

2. Probably the wife of Charles John Colville, first viscount of Culross (1818–1903).

3. Probably Arthur Rawson Ashwell (1826–79), principal of the Oxford Diocesan Training College in Culham, the Training College in Durham, and the Theological College in Chichester.

To Barbara Bodichon

Sunday ⟨March 1868⟩

Dear Mrs. Bodichon

Thank you much for you kind words.[1] I did not think you were losing faith in the cause, but I thought you were more discouraged than need be by other people's coldness, because you expected more from them than I did. You go about bravely talking to people & expecting sympathy from them, when I should not open my mouth, and so you get the cold water showered upon you. I did not think Professor Seeley was nearly so tired of the subject as I was. I had been talking about it all day & longed to get on to something else, & yet felt that I could not drag in the kind of things we should have liked to talk about without a greater basis of mutual understanding than we had to go upon. Mr. Seeley is very shy, swift to hear, slow to speak, and then his mother was lying almost insensible, & that must have haunted & *shadowed* him.

I am well used to the cool Cambridge manner. It is not half so pleasant as the kind, gushing way Oxford men have, but it comes to more. I could not go to Mrs. Lewes to-day. It would have interfered with family things. It is rather curious that she should be the only person who favours it to you.[2] I should not have wondered much if she had been against. In fact the only thing that ever surprises me is to find anybody for it. As Lady Augusta said—"Of *course* it is received with shouts." I expected no less, but that is because I got so used to them & to working really almost single handed thro' the Local Examns., & winning at last. Scarcely anybody cared. It was carried by the help of people who were dragged in, almost against their will. So now, we glory in tribulations also; knowing that tribulation worketh patience; and patience, experience: and *experience, hope*. All good things are done (and they *do* get done.) by faith & patience. The shield of faith quenches the fiery darts of the wicked. Let us run with patience the race that is set before us, looking unto Jesus the author & finisher of our faith; who for the *joy that was set before him*, endured the cross, despising the shame. Consider him that endured such contradiction of sinners (the Fawcetts &c) against himself, lest ye be wearied and faint in your mind. It is astonishing how much there is of parallel experience in old times. I often think of St. Paul, with his sensitive, highly strung, nervous temperament, and the amount of worry he went thro', with the care of all the churches upon him, all quarrelling and fretting and disgracing themselves, and he, *feeling* it all to the heart's core, held on, appealing & persuading & remonstrating, & every now & then coming out with songs of triumph. It makes one's own little vexations look very small.

You will forgive my quoting so many texts as it is Sunday—Sunday & churches & prayers & sermons are my sources of sweet waters (not the only ones.) and I think they will last my time whatever Science may do for the next generation. Edwin Abbott has been preaching about middle-class education & the Commissioner's Report & beseeching parents to give five minutes a week, or even five minutes a month, to looking after their children's minds.[3] I wished you had been there, tho' I am not sure that you would have liked it all.

Yours ever, ED.

I don't as much disapprove of early marriages. It is great disparity of age that I dislike.

GC: ALS ED B11

1. Bodichon wrote ED in early March 1868: "What really staggers me is the work before you! I can't lose faith in the cause that was in me before you were born & every expe-

rience of my life makes that faith more & more certain & more ardent.... I am astounded at the wonderful interest in the 'higher education' it is going on every where rolling about, this great wave of interest & your book partly set it going" (Chronicle 591).

2. On 4 March 1868, ED received a note from George Eliot containing a contribution of £50 and the message: "We wish to give our adhesion to the good work" (Chronicle 592).

3. Two Edwin Abbots are possible: Edwin Abbott (1808–82), who was principal of Philological School, Marylebone Road; wrote books and texts in Latin and Greek; and advocated better English training in schools; and Edwin Abbott (1838–1926), who was Assistant Master of King Edward's School, Birmingham; Headmaster of City of London School; Hulsean Lecturer at Cambridge University; and a writer of religious and educational texts.

To Anna Richardson

March 17th 1868

...I write a line to tell you that the negociations with the Voluntary Board have come to a bad end. Mr. Myers. (son of Mr. M. of Keswick) has written down to Miss Wolstenholme to tell her to get up a Memorial to Cambridge for advanced Examns. for women, to be signed by schoolmistresses, governesses, & ladies. He tells her what sort of Memorial it is to be, & warns her that 'of *course* it must not attempt to dictate the *kind* of examns.'

Mr. Myers seems to have great faith in the obedience of the Northern ladies, for he writes to me the same day, to tell me (without any qualification) that they are going to do it, conveying the impression that they have started it themselves. I am glad the matter has come to this point so quickly. I felt sure that the Voluntary was *tending* to a special scheme under University authority, tho' they kept asserting that it was 'merely a stopgap.'

Miss Clough it seems, goes about urging the scheme expressly on the ground that it *is* special & therefore likely to suit women better than a general one.

We shall be having a meeting of our old original Examn. Committee next week, & I shall bring the matter forward & get instructions from them.

GC: AMsS C593

To Anna Richardson

March 23rd 1868

...I have a word or two to say about the special Examn. scheme. I agree with you that it is not worth while to waste strength in opposing it, in so far that I wd. not think of getting up a counter Memorial or anything of that sort. But I think you do not quite know how much depends on the movement now going on. The new scheme has nothing about it of a stop-gap character. It is urged forward on the ground of female examns. for females, & if Cambridge is beguiled into granting it, it will be urged with equal pertinacity upon all the towns which have accepted the Lecture scheme. I have been talking to Mr. ⟨John⟩ Hales about it this morning & explaining to him that we did not want anything which wd. lead away from Degrees. He said: 'But Miss Clough & her section don't want Degrees.' And I have heard otherwise that she is pressing the scheme expressly on the ground that it will be specially adapted to women's needs. I have known this all thro', but it has not hitherto been necessary to dispute about it. *Now* however, the question is being put; Do practical, thoughtful & working women want Degrees & a common standard, or is it only the clamour of a few fanatics & women's rights people? The Memorial for an independent examn. will be an emphatic answer, one way or the other. That is why I am afraid of it. I do not think the case you mention is parallel. The idea of the new scheme is not that it is to be easy & a stop-gap, but that it is to be womanly. Miss Wolstenholme, who under the silently demoralising influence of working for a special scheme has quite changed her mind on the subject, means to go in herself. What it is best to do, is difficult to say.

...I don't mean to make up my own mind finally till after the Meeting of our Examn. Committee on Thursday.[1] The reason I write now is that in a letter from Miss Wolstenholme received this morning, she says 'Mrs. Butler heard from Miss Richardson about a week ago & certainly from her letter understood her to be favourable to our examn. plans.' You see it won't do to blow the trumpet with an uncertain sound. It only leads to misunderstandings, & the misunderstandings re-appear at Cambridge in the form of a unanimous cry from 'the North.' (they *dare* not include London.) for female examns.

GC: AMsS C594

1. The University Examinations Committee met on 26 March 1868 and resolved "that the institution of independent schemes of examns. for women exclusively, tends to keep down the level of female education." While they agreed reluctantly to recommend the new University of London examinations for women, they would not support a similar system proposed for Cambridge by the North of England Council (Chronicle 597).

To Anna Richardson

March 27th 1868

...Let me begin by answering your questions.
1. The &c. represents about £100. About £150 is actually paid in....
2. No site has been decided upon, but I think we are shut up to Hitchin as the

only place which combines the essential conditions of *rurality*, healthiness & accessibility.

3. Everything in the little report I sent you [re Conference, annexed] was agreed to. except that as Professor Seeley was prevented (by the illness of his mother) from coming to the Committee, it was agreed not to make any specific statement about the course of studies, beyond what is said in the circular. A 'Sub.Committee of Studies' (Mr. Seeley, Mr. Roby, Mrs. Manning, Mrs. Gurney, Mr. Bryce & Miss Metcalfe & myself) has been appointed. We have to agree upon the curriculum, the particulars of the Entrance Examn. & some 'Instructions' to intending students. & report upon the subject to the Executive Committee 4... 5... 6...

Lord Stanley is like me, a conservative, that is, a Liberal all the way round. He has always voted on our side. (even six years ago) in the London University. He is on the Senate. . . .

I think there is a great deal in what you say about getting the true thing for the *highest* education, which will naturally govern the lower. But we have not got it yet, & to have our best friends employed in working a false scheme wd. be a great injury. People so easily get to love the thing they are working at, & to think it the best thing possible. And if there was an efficient female examn. going on under University authority, the obvious thing wd. be to give us *that*, with abundant offers of raising it, to meet the needs of our higher students, instead of committing so great an innovation as to extend their own Examn. And we shd. not be able to urge our claim for the common standard, without pouring contempt on the existing University special examn. It is a dangerous thing to create an organisation. It has no idea of getting out of the way when its work is over. It seems very doubtful whether the Myers scheme can be carried. If it shd. be, we must make the best of it. . . .

I shd. be very sorry to have any reference to the College made in the Specializers' Memorial. It is not what you *say* in a Memorial but what people give their souls to working at, that tells. . . .

I don't know whether I have pointed out the undesirableness of detaching the young women who can never come to a resident College, from the London University. By & by we shall get Cambridge Degrees for residents, but the only common standard in existence for non-resident students is that of the London University. Anything got from Cambridge for non-resident women *must* be special. It seems to me our true policy to push our way with the London Examn. so as to link as far as possible the education of women in provincial towns with such institutions as Owens College & the Newcastle College of the future.

I think it is a thousand pities that the Manchester women do not try to attach themselves to Owens College, instead of setting up a new female machinery in an unsatisfactory sort of connexion with Cambridge. . . .

I am afraid it wd. be useless for you to write either to Mrs. Butler or Miss Clough. I tried talking to Mrs. Butler when she was in Town & she gave me to understand that she had no opinion on the matter, & wished I wd. talk to 'them', which I believe means Mr. Myers....

Miss Clough has been talked to by my friend Mrs. Heaton of Leeds, by Mr. Hales & by Mrs. Bodichon, without the slightest effect. (except making her angry.) To Mrs. Bodichon she spoke openly against both the College & the Local examn. I knew that was her feeling, tho' she has no doubt tried to keep it under. An objection that she brought to the College was that she did not like our having a Chapel & Chaplain! Mrs. Bodichon made her read the circular, as a penance. She fancies it was for the first time....

GC: AMsS C598

To Henry Tomkinson

April 1868

...I hope you were satisfied with the meeting.[1] I thought the mastery of the subject shown by the Executive Committee was quite remarkable. I expected every minute that somebody wd. be offering to sacrifice some vital principle, but nobody did. My brother thought your part was 'perfectly done.' The Dean thought it a capital meeting & wishes our religious meetings cd. be cast in the same mould.

Mr. Courtney has put down his name for £100. & a Mr. Shadworth Hodgson, who writes from the Isle of Wight, has sent £25....

GC: AMsS C608

1. On 28 March 1868, a public meeting was held in London to discuss the proposed College for Women. Over two hundred activists, educators, and reformers attended. Reporting on the meeting to Anna Richardson, Annie Austin noted that "all spoke as if their minds were made up, & of 'our College' & as if it certainly is to be done, which was very good to hear" (Chronicle 604).

To Anna Richardson

April 23 1868

...I did not go to the Hares' at Easter. My mother was so far from well that I felt I cd. not leave her. The old symptoms which troubled her last summer came back with the return of spring, & the remedies seem as before, to be ineffectual. Elizth. Garrett has insisted on a consultation, & she has seen Dr. Ramskill, who is considered an authority in nervous cases. Some new things are being tried under his direction, but hitherto without any permanent benefit. She fluctuates & some days seems decidedly better, but she does not on the whole, gain ground, & it makes us very anxious. Dr. Ramskill thinks the liver is affected, as well as the nerves. Paralysis, the fear of which has haunted me for a long time, is not, he thinks impending, & so far I feel relieved of a great anxiety. . . .

GC: AMsS C608a

To Anna Richardson

April 29th 1868

. . . My mother has seemed a little better the last few days. The most discouraging thing is that it is just the warm weather which does not suit her. She rallied during the winter months & fell back again on the return of Spring, without any assignable cause. . . .

. . . I am afraid she is not likely to be able to go North. She has a great horror of being so far from home that she cd. not come back at once if she felt worse. But thank you warmly for your kind thought all the same. . . .

GC: AMsS C609

To Anna Richardson

April 29th 1868

. . . I have been suffering much lately from Mr. Myers & Mrs. Butler. What they have done is.
1. To invent a very unwise scheme for petitioning Oxford & Cambridge to extend their Examns. for Degrees to non-resident women.
2. then to say that I proposed it (!)
3. then to get a number of men to write letters denouncing it.
4. then (without saying a word to me from beginning to end of what they were doing) to get the N. of E. Council to print and circulate these Letters.

I feel sure that they must have imposed upon Miss Clough, for tho' I know she is very strong on the Special side, I do not believe she wd. knowingly take part in misrepresentation.

I have had to write an official letter to her about it, in which I have expressed surprise, but not the indignation, which I cd. not help feeling. Unfortunately some Cambridge men have been led to commit themselves to narrow views about female education. However I dare say they will forget what they have said before the College Examn. come under discussion. The policy in this case has been to represent only two views as possible. either to ask for Oxford and Cambridge Degree Examns, or to ask for a special one. Some of the ladies at Leeds were however witty enough to see that there was also the alternative of not being for anything, & resolutely refused to sign the Memorial. I cannot help admiring their pluck, for with the pressure put upon them, it really was almost 'resisting unto blood.'

...I have been to Hitchin & seen desirable sites, & had much pleasant talk with Mr. Tuke & Mr. ⟨Frederick⟩ Seebohm....[1]

GC: AMsS C610

1. Probably James Hack Tuke (1819–96). He lived in Hitchin and was a partner in Sharples and Company, bankers, and chairman of the Central Education Board.

To Anne Jemima Clough

UNIVERSITY EXAMINATIONS. 17, CUNNINGHAM PLACE. LONDON. N.W.

April 29th 1868

My dear Miss Clough

I have this morning received from a friend, a copy of "Letters received and read at the North of England Council for the Higher Education of Women, held at Leeds on Wednesday. April 15th. 1868."

On reading these letters in the order in which they appear, it struck me with surprise that so many of them should treat almost exclusively of the question whether it would be expedient to open the Oxford and Cambridge Examinations for Degrees to women. I had not heard of "the scheme" to which reference is repeatedly made, and the pains bestowed in demonstrating its impracticability seemed to me superfluous. You may judge of my astonishment when on arriving at Mr. Bonney's letter, I discovered that the proposal purported to come from myself.[1]

Misunderstandings always have some origin, and in the present case it is possible (but this I offer only as a conjecture) that the mistake may have arisen out of a suggestion made by Mr. Myers last February, and which I supposed had long since been dropped. There was at that time, as you know, a proposal under consideration for establishing Examns. for women by a Voluntary Board. It was felt that such Examinations would labour under the great disadvantage of offering a new and unauthorised standard.

To myself and others with whom I am working, this objection seemed a fatal one. It was suggested by Mr. Myers that it might perhaps be got over by adopting the standard of some existing University Examn, and Mr. Myers mentioned the Cambridge Little-go as one which with the modification of making Greek alternative with German, might answer the purpose.[2] The idea was not mine, but it seemed to me that it offered an opening ⟨for⟩ compromise between the promoters of the Voluntary Board and the promoters of the Local Examination, and might meet the desire strongly felt on both sides to avoid anything like a division among the friends of female education, who had up to that time worked together with remarkable unanimity. I must add, that it was urged upon me with great emphasis that the new scheme was intended simply as a stopgap and would be withdrawn as soon as more satisfactory measures could be carried into effect.

Mr. Myers told me afterwards that he had consulted with his friends, and that his idea had been abandoned ⟨as⟩ impracticable. I was told also that instead of attempting a Voluntary Board, it was proposed to apply to the University of Cambridge for a Special Examn. for women, and a draft Memorial on the subject was sent to me. I took an opportunity of bringing the matter forward at a meeting of the London General Committee. (the Committee formed in 1862, thro' whose agency the extension of the Local Examns. was obtained.) and the following Resolutions were passed.

1. That this Committee, believing that the distinctive advantage of the Cambridge University Local Examns, consists in their offering a common standard to boys and girls, and that the institution of independent schemes of examns. for women exclusively tends to keep down the level of female education, cannot take part in the proposed Memorial to the University of Cambridge for advanced examns. for women above the age of eighteen.

2. That while regretting the special character of the examn. for women proposed by the University of London, the Committee recommend that women above the age of eighteen be advised to avail themselves provisionally of this Examination.

It appeared to us that it was on many grounds undesirable to ask Cambridge for examns. for women just at the moment when the London University, having obtained a supplemental Charter for this express purpose, is taking the matter in hand. As regards Examns. for teachers, as such, there is much to be said in favour of waiting until the important Recommendations of the Schools Inquiry Commission on this point shall have been fully discussed. In the meantime, governesses are in some respects better off than male teachers, as the diplomas given by the Science and Art Department and by the College of Preceptors are as accessible to women as to men, while governesses have besides, the Certificates of the Home & Colonial School Society, which in addition to such subjects as Arithmetic, Geography, Natural History, Modern Languages, Music and Drawing, certify also "Teaching power" and "Governing power."[3] There is I believe no institution which offers to male teachers of the middle class, certificates of corresponding value.

From what I have said, I am sure you will understand how far it has been from our thoughts to propose the "Scheme" alluded to in the "Letters." May I ask you (as Hon. Sec. to the North of England Council) to be good enough to take what means may seem to you best of making this known to their writers and readers.

I remain
Dear Miss Clough
Yours very sincerely
Emily Davies.

Newn: ALS AHEW(10)

1. Probably Thomas George Bonney (1833–1923), who was mathematical master at Westminster School; a Tutor at Cambridge in geology; secretary and president of the Geological Society; and Hulsean Lecturer at Cambridge.
2. See ED to Anna Richardson, 28 February 1868.
3. The Science and Art Department was established by the government in the 1850s to develop Science Schools, to regulate the payments by results scheme, and to award certificates to teachers. The Home and Colonial Institution was founded in 1836. It provided training for teachers of elementary and secondary girls' schools. For the College of Preceptors, see ED to Tomkinson, 18 November 1863.

To Anne Jemima Clough

UNIVERSITY EXAMINATIONS. | 17, CUNNINGHAM PLACE. LONDON. N.W.

May 1st 1868

My dear Miss Clough

Thank you for your note. I am quite sure of your readiness to oblige me in any matter, but this is not a matter of favour. It is simple justice, when a misstatement has been made of a nature to damage anybody's character, either of good sense or anything else, to make reparation as quickly as possible. I shall hope to hear from you by Monday. If not, I must consider what to do. In the meantime, perhaps I had better say that I do not think anything less than printing my letter *in full*, would answer the purpose. You say that the Letters are sent to people who want information. Surely we must all desire that such information should be accurate, whereas what is now in circulation is quite the reverse.

Please do not think that I am blaming *you* in the matter, or that I am making much of a trifle. For myself personally, I should not care about it, but connected as I am with educational movements, I am unwilling to run the risk of damaging *them* by letting people believe that I have been proposing a foolish & impracticable scheme.

And the worst of it is, that the more unlikely a story is, the more it seems to spread and the longer to be remembered. If *you*, who know me, believed this, how much more likely it is that others should be similarly misled.

When you come to Combe Hurst, I hope you will come and see us and have a little talk about this and other matters.

Ever yours sincerely
Emily Davies.
If you print my letter I shall ask you to be good enough to let me have a few copies.

Newn: ALS AHEW(11)

To Anne Jemima Clough

CLAREMONT, | LEEDS

May 2d 1868

My dear Miss Clough

I am really sorry to trouble you with another letter, but it has struck me that a phrase in my letter of the 29th may be misunderstood. I spoke of a compromise "between the promoters of the Voluntary Board and the promoters of the Local Examns." and I think it just possible that some people might take this as implying that *all* the promoters of the Local Examns. objected to the Voluntary Board, which would not be accurate. It is perhaps not very important matter, but I am anxious not to run the least risk of misconception, and I will therefore ask you to be good enough, in case my letter goes beyond yourself, to erase the words "between the promoters of the Voluntary Board & the promoters of the Local Examns." The sentence will make sense without this clause.

I shall be at home on Monday.

Yours very sincerely,
Emily Davies
"~~I have had sent me a copy~~"

Newn: ALS AHEW(12)

To Sedley Taylor

17 Cunningham Place. N.W. | May 16th | [1868]

Dear Mr. Taylor

I am sorry to find that my letter to Miss Clough, when read without the "Letters" which called it forth, conveys ^{almost} exactly the contrary impression to what I intended. There are 12 letters, all denouncing either directly or by implication, a "scheme' which one of them distinctly attributes to me, of memorialising "for the establishment of an examn. for female teachers *identical* with those now held for young men." *This* is the scheme my letter was written to disclaim. The proposal is I believe a pure fiction. It certainly was not brought forward by anybody at the meeting of the N⟨orth of⟩.E⟨ngland⟩. Council, & till these remarkable Letters appeared, neither I nor any one to whom I have spoken on the subject had heard a word about it. The Letters have been circulated as "information" among schoolmistresses & governesses, with a view to obtaining their signatures to the Memorial in favour of Mr. Myers's scheme. I send you a copy, that you may see what it is that I have repudiated in the last paragraph of my letter. It would perhaps have been as well simply to disclaim the proposal & say no more. But so much having been said on my behalf, I thought it might be useful to take the opportunity of explaining as quietly and inoffensively as possible, why the University Examns. Committee keep aloof from the Memorial. If you examine our Resolution, I think you will see that the language is general & very moderate. I am quite willing to hope that in the present case, the independent scheme may do good. We are taking no steps in opposition to it.

The originators of the College scheme, Mrs. Bodichon, myself & others, hold very strongly to the principle of a common standard, and we certainly should not have started the project on any other. One of the Resolutions adopted at the first meeting of the Executive Committee (the one proposing to connect the College with Cambridge) was intended to express this. But we are not at all anxious to put it forward unnecessarily or to press it in a fanatical spirit. I hope that when the Programme of the Entrance Examn. is agreed upon & can be circulated, it will show that we do not intend to exclude any subject of instruction in itself desirable, merely because it has not hitherto been made much of in the education of men. This sort of practical evidence will probably go farther than a great deal of discussion about principles, as to which it seems to me that the more explanations one gives, the more material one supplies for fresh misunderstandings.

If occasion should arise, I shall be much obliged if you will say for me that tho' I cannot see my way to asking for the new Examn. scheme, I & those with whom I have been working for the last six years, are not opposing it. For my own part, my great desire is to keep out of the whole thing, but that is scarcely possible when other people are determined to drag one into it.

With thanks for you letter,
I remain
Yours ever truly
Emily Davies.

CUL: ALS Add.MS.6258(E)37

To Anna Richardson

17 Cunningham Place. | May 23d. 1868

My Dear Anna

We had a meeting of the Executive Committee yesterday, & it was agreed to order two insertions of an advt. in the Literary Churchman. We have decided to issue a new *short* circular, to go with the old one, and to announce a system of nominations. What the system is to be is not yet quite decided, but the circular will answer for an advt. without it. We propose heading it with the names of *some* of the Committee. (All would make it too long.) Will you please tell me whether those I have marked are likely to be the best for readers of the Lit. Churchman. We considered what we could do about getting more orthodox names & agreed that Miss Yonge especially, was much to be desired, but no one knew how to get at her.[1] I have written to Lord Lyttelton to-day. We had a great deal to do, & did not get so far as to appoint Mr. Waterhouse as our Architect, but I hope it may be done at our next meeting. No one seems to wish for anybody else.

It is so long since I wrote last that I forget what I have told you. I have paid a visit to Hitchin & saw Mr. Seebohm whom I liked much. He has 4 daughters for us. There is a Mr. ⟨Fenton⟩ Hort also living near Hitchin, whose name Mr. Ashwell will know. He is a most accomplished scholar & may be a great help to us in teaching. In the meantime he & Mr. Tuke & Mr. Seebohm are ~~noting~~ looking after sites &c. for us.

The old circular is to be revised a little. I send you a copy, & I hope you will let me give your name as Local Sec. Would you ask Mr. Ashwell ~~also~~ to be good enough to act also? Yorkshire & Bristol are provided for, and St. Andrew's, Lancashire is I am afraid lost for the present. We cannot well do anything without Mrs. Butler and Miss Wolstenholme & they are too much absorbed in other schemes to have any interest to spare for the College. I think we shall get some help from Birmingham but we are waiting for the Social Science meeting to set things going there. Just now we are projecting a public meeting in London. It is a trial, but I fear a necessary one. A small Sub. Committee is to find out whether we can get good enough speakers to make it worth while. We propose trying for the Duke of Argyle to take the Chair. I suppose it will be in the second or third week of June. Perhaps Mr. Ashwell's article would come best before or after that. Will you ask him? Lady A. Stanley said yesterday that she thought the best way of promoting the scheme would be to get it "written up", & somebody else then said that people could write more easily if they had a meeting to refer to. I suppose it helps them in composing their first sentence. ~~Thank you for sending me the L. C.. I read the article & thought it likely to be useful.~~

~~I am glad Mr. Watson sees some hope for his scheme[2]. I shall tell Mr. Seeley about it when I see him.~~ (Mr. Seeley) ~~He has done a good deal at preparing our Entrance Examn. programme,~~ which is not quite finished yet.

~~What do you mean by Miss Clough's not being able to believe in the existence of parallel lines? I cannot imagine.~~

The Myers–Butler project has brought me much troublesome & painful & perplexing correspondence. Mr. Roby thinks that if it passes, which seems very likely, it will be almost fatal to our getting Degree Examns. from Cambridge. They will offer us a Myers Examn. instead. Mrs. Gurney thinks it will be seriously injurious to the College, as being regarded as a sufficient provision, in the shape of certificates. My impression is that it will be used as an excuse, but that we shall carry all our points in the long run. In the meantime, it is no doubt doing harm both in absorbing interest & energy, & stirring up strife. ~~It has been so unfairly worded that I should feel unwilling to accept help from its advocates. I should not like the College to be promoted by such means. Why have not you come up for the Yearly Meeting?[3] I have not seen a Friend. I wish I could have come to you. Many thanks. It would have been too pleasant for a wretched mortal who evidently wants much chastisement. My mother is certainly better. Love to Caro.[4] Ever yours~~, ED

GC: ALS ED GC1/6

    1. Charlotte Yonge responded: "I have decided objections to bringing large masses of girls together, and think that home education under the inspection or encouragement of sensible fathers, or voluntarily continued by the girls themselves is far more valuable, both intellectually and morally than any external education. I am afraid I cannot assist you" (Chronicle 622).

    2. Robert Watson's plans for a college, later the Newcastle College of Physical Science.

    3. The Quaker Yearly Meeting.

    4. Probably Caroline Richardson, Anna Richardson's sister.

To Sedley Taylor

17 Cunningham Place. N.W. | June 19th 1868

Dear Mr. Taylor

Mr. ⟨Henry⟩ Sidgwick's suggestion strikes me as exceedingly promising.[1] I will tell the Committee about it individually, and get them to think it over. I should not myself consider it a diversion of funds to spend some money upon it. It would seem to me to come in fairly under the head of preliminary expenses. I think however that the essential idea might be carried out without taking a house. The sort of women we have in view would not, I feel sure, like to be under superintendence, and it does not seem to me at all necessary that they should be.

I think it very doubtful whether they would even like to live together. That is a matter of individual taste, which I should prefer leaving open. The essential thing seems to be that our future teachers should both add to their own knowledge, and get ideas of what first rate teaching is. The difficulty I see is, that if our Committee acted officially in the matter, it would be almost equivalent to appointing our officers, & we are scarcely in a position yet to commit ourselves so far, especially as one advantage that strikes me in this plan would be that of finding out something about the qualifications of our teachers. So far as I see at present, I fancy the best thing to do might be something like this; to make known as widely as we possibly could privately, that any ladies who might be aspiring to take part in the College work by & by would find it to their advantage to go & reside at Cambridge for a time, and that they would find people there who would welcome them & help them. I suppose any of the Professors would admit them to Lectures, as a matter of course, but that seems to me much less important than the private class tuition of which you speak. There are plenty of Lectures going on in London, and they do not seem to be of very much use.

The kind of teaching given to a small select class would I should think be much more valuable as a preparation for our work. If it were done *very quietly*, I do not think ladies would have any real difficulty in living in lodgings by themselves. Miss Garrett spent a winter at St. Andrew's in that way, and afterwards she lived at Whitechapel for some months, while attending the London Hospital. Of course if two or more ladies chose to join, there could be no objection to their doing so. The great thing would be to avoid much talk about it before it was actually done. And we could scarcely take a house, & act officially as a Committee, without attracting a good deal of attention & incurring responsibility. I am assuming of course that the students should be old enough to take care of themselves, say women of five-and-twenty. If younger women wished to go, they might be put under some kind of charge of one of the older ones. Their submitting to advice might be made a condition of their admission to any classes that might be formed. I do not feel sanguine as to the prospect of finding *many* women ready to take advantage of the plan, but that would be of less consequence, as we shall want very few, perhaps not more than two resident teachers besides the head, for the first year. It would be an immense point gained to have even a small class of trained women to choose from, and those for whom we had no work, would be all the more valuable as teachers in schools for having had some more teaching themselves. It would of course be a contingent advantage of the plan that it would be the beginning of a link between the College & Cambridge.

We got thro' a good deal of business at the meeting yesterday—finally fixed upon the scheme for the entrance exam. appointed Mr. Waterhouse as our Architect. settled the nomination scheme. and decided to advertise to a considerable extent. Mr. Macmillan offers us a page in his Magazine gratuitously. The public meeting is postponed, as premature.

All the great people who were spoken to about it said they were not prepared to commit themselves.

I remain
Yours very truly
Emily Davies.

Are you going to the Social Science Meeting at Birmingham? We are to have half a day consecrated to the college in the Education Department.

CUL: ALS Add.MS.6258(E)38

1. Sidgwick had proposed taking a house in Cambridge as a residence for women who would eventually become officers at the proposed College for Women. See ED to Anna Richardson, 25 June 1868.

To Anna Richardson

June 25th 1868

... I have some progress to report. At our Committee meeting last week, it was agreed that Mr. Waterhouse should be our Architect & I have had a very pleasant letter from him accepting the office. ... I am delighted at the idea of meeting you at a sequestered public house. I have no fixed plans except *not* to leave home for any time till nearly the end of August, and I shall be charmed if you will come & take me to wherever you like, 'anywhere, anywhere out of the world.'

I have had the following suggestions from Cambridge. 'It seems highly desirable that when the College starts we should be provided with a certain number of women to act as its resident authorities who have themselves become personally acquainted with the methods of high education as employed by the best teachers. Such persons will however be most exceptionally difficult to obtain. With a view to secure them, Mr. Sidgwick suggests that we should hire a house in Cambridge with accommodation for say eight or ten (as a smaller number— four or five) and offer inducements to such persons as were likely to fill subsequently posts of importance in the College to take up their abode in the house in question under the superintendence of some competent lady—in order to profit by the educational advantages of the University, as far as they are yet attainable to women—and so fit themselves for discharging high educational functions hereafter with greater success than if they had seen only *school* teaching. Several of the Professors would I believe permit such female students to attend their Lectures, and private class tuition of quite the highest kind, could I am sure be secured for them.'

What do you think of it? The house & the superintendent seem to me quite unnecessary & objectionable, but the opportunity of getting class tuition of the highest kind & seeing the methods of high teaching, I should consider most valuable. Would it not be infinitely better as a preparation for the work you speak of than any kind of examns? What I ardently desire is that you should take advantage of this proposal, & persuade Miss Taylor, & others like her, to go too. I do not mean that all need live together. There need be no difficulty at all about living quietly in lodgings, & it would be better than the conspicuousness of taking a house. I am sure you would get every advantage in the way of Libraries & museums, besides all possible help & sympathy, & it would be the beginning of the link which we want so much to forge & to make very strong between the College & Cambridge. I don't think we could do anything more than make the proposal known as widely as we can privately, with the understanding that women who have had this training will be more eligible than others for the College offices by & by. We could not commit ourselves to anything like the appointment of our teachers at this early stage, but any for whom work could not be found in the College itself would surely find the training most useful for any kind of teaching, either voluntary or paid, which they might wish to undertake. Pray tell me what you think.

GC: AMsS C614

To Anna Richardson

July 15th 1868

...I cannot write to the papers, except when they make statements which want official rectification. You know I am almost incessantly writing quasi-private letters about the College, & when they are done—(which is *never*) I want to turn to something else. It is not so much that I dread monomania, as that I get too tired of the one subject to be able to think vigorously & freshly upon it.

... I seem to have given you the impression that the Cambridge scheme was more of a settled thing than it is. Mr. Sedley Taylor thinks it would not do for ladies, even the middle-aged, to live in lodgings at Cambridge, & the house would be a serious undertaking. If we could get a very nice lady of 60 to take a house on her own account, & if we could find some very nice students who would be her guests (paying, of course) it might work, but otherwise I doubt whether it could be done. The plan is to be discussed at a Committee meeting on the 30th, & till then it will be as well not to say much about it. I am not quite sure as to the good effect of living at Cambridge on *young* women. What you have heard of Oxford society applies I believe equally to Cambridge, & it is discouraging. The idea of student life at a University is as you say, most captivating, but when one comes to the working out, the risks begin to appear. Without much power of control, we should be responsible, & the smallest indiscretion on the part of any student would be disastrous. I am still however not without hope that something may be done.

As to our plans, I am very glad that you are willing to come to Birmingham.[1] We shall urgently want a little band of true believers to 'enlighten the ignorant, quicken the careless, convince the erroneous' &c. The chief use of the public discussions is to give occasion to private talks, which do real good.

... You will see no doubt that we have another boy to hope for.[2] He promises well so far, & Mary is getting on nicely. ...

GC: AMsS C618

1. The NAPSS meeting for 1868 was to be held in Birmingham.
2. Crompton Llewelyn Davies (1868–1935).

To Anna Richardson

17 Cunningham Place, N.W. Aug. 1st 1868

... I have a great deal to say to you & not much time to say it in, so I think it will be best just to give you a summary of what we did at the Committee meeting on Thursday. But first. I have had a very pleasant letter from your friend Miss ⟨Anna⟩ Lloyd. She seems zealous & hopeful & asked for more papers. She made a suggestion which I mentioned to the Committee that Mr. Ashwell's article should be reprinted. It was decided to print long extracts from it, & from some of the best notices in other papers, in pamphlet form. It is not to be done just yet, as we expect some more notices & we want variety in our extracts.

There was a serious discussion as to the desirableness of giving the undertaking more of a corporate character, by way of security to ~~our~~ contributors that our promises will be carried out, & a Sub. Committee (Mr. Roby, Mr. Sedley Taylor & Mr. Tomkinson.) were appointed to confer with a solicitor on the subject. They are also to get a legal opinion on the nomination scheme. If it is thought safer to issue it as it stands, it is to be printed & circulated at once. Then there was a discussion about the future programme of studies & the discipline, as to which people make constant inquiry, & it was settled that the 'Sub. Committee of *studies*' should draw up a curriculum of study & discipline. I hope to beguile Mr. Seeley into preparing a sketch of a plan of study, for criticism & discussion. The Committee have arrived at the discovery that we have not been definite enough in our statements about the College life. People do not *see* it, & they hesitate about giving money to a thing about which they feel so much in the dark. Mr. Roby suggested that in the paper to be read at Birmingham, I should give a sketch of the daily life of a student. The idea seems to me a good one, but rather difficult to carry out, as we do not know yet exactly what the life will be, & one has to steer clear between the temptation to make it look very pleasant, so as to attract students, & the risk of exciting the jealousy of parents.

... I had a visit on Saturday from one of our intending students.[1] She is nearly 19, ladylike & intelligent. She came for advice about the subjects to take up for the Entrance Examns., & decided upon Latin & Greek. Seeing her gave me a vivid impression of how delightful to teach, & how pleasant as companions, our students will be. When the Committee meets again, I mean to propose issuing a notice that intending students may send in their papers. I think we should get a good many & then we could make a 'case' of these poor young women panting for instruction & no one to give it to them....

My mother much enjoyed her day with you last week. What are you going to do in September? Shall you go to see the pictures at Leeds? Elizth. Garrett & I propose to be there on Sept. 26th, & to go from thence to Birmingham....

I suppose my mother would tell you all about our baby & its sponsors &c. He will be a very bad baby if he does not turn out well, with such advantages....

GC: AMsS C624

1. Emily Gibson entered the College for Women in 1869.

To Anna Richardson

Aug. 15 1868

Thank you for letting me see your brother's letter. It is very nice & very like him.[1]

... People bore me to death with asking how much money we have got. I cannot be always counting it up. There are a good many contributions under £50. I will send you a list some day. One reason why I want to get the Nomination scheme forward is that it will give an opportunity for bringing the pecuniary aspect of the case forward. People are so used to being *asked* for money that it does not seem to occur to them to give it spontaneously. And we cannot ask. As you see, I am strictly adhering to our principles & not saying thank you to your brother.[2] It costs me an effort. Mr. Seeley submits to his fate & is going to draw up a curriculum for consideration by the Sub. Committee of Studies. I suppose there is no one in England more competent to do it than he is. But don't you think it is good of him to undertake it?

I send you some papers of the Home Study Society & some copies of the Regulations for the London Examns. which are just out. . . .[3] I am particularly anxious to get good candidates for the London Examn., & I think there will be a good many. The Pall Mall has been pointing out that the Examn for women is substantially the same as the Matriculation Examn. for men, & lamenting that so good an opportunity of adapting an examn. to the female mind has been lost—ending with a prophesy that women will find it too hard & will not go in for it.

... Of course you will go with us to Birmingham. I wish you would persuade ever so many more good people to come. It is so much easier to work at anything when there is a little band than two or three alone. There will certainly be some people there whom it will be pleasant to meet.

... Are your questions of the sort that ought to be answered in my paper? I find it hard to write. The College is such an admirable scheme that when one begins to think of all that there is to say in favour of it, the task is endless. I am always looking out for the future officers. The Head is the great anxiety. So many qualifications are wanted.

You don't know how much pleasure it gives me to be working with you at this. It is a remarkable fact that all the people who take up the College heartily are the very best & nicest one knows. The pleasure of working with them makes up for a great deal of cold water from the inferior sort.

GC: AMsS C627

1. Richardson's brother had written to express support of the college and to donate £50.

2. Richardson told Davies that she ought not to thank people for their help with the college—that people ought to be grateful to her for providing them with the opportunity of helping (Chronicle 631).

3. On 15 July 1868, the Senate of the University of London adopted regulations for examining and certifying women. These were special examinations for which women received "Certificates of Proficiency."

To Jane Crow

17 Cunningham Place. | Aug. 21st. ⟨1868⟩

My dear Jane

I went to see Mrs. Lewes this afternoon, & tho' I did not stay very long, she said a great deal. We spoke of her health, which is such that she ^has scarcely ever had the feeling of being really well or can work without a sense of drag, but it does not come to an illness, & she is afraid she inherits from her father, longevity. The anxiety about Mr. Lewes's ~~sun~~ son upsets her a good deal, "but one hates oneself for being perturbed." Then she remarked how easily we fall back into any little vice that belongs to us, after being disturbed in it, & spoke of the state of perturbation as entirely caused by not being sufficiently occupied with large interests. I referred to something in Felix Holt about Mr. Lyon's preoccupation which set him above small cares, & said what an enviable state it must be. She said Yes, one only knew it by contrast, by the sense of the want of it. Somehow we got to talk of the Mill on the Floss. She said her sole purpose in writing it was to show the conflict which is going on everywhere ~~between~~ ^when the younger generation with its higher culture comes into collision with the older, & in which, she said, so many young hearts make shipwreck far worse than Maggie. I asked if she had known actual people like the Dodsons & she said "Oh, so much worse." She thought those Dodsons very nice people & that we owe much to them for keeping up the sense of respectability, which was the only religion possible to the mass of the English people. Their want of education made a theoretic or dogmatic religion impossible, & since the Reformation, an imaginative religion had ^not been possible. It had all been drained away. She considers that in the Mill in the Floss, everything is softened, as compared with real life. Her own experience she said was worse. It was impossible for her to write an autobiography, but she wished that somebody else could do it, it might be useful—or, that she could do it herself. She could do it better than any one else, because she could do it impartially, judging herself, & showing how wrong *she* was. She spoke of having come into collision with her father & being on the brink of being turned out of his house. And she dwelt a little on how much fault there is on the side of the young in such cases, of their ignorance of life, & the narrowness of their intellectual superiority.

Then we got to talk of fiction, & she was eager to explain the difference between prosaic & poetical fiction—that what is prosaic in ordinary novels is not the presence of the realistic element, without which the tragedy cannot be given ^shown—she herself is obliged to see and feel every minutest detail—but in the absence of anything suggesting the ideal, the higher life. She seems quite oppressed with the quantity of second rate art everywhere about. It gives her such a sense of nausea that it makes it almost impossible to her to write—"such a quantity of dialogue about everything, every hole and corner being ransacked, every possible incident seized upon." not *well* done, but done in such abundance that good art is discouraged & the higher standard works are thrust aside. She was anxious to impress upon me what she felt about the difference between prosaic & poetical work, because she thought I might disseminate it. She said in an appealing tone—"Then when you talk to young people & teachers, you *will* advise against indiscriminate reading?" She thinks she has done very little, in quantity. She cannot write what she does not care about. She has not that kind of ability.

Whatever she has done, she has studied for. Before she began to write the Mill on the Floss, she ~~read~~ ^had^ it all in her mind, & read about the Trent to make sure that the physical conditions of ~~an~~ ^some^ English river were such as to make the inundation possible, & assured herself that the population in the neighbourhood was such as to justify her picture. It is still amazing to me, tho' she seemed only to feel how *little* she had done, how she has managed to get thro' so much work, actual hard labour, in the time. A great deal of it must have been very rapidly done.

⟨damaged⟩

... must be so glad to have you. Give her my love please & I hope the waters are doing her good. I am very glad M. S. is perceptibly stronger. The Tukes have asked me to stay a few days at Hitchin, which I shall like. Esther is there now. I heard from Anna Lloyd a day or two ago. She quite means to come up, tho' trembling, for Examns. She is staying with a brother in law near Stratford on Avon. A⟨nna⟩.D.R⟨ichardson⟩.'s friend, Miss Taylor.

⟨damaged⟩

Mrs. Lewes said a good deal besides what I have put down. She thinks people who write regularly for the Press are almost sure to be spoiled by it. There is much dishonesty, bad people's work being praised because they belong to the confederacy. She spoke very strongly about the wickedness of not paying one's debts. She thinks it worse than drunkenness, not in its consequences, but in the character itself.

GC: AL ED III 5/15

To Anna Richardson

Aug. 22nd 1868

... It is on a Saturday, Oct 3rd that the Coll. is to be discussed at Birmingham. I do not think there is anything special to say. As to the London Examns. it seems to me that the great merit of the general Examn. (as they call it) is that as some of the papers have been complaining, a great opportunity of adapting an Examn. to the female mind has been missed. I believe the real fact was that when they came to discussing the subjects on their merits, it was found that there were no reasons for diverging from the curriculum laid down for men, from the point of view, of course, of those who consider the London Matriculation a good examn., as to which there is much difference of opinion.

I believe they have some examn. in Divinity for men. I suppose the New Testament would not naturally come into an examn. in *Greek*, as it is not good Greek. The examns. for higher proficiency seem to me very objectionable, as giving up the principle of a general education for women. It is saying in effect, 'So long as you know as much as we expect from boys of sixteen, that is enough for you in the way of general education. You may be examined besides in any particular subject that takes your fancy, but we have no idea that you could do anything equivalent to taking a B.A. Degree.' *Practically*, the certificates may be of some use, but I don't think they will come to much.

Mr. Seeley has only undertaken to prepare a curriculum on the understanding that he is merely making suggestions for the consideration of the Committee. I will try not to thank him too much, but really while so few people do anything like what they ought, it is difficult not to be grateful to those who come at all near fulfilling their duty.

I have just finished my paper[1] & feel like a free Briton—at least unless some of you make me write it all over again, which I rather expect. I shall ask for your criticism when you come. You will find many deficiencies to say the least, but I hope some of them will be supplied in the discussion....

GC: AMsS C630

1. For the NAPSS conference.

To Barbara Bodichon

PROPOSED COLLEGE FOR WOMEN. | 17 CUNNINGHAM PLACE. N.W.

Sept. 9th ⟨1868⟩

My dear Mrs. Bodichon

Will you please thank Miss Edwards for her kind note. I was very glad to have such a good account of you all. I am sending you by this post some College papers, & the reprint from the London Student, which you may find useful.[1] If *you* think it worth while, will you send the pamphlet to Mr. Mark Pattison & the Brodies. I would rather they did not get it from me.

I have been frightened about the College discussion at Birmingham but I hope it is all right now. They had been (by mistake) changing the day, & were going to mix up my paper with one by Mr. Myers about the Lectures &c. There is a talk of a joint paper by Mrs. Butler & Miss Wolstenholme, & another by Miss Becker. So we shall not be undisturbed, but I hope we may pull thro' without any unseemly clashing.

Miss Garrett has made up her mind to study for the Paris degree.[2] It seems to be necessary & she *likes* the hard work.

Ever your affecn.

ED.

GC: ALS ED B14

1. Emily Davies, "Special Systems of Education for Women," *London Student* (June 1868).
2. The Faculty of Medicine at the University of Paris had opened to women. In 1870, Garrett became the first woman to receive her M.D. from the Sorbonne.

To Barbara Bodichon

17 Cunningham Place. N.W. | Thursday evening | [Sept. 1868]

My dear Mrs. Bodichon

Your enclosure was forwarded to me at Birmingham, & I have sent it on to Jane Crow. I don't myself know anyone likely to suit Sir C⟨harles⟩. Lyell.

We had an encouraging week of Social Science & enjoyed it. The College was a very new idea, but it was well received. Judging by the size of the audience there was more interest about it than about anything else, except strikes. The discussion was poor, but it seems to have done no harm, which is something. I heard of some more girls who will come as soon as we are ready for them. I am going to propose to the Committee to enroll names. As to money, I think the time is come for beginning to collect small sums, & that as soon as ever we get enough we must buy the site and get the building planned & a picture of it.

I don't think collecting smaller sums will discourage large gifts & there are a great many people who might as well be employed in collecting. It seems to be a fact of ~~experience~~ observation that nobody gives anything without being asked. So we must ask.

Mrs. ⟨Charles⟩ Mathews (whom I like *much*) is to be Local Sec., & they will get up a Committee later on, when the girls' examn. is thoroughly established. There is a very nice sensible woman, a doctor's wife, who is working that, & she is a little afraid of starting anything else in the same line till after the first examn., which will be in December. She has got a capital Committee, & she is afraid they would some of them resign if they were dragged on too fast. She is going to start a Schoolmistresses' Association.

We seem likely to have a considerable increase in the number of girls examined at the London Centre this year, & there are some new Centres besides.[1]

I am sending you some papers. Please distribute them far & wide, & ask for more.

I shall be at Brighton next week for a few days. Dr. Hodgson's Lectures begin on Saturday.

Ever your affecn. ED.

GC: ALS ED B13

1. In December 1868, 241 Junior and 160 Senior girls took the Local Examinations in sixteen cities.

To Barbara Bodichon

THE KENSINGTON SOCIETY. | 17, CUNNINGHAM PLACE, N.W. LONDON. BRIGHTON.
Tuesday. | [1869?] | [Sept: 1868]

My dear Mrs. Bodichon

Thanks for your note. I should like very much to come & see you, but I *must* be back in Town for Dr. Hodgson's Lecture on Saturday & am to stay here to the last moment that I can. Have you heard of a capital article in the Guardian about the College?[1] I am getting it reprinted.

Dr. Acland has sent his name for the General Committee with a very pleasant letter. As to Lady Brodie, she probably does not know what Cambridge education is, *now*.

Mr. Seeley is working at our curriculum. There is nothing to stop us from making it the very best that the most enlightened people can devise. The discussion was at Birmingham was much better than it looks in the Daily News. To get a room full of people to listen attentively to a paper for more than an hour, is something; & the foolish parts of the speeches afterwards fell dead. Mr. Samuel Morley was present & seemed much interested. I wrote a letter to him yesterday which Mrs. Ernest Noel, who is a kind of cousin of his, promised to forward. He has £50,000 a year & does not spend £10,000, & gives largely to things that he approves. Mrs. E. Noel seems likely to be a capital ally. She has a large acquaintance & will diffuse information, as you are doing, among the clergy & gentry.

I am sure this is most useful work. We want to make as many friends as possible, not only for the present, but with a view to getting public money by & by. The Times article will do some good I hope.

There is a great deal to be done. I find people are much more interested in the College when they have *seen* somebody who is concerned in it. And prejudice melts away beautifully.

I believe we shall have about 100 girls for examn. this year. Last year we had 61. I have already had applications from 91, & there are several schools I have not heard from yet.

There are also 3 or 4 new Centres.

We had about 60 ladies & 2 gentlemen at Dr. Hodgson's Lecture on Saturday. Mr. ⟨Thomas⟩ Leslie (Professor of Pol. Econ. at Univ. Coll:) said it was the largest Pol. Econ. class he had ever seen.

Ever your affecn. ED.

GC: ALS ED B15

1. "A College for Women," *Guardian* (30 September 1868).

To Barbara Bodichon

PROPOSED COLLEGE FOR WOMEN. | 17 CUNNINGHAM PLACE. N.W.

Nov. 14th 1868

My dear Mrs. Bodichon

We shall be very glad to see a lady & answer questions about your servant's character.

I hope you are finding Ventnon pleasant & getting a little stronger. Mrs. ⟨Charlotte⟩ Burbury has asked me to let you see the enclosed copy of a letter which she sent to the Times but did not get inserted.

You may like to see too Mrs. Manning's note, which is as you will understand, quite private. Please let me have it back. Her conditions seem to me most liberal, & on such terms it may be possible to begin in a hired house. The first thing to do seems to be to find out how many students are ready to come. I have had letters from Hitchin about land. There is something to be said in favour of buying a site & getting a building planned, to exhibit in the Academy next year. Should you be willing to pay your subscription, or part of it, as soon as it is wanted for such an object? You are not bound to do it. It is entered on our Minutes that your £1000 is to meet £29,000. But it might be a step towards getting the rest of the money. We shall have to do something active in the way of canvassing. Mr. Roby says we want an enthusiastic person who will go about asking people. It is a sad fact, that people don't give to *anything* without being asked. We are working at the curriculum. Do you think the elements of Drawing might be taught to everybody, whether they have any taste for it or not?

Shall you be in Town about the 14th Dec.? I should like you to see our 136 dear girls.[1]

Yours affectionately
ED.

GC: ALS ED B16

1. Taking the Cambridge Local Examinations.

To Charlotte Burbury

17 Cunningham Place. N.W. | Nov. 17 ⟨1868⟩

My dear Mrs. Burbury

Thank you for your letter & its enclosure, which I have sent on to Mme. Bodichon. We shall be very glad of a favourable article in a Manchester paper. Perhaps it would be convenient to make my paper in the ^December^ Contemporary Review, the occasion for a notice, & Mr. Kennedy would find in it the points we have thought it most desirable to bring forward.[1] I am sending him some papers. I wish he could get some of the rich Manchester people to contribute. I will try & find out whether Miss Gaskell *cares* enough to make a good Local Secretary. I am sorry the Times did not put in your letter. The things they *do* put in, give one a low impression of the public taste. When we meet, I should like to have a little talk with you about the line of argument you have adopted. Of course I agree with you that it is justice, not gallantry, that we want. But I am not sure that it is well to say very much about justice. I think it may fairly be replied that the question is whether our claims *are* just. You see, the word justice has various interpretations, & I do not think we can assume as a matter of course that it means equal rights. Good men are not conscious of unfairness ~~in~~ in their dealings with women. They *feel* willing to give ample justice, & therefore an appeal to their sense of justice makes no impression, or if any, it only irritates & alienates. What I think we want to convince them of is that women are not so unlike men, that what is justice for one is injustice for the other. The theory that men & women are unlike, both in their nature & in the conditions of their lives, seems to me to have immense influence over good men. Without meaning the slightest injustice, they draw from it inferences which would follow from abject inferiority. To take an extreme case. (hardly arguable.) that angels were claiming the franchise. We should feel that to say that it is *just* for angels to vote because men do, would not be a tenable position. We should have to show ^if we could^ that the difference between men & angels was not such as to make equality of rights impossible or undesirable. I heard a man say, in a public discussion, that you might as well say animals ought to have votes because men have, as to say that women ought for the same reason. He did not argue that women were inferior, only totally different.

It seems to me that expediency is our best argument. If we take up the ground of justice only, we confound our case with that of minors, who might argue that it is unjust for 21 to have a privilege arbitrarily denied to 20. Even in the case of educational endowments, I feel that expediency is the surest ground. *If* it could be shown that it is for the *good* of the whole community that boys should be educated & girls not, I should not complain of the present distribution as unjust.

It seems to me rather important to be clear & guarded in what we say, on these points just now, because we are so liable to be misunderstood. You and I do not go for either equality or identity, but the claim for justice is understood to imply both. And I think we ought to hesitate in repudiating chivalry. Men feel that true chivalry is a good thing, & if we tell them we don't want it, they think we are putting an extinguisher upon a spirit which ought to be encouraged.

And as they are always thinking about what is good for men, this repels them. I think we ought rather to show them that it is *un*chivalrous, to take advantage of superior strength to keep an inferior sex, or inferior races, *more* inferior than they are by nature. The real question seems to me to be this. Is a state of subjection, the condition which is likely to bring out women's best, to produce their perfection, whatever it may be? And here I think we are on sure ground.

I hope I shall see you as soon as you come back to Town. I came from Gloucester Road by train yesterday, & found it very convenient.

Ever yours sincerely
Emily Davies.

GC: ALS Add.ED1.39.1b

1. Emily Davies, "Some Account of a Proposed New College for Women," *Contemporary Review* (December 1868).

To Barbara Bodichon

PROPOSED COLLEGE FOR WOMEN. | 17 CUNNINGHAM PLACE. N.W.
Nov. 23rd 1868

My dear Mrs. Bodichon
A lady has been here for your servant's character ⟨reference⟩. I was not at home, but my my mother saw her & said what you wished.

I seem not to have explained properly about the "small beginning" idea. I never thought of spending any of your money upon it, or mine either.

If it is done at all, which is very doubtful, my notion was to manage it very cheaply & make the student's fees cover the expenses. We should have to ask them whether they were willing to endure misery of various sorts for a year or two, rather than wait on indefinitely for perfect happiness. I am not in the least giving up the building project. Scarcely even postponing it. But I think it might help us to get the money, to come into existence in *some* shape, as soon as possible.

When I asked Lady A. Stanley if the Queen would do anything for us, she said she had no doubt she would as soon as we were on our legs, but not before. If we had a certain number of students actually ~~under~~ collected together & at work, we could proclaim the astonishing fact, & show that the thing is actually begun.

That is why I should like to buy the site. We want by every possible means to make ourselves look substantial. As you see I only propose the hired house plan for a year or two while the College is building, you will see that it would not do to have it at Cambridge. An insuperable difficulty would be that there is no house in Cambridge big enough. Even for a dozen or 20 students, an ordinary dwelling house would not be large enough. This is besides the other objection, of the strong feeling against us that we should stir up at Cambridge, just at the beginning when it will be pre-eminently necessary to conciliate. And the more I hear of Cambridge society, the less I regret the impossibility of going there. If the College was *strong*, it might reform the society, but at first it would be weak, & I think the social influence of the place would be not helpful, but very injurious.

Lady Brodie & the radicals will not help us, whatever we do. When we take one excuse out of their mouths, they find another. I am not altogether sorry for their defection, tho' of course it makes our work harder & slower. If they had been at all reasonable, we should have worked with them & been influenced by them, & the more I see of Radical women, the less I desire to increase their numbers. I went to a Radical dinner party last week, & the bold, unfeeling faces of some of the ladies & their reckless talk, quite shocked me. When I hear such things as that it is good for women to read Hepworth Dixon's books—& other similar sentiments—it makes me feel as if I had no common ground with people who think in that way. I don't want to judge them harshly, but I long to get away from them.

Our girls have increased this year from 232 to 401. They might be increased a great deal faster, if good women could be found to act as Local Secretaries. My very kind remembrances to Miss Edwards. I hope she is getting stronger.

Your affecn. ED.

GC: ALS ED B17

To Henry Tomkinson

PROPOSED COLLEGE FOR WOMEN. | 17 CUNNINGHAM PLACE. N.W.

Dec. 5th ⟨1868⟩

Minute to our Sub. Comee.
Dear Mr. Tomkinson

The Minute is as follows. "Read. A letter from Mr. Shaen, representing the desirableness of preparing a constitution providing for the future government of the College, before taking any further steps.

A Sub. Committee was appointed consisting of Mr. Roby, Mr. Sedley Taylor & Mr. Tomkinson, to confer with a solicitor & to report upon the following points. Whether it be expedient at the present stage of the undertaking to take steps, & if so, what steps, to give it a corporate character, & whether the Nomination scheme as already agreed upon may be issued without binding the Committee to anything which may hereafter cause inconvenience. The choice of the solicitor to be at the discretion of the Sub. Committee, the following names being suggested. Mr. Shaen, of the firm of Shaen & Roscoe. Mr. Wilson, of the firm of Bristow & Wilson."

You have not told me by what name to designate the Sub. Committee, & I cannot write Thursday's Minutes till the name is found.

I exhausted my invention in discovering the Sub. Committee of Studies.

Have you anything to remark upon the enclosed Proof?

Ever yours truly
Emily Davies

Will you see if the list of contributions agrees with the total amount promised?

GC: ALS ED XVII GC4/1

To Barbara Bodichon

17 Cunningham Place. N.W. | Jan. 1st | [?1869]⟨1869⟩

Dear Mrs. Bodichon

If I do not hear from you to the contrary, and if there is not a heavy fall of snow in the meantime, I hope to be at Robertsbridge on Saturday at 1.37. There seems to be no other train by which I can get to you before dark.

I am so glad you like the cold. I *bear* it.

Ever your affecn. ED.

Have not I got nice envelopes now?

GC: ALS ED B18

To Henry Tomkinson

17 Cunningham Place. N.W. | Jan. 6th 1869

Dear Mr. Tomkinson

Thank you very much for telling me about the Constitution as thought of. I am all the more obliged to you for letting me know the direction in which you are tending, as it is not exactly the line in which I am inclined to follow. I will tell you what strikes me about it, & you will not think it is from pugnaciousness if the points on which I differ come out rather conspicuously.

First, as to the Trustees. I suppose there is some reason for making them a separate body from the Governors? I fancied they would be the same, but as to that I have no opinion. I have a strong opinion that not less than half of every body connected with the College should be women.

The appointment of women as Trustees is no innovation. I am one of the Trustees for the Arnott Fund at Bedford College, & I happen to know of two instances of marriage settlements in which of the two Trustees, one is a woman. In these cases, they are unmarried, & there is no difficulty. In the case of married women, there is some complication, as the signature of a wife is not valid without that of her husband also. Mr. Shaen told me some time ago that whenever he drew up a Trust deed appointing unmarried women, he inserted a provision that in case of marriage they ceased to be Trustees, ipso facto. This seems reasonable, as otherwise you might practically be appointing as a kind of half-Trustee a man of whom you know nothing. When the husband already exists, you can take his qualifications into consideration before appointing the wife. I do not think Mrs. Bodichon would wish to act. She is in bad health, besides the difficulty of a French husband living at Algiers, &c. I do not think the Dean of Canterbury would be acceptable to Church people. Is not a traitor in the camp worse than an open enemy? On the other hand he is very popular with Dissenters, as is natural. In choosing the Trustees, I suppose the important things are that the names, being prominently before the public, would inspire confidence as regards characters, & that they should understand money. If there were *five,* perhaps it would be easier to combine these qualifications? Would not Mrs. Russell Gurney be good for one? Every one who knows her, believes in her, & her husband's name, & advice, would be a help rather than a hindrance.

As to certificates, it seems to me quite unnecessary to say anything about them. I hope the time will never arrive when we shall confer female Degrees.[1] I think the Sub-Committee ought to have had in their hands the fundamental Resolutions, passed at the first meeting, in which the distinctive character & aim of the College are defined. As to the religion question, it seems to me that we are bound by "the authorized Programme" to give some guarantee that there will be teaching "in accordance &c."

We are as much bound on that side, as we are, on the other, not to force the teaching on anybody who does not want it. ~~It would~~ But the less said about it on either side, the better I should like it.

I was thinking of the *Executive*, in what I said about the dismissal of incompetent officers. I see that that need not be discussed at present.

As to the composition of the Council, it seems to me that the proposal to represent *three* Universities departs altogether from the fundamental idea of the College, which is, to be at the earliest possible moment, a constituent part of the University of Cambridge, & adopts the totally different (not to say antagonistic) idea, of a new, independent, female University, pretending equality (perhaps superiority?) with "the existing and the venerable"—actually placing itself on the same footing with Queens College & the other excellent institutions which already give ladies' certificates.

Considering that the propelling motion for the foundation of the college was this—to obtain Degrees from one of " the venerable"—(the "the existing" having proved impracticable.) & that we were driven into starting a new thing chiefly because Queen's & Bedford refused to put themselves in the subordinate position of dependencies of Cambridge—you will understand that this proposal is surprising. All along, I have regarded the College simply as a measure of University extension. We chose to try to get the extension of Cambridge, because the London University (in which it would have been simpler & easier) refused, & because Cambridge seemed more likely than Oxford.

By some unfortunate accident, the Universities have hitherto ~~omitted to provide either~~ excluded women from education, examns. & attestation. We propose to remedy this deficiency. We are going to ask for the examn. & the attestation, & as a necessary preliminary, we undertake to provide the education, with the condition exacted from all members of the University of Cambridge that of residence. ~~in a~~ under some system of discipline approved by the University. This may be a wrong idea, but it is at any rate clear & intelligible & the one deliberately adopted at starting. Such an institution as the Constitution Committee propose could not be regarded as a kind of sister of say Trinity College.

It is more as if Trinity were to say—"We are the largest, the most liberal, & the most influential of the Colleges. We can afford to despise paltry University Degrees, & being ~~so~~ much more enlightened than anybody else, & also respected, we will cut ourselves off from "the venerable," & confer our own Degrees, representing our own ideas of what education ought to be, unhampered by the prejudices of Senate. But we don't want to be too Revolutionary or exclusive so the existing & the venerable shall each appoint a representative & so have a share in the government." Would Trinity gain, or lose, by such a course? This is putting it merely on the ground of expediency & prestige, which many people can understand. But *you* understand the real ground on which all separate schemes for women are objectionable. I mean the extreme undesirableness of drawing lines of demarcation & setting up artificial distinctions. And it seems to me that tho' there is an increasing disposition to give women fair play, there is also some tendency to increasing separation. We have not yet come to it in religion, but with Ladies' Committees, Ladies' Associations, Lectures to Ladies, & the rest, one does not quite see why we should not soon have also Ladies' Churches & Chapels, in which the duties of women as such, should be specially inculcated. We have the principle already, in the double moral code, which most people believe in.

I dare say this will seem to you an extravagant tirade on a very small provocation. Perhaps I exaggerate, but I think it is discouraging to see so many of the new things for women started on the basis of separation. It seems like getting into more of a *system* of separateness, & it makes one suspicious of anything like a step in that direction.

You know of course that my feeling against raising barriers between men & women has nothing to do with the assertion of equality or identity, in neither of which I believe.

To recur to the Council. Could Cambridge be represented by some ex officio people, such as the Vice-Chancellor & the Master of Trinity? Perhaps the Vice-Chancellor only would be enough, as of course the others might be Cambridge men. I think that not less than half of the whole body should be women. If there must be preponderance in one side or the other, it seems to me not unreasonable that in a College for women, it should be on that side, considering also the tendency of the age to give women, as such, less weight wherever they are.

If the Council is to be named for the beginning & to continue in office 4 years, I do not see any advantage in giving votes to subscribers. It would not be a provision with permanence in it, as the existence of subscribers is only a temporary evil. Have you "conferred" with Mr. Shaen? That is what the Minute requested you to do.

I have received four names of intending students, two aged sixteen, one nineteen, one 29: Two others are anxious to come, but not at liberty to put down their names. None of them are intending to be governesses.

~~I am so glad to hear of your being really better. I know you don't like saying how you are, but you ought to be willing to submit to the humiliation sometimes. I don't often ask it is an ungenerous revenge to taunt me with becoming mistress. What have I done to justify such a charge?~~

I am sorry to send you such a cross letter (& such a long one) but when you go so terribly astray, what can I do? It was very good of you to let me know what you were about.

Every yours sincerely
Emily Davies.

GC: ALS ED XVII GC1/7

1. ED was objecting to separate degrees for women.

To Henry Tomkinson

PROPOSED COLLEGE FOR WOMEN.
17 CUNNINGHAM PLACE N.W. | Wednesday ⟨January⟩ ['69]

Dear Mr. Tomkinson

It shows I fear a variable mind, but I have been thinking that perhaps 12 would be too small a number of Governors. I have thought of several eligible people, & I don't exactly see how we are to get them on, if we have only twelve.

I do not think we could very well spare any of the Executive Committee, except Mr. Hastings & Lady Goldsmid, who have seldom been present. We might eliminate them, by going on the principle of keeping those who have attended the largest number of meetings. But that would only give no one vacancy. I think as you say, we ought to have a scientific man. There is a Dr. Michael Foster, who seems to be a rising man, & who has given us advice thro' Mr. Seeley. Perhaps he would do? Then there is Mr. Seebohm, a father (of 4 daughters) a Banker, & a Quaker. & much interested. Would not he be a representation of three interests? I should like Mr. Hort, but I don't know that he would be representative of any fresh elements. There is a Mrs. ⟨Mary⟩ Ponsonby, who would I think join us, & whom I have met on another Committee. She is very sensible & pleasant & not a cipher. Lady Augusta ⟨Stanley⟩ could tell us more about her. She is a good deal taken up with Waiting on the Queen, but I don't think it would prevent her from being of use. I should rather like to have another representative (besides myself I mean) of the Miss Becker type. Miss Garrett would do, but I cannot say that she would *add* much, as she & I should probably always say the same things.

I begin to think we should be safer without the Vice-Chancellor. But please don't charge me with having any views about the governors. I am only making unsteady remarks.

Ever yours sincerely
Emily Davies.

I have an idea: Mr. Heywood might be made a Trustee, as you thought of, & so taken off the Ex⟨ecutive⟩. That would give us another vacancy.

GC: ALS ED XVII GC4/15

To Marian Bradley

17 Cunningham Place. N.W. | Jan. 22nd. 1869

Dear Mrs. Bradley

I have been waiting for a quiet morning to reply to your kind letter, as I wished to say something of the difficulty you refer to. It is one which has constantly been on my mind, & is *the* difficulty which cannot I think be treated as a mere prejudice. On the whole, however, I hope that it may be safe to leave it to be dealt with as occasions arise. You feel I think that those in whom the sense of duty was strong, would not let the passion for study interfere wrongly with home claims.

It might be an effort to put aside the one for the other, but it would be simply a case of doing what one ought instead of what one likes, which everybody has to do sometimes. The real difficulty perhaps is rather to decide which *is* the duty, as in some families the most trifling & useless faddles put on the air of home duties & are considered of more importance than any possible claim of any other sort. In these cases, a sound judgment is wanted, & it seems to me that wisely trained young women of twenty-one will be better fitted to decide, than girls of eighteen, suddenly thrown upon themselves after the strict routine of the schoolroom, often with no guidance worth speaking of, either from their mothers or anybody else.

Then as to the dulness of domestic duties as compared with study. Any one who cares much for learning would no doubt feel this, but she would probably be less discontented & troublesome than one who was dull from the opposite cause of emptyheadedness. Other things being equal, a dull & idle person is apt to be more actively annoying to other people than one who is only useless thro' being self-absorbed. With regard to the College, I cannot deny that it seems to me likely that the stirring intellectual & spiritual life will awaken a craving for *more* work than homes in the country can supply, where there are several daughters.

I am afraid parents must make up their minds to as much as this. that when home life manifestly does not supply more than enough work for one, while there are two able & willing to work, one must be allowed to leave home & find work elsewhere. It seems to me that where the home is what it ought to be, the home ties will be strong enough to bear as much strain as this. It looks like a consciousness of weakness and unsoundness, when there is so much fear that the home ties will snap at the least pull. Of course it would be a trial to parents to have to part with their daughters as well as their sons, but after all it would not be so hard as letting them marry & go away for ever.

And it is not considered a calamity when a girl is taken from her mother by marriage, even at eighteen. It is often spoken of as an advantage to the second daughter when the eldest marries, as "it brings her out." I have no doubt this is true & that the same result would follow from a similar cause produced in another way.

My paper in the Contemporary has been reprinted for distribution.[1] I send you a copy of it & also of an article written by Miss Garrett, which may perhaps interest you if you have not already seen it.[2]

We had a meeting of the Executive Committee yesterday & it was decided to open the College in a temporary way next October. We are now looking for a suitable house. It seems better to make a beginning in this way, as there are grown-up students ready to come, than to wait on indefinitely for the new building. The chief difficulty of the temporary plan is the expense. The students will probably be willing to accept inferior accommodation for a time, but we cannot offer them second-rate *teaching*, & the proportionate cost for a small number will of course be much larger. Only five students have actually put down their names as yet. We expect to hear of more now that the time is fixed, but I do not suppose we shall have any considerable number till we can publicly announce the place, as well as the time of opening. It is a little awkward to have to make provision in the dark. We shall be obliged to make a guess as to the number, & if more apply than we have room for, those who send in their names last, will have to wait, probably for two or three years, as the house will not grow according to demand.

We are beginning negociations for a site, professionally approved of by Mr. Waterhouse & very much liked by some of the Committee who have seen it.

I remain
Dear Mrs. Bradley
Yours very truly
Emily Davies

If you can make use of more College papers for distribution, will you kindly let me know?

GC: ALS Add.ED1.39.1j

1. Emily Davies, "Some Account of a Proposed New College for Women," *Contemporary Review* (December 1868).
2. In April 1867, EG's article "Volunteer Hospital Nursing" had been published in *Macmillan's*.

To Sedley Taylor

⟨January 1869⟩

Dear Mr. Taylor

Mr. Roby & Mr. T. have been good enough to let me see their draft ~~of the propose~~ report, on its way to you. May I trouble you with a word of explanation as to the clause I suggested—"that the College, should, as far might be practicable, occupy the same position in relation to the U. of C. as the existing Colleges." ~~This~~ ^Which you^ seems to have ~~conveyed &~~ understood ~~this~~ as ~~a pr~~ aiming at *affiliation*. This was not ~~at all~~ the idea I had in my mind, & ~~this~~ is not ~~seen to~~ I think implied, as the existing Colleges are not affiliated. but incorporated. Of course I have no idea that incorporation shd. be proposed at present, or for many years to come. It ^certainly^ would not be "practicable", now & perhaps the distance from C. wd. always be a difficulty.

But the ~~plans~~ distance is an accident, & might well be got over if necessary at some future time, by removal to Cambridge. But I am anxious to have a ~~definite~~ well-defined *ultimate* aim, & the wording of the Resolution passed at our first meeting is indistinct. ~~Manifestl~~ "Connexion" may mean ^either^ affiliation, or incorporation or almost anything else. & the different things are vitally different. There are two distinct & opposite ideas as to the position which it would be *desirable* if possible, for the Coll: ~~ultimately~~ ^eventually^ to occupy. One is that it shd. be adopted into the University ^educational^ system for the time being, sharing in all the reforms hoped for in the future. The other is that it should be a female University, connected, or not, with one or more of the old Universities, but substantially standing on a separate basis. ~~I believe that nearly all the people who are very much for the College & have promote it zealously, take the first view, & have worked for the College in the hope that this idea will be steadily kept maintained in view.~~ The ^first^ view is most strongly ~~held~~ urged by Mme. Bodichon, Miss Garrett, ~~Miss Manning,~~ & ~~others of the a speaking generally,~~ I believe it is the view of nearly all the people who care very much for the scheme. There are two reasons. One is, that on general moral grounds we think it very desirable that men & women should have substantially (tho' not necessarily in every detail) the same education. the other, that we think there is a better chance, looking at the matter from a practical point of view, of ~~getting~~ ^securing^ the best education for women by adopting whatever is authoritatively recognised for the time being as the highest for men, than by setting up a separate standard. You will understand that we do not in the least desire to bind the College to any ~~definite~~, immediate action. We should wish to leave the Council perfectly free. But we ~~also~~ do wish it to be clearly understood that the *humane*—not the female—theory is the governing idea. ~~of the College~~

It seems to me that simply as a matter of policy this would be the wisest course. ~~I don't want to fall into the error of~~ ^Would it not be a mistake to imitate^ the L⟨ondon⟩.U⟨niversity⟩., which seems likely to fall between two stools.

~~They have made~~ Their examn.^scheme is^ too hash for illiterate women, & at the same time ~~have made~~ it ^is^ impossible for the "humane" party to work with any heart at ~~this scheme~~ by limiting ~~it to women &~~ it, as they have not only made it Special but have insert~~ing~~ed a clause in their Charter providing that no male person shall be admitted ~~as a candidate to any such examns.~~ ^to it.^

We have already disgraced ourselves for ever with the Separatist party by adopting the Poll ⟨Ordinary⟩ Examns. It would ⁿᵒʷ be a pity to damp ~~the others by making an undecided statement about our general principles seeming to waver in our general aims~~. our friends ⟨by⟩ wavering.

GC: DAL ED XVII 4/9

To ⟨Sedley Taylor⟩

⟨late January/early February 1869⟩

I have had a talk with my brother about the definition of the aim. He does not like the form I proposed, which seems ~~thou~~ to him ᵗᵒᵒ ᵐᵘᶜʰ to ~~assume~~ ᵖʳᵉˢᵘᵐᵉ a kind of consent on the part of the U., but he thinks the same ~~meaning~~ ⁱⁿᵗᵉⁿᵗⁱᵒⁿ might be expressed in some better way. He suggested "that the College should *aim* at occupying the same position, &c..".

~~Perhaps~~ ᵂᵒᵘˡᵈ something like this ~~would~~ do? "that ~~such College~~ the ~~college~~ ᶜᵒᵘⁿᶜⁱˡ shall take such steps as from time to time may seem to them expedient with a view to placing the College in a position parallel with that of the ~~existing~~ Colleges which now form part of the U. of C." I don't mind how it is expressed ᵉˣᶜᵉᵖᵗ ᵗʰᵃᵗ the more modestly the better, so long as what we *wish* is made ˢᵘᶠᶠⁱᶜⁱᵉⁿᵗˡʸ clear.

v. back for what Mr. Roby proposes.

. . . creating & maintaining a College for the higher education of women.

. . . subject to the following provisions.

a. that the Council shall use such efforts as from time to time they may think most expedient & effectual, to place the College in connexion with the U. of C. & especially to obtain for the students of the College admission to the Examns. for Degrees of that U.

(. . . Mr. Tomkinson points out that ~~"connexion" might m~~ the mention of *Examns*. for Degrees rather implies that we are *not* to ask for the Degrees themselves.)

⟨incomplete⟩

GC: DAL ED XVII GC4/8b

To Henry Tomkinson

PROPOSED COLLEGE FOR WOMEN. | 17 CUNNINGHAM PLACE. N.W.

Feb. 5th ⟨1869⟩

Dear Mr. Tomkinson

Thank you for letting me see the draft. I have sent it on to Mr. Sedley Taylor at his sepulchral residence, with an explanation about affiliation. I have been studying the Cambridge Calendar, & what I have made out is that the clause I proposed excludes the idea of affiliation by expressly stating that of incorporation.

I agree with all you say about Resolution 4. Also I think it is quite clear that Mr. Roby's 2a. goes as far as Resolution 3 & of course no one is *bound* to go farther. I suppose however that it is a fair question for the Committee to consider whether in the Trust deed the aim might not be more exactly defined. I have had a talk with my brother about it. He does not like the wording I proposed, which presumes, he thinks, a sort of consent on the part of the University, & he suggests instead, "that the College should *aim* at occupying &c." I think with you that Mr. Roby's form seems rather to exclude Degrees, as any one might naturally say, "If they meant Degrees, why did they say Examns."? At the same time, "connexion" by itself, even with your addition of "closely & directly," might mean supervision by the University, Mr. Myers's Examn., & a female Degree, which "*the* Examns. for Degrees of that University," could not mean. I do not quite like your phrase about "members of the University," because it seems to claim something for individual students, whereas what we want is to secure the position of the College itself. I have proposed to Mr. Taylor to substitute for Mr. Roby's 2a. something like this. "that the Council shall take such steps as from time to time may seem to them expedient, with a view to placing the College in a position parallel with that of the Colleges which now form ^{constitute part} ^{of} the University of Cambridge." Should you like that?

I should have preferred if possible putting it simply in a declaratory form in Clause 1. but I cannot find any way of doing it which is not open to my brother's objection about committing the University. It secures I think a definite idea of the general aim, without binding the Council *ever* to go the full length, if it does not seem expedient. What I am anxious about is to pronounce distinctly between the rival principles of adoption into the University system, & setting up an independent system.

I see that in 1800 Downing College was incorporated by Charter. By about the year 1900, our Council may be prepared to ask for a similar Charter. I would rather wait a little for the true thing than take up with what is morally injurious. You understand what I mean by moral. I ^{have} had a talk with Mrs. Lewes since I saw you about this. She said she thought the great thing to be hoped for from the College was that it would modify the opinions of men about the education of women & assert in an emphatic way that whatever it is, it ought to be on a par with that of men.

On this ground she ^{inclined to be in} favou~~red~~ of the clause I had proposed, tho' she did not express a strong opinion on the immediate question.

It is a consolation to reflect that even if Mr. Roby's clause should be carried just as it is, we shall not be ruined. It would be a great deal better than anything that has ever been done before.

I enclose a cheque for
    Mr. Courtney   £20.
    Miss Emily Taylor   1.+
Ever yours truly
Emily Davies
From what is said in the Calendar, it seems that under the existing Statutes, we could not get Degrees for our students without a Charter of incorporation~~, but perhaps if~~

GC: ALS ED XVII GC4/8a

To Barbara Bodichon

PROPOSED COLLEGE FOR WOMEN. | 17 CUNNINGHAM PLACE. N.W.

Feb. 16th 1869

Dear Mrs Bodichon

The Committee have elected you a member. I told them you had refused, but Mr. Heywood thought you had changed your mind. The Trust-deed was passed with Mr. Roby's Clause 2a. I trembled even for that, Lady G. was so pertinacious against it, & Mr. Heywood wanted to prepare students for the London Female. Mrs. Manning came out strongly & was of *great* use. Mrs. R. Gurney & Miss Metcalfe were good, & so were Mr. Seeley & Mr. Sedley Taylor. Mr. Roby was not there.

Everybody likes the idea of the house at Hitchin, & it was almost decided to take it at once, but I am to make some further inquiries.

I shall be at home to-morrow *afternoon*, not in the morning.

Your affecn. ED.

GC: ALS ED B19

To Henry Tomkinson

Feb. 18th | ['69]

Dear Mr. Tomkinson

Is it all right about the £50? I *think* I told you, (but cannot be quite sure) that it was a draft on Barnatt⟨'s Bank⟩ signed Thomas Hodgkin & paid on the 22nd Jan.

I thought we got thro' the meeting on Tuesday wonderfully well, considering the untoward circumstances, but I could not quite make out whether the decision on the Trust Deed was understood to be final. I enclosed the revised copy. Could we now proceed to the appointment of the Trustees? Or ought the Council be chosen first? If you are not sure, would you ask Mr. Shaen? I am anxious to get preliminaries settled, partly because there is a chance of getting some public money. Lord De Grey has been talking to my brother about it. He expressed great interest in the scheme & said something about the application of the endowments. He said he wanted to know what point the project had arrived at, & is going to fix a day soon to have a thorough talk with my brother about it.

Will you think over the modifications I have suggested about the Examns.? I should have preferred having no *general* College certificate, but it seems to be a necessary concession.

Ever yours sincerely
ED

GC: ALS ED XVII GC4/14

To Barbara Bodichon

PROPOSED COLLEGE FOR WOMEN. | 17 CUNNINGHAM PLACE. N.W.

Feb. 20th 1869

Dear Mrs. Bodichon

If you have made up your mind about the Committee, will you kindly let me have a line before Tuesday. You were formally put on, so it is necessary either to accept or to refuse.

The further inquiries about the house at Hitchin are satisfactorily answered—gas & water laid on, &c. &c. If it is decided to take it, I shall propose a House Committee, with power to spend a certain sum on fitting & furnishing. Perhaps you would not mind being on *this*? I should like to have you, to help in making the house pretty & picturesque, & it would not want sticking to, like the Ex⟨ecutive⟩. Com⟨mittee⟩. I should propose having Mrs. Burbury & one or two other ladies who are not on the Ex. Com.

I mean also to propose on Tuesday to have a conference with the architect about the sites.

He ought to be able to advise, & perhaps in the meantime, some more people will go & look. Mrs. Manning inclines, as you & I do, to No. 3. rather than Mr. Wilshere's. I want to get on about the site, because I don't think we shall get more money if we *seem* to have no immediate use for it, & whatever happens, no harm could be done by investing what we have got, in land.

Your affecn. ED.

GC: ALS ED B20

To Marian Bradley

PROPOSED COLLEGE FOR WOMEN. | 17 CUNNINGHAM PLACE. N.W.

March 1st 1869

Dear Mrs. Bradley

You will see by the enclosed notice that we have decided to make a start next October. There are a good many difficulties in beginning on a small scale, but it seems on the whole the best thing to do, as the great difficulty is to begin at all, and we can only get over that by doing it. Shall you have a daughter for us? We have heard of a house at Hitchin which has many recommendations and will I think be taken. One advantage about it is that there is a house adjoining, which may probably be available for the second year's students. The pressure is likely to come in the second year, when experience has shown the working of the scheme, and before the building is ready. The students we have heard of so far, are very promising, so we may hope to have the advantage at any rate of good material to deal with.

I was very sorry to miss seeing you when you were in Town. Another time I hope I may be more fortunate.

I send you a copy of my paper which has been reprinted for distribution. I suppose you see the articles in Macmillan.[1] I know nothing at all of the writers on either side.

I remain
Yours very truly
Emily Davies

GC: ALS Add.ED1.39.1k

1. "The Ladies' Cry, Nothing to Do!" *Macmillan's* (March 1869), discussing an article in the *Saturday Review* about "girls of the period," and also referring to a piece in *Macmillan's* (February 1869), entitled "Two Girls of the Period."

To Barbara Bodichon

PROPOSED COLLEGE FOR WOMEN. | 17 CUNNINGHAM PLACE. N.W.

March 2d | [1869]

Dear Mrs. Bodichon

I have an engagement for to-morrow evening, if a troublesome cold gets well enough to let me go out, so I ~~am~~ ^{am sorry to say} I shall not be able to come to you.

From what Lady Goldsmid said the other night, & Mrs. Austin also tells me, I think there must be some misunderstanding about what was proposed at the College Committee. The estimate of expenses, as to teaching & everything else, was based on the supposition that there would be ten students to provide for. If there should be fewer, of course the estimate would be lower. Supposing ten students, & supposing that we pay well for teaching, the amount sacrificed the first year would be £500. If the number doubled, (and as the old students will remain & freshwomen come at the beginning of the second year, this is *naturally* to be expected) the second year's receipts would about cover expenses. So you see the risk is not very tremendous. If anything so astonishing should happen as that no-more students should offer themselves before October, we must modify our course accordingly, but it is quite impossible to make a conjecture as to the probable number, for months to come. I should think people would think they were doing very well if they let their daughters put down their names three months before hand. And here we are, at eight months' distance, & we have not so much as announced where the College is to be, or how much the students are to pay.

It is clearly a case in which some party must venture something, & evidently, it must be the promoters, who believe in the idea, not parents, who do not. It is no use putting off till we can be certain of a certain number of students.

"Great deeds are never done
By falterers who ask for certainty."

So please don't give way to despondency. I don't want to have to sing The Lost Leader over you. Do you remember? We shall march prospering, not thro' his presence

Songs will inspirit us, not from his lyre—&c.

Ever your affecn. ED.

GC: ALS ED B21

To Marian Bradley

PROPOSED COLLEGE FOR WOMEN. | 17 CUNNINGHAM PLACE. N.W.

March 9th 1869

My dear Mrs. Bradley

Thank you for your letter & for sending me the Miss ⟨Ada⟩ Bensons' circular. I am always glad to hear of good schools & to know good mistresses. Do you think it likely that either of the Miss Bensons would care to come to a meeting of our little Association of Schoolmistresses? If so, I would send them an invitation. Our next meeting is to be on Saturday the 20th at four o'clock, *here*. I am to read a paper on the training of the Imagination.[1] We discuss chiefly questions directly interesting to teachers, and in an unpretending, practical way, using the meetings also as an opportunity for friendly intercourse.

The house at Hitchin is not yet actually taken, but it is practically decided upon. We have been making inquiry lately about teachers, & are feeling very much encouraged on this point. We have already on our list, Professor Seeley, Mr. Hort, Mr. ⟨John⟩ Venn, Professor ⟨George⟩ Liveing, and I think I may add, Professor ⟨Joseph⟩ Lightfoot.[2] We feel it most essential to keep to a high standard of teaching from the beginning, & I am glad to say our prospects are very promising in this respect, as our students have also the intelligence & previous cultivation without which high teaching is almost thrown away. We fixed at our last meeting the rate of the students' payments, namely £35 a term, this covering board, lodging & instruction. We wish to make known also that those who cannot take the whole College course may come for shorter periods, say one year, or two.

I venture to enclose the school circular of a friend of mine who wishes to do for younger girls, the same sort of thing which the Miss Bensons seem to aim at with older pupils. The higher schools complain very much of the bad preparation of the girls who come to them. Mrs. Austin hopes to prepare for them by laying a good foundation in elementary subjects.

I remain
Yours very truly
Emily Davies

GC: ALS Add.ED1.39.1l

1. Emily Davies, "The Training of the Imagination," *Contemporary Review*, no. 9 (September 1869).

2. Liveing agreed to teach for the college, although a few days earlier he had joined a number of Cambridge lecturers in expressing an objection to locating the college at such a distance from Cambridge.

To Barbara Bodichon

PROPOSED COLLEGE FOR WOMEN. | 17 CUNNINGHAM PLACE. N.W.
Monday evening. | ⟨March⟩ [1869]

Dear Mrs. Bodichon

I tried to see you this afternoon chiefly to tell you that Mr. Seeley has been so good as to offer to take part in the teaching at the College. Mrs. Gurney thinks this is better than a gift of £1000 a year. I do not feel at all humble about our teachers. Those we have in view at present are all of the first rank, and I am not inclined to look lower.

I hear Lady ⟨Elizabeth⟩ Eastlake has offered £25 a year for four years if we would begin—which we shall now I suppose get.

There is a notice in this week's Athenaeum, of which is bringing me fresh applications for information.[1] A great deal of my life is consumed on doing up parcels. Have you seen The Ladies' Cry in this month's Macmillan?[2] I do not like it, but it gives us another pat on the back.

I hope you were not knocked up after Saturday's meeting. The room was rather hot.

You will be glad to hear that I had a very cheerful letter from Harriet Cook this morning. She seems really better.

Our little Charley is quite convalescent, but still very weak. He walked a few steps to-day for the first time.

Yours affectionately, ED.

GC: ALS ED B23

1. *Athenaeum* (6 March 1869).
2. Rev. D. Fearon, "The Ladies Cry: Nothing to Do," *Macmillan's* (March 1869).

To Barbara Bodichon

PROPOSED COLLEGE FOR WOMEN. | 17 CUNNINGHAM PLACE. N.W.
Thursday ⟨March 11⟩ [1869]

Dear Mrs. Bodichon

I have not the least idea of giving up trying for £50,000. Don't I keep urging that we ought either to buy the site, or definitively to fix upon it, in order that it may be clear that we are *not* giving up, or trying the experiment or anything of the sort?

It has never occurred to me to give up any part of the scheme. The reason for beginning with a house is that it seems to be the quickest way of getting the £50,000 & the building. Since we began talking, I have had a great deal of advice to this effect, from people who have done things. They all say, you *must* begin small & grow. And the Committee have all come to this view.

There is no difference of opinion. I entirely decline to name any exact number with which I wish to begin. If I said ten, & only eight came, you would be perpetually reminding me that I expected ten, & asking if I was not disappointed. The way in which you insist upon my being disappointed because money does not come in faster, really worries me. I try not to be depressed by it, & set it down to your being tired! but it does worry me a little. I cannot remember exactly what I expected, & I don't see that it signifies, unless I have betrayed anybody into doing anything which they would not have done, & I don't think I have.

I wish to begin at Hitchin in October with as many students as we can get, & to do it at the expense of the fund contributed towards building & preliminary expenses. If any one objects to his or her money being spent in preliminary expenses, we will keep it for building. There will be plenty for what we want. ^(from people who wish to begin.) I did not propose spending £*500 a year*. What I said was that according to a certain calculation, we should spend £500 the *first* year, & should cover our expenses the next. But I think it is attaching too much importance to a few hundred pounds to attempt very precise calculations such a long time beforehand. All we have to do is to keep well within what we have, & we are *miles* within. I decline to pledge myself to anything beyond taking the house ^(& paying for it) for two or three years, at the rent of £110 a year. For all the rest we must be guided by events. I ought to say that in promising to open in October, which we have done already, we do pledge ourselves to the students to some extent, but only a little way, as we could not be expected to keep the College open, at a tremendous loss—not that I have the slightest expectation of closing. It was because we felt so full of courage & confidence that we indulged in those jokes about a short life & a merry, which seem so completely to have misled you. If we had in the least contemplated failure, we should have had a very different tone. If there *is* a person who is *not* tired of the College, it is Mr. Tomkinson. You would have said so if you had seen him here the other night, talking over every detail for about two hours, & willing to take any trouble.

We have scarcely *changed* our way of working. I go on exactly the same, trying to get Local. Secs. everywhere & corresponding in all directions. But we have, *besides* talking, decided on making a step forward, because it seems to be the most effectual way of convincing.

I am confirmed in my opinion as to its being the best thing to do, by seeing how it works. Mr. Tomkinson said the other day that he found even people who ^(had) *dis*approved, were glad we were going to begin. It actually produces faith.

In practical working, one finds that the way to kindle faith, is to *show* it, by running risks. If, as Lady Goldsmid suggested, we gave notice that we would begin with less that ten, instead of stirring up anybody to come, we should suggest the expectation of failure, & every parent would say "Where are the nine?" before committing his daughter to the tenth. A parallel case occurs wherever a Local Examn. is started. Some cautious person suggests making the schools promise a certain number of candidates, before starting. Of course they won't promise. A Committee has to be formed & an announcement made that there will be an examn., & in due course the candidates appear.

I should have been well enough to come this evening, thank you. My cold is better. But I want my time & strength for other things. I am writing a paper on Imagination for the Schoolmistresses, & it uses me up. I *am* rather tired, but it is because I have not quite recovered the worries of last year, not present work.

I should think Mrs. G⟨odfrey⟩. Lushington much too good to misrepresent intentionally. It was the *party* that I was thinking of.

Ever your affecn.
ED.

GC: ALS ED B22

To Charlotte Burbury

PROPOSED COLLEGE FOR WOMEN. | 17 CUNNINGHAM PLACE. N.W.
March 18th 1869

My dear Mrs. Burbury

After leaving you yesterday it struck me that in my anxiety to repudiate the female Arnold, I had dwelt too exclusively on the negative side of my own idea. I think that besides the administration, for which a comparatively inferior person would do, there will be something for which I can find no better word than chaperonage, tho' that does not express exactly what I mean. I am not particularly anxious for the students to have a strong personal influence brought to bear upon them individually, but I *am* anxious that the Head should be a person conversant with the usages of society in our class & one who will give a refined and cultivated tone to the College society. This particular thing can be done only by the resident lady, & it will of course depend more on what she *is* than on anything she does.

I do not want to press this matter upon you, but I have one word to say about vocations.

It seems to me that when a thing comes in one's way which want doing, & which there is no one else forthcoming to do, that in itself constitutes as much of a call as one is likely to get. I think that if we wait for something which we feel quite cut out for, we run a great risk of losing opportunities of being useful. I often do things with great misgivings—things of an *overt* sort which I would much rather not do—& I am almost always glad afterwards to have done them. Nearly everything I do, I have to drag myself up to, against the grain. This you see, makes me sceptical as to one's own feelings being much of a guide as to what one ought to do.

Still one word more. If nothing unforeseen happens, I hope to be so much on the spot especially at first, that I should be able to take a considerable share of the work, & perhaps leave to the Head more of *being* than of *doing*.

Ever yours most truly
Emily Davies

GC: ALS Add.ED1.39.1c

To Marian Bradley

PROPOSED COLLEGE FOR WOMEN. | 17 CUNNINGHAM PLACE. N.W.

May 1st 1869

Dear Mrs. Bradley

I send you some copies of a new Prospectus, containing the contents of our scattered papers collected together, & of the notice of the Entrance & Scholarship Examns.[1]

This notice is already bringing out students, & I think there is little doubt that we shall have at least as many as we can accommodate.

You will be glad to hear that one of our greatest anxieties, that of the appointment of the first Mistress, is satisfactorily disposed of. Mrs. Manning, widow of the late Mr. Serjeant Manning, kindly consents to take the direction.[2] It is not to be a permanent arrangement, but we shall keep her as long as we can, & in the meantime we are greatly pleased that our start will be made under such good management.

Your report of Miss Simcox answers to my impressions of her, except that I think she must have moderated her tone since you saw her. Even as she is, I should be very sorry to have such a person in any position of authority. If she chose to come as a student, it would be a different thing. The discipline & the society of cultivated *ladies*, might give her what she wants.

I remain
Dear Mrs. Bradley
Yours very truly
Emily Davies.

GC: ALS Add.ED1.39.1m

1. The prospectus noted that the college would open in October 1869, and that the fee for students would be £35 per term for board, lodging, and instruction. The prospectus also stated that "application ... [would] be made to the University of Cambridge to hold Examinations of the Students of the College, and to certify proficiency according to the standard of the ordinary Degree" (First Prospectus of the College for Women, GC ED XIX/20).

2. On 16 April 1869, the committee appointed Charlotte Manning as Mistress of the College for Women at Hitchin. She served for one term.

To Barbara Bodichon

[May 1869?]

Dear Mrs. Bodichon

There is a bother about the house. The landlady wants us to take it for five years certain, & Mr. Shaen writes for instructions. It is vexatious.

The first candidate who has filled up her Form of Entry is a young woman after your own heart. She takes French, Mathematics, & Chemistry & declines Scripture. It is Miss ⟨Eliza⟩ Orme, sister in law of Professor Masson. She is 20.

I am asking Mrs. Benzon for Friday. Unless you wish it, I think you had better not bring Mrs. W. We have had scarcely any refusals and are afraid of being too many.

Your affecn. ED.

GC: ALS ED B24

To Barbara Bodichon

COLLEGE FOR WOMEN. | 17, CUNNINGHAM PLACE. N.W.

June 4th, 1869

Dear Mrs. Bodichon

Mr. Maurice gives a very favourable opinion of Mr. Oswald, in a delightfully cordial letter.[1] I have also had a delightful letter from Miss ⟨Louisa⟩ Lumsden, one of the most distinguished of the Edinburgh students.

She proposes coming up for examn. in October. She does not wish to hold a Scholarship, lest it should be depriving some one else who wants it more. She is 28, manifestly a lady, as well as an eager student.

Mrs. Manning has discovered thro' Mr. ⟨Sheldon⟩ Amos that Mr. Prine would probably like to let his house, one of the best at Hitchin, for a year or two. I have written for particulars.

I hope to go over & see the "angel" this afternoon.

Ever yr. affecn.

ED.

I am to see Mme. Sainton on Monday.

GC: ALS ED B25

1. Probably Eugene Oswald (?) a journalist and member of the Council of Working Men's College. He worked with F. D. Maurice; was German tutor to Princes Edward and Albert; German instructor at the Royal Naval College; Greenwich; and published on government and literature.

To Anna Richardson

June 4th [1869]

(a) My dear Anna

I have been seeing Mrs. Lewes to-day. They are in great trouble about a son of Mr. Lewes's, who came home from Natal with serious spinal illness. His recovery is very doubtful. & in the meantime, he is almost helpless & requires a great deal of nursing. Mr. Lewes is quite knocked down by it. Mrs. Lewes says that only people who have had some similar experience, realise what it means to have a sick person in your house, & how completely it puts an end to happiness "if we thought about that." She said humbly that as one got older one ought to be less easily excited & more able to make use of moments, and that she was better than she used to be at it. She talked a great deal about Italy. They seem to have been very much on your track. She has seen *now*, the frescoes at San Marco. She began talking about them before I had time to ask her, & in very much your tone. She has come to the conclusion that the Pre-Rafael's are right, and that the time of really high, noble art, was before Rafael. She thinks his great picture of the Transfiguration detestable & went from it with delight to Fra Angelico; and to Ghirlandaio, whom she seemed to care for almost as much.

It is Rafael's academical-ness that she dislikes so much; the want of effort after noble Nature.

On the whole, her impressions of Italy were sadder this visit than before. She thought the voices of the people harsh & that they seemed ill-tempered in their intercourse with each other, but the North she thought (partly from what she heard) more hopeful than the South. She thinks the dissolution of the monasteries right, but that the *present* monks ought not to have been expelled & that the confiscation is an example of the mean things government, like private people, will do when they are pressed for money. She spoke with great admiration of Giotto's frescoes at Assisi, and she went besides to the little church built on the spot where St. Francis is said to have been born, & had a long talk with an old monk. "As I listened with reverence, he quite understood that I believed all he said." She saw that he watched to see whether she crossed herself with holy water & would not pain him by not doing it, so he went on to give her a little book containing a life of St. Francis. She thought he seemed to have seldom had such a reverent listener & that it had been "quite a rich morning" to him. She admires the country very much & mentioned the Campagna as being to her peculiarly impressive, but she says the scenery is so different from that of England that you must tune your mind into quite a different key, to appreciate it. She has been to the English Lakes twice. Once, about 20 years ago, she staid ten days with Harriet Martineau & they made a delightful excursion to Derwentwater.

I did not pay a very long visit to-day. As usual, she desired me to come again. Mrs. Bodichon is sure she is writing something, as she is always at work, but evidently this illness of "Thorny's" has upset her very much. She is so bound up with Mr. Lewes that if one asks how *she* is, she answers by telling how *he* is. I don't tell you quite all that she says, because some things I fancy she might not like repeated, & she is so good in telling frankly that I feel bound to keep on the safe side.

Will you tell Miss Taylor that it is a fiction about Mrs. Bodichon's coming to Ambleside. Miss Napier has not even asked her.[1]

I went yesterday with Mrs. Burbury to a Flower Show at the Horticultural & was reminded of your unwise friend's deprecation of Grasmere rhododendrons. Those I saw yesterday were certainly magnificent, both in (b) ~~colour & size, but one was not allowed to gather, or to bring away anything, except the remembrance which is however a good deal. It is a glowing picture of colour to have before one.~~ It is mixed up with an economical discussion I was carrying on with a Miss ⟨Matilda⟩ Vernon from Manchester, another of the people who dreamed the College years ago. She was at the school Ruskin celebrates in Ethics of the Dust, & speaks highly of it in some respects. She hoped Miss Bell, the mistress,[2] would have been an ally of the College & would have stirred up her pupils to wish to come to it, but Miss Bell suggests that the women who come will be very much alike & that it is not good for people to associate with those who are like themselves.

I had a very nice letter this morning from Miss Lumsden of Aberdeenshire. She proposes coming up for examn. in October. She does not wish to come now, partly because it would be too great a hurry & partly because if she gets a Scholarship she would not wish to hold it, lest it should be depriving some one else. She *can* pay for herself, & will like to help the College, if only as a student. She is 28, manifestly a lady, as well as an eager student, & I should think eminently desirable for us to have in our first group. ED

~~A promising house has turned up, in~~

(a) GC: AL ED III 5/14

(b) GC: ALS ED XVII GC1/10

1. Probably Robina Napier, wife of Francis Napier. He held diplomatic posts in Vienna, Teheran, Constantinople, Washington, the Hague, and St. Petersburg; and was president of NAPSS, active in municipal reform, and a member of the London School Board.

2. Probably Elizabeth Bell, who was principal of a school in Newbury, and who signed the Local Examinations memorial.

To Barbara Bodichon

COLLEGE FOR WOMEN. | 17, CUNNINGHAM PLACE. N.W.

June 29th ⟨1869⟩

My dear Mrs. Bodichon

Thank you for your hint about Mrs. Lewes. I am glad to know that she does not want people, as otherwise I should have made rather a point of going, for the sake of showing sympathy.

The house we desired at Hitchin is offered to us, & the House Committee propose going to see it next week, after which we must have a meeting of the Executive, *probably* on Friday the 9th. I want to get something settled, if possible, before the candidates come up. We are to have the University of London rooms.

After the Examn. is over, on the 16th, we propose a little gathering of students, to meet their teachers & friends.

It is a long way to come up from Sussex to an At Home, but I venture to enclose a card, feeling that the assembly would be incomplete without you.[1] We are asking a good many of the Committee &c.

We cannot ask *everybody*, as we should like to do, our rooms being small.

Another student, not a candidate for Scholarship, has turned up, & there are rumours of others coming up in October. It looks like having twelve or fifteen to start with, if we could make room for them.

I suppose the Dr. is with you now. I hope you are both enjoying your world of rapine & prey.

Ever yours
ED

GC: ALS ED B26

1. After the entrance examination, Davies had a reception for students, which Bodichon attended.

To Barbara Bodichon

PROPOSED COLLEGE FOR WOMEN. | 17, CUNNINGHAM PLACE. N.W.
University of London[1] | July 13th | [1869]

Dear Mrs. Bodichon

We got thro' a great deal of work on Friday at the Committee. We appointed the rest of the teachers, decided to take the house, which is eminently desirable. (far more so than the old one we could not get.) and agreed upon a daily routine which practically determines the discipline.

Eighteen nice young women are under Examn. They vary widely in attainments. Some of the French and Latin papers are extremely bad, & some I *think* very good. This morning is devoted to the struggle with Arithmetic.

If you come on Friday (I doubt whether you ought to come at all) I think the least tiring way will be to come quite early & go away before the crowd if you find it too much.

Mr. ⟨Edwin⟩ Clark, one of the teachers, is coming at 1/4 to 4, to have some quiet talk with the students.

Ever your affecn. ED.

GC: ALS ED B27

1. The entrance examination was held at the University of London, Burlington Gardens.

To Barbara Bodichon

July 21st | [1869]

Dear Mrs. Bodichon

Thirteen out of the 18 candidates passed. The Scholars are Miss ⟨Isabella⟩ Townshend, and Miss ⟨Sarah⟩ Woodhead, a Quaker girl (very nice) from Manchester. Miss Scott was third, Miss Gibson fourth. One of the rejected, Miss Chambers, would like to try again in October, but I have rather advised her to wait a year, as she is only 18 & a long way behind the rest.

We are sure now of 8 good students to start with, and may probably have two or three more. I don't think the house will hold more than ten comfortably. We must devise during the first year, some way of making room for the new instalment coming up in 1870. I am so glad you were able to be here on Friday.

Part of the business at the next Committee is to consider a possible successor to Mrs. Manning.

Ever yours ED.

GC: ALS ED B28

To Barbara Bodichon

COLLEGE FOR WOMEN. | 17, CUNNINGHAM PLACE. N.W.

Aug. 2nd 1869

My dear Mrs. Bodichon

I am delighted to hear that you are coming up in a fortnight. I shall have got the ground plan of the house before then, and we shall be just at the stage of wanting to hear your ideas about furniture and fittings. Miss Gibson is certainly coming to the College. She is one of the adventurous five, of whom you have often heard.[1]

I get delightful letters from the students. There is not one as to whom there need be the least fear that she will do anything foolish.

I wish I could come to you for a few days, but I have already refused several tempting invitations. The chief reason is that I have spent all the money I have to spare for travelling.

I went to see Miss Edwards the other day & heard she was with you. I hope she is well—and the doctor too.

Ever your affecn.
ED.

GC: ALS ED B30

1. The first students at the College for Women were: Emily Gibson; Anna Lloyd; Louisa Lumsden; Isabella Townshend; and Sarah Woodhead. In the second term they were joined by Rachel Cook.

To Barbara Bodichon

COLLEGE FOR WOMEN. | 17, CUNNINGHAM PLACE. N.W.

Aug. 4th | [1869]

Dear Mrs. Bodichon

Thanks for Miss Edwards's note, & yours. We are not going to have any more College Committees at present. As everybody was going out of Town, the last meeting empowered the House Committee to do whatever is necessary till October. But I want to have a meeting of the old original University Examns. Committee, & I am calling one to meet *here* on Friday the 13th at 4 P.M.

I am going to propose to dissolve the Committee and to hand over the small balance in hand to Miss Garrett, to use in furthering the interests of medical women.

I dare say Miss ⟨Helen⟩ Taylor has told you that she did not write that letter in the Spectator. I was annoyed at the article the week before & wrote a to Mr. Hutton about it.

I am sorry to say I have not seen Miss E.'s article in the Pall Mall. How sad about your maid! She was such a pleasant looking woman.
Ever your affecn.
ED.

GC: ALS ED B31

To Barbara Bodichon

THE KENSINGTON SOCIETY. | 17, CUNNINGHAM PLACE. | LONDON. N.W.

Friday [August or July 1869]

Dear Mrs. Bodichon

Mr. Tuke's house is about half a mile from the Station. I think the least fatiguing plan for you will be to take a carriage from the Station & call on him first, asking for Mr. or Miss Tuke. His sister, who is a friend of mine, is staying with him. If he is at home, he will direct you to Mr. Radcliffe's site & Mr. Ransom's. There is nothing close that you need see. If Mr. Tuke is not at home, the driver could take you to Mr. Radcliffe's Park, & from thence to Benslow House. That is the name of our house.

Mr. & Mrs. Read are the tenants. If you get into Mr. Tuke's hands, it will be best to explain to him at the outset that you want time and strength for the house, or you may be led into spending too much on driving about first.

Please remember me very kindly to Miss Blackwell. You will not introduce her, I suppose as Dr. to the Tukes? It would be better not.

If Mr. Tuke says anything about the stables, will you say that Mr. Jackson *did* include them in his plan of the garden &c., but without giving the dimensions. I was going to write to Mr. Tuke, but will wait now till I have seen you. He gives £100 to the Building fund.

Ever yours, ED.

GC: ALS ED B29

To Barbara Bodichon

UNIVERSITY EXAMINATIONS. 17, CUNNINGHAM PLACE. | LONDON. N.W.

Aug. 21st [1869]

Dear Mrs. Bodichon

I have not yet seen anything of Mrs. Lewes. I meant to have called yesterday, but was prevented.

I suppose you may have had a letter from the sister of your Charlotte.[1] She was very anxious that I should write to you & I said I would, but I thought she might as well say to you what she said to me.

I don't think we shall be able to make very much of the house at Hitchin, but having a foundation of plainness & solidity, we may by touches of prettiness and originality here & there, save it from being ugly or depressingly commonplace. So please let us have hints if any come to you. Mrs. Burbury was here yesterday & made observations. She seems to know a good deal about household affairs.

I will call Miss Blackwell, Dr. or whatever she likes, if I ever go to America. I should take her opinion as to what might be wise at New York, but I don't think she knows enough of English society to be a good judge for us. Miss Garrett is quite determined never to be called Dr. She feels as I do about it, & as does Mrs. Gurney. I should not consider it an act of friendship to present any one to strangers under a title which excites repugnance.

Does thinking about the College make you tend more to Radicalism? It has not that effect upon me.

I am reading Kitty & find it very clever & amusing.[2] I cannot help wishing that there were some hint of some other kind of life. You know I believe very much in the influence of pictures of life, as determining or inspiring choice, & to have no suggestion of anything higher than the coarseness of Bohemia or the selfish luxury of Belgravia, seems to me directly lowering. By way of keeping up with modern literature, I am also reading Mme. de Stael's Delphine. It seems to me poisonous stuff.

Ever your affecn.
ED.
Mr. Eastly tells Miss Pipe that his daughter cannot be spared for the College.

GC: ALS ED B32

1. See ED to Barbara Bodichon, 4 August 1869.
2. Matilda Betham-Edwards, *Kitty* (London, 1869).

To Barbara Bodichon

17, C.P. | Aug. 23rd. [1869]

Dear Mrs. Bodichon

I saw Mrs. Lewes on Saturday. She is better, the boy is better, and they have got a good nurse. She sends you these three pieces of good news. She wishes me to go & see her when I can, & promises always to say if she is not well enough.

I have posted your letter to Henrietta. The two statements, that C⟨harlotte⟩. left three places on account of this kind of illness, & Marianne's, that she never left any till yours, are contradictory.¹ I should think she might do better in an easy place than at any other kind of work. If we wanted a housemaid, she would just do. I should not be at all afraid to take her, but this is rather an exceptional place. If I were Henrietta I should give her character as far as your experience has gone, & leave the past & the future alone.

I am glad Miss Edwards agrees with me about Dr.² I have finished the 2d Vol. of Kitty & I want to know what she is going to do with that wretched old Sir George. The 3d Vol. comes to-morrow.

I wish I *could* have a few days at the Cottage, the Traveller's Joy, but it is impossible.

The Tukes have asked me to stay a few days at Hitchin, which will be convenient & pleasant.

The newspaper slip is by Mrs. F⟨rederick⟩. Prideaux, a new ally, risen of herself, & doing all she can. She is propagandising at Exeter.

My kind rem. to Miss Edwards & the Dr.

Ever your affecn. ED.

GC: ALS ED B33

1. See ED to Barbara Bodichon, 4 August 1869; and ED to Barbara Bodichon, 21 August 1869.
2. See ED to Barbara Bodichon, 21 August 1869.

To Barbara Bodichon

COLLEGE FOR WOMEN. | 17, CUNNINGHAM PLACE. N.W.

Sept. 2d, 1869

Dear Mrs. Bodichon

This morning's post brings a bit of good news, & I hasten to share it with you. Miss Kershaw is going to buy two nominations for 500 guineas.¹ I believe they are for her nieces, & will not be used just yet. Besides the thing itself, it is capital as an example.

The House Committee has met, & by way of beginning with necessaries have commissioned people to buy a piano of the very best sort, china, and a bit of Indian carpet for the dining hall. Mrs. Gurney will choose the china and the carpet. We agreed that things which are to last for centuries, such as the china, might be good and pretty.

I mean that the *type* will last, being added to from time to time. Of course the individual will wither, but the race will be more & more. We are getting the Hitchin things valued, before deciding what to take.

You & Miss Edwards may like to see the enclosed letters. Please let me have them back. I hear a delightful report of Miss Lumsden. She has brothers & cousins who have distinguished themselves in India.

Is Nannie anywhere about? My love to her, if within reach. I am going to stay a few days with the Tukes, which will be convenient for looking after the house, but I am inclined to leave a good deal to be done in the Christmas vacation, when it can be done without hurry.

I have finished Kitty and I think the last Vol. is more moral & none the less amusing. It strikes me as very clever, & as showing that the author might do better still.

Ever your affecn.

ED.

GC: ALS ED B34

1. Probably a member of the Kershaw family of Manchester. James Kershaw (1795–1864) was a member of the Council of the Anti-Corn Law League; mayor of Manchester 1842–43; and M. P. Stockport, 1847–64.

To Barbara Bodichon

COLLEGE FOR WOMEN. | 17, CUNNINGHAM PLACE. N.W.

Sept. 16th 1869

My dear Mrs. Bodichon

In the summer you were good enough to say that we might have a room at Blandford Square for the Entrance Examn. If you could spare it for the October Examn. it would be a great convenience.[1] We shall have only three candidates so a small room will do. The Examn. will occupy 3 or 4 days, beginning on Tuesday, Oct. 5th.

I spent a couple of hours yesterday evening with Nannie and Isabella, & we had a nice talk. Nannie seems to me a great deal better in health & more interested in things. I am glad you are coming up before long.

Ever your affecn. ED.

GC: ALS ED B35

1. The College for Women had adopted the Cambridge University practice of having a matriculation examination twice yearly.

To Barbara Bodichon

COLLEGE FOR WOMEN. | 17, CUNNINGHAM PLACE. N.W.

Sept. 22d 1869

My dear Mrs. Bodichon

I am so glad to know that you can spare us your pleasant drawing room. It will be so cheerful to have the pictures to look at during the intervals of the Examn. Is there any chance of your being in Town that week (beginning Oct. 4th).

We have only one candidate in Drawing, and Mr. Roby proposes that instead of bothering Mr. ⟨John⟩ Sparkes who may not be at home, we should use an old Local Examn. paper. This would do very well, only that we must have some one to judge of the drawing, and of the answers to the paper in Perspective. Could you manage this? If not, I will try to think of some one else.

I have had a long talk with Nannie about the College &c. It is delightful to have got *herself* back again.

You will be grieved to hear that we have had a very bad account of Rachel Cook. She seems to have sadly failed in health while they have been abroad, instead of picking up strength as they hoped she would. Mrs. Cook thinks her quite too ill to come to the College, & it puts an end also to Mrs. Cook's coming after Christmas. I think it may not be very difficult to find some one else. The small number has compensations. It makes th it much easier to give the students comfortable accommodation, & also it will be possible to invite an occasional visitor. I think some of the students will very much appreciate the opportunity of getting acquainted with women worth knowing. We must get up some more Scholarships for next year. I am sure that is the thing to do.

Ever your affecn. ED

GC: ALS ED B36

To Barbara Bodichon

THE COLLEGE | HITCHIN

Oct. 11th 1869

My dear Mrs. Bodichon

I have been wanting to write to you, but I always know you will forgive silence, when the time is filled up otherwise. The candidates & I were very much obliged to you for the hospitality at Blandford Square. Nannie & Isabella represented you beautifully. Their cordial gracious ways were delightful. A *house* is certainly much nicer for an Examn. than a public room. Of the three candidates, Miss Lumsden passed with credit, Miss Lloyd just got thro', and Miss Chambers failed. She is an undaunted young creature, & will come up again next year.

We shall have only five to start with, but I think the Lecturers will feel that the quality makes up for the deficiency of number. If viewed as private pupils, they are not despicable, and the individual teaching will be valuable to them, as they are at various stages of progress. Miss Cook is better, & may probably be able to come after Christmas. Miss Garrett hopes her illness is not very serious. It was perhaps the sad experience ~~w~~ she has had which made Mrs. Cook take such a very anxious view of it. I have great hopes of the health of the students. Miss Tuke is looking forward to showing them the rides about. Besides good roads, it is permitted here to ride *any*where, over fields &c. Three at least of the students are fond of riding, & Miss Lumsden can also do the trapeze and is great at active games. She is a jewel.

Mrs. Austin spent last week here & did the worst of the settling. She went home on Saturday, but comes down again for a few days to-morrow. Mrs and Miss Manning come on Thursday or Friday. This really is a pleasant place. The flowers are most delightful. When will you come? Let it be soon, and bring Miss Edwards.

I enjoyed the first quiet Sunday very much. The Church is High, and the service most cheerful. I hope the undergraduates will like it. Three go to Church and two are Quakers.

Photographs of the College are already on sale in this town.

Ever your affecn.

Emily Davies.

GC: ALS ED B325

To Barbara Bodichon

THE COLLEGE | HITCHIN

Oct. 21st 1869

My dear Mrs. Bodichon

First let me ask a question. Can you tell me by about what time Nannie and Isabella were to reach Algiers? Our friend & ally here, Mr. Tuke, is going abroad with his daughter for a month's change. I have been recommending Algiers, & if they decide on going there, I should like to give them an introduction to Nannie. They talk of starting at the beginning of next week.

I have not written to you since our students arrived.[1] They all came duly on Saturday, & we have now had four Lectures. They work in together beautifully. Adelaide ejaculates "It *is* so pleasant to be at the College," and they all say the same in look and tone. I scarcely expected so much hilarity could come from so small a company. They seem to feel quite free, & quite docile. The mysterious difficulties seem very far off at present. We are most fortunate in our Lecturers, especially Mr. Clark, the Classical teacher, & Mr. Hort.[2] It is delightful to hear a language taught as Mr. Clark teaches Latin. It is so thoroughly intelligent & interesting. When are you coming to see us? We have not got salt spoons yet, & are using sticks for pokers in some rooms, but otherwise we are civilised. Mrs. Manning gives us plain food, well cooked and served, & it disappears like lightening. The gymnasium is in use, but they do not quite understand it. Miss Garrett talks of coming down on Saturday, & will I hope, give instruction in it. The Lecturers are very pleasant & do not despise their small classes.

Mrs. Manning sends you her love, and she finds the house as delightful & the air as salubrious, as she expected. I hope you will be able to manage a visit during our first Term. Miss Cobbe & Miss ⟨Mary⟩ Lloyd are asked for some day next week.

Ever your affecn.
ED.

GC: ALS ED B326

1. The College for Women opened on Saturday, 16 October 1869. The daily routine included prayers in the Library at 8:00 A.M. followed by breakfast. Lectures took place in the Library in the afternoons, and students dressed for dinner at 5:30 P.M. Dinner was served at 6:00 P.M., at which time the college gates were closed for the evening. Students were "allowed to have tea in their own rooms between 3 and 9 p.m." (Daily Schedule of the College for Women, 1869, GC ED XIX/24).

2. The first lecturers were Dr. F. Althaus, German; Edwin C. Clark, classics; Fenton J. Hort, divinity; George Liveing, chemistry; Gustave Masson, French; John R. Seeley, English; James Stuart, mathematics; and John Venn, moral science.

To Sedley Taylor

COLLEGE FOR WOMEN. | 17, CUNNINGHAM PLACE. N.W.

Oct. 23d 1869

Dear Mr. Taylor

I did not know when I wrote to you of the step you have felt it right to take, but it cannot make any difference as to your being a welcome visitor. I had gathered from something you said once at Birmingham that if you had had *then* to decide the question of taking orders, you would have remained a layman, and with that feeling it cannot be surprising that you should wish to withdraw from an uncongenial position.

I had to come home yesterday for a few days, but I go back to Hitchin on Tuesday, and will then consult with Mrs. Manning about the *time* of your visit, as she is, I know anxious that all her friends should not happen to arrive on the same day.

I am very glad you thought Miss Chambers so much improved in Arithmetic. It gives hope that with more time, she will make up in the other things.

I remain

Yours very truly

Emily Davies.

I use your clerical address, in case your friends should not yet have made any change.

CUL: ALS Add.MS.6258(E)48

To Charlotte Burbury

THE COLLEGE | HITCHIN

Nov. 17th ⟨1869⟩

My dear Mrs. Burbury

I did not answer your letter at the time it came, and I have since been almost afraid to write, having heard from Miss Crow that you were distressed by the serious illness of Miss Burchell.

Would you now send me a line just to say how you are; and what your plans are for the next few weeks. I feel quite in the dark about you.

I go home on Monday or Tuesday for about a fortnight. I shall have to "come down" again for a few days at the end of the Term. You will be glad to hear that Rachel Cook is so much better that she is quite hoping to come to the College after Christmas. We are going on most prosperously as regards the quality of the students and their thorough enjoyment of college life. The smallness of our number has not proved so great a drawback as I feared it might. There are of course some advantages in getting more individual teaching. Mr. E. C. Clark is a very successful teacher. We could scarcely have done better as to our Lecturers. The students are delighted with the teaching, which is different from anything they ever had before.

I hope your sister went home a great deal stronger. It would be very pleasant if you & your sisters would come and see us here. Perhaps we may be able to arrange something while I am in Town.

We have a Programme now brought down to November. Shall I send you come copies?

Ever yours sincerely

Emily Davies

GC: ALS Add.ED1:39. 1a

To Walter Clay

THE COLLEGE | HITCHIN

Nov. 18th 1869

My dear Mr. Clay

I send you, at last, some of the College papers, in case you should be asked for them. We have started with a very small number, but there is a good prospect of increase from year to year. As regards quality, the students are most satisfactory. They thoroughly appreciate both the teaching & the College life. I was afraid the smallness of the number would have been a serious drawback in the social life, but they could scarcely have been more hilarious than they are. It is delightful to see people able to keep up such an unfailing flow of good spirits without any amusement, in the ordinary sense of the word. We are fortunate in having a very healthy situation. I send you a photograph, but please understand that it is only the temporary house, and that the place is prettier & pleasanter than it looks in the photograph.

I saw your advertisement for a curate, in the Guardian, and I am afraid it is a sign that you are still not very fit for work. The process of recovery from that kind of illness is sadly tedious.

My relations in London are all well. I go up next week.

Pray remember me very kindly to Mrs. Clay, & Believe me

Yours very sincerely

Emily Davies.

A Miss ⟨Agnes⟩ Bulley of New Brighton is entered for admission here next October.

Duke: ALS MSJohnClay

To Barbara Bodichon

THE COLLEGE | HITCHIN

Dec. 5th 1869

Dear Mrs. Bodichon

I have forwarded your letter to Mr. Sedley Taylor, adding a line to explain that the Committee were not so much in the dark about the business in hand as your letter would lead him to suppose. I have had a very cordial acceptance from Mrs. Ponsonby.

The yellow books, ~~entitled~~ known as the Hitchin College Entrance Examn. papers, should be ordered from Macmillan thro' a bookseller. If you have difficulty in getting them, I will send you some copies gratis, but I cannot undertake selling them.

Mr. Sidgwick was the person who wanted the College to take a house at Cambridge.¹ He has shown no sympathy with our desire to be connected with the University. He was a leading supporter of the Female ⟨Voluntary⟩ Examn., & was specially put on to talk to me about it. He of course failed to convince me & I was equally unsuccessful in trying to bring him round to our view. Mr. Sedley Taylor has always seemed to me rather to *submit* to our aim at University connexion, than to support it at all warmly. I just mentioned Cambridge to Mrs. Gurney the other day and she said, "Oh, I *hope you* are not wavering." I said no, but I was being worried to death by other people going on about it. Mrs. Gurney feels, as I do, that a number of people like herself, Lady A. Stanley, &c. &c., who are now talking up the College & creating the public opinion which will induce parents to let their daughters come, would have their mouths closed. A whole system of propaganda would be stopped. Mrs. Gurney said decidedly that she should withdraw altogether. So should I. So would 5-sixths of the Committee & nine-tenths of our supporters all over the country. It would be breaking faith with the public ᵍᵉⁿᵉʳᵃˡˡʸ, & ~~with~~ more directly with a large number of people who have been & are, working for us on the distinct understanding that the College is *not* to be at Cambridge.

I noticed Mrs. Prideaux, a capital ally, who is now getting up a Scholarship, made a gesture of dissent the moment I mentioned Cambridge. I have considered what new supporters a change of plan might bring in, & I do not think it would conciliate even the Radicals. Their adhesion could only be bought by our promising to exclude religion, which, again, would drive off every one but the ultra set.

It seems to me that if, as time goes on, some of the supporters of a scheme change their minds & find that they can no longer loyally work at it, the only course is for them to withdraw, unless some great change of circumstances should induce the whole body to wish to withdraw the project & substitute another for it. This is not the case in the present instance. The main body are steadfastly bent on carrying out the original design. Mrs. Gurney remarked the other day that the talk about Cambridge might probably make it more difficult, & that seems to me likely enough, as it is always easy to damp & to discourage. It is possible, tho' I think not likely, that the ultras may start a small secular ᶠᵉᵐᵃˡᵉ place at Cambridge, with lectures given by University men, but not connected with the University. This might probably add to the difficulty of our getting University recognition, as it would tend to divide our small strength. But I don't suppose anything will be done at Cambridge beyond getting up some lectures for ladies living in the town. The Oxford lectures did not I believe attract a single student from a distance.

I do not care much about being what you call "in the vanguard." I suppose people who try to avoid "the falsehood of extremes" are always called cowards. It does not break their bones, and they ought not to let it break their spirits.

I saw Lord Lyttelton, who is Chairman of the Endowed Schools Commission, the other day.[2] He was very cordial about the College & said he would like to come and see it when it was more settled. He asked how much money we wanted for building—£50,000? and said, "Well, we must see."

I do not think we shall have another Committee meeting before the middle or end of January.

The Sub. Committee of Studies will have provisionally to appoint a Mathematical Lecturer, Mr. Stuart having resigned.[3] He suggests his substitute Mr. ⟨J.F.⟩ Moulton, & I think he is pretty sure to be chosen. He seems to me to be a very good man & the students would rather go on with him than have another change. I had a nice talk with him yesterday about the Mathematical studies. He spoke very highly of Miss Woodhead & Miss Gibson's ability & thinks it would be a great pity for them not to go in for the Tripos.

I have had a pleasant letter from Miss Shirreff, accepting her appointment.[4] The Wedgwoods speak of her most warmly.

I shall be sure to go & see Dr. Blackwell when I get back to Town. If you discuss College matters with her, I should like her to see this letter.

Ever yours affectionately
ED

GC: ALS ED B37

1. In December 1869, a meeting was held at the home of Henry and Millicent Fawcett. Those present included F. D. Maurice, James Stuart, Thomas Markby, and Henry Sidgwick. Sidgwick proposed situating a hall of residence or lodging at Cambridge, for students attending a series of Lectures for Women to be inaugurated in 1870.
2. Following the 1869 Endowed Schools Act, an Endowed Schools Commission—including Lyttelton, Canon H. G. Robinson, and Arthur Hobhouse, with Roby serving as secretary—was appointed to restructure the system of endowments to schools and to adapt the endowed schools to the educational demands of the present. The commissioners insisted on the importance of appointing female governors to schools and endeavored to extend to girls' schools the benefits of educational endowments.
3. Stuart resigned due to ill health and possibly also to the demands on his time imposed by traveling from Cambridge to Hitchin.
4. Emily Shirreff served as Mistress of the College for Women, Lent and Easter terms, 1870.

To Barbara Bodichon

COLLEGE FOR WOMEN. | 17, CUNNINGHAM PLACE. N.W.

Dec. 13th 1869

My dear Mrs. Bodichon

Your nice letter, which I found on my return from Hitchin, was very consoling to me.

I am so glad to know that the vital thing, the common standard, is still first with you, & the place second.

Fifty years is a long time. Mrs. Russell Gurney said the other day, 12 or 20. Mr. Roby, 10 or 12. The difficulty is to feel it worth while to build a beautiful house for 12 years only, but I think we ought to feel it. Nature makes a beautiful flower, to die in a few days, while the seed grows, and we ought to have our seed beautifully encased. The case will be used for something else, when we leave it.

I want *now*, not to build on a very large scale, but to begin as soon as possible. It will be hard enough to get even the second year's students into that house, & what we are to do in October 1871, I do not see. Sleeping about in outhouses would be very unpleasant, but it will have to be done. That house is the largest that we have the least chance of getting.

I think you would not long so much after Cambridge if you had staid at Hitchin. Enjoying & admiring it *as it is* helps to reconcile one to not having quite everything. Then the healthiness is a great point. I grew stronger while I was down there than I had been for years. And all that about the difficulty of getting teachers is quite fictitious. Mr. Moulton is delighted to come, & he is better than Mr. Stuart. I suggested the troublesomeness of the journey & he said "Oh yes, but it is so short."

I shall have a great deal to say to you when you come back.

We have had a busy afternoon with our 153 candidates under examn.[1] Mrs. Austin managed it beautifully. I have to be there from 9 A.M. to 9. P.M. tomorrow, so I must not sit up writing.

I sent you a few Programmes for immediate use. We are getting out a new Edition, which will be ready in a day or two, if you want more.

Ever yours affectionately
ED

GC: ALS ED B38

1. The Cambridge University Local Examinations.

To Charlotte Burbury

COLLEGE FOR WOMEN. | 17, CUNNINGHAM PLACE. N.W.

Jan. 25th 1870

My dear Mrs. Burbury

If nothing happens to keep me in Town, I go to Hitchin on the 1st Feb. & propose staying till about the 17th. If you should be passing thro' during that time, it would be very pleasant to see you, but I am not asking friends to come till later on, when they may see the place to more advantage.

Do you hear much for or against having the College at Cambridge? It seems to me that very nearly all the wisest people are against it, for the present & some time to come at any rate, but the others talk a great deal & insist that a Coll: *at* Cambridge would be more popular. It is difficult to prove, either way. If you can give any help in collecting evidence, I should be glad.

The questions are whether students would prefer & their parents be more willing to consent to their coming to Cambridge than to Hitchin. This is as regards support. But there is a further question to my mind, i.e. whether the prejudice against Cambridge is well founded. I think you may sometimes afford to f defy a baseless prejudice & find courage the best policy, but if the objection has real weight, it is another thing.

Is your cousin likely to be a candidate for a Scholarship? And can your friends at Manchester help Mrs. Prideaux? I should like Miss Vernon to know about the proposal.

I do not know what Mr. Green it is that is appointed to the Church you speak of. The Saturday Reviewer is J. R. Green. I believe he has left off his evil deeds.

Ever yours most truly
Emily Davies.

GC: ALS Add.ED1.39.1d

To Barbara Bodichon

COLLEGE FOR WOMEN. | 17, CUNNINGHAM PLACE. N.W.

Jan. 31st 1870

Dear Mrs. Bodichon

I shall be much *more* than satisfied with V.'s choice. I knew you would not forget the pictures, so I told Miss Shirreff they were coming & promised not to begin to "hang" before her arrival. I go to-morrow, Miss Shirreff on Friday, the six students on Saturday, Miss ⟨Julia⟩ Wedgwood on Tuesday. I mean to stay a fortnight or so this time. I should like ʸᵒᵘ to come while I am there if the weather is tolerable.

I will write to Miss Elliot. Miss Townshend was not very well when she came in October, but picked up wonderfully while at Hitchin. Her relations noticed how much better she was looking.

I am sorry you are sorry about Elizth. Garrett's paper. It was my brother's doing to get it into the Pall Mall & she is gaining great credit by it.[1]

Ever your affecn.
ED.

GC: ALS ED B39

1. Elizabeth Garrett, "The Contagious Diseases Acts," *Pall Mall* 11 (25 Jan 1870): 6.

To Barbara Bodichon

COLLEGE FOR WOMEN. | 17, CUNNINGHAM PLACE. N.W.

Feb. 25th [1870]

My dear Mrs. Bodichon

I received your letter, which gave great & diffused pleasure, just before leaving Hitchin. I have since heard from Miss Shirreff of the arrival of the first instalment of pictures. She was putting off hanging them till she had them all together. None of us knew anything about autotypes.

Miss Wedgwood is very useful & enjoys her work extremely. The students also enjoy reading with her, & she is delightful to have there. Everybody likes her.

I will send or take Miss Potticary's book at the first opportunity.

We are hearing of candidates for the next Entrance Examn., chiefly friends or acquaintances of the present students. I have been very busy since I came home, with Schoolmistresses &c. or I should have tried to see you before now. We have been grinding at a paper of Suggestions about Endowments, & have I think produced one which is likely to be useful. Miss E. B. C. & I have been working together at it. I like her very much. The prospect of getting something really good in the way of high schools is better than we expected.

I hope you have not suffered much from the winter weather. Hitchin keeps up its health & spirits delightfully.

Ever your affecn. ED.

I have not expressed sufficiently *how* welcome the pictures are.

GC: ALS ED B40

To Lord Lyttelton

March 1870

My Lord

I am much obliged to you for your letter & for the consideration you have given to my rather free criticisms of the Girls' School Scheme.[1]

I have put down a list of subjects which might I think work well. It is very true that the question of fit subjects ⟨of instruction⟩ for girls is unsettled, but so it is ~~for~~ ⟨in the case of⟩ boys, for whom a curriculum is laid down. It seems to me that leaving the choice to the governors turns over the difficulty to people who are even less fit to solve it for girls than they would be for boys. I suppose I look at the matter rather from the point of view of the sch⟨ool⟩. m⟨istresses⟩., who are quite distracted by the ⟨contradictory⟩ advice ⟨they get⟩ from ed⟨ucational⟩ ref⟨ormers⟩r. each proposing his favourite subject. It is almost pitiful to hear them constantly asking how all the ~~subjects~~ ⟨things⟩ are to be got in, each being evidently good in itself. They really need guidance, & I believe that a curriculum recommended by authority might be of great use to private schools. I do not think there would be any difficulty in carrying it out, especially with the discretion ~~is I suppose~~ given to the Headmistress as to classification & arrangements. ~~I suppose this~~ ⟨which⟩ would include ⟨I suppose⟩ the power of exempting individual girls from studies, which the Mistress found undesirable for them. I shd. think it would be ~~better~~, ⟨well⟩ so far as possible, to leave the question of aptitude ~~rather~~ to the teachers, who will have experience to guide them, rather than to the governors. ~~who, for the most part will have nothing but prejudice.~~

I am sorry you object to Greek. Judging by the no. of ladies who study it for mere pleasure, it wd. seem specially ~~adapted~~ ⟨congenial⟩ to the female mind. But if other languages have been well taught it can easily be taken up after by those who care for it.

The subjects I have omitted, (Moral Phil. &c.) are of course valuable for everybody, but there would be a risk I think of their being superficially taught, either by catechisms, or ⟨by⟩ ~~courses of~~ popular lectures, which may be useful for grown up people, but are not good as mental training. I asked Miss Garrett's opinion (in reference to another case) about ⟨teaching⟩ the Laws of health. She believes very little in direct teaching ~~of~~ but very much in enforcing healthy habits. And I have been wondering whether ~~it would be possible to insert a clause, for both boys & girls, making provision~~ ⟨something more⟩ ~~definite~~ ⟨explicit⟩ could be said about the sanitary arrangements. Girls' boarding schools are ⟨almost always⟩ often scandalously deficient in ~~means of~~ ⟨provision both for⟩ ventilation & for washing. It is also extremely to be desired that each girl should have a ~~separate~~ bedroom, or partition ⟨to herself⟩. People who know what boarding schools are, speak of this ~~condition as making a~~ most essential point.

Poetry & Composition might I shd. think be considered as included in L⟨anguage⟩. &.Lit⟨erature⟩. I rather thought that specifying poetry was a tribute to the imaginative nature of women, & feared it was undeserved. Most of us I think are lamentably unpractical. But perhaps it is ~~because our imaginations were not trained in our youth~~ ⟨from want of training⟩.

I am glad you do not think it necessary to require a certif. from mistresses.

In the other case, the difficulty would of course be much less serious, but I cannot help thinking it needless to impose ^{as} a qual⟨ification⟩. what is really no qual. at all. The Examns. of the Soc. of Arts are in single subjects & primarily intended for artisans. The Local Examns. ~~guarantee~~ test boys & girls ~~of~~ under 18. The London ^{U.} Examn. is a stage higher, but it has no pretension to be considered a test of adult education. The Coll. of Preceptors stands so low that ^{nearly any} Preceptors of any standing will take its certificates. ~~It do~~ Would it not be better to postpone recognition till something exists which deserves it?

I suggested the word "undue" for the sake of leaving the governors free to ~~act~~ use their discretion, "publicity" being ~~also a rather vague word or expression~~ ^{a word which *might* be interpreted in a very extreme sense.} But I ~~suppose~~ do not think it ~~very~~ important.

The ~~public~~ occasion I referred to was at Burlington House ^{not Miss Buss's school.} Mr. Roby was

GC: DALS ED V SIC-31

1. Lyttelton was the chair of the Endowed Schools Commission.

To Charlotte Burbury

THE COLLEGE | HITCHIN

May 6th 1870

My dear Mrs. Burbury

I shall not be here on the 13th. Miss Shirreff has home calls which make it difficult for her to remain here, so I have arranged to take a few days in Town next week & then to be responsible here for the rest of the Term. I go up on the 10th or 11th & probably shall return on the 16th. As I suppose you will at any rate stay over Sunday & Monday at Cambridge, I hope I may have the pleasure of seeing you here on your way back. If your sisters would come with you, we should be very glad either to see them then or on some other day.

There is one thing I should like to know about the Cambridge Lectures to Women. i.e. how the Lecturers are paid. I fancy we pay at a higher rate here, & if we *are* extra liberal, it would be satisfactory to be aware of it.

We have had some difficulty about the Latin Lecturers. Those we had fixed upon had all their time filled up. I suppose we ought to have made the arrangement before the end of last Term. However we are to have Mr. Green, who stands very high as a scholar, & whom I liked when I met him at Cambridge, so I hope we shall do very well after all.

You must have been amused by the debate on the Franchise bill. There is an astonishing amount of *confusion*, both in the speeches & the Times article.

Ever yours sincerely
Emily Davies

GC: ALS Add.ED1.39.1e

To Marian Bradley

17 Cunningham Place. N.W. | July 4th 1870

Dear Mrs. Bradley
       Many thanks for your most kind invitation.
   It would be very useful to me to have some instruction in the system of keeping accounts, and very pleasant to see you again. So if nothing intervenes in the meantime, I shall be very glad to pay you a little visit in September. How much you must want a holiday after all your trouble. I have often been thinking of you during this most trying time. I suppose the *worst* was soon over, but the anxiety must have haunted you long, & perhaps only a thorough change will quite take it away.
       I remain
       Dear Mrs. Bradley
       Yours most truly
       Emily Davies

GC: ALS Add.ED1.39.10

To Barbara Bodichon

COLLEGE FOR WOMEN. | 17, CUNNINGHAM PLACE. N.W.

July 7th | [1870]

Dear Mrs. Bodichon
   The expedience of a supplementary house has been very fully considered & I came to the conclusion some time ago that it would not do.[1] The objections are too serious. I cannot go in to them in writing, & it is the less necessary, as, so far as I know, there is no suitable house to be had. Any difference that there may be in comfort in the iron rooms will I think be made up for by the greater healthiness of the situation.
   The Tukes are always complaining that they live in a hole, & wishing they could be on our hill.
   Mrs. Austin is going to inspect the Workhouse wards this week. She knows so much about houses, from her husband having been an architect, that her going may be of real use to us, tho' mine would not be. I think it must be pos-

sible to make iron buildings sufficiently comfortable, or they would not be so much used.

I grudge the money, but after all, the sum we propose spending, (especially if we have only four or five new students) is microscopically small, compared with what is spent in launching other undertakings, both public & private. I don't think we need be dispirited at having to sink a few hundred pounds in starting. Did I ever tell you about Marlboro' College, which offered Scholarships out of its own funds, when it was £40,000 in debt? It was an audacious policy, & it answered. I believe even private schools scarcely expect to pay their expenses for the first two or three years.

I am going to-morrow to see Miss Beale of Cheltenham, who is on a visit to a schoolmistress sister at Barnes, & I shall see if I can learn anything from her of the Cheltenham experience as standing. The Miss Beale of Barnes is preparing a pupil for Hitchin. I have heard already of three or four students likely to come next year.

Yours affectionately
Emily Davies

GC: ALS ED B42

1. While it was never the intention of the College Committee to remain at Benslow House permanently, it was necessary to extend living space temporarily while plans for building a college continued. The committee achieved this by purchasing a small iron house, which was erected on the grounds of Benslow House. The students referred to this building as the "Tin Tabernacle."

To Barbara Bodichon

COLLEGE FOR WOMEN. | 17, CUNNINGHAM PLACE. N.W.

July 6 [1870]

My dear Mrs. Bodichon

I find Mr. Roby cannot come to a meeting on the 16th, & he can on the 23rd., so we will fix that day at four o'clock as usual. Morewood refers us to two Workhouses, Westminster & Kensington, for specimens of iron houses, but I should think Mrs. Gurney's & Miss Metcalfe's information will be the most useful.

I am going to ask the Committee to fix the definite sum to be raised before we begin building. I do not care to print anything fresh or to make any public demonstration at present, but I want to have something definite to say, when occasion arises. Our experience with Scholarships has shown that people will give to a specific object when they are asked, but they are not likely to come up & offer ~~it~~ money, when we show no sign of intending to make any immediate use of it. I do not want to build on a large scale. Comfortable accommodation for 20 students would satisfy me for the present, & the sum required for that could not be very large. What I cannot endure is the prospect of going on from year to year spending money in putting up temporary things on other people's ground. We *must* do it this year, but the sooner we stop such wasteful expenditure the better. It seems likely that we may not have ~~four~~ more than four new students to provide for, as Miss Richardson tells me she cannot be ready for examn. by October & another of the uncertain ones will also, she thinks, come up in June. One would rather have had them this year, but the time will be well bestowed on preparation, & it will save some expense in rooms. There is this consolation in spending our money on the iron rooms, that it gives us a capital *case*, in asking for money.

The Medical Scholarships are not awarded. There were only two candidates & neither of them has satisfied the Examiners. I wonder whether the time is come for asking the Queen & Princess to support the College. We must consult Lady A.S⟨tanley⟩. & Mrs. Ponsonby.

We are still enjoying your beautiful lilies.

Yours affectionately

ED.

GC: ALS ED B41

To Charlotte Burbury

17 Cunningham Place. N.W. | Aug. 2nd ⟨1870⟩

Dear Mrs. Burbury

I enclose a Local Examns. letter. All that is necessary is to send the Regulations & the local circular. I used generally in such cases to write a note, expressing willingness to give further information, but that is supererogatory. Lady Goldsmid called here a few days ago, & left with me the money for her prize, which Mrs. Austin had asked her to send to you. She had not faith to send to the address given her, as she could not find it in the Directory. Shall you be in this neighbourhood before your leave Town? If not, I suppose I had better open the packet & send the money by Post-office order.

I have my hands full just now, being instructed to send the Resolution of the College Committee to supporters generally. Its purpose is that as soon as we can raise £7000 we are to build for 30 students, either at Hitchin or near Cambridge, but not in or close to Cambridge. I fancy that "near Cambridge" would bring together the greatest number of supporters. I should like to know from people in a position to judge, whether at a distance of three or four miles, we should be tolerably secure from the ravages of Cambridge *ladies*. I am not so much afraid of undergraduates, &c. I think we might protect ourselves from them, while still giving the students ~~more~~ ᵃˢ ᵐᵘᶜʰ freedom ~~than~~ ᵃˢ at their age (from 18 to 21) would be desirable for them.

But we could not make rules against decorous, but distracting visits, from & to Professors wives & daughters. Your sisters may perhaps know how far Cambridge people are likely to wish to entice our students into their society.

Ever yours sincerely
Emily Davies

GC: ALS Add.ED1.39.1g

To Charlotte Burbury

HITCHIN COLLEGE. | 17, CUNNINGHAM PLACE. N.W.

Aug. 23d ⟨1870⟩

Dear Mrs. Burbury

Thank you for thinking about the stamps. I return them as I had a store standing over which are not yet used up. I think the cousin you have lost must be one of whom I did not know. I do not remember hearing you speak of him.

I enclose another Local Examn. letter. Candidates who mean to be examined at the Cambridge Centre, must of course get their Forms of Entry from the Cambridge Local Secretary.

Mr. Clark mentions a tempting site for the College, near Grantchester, rather more than three miles from Cambridge. Do you know that neighborhood? I have had a satisfactory talk with Mr. Waterhouse about the iron building.

Ever yours truly
Emily Davies

GC: ALS Add.ED1.39.1h

To Marian Bradley

17 Cunningham Place | N.W. | Sept. 17th [1870]

My dear Mrs. Bradley

Thank you very much for your kind note. It is very good of you to remember my want of instruction when so much has been happening to put everything out of one's head. Any time next week or the following would do for me.

If I went down ~~on~~ ⁿᵉˣᵗ Friday afternoon, would Saturday morning be a convenient time for seeing the accountant? If this should be convenient to you, I will write again about the train. I might be either coming to you from ~~Reading~~ ᵂᵒᵒˡʰᵃᵐᵖᵗᵒⁿ, or going on there on Saturday.

I shall want to ask you a good deal about the hostel system. There is some question going on as to how far it may be desirable to adopt it in the new girls' schools which are being funded under the Endowed Schools Commission, and I do not feel to know enough about it to have an opinion.[1]

I remain
Dear Mrs. Bradley
Ever yours sincerely
Emily Davies.

GC: ALS Add.ED1.39.1p

1. Some of the first public schools for girls, founded at this time, were modeled on boys' boarding schools. Bradley's advice was being sought because her husband was the Headmaster at Marlborough College, a prominent public school for boys.

To Charlotte Burbury

THE COLLEGE | HITCHIN

Oct. 14th 1870

My dear Mrs. Burbury

~~If~~ Thanks for your letter & cheering information. You will have enough to do with such a crowd upon your hands.[1] Mrs. Austin has given me the balance & account-books, & I will deliver them to you with Mr. Cromwell's cheque, when we meet.

When you write to Dr. Carpenter, I should think it would be worth while to impress upon him that a *great deal* of waiting room will be wanted. These two hundred girls will probably have 50 attendants, at least, waiting about for them, & it makes a great difference to the facility of keeping order, whether they are very much crowded. It is a point of difference between boys and girls. Boys come & go by themselves, & in that way, are much less trouble.

Miss Garrett has been chosen by the Working Men's Assn. (*not* the League) as one of their candidates for the Metropolitan Education Board.[2] They chose by ballot from a long list, & she was far ahead of all the others, including ⟨Thomas⟩ Huxley. I solicit your interest, as you have no votes for Marylebone, in her behalf.

We are rather busy here, preparing for the students' arrival to morrow. Mrs.

Austin is very well & hopeful. The iron rooms are not bad. And we have got all the Lecturers satisfactorily arranged.

I hope you will get a good rest next week. You must be very tired.

Ever yours sincerely

Emily Davies

GC: ALS Add.ED1.39.1i

1. Burbury was coordinating the Cambridge Local Examinations for girls.
2. The Elementary Education Act of 1870 allowed women to vote for members of newly constituted local school boards and to serve on those boards. Four women were elected in the first years of these school board elections: Elizabeth Garrett and ED in London, Flora Stevenson in Edinburgh, and Lydia Becker in Manchester.

To Barbara Bodichon

THE COLLEGE | HITCHIN

Oct. 18th. 1870

Dear Mrs. Bodichon

Your note has been forwarded to me here.

Contributions for the College should be sent to the *Treasurer*. His address is "H. R. Tomkinson, Esq.

24 Lower Seymour Street

⟨London⟩ W."

I will send Mrs. Scott the Programme with full particulars about nominations.

Henrietta was good to us at 5 Bl. Squ. during the Entrance Examn. I was very glad to be able to hold it in such a pleasant house. One of the candidates, Miss ⟨Gertrude⟩ Slade, spent odd moments in sketching from the busts &c. She passed & is now here. One other passed, but is uncertain as to when she will be able to come. The third failed. She will probably come up again in June. The Entrance Examns. reveal a terrible want of preparatory education. It is evidently a very serious bar, & must keep the College back as regards number. And yet it could not be made easier without admitting people quite unfit for higher teaching.

I think I have not told you that a student whose name has been down nearly a year, (a very nice pupil of Miss Pipe's) is prevented from coming this year by illness in the family. This mischance, with Miss Millington's resignation, reduces the new students to three.[1] The old ones are all returned except Miss Lloyd, who has been rather seriously ill, but hopes to be here by the end of the week.

The occupants of the iron rooms like them. I wish you could come down, but I suppose it would be difficult to manage it just now. Henrietta told me about your exchange of houses.

We must have a Committee meeting in about a fortnight. The Lecturers here think there is very little fear but that we shall get what we propose asking for as to the Little-go.

Yours affectionately
Emily Davies

GC: ALS ED B43

1. The three new students who entered the College for Women in 1870 were Isabella Gamble, Gertrude Slade, and Ellen Tidman.

To Barbara Bodichon

THE COLLEGE | HITCHIN

Nov. 2d. 1870

My dear Mrs. Bodichon

Mr. Tomkinson showed me your letter to him about your subscription. He thinks I ought to ask you ~~whatever~~ what you wish about your name on the list. i.e. whether you wish it taken from its present position & put down for what you have paid, or for anything else. It is entered on the Minutes that your £1000 was offered to meet £29,000, & the College has no claim upon you for any part of it till the £29,000 is forthcoming, which is likely to be a long time hence. For that reason, you have never been asked to pay any of it, as the other contributors have been from time to time, as money has been wanted. We have not found the idea so well supported as you hoped we should when we first began to talk about it. Evidently our plan of preparing a "fair and civil building", as Disraeli would call it, to receive a flock of 100 students, cannot be carried out. The little band of pioneers must accrete a modest building round them. Is there not some animal that develops a shell? If not, there ought to be.

I am in favour of building on a very small scale, within a walk of Lecturers, in time to migrate when this lease expires, & I believe that if we cannot get enough money, it would pay to borrow what is deficient. The saving of rent and on the cost of Lectures would be so considerable that I believe we should at least cover expenses with only ten students.

We are all here now, the six old students come back & three new. The old & new harmonise pleasantly, & the new Lecturers are much liked. I am hoping that the Little-go Examn. may give us a lift as regards outsiders. It seems that it will be much more convenient to have it at Cambridge than here, and I believe it can be easily managed for the students to go.¹

Yours affectionately
ED.

I go home on Friday.

GC: ALS ED B44

1. Plans were under way for the students to take the Little-go. The College Committee had to request formal permission from the university for the students to take this examination.

To ⟨James⟩ Cartmell

⟨November 5, 1870⟩

~~THE COLLEGE~~ HITCHIN College.
17 Cunningham Place, | London N.W.

To the Vice-Chancellor and the Council of the Senate of the University of Cambridge

Gentlemen

The Executive Committee of Hitchin College, desiring an opportunity of testing the attainments of the students in an Examination which shall be equivalent to the University of Cambridge Previous Examination respectfully request permission to make use simultaneously of the papers to be issued for the approaching Examination, and to make a private arrangement with the Examiners for looking over & reporting upon the Answers, and for conducting the vivâ voce part of the Examn.

In the event of this application being granted, the Committee will appoint a responsible person to take charge of the papers, & will be answerable for any expenses that may be incurred. It is proposed to hold the Examination in a suitable room at Cambridge, under the superintendence of a lady.

Five students, who have been in residence at the College during four Terms, are prepared to present themselves for Examination. ~~I beg~~

I beg to forward herewith a copy of the College Programme.

I have the honour to be
Gentlemen
Your obedient servant
Emily Davies.
Hon. Sec.

GC: ALS ED AC 2/3/11

In 1869, Jacob Bright, M.P., slipped through an amendment to legislation on borough electoral qualifications, giving women taxpayers the local vote. In 1870, the Elementary Education Act provided for new school boards to establish Board Schools that were intended to supplement existing voluntary schools. Women taxpayers were eligible both to vote and to stand for these boards. Towns with developed women's suffrage organizations such as London, Manchester, Bristol, and Birmingham were the first to support women candidates.

To Henry Tomkinson

17 C.P. Nov. 7 | [1870]

Dear Mr. Tomkinson

Would you be kind enough to criticise the enclosed in case I should rise to the point of issuing an address to the City electors. My inviter is Mr. P⟨aul⟩.F⟨rederick⟩. Tidman, 34 Great St. Helen's-^(of the Kershaw tribe.) uncle of one of the Hitchin students. He thinks success will depend very much on personal exertion & he ^{and his friends} offer to take all the trouble and expense. They do not want me to do anything but to write an address. I am torn in two between rival advisors. My mother & Miss Garrett urge that if a woman is wanted to try it, I ought not to lose time by holding back. My brother insists that it would be *too* audacious to offer to stand for the "greatest constituency in the world" without *more* invitation.

He thinks if there were any chance, it would appear in the form of a requisition, or something of that sort. Miss G. says that it too much to expect, & ought not to be waited for. What do you think? If one could be tolerably sure of a respectable failure, it would be enough. An ignominious & ridiculous defeat would do harm. I have promised to stand if there seems to be any chance, but I am waiting for more encouragement before issuing an address.

I left Hitchin in excellent spirits. The Mathematicians have come to a block again. Miss Woodhead regretted that they had not asked you to help them over their Trigonometry. She thought you would have explained the sums "in a calm way."

My brother was so excited all last week about Miss Garrett's candidature that he could not write his sermon & was obliged to preach an old one. (to which Miss G. and I found ourselves unable to listen.)

Do please give me some advice directly about the City. It strikes me as preposterous to think of. But preposterous things sometimes get done.

Ever yours truly
ED.

GC: ALS ED IV LSB-16

To City of London School Board

[Oct ~~Nov~~ 1870]

Gentlemen

In compliance with a request from some of the electors, I beg to offer myself as one of the candidates for the representation of the City on the London School Board.[1] I have had some experience in the management of schools for the artisan & labouring classes, & in other ways have had opportunities of becoming personally acquainted with the homes of the poor.

I believe that the education of neglected children can only be secured by compulsory measures, but in order that such measures may ~~be effective~~, not be a dead letter it will be necessary to act with considerate regard to the circumstances of those whom it is desired to benefit.

In seeking to ascertain in what manner & to what extent it may be possible to enforce attendance at school, & in the discussion of other points of detail, it is hoped that the assistance of women on the Board might be found practically useful.

I should be sorry to see religion excluded from the schools. I believe that such religious ~~instructio~~ instruction as is suitable to children may be given without entering into doctrinal differences, and that for ~~the~~ practical teachers the "religious difficulty" can scarcely be said to exist. At the same time I should wish to see loyally carried out the provisions of the Act which enable parents who desire it to obtain education for their children in all the secular subjects without sharing the religious instruction.

I have the honour to be
Gentlemen
Your obedient servant
Emily Davies.

GC: DALS ED IV LSB-17

1. The London School Board, established by the Elementary Education Act of 1870, supervised elementary schooling for boys, girls, and infant children. At the time of ED's candidacy, London had a population of five million, yet just over 220,000 children were attending schools regularly.

To Barbara Bodichon

HITCHIN COLLEGE. | 17, CUNNINGHAM PLACE. N.W.

Nov. 8th 1870

My dear Mrs. Bodichon

I am glad you wish your name to remain as it is. It might have been perplexing to people to see it altered. The Committee agreed on Saturday upon an application to Cambridge for the Little-go papers & have asked Professor Lightfoot to take charge of it. The Examn. is to be held at Cambridge, as being much more convenient than doing it at Hitchin. The Cambridge Committee are formally asked to look out for a site, or, by Mr. Heywood's suggestion, for a house which could be adapted to our purposes, not less than three miles from Cambridge.

The Lecturers say this will be quite near enough for them. It is important not to lose time in getting the site, as preparing the plans & considering them will be a long process. I left the College in very good spirits. Mrs. Austin is much liked. I shall have to stay in Town over the 29th, the School Board Election. I find myself put down as head of Marylebone parish under Miss Garrett's Committee, which means that I am expected to organise a personal canvass of 16,000 electors (there are 55,000 in the whole Division) during the next three weeks— of course one can *try*, & do what is possible.

I have been asked to stand for the City, my inviters promising to take all the trouble & expense, if I will write an address. I am waiting to see if there is enough of a chance to be worth trying, before taking any public step. There are about 12 candidates already in the field. It was a Mr. Tidman, a member of Sir John Lubbock's Committee, who came to me.

I will send Programme &c. to Miss G. Martineau.

Yours affectionately
ED.

GC: ALS ED B45

To Henry Tomkinson

Nov. 10 [1870]

Dear Mr. Tomkinson

Your letter made me feel for a minute as if I had been doing a base thing. Please let me explain. I thought that putting in the word "comparatively" would show what I meant. Of course I think elementary education a desirable thing. It does not seem to me the greatest & most pressing want at this moment. If it had, I should naturally have been working at that, for which there are plenty of opportunities in my brother's parish, instead of on anything else. But surely it is not necessary to regard a thing as of primary importance, to be able to work at it honestly at all. The question to my mind in such a case as this of the School Board is whether one is prepared to give a fair amount of time & thought to the specific objects, not the degree of interest (by comparison with other things) that one feels in one's inmost heart. My impression about most of the people who take part in the College is that they do not really care for it a bit, but I should be very sorry if for that reason, they refused to have anything to do with it.

What I meant about the address being nonsense was that when one comes to think of Roman Catholics, it is nonsense to say that you can teach even small children without entering into doctrinal differences. But as they cannot, with any consistency, send their children to anything but a purely Roman Catholic school, it is perhaps not worth while to think of them.

I do not feel guilty of having "sought a conspicuous place" in connection with elementary education. I should not have thought of standing for *any* constituency, least of all the City, except on the conditions proposed to me, that the people who *asked* me to stand would take all the trouble & expense. I am not sure that it would not have been better to refuse at once, without saying anything about it, but it is possible that some small good may ~~have~~ be done by accustoming people to thinking of it.

It will be a relief to me personally, tho' I shall be sorry on public grounds, when Mr. Tidman reports that there is not enough encouragement to make it worth while to go on. I send you some more of Mrs. ⟨Maria⟩ Grey's addresses.[1] It is very inconsistent of you to ask for mine & I am not going to let you have any.

The object of getting questions put to Miss Garrett is to avoid her having to make a set speech. The Chairman is to invite the meeting generally to ask questions. If the invitation is met by dead silence, he will then ask Miss Garrett to state her views, which will be more difficult & disagreeable for her than having them drawn out. We had not any of the crafty designs you attribute to us.

I was not exasperated by Professor Lightfoot's suggestion—only grieved & disappointed that such a good & sensible man should take that view. The new names on the Council struck me as promising for us.

I am afraid you will find this a very cross letter, but am really grateful to you for saying what you thought. I have been trying to remember ~~about~~ the text about the reproofs of the wise. Does not it say that they break one's head, or something of that sort? It is quite true.

Yours very truly
ED.

GC: ALS ED IV LSB-23

1. Maria Grey had been nominated to the school board for Chelsea.

To Henry Tomkinson

Saturday. [12 Nov? 1870]

Dear Mr. Tomkinson

My candidature is at an end, if it ever began. Mr. Tidman thinks there would be a better chance at Greenwich & is trying to get up a Committee there, but I have written to decline standing. One reason is that I should be brought forward by Radicals in opposition to what they call a clerical & sectarian list, and it would be a false position—more false to my mind, than working on the Board without enthusiasm. I did not see you or Mrs. Tomkinson last night. It was a most successful meeting.

Mr. Leader has sent back the Ledger and I think I see my way to the Books now. I like Mr. Ledger's way of teaching. He wants no understanding—only slavish submission, which is so much easier.

Yours ever truly
ED.

GC: ALS ED IV LSB-25

To Henry Tomkinson

17 C.P. | Nov. 14th | [1870]

Dear Mr. Tomkinson

I am going to do it after all. Mr. Tidman came up on Saturday evening & again yesterday & made out such a moving case of the anxiety of the electors of Greenwich to return a woman (what woman being a secondary consideration) that I thought I ought not to refuse. I am not to pretend to represent the Secularists. It is a coalition of very respectable ladies, "Low-Church persons," (perhaps High Church too) & Mr. Mill.

Four meetings are proposed. The first to be at Greenwich on Thursday evening, the second a four o'clock thing at Blackheath on Saturday. There will be plenty of opportunity for practicing the Op. Fal. doctrine, but I am assuring myself that these meetings cannot be worse than those terrible drawingrooms about the College at Mrs. Russell Gurney's, which I *did* survive. You never told me how you liked the Warwickshire occasion.

I am very sorry you & Mrs. Tomkinson do not approve, but I think perhaps you would if I could explain exactly with what intentions I am going into it.

I should like to see the Catechism of Health, but I know Miss Garrett does not believe much in direct instruction on sanitary subjects. There was talk about a Professor of Hygiene [for Hitchin] & I consulted Miss Garrett & Mrs. Lewes about it. They both said the same thing—that as much as it is necessary to know about the laws of health could be taught in an hour, & that the great thing would be to enforce healthy habits. I should think it possible that some little teaching might also be useful in elementary schools, the ignorance of the class from which the children come, being so great.

I was between Mrs. Christie the white haired lady, and Miss ⟨Susan⟩ Durant, the sculptor—Could not you have put your question after the swimming man?[1]

I am so afraid some tiresome Greenwich person may be asking about industrial schools, of which I know nothing.[2]

Yours ever truly
ED

GC: ALS ED IV LSB-26

1. Probably the wife of William Dougal Christie (1816–74). Christie was an M.P. who advocated admitting Dissenters to Cambridge and Oxford; a member of the Council of University College; and vice president of the Working Men's Club.
2. The Industrial Schools Act of 1866 legislated that "mendicant, vagrant, destitute, and refractory" children were to be admitted to fully residential institutions that provided industrial training in addition to some literary education.

To Adelaide Manning

Nov. 15 [1870]

Dear Adelaide

I consented to stand for Greenwich, as some of the electors are vehemently desirous of returning a woman & have fixed upon me. My invitor Mr. Tidman makes himself responsible for the expenses & will give up his whole time till the election. He is uncle to Miss Tidman ^{student} of Hitchin & a friend of Mr. Mill's. He relies chiefly on public meetings. The first is to be at Greenwich on Friday, 8 P.M. A Low Church clergyman is the Chair, Mr. Hughes & Miss Garrett to speak.

One at Blackheath on Saturday at 4. Mr. Abbott & Mr. Roby promised, & Dean Alford asked, to speak. There are to be as many as possible next week.

Greenwich includes New Cross, Lewisham, Forest Hill &c. Mrs. Powell is a warm supporter and so is a Miss Stephen of Blackheath, whom Mrs. Gurney describes as "a wise woman."

I have no Committee work to do, & Mr. Tidman is managing for me in the most considerate way. I wish you were going to be on the Board.

Yours ever
ED.

GC: ALS ED IV LSB-31

To Adelaide Manning

17 C.P. Nov. 17 [1870]

My dear Adelaide

Many thanks for your cordial note. I send the Addresses. Of course I am not responsible for the wonderful statement of qualifications, which I did not see before it was printed, & in which I do not like to correct anything, partly because as I am doing no Committee-work I am unwilling to interfere, & partly because if I corrected *some* of the statements I might seem to be guaranteeing the rest.

You will notice the long list of places included in the Division. I think you must have friends in some of them. My Committee are working energetically. They meet twice a day.

We hear from Cambridge that as we have more than 200 girls for Examn. this year, we are to have 3 Conducting Examiners.[1] Mr. ⟨Arthur⟩ Holmes, who came last year, is to be one, & I am appointed, but they want another lady, who is to be nominated by our Committee in London. Would you like to undertake it? The Examn. begins at 2 P.M. on Dec. 12th & continues more or less for the six days. The Fee is £10.

As far as qualification goes, I am sure you could manage it, as I shall be there constantly (besides Mr. Holmes) to answer any questions that you don't know about. The only question is as to fatigue. I used to find it extremely tiring, when it was new & I was anxious. Last year I got thro' pretty easily. It is not necessary for all the Examiners to be there all the time. We can relieve each other. I have mentioned you to Mrs. Burbury (who is now Sec.) but it would be well to know before the Committee meets whether you are willing. I always enjoy the week. It is to be at the London University this year.

Yours ever
ED.

GC: ALS ED IV LSB-33

1. The Cambridge University Local Examinations for 1870.

To Henry Tomkinson

HITCHIN COLLEGE. | 17, CUNNINGHAM PLACE. N.W.

Nov. 21st. [1870]

Dear Mr. Tomkinson

I suppose the spot the Ex. Comm. propose only means somewhere more than three miles. We must of course have a Committee meeting to discuss the

Cambridge Resolution, but I do not think it can be till after the Local Examn. I should like to have a talk with you about it some time.[1]

I saw you at Blackheath & looked for you afterwards. I did not retain any clergyman to vouch for anything. Except asking people from London to go & speak I am not expected to do anything more than attending the meetings, & I am not responsible for what the Greenwich people say or do. It is necessary to explain this, or you will take for granted that I wrote the remarkable statement of qualifications which I enclose.

I am a little disappointed at finding that speaking does not get easier as one goes on. It was quite easy at Greenwich, but at Blackheath I found it hard & I had an uncomfortable sense of failure when it was over. I felt that I had been nervously hurrying on to get it over, & I am afraid the audience must have felt the same. The chilling reception to the opening speeches was depressing, but of course one ought to be able to resist such influences. I thought Mr. Roby's speech *very* good I mean the point about the value of *direct* influence. There was more opposition near the end, of a more vulgar sort, & I could not judge as to how far it called out sympathy on the other side. The chief feeling I have thro' it all is a kind of sense of being half asleep & having nothing to do with it. But I cannot help wishing you had been at Greenwich instead of Blackheath. You would have liked Miss Garrett's speech—it was only too generous—& the meeting was enthusiastic. The Hall was fuller than it would hold (it holds 1000) & the women came crowding into the Committee room at the end to shake hands & promise their votes.

Shaking hands seems to be a chief part of a candidate's business.

There are to be meetings at Lewisham to-night, Woolwich to-morrow, Sydenham on Wednesday, Eltham, Friday & a three o'clock meeting at the Crystal Palace is talked of for Saturday. I am afraid Sydenham & the C.P. may be something like Blackheath. Those rows of ladies with apathetic faces, from which one cannot guess whether they are agreeing or contradicting, are hard to encounter.

Do you still regard my standing a Hepworth-Dixon-adventure? I should like to know. Feeling disapproved of tires me more than the "rounds", as you call them.

Yours very truly
ED.

GC: ALS ED IV LSB-35

1. On 15 November 1870, a committee of Cambridge men resolved that the College for Women ought to be located in or near Cambridge. The committee of the college, however, had been looking at sites as far as three miles from the town.

To Henry Tomkinson

HITCHIN COLLEGE. | 17, CUNNINGHAM PLACE. N.W.

Nov. 25th. [1870]

Dear Mr. Tomkinson

I want you to read what Mrs. Gurney says & to let me know whether you are likely to be able to come to a Committee on Saturday, Dec. 17th. It is the last day of the Local Examns., but the girls generally finish before Saturday afternoon, so I shall be able to get away. I think we ought to get the Cambridge question discussed & settled, if possible, before Christmas.

The Little-go Examiners consent to examine, but they won't take any fees & they wish it to be distinctly understood that they do it in their private capacity.[1] There was a sharp fight over our application in the Council, & the decision was only carried by the casting vote. This seems to show that the step was felt to be an important one. No fit lodgings can be got, so the students will be received by friends. It promises to be all smooth & pleasant.

You ignore the philanthropic period of my history. The twenty years at Gateshead were *all* schools & District visiting & I feel that the experience counts for a good deal as a qualification for the School Board. The meetings have been very successful, but I cannot help rejoicing that six of them are done, and that only 4 more (including 2 to-morrow) can possibly be got in before Tuesday. The arena is a dull place.

Yours very truly
Emily Davies.

I hope Granny will see that her terrified ladies go to the Poll on Tuesday.[2]

GC: ALS ED XVII GC5/6

1. ED had written to the university on 5 November 1870 to request that students at the College for Women be allowed to take the Little-go Examination. The council of the senate responded that it could not give formal permission, but that it would not object to the College for Women's making private arrangements with the examiners. Copies of letters written to the examiners to make arrangements for the Little-go are not extant.

2. The elections for the London School Board took place on 30 November 1870. Davies came in at the head of the poll in Greenwich, receiving more than 12,000 votes. Elizabeth Garrett received 47,858 votes in Marylebone.

To Marian Bradley

17, Cunningham Place N.W. | Dec. 20 | [1870]

My dear Mrs. Bradley

Mrs. Tomkinson has given me your kind message. I had been wishing to offer you my congratulations and good wishes on Mr. Bradley's promotion, &

refrained, partly because I felt sure that you would scarcely have time even to *read* the flood of letters that would pour in upon you, and partly because I felt that there must be so much to regret in leaving Marlborough that congratulations might be scarcely in place.[1] You must be glad to look forward to the comparative rest of Oxford for Mr. Bradley, tho' I should imagine that no place occupied by him is likely to be a sinecure, and no doubt there will be great interest in his work, and in yours, there.

I suppose there is no chance of your being in Town at all just now. I shall look forward to seeing you later on when you are settled in your new home & are allowed to breathe. I will only add my sincere & hearty sympathy in *both* sides of what the change must be to you. I remain

Dear Mrs. Bradley
Ever yours most truly
Emily Davies.

GC: ALS Add.ED1.39.1q

1. Bradley left Marlborough when he was made Master of University College, Oxford.

To Frances Mary Buss

17, Cunningham Place. | N.W. | Jan. 5 | [?1870] ⟨Jan. 5 1871⟩

Dear Miss Buss

I am sorry you should have had the trouble of reminding me of your question. I am quite willing to accept the honour of being patron, tho' I am afraid it will be of little use without work, which I cannot give.

I am glad you have three such good Trustees as Mrs Burbury, Miss Edwards & Miss Vincent Thompson. I noticed in one of the circulars that Latin was only an extra, even in the highest school. I suppose this could not be helped.

I think the omission lowers the character of the school rather seriously, but you must know best what is possible under the circumstances.

Do you remember beguiling me into being Auditor to the Sch. Reg. Assn., & assuring me that it could not be much trouble, the annual income being so small? I went to a meeting last night to look over the accounts, which after three hours, ended in something like despair, the accounts of the Sec., Finance Sec. & Treasurer being irreconcilable. I am to go again on Saturday, to receive explanations. I thought of resigning, but as there is difficulty in getting anybody else to do it & the trouble only comes once a year, I suppose I must go on.

The School Board seems likely to absorb much time. Besides meetings once a week (lasting four hours!) there will be Committees, at which probably the most useful part of the work will be done, & other subsidiary business.

Have you heard of Miss Garrett's engagement to Mr. ⟨James Skelton⟩ Anderson, an East-end ship owner?[1] I like him much, & am very glad about it altogether. They have no idea of her giving up her profession.

Every yours sincerely,
Emily Davies

NLCS: ALS ED FMB1

1. Elizabeth Garrett and James Skelton became engaged on 23 December 1870.

To Frances Mary Buss

THE COLLEGE | HITCHIN

Feb. 13. 1871

Dear Miss Buss

I do not like Mrs. Grey's appeal. There is something plausible about it, but it, but it strikes me as the work of a person who knows very little about elementary schools.

The Board school will be obliged to satisfy the requirements of the Education Department, *first*, & if this was not the case, I do not believe that a Committee of ladies are likely to suggest anything much better than what we have already, except that of course if we can get *regular* attendance by compulsion, the schools will be able to do better and more than they can now.

I should like to know whether my going to Miss Robins's meeting is of real importance. It will most likely involve giving up something which I shall be very sorry to lose, but I will keep to my engagement if you feel that it will make any serious difference.

Will you kindly send a line in reply to Cunningham Place. I hope to send out the notices for the Sch. meeting to-morrow. It is not at all inconvenient to us to have it, thank you.

Yours very truly
Emily Davies.

NLCS: ALS ED FMB2

To George Reyner

HITCHIN COLLEGE. | 17, CUNNINGHAM PLACE. N.W.

Feb. 18. 1871

Dear Sir

Mr. Bowling has I believe mentioned to you that the Committee of Hitchin College are looking for a building site at a distance of about three miles from Cambridge. We shall not at present want more than four ~~of~~ or five acres, but we should wish to have the option of purchasing later, to the extent of ten or twelve acres. As to locality, we wish for a high and open position, within reach of a plentiful supply of water. If there are any sites answering to this description belonging to St. John's College, may I ask you to be good enough to let me know whether, and on what terms, the College might probably be willing to sell.

I remain, Sir
Yours obediently
Emily Davies.

JCC: ALS SB21

To Barbara Bodichon

HITCHIN COLLEGE. | 17, CUNNINGHAM PLACE. N.W.

March 16. | [1871]

Dear Mrs. Bodichon

On coming home, I found Mrs. Austin here.[1] We agreed that the reference to the Committee, which the students greatly shrink from, should be postponed at any rate for the present. Mrs. A. thinks nothing wd. do so much good as a visit from you. She said Miss Gibson had written, or was writing to you. In answering her letter, it would be as well not to mention having seen me. Miss Townshend has come out very well in the last few days.

Yours affectionately
ED.

GC: ALS ED B46

1. Emily Shirreff had resigned as Mistress of the College for Women. Annie Austin took over as Mistress temporarily, leaving in the spring of 1872 due to illness. In April 1871, Charlotte Manning died.

To Marian Bradley

HITCHIN COLLEGE. | 17, CUNNINGHAM PLACE. N.W.

May 8 ⟨1871⟩

My dear Mrs. Bradley

It is some time since I heard of you & I feel rather in the dark, but I suppose a letter addressed to you at Oxford will always reach you. I am writing now on the chance of your being likely to be in Town this month, to tell you of a College Public Meeting to be held next ~~month~~ Monday, & of a little gathering of friends which we are to have at Mrs. Russell Gurney's, 8 Kensington Palace Gardens, on Thursday, from 4 to 7 o'clock.[1] Mrs. Gurney desires me to say that if you should happen to be in Town, and could manage to join us, it would give her much pleasure. It is to be what Mr. Tomkinson calls "a social struggle", not a drawingroom meeting, and I should most particularly like you to come, if you can without too much trouble.

In any case, I hope I may see you before long. I have not heard anything of how you like your new Oxford life. There must have been much to regret in leaving Marlboro'. I have been much interested in reading about it & other things in Bishop Cotton's Life.

I remain
Yours very sincerely
Emily Davies

GC: ALS Add.ED1.39.1n

1. The College Committee had decided to buy land and build a new College, and thus embarked on a campaign to raise £10,000 to cover construction costs. As part of this campaign, a public meeting was held at St. James's Hall in Piccadilly, on 15 May 1871. It was chaired by Cowper Temple, M.P., and among those present were Lyttelton, Garrett Anderson, and Joshua Fitch. As a result of this meeting £600 was promised, and the committee planned to continue with the campaign of meetings in the provinces.

To Barbara Bodichon

HITCHIN COLLEGE. | 17, CUNNINGHAM PLACE. N.W.

June 4 [1871]

Dear Mrs. Bodichon

I was relieved to get your note. I was so afraid the cold wind might have brought back your tic. Do take plenty of port wine & quinine & keep it off.

We added Mr. Anderson to the Committee yesterday, & appointed him, with Mr. Tomkinson & myself, a Sub. Committee to settle about a City meeting. I hope it will come off, but we have not yet quite information enough to decide upon. By Mrs. Gurney's suggestion, we are to have a circular letter printed, giving more detail of the College life than anything we have had yet, & winding up with an appeal. It is intended to be signed by all the Executive Committee. A draft I had prepared was agreed to, subject to improvements when seen in Proof. I hope to have a Proof to send you to-morrow. The Committee, those of us who were there—agreed that as we have enough money in hand, we had better buy the site & get plans. I shall give notice before the next meeting that it will be to decide upon the site. Mr. Roby & Mr. Tomkinson have seen another at Cherry Hinton, which has merits. From what they say, I should think either that or the one near Girton would do equally well, & I should be guided a good deal by price. But I should like you to see both if you could. The Miss Metcalfes are thinking of going this week. If you would write & find out their time, perhaps you would join them. And if after all you could not go with them, you & I might manage to go together some day next week. I go to Hitchin on Wednesday evening, (for the internal Examn.) to stay till the end, i.e. the following Wednesday morning. I am afraid I may have to come up for the day on Friday, for School Board business.

I hope Nannie will stay long enough in Town for me to see her quietly, after the present stress is over.

Your affecn. ED.

About £600 has now been promised as the result of the meeting. There have been very favourable articles in the Saturday & the Guardian.[1]

GC: ALS ED B47

1. "Cambridge," *Guardian*, no. 1328 (Wednesday, 17 May 1871): 588; "The Profession of an English Matron," *Saturday Review* 31, no. 812 (20 May 1871): 626–28.

To Barbara Bodichon

HITCHIN COLLEGE. | 17, CUNNINGHAM PLACE. N.W.

June 6 [1871]

Dear Mrs. Bodichon

I send you this Proof, full of misprints as it is, not to lose time. Please suggest any improvements that occur to you. I go to Hitchin to-morrow evening & stay, School Board permitting, to the end of the Term, i.e. the 14th. Would it be any way possible for Nannie to come down? She could have a comfortable bedroom, if the double journey in one day would be too tiring for her. You know how heartily welcome she would be. Please give her my love, & say I will *hope* for her. It is in accordance with the fitness of things that she should see the College, and "the happiest women in England," as Mr. Mayor[1] of St. John's calls the students.

Your affecn. ED.

GC: ALS ED B48

1. Both John Eyton Bickersteth Mayor and his brother, Joseph Bickersteth Mayor, were connected to St. John's College.

To Frances Mary Buss

THE LONDON ASSOCIATION OF SCHOOLMISTRESSES
17, CUNNINGHAM PLACE. N.W.

Nov. 9. 1871

Dear Miss Buss

I find from Miss Metcalfe that she is engaged on the ~~17~~ 16th, and would have difficulty in being present on the 15th. In any case I think the notice for next Wednesday would be too short, as our rule says we are to give at least a week's notice of new members proposed, & as you see, we have four this time.

I hope it will not be inconvenient to you to be in Town on that day, so I will send you the Minute book and Agenda paper, & perhaps you will kindly take my place as Secretary. I go to Hitchin to-morrow & propose staying ten days or a fortnight, if I am not obliged to return earlier.

Yours very truly,
Emily Davies.

NLCS: ALS ED.FMB3

To Barbara Bodichon

THE COLLEGE | HITCHIN

Nov. 11 [1871]

Dear Mrs. Bodichon

I hope Wednesday will suit you for the Coll: Com., as I particularly want you to be present. The point to be discussed is the clause about the religious instruction & services.[1] We are told that this ought to be inserted in the *Memorandum*, not the articles, as it is the Memorandum that answers to a Trust-deed, & we have been announcing for two years that certain clauses including this one, would be in the Trust-deed.[2] If it were in the Articles, it could be reversed any day, at the pleasure of the members of the College. It seems to me that we are distinctly bound to put the clause in the memorandum—very nearly, if not quite, as much so ⁽ᵐᵒʳᵃˡˡʸ⁾ as if the deed had been executed two years ago, as it would have been, only that we had not a large enough sum to be worth investing in Trustees. But some of the Committee think that we might free ourselves by sending a notice to all the subscribers & returning their money if they objected. I do not agree, as people have given names & work & influence, which cannot be returned to them, on the strength of our promise, & I don't see what right we should have ever to be trusted again if we changed on a point which is felt to be as important as this. But apart from that, I think it would be most undesirable to bring the question forward in connexion with the College, as we should do if we wrote to all our miscellaneous body of contributors about it. If we had to begin again, it would be a different matter, but I should still, on the whole, prefer making the clause permanent. This is not because I want to bind posterity. I feel certain that the letter of a Trust-deed would not bind them, if such a change ⁱⁿ ᵒᵖⁱⁿⁱᵒⁿ took place as would make this clause hurtful. It would either be disregarded, as obsolete, or there would be an Act of Parliament to alter it. But I should like the matter to be considered *settled*, for the present. If it were known that the members of the College could make a change at any moment, some restless person might feel it his duty to be continually proposing it & we should be in constant hot water. The compromise has been accepted by moderate people on both sides, & I think we had much better stick to it.

I send a copy of a letter to Mr. ⟨Henry⟩ Crosskey of Birmingham, who raised the question there. We had only time just to send the report of the Building Committee. It will come on, if there is time, on Wednesday. I would rather do all that work at once in January, if we could rely on having Mr. Waterhouse at our command, but I am sure it is not safe to postpone the preliminary part. There are such incessant delays at every point.

I stay here perhaps ten days or a fortnight, going up for the day on Wednesday.

Ever yr. affecn.
ED.

GC: ALS ED B49a

1. While the University of Cambridge was moving conclusively away from religious tests, ED was insistent that students at the College for Women have the opportunity for religious observance according to the Church of England. This insistence alienated some supporters, including Sidgwick. In the summer of 1871, Sidgwick rented and furnished a house at Regent's Street, Cambridge, and under Clough's supervision the residence accepted its first five students in October 1871. Originally known a Merton Hall, it later became Newnham College.

2. The fundraising efforts had not generated sufficient money to build the new college.

The committee decided to incorporate the College for Women under the Board of Trade, and the college (hereafter Girton College) then borrowed on the security of a number of friends, who acted as guarantors. The College for Women was incorporated on 15 May 1871.

To Sedley Taylor

HITCHIN COLLEGE. | 17, CUNNINGHAM PLACE. N.W.

Nov. 28. [1871]

Dear Mr. Taylor

I am afraid none of us are in a position to incur unlimited liability on behalf of the College.[1] From what you say, I think you have not noticed that the liability would not exceed £5, unless we had been dividing the profits of the College among ourselves. If we had arrived at such a state of prosperity as to be thinking of doing that, any member could relieve himself of responsibility by resigning.

The Committee have no choice about clauses 5 & 6, as they are required by the Board of Trade, & it was thought that they would be quite harmless as we are never likely to act in contravention of clause 4. Could you persuade Prebendary Brereton to include girls in his Norfolk School scheme?

I am sorry I shall not have an opportunity for a talk with you about the Part Singing at the College. It will evidently not be worth while to go to great expense about it, as the students will not have much time to spare for practising, but they could scarcely get on without a start & some direction & stimulus. I thought I might perhaps have beguiled you into coming from Cambridge for an evening two or three times in the course of the Term, which would have been enough to keep the class going. If this is impossible, we might perhaps persuade Miss Metcalfe to undertake it. A regular teacher coming once a week from London would be very expensive, & the results would probably be inadequate, as we have no very good voices or great musical gifts. I believe six or eight of the students would like to join a class in a humble way & would enjoy it much. As a preliminary step, could you kindly advise about music? If you could name some three or four pieces, not difficult, & which could be done by women only, they might be practising their parts during the Vacation, so as to be able to do something together when they come back.

I shall be in Town till the end of this week.

Yours very truly

Emily Davies.

CUL: ALS Add.MS.6258(E)71

1. See ED to Barbara Bodichon, 11 November 1871.

To Barbara Bodichon

HITCHIN COLLEGE. | 17, CUNNINGHAM PLACE. N.W.

[Nov. or Dec. 1871]

I think the 3d. of January would be better than the 23d. Dec. That being a Saturday would practically be the day before Christmas Day, which is always a time of great distraction. Could you give a choice of the 3d, or 4th, of January. I was going to add the 6th, but that is Twelfth Day, which may be a day for parties in a place like Hastings. I am very glad Mr. Brassey[1] chooses after the 18th, as Mr. ⟨John⟩ Percival of Clifton wishes our meeting there to be before that, & I was afraid they might be fixing on the same day. Mr. Percival is the Headmaster of Clifton College & has a good deal of weight. He writes in a most friendly tone & Miss ⟨Amelia⟩ Edwards now thinks our prospects are good.

I will send papers to Mr. Brassey & will write, offering any further information that he may desire. I suppose he will get the Birmingham paper, which contains all I have got to say.

I should not think it necessary to pay the expenses of speakers from London, as the journey is not very expensive & it is a nice lark to go to such a place as Hastings. I shall see Mrs. Grey this afternoon & will ask her. I will ask Mr. Abbott as soon as the day is fixed, if you think it worth while. He is a clergyman & pretty well known in one way or another & speaks well. Mr. Percival wants Conservatives for Clifton, so I am going to ask Mr. ⟨John⟩ Gorst.

ED.

GC: ALS ED B50

1. See ED to Barbara Bodichon, 26 December 1871.

To Barbara Bodichon

HITCHIN COLLEGE. | 17, CUNNINGHAM PLACE. N.W.

Dec. 12. [1871]

Dear Mrs. Bodichon

I do not know which "College papers" you mean, but I send some Programmes & letters. Will you please attend to Dr. ⟨William⟩ Greenhill. What does Mr. Brassey say about Mr. Goschen?[1] I think it might be well to get a new edition of the Hastings circular, with the names of speakers. But if there is a chance of Mr. Goschen, we had better wait for him. I have sent circulars to Mrs. Andrews (née Hare) & she promises to forward them to her friends at Hastings.

Besides the public meeting at Clifton, there is to be a drawingroom meeting on Monday. I am to dine with the Hills on Sunday.²

I shall be at home till Friday morning & I hope back again on Monday night. My address at Clifton will be

Care of Miss Edwards
1 Cambridge Place
Clifton
Bristol.

Have you found anybody to receive subscriptions at Hastings?³ Mr. ⟨Samuel⟩ Morley, M.P. promises £100. And I have heard of two more students likely to come next October.

Yr. affecn.
ED.

Let me know if you want more of anything.

GC: ALS ED B51a

1. Probably George Joachim Goschen (1831–1907), who was M.P. for the City of London; president of Poor Law Board; and an advocate of opening Oxford and Cambridge to Dissenters.
2. The Davenport Hills—Mathew, Florence, and Rosamund—lived in Bristol.
3. See ED to Marian Bradley, 8 May 1871.

To Barbara Bodichon

HITCHIN COLLEGE. | 17, CUNNINGHAM PLACE. N.W.

Dec. 20 | [1871?]

Dear Mrs. Bodichon

Will you tell me whether you will want the enclosed circular, adapted to Hastings. We could of course have it printed without any Local Sec.'s name, if no suitable person has arisen.

Would it be possible & useful to have a drawingroom meeting a day or so after the public meeting? At Clifton we had the public meeting on Friday, Schoolmistresses on Sat. afternoon, a party in the evening, private visits on Sunday & a drawingroom on Monday. And it seemed to me that all put together was none too much to dispel the thick darkness. They are forming a Local Committee to go on working, & have started a Scholarship to pick up small sums. Florence Hill said she would rather contribute to that than to the building. She has become much more friendly & altogether I felt that there was a great deal more sympathy than that dreadful day when you and I sat with all their stony faces before us & failed to move them at all.

I have not heard from Mr. Goschen yet. I have a letter to-day from Mr. ⟨Robert⟩ Quick, who is at Brighton. I shall ask him to come to the meeting if he can.

Yours ever
ED.

GC: ALS ED B52

To Barbara Bodichon

~~UNIVERSITY EXAMINATIONS.~~ | 17, CUNNINGHAM PLACE. LONDON N.W.

Dec. 26. [1871]

My dear Mrs. Bodichon

I hope you have been having a merry Christmas. I am sure you have contributed to the mirth of the Crowham household, & have enjoyed having the children to amuse & please.[1] I appreciate my little relatives more at Christmas than at any other time. We won't be anxious about the Hastings meeting. I never expected a great success. If there was enough interest & goodwill to ensure successful meetings, it probably would not be necessary to hold them. The more ignorance & prejudice there is to overcome, the more necessary it is to have a meeting. We must consider a little about the order of proceedings. Perhaps it will be best for the strangers to speak first all in a row, & then to have a Resolution approving of the scheme, moved & seconded by two Hastings men. Would Dr. Greenhill & your Cambridge tutor do? Then there must be a vote of thanks to the Chairman. You might do that? Please let me know when you go back to Hastings.

I am sending notices for a College Committee on Thursday Jan. 4. at five. I suppose you will be back in Town by that time. I hope Mr. Waterhouse may have the plans ready.

I have no answers from Mr. Goschen yet.

If not premature, I wish you all a happy New Year.

Yours affcn. ED.

Mr. Waterhouse is going to build a house for Mr. Albert Brassey which is to cost £100.000.

GC: ALS ED B53

1. The household of Bodichon's brother William Leigh Smith.

To ⟨Matilda Betham-⟩ Edwards

HITCHIN COLLEGE. | 17, CUNNINGHAM PLACE. N.W.

Dec. 31 [1871]

Dear Miss Edwards

Many thanks for your letter & information about the trains. Will you kindly give the enclosed to Mrs. Bodichon, when you see her. I hope you may be able to persuade her to move the vote of thanks. I think it would come appropriately from her, as she is the author of the meeting & that it would please the Hastings people for her to say just a word or two.

I have seen Mr. Abbott & have told him about trains. He is going to lunch with an old pupil. He will speak about the enormous benefit that would result to the whole nation if mothers were sufficiently instructed to be able to teach their children, as the maternal instinct would prevent them from cramming. Is not this good?

I hope you & Mrs. Bodichon will not be disappointed if the meeting should be rather small. We never get a crowd, the subject is not attractive enough, but the people who *do* come pay attention. I am satisfied that the Clifton meeting did great good, tho' it was not large.

Ever yours truly
Emily Davies

I suppose there will be reporters.

GC: ALS ED B54

To Barbara Bodichon

HITCHIN COLLEGE. | 17, CUNNINGHAM PLACE. N.W.

Jan. 15 ⟨1872⟩

Dear Mrs. Bodichon

I am delighted to hear of Mr. Mocatta.[1] So we go on, here a little & there a little.

I have taken the liberty of telling Mr. Bryce that you will be glad to see him on Wednesday. I don't think we shall be able to get a Committee meeting before to-morrow.

I go on Monday to the West for a week.[2]

Mr. Enfield has been here this morning. He sees the desirableness of the Guarantee fund & will let me know what he will do. I never thought of departing in peace till the College is incorporated, in its own building, & able to pay its way. To that I look forward.

You are a perfect treasure on the Building Committee.
Yours ever
ED.
I enclose cheque.

GC: ALS ED B55

1. Probably Frederick David Mocatta (1828–1905), an Anglo-Jewish philanthropist and linguist.
2. ED spoke at the Assembly Rooms, Bath, on "The College for Women at Hitchin" on 24 January 1872.

To Barbara Bodichon

HITCHIN COLLEGE. | 17, CUNNINGHAM PLACE. N.W.

Jan. 16. ⟨1872⟩

Dear Mrs. Bodichon

I am very sorry you are troubled about the plans.[1] We cannot break off from Mr. Waterhouse, but I am sure he will pay attention to all that you have to say. I have been struck by his willingness to listen to & *adopt* my amateur suggestions. I think we ought to be careful what we say to outsiders, or there will be a report that we are wasting money on an unhealthy building, which would be quite untrue. I don't believe in Mr. Chadwick's healthy building for £6000 & if I had to listen to him, I should die of despair before the first stone was laid.

I have not the least doubt in the world that the College will be a Temple of health, at any rate as compared with the houses most of the students will come from. It may not attain the highest ideal, but one cannot expect that. Private people must ruin themselves in trying the ideals before public bodies can adopt them.

It *is* vexing about E. F., but I don't see what we can do. You might explain to Mrs. B. that she is not a friend of yours. I should not like ⟨to⟩ make such an adroit manager of people our active enemy.

If not too late, would you ask Mr. Albert Dicey for to-morrow. I will take our notes to Mr. Waterhouse & perhaps you will fit yours in, that he may dispose of one point at a time.

Yours ever
ED.

GC: ALS ED B56

1. Waterhouse designed the first stage of the building at Girton in close consultation with ED. The guiding principles were that the buildings should allow for easy expansion and be both secure and hygienic. The college was built in long wings with corridors down

one side, rather than in the traditional "staircase" system used in the older Cambridge colleges. The corridor system had its critics, but ED recognized that it provided a secure layout that would appeal to the parents of female students, and that it provided for healthy rooms by allowing good cross-ventilation. The first building, known as Old Wing, cost £12,000 to build.

To Barbara Bodichon

HITCHIN COLLEGE. | 17, CUNNINGHAM PLACE. N.W.

Sunday. Jan. 21. | [1872]

Dear Mrs. Bodichon

Thank you for sending the plans &c. Mr. Tomkinson has invented one on the "well" system, without attics, & will try to see Mr. Waterhouse before we meet on Wednesday & find out what difference it would make in the cool. It involves having eight pairs of rooms with a North-east aspect!

If it would save *much*, I suppose we must reconcile ourselves to that & other drawbacks.

I have thought of a modification of the original plan which would get rid of the objectionable arrangement under the staircase & make the entrance more open & cheerful. It would not save anything.

Mrs. Prideaux has undertaken to write to the rich Mrs. Holland about the Guarantee fund. She said she had friends at Leicester, no doubt the Miss Ellis's.[1] I know them (tho' not personally) thro' two or three channels, & was intending to write as soon as the Leicester arrangements are settled.

I will be with you, with the plans, a little before eight on Wednesday & will bring also the iron rooms & the present house, with all measurements marked, which I find useful for comparison.

Yours ever
ED.

GC: ALS ED B57

1. Margaret, Eliza, Charlotte, and Isabella Ellis.

To Barbara Bodichon

THE COLLEGE | HITCHIN

Feb. 2 ⟨1872⟩

Dear Mrs Bodichon

I am forwarding your letter to the nicest & kindest people I know at Newcastle. They are likely to like to show friendliness to a foreigner.

I am very glad to hear of Miss Swanwick's additional £50, & have entered it in the new edition of the Programme. Miss Eccles has sent another £100 instead of taking part in the Guarantee.[1] Mr. Westlake will guarantee £500.

I think it may not be necessary to guarantee more than £4000, as we are now close upon £8000 in promises. I wonder whether we said anything imprudent at Hastings about Cambridge. A rich lady who was at the meeting objects on the same grounds as Mr. Shuttleworth.

I find Mr. Tomkinson has an engagement on Wednesday evening so we must put off the Building Committee. Would ~~you~~ Monday (the 12th) or Tuesday or Wednesday in the following week suit you? I should like Tuesday the 13th best.

I have been spending a night at a house lately enlarged under Mr. Waterhouse's direction. It is very pretty & pleasant & convenient.

I shall be here till Wednesday. Mr. C. Russell Scott is to pay his visit on Monday.

Yr. affecn.
ED.

GC: ALS ED B58

1. Probably Charlotte Eccles (?–1911), Irish author and journalist.

To Barbara Bodichon

⟨late February/early March⟩ Thurs: | [1872]

Dear Mrs. Bodichon

I am anxious to hear what Mr. Waterhouse says. I fancy pressure will make a good deal of difference to Mr. Loveday, as he is doing other building at Cambridge & can give precedence to ours if he understands that he must. There was not half time for all the things that I wanted to talk to you about. I meant to have told you of an idea of getting the little house in which the foreman lives kept standing for James. It is the only chance of having him near, as no house can be got at Girton. I suppose we should have to pay something for it.

Miss Bulley & Miss ⟨Jane Francis⟩ Dove came to me last night with the enclosed paper. I should like to know what you think of it. I think there is some reason for their wish for more variety, but it looks as if there must be a marked deficiency of real grievances when having to drink out of a teacup is considered a hardship worth mentioning. The list on the left hand side is of things that they want to have occasionally. I promised to give Hammond receipts & to stir her up to a little more variety, but did not give them much encouragement otherwise.[1]

Please return the paper:
Ever yours
ED.

GC: ALS ED B59

1. Hammond was the housekeeper at both Hitchin and Girton.

To Charlotte Burbury

The College

March 26. ⟨1872⟩

My dear Mrs. Burbury

So far as I know at present, there is nothing to prevent my attending a L⟨ocal⟩.E⟨xaminations⟩. Committee meeting during the Vacation, but I hope you will fix the day without reference to me. I shall have to be back here about the 16th April.

The last account of Mrs. Austin was decidedly better. It seems likely that the attack will be short & slight, & that it may pass by without any more serious break in her life than is involved in the necessity of giving up this place. The Committee have agreed to my taking charge for next Term.[1] I did not find it necessary to say anything about the nature of the illness which had obliged Mrs. Austin to leave.

There is no foundation for the story about my brother's plucking. I doubt whether he knows himself where St. Paul was born.

When you go to Cambridge would you thank Marian for her kind letter to me & tell them that I am giving up thinking of a stone laying ceremony.[2]

Ever yours sincerely
Emily Davies

GC: ALS Add.ED1.39.1f

1. See ED to Barbara Bodichon, 16 March 1871. After Austin fell ill and had to resign as Mistress, ED accepted the position of Mistress, which she held until 1875.
2. Construction was about to begin on the new college building in Girton. See ED to Barbara Bodichon, 21 October 1872.

To Dr. William Carpenter

HITCHIN COLLEGE. | 17, CUNNINGHAM PLACE. N.W.

March 30. 1872

Dear Sir

I am desired to ask you to be good enough to bring before the Trustees of the Gilchrist Fund the claims of the College for women upon their support.[1]

This College was opened in October 1869 and is for the present carried on in a hired building & on a small scale, at Hitchin. A site has been purchased in the parish of Girton, near Cambridge, and it is hoped that the institution will be established in its own building in the course of next year.

We understand that it is not the practice of the Trustees of the Gilchrist Fund to make grants for building. I am therefore desired to request you to call attention to the need of Scholarships, enabling the holders to carry on their education without cost to themselves, or at a lower cost than that of the whole of the College fees.

Particulars respecting Scholarships already given will be found in the Programme, of which I send copies. The Examinations for Scholarships have always attracted a considerable number of candidates, many of whom are intending hereafter to make teaching their profession. It is believed that by affording to such persons the opportunity of obtaining a thorough education, not otherwise within their reach, the most effective means will be adopted of improving girls' schools, which now suffer at all stages from the want of a supply of competent teachers.

The College for women has hitherto been carried on under the direction of an Executive Committee. With a view to acquiring a legal status, steps are being taken & are nearly completed, for obtaining incorporation by license from the Board of Trade.

If there should be any point on which the Trustees may desire further information, I shall be glad to give it.

I am, Sir
Yours obediently
Emily Davies
Hon. Sec.

GC: DALS ED AR 2/6/14a

1. The Gilchrist Scholarship of £50 a year for three years was first offered in 1873. It was awarded on the basis of the candidate's performance in the London University General Examination of Women and could be used at Girton. (The scholarship was discontinued at Girton in 1878, when women were admitted to degrees at London University.)

To Barbara Bodichon

GIRTON COLLEGE.

Hitchin | April 21. | [1872?]

Dear Mrs. Bodichon

After talking to Mr. Waterhouse to-day, we decided not to recommend any alterations, but to be satisfied for the present with the room over the kitchen for recreation.

This is 24 X 20, which is a very good size, I suppose, for dancing. As to the iron bars, they would be a great expense (£60 at least) & not an effectual protection after all. It was concluded that we had better have a catch in the windows, & for our principal protection rely upon a little dog running about the corridors.

Under these circumstances we have nothing particular to report & shall not want a Committee next Monday.

Eight students & Miss Lumsden are arrived. The other two are due tomorrow. Miss W⟨oodhead⟩. writes to say that she cannot come till Wednesday, giving no reason. She does not seem to understand the nature of an engagement. Miss Lumsden virtuously gave up a dinner party in order to come back to time.

I wish we could get her some pupils in Town. There was a chance of some in a school, but she would have had to go to them every day which she could not do from here.

It is beautifully fresh & pleasant & the flowers are delightful.

If I am to write to W⟨illiam⟩.B⟨ell⟩. Scott, would you please let me have his address.

Your affecn.
ED.

GC: ALS ED B60

To John Stuart Mill

THE COLLEGE | HITCHIN

April 26, 1872

Dear Sir

It is the practice in this College to hold an Examination at the end of each Academical year in the subjects which have been studied during the year, the work of examining being kindly undertaken by friends of the College not concerned in the teaching. This year we have had a class in Political Economy, and I am desired to say that the Committee would consider it a great favour if you could be good enough to set a paper & report upon the answers. The latter part of the work would not be burdensome, as there are only four students in the class at present. Our Lecturer, Mr. Venn, instructs me to describe the subject of his teaching as "The principles of Political Economy, taking Mill's treatise as the text-book, but stopping short at the end of the third book." We should be glad to have the paper in the course of next month. I hope it may be possible for you to do us this service.

Two of the students in this class look forward to taking (informally) the Examn. for the Moral Science Tripos, which includes Political Economy. We hope by & by to have a much larger class. At present the whole college is on a very small scale, & it is impossible to find time for the many subjects which it is desirable to learn. We are just now on the point of being incorporated as "Girton College" & hope to begin building within the next few weeks.

May I ask to be very kindly remembered to Miss Taylor.
I remain
Yours very truly
Emily Davies.

JH: ALS JSMill HUT4

To Barbara Bodichon

17, C.P. | Sept. 12. | [1872?]

Dear Mrs. Bodichon

Miss J. Boucherett told me to see a Miss Hill at Brighton, who greatly desires to prepare her pupils for Girton. She looked pleasant, but I do not know enough to say anything more. I have not the address. Miss Boucherett's is 8 Mill Terrace, Cliftonville. A day or two ago I had a letter from Miss ⟨Laura⟩ Soames, Tranmore Lodge, Brighton, asking about our Schoolmistresses' Assn. She wants to "persuade some of the best schoolmistresses to form such an Assn." at Brighton. This looks as if she had some kind of access to the best, & she might be willing to give information.

Please send me your opinion on the enclosed letter. I don't mind going up & down a few steps, & I would rather keep to the old plan than reduce the size of the rooms.

The October Entrance Examn. has fallen thro' for want of candidates. I suppose they found it a bad time for working, as only one returned her Form of Entry & she will not be 18 till April. It is a most inconvenient time for an Examn., in many ways. A Miss ⟨Frances⟩ Müller (half German) living near Barnet, wants to come to the College as soon as she can, but she could not be ready for Examn. in October.

My letter to the Spectator brought £20 from Mrs. Sheffield Neave, of whom I never heard before, & 10 guineas from Dr. ⟨Montague⟩ Butler of Harrow. He hopes to add to it next year.

It is rather bad of us not to go to Plymouth.[1] Mr. Hastings has promised to talk about the Coll: in his Address & Miss Shirreff will mention it in her paper.

Your affecn.

ED.

GC: ALS ED B62

1. The NAPSS annual congress was being held in Plymouth, 11–18 September 1872.

To Barbara Bodichon

~~PROPOSED ADMISSION OF LADIES TO THE EXAMINATIONS FOR DEGREES OF THE UNIVERSITY OF LONDON.~~ | ~~17, CUNNINGHAM PLACE, N.W.~~

Hitchin. | Oct. 14 [1872]

Dear Mrs. Bodichon

The pamphlet seems to me all right. I suppose you have some evidence as to the good of the School Board elections. I have not seen women showing an interest in the candidate's opinions, & it is disappointing to see how entirely unconscious the members are of being partly dependent on women for their return, but one cannot expect these things to come all at once. I would leave out Miss Marsh's name, & perhaps insert some more modern one instead. Miss M. has not been before the public much, & think most people would wonder who she was.

I am glad you felt as I did about those people's forgetting the College. Disapproval one can understand, but that they should *forget* it after all we have said to them! There are two candidates now who want to come as soon as they can, Miss Müller & Miss ⟨Amy⟩ Mantle, but they have not passed the Entrance Examn. & we have not room for them. It is very fresh & sweet down here, & it is a great rest to have no Committees to attend.

I expect about 8 students to-day & the rest to-morrow.[1] The domestic arrangements are going smoothly & give me very little trouble. I think this is greatly owing to Mrs. Austin's having organised the service thoroughly well once for all. It is easy to keep it right, when well started.

Mrs. A. is much better, but not quite satisfactory. She has taken lodgings for herself & her boy in London, against the urgent advice of her relatives, one of the objections being that on the plan she has laid out she cannot possibly live on her income. It is of course uncertain how long she may wish to stay.

Your affecn. ED.
I rather tremble as to the answer from Venice.

GC: ALS ED B63

1. Three new students entered Girton in 1872: Eliza Barker, Constance Maynard, and Constance Shorrock.

To Barbara Bodichon

GIRTON COLLEGE. | 17, CUNNINGHAM PLACE. N.W.
Hitchin | Oct. 21. | [1872]

Dear Mrs. Bodichon
    I hope Nov. 6. will be convenient to you. The Ex. Com. will meet at 5 P.M. I have found out about the Little-go & Mathematical Examiners. The latter are believed to be friendly. I think we have a fair chance of getting what we want.
    The 13 are setting to work in good spirits. Next Term I expect we shall be preparing candidates for the Natural Science, Moral Science, Classical & Mathematical Triposes.
    Let no one say we lack variety when out of ten students we have candidates for four Triposes, besides the students who follow their own bent, unfettered by Examns.[1]
    Mr. Venn told me to-day that he & Mr. Seeley had been out to Girton & met six or eight Cambridge men who said they had all been helping to lay bricks. They had each written their name on a brick & laid it. The walls were about the height of the Mantelpiece. I am trying to stir up Mr. Waterhouse about the planting.
    Miss ⟨Constance⟩ Maynard says her neighbour Miss ⟨Constance⟩ Herschel is quite looking forward to coming, next year I believe.
    Ever yours affn.
    ED

GC: ALS ED B65

1. At Girton College, University Examinations were "open to, but not enforced upon, all students" (Programme for a College for Women, GC ED VII/GC1/4). Thus while the college encouraged students to take university-level examinations, not all students chose to do so.

To Barbara Bodichon

Hitchin. | Oct. 23. [1872?]

Dear Mrs. Bodichon

Will you please tell me, by return of post if you can, whether you think it desirable to put the hot water furnace under the gyprooms, instead of the housekeepers' room.[1] Mr. W. suggests it on the ground that the dry earth will on the present plan have to be carried to the gyproom. On the other hand we could take the provision for drying boots & clothes, & I think the loss would be greater than the gain.

Could you ask Mr. ⟨Charles?⟩ Darwin to give us his Works? We want also the Works of Goethe & Schiller, & could take some other books. Would it be well to make a list for Lady Goldsmid? The weather is enchanting & our many coloured trees a sight for to see.

Yr. affecn.

ED.

Don't you think we had better at once order the planting of the corner opposite the farm buildings? Any trees anywhere would be better than none.

GC: ALS ED B66

1. A *gyp* was a domestic servant who was responsible for students' rooms.

To Edmund H. Morgan

Girton College.
17, Cunningham Place ^London^ N.W. | Oct. 24. 1872

Sir

I am desired ~~by the Executive Committee of Girton College~~ to ask you to be good enough to lay before the Examiners for the ensuring Previous Examination of the University of Cambridge a request for the favour of their assistance in examining some of the students of this College.[1] We propose to hold the Examination simultaneously with that of the undergraduates of the University, in the same papers, and we shall be ~~greatly~~ ^much^ obliged if the Examiners will undertake to look over the answers & report upon them according to the University standard. We have also to request that the vivâ voce Examiners will be good enough to conduct this part of the Examination, at such time as may be convenient to them. The Examination will be held at Cambridge under the superintendence of a lady. We shall have five candidates, all of whom have been in residence for not less than four Terms. Four of the candidates will wish to take the Additional Subjects.

I am desired to add that the ⟨Executive⟩ Committee ⟨of the College⟩ will be obliged if you will kindly advise them as to the fees which should be offered to the ~~respective~~ Examiners.

I send a copy of the Memorandum and Articles of Association of the College, and also of the Programme, containing a Certificate received from the Senior Examiner on a similar Examination held with the cognisance of the Council of the Senate in 1870.[2]

I have the honour to be
Sir
Yours obediently
Emily Davies.
Hon. Sec.

GC: DALS AC 2/3/12

1. Each year, ED had to request individual permission from each university examiner for the students at Girton College to take the university's examinations. See ED to James Cartmell, 5 November 1870.
2. The 1872 Girton College Programme noted that "since the opening of the College, eleven students [had] passed informally the Cambridge Examination known as the Little-go, nine of whom attained the standard required for a First-Class."

To William Davidson Niven

Girton College.
17, C.P. London. N.W. | ⟨October 1872⟩

Sir

I am desired to ask you to be good enough to bring before the Examiners for the ensuing Examination for the Mathematics Tripos, an application on the part of Girton College for the favour of their assistance in examining S⟨arah⟩. Woodhead, a student of this College.

Miss Woodhead has entered upon her ~~tenth~~ ninth Term of residence in the College, & we believe that she has fulfilled so far as has been practicable, all ~~the~~ conditions imposed by the University on candidates for the Mathematical Tripos Examn. I enclose a copy of a Certificate received from the Senior Examiner for the Previous Examn. upon an Examn. of ~~our~~ some of our students, held with the cognisance of the Council of the Senate in 1870.

In the present case, we propose to hold the examn at Cambridge simultaneously with that of the undergraduates of the University, in the same papers, and our request is that the Examiners will kindly undertake to look over the ~~papers~~ answers & report upon them according to the University standard for the several classes of the Mathematical Tripos. The Executive Committee of the College are desirous to offer a suitable fee, and we shall be ᵐᵘᶜʰ obliged if you will inform us with your advice on this point.

I send herewith a copy of the Memorandum & Articles of Assn. of the College.

I have the honour to be
Emily Davies

GC: DALS ED AC 2/3/12

To Arthur Holmes

Girton College.
17, C.P. London N.W. | ⟨October 1872⟩

Sir

I am desired to ask you to be good enough to bring before the Examiners for the ensuing Examn. for the Classical Tripos an application on the part of Girton College for the favour of their assistance in examining R⟨achel⟩. S. Cook & L⟨ouisa⟩. I. Lumsden, students of this College.

~~We believe that~~ They have entered upon their ninth Term of residents in this College, & we believe that they have fulfilled, so far as has been practicable, all the conditions imposed by the University on candidates for the Classical Tripos Examn. I enclose a copy of a Certificate received from the Senior Examiner for the Previous Examn. upon an examn. of some of our students, held with the cognisance of the Council of the Senate, in 1870. Miss Cook & Miss Lumsden were examined by one of the University Examiners in the Additional Subjects in ᴰᵉᶜ· 1871 & approved.

In the present case, we propose to hold the examn. at Cambridge, simultaneously with that of the undergraduates of the University, in the same papers, & our request is that the Examiners will ~~kindly undertake~~ ᵇᵉ ᵍᵒᵒᵈ ᵉⁿᵒᵘᵍʰ to look over the answers & report upon them according to the University standards for the several classes of the Classical Tripos.

The Ex. Committee are desirous to offer a suitable fee, & we shall be much obliged if you will favour us with your advice on this point.

I send herewith a copy of the Memorandum & Articles of Assn. of the College.

I have the honour to be
Emily Davies.

GC: DALS ED AC 2/3/12

To Barbara Bodichon

The College.

Hitchin. | Oct. 26. | [1872]

Dear Mrs. Bodichon

The enclosed particulars about German Works are from our German teacher, Fr: V. Bohlen. We could take Goethe, Schiller & Lessing. I wish Sir A⟨rthur⟩. Helps would give his works.

Mr. Brassey might send us his book.

Miss Metcalfe agreed with me that we could not give up the drying closet, & what you say about the ashes tells on the same side, so I have written to Mr. W. to that effect. I have urged him about the planting & asked him to find our whether the trees you speak of would be worth the carriage from Sussex. Please don't send them to *me*. What could I do with them? Mr. Scott's letter is nice. I am glad you will be up on Nov. 6. Lady Stanley is back & ready to be active. I want you to reign here in my stead during the Classical Tripos Examn., i.e. Feb. 17–26. I might if necessary ⟨to⟩ come back for the intervening Sunday. All the students will be here then except the two under examination. I think I can provide more easily for the Little-go absence, which will come just at the end of this Term. The Mathematical Tripos will be in January, during Vacation time.

Why do we spend so much money on food? Our cook here is the daughter of a Wiltshire labourer who brought up ten children on 10/. a week.

Your affecn.
ED.

GC: ALS ED B67

To Barbara Bodichon

Hitchin. | Oct. 30. [1872]

Dear Mrs. Bodichon

Could you arrange to stay a little after the College meeting on the 6th for a Building Committee, to consider suggestions on enclosed plan. No access for a coal-cart to the gyproom basement has been provided. I mentioned it to Mr. W⟨aterhouse⟩. the other day & he proposed a road outside the yard wall. This would be very circuitous & could also prevent our using the wall later on for additions.

The Mathematical Examiners consent to examine Miss Woodhead & suggest that the examn. be conducted by an M.A. appointed by us & approved by them. The letter is very friendly. I have not heard yet from the Little-go.

Yours ever
ED.

GC: ALS ED B68

To Barbara Bodichon

Hitchin. | Nov. 1. ⟨1872⟩

Dear Mrs. Bodichon
    Mr. Waterhouse has sent the plan. I like the planting part of it, but not the gymnasium &c. I am sending it to Mr. Tomkinson & asking him to forward it to you, with Mr. W's letter. Would you please bring both, & the enclosed, which Mr. W. wants back, on Wednesday to Victoria Street. I am asking Mr. W. if he can see us at his office on Thursday (the 7th) at five o'clock, or if not, on what other day. I will let you know directly I hear from him. We must have a talk over the plans & make up our own minds on Wednesday, & after that, the sooner we see Mr. W. the better.
    Ever yours
    ED.
I have a very propitious letter from the Senior Classical Examiner. He will see his colleagues as soon as possible.
    I forget whether I noted on the plan I sent you that "Ashes" could be transferred to basement under pantry, already allotted to cinders. Could you kindly bring with you Robinson's Wild Garden?

GC: ALS ED B69

To Barbara Bodichon

HITCHIN COLLEGE. | 17, CUNNINHAM PLACE. N.W.
Friday [O̶c̶t̶ ̶3̶1̶?̶ 1 Nov. 1872]

Dear Mrs. Bodichon
    I have been studying the plans & comparing them with that of the present house at Hitchin which I have here. This plan gives the measurements of all the rooms & as they have been lived in, we can judge exactly how they work. The result is that I have hit upon some ideas which I hope will meet some of your difficulties & Miss Metcalfe's. I should like very much to have a talk with you about them before Wednesday & could come to you at any time to-morrow up to f̶i̶v̶e̶ six o'clock. I mean that I should have to leave by six, for some people from Plymouth who propose calling in the evening.

In the case of these plans I find the advantage of not having an original mind. I could not *invent* so much as a cottage, but I can enter into other people's views & suggest little modifications of them.

I do not agree with you as to the *amount* of time & attention that people are bound to give to public business, *if they give any*. On your principle nobody ought to do anything unless they can do a *great deal*, which would be a fatal hindrance. It might be better if you or Miss Metcalfe could give your *whole* minds to the College work, but you cannot. And what you can give is an immense deal better than nothing. Of course we shall make some mistakes, but I don't believe they will be bad ones.

Ever yours
ED.

GC: ALS ED B70

To William Davidson Niven

Nov. 13 1872
Dear Sir

I am desired to acknowledge with many thanks your letter & the kindness of the Mathematical Examiners in ~~undertaking~~ consenting to look over our student's papers. The Committee gladly ~~accede to~~ accept the suggestion that the Examn. should be conducted by an M.A. member of the University.

~~If the Examiners would be good enough to make the appointment,~~ The Committee would prefer that the appn. should be made entirely by the Examiners, but if this would involve more trouble that they can conveniently undertake, the Committee will nominate, subject to ~~their~~ Examiners' approval. It is proposed to offer a fee of not less than £5.

E. D.

GC: DALS ED AC 2/3/12

To Edmund H. Morgan

Nov. 21 [1872]

Dear Sir

I have to acknowledge with thanks your letter, communicating the official decision of the examiners for the Previous Examn. respecting the admission of our Students.[1]

You were good enough to say in your former letter that some of the Examiners would be willing to ~~help~~ ^{oblige} us in their private capacities. May I ask if you can kindly arrange this for us with the Examiners?

~~The vivâ voce p~~ In that case, we may perhaps be allowed to send you our students' papers, to be forwarded thro' you to the Examiners who are kindly willing to look over them.

We should have to ask the Vivâ voce Examiners to be good enough to come, at whatever time might suit them best, to the place at wh: we hold the Examn. This will probably be a room in the University Arms Hotel.

If what I am asking would be giving you too much trouble, would you favour me with the address of the Examiners who have so kindly expressed their willingness to help us.

ED.

GC: DALS ED AC 2/3/12

1. Morgan, the senior examiner for the Previous (Little-go) Examination, advised ED that the council of the Senate had decided, on 18 November 1872, that the examiners could not admit students of Girton College to the Previous Examination. However, the council did not explicitly forbid examiners from acting privately to examine the Girton students.

To Mrs. Oliver

GIRTON COLLEGE. | 17, CUNNINHAM PLACE. N.W.

Hitchin. | Nov. 22. [1872]

Dear Mrs. Oliver

Queen's College and Girton College are so very different that one scarcely knows how to make a comparison between them. Queen's College is a system of classes for girls living at home or in boarding houses. Pupils are admissible at thirteen, & tho' there are probably few or none so young as that, the great majority are under or about eighteen. Here we admit none under eighteen, & our students' ages range from that to over thirty. The classes are very small, & where necessary, we allow individual teaching. All our students are of course resident. I send you some papers, giving fuller particulars. With regard to the particular point as to which you ask, I think it would be rash, in these days of shaking & change, to give any sort of guarantee for the security of faith anywhere, but I should feel less apprehension here *now* than in our first days. At the very beginning, we had, not unnaturally, some students who were not at all orthodox. These have left or are leaving, and those who have come the last two years are of a different type. It is not a subject on which I should like to say much, but I observe that they go regularly to Church or Chapel. (of those who have come the last two years all but one attend Church.) and scarcely ever miss our Morning Prayers at eight o'clock. I offer the loan of a sermon or a theological book sometimes, & find it gladly accepted.

But ~~then~~ in such a place as this there must always be the chance of hearing free discussion, and I can not say positively that our standard of orthodoxy is such as your friend would approve. We hope to be in our new building by next October.

Yours very truly
Emily Davies.

GC: ALS Add.ED1.39.1r

To ⟨Edmund H. Morgan⟩

GIRTON COLLEGE. | (17, CUNNINGHAM PLACE. N.W.)
Hitchin. | Nov. 23. 1872

Dear Sir

It was quite understood that the Examiners would not *give* us the papers in sense in which official ~~permission~~ ^authority^ could be required. We have always sent to the Senate house for them half an hour after they have been given out, at which time I believe anybody that applies may have them. Taken in this way, I suppose there could be no more objection to looking over this year's papers than ~~to~~ any others. It is entirely a private matter between the College and the Examiners who may be good enough to undertake it. To have fresh papers set would give the examiners unnecessary trouble & would not be satisfactory to the College.

As time presses, I am obliged to write without waiting for direct instructions, but I have no doubt that this ~~is~~ ^would be^ the view ~~that would be~~ taken by the College. We have always ~~taken for granted that whatever happened, we could~~ ^reckoned upon^ having the use of the papers ^in any case^ as it was not any special privilege accorded to us.

I am sorry that any ambiguity in my letter should have given you the trouble of writing on this matter.

GC: DAL ED AC 2/3/12

To Edmund H. Morgan

GIRTON COLLEGE. | ~~17, CUNNINHAM PLACE. N.W.~~
Hitchin. | Nov. 25. | [1872]

Dear Sir

Thank you very much for writing at once in reply to my letter. I am afraid it must too troublesome to you to have this matter on your hands at such a busy time, but you will understand that ~~there is we are obliged to look to you~~ there is no one else to whom we can look to help us out of our difficulty. I was not at all aware that the practice of distributing papers half-an-hour after they had been given out, had been discontinued.

This ~~of course~~ would I presume make it improper, as well as useless, for us to send to the Senate house for them, as we have done hitherto. I suppose however that the papers may be considered the property of the Examiners who set them, & that at some later hour, to which we should accommodate ourselves, they might be able to send them to us.

I quite feel the difficulty of doing anything which might have even the appearance of contravening the decision of the Council. But ~~I understand~~ a member of the Council ~~assures us~~ who was present when the subject was discussed assures us that the Council carefully abstained from expressing any disapproval of the Examiners acting in their private capacity, & that the decision come to upon our application in 1870 was not ~~reversed~~. You may perhaps find it of some use to be in possession of the letter received from the Vice-Chancellor on that occasion, & I therefore enclose a copy. You will see that we have been all thro' entirely dependent on the personal kindness of the Examiners & it is to this only that we were trusting ~~on the present occasion~~.

~~Perhaps you will kindly let me know when you have time to write, what arrangement you are able to make for us~~. We are of course anxious that the Examn. should be as nearly as possible equivalent to the Little-go, & that it should be conducted on such a way as to be above suspicion, but you must yourself be the best judge as to how far this can be managed without compromising the University. I am sure we may rely upon your making the best arrangements that you can for us, & we should like to leave it entirely in your hands. We are very sorry to be obliged to give so much trouble.[1]

GC: DAL ED AC 2/3/12

1. Morgan facilitated ED's request by arranging for women students to have access to the Little-go papers not less than two hours after the time at which the University students had commenced answering the questions. He later arranged that the papers would be available to the women students half an hour after they had been given out to the men. See ED to Morgan, 30 November 1872; and ED to Morgan, 20 December 1872.

To Charles Smith

17, C.P. | Nov. 27 ⟨1872⟩

Dear Mr. Smith

I have heard to-day from Mr. Miller that he does not see his way to taking part *in* ~~the~~ examining our Student ~~in the Math. Tripos papers~~.[1] We are to have a meeting of ~~the~~ our Committee on Friday, at which I shall have an opportunity of asking for ^further^ instructions. In the meantime, can you kindly advise us? In an analogous case as to the Previous Examn, the Examiners who were favourable ~~to the application managed~~ ^arranged^ for us, disposing among themselves of the work of the Examiner who declined. Cd. this now be managed, or ~~shd. you think it better to~~ ^must we^ ask some external Examiner of sufficient standing & experience? ~~Mr. Courtney, Senr. Wrangler~~ This is a possible resource, but I feel no doubt that our Committee wd. much prefer to keep the Examn. entirely in the hands ~~for~~ ^of^ the Examiners for the year, if ~~they a~~ you could kindly make the necessary arrangements.

GC: DAL ED AC 2/3/12

1. Probably Robert Kalley Miller (1842–89).

To ⟨Edmund H. Morgan⟩

GIRTON COLLEGE. | ~~17, CUNNINHAM PLACE. N.W.~~

Hitchin | Nov. 30. 1872

Dear Sir

We are very much indebted to you for the trouble you have taken about our Examn. It is a great satisfaction to know that the work will be undertaken by such competent Examiners. If you will kindly favour me with the printed Timetable I will send to the Senate house for the papers on each occasion between two and three hours after they have been given out to the undergraduates.

May I send our students' papers to you, to be distributed to the other Examiners? If not, I am afraid I must ask you to let me know which subject is taken by each respectively. We should wish to have the final classification done for us & a certificate given by one of the Examiners.

From what you say, I understand that you would prefer that this should be done by Mr. Cartmell. Otherwise we should have ventured to ask you to be good enough to undertake it.

With many thanks for your most kind and friendly help.

I remain

Dear Sir
Yours very truly
Emily Davies.

GC: ALS ED AC 2/3/12

To James Porter

GIRTON COLLEGE.

Cambridge. | Dec. 2 ⟨1872⟩

Dear Mr. Porter

Many thanks for your note. I write one line just to express the hope that in case the Examiners should not ~~see fit~~ all as a body see fit to grant our application, which we should of course prefer, ~~they~~ a sufficient number of them may be willing to undertake the work individually. It would not be necessary to trouble them all, ~~even if they consent as a body~~ in any case, & we have been very careful not to commit the Examiners to anything beyond the ~~unofficial~~ informal examn. which they have been good enough to give us.

ED.

GC: DALS ED AC 2/3/11

To Arthur Holmes

Cambridge. | Dec. 11 ⟨1872⟩

Dear Mr. Holmes

Since writing to you the other day I have been reading your official letter again, & I begin to fear that ~~my first interpretation was too favourable~~. ~~I may have given it too favourable a meaning~~ I see you say that the examiners will give their private opinions of the performance of our candidates "such opinion being worded so as to make no reference to the University standard of the several Classes of the Classical Tripos." I took this as meaning the same thing that had been arranged for the Little-go, i.e. that each Examiner would give us his verdict separately, leaving it to us to deduce the collective result as to the Class taken. But I am afraid now that the meaning of the Classical Examiners may be that they do not intend to *mark* at all, but only to make general remarks, which for our present purpose would be useless. Miss C⟨ook⟩. & Miss L⟨umsden⟩. are candidates for our "Degree Certificate" & by our Bylaw 1. (of which I enclose a copy) this cannot be conferred without reference to the University standard. If the unfavourable interpretation is the right one, I think the course adopted by the Committee would be to ask the Examiners individually to mark the papers, & in case any one should refuse, his place would be supplied by some other Classical scholar, if possible, of equal experience, in examining for the Tripos. This is practically what has been done in the case of the Little-go. One or two of the Examiners (I am not sure how many) declined, & Mr. Morgan, the Senior Examiner, who kindly took the business in hand for us, ~~has~~ got their places supplied.

~~We are to hear the result~~

You know I dare say that all the Mathematical Examiners have consented to examine & report for us. After explaining that the examn. of our candidate is undertaken by them as private individuals & not in their official capacities, they go on to say that they think it is undesirable to indicate the exact place in the Tripos list which her papers might entitle an actual candidate to, but they will inform her what class she takes & give their opinion on her performance generally.

~~I am very sorry to have to trouble you about this, but~~ The Coll: Committee is to meet next week, & it might save some time if you could kindly let me have a line before then to make us quite sure ~~as to~~ how we stand.

GC: DAL ED AC 2/3/12

To Edmund H. Morgan

~~Nov.~~ Dec. 17. ⟨1872⟩

Dear Mr. Morgan

I hope I shall not seem impatient in writing to you about the report on our ~~students'~~ examn., which may probably be now on its way, but I am a little puzzled by having received a Certificate from Mr. Josling evidently written under misapprehension.[1] Mr. Josling certifies that our students passed "a satisfactory Examn." in the Plato. This is of course not at all what we want. ~~to know.~~ Opinions may differ as to what is "satisfactory," & what we want to know is whether they reached the standard for a B or a C in the Little-go. If any Examiner ~~objects~~ is unwilling to give us this information I think the course we should have to adopt would be to ask some one else on whom we could rely to look over the papers. The reason I am obliged to trouble you about it is that as we should in that case have to ask for the return of the papers. I am anxious to provide against their being in the meantime destroyed.

I earnestly hope however that there may be no such ~~difficulty~~ complication to meet.

I am heartily sorry for having to trouble you once again, but your kindness hitherto encourages me to hope that you will now come to the rescue & carry us thro' to the end, if there should still be difficulties to overcome.

Our students much enjoyed their week at Cambridge, in spite of a good deal of nervous trepidation. It must have been a less agreeable time to the Examiners tho' they certainly seem to get thro' their work with wonderful ease & despatch. I am going to-morrow to see some of the Local Examn. candidates whose work will be coming under your inspection.

GC: DAL ED AC 2/3/12

1. Probably William James Josling (1839–1906), Scholar and Fellow of Christ's College, Cambridge.

To ⟨Edmund H. Morgan⟩

Dec. 20 1872

Sir

I am desired to acknowledge with thanks the reply of the C⟨ambridge⟩. T⟨ripos⟩. Examiners to the application ~~for~~ of the G⟨irton⟩. C⟨ollege⟩. Ex. Committee on behalf of Miss Cook & Miss Lumsden.

The Committee desire me to ~~express~~ convey their ~~sense of the~~ cordial thanks to the Examiners for their courtesy in consenting to allow the use of the examn. papers to our students half-an-hour after they have been given out, & also ~~of~~ for their ~~great~~ kindness ~~of~~ in ~~consenting~~ undertaking as private individuals & unofficially to look over our students' papers & to express an opinion upon them.

The Committee have now only to request that the several Examiners will be good enough to indicate their opinion of each paper by assigning to it the proportion to which they consider it entitled of the maximum number of marks.

I have the honour to be
&c.
ED

GC: DALS ED AC 2/3/12

To Adelaide Manning

⟨January 1873⟩

My dear Adelaide

I am very sorry I cannot attend your party on the 18th. I shall be obliged to do something more fatiguing & less pleasant. i.e. a Tea party given by Mr. ⟨John⟩ McGregor at Lewisham to all sorts of School Board people, at which he wants to have all the members for the Division present, & I have promised to go.

I go to Cambridge on Wednesday evening & stay till Friday—then the night at Hitchin—& home on Saturday in time for the Teaparty.

I am afraid we have not gymnastic appliances enough to make it worth while for Capt. Manning to take us in hand.[1] If they jump high, they hit the ceiling with their heads. But thanks all the same.

Mr. Waterhouse proposes for the clock a panel of glass mosaic work, (either above or beneath the dial, which itself will be a piece of glass mosaic) bearing the initials or anything else that we like.[2]

Should it be "In Memoriam C.⟨harlotte⟩ M.⟨anning⟩"? Or is there anything else that you would prefer? The Committee likes the idea of the panel, but they wish to know whether you like it, & which inscription you would choose. Please let me hear before long, as the building is growing. Kind remembrances to Miss Solly.

Ever yours, ED.

GC: ALS ED XVII GC-9/1

1. The architect's plan of 1872 included a gymnasium to be built at a cost of £400 (Plans of Girton College by Alfred Waterhouse, 1872). The gymnasium was not built until September 1874. See also ED to Barbara Bodichon, 1 November 1872; and ED to Barbara Bodichon, 5 September 1874.

2. A clock dedicated to Charlotte Manning was mounted over the original main entrance to the college (now Emily Davies Court).

To Barbara Bodichon

GIRTON COLLEGE.

Hitchin. Feb. 8. [1873]

Dear Mrs. Bodichon

I have been wavering in my mind as to whether I should beg you very much to come for the two nights, & I really think it would be worth while to give up something for it. This matter of the letter is very troublesome & think it would be useful to give the students the opportunity of talking to you about it.[1]

You might say things to them which either I could not say so well or they want saying again by other members of the Committee. They were greatly aggrieved at the reception of their letter. Their intention had been to send round copies of it to all the Committee beforehand. I persuaded them not to do this, telling them that people would not understand what it was about & that the matter would almost certainly be referred to the Studies' Committee & at any rate would not be decided hastily. Miss Woodhead told me yesterday that they had only given up sending the letter round out of politeness to me, on my distinct assurance that it would not be decided upon at once. I explained that of course I had no right to make any such promise, ~~but~~ & that the matter had been referred to the Sub-Committee of Studies, in so far as that they had been asked to consider the certificates of proficiency with a view to defining the standard. She asked who were present & whether it was an Ordinary or Special meeting, & had "observed" (she copied the notices) that the notices did not mention this business or say whether it was Ordinary or Special, as the Article required. I suppose they had been calculating upon appealing against the decision on the ground that the meeting was irregular. I explained that it was not a College meeting at all (to which those rules apply) & of course that design, whatever it was, fell to the ground.

~~It~~ Is not it vexing to see such a spirit shown? I am afraid we shall have no lasting peace while any of the pioneers remain. Miss Shirreff, it seems, told them she had never heard the question discussed by the Committee & gave the impression, of course by mistake, that it was quite open. Miss W.⟨oodhead⟩ said "Our Lecturers" agreed with them, but declined to give names or particulars, except that "some of us" had written to "some of them." I objected to the Lecturers' time here being taken up in discussing this, & she promised not to do it, with an intimation that probably nothing wd. be done at present. But they sadly want bringing to a more reasonable mind.

Yours ever
ED.

GC: ALS ED B71

1. In February 1873, all thirteen students at Girton College sent a petition to the College Committee asking that henceforth students be allowed to take the Tripos Examinations without having first passed the Previous (Little-go) Examination. This proposal was consonant with reforms underway at Cambridge and therefore had the support of seven of the Girton College lecturers. ED believed that the Previous Examination offered the students the experience of being tested before they advanced to the Tripos, and that it helped them shape their academic decisions. The student petition quickly was rejected. See ED to Barbara Bodichon, ⟨early February⟩ 1873; and 13 February 1873.

To Barbara Bodichon

GIRTON COLLEGE.

Hitchin. Feb. 11. ⟨1873⟩

My dear Mrs. Bodichon

I am sorry you cannot come, but ~~will~~ it will be possible to make some other arrangement. It would not do at all to ask Miss Dove to be Chaplain. I think that the less that is said about the students' letter to any one not on the

Committee the better. They have accepted I believe the decision, at any rate for the present. I had a letter from Mr. Graves yesterday, which I was glad of, as it gave me an opportunity of explaining. He ~~said~~ spoke in his letter of the desirableness of not requiring all students to take the whole University routine, so I told him we did not require it, & that there were three other courses open to every one who comes here. I think many people, when the matter is explained to them, will see that it is an unreasonable claim to want *University Honours*, without fulfilling the conditions. This is what the students asked for.

I am half sorry now that I prevented them from sending the letter round to the Committee beforehand, ~~but~~ as it puts a little grievance into their hands, but I think they know that it would not have made any difference. I don't think *all* the Committee would agree with us, but I think there would be a strong majority. It was unfortunate that the meeting was so small, but it included those who have done most for the College.

It will be a great honour to us to have Mrs. Somerville's legacy.[1] But when I see such a spirit as Miss Woodhead showed the other day, it makes me feel terribly out of heart about our work.

I will send you Mr. Graves's letter & a copy of my answer in a day or two. In the meantime I am sure that the fewer people hear of our troubles the better. We are quite quiet here now.

Ever yours,
ED.

N.B. I think we ought not to consider that most of the students are seriously implicated in this matter. I fancy a good many signed because they were asked, not ~~thinking~~ understanding what they were doing. They have not looked at all conscious of having done anything unpleasant.

GC: ALS ED B75a

1. Her mathematical library.

To Barbara Bodichon

GIRTON COLLEGE.

[March | 1873?] ⟨early February⟩

I don't think there is any fear of losing any of our students.[1] They are ~~all~~ working quietly for their Triposes & Little-go, as if nothing had happened. It is in the natural order that Miss Bulley should leave at Midsummer, but I should not wonder if she asks for the additional year, & Miss ⟨Isabella⟩ Gamble is very likely to do the same. What you say as to the giving of 4 years leading to idling one year, is very much to the point. It is because Miss Bulley lost her first year that she wants one added now. I remember Mrs. Austen's remarking how little she worked when she first came, besides staying away altogether the first term.

We ought to announce about Mrs. Somerville's legacy. Would you send me an exact statement?

Miss Woodhead has made up her mind to ^(try to) get~~ting~~ teaching in London, chiefly of Arithmetic, & would like to leave here at Easter, if she can get enough to do.[2] I have written to Miss Buss & have given Miss W. names of people to write to herself. I should be very glad if she could be provided for so as not to need her here next Term. We shall probably be wanting very little Mathematical teaching here after Easter, for this year.

I think Miss Pipe has encouraged Miss Bulley in idleness & is over estimating her ability. She is intelligent & can talk well, & has very good qualities, & is interested in study. But she does not stick to work in the steady way that is necessary to do well in examns. Or perhaps it is rather that she works regularly, but not enough of it. She gives a good deal of time to Music, & ~~tries~~ other things—e.g. there was a debate the other night, which she opened, on Ancient & Modern Tragedy—& there is a Shakespeare reading now arranged for. And Miss B. always seems to be trying to lure ~~the~~ others away from their regular work. I don't mean to object at all to music & other things. I think they are a useful change. Only if people are not clever enough to do them besides doing well in serious study, they ought not to expect Honours. Miss Bulley's difficulty in the Little-go was Arithmetic ^(not Latin or Greek). I believe she narrowly escaped being plucked in it.

Your testimony ~~from~~ —about Dr. E⟨lizabeth⟩.B⟨lackwell⟩. in America is very important & likely I think to have influences. What our students proposed is somewhat analogous to what it would be if Miss Buss's pupils were to send a Memorial to the Board of Governors asking that they might go in for the Local Examns. & take distinctions in Languages &c. without passing the Preliminary Part of the Examn., without respect to the limit of age. This would exonerate them from the Arithmetic, which is so terribly fatal to girls. The answer they would get would be the same as ours—that they are obliged to take the Examns., but if they do, it must be on the usual terms. Of course the other side would reply that the Preliminary Local Examn. is good & the Little-go is bad. But I think the Little-go as it is *now,* (it has been a good deal improved, I believe) & *as we work it,* is not at all bad. People like Miss Buss's pupil, Miss ⟨Eliza⟩ Baker, can prepare for it by sound steady reading, without over-pressure, even when the subjects are quite new to them. Miss Baker had not done anything on Classics or Mathematics till after the Entrance Examn., but she will be able to take the Little-go without difficulty. And in the course of preparing for it, she will find out something of her powers and tastes, so that she can choose a Tripos intelligently. She would have chosen almost completely in the dark when she first came, & if students were *allowed* to ~~cho~~ work for ~~the~~ [a] Tripos from the beginning, they would be almost compelled to do so, as otherwise those who took the Little-go would be at a great disadvantage in competing with the others.

GC: AL ED B79

1. Agnes Bulley was the only student to leave Girton at this time. She moved to Newnham College.
2. Woodhead left Girton in 1873 to become mathematics Mistress at Manchester High School.

To Barbara Bodichon

GIRTON COLLEGE. | Hitchin.

Feb. 13. | [1873]

Dear Mrs. Bodichon

I do not quite understand Miss ⟨Mary⟩ Lloyd's letter. It sounds odd for a valuable Mathematical Library to be contained in one package, & if there is at all a considerable quantity of books, it would be a pity to have them sent here.[1] They had better wait somewhere in London till they can go to Girton. Also, there ought to be some kind of offer to & acceptance by the College. Important public bodies do not get great gifts smuggled in thro' individual members. I dare say you can arrange to get an offer made to the College which can be acknowledged in some proper way.

I do not think the students' letter at all implied being a College of the University. It proposed getting University Honours, but repudiating University conditions—in other words, getting men's Honours on cheap terms for women. But they don't put it to themselves in that way. What they want is to be ~~quite~~ unchecked in the selection of their course of reading, but at the same time to have the advantage of an Examn. of the highest character. This is plausible, but will not stand. When they come here they are not fit to fill up their whole time, & there is no one competent to advise them. The Little-go gives them time to test their powers & tastes before deciding on their Tripos. If they chose beforehand, it would probably be the Moral Sciences, which would be the worst they could make. It is not the kind of reading for young persons from 18 to 21 to give their main strength to during the whole of their College course. I had a little talk with Mr. Graves yesterday. He said he should like to develop the Certificates of proficiency, but was able to see difficulties & objections.[2] He apologised for offering advice & I said I was very glad to talk with him about it. I fancied he looked a little guilty when I said we were sorry about the students' letter, but

I don't think there has been much conspiracy. ~~I did not know Mr. Milton was anti-Christian. I had heard of his being a Republican I think.~~

~~I don't think the Club will be a scandal but I think its influence likely to be bad rather than good, so I should not wish to have any part in it.~~[3] ~~I am certain none of us could control it, & we should scarcely have any right to attempt it. I suppose it may be something like Mrs. P. Taylor's parties. I think women are too poor & scattered & too fond of staying at home to make much of a club, & men prefer their own. I have asked Lady Rich to~~ send you Mr. Graves's letter & my answer. Will you please forward them to Miss Shirreff. Mr. Roby is too busy to attend to this matter. A Select Committee has been appointed to inquire into the working of his Commission.

Yours ever
ED.

How many Appeals shall I send you?[4]

GC: ALS ED B72

1. Mary Lloyd, with whom Frances Power Cobbe lived, was a friend of the highly regarded mathematician Mary Somerville, after whom Somerville College, Oxford, was named. Lloyd gave Mary Somerville's mathematics books to Girton.

2. The students who petitioned in favor of dropping the Previous, or Little-go, Examination had objected to being awarded College Certificates that had no value within the university. Although Graves suggested that the College Certificate could be improved, the committee did not pursue this.

3. Possibly a reference to attempts by Girton students to form a university club for women. On 5 May 1883, Louisa Lumsden chaired a meeting of women including those associated with Newnham and Girton, which eventually led to the formation of "The University Club for Ladies."

4. The text of this letter was probably scored through by Davies in 1904, when she edited some of her papers for inclusion in the Family Chronicle.

To Barbara Bodichon

GIRTON COLLEGE.
University Arms Hotel. Cambridge. | Feb. 17. [1873?]

Dear Mrs. Bodichon

I am very glad you agree with my letter to Mr. Graves. I should like you to talk to Mrs. Lewes, tho' I think it is difficult for any one to form a judgment on the matter without knowing a good deal about the details of education. One thing that I feel strongly is that our students do not when they come know at all what they are fit for, or what is best for them. The Little-go gives them time to try, & worked as we work it, i.e. not making the learning altogether subordinate to the examn., it seems to me to be a very fair process of mental discipline to go thro'. So little is the Examn. pressed ~~that~~ into prominence, that when we were up for the Little-go, one Lecturer Mr. Clark, whose pupils were taking it, asked what we were here for, having forgotten all about it. Your talking to Mrs. Lewes is not likely to do any harm, as she will not spread it abroad & make a fuss. What I have been afraid of is that, seeing how easily things are magnified & distorted, a story might be got up that there was a quarrel going on, with all the students & Lecturers on one side, & the Committee on the other. This would be unpleasant. Our candidates are at work, the examn. having begun this morning. We shall be here continuously till Wed: week.[1] Lady Rich has kindly promised to stay all the time, & I think this will work well. I left her at Hitchin on Saturday, feeling at ease in my mind.

    Yours ever, ED.

If our students were allowed to take Honours without the Little-go, they wd. ~~of course~~ naturally choose their Tripos on starting, and wd. probably choose Moral Sciences, as Miss C⟨lough⟩'s young people are doing. I think ~~that~~ it wd. be about the worst choice they could make, to spend the whole of their College course on subjects peculiarly unsuitable for immature, undisciplined minds. They might also want to change about from one thing to another, especially if the time were also unlimited.

GC: ALS ED B73

    1. Two students, Louisa Lumsden and Rachel Cook, sat for the Tripos Examinations in February 1873. Lumsden recalled that ED chaperoned them throughout the examinations, and that while the week was arduous, friends entertained them with dinner parties. Lumsden attained the equivalent to Third Class Honors, and Cook's result was the equivalent of Second Class Honors. When the telegram brought the results of their success to Girton College, the students rang the alarm bells and tied flags to the chimneys in celebration.

To Barbara Bodichon

GIRTON COLLEGE.
University Arms Hotel | Cambridge. | Feb. 18. | [1873?]

Dear Mrs. Bodichon

    I am glad Mr. S⟨edley⟩. Taylor has written to you. He has written also to Mr. Tomkinson, asking how much we have guaranteed, &c. apparently in a fright about money, & adding a postscript about the other business. We might as well have let him go a year ago, when he took fright about the pecuniary responsibility & proposed resigning. I think it rather too bad of people who never come to a meeting & do nothing at all for the College, to take advantage of their position on the Committee to worry those who are doing the work. You must use your discretion about talking to people. The Clough faction naturally are informed of it already, as the whole thing can be ultimately traced to their influence. The irrepressible Miss C⟨lough⟩. came to call here the day after our arrival full of kindness & hospitality. It is not soothing to me, when people are flying at our throats to have them beaming with benevolence all the time.

However, it is no doubt best on the whole that they don't want to quarrel. If anything is said about there being no mention of the students' letter on the notices of the meeting, it can be replied that it was not put into my hands till after the notices had been issued.[1] Mrs. Bulley's letter was, but that had nothing in it about being excused the Little-go. It was an application for an additional year—really, to make up for a lost year at the beginning. These Cambridge people have not taken up that point at all.

I wonder what would be thought if the undergraduates of a College, including all the freshmen, took upon them to make such a "suggestion" as that of our students, to the Master & Fellows. I think it is unfortunate that we are obliged to call our young people "students". It sounds older & more important than undergraduates. We have come now upon one of the special difficulties of a women's College. Our young people are talked to by men, I feel sure, in a way that they would not talk to undergraduates. And it is useless to shut our eyes to the fact that any one of our unmarried Lecturers may, for all we know, be at the feet of some one of our students. It makes discipline a complicated matter.

Lady Rich knows the O. Smith set & might talk to them. She is quite sound & very nice. Yours ever,

ED.

Mr. Taylor is not on the Studies' Committee. I remembered to Miss W⟨oodhouse⟩. that I saw all had signed the letter but I supposed some did not know much about it. She smiled and said nothing.

GC: ALS ED B74

1. ED had not circulated the students' petition to the Executive Committee prior to the meeting at which it was discussed. See ED to Barbara Bodichon, 11 February 1873.

To Barbara Bodichon

Tuesday evening. ⟨late February/early March 1873⟩

I have had a friendly little note from Mr. Graves, in acknowledgment of my letter. He says there are one or two points he would like to discuss. I think very likely ^{many of} the Lecturers may have said *something*, but it may have been under some misapprehension. I still feel that we had better keep as quiet about it as we can. If the students tell everybody they know, it won't amount to many people. I don't see anything to regret on behalf of the College in Miss Gibson's engagement.[1] As to our controlling anything in which these young people are concerned, you cannot know them if you think they would listen to us. Miss Townshend's quietness & civility was refreshing on Sunday, but I doubt the success of the club. Of course they would be glad to get names of weight to back them up, but they would never submit to guidance.

Heaven defend me from attempting it—I should like you to see Mr. Tomkinson. He will be at home by Thursday evening.

GC: AL ED B75b

1. Emily Gibson left Girton College in 1872, without taking the Tripos. She married Chambrey Corker Townshend, an architect and the brother of fellow Girton student Isabella Townshend, on 8 May 1873.

To Barbara Bodichon

GIRTON COLLEGE.
Hitchin. March 5. | [1873?]

Dear Mrs. Bodichon

I am sorry to hear of fighting going on in London.[1] We are so quiet here that I have been hoping the matter might be considered as done with. I sent the copy of my letter to Mr. Graves to Miss Metcalfe via Miss Shirreff & it has not yet come back. I do not think it would be quite the thing for Miss Pipe to see. It was written to a man who delights in a joke, & if I am not mistaken Miss Pipe is destitute of humour & not to be joked with. Also I should not like to bring outsiders in to look on at anything like a correspondence between us & our Lecturers. If they are quoted against us, their names ought to be produced. No one but Mr. Graves has said a word to me, & when I talked to him a little *after* my letter, he was very moderate & reasonable, & saw the difficulties of giving up our policy.

I doubt whether the Lecturers generally would support the students' suggestions, if the matter were made clear to them. There is a great feeling at Cambridge against the Little-go, & people who have not thought much about it, don't see why we should make a point of keeping it. There is much less sympathy I think with the demand for extra time.

I think it would be worth while to talk to Miss Pipe, & remove misapprehensions, tho' I don't think there is any chance of converting her. What I think we ought to urge is, the unreasonableness & almost baseness of grasping at men's

Honours on women's terms—& that we are willing to give a good education without reference to men at all. People think it hard to force men's terms upon women, but they ought to see that we don't force them. It is only that we won't give false decorations.

Yours ED.

GC: ALS ED B76

1. Hannah Pipe, Headmistress of Laleham School, Clapham Park, London, had argued in support of the students' petition and had suggested that ED had been underhanded in her dealings with the students. See ED to Barbara Bodichon, 11 March 1873.

To Barbara Bodichon

[1873]

I think the notion that any of the students are likely to go off to Miss C⟨lough⟩ (except of course Miss Bulley.) is an entire mistake. They want to have the College governed according to their ideas, but I don't believe it ever enters their head to desert. It would be quite out of keeping with the incidental remarks continually made, showing how entirely they identify themselves with the College. Their tendency is rather to treat themselves as *the* College, and us as interferers. ⟨incomplete⟩

GC: AL ED B81

To Barbara Bodichon

GIRTON COLLEGE.

Hitchin. | March 11. | [1873]

My dear Mrs. Bodichon

I heard from Jane Crow yesterday of this blow.[1] At the best, it must have been a great shock, & I can understand what a closing of the door of hope it must be to you, & how it must throw you back in thought to the old days before the trouble came, when she was so bright and sweet and loveable. I am glad to have known her early enough to know what she was. Do you remember that she gave me three pictures, to pin up in my room, as she said. I have one of them here, & am glad to have the remembrance of her.

Thank you for your dear loyal letter.[2] Miss Pipe's was a great blow for the moment but there is much evidence here that it is to say the least exaggerated, & that helps one to bear it. I think I must ask Miss Bulley to stop Miss Pipe from saying that "the girls" think I have been underhand. I do not believe they think so, tho' in their disappointment at the decision, one or two may have said so rashly. You will have received Mr. Taylor's manifesto by this time. Lady Stanley owns that she does not understand it. I think it would be very useful for you to see her, & also Lady Rich. Her impressions of the students are entirely favourable, & it is pleasant that it should be so, but she ought to know, as you do, what they *can* be, when they are contradicted.

Only 3 of the signatures to the statement are those of Lecturers permanently appointed & on our printed list. The others are assns. or substitutes. Some of the things they say are either not true or quite unsupported by evidence. I am glad they altogether reject the Bulley proposal. Something like what they ask is not incompatible with our Resolution & the reference to the Sub. Committee. Mr. Bryce thinks your views sound & clear. I think we shall pull thro'. Ever yr. affecn. ED.

GC: ALS ED B77

1. Bodichon's sister, Isabella Leigh Smith Ludlow, had died of consumption.
2. Bodichon had written to ED saying in part that she wanted to discharge all of the college's lecturers, because "my opinion is they are all wrong about *the idea* of the College. I have been boiling with rage at some of the things I have heard" (GC XVII/GC 10/6).

To Barbara Bodichon ⟨?⟩

Tuesday evening. | [March 11? 1873 ?]

Mr. S. Taylor has been here. He said his view was different from that taken by the Ex⟨ecutive⟩. Com⟨mittee⟩. & he thought it an important matter to have been decided by a small Committee, without notice. This I explained. I remarked that there would be an opportunity of going back to the matter when the Minutes are read at the next meeting, & explained that the Com. partly decided at once because they did not wish to make too much of it, feeling that such very young people as the students were not the people to propose a grave constitutional change. That he saw and had sympathy with. He had not seen that their letter asked for more time, & does not care about that. Finally, I agreed to put this down on the notices for next time. He said he should probably send something round to the Com., an expression of local opinion.

I made no opposition, not wishing to seem anxious to stifle discussion. But if you shd. see your way to it, perhaps you could indicate the uselessness of putting on Camb. men to bother us, wasting time & strength on an agitation which can only damage the College without producing any other fruit, our majority being as I believe quite overwhelming. I wonder it does not seem to occur to people who *do* nothing that they have no *right* to bother. The interview was friendly & calm.

GC: AL ED B78

To Edwin C. Clark

GIRTON COLLEGE.

Hitchin. | March 15. ⟨1873⟩

Dear Mr. Clark

Many thanks for your kind letter. The printed statement was sent to me & to the rest of the Committee a few days ago & will be considered at a meeting to be held on the ~~24~~ 6th. the matter is now, as it has always been, in the hands of the Committee, & I hope that whatever decision may be arrived at, it will be clearly understood that it is that of the College as a body, not of any individual members.

With regard to the students' Memorial, I think it was felt by the Committee generally, that as persons *in statu pupillari*, & most of them ᵛᵉʳʸ young & inexperienced, they were scarcely in a position to make as a body, a formal suggestion to the committee on a grave question of general policy. Some certainly signed knowing very little about ~~what~~ they ᵐᵃᵗᵗᵉʳ ~~were doing~~. ~~And we cannot help regretting that some of~~ the Lecturers should in this case have discussed the Colleges policy with the students, apart from the Committee, & endorsed *their* action, instead of addressing the Committee, if they thought it desirable to do so, on their own account. I feel however that in ~~doing so~~ ʷʰᵃᵗ ʰᵃˢ ᵗᵃᵏᵉⁿ ᵖˡᵃᶜᵉ the Lecturers were ᑫᵘⁱᵗᵉ unaware of the difficulties we have had to contend with in the internal management of the College, & that consequently it did not occur to them that there would be risk of harm in the sort of encouragement they were giving to the students in urging their opinions. We have not talked about our troubles, ~~because we have felt that such things were liable to be greatly exaggerated, & that it would be more damaging to the College for reports to get about~~. & I do not wish to do so now, even to you, but it has not been by any means uniformly smooth sailing. I suppose it was not to be expected that it should be in launching so new an enterprise. but they have not been wanting. I will mention one case which occurred only last Term, as perhaps giving a little idea of the way some of the students look at things. It was a deliberate attempt by Miss Woodhead to get rid of our morning marking ⁽ⁿᵒᵗ ᴾʳᵃʸᵉʳˢ⁾ by ˢʸˢᵗᵉᵐᵃᵗⁱᶜᵃˡˡʸ absenting herself.[1] I let it run on for some time, not wishing ever to press a rule more than necessary. When at last I spoke to her, she told me candidly that she had thought I should not say anything, & that she should have established a precedent by staying away. It was only *Marking* that was in question, as attendance at prayers is not required, but she did it on principle. This was an individual case & she gave in without much difficulty. Two years ago we had a far worse trouble, of a different sort, in which all the students but one were concerned.[2] I feel sure that in that case you would have agreed with the authorities & have been astonished & grieved at the spirit shown by some of the older students. That is past, & I hope nothing of the kind is likely to come again, but looking forward to Girton, I feel that fresh perplexities may arise from being near Cambridge, & that we may need the moral support of the Lecturers & other Cambridge friends in maintaining authority, as such, if unfortunately it should be necessary to go against the opinion of the students, or of some of them. I wish sometimes that I could have a good talk with Mrs. Clark about things here, especially with a view to Girton. I feel as if her clear good sense might be a great help. But it is not easy to get opportunity for a quiet talk.

Miss Townshend's case was simply this. She had a Scholarship for three years & less when it expired. If she had been a qualified candidate for the Tripos, I believe she would have stayed on for it, but on the other hand, Miss Gibson, who *was* qualified, did not think it worth while to stay for the Math: Tripos. After passing the Little-go, Miss Townshend told me she did not intend to take any more examns. & left off working with reference to them. Later on she changed her mind, but as you know, industry was not her strong point. Hers is the only case of failure we have had, & we cannot expect to pass every student, whether industrious or idle.

Looking at the matter practically, it seems to me that for those who wish to take a U. course, which is really quite optional, & in my opinion is not in all cases desirable, the Little-go has the advantage of giving a student the opportunity of testing her powers & tastes before deciding on her whole course. As a rule they come with no "special object", & if they were practically obliged, in order to compete with each other on equal terms, to choose a Tripos on starting, I should think disciplinary subjects, such as Classics & Mathematics, would scarcely ever be chosen. I certainly should not like to advise such a choice on starting, quite in the dark. Physiology & Political Economy would perhaps be most usually fixed upon, if there were a Tripos combining them. No doubt we may have a case now & then like Miss Lumsden's, who was old enough & pronounced enough in her tastes to be quite clear as to her special object. Such exceptional cases we have always been ready to provide for by single Certificates.

I doubt very much whether the dislike to the Little go is so strong & universal here as you have been led to believe. Of the four who have not yet passed, one is not going to take it, one might almost be said to have been attracted by it, as she came at first only for a year & another Term has been added on purpose for the Little go, it being still uncertain whether she will stay on after it.

The other two are taking it entirely of their own free will ^(without any pressure.) It seems to me that we may fairly claim to have shown that even the Little go subjects can be made interesting when well taught & intelligently learnt, without incessant & servile reference to the Examn.

However, I am not going to extol the Little-go & will only add how entirely I believe what you are good enough to say of the personal friendship of the Lecturers. Their unvarying cordiality & kindness have been the greatest possible comfort thro' the difficulties & dangers, external & internal, which our struggling little institution has had, & still has I am afraid, to go thro'—

Ever yours most truly
Emily Davies.

GC: DALS ED XVII GC 10/8

1. From the inception of the college, part of its daily routine included marking a roll book at 8:00 A.M. following prayers, again at noon, and in the evening before dinner (Daily Schedule at the College for Women, 1869 GC EDXIX/24).

2. In early 1871, a group of students planned to perform some scenes from Shakespeare. They invited lecturers and ED, Julia Wedgwood, Annie Austin, and the servants to a dress rehearsal on 7 March 1871. Some of the students wore men's costumes for the production, and this provoked a heated response from the College Committee.

To John Stuart Mill

GIRTON COLLEGE.

Hitchin | March 17. 1873

Dear Mr. Mill

Some weeks ago a letter addressed to you at Avignon was returned to me covered with postmarks. I have waited to write again till I heard of your being in London. The former letter was to convey to you the hearty thanks of the College Committee to you for your kindness in examining for us last year in Political Economy. I now send you a copy of the Examiners' reports printed.

Since Miss Woodhead's examination, we have sent in two candidates for the (unofficial) Classical Tripos Examn, & are hoping to hear the results by the end of this week.

May I ask to be very kindly remembered to Miss Taylor.
I remain
Yours very truly
Emily Davies.

LSE: ALS Vol.II247

To Joshua Fitch

GIRTON COLLEGE.

Hitchin. | May 27 [28/5/79] ⟨1873⟩

Dear Mr. Fitch

We are arranging now for our June Entrance Examn. & are hoping that you may be able to set papers for us in English Grammar & Composition, as you were good enough to do last year. The Examn. begins on June 24. As there are only six candidates, the work of looking over the papers will not be very burdensome.[1] We shall be very much obliged if you can kindly help us.

We are looking forward to getting into our new building in the course of the summer & when we are settled there I hope to be able to persuade you & Mrs. Fitch to pay us a visit. We shall have a spare room there.

Yours very truly
Emily Davies

St. A: ALS MS30716

1. In 1873, six new students entered Girton College. They were: Alice Betham, Malvina Borchardt, Elizabeth Burgess, Amy Mantle, Frances Müller, and Annie Wallace.

To Barbara Bodichon

Hitchin.
May 25. [1873]

Dear Mrs. Bodichon

It occurs to me that I ought to have explained more fully why I think it would be better not to cluster old students together at 5 Bl⟨andford⟩. Squ⟨are⟩., making it a sort of College house.[1]

It is not only that I think it would be better for them to get some experience of the world & its bothers thro' *other* people, not members of the Committee, tho' that is one consideration.

What I shrink from is the gathering together what Rachel calls "the first five" into a kind of body, & presenting them, with their "free discussions" to the world as a specimen of College training. You see if your house was to be made this kind of centre, it would naturally be the resort of the Gibsons and Townshends & their friends, & they are not the sort of people by whom we want to be represented. You could not tell them that they must not invite this or that person, e.g. Miss Gibson's sister, Mrs. Brown, tho' you would not invite her yourself. From what I have heard from Miss Metcalfe & Miss ⟨Jane⟩ Chessar &c., I think there can be no doubt that the sayings & doings of that set are very damaging to us.

Miss Chessar told me that she met Mrs. Brown, (I think that is her name. Miss Gibson's married sister.) at a party & her dress was so unpleasantly low that a young man whom she was inviting to her house told Miss Chessar he did not like the look of her & should not go. Miss C. hears a good deal about the Gibson set & has been most anxious to protest against the College being identified with them. It would be more difficult I think to ~~maintain~~ ^justify^ this protest if they were the leading spirits in a sort of College house. I don't feel this difficulty in recommending those who wish to teach. I think we can safely make ourselves partially responsible for them so far as that goes. And in that case, each is taken by herself alone, whereas if any of us were to give them a sort of social organisation, the objectionable eccentricities of each (& they have a good many among them) would be charged upon all, & upon the College. It will be different by & by, when the later ones come to the front. They are very hopeful in many ways. Even as regards public spirit, I see signs of improvement. ~~Two or~~ three ^or four^ of them are teaching in Sunday schools here, which I think is very good of them to do, instead of wandering about for long walks or reclining on the grass these fine summer days. Miss ⟨Rose⟩ Aitken, who grows more & more into leadership, is very satisfactory. In fact all the later ones are, in some ways. I hope we shall have no more of Miss Pipe's old pupils. I would so much rather get them from other schools.

There is some chance of selling the iron building to a school at Bedford in which Mr. Seebohm is concerned. He is coming to look at it.

I go to Girton on Wednesday. Is there anything particular to look after?

Ever yr. affecn.

ED.

GC: ALS ED B82

1. See ED to Barbara Bodichon, 13 February 1873.

To Barbara Bodichon

17, C.P. July 26. | [1873?]

Dear Mrs. Bodichon

There is no hurry about fixing a day. I hope to go to Normandy with Miss Manning on Aug. 5. for a week. Some day after that will do. Do you know this nice Mrs. Rathbone?[1] I fired into the air, supposing my correspondent to be the wife of Mr. W⟨illiam⟩. Rathbone. Miss Mitchell (the astronomer) has been to Girton & was delighted with it.

It is not worth while to come up for Aug. 1. If you are coming up for anything else, I should like to go with you to Mr. Waterhouse (he is away till the end of this month) to talk about several things. I wonder whether Nannie has any notions about stuff for curtains. She made a capital suggestion for Hitchin, of Indian tissue, which has turned out most satisfactory.

Ever yours
ED.

GC: ALS ED B83

1. The Rathbones were a prominent extended family of Unitarians and reformers from the Liverpool area.

To John Venn

GIRTON COLLEGE. | 17, CUNNINGHAM PLACE. N.W.

July 26. 1873

Dear Mr. Venn

I am very glad to know that you are likely to be able to lecture for us twice a week next Term. I shall have to ~~ask~~ ᵂʳⁱᵗᵉ ᵗᵒ you ~~to advise~~ as to the amount of time &c. later on, when I know more certainly what pupils there will be. I expect that we shall now have a permanent class of three. Miss ⟨Mary⟩ Hoskins has recd. Perm⟨ission⟩. to ⟨defer⟩ on account of ill health, & will therefore be able to read with Miss M⟨aynard⟩. & Miss B⟨aker⟩. for the Tripos of 1875. The two last will however be pretty taken up with their Little-go subjects next Term.

The Mem⟨orial⟩: to which you refer, signed by many of our Lecturers, was sent to members of the Coll: but it was not formally presented to the Com: & no formal answer was returned. I wrote to Mr. ~~E.C.~~ Clark whose name was at the head of the list, after the ~~meeting~~ at which the subject was discussed, telling him something of what had taken place. The reasons for the decision cd. scarcely be stated fully without entering upon a wide controversy, but I may say ~~generally~~ that the suggestion was regarded as contrary to the fundamental policy of the Coll: which aims at obtaining Univ: Degrees in a regular way. ~~It We~~ It cd. scarcely be expected ᵒᶠ our students ~~to~~ ᵗʰᵃᵗ ᵗʰᵉʸ ˢʰᵈ· go thro' the ~~Classical & Mathematical~~ study ᵒᶠ Cˡᵃˢˢ: & Mᵃᵗʰ· required for the Little-go if ᵗʰᵉʸ ᶜᵒᵘˡᵈ ᵒᵇᵗᵃⁱⁿ Honours of apparently equal value ~~could be obtained~~ without it. ~~It seemed There would seem to~~ ᴵᵗ ʷᵃˢ ᶠᵉˡᵗ ᵃˡˢᵒ· ᵗʰᵃᵗ ᵗʰᵉʳᵉ ʷᵒᵘˡᵈ be great risk of confusion, to say the least, if it were announced that ~~of~~ candidates had passed a Tripos Examn., which in the ~~ordinary~~ case of ~~men~~ ᵘⁿᵈᵉʳᵍʳᵃᵈᵘᵃᵗᵉˢ· implies some knowledge of Classics & Mathematics, besides the specific subjects of the Tripos ~~Examn.~~, unless it were ~~very~~ clearly explained that in the case of women this knowledge was not included, & it would be ~~very~~ difficult to be perpetually explaining, ~~as~~ ⁿᵒ distinctly as ~~honesty would seem to require~~ ᵗᵒ ᵇᵉ ᵘⁿᵈᵉʳˢᵗᵒᵒᵈ that the Tripos did not mean the same thing for our students as for the ~~regular Univ~~ students in the Colleges of the Univ: As it is entirely optional with our students to take Degree examns. at all, we do not feel that there is anything oppressive in requiring those who choose to go in for them, to fulfil the regular conditions. The case of those who wish to have their knowledge certified without taking a regular University course is provided for by a College certificate & certificates of proficiency in single subjects. A ~~regular~~ ᶜᵒᵐᵖˡᵉᵗᵉ scheme for single Certificates has now been ~~drawn up~~ ᵃᵍʳᵉᵉᵈ ᵘᵖᵒⁿ. ~~I send you the Report of the Sub. Committee~~ It is contained in a of Studies, which I enclose: I send you ᵃˡˢᵒ extracts from the Minutes of the Meetings ᵒᶠ ᵗʰᵉ ᴱˣ· ᶜᵒᵐ: at which the ~~whole~~ subject ᵍᵉⁿᵉʳᵃˡˡʸ was discussed. ~~& also the report~~

GC: DAL ED XVII 10/11

To Barbara Bodichon

⟨Autumn⟩ [1873?]

I wonder whether it would suit Miss Edwards to come on some such plan as I have suggested for the Lent & May Terms. There would be only the short Easter Vacation of three weeks between, so that she would be able to give up her lodgings at Hastings after Christmas. We could have an Entrance Examn., for her in January. There would be the risk of the cold being too much for her in February. We shall be better able to judge of that after we have been there a Term. I should think it ought to be possible to guard against it in a well-built house on a dry soil, by keeping indoors in bad weather.

GC: AL ED B84

To Barbara Bodichon

17, C.P. Sept. 2. | [1873]

Dear Mrs. Bodichon

I forwarded the cheque to Mr. Howard & have received his receipts.

What do you think about the tiles? Mr. Willey says if Mr. Waterhouse had known that they could be had for £50 more, he would have recommended them before. He thinks Mr. Loveday has some special facilities for making a good bargain. He is building the Physical Science place at Cambridge & would order their tiles & ours together. Mr. Tomkinson thinks the Building Committee can decide & that we had better have the Staffordshire. If you think the same, I will write to Mr. Willey accordingly.

I was at Aberley the evening you were in Town & at Woolwich the next day; seeing parents about their children. A great part of the population are escaping to the hoppings, but we shall be down upon them as soon as they come back.

It was a great pleasure to me to direct the summons of a top sawyer who makes money by "booking" at races. He professed only to attend races for pleasure, & thought it odd that ~~we~~ he should be "shut up" in order that his little boy might go to school. His excuse was that he could not do without the child's work. I begin to respect the School Board more, now that we are doing *the* thing which was wanted & could not be done before.[1]

Ever yr. affecn.
ED.

GC: ALS ED B85

1. The By Laws Committee of the London School Board, on which ED sat, was enforcing compulsory school attendance legislation.

To Barbara Bodichon

GIRTON COLLEGE. | 17, CUNNINGHAM PLACE. N.W.

Sept. 3. | [1873]

Dear Mrs. Bodichon

Will you please add your ~~address~~ signature to this cheque & forward in the enclosed envelope.

Mr. Loveday asks £60 for the cottage.[1] I have suggested to Mr. Waterhouse to try £50. I suppose we must give £60 if he will not take less. Jane Gregory has not called. I think we should get a good boy and girls from Mrs. R. Martineau, but there is no sign of a housemaid yet.[2]

I am going to Girton on Friday, & shall have a look at the fents.

I am to see Professor Liveing for a talk about the Natural Science Lectures. It takes a good deal of arranging, for so many branches. I forget whether I asked you before to tell Miss Edwards that Botany will probably be postponed till the May Term. I am afraid the Arithmetic can only be got over by learning it, but you know it is not really at all a hard Examn. for any one who has been properly taught.

I am rather afraid of middle-aged students. Even when they are as nice & sensible as Miss Lloyd was, they are apt to make rules which are manifestly reasonable for 18, look unreasonable, & if we happen to get a Miss ⟨Gertrude⟩ Slade, the mischief is serious. But I think we might perhaps meet the difficulty by creating a new caste of students over 28, answering to Fellow-Commoners in the old Colleges. They might sit at the Mistress's table, & be distinctly recognised as under a different regime from the younger students, perhaps paying a little extra.

Miss ⟨Annie⟩ Wallis has been here with her mother, & I was much pleased with what I saw of them. She is not distinctly destined for teaching, tho' she has been taking classes, including the Latin class, at her old school, & I am afraid she will not satisfy Miss Soames's requirements, but I have made up my mind to manage for her to come somehow. They are afraid they cannot pay more than £30 a year themselves, having 5 other children to educate.

Mr. Potter has sent Prof: Rogers' address & I am going to write to him.[3] Miss Woodhead is appointed to the second Mistresship of the Manchester school, my answers to some questions from the Committee being considered entirely satisfactory. There must be a great prejudice in favour of Girton students. She sent in no testimonials & did not even refer them to me. I am glad she has got it, in spite of herself.[4]

I find I have left the pamphlet about Vassar at Scalands. Will you kindly return it before you leave. I suppose your chairs are for the *College*. If you use that vicious expression "for you" again, I shall keep the things for myself.

Ever yours,
ED.

GC: ALS ED B86

1. See ED to Barbara Bodichon, late February/early March 1872.
2. Probably Mrs. Russsell Martineau (1831–98). Russell Martineau was educated at Heidelberg and the University of London and worked at the British Museum.
3. Probably Thomas Bayley Potter (1817–98), chairman of Manchester branch of Complete Suffrage Society; and M.P. for Rochdale.
4. See ED to Matilda Vernon, 31 October 1873.

To Barbara Bodichon

GIRTON COLLEGE. | 17, CUNNINGHAM PLACE. N.W.

Sept. 6. | [1873]

Dear Mrs. Bodichon

I went to Girton & Cambridge yesterday & had a long talk with Professor Liveing about the Natural Science studies, which ended in our deciding that our three Students (Miss ⟨Mary⟩ Kingsland, ⟨Jane⟩ Dove & ⟨Isabella⟩ Gamble) had better attend his ^{Professorial} Lectures on Chemistry, & Professor Humphrey's on Anatomy & Physiology.[1] Prof. L. thinks the course he is to give will be suitable for them & it will take less of his time & he can do more for them than if he came out to Girton. I don't think he has had any women in his class before, but Prof. Humphrey had one last year. In speaking of his, it would be best to call it Physiology, as the word Anatomy may give the impression that the Lectures are different from what they are.

Prof. L. has attended them himself & thinks that as to the subject, there is no reasonable objection to a mixed class. I should go with them at first & occasionally.

I could not undertake to go always, as between the two Professors there will be a Lecture (of an hour) every day. We must let them have a fly both ways, which will cost 4/. a Lecture for the three students. The Lectures cost nothing, as the Professors are not paid by fees. The Students by attending the Lectures will come in for other privileges, such as the use of University skeletons. I have written to Professor Humphrey about his Lectures. He has always been a friend of the College & is sure to be pleasant. Prof. Liveing went into the matter in the kindest way, taking it up as if it was quite his business to do the best he could for our Students. It is certainly a great thing to come within range of these nice friendly people. We shall want Mr. Hicks at Girton besides, & probably some more apparatus, which we can the better afford as we shall be paying so little for the teaching.

I had not time to open the Japanese parcel yesterday, but a question has occurred to me. How will it look on the outside, to have the linings for the sitting & bedroom curtains alternately blue & white? Would it be better to have them all alike? I should incline to white. (as I am so afraid of not being able to get a blue that won't kill the Japanese. the Butcher's blue at Shoolbred's would not do at all.) but I don't know how that would look in a sitting room & on the outside. If it were glazed white stuff, perhaps it would do. Please advise. I came across a difficulty about the planks. The bedroom windows come down to the within 2 ft. of the floor, so that tables of 2ft. 6. would prevent the casement from opening, if the tables were close to the wall. If they were, say two inches from the wall, they would open a little way, & of course at the top besides, which is what one wants most in a bedroom. I don't like giving up the planks. Seymour will make them for 18/. each, & they would be much nicer than even tolerably good dressing & washing tables. Shall we try five or six? Mr. Howard told me that the windows for the bathrooms &c. are to be ground glass, so we shall not want curtains for them. I showed the linen rep to Mrs. Liveing & she liked it very much. She gave me a good deal of useful advice about shops.

Mr. Waterhouse has bought the Cottage for us.[2] Mr. Loveday proposed £60. we offered £50. & he accepts £55. with immediate possession. I am telling James to get in as soon as he can. Mrs. Martineau has heard of a boy for us, a lad of 20, her gardener's son. If he comes I shall ask her to send us things for the garden by him. I have been offering gardens to the students, but so far, they have been declined. Miss Dove ~~& Miss Maynard~~ says ~~they~~ ^{she} has not time, & Miss Maynard that the winter is not a good time for working, which is true.

I have been seeing Miss Edwards of Clifton & she told me she heard from a Bristol lawyer last May that he had been making a will containing a handsome legacy to the College.[3] We have no idea who it can be.

I have written to Professor Rogers to-day.

I shall be going to Girton for the first night there on the 15th, the day you begin your travels. There will be perpetual reminders of you at Girton. Howard has achieved the iron bar with holes in it for the windows, & it works well. He is certainly very thoughtful& ready to do what we want.

Bon—(or best possible) voyage—if I don't write again.

Ever your affecn.

ED.

Thanks for the Vassar pamphlet.

GC: ALS ED B87

1. Probably Henry Humphreys (1844–1917), St. John's College, Cambridge, Scholar and Fellow; M.D. and assistant physician, Middlesex Hospital. He was also a physician in Manchester (1877–80) and in St. Leonard's (1880–90).

2. See ED to Barbara Bodichon, 3 September 1873.

3. Possibly Laura Edwards, who was a schoolmistress from Clifton.

To Adelaide Manning

GIRTON COLLEGE. | 17, CUNNINGHAM PLACE. N.W.

Sept. 6 ⟨1873⟩

My dear Adelaide

I have just been writing to Hammond to tell her that her room will be ready for her by next Saturday, & to James to ask him to get into the Cottage, which we have brought from Mr. Loveday for £55, as soon as he can. I go myself on the 15th. My own rooms are to be ready by that time.

I think we need not trouble Miss Solly to look out for ⟨servant⟩ girls as I expect to get them from Walsham, which is much nearer than Islington. Mrs. Martineau has already written about a boy, who seems likely to suit. He is her gardener's son, a lad of 20, & has been a tailor, but wants to go out into the world. Mrs. M. thinks that coming to us for two months at first would be a trial for him, & he can revert to his tailoring if he likes it better. We do not hire girls by the year & send them home for the Vacations. We engage them for ten weeks or so, with a prospect that if they do well & wish to come back for the next Term, they may. Hitherto they have wished it. It is a little more awkward with grown-up servants, but it has not been much of a difficulty yet. Should you propose keeping seven servants doing nothing in an empty house for seven weeks at a time?

I do not know of a governess for the Max Müllers. Would it not be a pity to trouble Miss Buss about it? She has much more than enough on her hands, without keeping a gratuitous Registry, & the Max Müllers have no sort of claim on her, public or private. Perhaps you scarcely realise what it is to be overdriven every day, & how cruel it is to add a straw to the back-breaking burden. The mere trouble of opening & reading a letter, reading the details, trying to think whether one knows somebody & deciding that one does not, is an appreciable weight to any one already over tried & worried, as Miss Buss generally is. She is the last person to protect herself from encroachment, being only too ready to undertake more than she ought, but she is visibly the worse for it. The difference in her at the end of a holiday is enough to show that.

Thank you for seeing about Cooperation. I think it will be time enough to talk to Hammond at Girton. I got a great deal of good advice from Mrs. Liveing yesterday. She told me the right shop to go to for linen &c. & thinks they will recommend us a workwoman.

I can do without Luther, thank you, as he is difficult to get.

I thought I might get something from him to quote in my School Board discourse, but there would very likely be nothing appropriate. This is to come off about the beginning of October, & I have also to speak on a Motion about the deficient supply of Schoolmistresses on Oct. 1., for which it is necessary to learn up some facts. I have been corresponding with Miss ⟨Louisa⟩ Hubbard of Otter College about it, & she wanted me to go to Chichester to-day, to see the place, but I could not spare time & strength.[1]

I ought to be at Girton during the first week of October, if it were possible, but I must be in Town, for the Entrance Examn. as well as other things. A Schoolmistresses' Meeting must come in about that time. You will see I hope, that I cannot go to Norwich.[2] I am not very hopeful about a Sub. Committee for talking about the higher education of women. If Miss Howell is pressing for Lectures, it will probably take that direction.[3]

They have had the Local Exams. at Norwich for many years. I wrote to Mr. Hinds Howell about the College, & he disapproved, but they may be coming round by this time. At any rate, if there is to be talk, I am glad that you should be there to say something sensible. I do not think Miss Beale would leave her school, & she is useless in a general discussion. Miss Morgan knows nothing I should think, of higher English education, & I have not found her wise on non-professional subjects, so far as I have seen, which is not much.[4] I should not think it worth while to trouble good people to go to Norwich on purpose, tho' perhaps no opportunity ought to be slighted.

Perhaps you will entice Miss Bateman to Girton. I had a very interesting talk with Professor Liveing yesterday about the Natural Science for the coming year, which ended in deciding that our Students (three) must attend his University Lectures on Chemistry, & another Professor's on Physiology. I will tell you the details when we meet. We must let them have a fly both ways, which will cost 4/. a day, but we need not grudge that as the Lectures will cost nothing. The Professors are paid by stipends, not by fees.

I have had a heavy week's work, including the School Board. At Woolwich on Wednesday, I had 45 cases for prosecution to decide upon, & nearly all the people appeared. It was rapid work to get thro' in three hours, & I did not get home till nearly 11.30 at night.[5] To start with a headache next morning was not surprising. I feel that like St. Paul, I speak as a fool in dilating on what I have to do, but it seems the only way of making it understood that invitations to Norwich & commissions to get governesses are supererogatory. Ever yours
ED.

GC: ALS ED XVII GC-9/2

1. Bishop Otter College, Chichester, was founded in 1839 for women who wanted to become elementary schoolteachers.
2. The NAPSS Annual Meeting was held in Norwich, 1–8 October 1873.
3. Probably Agnes Howell (?), from Norwich, a writer and poet.
4. Probably Emma Morgan, Mistress of a school in Bath.
5. The new London School Board was charged with creating new spaces and schools; enforcing recently passed rules making school attendance and fees compulsory; and finding and training new teachers. Davies sat on the By Laws Committee and drafted the plan to enforce compulsory attendance. Parents who failed to send children to school could be brought to court. In her division in Greenwich, an additional 5,500 children began attending school.

To Adelaide Manning

GIRTON COLLEGE. | 17, CUNNINGHAM PLACE. N.W.

Sept. 12, 1873

My dear Adelaide

There is to be an opening of Board schools at Deptford on Saturday the 27th, at which I suppose I ought to be present. This may oblige me to come home on the 26th, so if it would not be troublesome to you to come to Girton a day earlier than we proposed, I should be very glad. There will be a great deal to talk over, & you are a friend indeed to be ready with your valuable help just now.

We are rapidly engaging servants. Jemima's sister wishes to come as housemaid after all, & we are glad to have her with the prospect of her taking the cook's place when Jemima goes. I had heard in the meantime of another, recommended by the Harts, who did not at all object to coming home for the Vacations. As we shall not have her now at Girton, my mother thinks of taking her for ourselves. So there are now only the two girls to get—who are comparatively easy—and, you will be surprised & sorry to hear, a gardener. Our treasured James is going. It is his wife's doing & I think her dislike to the Cottage & an exaggerated estimate of James's value, are at the bottom of it. I will tell you the details when I see you. I am sorry to lose him, but it would not have done to give in to his demands. With his uncertain health, he might be ill at any time, & they would have been sure to attribute it to the Cottage. They are to go next Thursday. There will be no difficulty in getting a gardener from Girton temporarily. In fact one who has been employed in the garden applied for the place some time since.

Miss Soames will give £40 a year ⟨scholarship⟩ for Miss Wallis. I have asked Mr. Tomkinson about nom⟨inatio⟩/ns. & I think he would not object to using two, if necessary, but he thinks people would help Miss W. to come who would not give to the College, & he is asking Lady Rich to see if any of her friends will contribute.

You have had notice perhaps of a conference of Mrs. Grey's Union on Oct. 3 & that there is to be a Union meeting on Sept. 22 at Bradford.[1]

So I am afraid I shall not get such a quiet time there as I was hoping for. This crush of work is however only temporary, & the autumn is my best time. Thanks for your kind solicitude. The Greenwich meeting is to be on Oct. 6.

Ever yours
ED.

GC: ALS ED XVII GC-9/3

1. In the early 1870s, ED and Maria Grey promoted the efforts of the National Union for the Education of Girls of all Classes above the Elementary, the organization from which the Girls' Public Day School Company evolved. The Union met with strong opposition over the issue of mixing social classes in large day schools.

To Adelaide Manning

GIRTON COLLEGE.

near Cambridge. | Sept. 16 1873

My dear Adelaide

I do not like the idea of your being routed up at unearthly hours for the sake of getting here two hours earlier. Having receded from Greenwich by 60 miles more, my sense of obligation to it has diminished & I begin to think that I shall not go to the school opening.

I have written a farewell address, explaining that I cannot attend to their interests, so my absence will I hope be understood.[1]

I should have made more of a point of going if Miss Guest could have been there too, but she is away in Monmouthshire & wants the rest, being knocked up with neuralgia. So I think I shall stay here till Saturday evening, or perhaps Monday morning. And that will give us more time for talk.

It is a relief to have put off Bradford till Thursday. I shall probably come back here on Tuesday. Hammond is setting to work in good spirits. She thinks the girl you wrote about would not suit. We are going into Cambridge this afternoon, to get material that Hammond may be going on making curtains, & I am expecting the joiner presently to make measurements for blinds &c.

I have been writing to Mr. Waterhouse to see if he can get more men put on, as the work might get on faster if there were more of them. I am occupying the Mistress's rooms & find them very pleasant. It is excessively airy. I could not sleep for the whistling of the wind last night. My address after to-morrow will be care of.

Grach, Esq.
Crag Wood
Rawdon
near Leeds

I have been writing to decline an invitation (provoked by Mr. Hinds Howell) from a Mrs. ⟨Joseph⟩ Blake of Norwich.

Ever yours affecn.
ED

I am telling the enclosed that if she goes to Norwich, you would be pleased to make an acquaintance. (she is a friend of Mrs. H⟨orace⟩. Davey's.) & that I have not time to read her MS. Mr. Deane's is useful.

GC: ALS ED XVII GC-9/4

1. Both ED and Garrett Anderson decided not to stand for re-election to the London School Board when their term of office expired in 1873.

To Barbara Bodichon

GIRTON COLLEGE.

Cambridge. | Sept. 25. | [1873]

Dear Mrs. Bodichon

It is very nice to have your address & to be able to send you word how we are getting on. I always feel sure of you, that your interest in the things we are about does not die away when you go into quite different spheres. I hope Switzerland has been fresh & reviving & the perfect one a congenial companion. We have been having very nice weather here. I enjoyed my visit to Bradford. The ⟨Titus⟩ Salts were suddenly prevented by illness from receiving guests, so I went instead to some other people & had as fellow-guest Mr. F⟨rancis⟩. Galton the African traveller, who is delightful company. I saw a good deal too of the ⟨Rutherford⟩ Alcocks of Japan, & Miss ⟨Eleanor⟩ Smith of Oxford & her brother ⟨Henry⟩, & ended with a night at the Forsters pretty quiet unpretending place on the Wharfe. You know Mrs. W.E. Forster was a Miss ⟨Jane⟩ Arnold. I found both place & people charming.

I came back here on Tuesday, & found happily a good deal of progress made. Mr. Waterhouse is here to-day, & he says *all* the rooms necessary for immediate use will certainly be ready. I like the building more & more. Mr. W. says the builder has done his work *very* well.

The blue carpets are here & look nice, & Mr. W. is delighted with the Japanese curtains. I could not get blue lining that would do, so they are all lined with white *twilled* glazed lining (very nice) & the sitting rooms have a border on which matches wonderfully & is a halfpenny a yard! It is really amusing to get things so cheap. (I enclose a bit.) I like the Cambridge shops, & Hammond does not find provisions specially dear. She is full of admiration of the building. Would that it were paid for! I am afraid we shall soon have to offer greenbacks or something of that sort instead of money to pay our bills. I spoke about the College at a meeting at Bradford & quite forgot to say anything about money. What shocking *heedlessness* Miss Shirreff would think it. However, I asked for support, which I suppose meant the same thing.

I forget whether I told you that it is arranged for our Nat. Science students to attend the University Lectures of Professors Liveing & Humphrey on Chemistry & Physiology. Both Professors have been very kind about it. It is quite settled for Miss Wallis to come. (Miss Soames contributes £40 a year) & I think we are sure now of six new comers.

I hope I shall hear of you when you get to Algiers. Ever yr. affecn.
ED.

GC: ALS ED B88

To Adelaide Manning

Sept. 30 ⟨1873⟩

My dear Adelaide
    Thank you for forwarding my letters & other favours.
    I am going to write to Hammond about the servant. She was right & I was

wrong about the wages. I don't know how I got 1/6 a week into my head. Would you kindly tell Mrs. Martineau that it is 3/. & that we shall not want the girls till about the 13th. Miss Solly has 3 or 4 wanting places & I am sending her our exact terms, which she asks for, but I shd. prefer getting country girls from a shorter distance if we can. I have a very good character of Jemima's sister. It has been understood all along that *she* is to succeed Jemima, & I shd. not like to promise it to C. Papworth.

Thanks for arranging about the laundry. I hope you saw the baker's wife with her hat on. She wears it much as you did at St. Malo. *Do pray* be precise in your appearance at Norwich. Please tell Mrs. Martineau how much obliged we were for the plants & seeds, & Wm., & all the trouble she has taken.

Miss Chessar has decided to stand for the School Board. She gives a very bad account of other Colleges. Miss Trevor quite unfit for the position & Miss H. well-meaning but destitute of judgment.

My mother had a better night, but has been suffering much this morning. I am not going to Deptford on Friday, or doing anything extra that I can avoid.

Ever yr. affecn.

ED.

GC:ALS ED XVII GC-9/5

ED moved into the new college building in Girton on 14 October 1873. The students arrived for Michaelmas term, despite the fact that construction of the building was still far from complete. According to Jane Frances Dove: "There were no windows or doors on the ground floor, the staircase was covered with planks. . . . There were no door-posts up, no blinds or curtains. . . . [However,] Miss Davies' pluck was contagious, and after a few weeks she gave a big party" (Jane Frances Dove, Girton Archives, GC PP Stephen).

To Matilda Vernon

GIRTON COLLEGE.

Cambridge. | Oct. 31. 1873

Dear Miss Vernon

Miss Woodhead might be described as a "Certificated Student in Honours of Girton College". or as "holding a ^{Girton College} Degree Certificate in Honours"—or, if you are not afraid of making your story too long, you might add, "her proficiency having been certified to the satisfaction of the College as equivalent to that of candidates who have been declared to deserve a place in the Second Class of Mathematical Honours according to the standard qualifying for such Honours in the University of Cambridge in the Mathematical Tripos ~~in~~ Examn. in the year 1873."

This last statement might of course be abridged, but it is important to say nothing which implies that the Certificate was given by the University Examiners.

They were anxious not to commit the University by any formal act done in their official capacity, & we are of course anxious not to commit them, or to make any statement beyond what the facts strictly justify. For the present we are obliged to be satisfied with an unofficial guarantee of the standard, the College giving the formal Certificate. I suppose people will believe that we should not make a formal statement of this sort without sufficient authority.

I am glad to hear that you have succeeded in getting a house. You will no doubt have much to do in getting things into order at first, as we have here. We are greatly pleased with our building & the situation. Miss Borchardt is one of the six new Students who have begun this Term. We are trying to persuade her not to overwork. With her liability to severe headaches & her eyes too not being strong, I am sure she ought not to work very hard, but it is not easy to restrain her eagerness.

Yours very truly
Emily Davies.

MHS: ALS Misc. Papers

To Adelaide Manning

THE LONDON ASSOCIATION OF SCHOOLMISTRESSES.
17, CUNNINGHAM PLACE. N.W.

Girton College, Cambridge. | Nov. 23. ⟨1873⟩

My dear Adelaide

As I shall not get home till just before the Local Examns. week, which would be an inconvenient time for a Schoolmistresses meeting, the next must be held without me & I shall be very much obliged if you will kindly take my place as Sec. It will be at Miss Buss's, as Miss King is away & does not wish the first meeting at Berners Street to be held in her absence. Miss Dorech proposes either Tuesday the 9th Dec. or Friday the 12th. If you will kindly let me know which, if either, will suit you, I will send notices accordingly.

I have had a letter from Miss Solly about Rose, & a consultation with Hammond, & a talk with Rose—the result of which is that if she does better for the next three weeks, we will have her back after Christmas. She *can* do, if she chooses, & has been better the last two or three days. I have been talking to Mitchell too. She has been very forgetful lately, & it is too bad for Hammond to have to be always running after her.

I went up to Town on Friday for a School Board dinner & for a meeting at Blackheath on Saturday. If you care to hear about them & will take the trouble to call at C⟨unningham⟩.P⟨lace⟩. my mother will be pleased to tell you that & other news.

Poor Miss Shirreff is at Cambridge to nurse a sick nephew at Caius College. They are an afflicted family.

Mrs. Lestourgeon called again while I was away, & left a very kind message that she had a spare room at my disposal for any visitor here.[1] It was very considerate.

We have not had many callers yet, but I feel that keeping up with them will be an arduous business when it begins in earnest.

Ever yrs. affecn.
ED.

GC: ALS ED XVII GC-9/6

1. Probably wife of Charles Lestourgeon (1808–91), Trinity College, Cambridge, surgeon at Addenbrooke's Hospital, Cambridge, and member of the board of medical studies.

To Dr. William Carpenter

GIRTON COLLEGE. | 17, CUNNINGHAM PLACE. N.W.

Dec. 22. 1873

Dear Dr. Carpenter

There was a meeting of the ^Girton^ College Committee last week, at which your letter ^relating to the G.R. Scholarship^ was read. I was desired to explain that the "veto" to which you refer would apply only to character, not to the intellectual qualification, which would of course be guaranteed by the Examination. & that a similar veto would be claimed in the case of every Student applying for admission to the College.

The Committee were rather puzzled to know why ~~th~~ a form of announcement which exactly corresponds with that adopted in the case of University Hale, ^&c.^ should be objected to.

In the meantime however the notice issued by the College does not refer to the veto.

Yours very truly
Emily Davies.

GC: DALS ED AR 2/6/14b

To Barbara Bodichon

GIRTON COLLEGE. | 17, CUNNINGHAM PLACE. N.W.

Jan. 6. 1874

My dear Mrs. Bodichon

To think that I should have let all this time go by without sending you any word about anything. I have been half expecting to hear from you, & then one always puts off foreign letters, as they are so much more serious. I was very glad to hear from Rachel Cook the other day that you talk steadfastly of March 1. I hope you will give Girton an early place among your necessary visits, so that we may see you there before the end of next Term. There are such endless things to talk to you & to consult you about which can only be done satisfactorily on the spot. You don't know how I miss you. I had got so much into the habit of looking to you for advice & help about all sorts of things that I am always feeling after it still. However I hope your absence is working well & that you are not thrown away elsewhere. & you may come back all the richer & fresher. In the meantime we have Mrs. Gurney safe back. She came to the last Committee meeting for the first time after her long absence. It is very nice to have her back again.

We pulled thro' our first Term bravely in spite of difficulties. Many windows were wanting & it was long before we had outer doors. To the last there was neither bell nor lock to our principal door. However we escaped burglars, & we had no trouble from damp, which was of course the great fear. The walls have dried beautifully & the ~~hot~~ warming apparatus works well. Altogether the building gives great satisfaction & I think the Students were agreeably disappointed in the pleasantness of the situation. There are such pretty walks about, & the views are really fine at sunset time.

There is no difficulty about attending Lectures at Cambridge. The Naturalists have been attending Professor Liveing's & Professor Humphrey's in Chemistry & Physiology, & getting the use of apparatus, microscopes, skulls, &c. Next Term they will attend the same Courses & some others. They had a fly or waggonette, (according to weather. generally an open waggonette.) always to go in, & either walked or drove out, as they found best. The expense came to about £8 for the Term. The proximity to Cambridge—& also having Miss Lumsden. has made a great reduction in the cost of the teaching.[1] We shall certainly have a balance of Profits to show next June, & to help towards the Capital fund. Miss L. has been most useful & very pleasant to do with. I wish we had a Mathematical Resident Tutor besides. We have not made much way in getting money lately, but are hoping to do something at Liverpool. There is to be a meeting there on the 20th, got up by the Rathbones, who seem to be very zealous. I am to stay with them & Lady Stanley will probably go too, & Mr. Heywood, who has rich cousins there. The Cooks are greatly enjoying Bl⟨andford⟩: Squ⟨are⟩.

Rachel has some pupils, among them Miss Herschel. Miss Woodhead has been staying with them. The Manchester school is to be opened this month. I hope it will get on, but I expect it will have to make its way by degrees, like other schools. There is a prospect of reform at Queen's College. My brother has been made Principal, & he is aiming at getting it re-constituted on the model of University & King's. i.e. having a good *school* for girls under 18, & making them pass an Entrance Examn. for admission to the *College*, which might then be a place of advanced teaching, preparing for London Univ: Examns. The London Univ: is moving a little bit. Dr. Carpenter says the Women's Examn. is likely—(he thinks quite certain.)—to be made identical with Matriculation, & he thinks this will be a step towards getting Degrees. He says the feeling is decidedly growing more favourable to this than it was. It seems to me that his own is, at any rate, which is something. You may have seen that the Cambridge Women's Examn. is extended to men. We have been considering whether to accept it now, & have decided to postpone it for the present. The Time-table is so arranged that the same candidate cannot take both Latin & Mathematics, which would not do at all for us. This is likely to be altered. You will have seen that we have still two women on the School Board. It is vexing to have lost Greenwich. Isa worked very hard for Miss Guest & heard a great deal of talk—among other things, that I did not fight enough for the Church & did not care for needlework but left it to an old bachelor—(presumably Mr. MacGregor.) Mr. Legge, who has taken my place, is a very good member, but it is a pity so many votes were wasted upon him. He had more than enough to have brought in Miss Guest, whom he hoped to have had as a colleague.

Now I think I have given you a *good* cram of news. We go back to Girton on the 27th. I expect there will be a great deal of receiving to do. People swarm out to see the place. Hammond heard a party in the Dining Hall one day & went to look after the spoons, & found a Bishop: (Colonial.) Lady Rich is coming on a visit. Kindness to the Dr. Ever yr. affectn.

ED

My mother has been *much* better these last three months. It is such a comfort.

GC: ALS ED B89

1. Lumsden took the Tripos in 1873 and stayed on at Girton as Tutor in classics until 1875.

To Barbara Bodichon

GIRTON COLLEGE, | CAMBRIDGE.

March 9. | [1874]

Dear Mrs. Bodichon

Miss Manning tells me you would like to pay your promised visit next Monday. Except that just the end of the Term is rather a busy time for talking over the Students' work & arranging the next Term's Lectures &c., it would be quite convenient, but if you are thinking about furnishing, I am afraid nothing can be done till my chimney has been seen to. The soot has been blown down the chimney four times this Term, & naturally the carpet is in a horrible state. Could you get to see Mr. Waterhouse *himself* & make him understand that something *must* be put on outside? No blower or inside remedies will protect from these falls of soot in the night, when there is no fire. We cannot do anything without Mr. Waterhouse, because one builder does not like to interfere with another man's work, & Loveday won't act without Mr. Waterhouse, even if I knew exactly how to instruct him. I have made notes of the quarters of the wind which affect the various chimneys.

It is all at my end.

Fortunately the rooms along the corridors are all right, & there is no trouble in the Dining Hall. Mine is the worst, as regards these falls of soot. I am now keeping the register down till the wind moderates.

Ever yr. affecn.
ED

GC: ALS ED B90

To Barbara Bodichon

GIRTON COLLEGE. | 17, CUNNINGHAM PLACE. N.W.

March 28. | [1875?] ⟨1874⟩

Dear Mrs. Bodichon

I am afraid we cannot manage the papering just now. Hammond is away for a holiday, & I should not know whom to send an order to, as we have never had any work of that kind done yet, & I do not know whether people we employ for other things would undertake paper hanging. We shall have to see to the whole business when we get the ~~plas~~ walls coloured & the Cartoons put up. Do you mean by "the sofa covers," fresh covers for the existing sofa & chairs? If they are to be simple things of chintz or some material of that sort, Hammond can manage them. ~~They~~ The maids will not have much time, but one can get a workwoman if necessary. I do not think Hammond could undertake upholstery that required much fitting, but she has done chair covers, & these seem to me the most pressing thing, as the frocking is not clean, besides not matching the other stuff.

I did not know you meant the book-case for the Mistress's room. Do you see a place for it in your mind's eye? The carpet had arrived before Hammond left.

If there are any directions about putting it down, please let me know. Hammond will be back on Thursday. I am sorry we cannot make the room quite nice before the new Term, but I do not think it matters very much, as there is nothing characteristic about the room. It is not a *feature*, for strangers to notice & remember.

I was with the Goldsmids yesterday & Lady G. asked a good deal about money & our debt. Sir Francis too talked about the College in a friendly way. Do you think it is want of presence of mind, or what, that prevents him from making his Guarantee of £300 a gift? He is not at all well & is suffering from depression.

Ever yr. affectn.
ED.

GC: ALS ED B91

To Barbara Bodichon

GIRTON COLLEGE. | 17, CUNNINGHAM PLACE. N.W.

April 14 | [1874]

Dear Mrs. Bodichon

I enclose Miss Hoskins's letter about the blinds. I have told her she had better have a talk with you & suggested to her to write & ask when you can see her. It seems likely to cost a great deal of money for what will only be practically useful during a few days of the year, but one cannot of course dictate gifts, & if we do have any hot weather the sun will be very strong on the S⟨outh⟩. W⟨est⟩. front.

Yours ever
ED.

Whatever we have in the way of outside structure ought to be very strong, as the wind is so powerful up there.

GC: ALS ED B92

In April 1874, Dr. Henry Maudsley published in the *Fortnightly Review* a long article, "Sex in Mind and in Education," claiming that higher education posed a threat to the health of women students. He argued that women were physically and mentally unsuited to college education, as there were "significant differences between the sexes ... [and] the development of puberty ... [drew] heavily on the vital resources of the female constitution." In May 1874, Elizabeth Garrett Anderson wrote a refutation of his claims in the same journal, entitled, "Sex in Mind and in Education: A Reply." In her reply, Garrett Anderson questioned Maudsley's motives in "placing such medical and physiological views before the readers of a literary periodical" and highlighted a series of inaccuracies in his article.

To Barbara Bodichon

GIRTON COLLEGE.

Cambridge. | May 16. [1874]

Dear Mrs. Bodichon

The time for the Entrance Examn. will I believe be June 23. & three following days. Will that be a convenient time for us to be at 5 Bl⟨andford⟩ Squ⟨are⟩.?

I am feeling puzzled about the walls. The son of our Clark of the Works was up here the other day, & hearing some talk about colouring, suggested that it was too soon & said his father always advised waiting a year. Lady Stanley was here yesterday & was anxious that we should not be in a hurry. Do you think it is safe for the Cartoons? The groundfloor corridor was the last part plastered. There is not the least sign of dampness. Then about the colouring. Our gardener Chalkley wants to do it. If he does, it will be necessary to keep on our boy, so-called, but really a man, for some weeks longer than would otherwise be necessary. His wages, after we leave, will be 15/. a week. Do you think non-professional people can be trusted for such work, & that it would be cheaper than having it done by a regular man? The reason I ask now instead of waiting till you come, which would be much better, is that if Chalkley is to do it, I think he ought to try upon one of the rooms upstairs. And in that case he ought to have a pattern ^(from you) for the colour, & get one done before you come, for you to see.

We are having a succession of visitors & I am hoping & believing that the results are equal to the time & exertion consumed.

Isn't it delightful of the London Univ: Convocation? It takes one back to 12 years ago.[1]

Ever yr. affecn.
ED.

GC: ALS ED B93

1. See ED to Anna Richardson, 15 August 1868; and ED to Barbara Bodichon, 6 January 1874.

To Barbara Bodichon

GIRTON COLLEGE, | CAMBRIDGE.

May 18. | [1874?]

Dear Mrs. Bodichon

Mrs. Roby was prevented from coming on Saturday & hopes to be here to-night. I do not know whether she will stay over Thursday, but I am having another room got ready, in case she should be occupying the spare room. I should be glad to know what time you are coming & whether it is arranged for Miss Buckley & Miss Kingdon to stay to dinner.[1] I suppose they will be here at lunch.

Yours affecn.
E. Davies.

GC: ALS ED B94

1. Probably Arabella Burton Buckley (1840–?), a scientist and secretary for Sir Charles Lyell; she wrote popular scientific texts and edited Mrs. Somerville's *Physical Sciences*. Probably Emmeline Maria Kingdon (?–1890), who was superintendent of the Royal School for the daughters of officers in the army.

To Barbara Bodichon

GIRTON COLLEGE, | CAMBRIDGE.

Wednesday. | [20 May ?1874]

Dear Mrs. Bodichon

I have heard this morning that two schoolmistress-friends of mine who have long looked forward to a visit here propose coming to-morrow by the nine o'clock train. I cannot put them off, & I should like to have a little time free for them only, so perhaps you will kindly arrange—in case you should also be coming by that train—to take anything you have to do in Cambridge first, coming up here later. Perhaps you can let me hear by to-night's post at what time I may expect you.

Yours affectionately
E. Davies

Mrs. Roby arrived yesterday & stays till Friday.

GC: ALS ED B95

To Barbara Bodichon

GIRTON COLLEGE.

Cambridge. | May 20. [1875⁴]

Dear Mrs. Bodichon

I am not in a hurry about the colouring. If it is put off, it will be one thing less to attend to just now. For the cartoons at any rate it seems safest to wait.

We shall be taken up on the afternoons of the 2d & 3d by the Concert in which some of our students are to take part, so that it would not be of any use to be here before 5.30 on Tuesday or after 2 on Wednesday. Miss Blackwell can have Miss Hoskins's or Miss Gamble's late room.

Can we have the Examn. on the 23d & three following days at 5 Bl⟨andford⟩. Squ⟨are⟩.? Another candidate, a Miss ⟨Jessie⟩ Arthur, a clergyman's daughter, has written for a Form of Entry. She came with her mother to see the place the other day, & Hammond, who showed them about, liked them. This is all I know. We have many visitors, who are welcome, tho' fatiguing, coming on the top of one's regular work. Mr. ⟨Samuel⟩ Morley, M. P. came yesterday & was very pleasant.

Ever your affecn.

ED.

There are 2 candidates in the Honours Div: of the London Univ: Examn., one of whom will I know be glad of the Gilchrist ⟨Scholarship⟩, if the other either does not get it or does not wish to hold it.

GC: ALS ED B96

To Barbara Bodichon

GIRTON COLLEGE.

May 27. [1874]

Dear Mrs. Bodichon

I have given directions to Hammond about the pictures & she will send them to-day if she can.

I suppose neither you nor Miss Blackwell wd. care to go to concerts at Cambridge? I have two extra tickets for each day. (the Concerts are at 3.30 on Tuesday & Wednesday) which are at your service. Please let me know whether you care to use them, & also what time you propose to spend here. With so many people to be received, one wants a little notice. There were 6 parties shown over the place yesterday & ~~seven~~ more are expected to-day besides other engagements, & work.

Ever yr. affecn.

ED.

GC: ALS ED B97

To Barbara Bodichon

GIRTON COLLEGE.

Cambridge. | Saturday. | [1874]

Please burn this

Dear Mrs. Bodichon

I am sending papers to Miss Greatorex. I had written some days ago to Mr. Rowsell pretty fully. What wants to be said & cannot well be said in *writing* is that if they give similar sums to us & to Merton, it *means* much less to us, as our fees being higher, owing to the superior quality of the teaching, it leaves much more for the student to pay for herself. Miss Creak comes to Lectures here three times a week.

Old Mr. ⟨Thomas⟩ Bastard came here the other day & promised £100. He wants to give it in some way which would entice other people into giving, as e.g. that for every £15 he will add £5. I don't think it would be of any use in such a case as ours, & it would be rather troublesome. However I said it could be considered. He talked of seeing Mr.
⟨damaged⟩
that if fathers could see the place, they could not help sending their daughters.

Lady Herschel has written for a Form, so I hope Miss H⟨erschel⟩. is safe. A Miss Parlby (over 30) means to come if she can pass the Entrance Examn., but cannot be ready for it before October.

Our Students are to attend a valuable course of Lectures on Biology by Dr. M⟨ichael⟩. Foster

GC: AL ED B98

To Barbara Bodichon

GIRTON COLLEGE.

June 12. 1874.

Dear Mrs. Bodichon

Miss Lumsden gave Dr. Blackwell's message to Miss Wallis & also told me about it. I thought she had better give up the examn., but when I got her to come & talk to me about it I found her very unwilling to take the advice. She urged that she was better—(as she certainly seemed to be.) that Dr. Blackwell had only just seen her & had not asked her much about her health—that she did not know how prepared she was for the examn., knowing the Herodotus almost by heart, &c. I felt that it was true that Dr. B. did not know anything about the examn. & that what she knew of Miss Wallis was only indirect. Finally,

I consented to her trying it, on condition that she should judge for herself & stop at once if she found it was trying her head. She seemed particularly bright & well while it was going on & thinks it has not done her any harm. I have had talks with her about her health generally, & urged her to have advice & try to learn how to manage herself. She said that was the difficulty—that she did not know at all how to manage herself. I suggested her having more frequent advice, & offered, if the expense was a difficulty to arrange about it with Mrs. Anderson. (Mrs. A. offered not to take the fee when I took her to her.) She is to write to me from home & I hope she will go to Mrs. Anderson regularly & get into a good system of taking care of herself. She had very bad habits when she came, as to eating & sleeping, & I think her constitution was misunderstood at home. We have been trying to get her into healthy habits, but it takes time & it has been confusing for her to be told one thing here & the opposite at home.

As to the general question, I should like to tell you how I look at it, & then perhaps we shall see better where & how much we differ.

I do not think that I undervalue the importance of taking care of health—only it seems to me that even quite young people can do it better for themselves, if they are taught how, than any one else can do it for them, & that the thing to aim at is not to be constantly looking after them about every detail, but to have a generally healthy system going on, & only to put in a word now & then, & to be ready of course to advise & help & even to nurse, when any special need arises. I think that if girls of 18 have been well trained either at home or at school, this will be enough. We have found it so here, as a rule. But of course exceptions may come & we must deal with them in an exceptional way, taking care that they do not suffer seriously, but not altering our whole system on their account. This is what we have tried to do with Miss ⟨Elizabeth⟩ Burgess & Miss Wallis, & I feel quite satisfied that they have not suffered from want of care. No doubt the College life has made some demand upon their self-control, but that they have not felt it too much of a strain has been shown I think by their extreme unwillingness to go away, even when they were quite ill. Whenever sending them home was talked of, their countenances fell, & they seemed ready to do anything if they might only stay. Perhaps more care was taken than you know of. e.g. when Miss Wallis was out of sorts in her first Term & I thought it was too long to put off getting advice till she went home, I took her myself to Mrs. Anderson & got directions as to what to do for her. And when Miss Burgess had to go home ill, I took her to Town & did not lose sight of her till I had given her into her father's hands. Mrs. Burgess has spoken most gratefully & pleasantly of the kindness shown to her daughter, & what is more—tho' she is so delicate that I should be almost afraid to let her go from home at all, the parents do not seem to have a thought of taking her away. Mrs. Burgess has talked to me of the great advantage her younger daughter would have in coming here from school & having had some experience of discipline. The elder one had completely run wild at home & it was hard for her to get into orderly ways.

It is not a question of age. Miss Mantle & Miss ⟨Constance⟩ Shorrock were about the same age as Miss Burgess & Miss Wallis, & I am sorry to say they are very far from strong, but they had both been at good schools, & tho' I have talked to them now & then about their health & given them bits of advice, it has not been necessary to watch them like babies. I should not call Alice Betham a baby. She gets on pretty well, but if she had been at Miss Buss's *house*, instead of only at the day school, it would have been better. If you bring up your nieces in the way they should go, I dare say they will keep to it, but if they really are babies at 18, as you prophesy, I think you should send them to a good school for a year before they come here. Our College is not a place for "young girls", any more than the other Colleges are for young boys. It is a place for young women. As to their sometimes feeling lonely, I am afraid that cannot be helped. I am only surprised that they seem to feel it so little. It is surely inevitable that human beings should often in the course of their lives feel very lonely. Don't you know how terribly young wives often suffer at first, & even those who are not young, till they get used to the change of being away from their mothers or their homes? I have wondered sometimes what would have become of Miss Burgess if she had married, as so many pretty girls of her age do, instead of coming here. We must remember that the young women who come here are considered old enough to take care not only of themselves but of husbands & households & children, with very little help from anybody. The Students here are a great deal to each other, & I think it is good for them that it should be so, & that they should feel a certain responsibility for each other. When your friend Miss Herschel comes, Miss Maynard will naturally be her guide, philosopher & friend. If anything should turn up that the Mistress ought to know, she will hear of it, either directly, or from Miss Maynard, or perhaps thro' Miss Lumsden.

I have found that things come round to me in one way or another. I am not so much in the dark as you imagine.

The drawingroom can be got I think by a little re-arrangement of things such as I spoke of when you were here. We can make the Library, which we now use occasionally for Lectures, the Classical Lecture-room, & the Classical room the Reading room, using it for Lectures when wanted. The piano must I am afraid stay upstairs, but we can alter its place, so as to make room for the Classical books & have Prayers in the Playroom, to which there will be no objection when we get the covered place out of doors for play. I have talked to Miss Lumsden about this & she thinks it a good plan.

The attractiveness of the Reading room seems to depend very much on its locality & if we have it close to the diningroom it will be easy to turn in after dinner.

There are two or three reasons why I do not care for mixing with the Students in that way. One is that it does not suit my "genius", as you would say, to talk to a multitude at once. I can do better with one or two. And towards the end of the day I am often very tired & not feeling up to more talking than is wanted in other ways, which is not a little. And also I cannot sit in two rooms at once, & after dinner, I "receive" in my own room. The Students come of course at all hours of the day besides if they want anything, but at that time they know that they can come without fearing to be an interruption. And there is no other hour that would be so convenient.

I am always hoping that some day Miss Lumsden may be able to be Mistress. I think she would carry out our ideas, or mine rather, which I am clearer about than I can be about any one else's. When I talk over things with her, as I have been doing constantly more & more, we almost invariably agree. But that may be partly because she is so much influenced by any one that she happens to be with. I think her spirits & want of readiness & adroitness would be against her, & I do not see how she could get thro' the work as it is now. She has so little power of mastering the details of business. But we shall never get all we want from any one person. What I look forward to is the larger staff, each having her own gifts & affinities, all working together & among them supplying many & various needs. My "idea" of the College is that of a society, not a family. The Students have their family life already, without us. I think we ought to supply something different from a home, not an inferior imitation of it, as a family composed of women only must be. I should not like the college to be a sort of widow with a great many daughters all almost the same age. I think that the society is gradually shaping itself in the process of growth. As far as I can see, things have gone more smoothly & happily this year than ever before. I attribute this to various causes but chiefly to our having had Miss Lumsden, who has been a great help both to the Students & to me. I think that people who just look in upon us for a little while can scarcely judge quite fairly of things as a whole, & may be in some danger of both giving & receiving wrong impressions.

Do you know, you have given an impression that you have a dislike to some of the Students—that you like eccentric ones like Miss Gibson & Miss Townshend & do not care for those that are steady-going & like other people. I know this is not true & have said so, but it just shows how easily mistakes may be made.

I am glad that this question has been raised & seriously discussed. I have for some time felt that some of the Committee were dissatisfied & have been harassed by it without knowing how to meet it. It seems best that the differences of view should be brought to a definite issue & there could not be a better occasion than the appointment of the Mistress for the ensuing year. I should like it to be understood that I am not ready to carry out any other "idea" than this which I have tried to explain & which I have had in view, more or less distinctly, from the beginning. One of the chief reasons for my being here has been that having worked so long with most of the Committee, it seemed likely that I could represent their mind better than a stranger. If this is not the case—if the Committee generally have different views from mine, some one must be found who can work them out cordially. The Committee & the Mistress must not be at cross-purposes, working against each other. If they cannot work together, one or the other must go, & clearly it cannot be the Committee. Apart from this, there is another reason for my giving up.[1] It would be an advantage in some ways to have a Mistress without home ties, who could live here all the year round. And as you know, it is not likely to be more easy to me, but rather less, as years go on, to be away from home even during Term time. I am afraid the change would involve also a change of Secretary. We seem to have reached the stage at which it is almost essential for the Secretary to be resident, & it could scarcely work for me to reside here, with some one else as Mistress, put here on purpose to carry out a different idea from mine, even tho' the actual changes made might not be very conspicuous.

There will be time to think over these things during the next few weeks, before the annual College meeting. I go home to-morrow, & I dare say I shall see you before long. There is nothing very important for the Committee on Monday.

Ever yours affectionately
Emily Davies

GC: ALS ED B99

1. For two years ED had been Mistress of the college; secretary to the College Committee; and a member of the Executive Committee, in addition to other responsibilities with other organizations. When she accepted the role of Mistress, she did not expect to be in the position for more than one term, and she did not believe that the Mistress should also be a member of the college's governing body. By April 1875, she was planning to resign as Mistress. See ED to Barbara Bodichon, 22 April 1875.

To Barbara Bodichon

GIRTON COLLEGE. | 17, CUNNINGHAM PLACE. N.W.

5 Bl. Squ. | June 26. 4.45 P.M. | [1874]

Dear Mrs. Bodichon

I must send you a line from this nice place. It makes the superintendence easy & pleasant, when the ⟨entrance⟩ examn. goes on in such comforts & with plenty of nice things about. Some kind person sends us in tea, which is very refreshing, especially on a close day like this. I think all these will pass & that we shall get 4 good Students from among them. Only one of the Miss Grüners will be able to come. The other will help to pay for her out of her salary as a governess. They all strike me as sensible & businesslike, except Miss ⟨Mary⟩ Kilgour, who is very helpless. She is childish, by comparison with Miss Herschel & Miss ⟨Jessie⟩ Arthur, tho' several years older than they are. On the other hand, I fancy she is better prepared than any Student we have had & likely to do creditably in the Math: Tripos—which is very important. These 4, (I am assuming that Mme. ⟨Leonie⟩ Blumenthal's £25 will be available for Miss Kilgour.) with Miss ⟨Elizabeth⟩ Brown, & the Gilchrist Scholar (not yet determined) will make six, & I think the American means to come.[1] If we could get one more, we shd. be *crowded*.

I hope Dr. Bodichon is better. We must have a Committee before very long, perhaps in about ten days. The last payment has been made for the building & there is some money (borrowed) left in hand.

Ever yr. affecn.
ED.

GC: ALS ED B100

1. Probably Eliza Theodora Minturn, an American who entered Girton in 1875.

To Barbara Bodichon

GIRTON COLLEGE. | 17, CUNNINGHAM PLACE. N.W.

July 1. 1874

Dear Mrs. Bodichon
 Miss Kilgour did very well in the examn. & is recommended to the Clothworkers for their Scholarship.[1] Mme. Blumenthal's £25 will not be wanted for her. The Miss Ross's called here yesterday & I told them about Miss K. & they said they wd. make up the 50 guineas a year. The marks are

 667 M⟨ary⟩. Kilgour
 572 C⟨onstance⟩. Herschel
 501 A⟨lice⟩. Grüner
 496 J⟨oan⟩. Grüner
 379 J⟨essie⟩. Arthur

Miss Arthur did not do well but pulled thro'. The Examiners say that Miss Herschel & the Grüners are all qualified for Lady S⟨tanley⟩.'s Scholarship, as to attainments.

 I have communicated this to Miss H⟨erschel⟩. & told her Lady S⟨tanley⟩. meant it for one who could not come without it, & that I supposed she was disqualified by this condition, but we wished to hear definitely. It was thought necessary to do this, as Examiners are not supposed to know circumstances without inquiry.

The Gilchrist is accepted by Miss ⟨Fanny⟩ Harrison of Brighton, who was with Mrs. A. Bennett.

Yrs. affecn.
ED.

GC: ALS ED B101

1. The Clothworkers Company founded the Mary Datchelor School in 1877 and was known for its support of education for girls and women. In 1874, it established scholarships for Girton College students. The sums varied from 50 to 80 guineas.

To Barbara Bodichon

GIRTON COLLEGE. | 17, CUNNINGHAM PLACE. N.W.

⟨before July 20⟩ [1874]

Dear Mrs. Bodichon

If this is the kind of thing wanted for Mme. de Noailles, will you kindly forward it. I have not her address.

I have come to the conclusion that we had better not prescribe one ⟨gym⟩ dress, as there seem to be many harmless varieties, but to make it subject to the approval of the Mistress, & I am inclined to make essential these points. full trousers to the ankle, skirt, blouse or tunic to the throat with long sleeves & 2 or 3 inches below the knee.[1]

These conditions would exclude the things we dislike. Would it be worth while to send a line to Lady Rich, telling her exactly what you saw. She talked as if she was quite in the dark, & it would not be pleasant to have those questions coming over again next time.

Your affecn.
ED.

GC: ALS ED B103

1. In the Maudsley-Anderson exchange in the *Fortnightly Review*, Maudsley had accused reformers of women's education of neglecting physical training. Garrett Anderson had responded that schoolmistresses associated with the Oxford and Cambridge Local Examinations wholly supported physical education. ED was equally supportive and the first paper of the London Association of Schoolmistresses, of which she was secretary, was entitled "Physical Exercises and Recreation." In European schools and colleges at this time, it was becoming commonplace to erect gymnasiums, and calisthenics were a feature of female education

and training. Gymnasium dresses were designed to facilitate comfort and mobility without compromising modesty.

To Barbara Bodichon

GIRTON COLLEGE. | 17, CUNNINGHAM PLACE. N.W.

July 16. | [1874]

Dear Mrs. Bodichon

The Ex. Committee appoint all the officers except the Treasurer & Secretary, so that in some sense next Monday's meeting is the most important of the year. I think it would be rather a pity for you to be absent, as a full meeting seems to give more weight to what is done, even tho' there may be no discussion of much importance.

I had been thinking that if the Committee should decide to leave the dress open, subject to approval by the Mistress, we might perhaps manage for two or three of the ladies to meet—say yourself, Lady Rich, Mrs. Ponsonby if possible, or Miss Metcalfe & myself. on Tuesday morning, to agree if we can as to what should be made essential. I want to be in a position to tell the Students, as soon as possible, as I may be seeing some of them, & at any rate it ought to be settled before October, which means *now*, before every one leaves Town. You may like to see this note about it from Miss Manning. I am going to ask Mrs. Ponsonby about the length of the blouse in the dress she spoke of.

Your affecn. ED

GC: ALS ED B104

To Barbara Bodichon

July 21 ⟨1874⟩

Dear Mrs. Bodichon

You will like to hear about yesterday's meeting. The only appointments achieved were mine & the Local Secs. Mr. Roby was absent, on Commission business, so we were obliged to postpone the Lecturers & Miss Lumsden. We want to alter her payment & to increase it. There were only Miss Manning, Miss Metcalf, Mr. Tomkinson & Lady Rich there. It was decided not to prescribe a uniform gymnastic dress but to make it subject to the approval of the Mistress. If we allow such an one as is described by Mrs. Ponsonby—i.e. the blouse to or below the knee, as I think we may do, with long full trousers, (considering that it is worn somewhere in London, as well as at Miss L⟨umsden⟩.'s Belgium school) there will be no difficulty in getting it adopted. Miss Müller, who was here yesterday, made not the least objection to altering hers to whatever might be decided upon. Miss Harrison (the Gilchrist) has the German one.

We admitted the 6 new students, their certificates of character being all properly filled up. Do you think this Miss ⟨Hertha⟩ Marks is Miss De Morgan's friend? I have explained about Scholarships & asked what amount of assistance wd. do, & whether she has passed any qualifying examn. Would Miss ⟨Mary⟩ Ewart help anybody to come? I think we ought not to promise anything to Mrs. ⟨Fanny⟩ Tubbs till we see how the girl does in the Local Examn., but to hold out hopes. I have received & acknowledged Mme. Blumenthal's £25. I want very much to get some one to use it *this* year. Let nothing in heaven or earth prevent your coming on Wed. the 29th.

Ever yr. affectn.
ED.

GC: ALS ED B106

To Barbara Bodichon

GIRTON COLLEGE. | 17, CUNNINGHAM PLACE. N.W.

July 28. ⟨1874⟩

Dear Mrs. Bodichon

Miss Marks has just been with me. She has been maintaining herself by teaching for five years, (since she was 15) & could not come unless the whole fees were paid. She thinks of trying for the Gilchrist & Lady G⟨oldsmid⟩'s Scholarship next year, & wd. rather prefer writing for them, so as to come better prepared. I told her if she got one, we might probably be able to make up the rest. She is pleasant & I should think promising. I am rather inclined to think of that other one, Miss Benton, for this year. Would it suit you for me to be at Scalands for a few days toward the end of next week? My brother will be going away on the 10th, & I want to be back by that time. There is a great deal to consult you about—the new furniture &c. I expect to go to Girton next Monday with Mr. Tomkinson, to see about the gymnasium, garden, &c. It is not a very good day, being the Bank Holiday, but he cannot get away just now at any other time, except for Sat. afternoon & Sunday. Is there anything that you think of to see about at Girton before we have our talk?

Will you tell me tomorrow whether you agree to what I propose about the Gym: dress. i.e. high to the neck & wrists, full trousers to the ankles, blouse, skirt or tunic to or below the knee, & leather belt.

Yrs. affecn. ED

GC: ALS ED B105

To Barbara Bodichon

17, CUNNINGHAM PLACE. N.W.

Aug. 12. [1874]

My dear Mrs. Bodichon

I got home quite comfortably & found my mother pretty well. She was rather full of a message from Lady ⟨Mary Catherine⟩ Hobart, thro' my brother, asking me to send all College papers since she left England. Her husband is Governor of Madras. I found a pleasant letter from Miss Aitken, about what she is doing & thanking me for letting her now about the Gym: dress. The one I have been anticipating from Miss Lumsden came this morning. She has been anxious about her mother, who is ailing, & would not leave her, except as a duty, but as she supposes there is no one else to fill her post, she will come for two Terms on condition that she may resign at any moment if her mother's health or her own shd. require it. She cannot promise to stay thro' the May Term, as the heat knocks her up. She is grateful for the proof of esteem & satisfaction given by offering to raise her pay, but feels that it is merely just, as her teaching must be worth more than it was a year ago. She wd. prefer paying for her Board, & having her fees for teaching raised.

She proposes 7/6 an hour (i.e. more than we pay the Lecturers, counting the time they spend in coming & going.) & £1.10 per week for Board.

This wd. give her more than the most that we proposed. I don't suppose she has calculated how much it would come to. She asks for more generous & nourishing dish, but not for Hammond's dismissal. It is not nice altogether, but we must make allowances for her being with a mother & sisters who are no doubt making a martyr of her.

She is sure the Gym: dress will be found satisfactory.

I hope you will get into Cornwall, & before the season gets too far advanced. I hope too that Miss Edwards is picking up. I must go off now to the printer about the Programme.

Yours ever
ED.

GC: ALS ED B107

To Barbara Bodichon

⟨late August 1874⟩

The address given at the end of the list is 66 Riviera di Cheassa
Naples

On consideration I enclose the last sheet, that you may see exactly what is said.

You may like to see this letter from Mr. Rathbone, & my answer. ^{Please return.} It looks as if something might be done at Liverpool. Some fresh person like your Mr. Cross, is always arising to keep us from sinking. All is well here. When are you coming to see us?

GC: AL ED B108

To Barbara Bodichon

GIRTON COLLEGE. | 17, CUNNINGHAM PLACE. N.W.

Sept. 2. 1874

Dear Mrs. Bodichon

I wrote on Monday to Miss Müller, who is I hope, still at Cambridge, asking her to find out the best blindmaker & to get him to meet herself & me at Girton to-morrow. I don't think it will be much trouble, thank you, & it will be a good thing done.

Hammond came up yesterday, full of energy & enterprise & goodwill. My mother thought her looking younger than when she saw her some years ago. She is quite ready to do things on a more luxurious plan, & to give herself more to superintendence & to foraging expeditions to Cambridge & the neighboring farms, instead of helping at servants' work.

No one had complained to her except Miss Lumsden & Miss Dove & she told Miss L. we would change the butcher if the meat continued to be tough. She says the mutton was not, but the beef was, & is not sure whether it was owing to the cooking. She is hopeful about Caroline & what she says sounds promising. We know she is steady & docile, & Hammond says she wants to rise in her profession, so she is likely to take pains. Her last place before she came to us was as general servant, where there was a good deal of plain cooking to do. It was a respectable place & she was there three years. She says she can make pastry &c. Hammond seems to have had a good many little compliments which she mentioned incidentally. I did not tell her how she had been vilified, as it could do no good. She entered into what I said about succession of change, & also as to specially good things being wanted by people leading a sedentary life. Poultry seems to be as dear as fish. In June nothing cheaper than 4/6 for one fowl was to be heard of. H⟨ammon⟩d. is going to Girton on the 15th & I shall go on the 21st for a few days to make a complete catalogue & supply what is wanted of extra furniture, & china & glass &c. I have tried to make the catalogue during Term time, but have never been able to manage it.

You will be interested in the enclosed. I would rather see Mr. Roby in business at Manchester than master of a school at Bedford. Two Miss Days came to see me yesterday, the Man⟨chester⟩ Mistress & the possible Student. She would not come *this* year, for various reasons, & probably not at all. The elder sister would be willing to help, & Girton would have been an immense temptation to her, but the younger does not much care & did not look promising. The Manc⟨hester⟩ school prospers. Miss Day likes Miss Woodhead except her dialect. Miss W. felt the work so much that Miss Day was afraid she would have broken down. Miss Day herself found it less hard than what she had been used to before.

Ever yr. affecn. ED

What do you think of giving Mme. Blumenthal's money to Miss Grüner? She certainly wants it, & it wd. not be doing more for her than for others. I have been thinking of asking some one for a Nom⟨ination⟩. for her, which wd. be taking it out of the College.

GC: ALS ED B109

To Barbara Bodichon

GIRTON COLLEGE. | 17, CUNNINGHAM PLACE. N.W.

Sept. 5. 1874

My dear Mrs. Bodichon

Before I forget it—may I take 2 Miss Richardsons, friends of mine who are staying in London, to see your pictures at Bl⟨andford⟩. Squ⟨are⟩.? I mean those that are hanging about within sight.

Miss Müller will not get a book at Girton till she goes back in Oct. She leaves Cambridge I think to-day. I am glad you like to give the £25 to Miss Grüner. I am sending her word. It would be hard that she shd. have much less help than the others, only because she & her sister were so ready to help themselves & were not grasping.

I hope you will like Miss Marks, & I hope she will not get spoilt. It is very disappointing to find that it injures people to do a great deal for them.

Miss Müller got a good man to meet us about the blinds. There is not enough woodwork to do them as was intended. We almost despaired of being able to have any at all, but happy thoughts came, & something inconspicuous & tolerably effectual may be managed. The man is to send an estimate & patterns of stuff, which I suppose Miss Hoskins had better see before the order is given. She is due at Dr. ⟨Mathias⟩ Roth's on the 15th. I found on looking at the attic windows that the sill projects about 6 inches beyond the curtain pole, so they wd. scarcely do to come down to the ground, & for short curtains, the felt wd. be too thick. It wd. also take too much room, as the roof projects in so that the curtains cannot be drawn *past* the window at all. I went to Shoolbred's today, & decided upon the fleur de lis (they have only one pattern & size. the same as yours I think.) for the portières & on the grey felt for the floors. I thought Indian tissue with a good deal of red in it might do for the window curtains, but the patterns were too large & obtrusive. I tried cretonne, but saw nothing that wd. do well. The man strongly recommended wool damask & it seems to me on the whole the best we can do. I enclose pattern. Please tell me what you think. It is 4/3 a yard, width 1 1/2 yards. One breadth will make a curtain. They will be two yards long. If we have this, & chair covers of brown holland bound with red, it will I think be harmonious. The damask of course matches (sufficiently) the fleur de lis felt.

I have to go to Girton again on Tuesday about furniture. The Gymnasium walls are rising. Miss Müller hopes her father will give some money for it. She asked about Miss Lumsdsen, & I explained that the heat was too much for her in May. She said she thought Miss L. did not manage herself very well & went on to speak of her *very* anxious temperament. I saw Miss Borchardt too & they both seemed as cordial & contented as could be. Miss Beale of Cheltenham was here with me this afternoon, & I have some hope that she may take Miss Dove after Christmas. (Don't mention this.) It depends partly on what Miss Kilgour (of whom Miss Beale gives a promising account.) may report of her.

Ever yr. affecn.
ED.

GC: ALS ED B110

To Adelaide Manning

17, CUNNINGHAM PLACE. N.W.

Sept. 7 [1876] ⟨1874⟩

My dear Adelaide

Thanks for the Morals. The sketch of the course looks interesting. I don't think anyone would object to your including the relation toward God. I suppose you would put it first of the series. Shall I add it in? I am not sure whether it is wise to choose such a very difficult & disputed subject as Justice for the specimen lesson. My brother & Mr. Mill had a ^little^ controversy as to the meaning of the word, in which Ll⟨ewelyn⟩: thought Mr. Mill erred thro' want of exact scholarship. You know of course that the whole of Plato's Republic is a discussion ~~of~~ on what is justice. If you like to take the risk of criticism, I don't object. I shall not want to print this just yet, as I have made very little way with the compilation. I am beginning to look forward to the Christmas Vacation as the time for rest. There will be plenty to do now till Term begins.

I have seen H⟨ammon⟩d. She was looking remarkably well & young, & is quite ready to charge the butcher, increase consumption of delicacies, &c. She gives a promising account of Caroline. She did a good deal of plain cooking at the place she was at before she came to us, & she was there three years. Hd. is to go to G.⟨irton⟩ on the 15th & at once to inquire for servants, whom I am to see the following week. I go on the 21st for a few days. I went for a day last week & saw Misses Borchardt & Müller. Both seemed as contented & cordial as could be. Miss M. said she thought Miss Lumsden did not manage herself very well, & spoke of her very anxious temperament. She did not seem to have an idea that there was anything at G. to make anybody ill.

Hd. is evidently quite unconscious of unpopularity & I did not tell her, as it wd. only have been discouraging. The extract you sent must be from Miss Borchardt. It is in bad taste to publish it. I have been seeing Miss Beale of Cheltenham. She is going to send a paper to Glasgow on Univ: Degree. May I tell Mr. Brooke Lambert that you will read it? he has written to me about bringing the Coll: forward at the Meeting.

Miss Beale gave a nice account of Miss Kilgour.

Ever yr. affecn.

ED.

I hope you are getting stronger. Is the chronic cold gone?

GC: ALS ED XVII GC-13/2

To Barbara Bodichon

GIRTON COLLEGE. | 17, CUNNINGHAM PLACE. N.W.

Sept. 10 | [1874]

Dear Mrs. Bodichon

I went to Shoolbred's yesterday & looked at blind stuff. The pattern I liked best for our purpose is the enclosed, which as you see matches the felt carpet as nearly as worsted & cotton are likely to do. They both look better in the piece than in the small scrap. The blind stuff can be had in three various widths. Would you tell me whether there is any fulness in your frocking curtains when they are drawn. Our windows are 7. ft. 6 in. wide. i.e. 90 in: or 3 1/2 yds. If we had the stuff 48 in: wide, 1 breadth in each curtain would be quite plain, when hems are allowed for. One breadth of 54 in: would give a little fulness. Or if much fulness is desirable, we might have 1 1/2 breadths at 42 in: making each curtain 63 in: wide.

If you approve of this stuff, perhaps we might have the chaircovers of the same. There will be only one easy-chair to each room, so it would not make a great deal of it, & I fancy it would look better than the brown holland, which would be a sort of patch of buff, not repeated anywhere else. The blind stuff is 2/2 a yard at 42 in:. The 54 in: is 2/9. It would ~~be~~come to 11/. for each room. If it did not work well, we might use the stuff for chaircovers or blinds elsewhere, as it would not clash with anything that we have already. I have ordered the carpets & portières at Shoolbred's, & bedsteads, bedding, chests of drawers, tables. &c at Cambridge. The bedroom furniture is all to be painted white with a suspicion of cream in it.

I enclose the letter about the outside blinds, omitting some impossible patterns. I like the one with the narrow red & white stripe, like the one you sent, best. It would look well I should think, with the red bricks. If you will give me your opinion I will try to see Miss Hoskins next week. She is due at Dr. Roth's on the 15th.

I have a cordial & cheerful letter from Miss Kingsland to-day. partly about the work for next Term, which I am beginning to arrange for.

The sunflowers at Girton are glorious. One that I brought home measured 5 in: across. There are so many buds still that I hope they will last till we get there. The china asters also are beautiful.

The enclosed lady has just called, to ask for information about examns. She cd. not come to Girton but wd. like to get a Certificate. She & her mother have a little school, chiefly for Indian children.

Yrs. affecn. ED.

GC: ALS ED BIII

To Barbara Bodichon

GIRTON COLLEGE. | 17, CUNNINGHAM PLACE. N.W.

Sept. 14. [1874]

Dear Mrs. Bodichon

I wonder whether you have realised how small the outside blinds will be. Each window, i.e. each *pane*, has to be provided for separately. There cannot be side-pieces, & the top (arched) part of the windows cannot be done at all, as there is not enough woodwork for fixing. The proposed box would be as nearly as possible like the one given on Mr. Waterhouse's sketch. ~~(and Box for blind.)~~ which you no doubt remember. It would not show at all inside when the windows are shut, & only a little bit of blind when they are open. Would it not be best to let the man make & fix one, as he proposes, & let the rest stand over till you can see it?

I await further orders as to curtains & chaircovers.

Will you let Mme. Blumenthal know about the disposal of her money? I suppose she ought to be told.

I have heard from Miss Dove. She says she is very well, & seems in better spirits. I have a sensible letter from Miss Wallis too, about her Lectures for next Term. I am thinking of trying to persuade Miss ⟨Elizabeth⟩ Welsh to get good medical advice in London before she returns to Girton. We could then go by the orders, whatever they might be. I have had further talk with Mrs. Anderson & she speaks strongly about the injuriousness of too much food, especially animal food, for people who are engaged in brainwork. Dr. Radcliffe, who is much resorted to by overworked barristers, at once cuts them down to meat once a day & abolishes beef-tea &c.[1] If anything of this sort is really wanted for our cases, it would be worth while to get it ordered, as it is important for Miss Welsh to keep as well as possible for the next few months. On the other hand, if feeding up was ordered, we need have no hesitation in taking that line.

Mrs. Anderson speaks particularly of depression as caused by taking more food than can be properly digested. Her father was so ill in that way that she was afraid he was going to have softening of the brain, & was cured (or as she put it "went up like a shot") under Dr. A⟨ndrew⟩. Clark's reducing system.

Ever yours
ED.

GC: ALS ED B112

1. Probably Charles Bland Radcliffe (1822–89), who was physician to Westminster Hospital and wrote on the nervous system and epilepsy.

To Barbara Bodichon

GIRTON COLLEGE. | 17, CUNNINGHAM PLACE. N.W.

Sept. 16 [1874]

Dear Mrs. Bodichon

If there is an Oct. ⟨entrance⟩ Examn. at all, it will be here, beginning on the 6th. But there is only one candidate, [Miss Minturn]. & there is doubt as to whether she can be ready. She is in Miss Chessar's hands now, & I hope to hear in a day or two, what she advises.

Before I give the order for the box, would you tell me what is the objection to the Venetian shutters. I showed Mr. W.'s sketches to friends yesterday, who thought the shutters much the best.

They say blinds suffer so much from weather, & I should think that without side pieces they will not do very much in keeping off the sun. The shutters wd. of course exclude air, but with windows & ventilators wide open, & corridor windows open too—(the corridor is not exposed to the sun.) there wd. be a great deal of air. & the shutters wd. be more effectual against the glare. As regards the outside appearance I shd. think they wd. be rather better than the boxes.

We went to Bl⟨andford⟩. Squ⟨are⟩. yesterday & my friends were greatly pleased. Mrs. Anderson has another girl—"conspicuously vigorous", & all going well.[1]

I go to Girton on Monday for a few days.

Ever yours

ED.

GC: ALS ED B113

1. Margaret Skelton Anderson was born 9 September 1874. She was Garrett Anderson's second child.

To Adelaide Manning

17, CUNNINGHAM PLACE. N.W. | Sept. 16 ⟨1874⟩

My dear Ad:

Would you kindly let me know, by return of post, if possible, whether any & if so, which evening from Oct. 5–9 ~~to~~ inclusive would suit you for a Schoolmistress meeting. I am ^specially^ anxious to have you, but I am afraid it cannot be later than that week. I want a College Committee most likely on the 12th, & must go to Girton if possible, on the 13th.

I am so glad you are better. I do not want Dr. H.'s book back. I sent the copy with my name in it as it was the only one I had.

I go to Girton on Monday to stay as long as I find to be necessary. probably till Saturday.

Mrs. Anderson has another little girl "conspicuously vigorous." All was going well when we heard yesterday. It occurs to me to say, as it comes into my head, as it often does, what a comfort you are. I can open a letter from you without fear, & about many things one can feel confident & at rest with you. There are not many people who have both judgment & good heart.

Yours always

~~ED.~~

Emily Davies.

The ~~paper~~ ^sketch^ on justice is a good specimen of the difficulty of giving lessons on Morals. I think it is open to question at every turn & implies about all the hardest points of controversy in Moral Philosophy.

GC: ALS ED XVII GC-13/3

To Barbara Bodichon

GIRTON COLLEGE, | CAMBRIDGE.

Nov. 4 ⟨1874⟩

Dear Mrs. Bodichon

I am sure you must be wanting to know how we are getting on here, & I am glad to be able to give you a good account. We made a good beginning with our nineteen. Miss Welsh came back in better health & spirits than I expected & thinks Girton suits her better than her own home. The new ones are a nice set, in some respects the best prepared & most promising we have had at all. Miss Herschel is particularly pleasant & well-bred, & as Miss Maynard observes "a very satisfactory Student." She seems likely to do well in Nat. Science, & we have two good Mathematicians in Miss Harrison & Miss Kilgour.

There is some chance of another new Student next Term, besides Miss Minturn. It is the sister of an undergraduate named Ireland. He came up to make inquires & compare with Merton, & as he looked round, said to himself. "I think this decides it." He seemed greatly pleased, & gave a promising account of his sister. She passed the Senior Local 3 or 4 years ago, & he said would probably take a Mathematical Degree, if she comes.

I have talked to Miss Kingsland about the possibility of her st coming back to us next Term & taking part in the teaching.[1] She wishes it much, but referred the decision to her parents, who are considering it. I asked of course merely whether in case the offer should be made by the Committee, she could accept it. The instinct of loyalty induced her to tell Miss Dove, as she knew she wished for it herself. & she told Miss Lumsden, who thereupon came to me to ask if Miss K's position would be the same as hers, as if so, she must resign. I told her that Miss K. being so much younger, her position would of course be different, but I was not prepared with exact definitions. Accordingly she suggested that she should not sit at our table, & should otherwise remain in the position of a Student. I think this unreasonable, & I am not at all afraid of Miss L.'s resigning. She seems quite bent upon staying. I am afraid we must give up our hope of her ever being fit to be Mistress. She has come out very badly in this business, having been so indiscreet as to discuss it, not only with two or three of the older Students, but with Miss Kilgour! On the other hand Miss Kingsland's way of receiving the idea made me wish for her still more than before. Miss L's objections to her are her social inferiority & the ignorance of conventional manners that it entails, & her alleged childishness—(which I do not see.) There is a prospect of a position for Miss Dove at Cheltenham, with Miss Beale.[2] The carpets & curtains have turned out well. The fleur de lis is much liked & the red is not overpowering. We have had about £100 in fresh subscriptions lately. All Students' fees are paid except Miss Betham's.

Ever yr. affecn.
ED

P.S. I had written so far, when the midday post brought a letter from Lady S⟨tanley⟩., in which she mentions having seen you & Miss Shirreff. It seems necessary now to have a Committee meeting, as it would not be right for me to be practically settling the matter according to my own judgment in opposition to that of others, without giving the committee an opportunity of deciding. I saw that Lady S. was impressed by what the Students said, but she said to me that she could give no opinion herself. We need not attach too much importance to Miss Kingsland's having said ^{to Lady S. that} she could not come back in October. She said just as positively before that she could not leave home at all. It seems to be forgotten that from Miss Woodhead's leaving till this Term, we have managed to get on without a resident Mathematical teacher, & the want was more serious than that of a similar teacher for Classics would be. I have often wished for a good teacher of elementary Mathematics but never for a moment regretted having let Miss Woodhead go.

I am sending this via Mr. Tomkinson & asking him to see you if possible this week. He is coming here on Sat: & could tell me anything you may have to say. We cannot have a committee meeting till the Tripos is over.

GC: ALS ED B114

1. Kingsland was the resident lecturer in natural science at Girton College, 1875–76.
2. Dove became the Assistant Mistress of Cheltenham Ladies College, where she served from 1874 to 1877.

To Barbara Bodichon

GIRTON COLLEGE.

Nov. 10. | [1874]

My dear Mrs. Bodichon

The Kingslands think it would be a great advantage to their daughter to stay on here for a time & will be pleased that she should do so if I can arrange it with the Committee. I have had a little further talk with Miss L⟨umsden⟩. about it, & it seems she did not tell Miss Kilgour & when she discussed Miss Dove & Miss Kingsland with her, did not know that she had been told. That was Miss Dove's indiscretion. Miss L. herself told Miss Welsh & treated it as a matter of very little consequence whether the Students knew it or not, as she supposed it would be made public very soon. I said it would not, as I did not think we should have it discussed in Committee till after Miss K.'s examn., in December. She was glad to hear that, as it will give her time to see her mother &

talk it over with her. I told her I meant to propose an arrangement similar to that made with Miss Woodhead on her coming back to us immediately after her final examn. She said she did not agree with my view of the matter. If she was mistaken, she must take the consequences. She was not vehement, this time.

Miss Edwards is here & I hope enjoying herself. Alice is showing her about Cambridge this afternoon.

Mr. Russell Gurney is going to give us ten *large* trees, such as may be sat under next summer. I am much occupied with considerations as to the planting of them & where they should go, &c.

The Gymnasium is already in use for play, tho' not quite finished, & is much enjoyed. & admired.

Ever yr. affecn.
ED.

GC: ALS ED B115

To Barbara Bodichon

G.C.C. Nov. 19. | [1874]

Dear Mrs. Bodichon

I hope the 30th will suit you. I want to get Miss Ki⟨lgour⟩.'s business settled before we separate, as it will be convenient to make some arrangements beforehand.

Miss L⟨umsden⟩. came to me the other day & said that she had thought over the matter & should not offer any further opposition. I think I told you that Miss Dove is to go to Cheltenham College in Jan. & to have £60 for two Terms, working only half-time, after which a fresh arrangement will be made. She is to teach Physiology. The Gym: is I believe quite finished to-day. It has been in use for Badminton, which is all the rage, for some time, & is very valuable. I don't know why you shd. call on Mme. de Noailles for my sake. She has never done anything for me & I have no expectations from her. We have got the trees in. They are not very large, but a good deal bigger than what we had before. Hammond is shut up with bronchitis & the parlour-maid, Mitchell, after troubling us for some time, became so hysterical that we were obliged to send her home. So the service has been, & will be to the end of the Term, somewhat of a struggle. Miss Herschel, whom I like much, goes with me to dine at the ⟨John⟩ Adams's this evening.

Yours ever, ED.

GC: ALS ED B116

To Frances Buss

GIRTON COLLEGE. | 17, CUNNINGHAM PLACE. N.W.

⟨incomplete⟩

the sort of thing Boards do. You have scarcely made up your mind yet, I think, to the fact that you cannot have the advantages of public & private schools, both at once. You were very anxious to have your school, which you had *made* as a private one by your own exertions, turned into a public school. You have succeeded. It has brought you great honour, & you have enjoyed the position it has given you. But you are not willing to accept the inevitable drawbacks, (tho' you try hard to do so.) I have had rather a strong sense of these drawbacks, & it has made me less enthusiastic than perhaps I might have been, in advocating public schools. Of course, I recognise that *on the whole*, they are to be desired, & can heartily rejoice in the success of your efforts. But the loss of the freedom and promptitude of action which only the *owner* of a school can finally claim, is I think serious. To a person of your eager & ambitious temperament, to be under a slow, bothering Board, must be particularly trying, & besides the personal annoyance, it touches you where you have a right to feel strongly, i.e. the interest of the school. You say to yourself probably—"I should not mind it for myself, but it is the school & the cause generally, that suffers." That may be true, but it must just be accepted. If I were in your place, I think I should often have to say to myself—"I think this decision a mistake, & likely to prevent good, if not to do actual harm. But it is not ruinous, & as on the whole, I am satisfied that this gain has been greater than the loss, from changing the character of the school, I must not dwell upon it." I should probably be able to push it aside. But if they were overwrought & irritable, I should not be able to help thinking about it a great deal too much. I think this applies to such a case as that of the swimming. If I had been there, I should probably have voted with you, but it was clearly a case on which there might be a difference of opinion. I think it was a mistake, after the point had been argued & carried against you, to write to Mr. ⟨A. W.⟩ Thorold about it, & that it partly justified his impressions that you could not bear to be opposed.[1] You see, after all the years you have spent in that work, your attitude is naturally & almost inevitably, on every point—"I know more about this than any one else can know. My opinion is worth more than all the rest put together." And you are, to say the least, "surprised" when others *maintain*, as well as express, a contrary opinion. Then as to Dr. S⟨torrar⟩.[2] You know how far he is from being a favourite of mine, but it does seem to me that it was an unfortunate piece of discourtesy which he might fairly resent, to take no notice of the letter he sent you at Christmas. And I think you do not sufficiently remember that it was your own mistake to put him on. I think you ought to think less of your own annoyance, (tho' no doubt you are the greatest sufferer) & more of the annoyance that you have brought upon other people, & that instead of being angry with members of the Board for not supporting you more warmly against him, you ought to be grateful to them for putting up with him & not turning upon you with reproaches for what was certainly an error of judgment. This is a terribly faithful letter, but I know you want help, & in a case like this I feel that plain speaking, painful as it must be, & trying to do justice to the other side, is the best help one can give. I know that what I have said must hurt you. You would not be human if it did not. But you know too how much I sympathise with you. If I had to put *your* side, I should have a great deal to say upon that, & you may be quite sure that if I have an opportunity of saying a word anywhere that may be of use, I shall be only too glad to use it.

I do not think an Assn. of the mistresses of public schools would do good just now. And I do not quite like to interfere about Milton Mount without being asked, tho' I should be ready to protest against a Ladies' Committee if occasion should arise. I do not feel sure that the fault is all on one side in that case. Miss H's stipulation as to being called Principal does not sound very wise. And I did not entirely like her address at the meeting.

Thanks for the list of salaries. We quite look forward to seeing those posts occupied by Girton Students by & by. The death of the Commission is very grievous. I am afraid that even when reconstituted, as is said to be certain, it may be without the friends to whom we owe so much.[3]

Ever yours most truly
Emily Davies.

Girton accounts are waiting to be made up, & ought perhaps to have come before this long letter. One cannot always practice what one preaches!

NLCS: ALS ED FMB6

1. Anthony Wilson Thorold (1825–95) was vicar of St. Pancras and later bishop of Rochester. He was a member of the Schools Inquiry Commission and served on the board of the North London Collegiate School.

2. Dr. John Storrar of University of London Convocation was chair of the governing board of the North London Collegiate School from 1870 to 1874. He and Buss had a troubled professional relationship.

3. By 1875, the distribution of ancient endowments had brought criticism on the Endowed Schools commissioners. In 1874, legislation was passed to give the Charity Commission power to deal with the reorganization of endowments.

To Louisa Hubbard

GIRTON COLLEGE, | CAMBRIDGE.

Nov. 27. 1874

Dear Miss Hubbard

I have made some corrections on your Proof, put in such a form as to be understood by the printer.[1] I must add a few words of explanation.

Sheet 1. It seems to me a pity to say *Colleges*, when you really mean Schools. Your two first pars: under this heading cd. not apply at all to such Colleges as Girton or Queen's or Bedford. On the other hand I am afraid it is useless to try to restrict the use of the name to adult places, as it is in thoroughly established use for many schools for boys as well as girls. e.g. Cheltenham & Marlboro. I do not know whether Sheet 1 is the place to insert the Table of Salaries which I send, but I am sure you will like to put it in somewhere. It is like a new era for women, when such prizes as ~~as~~ a Mistresship of £2000 a year can be spoken of even as a possibility.

On the sheet headed Ten—I have suggested considerable alterations. It seemed to me best to put the information as to the various Certificates & the means of preparing for them, together & to arrange them in the order of difficulty, which I suppose may be assumed to imply merit. There are very good Courses of Lectures at Edinburgh, & Certificates are also given, but I cannot undertake to supply information about anything out of England. It might be obtained as to Edinburgh from Miss Dundas, Polton, Lasswade, Edinburgh.[2]

Miss Clough has been turned out of Merton Hall. (The landlord is I believe living in it himself.) They are building a house, to be called Newnham Hall, & in the meantime are occupying houses in Bateman St. to which they give the name "The Hall."

The Local Examns. are not "for girls". It is one of their great merits that as they were primarily for boys, & a vast number of boys go in for them, ~~th~~ in such subjects as Arithmetic &c. they are kept up to the male standard. As this makes it much harder work for the girls, it is fair that the fact should be kept in mind.

I hope I shall not have put you to inconvenience by the delay in returning the Proofs.

Yours very truly
Emily Davies.

Faw: ALS 12.A.1

1. Hubbard was editing *The Year-Book of Women's Work* (London, 1875).
2. Probably Anne Dundas, a friend of Louisa Lumsden, who was active in the Edinburgh Lectures for Women.

To Barbara Bodichon

GIRTON COLLEGE, | CAMBRIDGE.

Dec. 9. 1874

Dear Mrs. Bodichon

I will see about the Cartoons & either bring them up myself or get them sent.

The wine is come & cost 6/8 for carriage. I do not know whether we may not have to make some rule about presents. Clearly we must not be at the mercy of any one who chooses to send us a white elephant & in some cases it may be only some one on the spot who can judge as to whether a thing is really desirable or not.

The Examns. are going on now, & we hope successfully. Miss Gamble is here & makes herself useful & pleasant. I am rejoicing greatly in the prospect of having Miss Kingsland's help. It is such a valuable thing in a place like this to have the influence diffused about of a person who is always calm & bright & reasonable.

There will be plenty for her to do. I shall have to take care that it is not too much. I have had a little talk with Miss Herschel about her work for next Term. She said she should like to do anything that Miss Kingsland thought best. When I spoke of her being here, she said she was so glad, it would be such a help. I was pleased to find her tone so respectful, as well as cordial.

There is a chance of getting something from the Mercers' Company. Miss Müller, under the direction of the Master of the Company, whom she knows, sent in a Petition from the Students here, & on Sunday a letter came from Mr. D[aniel]. Watney to say that he had promised to investigate & asking her to put his letter into the hands of the proper person. He spoke of paying a visit to the College, so I asked him to come to-day & we expect him this afternoon. It is a howling day, but fortunately it is not the wind that makes my chimney smoke. I do not think you have realised how serious the plague has been, first one room & then another. The builder I consulted refuses the job & says the architect ought to be consulted. I have seen Loveday & written to Mr. Waterhouse.

Ever yr. affecn.
ED.

GC: ALS ED B117

To Barbara Bodichon

GIRTON COLLEGE. | 17, CUNNINGHAM PLACE. N.W.

Dec. 24. [1874]

Dear Mrs. Bodichon

There is business for the Building Committee & I should like to have a meeting either Thursday *evening*, Jan. 2. or at any time on Friday the 3d. Will either of these do for you? Please give me as much latitude as you can, & would you tell me whether you *prefer* to have the meeting at 5 Bl⟨andford⟩. Squ⟨are⟩.

If not, I dare say Lady Stanley will like us to go to Dover St., or we can meet *here*.

The report about the Addnl. Subjects came the next day. All our candidates passed & are set free for their Triposes, so we shall have to prepare for the Classical, Mathematical, Natural Science & Moral Science.

There is a satisfactory letter from the Classical Tripos Senior Examiner. He cannot get a meeting before the end of January, but quite expects to be able to give us such information as will put us in a position to confer or withhold our Degree Certificate. I wish you & yours a Merry Christmas. Our family festivities are postponed till New Year's Day.

My mother has been suffering much, but we are now trying galvanism for the neuralgia & it seems to be doing good.

Yours ever
ED.

GC: ALS ED B118

To Barbara Bodichon

17, CUNNINGHAM PLACE. N.W.

Wed: evening | [1875?]

Dear Mrs. Bodichon

Please let me have the enclosed back as soon as you can. Mr. Greenwell seems to have quite misunderstood me. I asked when I could see him. It was not at all a note intended to be shown to Mr. Holloway.[1] I scarcely know what to try next.

I have told Mrs. Betham that Alice can have an extra week, & after that if her Aunt will write & tell me how she is getting on, we can decide accordingly. I am afraid Miss ⟨Amy⟩ Mantle must be threatened with consumption. I spoke to her strongly about seeing a doctor last summer. I shall try to see her & hear more particulars before I go back to Girton.

"Jane" has not appeared yet.

Ever yours

ED.

GC: ALS ED B119

1. Probably Thomas Holloway, (1800–83), a businessman and philanthropist who built and endowed Holloway College for Ladies in 1866.

To ⟨Charles Edward Graves⟩

GIRTON COLLEGE, | CAMBRIDGE.

Jan. 28. 1875

Dear Mr. Graves

Our committee were much pleased to hear of the favourable answer from the Examiners for the Classical Tripos to our application. With regard to the desire expressed that a member of the Senate should be present at the Examination of our Students, I am desired to say that we ~~should~~ shall consider it a favour if the Examiners will themselves be good enough to nominate a Conducting Examiner. This was done in a similar case by the Examiners for the Mathematical Tripos & we found it a satisfactory arrangement. ~~The fee was in that case £5, but we take for granted that this~~ We propose to hold the examn. at our own College.

GC: DAL ED AC 2/3/12

To Barbara Bodichon

GIRTON COLLEGE, | CAMBRIDGE.

Feb. 1. 1875

Dear Mrs. Bodichon

Would you kindly return the Library Catalogue. There are some additional books waiting to be entered. Do you remember that long ago, you & Lady Stanley & Mr. Bryce, (I think) were appointed as a Committee to make a device for sticking into the books. Could you do it now? Perhaps you could manage the reducing of the view on the small photograph, which we thought might have done for the Seal, if Mr. Waterhouse had encouraged it.

We have had a good deal of wind & no smoke to speak of yet, except in

Miss Kingsland's room, where it has not I think been really bad. The drains were beginning again, but I got Loveday's men to come on Saturday & they did what was wanted at once. There is still something to be done in the front, for which we must wait for the plan (I have written again for it) but there is no trouble there at present.

You will like to see this nice letter from Lady Herschel. Please return it. The oaks are planted temporarily in a sheltered spot. Chalkley is very doubtful of their growing. They seem to be very tender.

Miss Dove has been heard from & seems to be getting on well, on the whole. Miss Kingsland is fitting in nicely I hope, but there has not been time yet to judge about the teaching. Miss Minturn is happy. Hammond is much better & the new maids are promising. Lady Stanley will come on the 18th & I am going now to send out At Home cards for the 19th. I have to-day corrected the Proof of my letter to Mrs. Mathews & hope to send you some copies soon.

Miss Burgess's sister is to come in Oct., if we will admit her about three weeks under age.[1]

Ever yours
ED.

GC: ALS ED B120

1. Mary Ann Burgess entered Girton College in 1877.

To Louisa Hubbard

GIRTON COLLEGE, | CAMBRIDGE.

Feb. 3. 1875

Dear Miss Hubbard

Many thanks for your kind letter & the Year-book, which have been forwarded to me here.[1]

I am very glad that the little help I was able to give was of some use.

The compilation must have been a very troublesome business.

Miss Buss, the Head-mistress of the North London Collegiate School, drew up that surprising paper, & I believe the information was taken from the published Schemes of the Endowed Schools Commission. Miss Buss told me the other day that she had heard that there were more Schemes which might have been included, & that under the new regime, which we feared might be less favourable to women than the old, we are likely to be as well treated as before. But we must remember that many of these Schemes have not yet become law, & also that a good deal is left to the Governors in each case who will probably keep down the mistresses' salaries as much as they can. Still, it is a great thing to have such things gravely proposed by responsible people.

Yours very truly
Emily Davies.

Faw: ALS 12.A.2

1. See ED to Louisa Hubbard, 27 November 1874.

To Anne Jemima Clough

G⟨irton⟩. C⟨ollege⟩. C⟨ambridge⟩. Feb. 3 1875

Dear Miss Clough

We always hold our Examns. here, unless there is some special reason to the contrary & intend to do so in the case of the Class: Tripos. By the desire of our Committee I wrote a few days ago to the Senior Examiner, asking them to nominate a Conducting Examiner & I mentioned that we proposed to hold the examn. at our own Coll:. I have not had an answer yet, but it was settled that if they declined to nominate, I shd. do so on behalf of the College. So you see, our arrangements are decided upon, tho' not completed.

If it will be of any accommodation to you, I shall be very glad to receive Miss Creak here & to do the same for her as for our own Students.

The Examn. will begin each day as soon as we get the papers, which will probably be about ten o'clock. On the We should hope to have Miss Creak with us at lunch, on the & to keep her for the whole day on the days on which there are afternoon papers. We have plenty of room & it wd. be a pleasure to have her.

If you shd. still wish to have a little talk about it I will make a point of being arrange to be at home on Friday afternoon, but it is perhaps scarcely worth while for you to have the trouble of coming up. If you decide for Miss Creak to join us, I will be sure to let you know our arrangements in good time.

GC: AL ED AC 2/3/12

To Barbara Bodichon

GIRTON COLLEGE, | CAMBRIDGE.

Feb. 4 [1875?]

Dear Mrs. Bodichon

I forgot to send you in my last letter the dimensions of my room. It is 17.6 x 15. It is a good thing we had done no papering or colouring, as the damp, consequent upon the bursting of the pipes I suppose, has discoloured the walls. We are all right now as to pipes & not troubled with the drains.

The *Seal* is you know a settled thing. It was a device to stick in the books that was to be seen about. I don't think consulting wd. be of any use. If you can *make* a device, that is what is wanted. I have recd. the Catalogue. I wish those people had the trouble of keeping & not losing a lot of books that no one ever opens. However I don't so much mind keeping what we have got, if people can be stopped from sending us more things that are not wanted.

Wd. valuable people care to come all the way to Cambridge to an evening party? We could not do with them here either before or after it. Lady Stanley & Mrs. Lyulph will be staying here & it will be as much as we can do to get along.[1] A party is so much more difficult here because we have to use rooms which are wanted for other purposes, & must take care not to disturb Lectures or the routine generally more than we can help. The furnishing of the Dining Hall as a drawingroom on picnic principles just before the people come will be rather a business tho' we make it a joke. We must turn the Laboratory into a Cloakroom, the Reading-room into a Tea room, & the Classical Lecture room (upstairs) must be used for supper. I have asked about 75 (besides the 20 here) but of course a great many will not come.

I am sorry to say the two new maids have both given notice. They complain of nothing, but cannot stand being so constantly on the go. I had been rejoicing in having [2] trained people, among the raw crew, & still hope to get successors of the same sort, but with stronger muscles. There is a great deal of walking about. We have been here a week & have had 6 breakfasts & one dinner in bed. It sounds like a sickly lot, but I think it is really that it is a place where it is considered essential to be quite well, & so instead of putting up with a headache or a cold, efforts are made to get rid of them. Miss Müller came back with a cold, Miss Welsh has had some headaches & Miss Borchardt toothache. Miss Shorrock is laid up at home with diphtheria. A. Betham is to come back on Monday.

 Ever yours
 ED

It wd. be very nice to have you with us on the 19th. We shd. all enjoy it, but you will see that we cannot be hospitable.

GC: ALS ED B121

 1. Lyulph Stanley was Lady Stanley's son.

To Barbara Bodichon

GIRTON COLLEGE, | CAMBRIDGE.

Feb. 9. [1875?]

Dear Mrs. Bodichon

I send the dimensions of my window. The existing curtains are one breadth ^{each} of the fleur de lis stuff & each took 3 1/2 yards of stuff.

The length of course depends on how much you like to have lying on the floor. We could not do with workmen in or any avoidable extra during Term. If you remember, the Easter Vacation was the time we thought of for the furnishing. The two new upper servants have given notice because they cannot stand the drive even of the daily routine, which is carefully arranged so as to be as little driving as possible. Hammond keeps up so far. I hope she will not knock up with the Party. We shall have extra help for that & Lady Stanley's visit, but the difficult here is to get *skilled* help. Trained servants who know their work like a quieter sort of place. Miss Betham came back yesterday looking much better, but by no means clear of cold. I have urged her to be very careful & I hope she will not get worse. Miss Müller brought a cold with her which is still troublesome. Mine is almost gone.

I will ask my mother to send you the Reports.

It is quite settled for Miss Aitken to go to Miss Buss after the Easter holidays.[1] She is to have 100 guineas a year to begin with, besides board & lodging. It will be pretty hard work.

Ever yr. affecn.

ED.

I have to-day received & answered the enclosed letter. Please return it.

GC: ALS ED B122

1. In 1874, Rose Aitken became classics Mistress at North London Collegiate School.

To Barbara Bodichon

GIRTON COLLEGE, | CAMBRIDGE.

Feb. 22 [1875]

Dear Mrs. Bodichon

You will be glad to hear that the Party passed off pleasantly, or as Lady Stanley said, brilliantly. The Dining Hall was converted into quite a home-like looking drawingroom. We found the advantage of a very large room in being able to accommodate a large number & yet have plenty of room for chairs & sofas, so that it could be conducted in a sociable style. The weather was so bad & there is so much illness about that we doubted how many would come, but we had 47, which with our own party were enough to occupy the room comfortably. The M. Fosters came all the way from Shelford, & the Clarks from Grantchester, which seemed to show great goodwill. Lady Stanley was very useful & agreeable, & our Students presented a prepossessing appearance. They enjoyed themselves much, & the guests seemed generally pleased. Hammond has had no return of illness, which is a great blessing considering the weather.

The Tripos Examn. has begun to-day & will not be over till Wednesday week. Miss Welsh has been suffering from neuralgia & was kept awake by it last night till one o'clock, but she seems pretty well to-day. They will leave on Thursday or Friday week. Miss Aitken is to go to Miss Buss after the Easter holidays & is to have to begin with, 100 guineas a year with board & lodging, & of course a very good prospect of speedy advancement. Miss Welsh will not I believe do anything at present. I told her she might perhaps be asked to come here for the May Term, but she put it aside on the ground that it would be dishonourable to take Miss Lumsden's place, unless she had distinctly refused to stay.

Thereupon Miss L⟨umsden⟩. came hot & angry, & intimated that she had not intended to go, but that there might be no difficulty on that score, tendered her resignation. I told her quietly that it had been quite understood that she accepted her appointment for two Terms only—& not very much more was said. She wants to stay, which is natural enough, as the post is about the easiest & pleasantest that could be invented, but I incline more & more to let the old ones go & ~~bring~~ make room for the younger & later ones, who are in some respects so much more satisfactory. It is evident that Miss Lumsden, by simply staying on & doing what she likes, is ~~supposed~~ considered to be establishing a claim upon the College & ~~that~~ we are supposed to be under an obligation to keep her as long as she likes to stay. This makes it desirable to assert our freedom of action before going farther. Miss Welsh's case is different. She has never shown ~~Miss~~ the self-asserting temper which is such a serious drawback in Miss L., but her uncertain health is against her. It is in both of them, not only the not being strong, but the *kind* of ill health that is so much out of place here. It is bad enough to have delicate Students. That we cannot help, but we need not add to anxieties by having resident teachers who are subject to disabling attacks of nervous illness. One must not forget of course the Students' needs in the way of teaching, but I think I see means of supplying them. In the May Term, there is very little Classical teaching to do apart from the Lecturers. In October, there will be the new ones coming in, but I think we shall be able to provide for them. Miss ⟨Eliza⟩ Baker who is I believe an excellent teacher, will then have comparatively little to do, & there will be besides, Alice Betham & perhaps Miss Wallis, to lend a hand. They will only have one subject to prepare for examn. during the whole of their third year, & it will be a matter of choice whether they should spend their spare time in taking up other subjects or in teaching. For those who are to be Schoolmistresses it would seem to be the best thing that they should use the opportunity of practice in teaching, & what the beginners want is so elementary that they could very well undertake it. I mean of course that it should be organised in a regular way. They might perhaps be paid some small sum for it, tho' I believe it would be considered that they were sufficiently paid by the advantage to themselves. Miss Kingsland is getting on very nicely. I hope we may be able to keep her some time longer. I look forward to drawing her out a little more, when she is not overshadowed by the superior 'social position." I told Lady S⟨tanley⟩. about that business & she was much struck by the folly & *vulgarity* of it, & thought it showed that Miss L. cared for herself & not for the College. She said too that she thought Miss L. had done us harm in Scotland by complaints of the food. She had heard complaints there, & had always been able to trace them to Miss L.

I feel as if I had been writing rather uncharitably, but I want you to understand that I have not come to a conclusion against poor Miss L. without looking well at it all round.

Can you do anything to help about Scholarships. Miss Buss has five pupils who cd. come next October with help, & there are others.

Ever yours
ED.

GC: ALS ED B123

To Barbara Bodichon

GIRTON COLLEGE, | CAMBRIDGE.

Feb. 28. 1875

Dear Mrs. Bodichon

I had written the notices for the Committee meeting before receiving your note this morning. I find that several of the most active members of the Committee, including Miss Manning, who knows more than most people about things here, are in favour of asking Miss Lumsden to come back in October, & I do not intend to oppose it. I should be sorry to have her here during the coming May Term, & I believe this is not proposed.

Yours affectionately
ED.

GC: ALS ED B124

April 1875 457

To Barbara Bodichon

GIRTON COLLEGE, | CAMBRIDGE.

April 12. | [1875?]

Dear Mrs. Bodichon

Did you want to see me before I came away? Miss Manning thought you gave her some sort of message but could not be sure.

I wanted to tell you about Miss Mantle. You know I had not calculated on her coming back, & had rather thought of suggesting that she should ask Miss Lumsden to take her in hand instead. I suppose she might have been willing to do so, as she had offered to teach her during the Christmas Vacation. Miss Mantle however seemed to have no such thoughts in her mind. She was quite bent on coming back & not upset at the prospect of getting her teaching from the Lecturers. I hope to be able to manage satisfactorily for her, & if so there need be no anxiety about any one else. I want you to know about it, as from something Miss Manning said, I am afraid you have been really uneasy about losing Miss Lumsden's teaching. You will be glad to hear too that Miss Kilgour is to be here after all. She has not been well & her father though if she staid at home they would have two invalids instead of one, & that she had better come back. So I hope she will arrive to-day & Miss Shorrock is due on Friday. It ~~is~~ will be very nice to have our 16 safe. I should have been very sorry for Miss Kilgour to lose this Term. Miss Borchardt has taken French leave not to come back till tomorrow, if then. It is too bad, after the solemn talk we had just before the Vacation. It will be a good thing for the Coll: when the time comes for her to leave.

I have again had a very pleasant letter from Lady Herschel. She says Constance speaks of Girton as "a Paradise of a place," & they hope they have "won another pupil" for next October.

We need not trouble about chaircovers, as the blue & white goes well with the forget-me-nots in the carpet.

Ever yr. affecn. ED.

GC: ALS ED B125

To Barbara Bodichon

GIRTON COLLEGE, | CAMBRIDGE.

April 22. 1875

Dear Mrs. Bodichon

You may like to see this letter from Miss Buss. Please return it soon. Miss Buss's opinion on the question of whether the Mistress should be on the Committee has the weight of experience, as she is on her own Governing Body.[1]

An *in*experienced person would I think be almost sure to wish to be on, fancying that it would give her a better position, but it does not follow that she would really find it so. It is certain at any rate that being on the Committee does not secure the desired effect of making things easy & pleasant for the Mistress. I do not consider this a vital question, but I should like to do what experience says is most likely to work well.

The point that seems to me most important is to secure to the Mistress the nomination of the resident teachers, the Committee retaining only a veto. This is what Head Masters & Mistresses are ready to die for, & in a case like ours, where it is not a matter of being only a fellow-worker during the hours of study but an actual inmate, holding constant intercourse with both Mistress & Students, it is surely still more important. It does not seem to me that it would at all answer the purpose to say that we shall consult the Mistress & that it is not likely we should go against her. The essential thing is, not that she should gain her point after a fight, but that agitation & disturbance should be altogether excluded, which cannot be when a dozen people have a voice in the decision, every one of whom may be more or less open to pressure. You know experienced people say that if a Mistress has an assistant forced upon her of whom she does not approve, she has no alternative but to resign. It seems to me that those who feel the force of this view will have to consider whether they are not bound to avoid having any part in obliging a Mistress to resign on any particular case, by resigning themselves beforehand on the general principle, if the policy they so strongly disapprove should be decided upon.

Miss Metcalfe's notice about Miss Lumsden came too late, but I hope it may still be possible to get the discussion over on May 3, if no one objects.[2] To put a subordinate officer on the Governing Body seems so manifestly objectionable that I should hope not many would wish for it. You know I do not consider Miss Lumsden a suitable person in any case to be on a body which ought to be specially wise & self-restrained. If people will only have a little patience we can before very long put on a really satisfactory old Student, who will be able to attend meetings & will I hope by & by be of great use to us.

Miss Kingsland is giving some Lectures on Physiology with the microscope & black board. Her teaching will be a great loss as to Natural Science, as we have no Students nearly ready to take that up. But I cannot attempt to persuade her to stay on & miss the chance of the appointment at Bradford.[3] It would be a relief to me if Miss Lumsden would at once make up her mind not to come back. I could then be preparing, before the Vacation, for supplying the teaching. The three who might be made pupil teachers are nice young creatures.

We have all the sixteen here now, & tho' Miss Shorrock looks sadly pulled down, there is a great improvement in general as to health, & as usual much vivacity. Miss Kingsland has been remarking how the liveliness at table keeps up, in spite of Miss Welsh's absence. Mr. Pretor has been telling Miss Minturn that she might get a First Class in Classics & she is inclined to try.[4] It will be a feather for the Americans if she is the first Student who gets a First Class in anything.

I am 45 to-day. a good age for retiring into private life.

Ever yr. affecn.

ED.

GC: ALS ED B126

1. Plans were underway to hire a new Mistress for Girton College, since ED was preparing to step down, which she did at the end of the Easter term, 1875. See ED to Barbara Bodichon, 12 June 1874.

2. The students expressed a desire to be represented on the Executive Committee of Girton College. Bodichon and Metcalfe proposed the election of Louisa Lumsden to that committee, but ED opposed it strongly and the proposal was eventually withdrawn. Lumsden resigned in the spring of 1875. See ED to Barbara Bodichon, 12 April 1875.

3. Kingsland left Girton College in 1876 and joined the staff of Bradford Girls' Grammar School.

4. Probably Alfred Pretor (1840–1908). He was educated at Trinity College, Cambridge, moved to St. Catherine's; and was the classical lecturer at Trinity Hall and Emmanuel College. He edited classical satires and wrote short stories.

To Fanny Metcalfe

GIRTON COLLEGE, | CAMBRIDGE.

April 24. 1875.

Dear Miss Metcalfe

You will by this time have received the supplementary notice. As no one is likely to object, I hope there will be no further difficulty in the matter. I understood from what passed at the meeting that you were *intending* to give notice, but certainly not that it was given then, or I should of course have put it on the business paper without waiting to hear from you.[1] I postponed issuing the notices till the latest day, a Sunday. & when the last moment came there seemed nothing more that I could do. The fact that you intended to send a notice seems to imply that it had not been formally given, as it would not have been necessary to give it twice, & in all matters connected with the *College*, as distinguished from the Executive Committee, I feel bound to be strict in adhering to forms. It is quite an anxiety to me whenever a College meeting is coming on, lest I should commit some irregularity & invalidate the proceedings.

Yours very truly

Emily Davies.

GC: ALS ED B128

1. Metcalfe had intended to propose the election of Louisa Lumsden to the Executive Committee. See ED to Barbara Bodichon, 27 April 1875.

To Barbara Bodichon

Private.

GIRTON COLLEGE.

April 27. | [1875]

Dear Mrs. Bodichon

If Miss Metcalfe gave me a verbal notice I did not hear it. I do not suppose any one will object to taking the discussion on May 3. I should think everybody will wish to get it over.

I am very sorry & disappointed to hear that you are going to vote for Miss Lumsden. I think you are in much too great a hurry to get an old Student put on. It would be far better to wait till we can have one who will represent the good feeling that now exists, undisturbed by rankling memories of past battles & discontents. It is quite possible that occasions might arise when Miss Lumsden's presence would be embarrassing & a real hindrance to free discussion. I should not feel this in at all the same way with Miss Aitken. I hope however that you will not speak of her to old or new Students at present. It might make difficulties, & in any case such matters ought not to be talked about with Students before they are settled.

I think that if a member of the College should be appointed to any office in the internal administration, she should resign her position on the Governing Body. I do not know whether you may be thinking of my own case. I should be sorry for any one to be put in such a position as mine. It has been a very painful one. I don't want to dwell upon it, & it would be difficult to explain all the causes of discomfort, but in planning for any one else I am anxious that my own & other experience should be turned to account & the post made if possible less wearing than it has been to me. I don't think you can have any idea of how the annoyances & anxieties of the last few years have sickened me of "public life." I suppose I don't show illness much, for it seems impossible to make people understand how worn-out I am. I have often felt as if I could bear it no longer—(I mean being the object as public servants are, for every one to stick pins into.) & must throw it all up. It may be impatience. People *can* bear a great deal, but it is not always the wisest & best thing to do. I am not proposing to give up being Sec. at present, but I shall not undertake to go on at all costs, if fresh sources of trouble are introduced without necessity. I have the strongest objection to this movement for putting the Mistress under the control of the Students—for that is what it comes to. I think the part taken by some of the Committee about Miss

Lumsden & other matters has been most ill-judged & that such things ought never to be done again.

If the work is to be embarrassed by such difficulties as these, the people who create the difficulties must expect to be left to carry it on themselves. It is only fair that they should. I hope however that we may still be able all to pull on together.

Ever yr. affecn.
ED.

GC: ALS ED B129

To ⟨Barbara Bodichon⟩

⟨late April 1875⟩

Miss Herschel was carried off by Mr. & Mrs. Müller to a Ball (I think a Bachelors' Ball) at Cambridge. I had gone up to Town & when I arrived at the Cambridge Station, rather late at night, I was met by a note from Mrs. Müller, telling me what she had done. Miss Herschel was with her, at an Hotel or Lodgings. She rose early the next morning & appeared at Prayers at Girton. Directly after breakfast, she came to me & said she was afraid she had done wrong. I told her that if she wd. make known to the students that she recognised this, no notice wd. be taken. She had gone to Miss Kingsland then resident as Art Lecturer, who had told her she wd. say nothing. She did not consult Miss Maynard, who did not know of it till she was gone, & who considered that the Müllers had taken unfair advantage of Miss Herschel's youth and inexperience.

GC: AL ED XVII GC-12/6b

To Barbara Bodichon

GIRTON COLLEGE, | CAMBRIDGE.

May 14. [1875]

Dear Mrs. Bodichon

I enclose a cheque for Morris's bill. I suppose you will bring the serge & explain it when you come.

I will tell you my engagements, as far as they are as yet fixed & you will see where the vacancies come. Mrs. Roby comes to-morrow & will stay till Wednesday at any rate, probably some time longer. The Hills (Rosamond & Florence) come on Friday for one night. I shall be engaged on Saturday evening the 22d & on Sunday.

The week following is clear till the 29th, when I am to dine at the Clarks to meet the Westlakes, & they all dine here on the 30th. On the 31st, ⟨entrance⟩ Examinations begin. If you are thinking of coming for the day only, it would not matter about other people being here. Aunt Julia came the other day with two of Miss Clough's young people & made a pretty comprehensive inspection. She mentioned that Miss Edwards was to be with her soon. Alice ⟨Betham⟩'s fees have not been paid for this Term again.

I have had six letters of inquiry about the Mistresship elicited by the advt., & two others, from Miss Samson & Miss Buckley, whom you have seen.[1] I have asked Miss Buckley to come & see the place if she likes.

Things are going on well. We have 13 Lecturers this Term, all First Class men, three Senior Classics & one Senior Wrangler.

Ever yr. affecn.

ED.

GC: ALS ED B130

1. Marianne Frances Bernard was appointed Mistress of Girton in 1875. She held this post until 1884.

To Barbara Bodichon

GIRTON COLLEGE. | 17, CUNNINGHAM PLACE. N.W.

June 26. [1875]

Dear Mrs. Bodichon

I went this morning to Mr. Waterhouse's office, intending to see if I could make an appointment for us to go to him on Tuesday morning. He is however away for his holiday & will not be back till the middle of July ^{at the earliest.} Under these circumstances I do not know what to do about the Dining room &c. & must ask the Committee.[1]

The part you undertook was the putting up of the cartoons; & the Mistress's room & Reception room. As far as these go there is no need to consult Mr. Waterhouse, as it was left entirely to your discretion. If you are willing to undertake the rest, I should be only too glad, & I have no doubt the Committee would be glad to put it into your hands, without reference to Mr. Waterhouse. People seem chiefly anxious about the dining room. Perhaps, you might be able to undertake that, if not the rest.

I will let Hammond know about the time for your going. I suppose she had better get the Mistress's & Reception rooms pulled to pieces. i.e. put ready for workmen.

Would you let me know which rooms you would like to live in, that she may ~~get~~ make or keep, them habitable. Hammond reports that some large pictures have arrived. Do you know anything of them?

The rooms were very pretty & cheerful for the Examn. & the servant was very good. One of the candidates said her father had promised to send her, irrespective of a Scholarship. Miss ⟨Esther⟩ Case, a niece of Mrs. Dixon of Birmingham has accepted the Gilchrist ⟨Scholarship⟩.

Yr. affecn.
ED.

GC: ALS ED B131

1. The dining room (Old Hall) was not extended until 1883.

To Barbara Bodichon

GIRTON COLLEGE. | 17, CUNNINGHAM PLACE. N.W.

July 2. 1875.

Dear Mrs. Bodichon

I return M. Blumenthal's cheque, as it wants your endorsement.

I enclose the card of the Cambridge paper-hanger. He is employed by a respectable joiner & under him did our varnishing, but prefers of course working for himself. Have you realised the extent of wall & the time that it would take for one man to do it all? Perhaps you can give part of the work to Collingwood. I enclose my notes of his conversation. He seemed to me to understand his business but I know too little about it to be much of a judge. It is very good of you to take this work in hand. I should feel more ashamed of handing it over to you if it were not that you know so much more about it, & it is acting upon the maxim "A chaque production l'ouvrage auquel il est propre."

I have got the Bank-book to-day & I find we have ~~again~~ a small surplus on the Maintenance Fund. You have not said whether you sent the pictures Hammond wrote to me about. There is a charge of 6/9 in Hammond's accounts for the carriage, which I ought scarcely to pay out of the Coll: money without knowing where they came from. I am thinking of proposing to revise the Library & to give it the authority for also accepting or not, pictures and scientific objects, reserving definitely to the Mistress the discretion as to gifts of furniture or anything belonging to the housekeeping department. It seems clear that it won't do to let anybody that likes send presents in kind, any more than say, to offer prizes, without reference to some authority & as the Mistress is responsible for keeping the place nice, it seems best that she shd. have the option of refusing objectionable gifts. Don't you think so?

I have talked to Miss ⟨Marianne⟩ Bernard about Miss Kingsland, & as she quite wishes to have her back, I shall nominate her at the next meeting. You know it is arranged now that the Mistress is to have the nomination of all the resident teachers. It is part of the Contract with the new Mistress. There is no old Student available whom I shd. think it well to have, except Miss Kingsland & after the experience of last Term I am more satisfied than before to do without any one else for the present. Miss Mantle, who is I think the weakest Student we have ever had in Classics, got on so wonderfully well with Mr. Roberts. She told me she cd. not have believed that any Camb. man could have so brought himself down to her level.

I cannot propose Miss Aitken as a Member of the Coll: I found your letter on coming home from an evening with Miss Manning, when we had been talking over possible new members & congratulating ourselves that Miss Aitken had not been mentioned. Miss Manning thought it wd. be very undesirable just now & I doubt whether she wd. wish it herself. I shd. like to have her by & by, if she goes on well, but not yet. I think it is too soon—not six months since she was *in statu pupillari*, besides other reasons. I have thought of two or three new members, but have not quite made up my mind about them yet. I think we all agree that we want more *men*, if we can get good ones, & I am anxious not to fill up all the vacancies now, but to leave room for Miss Aitken, Lady Hobart, or any specially desirable person that may turn up. I could not say much about Mr. Venn at the meeting, but I don't think you wd. wish to choose from among the Lecturers one who went so far as to advise a Student, as he did Miss Maynard, not to go in for any examn. I am afraid Mr. Jackson is likely to be of the same way of thinking.

I am delighted with Miss Bernard—herself, & her way of taking up her work. She seems to me of a different type from any of the others & a higher sort of person than we could have ventured to hope for. I hope she will carry out the best ideas, whatever they may be. Are yours & mine the same? You know it is not mine at all to put the Mistress or any part of the working of the Coll: under the control of the Students. If Miss Aitken or any one else were to be regarded as the mouthpiece of persons in statu pupillari, it wd. be a sufficient reason for my objecting to the election. It will be quite a different thing when *Certificated* students choose some one whom they know & have confidence in. Most of them will have been out in the world long enough to have had time to learn a good deal & to look back upon their undergraduate experience with the light of wider knowledge, & we may fairly hope that there will be some among them whose zeal & attachment to the College, as well as their intimate knowledge of its working, may make them specially valuable. I should like to invite Miss Aitken to join us with as little delay as wd. be consistent with prudence, but if her election were likely to be taken as an act of grace to the present students & as implying that thro' her they might have a check upon the Mistress, such a consideration wd. to my mind outweigh any help that she might be able to give. I look at it in relation to the Mistress, because it is only as to internal matters that Students can be supposed to have any special knowledge. The Mistress's post is difficult enough, without adding a single unnecessary worry, & the mere fact of giving Students any sort of voice in the government, would tend to make it harder for her to keep on the right sort of footing with them.

As to your saying the Coll: is mine, you know that is nonsense. It has taken all of us to get so far, & it wants us all still.

Ever yr. affecn.
ED.

GC: ALS ED B132

To Barbara Bodichon

GIRTON COLLEGE. | 17, CUNNINGHAM PLACE. N.W.

July 3. [1875]

Dear Mrs. Bodichon

I have thought of three new members to propose, & should like to know what you think. They are, Mr. E⟨rnest⟩. Noel, who read your paper at Manchester. He is in Parliament now. He knows something about us, thro' Social Science. I think he would not be difficult to do with. He is a talkative man, & would talk in a different circle from the rest of us—supposing he wd. join, which is doubtful.

Then. Dr. Abbott. Mr. Bryce mentioned him some time ago, but I fancy has forgotten him. He is friendly & I fancy wd. do more if he belonged to us.

Third. Isa Craig Knox. Miss Manning inclines to wish for her, & Mr. Tomkinson also. He remembers meeting her on the Examns. Committee long ago. She is very full of life, & could write letters & articles. Her being a woman is an objection but she is so unlike the other ladies on the Com: that she wd. be almost as good as a man. These three, with Mr. Jackson & Mr. Courtney, wd. be five new members. There are only seven vacancies.[1]

Ever yr. affecn.
ED.
Do you see your way to a device for the label in the Library books?

GC: ALS ED B133

1. The new members appointed to the Executive Committee by 1876 were L. H. Courtney, Edward Enfield, and William Rathbone.

To Barbara Bodichon

GIRTON COLLEGE. | 17, CUNNINGHAM PLACE. N.W.

July 6. 1875

Dear Mrs. Bodichon

I have received the cheque. I have written to-day to the three people that I mentioned, to ask if they would serve. It is adding a large proportion of new members at once, if they all consent. From what you say I think I must have failed to convey my view of the case, as regards Students, but I will not attempt further explanation in writing. Only I cannot help saying that I am sure you are mistaken in supposing that their feeling toward the College is unfriendly. There is an abundance of unmistakable evidence that they are much *more* than friendly. I think it must be because you always mean what you say & never tell stories, that you believe so much too easily anything you hear & attach too much importance to careless talk. Most of us say one thing one day & another another, & cannot afford to have much weight given to our hasty expressions.

If I do not hear to the contrary I will put you down as seconding Mr. Noel, if he consents to be proposed.

Yr. affecn.
ED.

GC: ALS ED B134

To Barbara Bodichon

Sunday | ⟨July⟩ [1875]

Dear Mrs. Bodichon

On further reflection I am much inclined to postpone the work at Girton. I quite feel as you do, that if we do anything, we had better do it all when we are about it & in a way that will last. If it cost £300 we should have only £70 left in the Bank. I should like to keep the £370 & try to add to it as fast as we can at least enough to make up the £1000 for which we are paying interest, & pay that off. It does not seem as if this work was of urgent necessity. Of course the place looks unfinished, but that is not altogether a disadvantage. It brings home to people that we have not money. When everything looks smooth & nice, it does not occur to people that it is not paid for. And for the Students it is not amiss I think to have a reminder that the place did not grow up of itself without any trouble.

Another reason for putting off is that the time is short. Another year we might begin a month earlier, ~~wh~~ & get more of the long days.

The only thing that seems to me urgent is the Mistress's sitting rooms, & perhaps the closets. The Mistress's rooms are much worse than the rest, from an attempt having been made upon them too early. Could you, if you decide ~~not~~ against doing the whole, instruct Brimley to do the Mistress's room only? I suppose he could do that this week.

It seems a pity that you & Miss ⟨Gertrude⟩ Jekyll should have had all the trouble of preparing for action & then not to act, but the preparation won't be thrown away. We know now what is wanted, & can do it whenever we have money.

Yr. affecn.
ED.

GC: ALS ED B135

To Barbara Bodichon

17, CUNNINGHAM PLACE. N.W.

July 22. | [1875?]

Dear Mrs. Bodichon

Brimley came to me on Monday. I had of course no authority to give him any orders, but I told him I should not mind giving an order for the Mistress's room only, if he cared to take it, but he did not wish to do that. I suppose you will ask the Committee to-morrow what they wish done, & if they decide to postpone the work, perhaps you will be able to say what ought to be paid to Brimley for his time at Girton. Have you given up the idea of doing the Mistress's & Reception rooms yourself? If so, perhaps I had better ask Miss Bernard what colour she would like, & let the Cambridge man do her sittingroom. I could manage a small affair like that, & if it was not well done, it would not be ruinous.

I begin to feel the building question a pressing one. Two candidates are preparing for the October Examn. besides the San Franciscan, & there are two Exhibitions not yet awarded. This makes a possibility of 26 in October, & if we have as many new ones next year, it would bring us up to 30 or more & 6 additional sets of rooms would not be enough. It looks as if we were at last beginning to make way. The numerous Exhibitions account partly for the increase this year, but in every case but one, the Student has to pay some £50 a year for herself. And I have already done 8 or 10 possible for next year.

Mrs. Tubbs accepts with effusion.

Yrs. ED.

Hammond says something I don't quite understand about your having told her you were going to send cocoa matting to Girton.

GC: ALS ED B136

To Barbara Bodichon

Friday. [1875?]

Dear Mrs. Bodichon

I was just going to write to ask you to let me know whether I should be wanted at Girton, when your note came.

I suppose some one will be responsible for carrying out the whole of the work & getting it done in time to be dry by the end of September. If anybody is wanted to look after things, I must go myself, as Hammond cannot stay.

Yr. affecn.

ED.

Wd. you please address the enclosed

GC: ALS ED B137

To Frances Buss

GIRTON COLLEGE, CAMBRIDGE.

17, CUNNINGHAM PLACE. | N.W. | Sept. 9. 1875

Dear Miss Buss

I am sorry to trouble you about Miss [Adèle Emily] Martin, but it seems necessary to be clear as to the responsible party. If Miss Soames undertakes the responsibility instead of the parent, she ought to send a communication to that effect to me as Secretary, & also to understand that she is bound to pay one-third of the sum due for the year on the first day of each Term. The necessity of having the responsibility fixed somewhere has been brought home to me by the difficulty I have had about A⟨lice⟩. Betham's fees. The family ignored responsibility, & Miss Warne of course could only pay what she received. Miss Betham Edwards took an easy line, apparently assuming that if subscriptions did not come in, she was sorry, but not recognising that the fees must be paid. I was obliged at last to bring the matter before the Committee, & was instructed to ask her whether she would take the responsibility, & she has agreed to do so for the next two Terms. Last Term, the whole amount had not been paid up to the end, & to avoid bother in the College accounts, Mr. Roby paid the balance.

It would save trouble if Miss Soames would pay for the whole year, at the beginning, but I do not suppose she will do this. She helps another of our students & I have to write for the money every time. This is of course troublesome, but as in that case I undertook to get the money, it is my business to collect it.

You will be glad to hear that if three candidates for the October Examn. pass, we shall have ten new students, making 24 altogether, & there is a good prospect for next year also. One of the new comers is a Miss ⟨Anna Elizabeth⟩ Tuthill of San Francisco. She knows your cousin Miss Burgess & has heard of you from her.

It is something like lengthening our cords, when they reach to California.
I hope you have had a good holiday.
Ever yours sincerely
Emily Davies

NLCS: ALS ED FMB4

To Barbara Bodichon

GIRTON COLLEGE, | CAMBRIDGE.

Sept. 14 [1875]

Dear Mrs. Bodichon

I received your letter, with one from Miss L. Boucherett yesterday before leaving Town. I will call at No. 5 some time before the Examn. It begins on Oct. 1.

We must have a Committee on Oct. 6. 7, or 8. I am not sure yet which day, to admit new Students formally. I am afraid that even by that time scarcely anybody will be in Town. I have not heard what Mr. Waterhouse has said to Lady Stanley. I shall be sorry if she wants to have another architect. I cannot see how a change of *architect* can lessen the expense, if the rooms are to be exactly the same, as is proposed. An expensive architect may of course put on unnecessary ornament, & I have heard that Mr. Waterhouse is apt to do that when he has money at command, but he has not done so in our case. I should think professional etiquette would prevent a respectable architect from taking up another man's work under such circumstances. I am here to revise the inventory & wind up generally. The Mistress's sittingroom is improved by the papering. Hammond thinks the man has done his work well, but that remains to be proved.

I have been at home during the summer till now & very glad of the rest, present & prospective. The little bit of work I am doing here now brings home to me what a small stock of strength I have to draw upon. I expect to get home on Friday or Saturday.

Miss Müller is now staying with the Philip Rathbones. I have heard again from Miss Minturn. It is a much better account of her mother & she now speaks quite hopefully of coming back by & by.

Ever yrs. affecn.
ED.

GC: ALS ED B138

To Frances Buss

GIRTON COLLEGE, | CAMBRIDGE.

Sept. 18. [1875]

Dear Miss Buss

Thank you for attending so promptly to Miss [Adèle Emily] Martin's business. You stirred up Miss Soames so effectively that she sent the sum due for the year, £35, at once. If only £25 is wanted from her, perhaps the best way of putting things straight will be for Miss Martin to send the Gilchrist £10 to her, instead of to me.

I came here on Monday to revise the inventory of our effects & supply what is wanted for the new students, &c., & hoped to have got home to-day, but I find I shall not be able to get away before Thursday. I spent yesterday afternoon with Mrs. Burbury & Miss ⟨Julia⟩ Kennedy & we had a little talk about the subject proposed for discussion at our next Schoolmistresses meeting, School Organisation. I think it may be the best plan to take Miss Beale's paper on the Cheltenham organisation as our starting point, & after a discussion upon that we might see our way further.

I am afraid I shall not have time before the *next* meeting to go into the subject enough to collect materials for a paper of our own.

I am grieved to hear of the death of Miss Doreck.[1] She will be a serious loss to our Assn. & to education generally, & to many of us she was a valued personal friend.

Ever yours sincerely
Emily Davies

I hope Miss Aitken has come back in good ease. I shall hope to see her at Cunningham Place before very long.

NLCS: ALS ED FMB5

1. A kindergarten teacher and long-time colleague of Frances Buss, Doreck was also a member of the Council of the College of Preceptors.

To Barbara Bodichon

GIRTON COLLEGE, | CAMBRIDGE.

Sept. 20. [1875]

Dear Mrs. Bodichon

I am here still, the inventory business having taken longer than I expected. It is after all not quite so full & minute as I could have wished, but I hope it will be enough. You have still I believe the fossils which you took away in the

Spring. I should like to hand them over to Miss Bernard with the rest of the College property at Michaelmas, but I am afraid there may be difficulty about sending them. If you can get them to Cunningham Place, I will take charge of bringing them here.

I expect to see Miss Bernard in Town on or before the 30th, for transferring the accounts &c., & she has asked me to come here at the beginning of the Term to arrange the Lectures, so I shall be here for a few days from Oct. 11

I am going home to-morrow.

Ever yr. affecn.

ED.

GC: ALS ED B139

To Barbara Bodichon

GIRTON COLLEGE, CAMBRIDGE. | 17, CUNNINGHAM PLACE. N.W.

Sept. 24. 1875

Dear Mrs. Bodichon

Sir F. Goldsmid guaranteed £300 & of course paid it. I should certainly ask him to "surrender" it, which is equivalent to giving it towards the debt. How easy it must be to him when he does not ever know whether he has paid it or not. I wish it had been £1000. There is a Form of surrender to sign, which you can get from Mr. Tomkinson. He is out of Town now, but expects to be back in about a week. Perhaps it will be best to wait till he comes back, & then you can send the Form with the advice & it will be one trouble.

I have asked Lady Stanley whether she has any proposal to make about building at the next Committee & keep the papers you have sent, on the chance, but I have no doubt that in any case, any discussion would be postponed till more people are in Town. If so, there will be no business at the next meeting worth coming up for. I only call it at that time because it is wanted for the formal admission of new Students.

I do not quite understand about the fossils & bones. Perhaps I ought not to have said fossils? I only meant whatever it is that belongs to the College. There were some things dug up which Professor Hughes thought worth preserving.[1] He told them Miss Müller where they were, in our shed. & she found them & took care of them, till you took them away. I ought to have entered them in the Catalogue & looked after them more. I hope Miss Bernard will be more careful. In the meantime, would you be so good as to put me right by writing a little memorandum to give to Miss Bernard, stating what you have & acknowledging it as in your charge. You see the agreement with the Mistress puts under her charge "the Library & the scientific apparatus, &c." & I am bound to give her an account of what she is responsible for. I got Miss Kingsland to look over the science things, & I think I have done everything else of any importance, except these exhumations—& the pictures, which I have not catalogued. I thought it would be easier to do room by room, when they are all hung, & I have left the hanging to Miss Bernard, that she may use her own taste & judgment: She seems fond of pictures. I ought to tell her which belong to the College & which are loans. I noticed on the back of one of yours a memorandum that it was lent, but I think there was no mark on most of them. Would you kindly send me a list? It need only be of those that are *lent*, if the others are to be entered as belonging to the College. I should like to have the list by the 29th, as that is the day for the transfer of responsibility & Miss Bernard will I hope be here on the 30th, & take all the documents into her own hands. But if it is inconvenient to you to do it just now, I can let it stand over till I go to Girton on the 11th (explaining to Miss Bernard) & then send you a list of what there are, for you just to mark. I am anxious to leave things as orderly as I can. The inventory was a tedious business, but I got rather interested in trying to make it as perfect as possible.

    Ever yr. affecn.
    ED.

GC: ALS ED B140

    1. Probably Thomas McKenny Hughes (1832–1917), of Trinity College, Cambridge. He was a member of the Geological Survey of England; Woodwardian Professor of Geology; and president of the Cambridge Antiquarian Society.

To Lady Jenner

~~GIRTON COLLEGE, CAMBRIDGE.~~ | 17, CUNNINGHAM PLACE. N.W.

Sept. 27. 1875

Dear Lady Jenner
    I shall be very glad if I can give you any help in finding a good school for your daughter. I send you a list of members of the Schoolmistresses' Association, with some addresses marked, & two of the papers issued by the Association, which may give you some idea of the way of thinking that prevails among its members.
    Of the names that I have marked I should perhaps put Miss Buss's school highest, if not *too* large. It is a dayschool of 400 girls, with boarding houses attached. Miss Buss's own house is near Primrose Hill. I think there are about 30 girls in it. As to the arrangements for daily baths &c., you could see & judge

for yourself. One of the best of the Girton Students is an Assn. Mistress in the school & lives in the house, helping to take care of the girls. Miss Buss finds her a very valuable ally. I think the teaching might be relied upon in all the schools that I have marked. Miss Brown's is perhaps the least advanced, tho' she is herself so intelligent & sensible that I think it must be fairly good. All that I have named are Churchwomen, of I should say a thoughtful & liberal cast, except Miss Janion who is I believe a Wesleyan, but of a very enlightened type. I have specially liked both Miss Janion & Miss Leighton, judging by what I have seen of them during a sort of professional acquaintance of many years' standing. Their schools may however be smaller than you would like. The Miss Metcalfes have sixty, all boarders. A young friend of the Aldridges' is there, & I believe she & her family are quite satisfied with the school.

I suppose you would write for circulars & then see the people, before coming to any decision. I always hesitate in recommending *too* confidently, because I have little means of judging beyond what I know of the mistresses personally, & that is not knowing the *school*. I mean this as to the tone among the girls, &c. Of the teaching one can judge to a considerable extent by the results of examns. I hope you may be successful in your search, which must be a somewhat anxious one.

Ever yours truly
Emily Davies

GC: ALS ED ADD NL 3

To Barbara Bodichon

GIRTON COLLEGE, | CAMBRIDGE. | 17, CUNNINGHAM PLACE. N.W.

Oct. 16. | [1875]

Dear Mrs. Bodichon

Would you please read the enclosed. Miss Chessar is on the School Board, & in other ways a most valuable person. I am giving her an introduction to Miss Thurshaw, who is in Town now & will be able to help her with recent experience. If you can ^{by introductions or} in any other way, help her, I shall be glad & obliged.

I went to Girton on Monday for the beginning of Term & left it on Thursday in a most cheerful & promising condition, Miss Bernard setting to work in good heart & great rejoicing going on over the increase of numbers.

There are 23 Students in residence now, & according to present intentions, there will be 21 coming back next October, i.e. one more than we can properly accommodate, without any new ones, & without counting two probable Assn. Lecturers. Miss Arthur now hopes to stay on for a full course, & is setting to work at preparation for the Little-go, with a view to the Moral Sciences Tripos. Every Lecturer that we wanted is able to come & to give as much time as is necessary.

The 3 candidates all passed the Entrance Examn. but Miss ⟨Anna⟩ Tuthill, of San Francisco, will by my suggestion, spend the winter at some warm place & enter at Easter. She had a cough & looked I thought unfit to begin work in cold climate & she thought herself that she would start at better advantage in the Spring.

When shall you be at hand for a Committee meeting? We ought to have one as soon as we can after Oct. 26. When Lady S. is to be back.

Yr. affecn.
ED.

GC: ALS ED B142

To Barbara Bodichon

GIRTON COLLEGE, CAMBRIDGE. | 17, CUNNINGHAM PLACE. N.W.

Oct. 23. 1875

Dear Mrs. Bodichon

I think we can have the meeting at 3 on Nov. 8 & I hope this will make it possible for you to come. I suppose you are not likely to be coming up for a day before then? Miss Manning & I should like to have a talk with you about the building scheme.[1] We think that when we are about it, it ought to be on a tolerably large scale, to meet the immediate need & a little more, so as not to have to begin again at the whole thing the next year. But for this it would be necessary to have the scheme worked by the Committee as a body, & this is incompatible with the plan of attaching my name to some part of the fund—unless I were to resign the Secretaryship, which would I am afraid be inconvenient.

Should you mind withdrawing the testimonial part of the scheme? I do not see that there need be any difficulty about it, as it has not been made public, & in fact I suppose not half the Committee have heard of it.

Lady Goldsmid might perhaps not care to give her £200, but the loss would be more than made up by the advantage of being able to work freely on a broad basis, applying to City Companies &c. I do not suppose we should get at once all the money that would be wanted, but we could borrow part, & pay the interest out of profits. I think it is more desirable to extend our number, even from the commercial point of view as it brings in more people who may become contributors. We are ready now to pay off the £1000 as soon as ever the mortgagee will take it, & the debt to the Guarantors is reduced to £3000. So we are making way in getting rid of the existing debt.

It would be a relief to me if you & Lady Stanley could agree to withdraw the proposal of a testimonial before the meeting, & it would save the Committee from an uncomfortable dilemma. As it stands, they would have to choose between declining the proposal, or accepting it while it was clear that it would stand in the way of a necessary development. I should think it might easily be explained to the three or four people who are concerned that complications have arisen which were not foreseen when the proposal was first made. Miss Manning had an idea of in some way setting apart the £1000 that has been promised, but it will not work. We have talked it over & it will not do.

I rather think Lady Stanley is at St. Leonard's with an invalid friend, so perhaps you may be able to see her. I am writing to her about this matter. If you can get it settled, I will try to have some sort of plan ready to submit to the Committee on the 8th. If the rooms are to be ready for next year's Students, we have no time to lose.

It is very pleasant to hear of Lady Herschel's warm approval of the College.
Ever yr. affecn.
E. Davies

GC: ALS ED B143

1. In 1875, Girton College established a Building Committee to raise funds and to plan extending the college premises. The next stage of building began in 1876 when the original building, known as the Old Wing, was extended to the west and two lecture rooms, a classroom, and eight sets of student rooms were built.

To Barbara Bodichon

~~Monday.~~ | Wednesday. ⟨October/November 1875⟩

Dear Mrs. Bodichon

I am glad to have your letter & one from Lady S⟨tanley⟩. to the same effect.

You will see that I have named *five* for the Committee. It seems doubtful whether you can come in any case, & I am unwilling to alter time or place except for some very strong reason.

The ᵉᵃʳˡʸ afternoon is a very awkward time for men, & as we want them to come, we must consider their convenience. I think too it would be of as much use, or more, for me to see you *before* the meeting. I do not understand your objection to lengthening the corridor, & I should like to talk it over with you, with the plans before us—& to propound my views for the remote, as well as the near, future. I have no objection to Mrs. Tubbs' seeing my letter.

I suppose it would not help you, as to coming up, to have a bed here? We have one to spare while Jane Crow is away.

Lady S. is at St. Leonard's till Nov. 3. but does not say where.
Yr. affecn.
ED.

GC: ALS ED B144

To Barbara Bodichon

GIRTON COLLEGE, CAMBRIDGE. | 17, CUNNINGHAM PLACE. N.W.

Nov. 5. [1875?]

Dear Mrs. Bodichon

Miss Lawrence has just been here bringing the enclosed cheque. I promised to return it to you with a message that she wishes to give it to the building. You will see that the plan for additions includes a staircase, which I suppose removes the fire objection to lengthening the corridor. Have you any other?

According to the Plan, we continue our present line for 3 more pairs of Students' room $^{\text{per story.}}$ Then comes necessarily before turning the corner, a square space, to be occupied by a new staircase. then 4 more pairs of Students' rooms per story. Only that the two ^{pairs} on the ground.floor which would respectively meet the staircase at the corner, we propose to make Lecture-rooms, as we already rather want them, & it is well to utilise some of the groundfloor, in a quiet spot, for that purpose. I sent the Plan to Miss Bernard, to see if she had anything to suggest. She likes it much. It has been ascertained by digging that the gravel extends to the limits of the proposed extension, which will be within about 7 ft. of the road which crosses our field. Mr. W. estimates the cost of building at £4.800, & we must allow £1200 for additional furniture &c. The reason for proposing this number of rooms is that just up to this limit, & no farther, we can do without a new "Gyp-wing." We can reduce by cutting off either one or two sets per story, if the scheme is considered too large.

Ever yr. affecn.
ED.

Mr. W. said we cd. have either a wooden or stone staircase. & either sash or casement windows. If the latter, they must of course open outwards. I do not know whether these points will have to be decided on Monday. A wooden staircase wd. be a little the cheapest.

GC: ALS ED B145

To Dr. William Carpenter

Nov. 9 1875

Sir

I am desired ^(to ask you to be good enough to) to make application on behalf of ^(the Ex. Com: of) Girton College ~~for~~ ^(to) the ~~renewa~~ Trustees of the G⟨ilchrist⟩. Ed⟨ucation⟩. Fund for ^(the gift of) a Scholarship tenable at the College for three years & awarded in connexion with the L⟨ondon⟩.U⟨niversity⟩. Gen. Examn. of Women, as in the case of the ~~two~~ Scholarships already conferred by the Trustees on students of G⟨irton⟩.C⟨ollege⟩.

The Com: venture to express the hope that as the Coll: is now established on a secure basis, having been at work for 6 years, & formally incorporated for mo three years, the ^(annual) offer of the Gilchrist Scholarships may ~~also~~ be made permanent, so that promising candidates may ~~be encouraged to~~ have sufficient notice of it to spend a fair share of time on preparation.

I am also desired to request you to ~~b~~ ^(have the) goodness to lay before the Trustees the needs of Girton College as regards books & scientific apparatus. The College Library ~~I~~ is almost entirely composed of gifts presented from time to time by individuals & it is deficient on the scientific side. There is also an immediate want of ~~a supply of~~ scientific apparatus for the use of Students of Chemistry & Physiology. There has been an increase ~~during~~ this ~~present~~ Term ~~of~~ ^(in) the number of Students, who are taking up Natural Sciences, causing requirements which the ~~very~~ limited resources of the College make it difficult to meet. Some of the Students ~~of the College~~ are in a position to ~~provide for~~ ^(supply) their own wants, but there are others, especially those who are intending hereafter to become ~~professional~~ teachers, to whom the difficulty of procuring costly scientific ~~apparatus~~ ^(appliances) must be a serious hindrance ~~to progress~~, unless ~~it can~~ what is needed can be provided for them while pursuing their course of study.

ED
Hon Sec

GC: DALS ED AR 2/6/14c

To Barbara Bodichon

GIRTON COLLEGE, CAMBRIDGE. | 17, CUNNINGHAM PLACE. N.W.

Dec. 10. 1875

Dear Mrs. Bodichon

I was very sorry to receive your note on Wednesday morning. Miss Metcalfe has written to me since enclosing notes from yourself & Lady Stanley. Your own might seem almost to imply that Lady Stanley was empowered to appoint members of the Sub. Committee. As you know, this was not the case. The Sub. Committee of three were formally appointed & we had no power given to us, either individually or collectively, to add to our number. It puts a Secretary into a very awkward position, when members of a Committee take matters into their own hands & act without regard to the decisions of the Committee. I suppose it might be considered my official duty to report what has taken place & bring the matter before the Committee, but I should prefer to avoid, if possible, an uncomfortable discussion, & I am telling Lady Stanley that as no votes were taken & Miss Metcalfe's presence made no difference in any conclusion arrived at, I think it might be treated as an accidental circumstance, & if you both wish it, I would say nothing about it. But in that case I should wish to have some sort of understanding that what has been done will not be made a precedent. You will I hope feel that this is reasonable. I do not see how a Committee can work if its members are not prepared to abide by its decisions & it seems to be specially the duty of a Secretary to take care that the business is carried on in conformity with the instructions given.

There will of course be no hesitation in putting Miss Metcalf on the Sub. Committee if she is well enough to attend & I have told her that I shall myself be glad to propose the addition of her name at the next meeting of the Executive Committee.

Yours affectionately
Emily Davies.

GC: ALS ED B146

To Barbara Bodichon

GIRTON COLLEGE, CAMBRIDGE. | 17, CUNNINGHAM PLACE. N.W.

Dec. 19 | [1875]

Dear Mrs. Bodichon

I ought to have told you yesterday that Miss Minturn does not wish her name mentioned in connexion with the proposed Scholarship.[1] She did not like her former gift having been noticed in the papers.

I think it will be best to say nothing ^{beyond ourselves} about this £2000 till the Sub. Committee have reported & some decision has been come to.

If you come across devotees of Natural Science who support Newnham in preference to Girton, they might be asked, what has Newnham done for the encouragement of Natural Science, & informed that already two Certificated Students of Girton have been teaching it for a year. (Miss Dove & Miss Kingsland) & are going on. This is besides Miss Gamble, who has done something, & the others who are coming on.

Let them ask Dr. M. Foster, Mr. ⟨Henry⟩ Martin, Mr. Hicks, &c., whether their pupils belonged to Girton or Newnham.

Mr. Jodrell might perhaps be got to give some apparatus.

Yr. affecn.

ED.

GC: ALS ED B147

1. Minturn had been a pupil of Jane Agnes Chessar, and in 1876 she established the J. A. Chessar Classics Scholarship.

To Barbara Bodichon

GIRTON COLLEGE, CAMBRIDGE. | 17, CUNNINGHAM PLACE. N.W.

Dec. 29. | [1875]

Dear Mrs. Bodichon

The Girton Students whose homes are in or near London are Misses ⟨Alice⟩ Betham, ⟨Amy⟩ Mantle, ⟨Frances⟩ Müller, ⟨Annie⟩ Wallis, ⟨Jessie⟩ Gill, ⟨Janet⟩ Wood, & ⟨Esther⟩ Case. I do not know whether they are at home or whether any others may be staying in Town.

I hope you will not mind my not going to your parties. I have made a rule not to go anywhere, & it is awkward to make exceptions. You will wonder why I am giving up society, so I had better explain that ~~there~~ I prefer other ways of spending my money, which is not redundant, & also I do not care to undergo the fatigue. I went a few weeks ago under urgent persuasion to a party at Miss Mannings's & it tired me so much that it took two days to get over it.

Miss Minturn's Scholarship business is in the hands of the Sub. Committee, to which it was referred. I am asking Mr. Roby whether there is any chance of their being ready to report during the first half of January. We must have a Committee meeting before very long. I do not expect to hear anything from any City Company till after Jan. 5.

I thought over your idea of a drawingroom meeting at Lady Stanley's, & I think if she is inclined to take the trouble of it, it would certainly be helpful to the College. I do not know whether there is any distinctive way of arranging such meetings. Except those we had at Mrs. Russell Gurney's & the Kennedys, I only remember being present at one, & then I had the misfortune to be in the Chair. It was for the Franchise & was like a public meeting, except that people had tea offered them in another room as they went away.

Yours affectionately

ED.

GC: ALS ED B148

Biographical Register

When we are reasonably certain of the identity of a person mentioned in the letters, the first name of that person appears in angle brackets ⟨ ⟩ after the first reference in the letters. Biographical information for these people is listed in this biographical register. When the identity of a name mentioned in a letter is not conclusive, a footnote provides our best guess as to the probable first name and brief biographical information for that person. Names of people for whom we could not find plausible identities are not listed in the register or footnoted in the letters.

In many cases—especially for women and for servants—we have not been able to locate any biographical information. Wives of all social classes, including the aristocracy, are usually erased in standard biographical resources, their identities subsumed by that of their husbands, while unmarried women who were neither wealthy nor published authors are also often invisible in the public record. In addition, many of the actual sources of biographical information for women differ significantly from those for men, and their style and content are also distinctly different. Pratt, Bose, and the older *Dictionary of National Biography* list public schools, universities, and public accomplishments, while obituaries in the *Englishwoman's Review* describe personal lives and personalities. Gender and class thus shape and determine the kind and extent of biographical information available. For example, Anglican men are better represented in biographical references than many Dissenters, and even the feminist work of many of the men of all religions who were active in the women's movement of the nineteenth century is frequently erased in standard biographical references. Thus the nature and extent of information available differs widely according to gender, marital status, class, and religion.

Names of women, married or single, are listed as they initially or primarily appear in the letters. Thus Isa Craig is listed under "Craig" with a cross-reference under her married name, Knox, since she appears initially and most often as Craig rather than Knox in the letters. And Barbara Leigh Smith Bodichon is listed under "Bodichon," since that is the name by which Davies knew and wrote to her.

Acland, Sir Thomas Dyke (1809–98). Christ Church, Oxford; Fellow, All Souls' College; Conservative M.P. from West Somerset until 1846; worked for the journal for Bath and West of England Society; helped establish Oxford Local Examinations system; member, Local Examinations Committee in Exeter; member, Schools Inquiry Commission; proponent of separate exams for girls.

Adams, John Couch (1819–92). Astronomer, Fellow, and Tutor, St. John's College, Cambridge; Fellow, Pembroke College; discovered information about planet Neptune; catalogued Newton's unpublished writings.

Aitken, Rose (1848–1923). The College for Women, Hitchin, 1871–75; Classical Tripos, 1875; Classics Mistress, North London Collegiate School for Girls; Assistant Mistress, Redlands High School for Girls, later Cavendish House School.

Alcock, Rutherford (1809–97). King's College, London; surgeon, Marine Brigade in Portugal; consul-general, Japan; envoy to China; wrote books on Japanese grammar and culture; president, Royal Geographical Society; investigated London smallpox and fever hospitals.

Alford, Henry (1810–71). Trinity College, Cambridge; Hulsean Lecturer, Cambridge; examiner in logic and natural philosophy, University of London; published poetry and an edition of Greek Testament; edited *Contemporary Review*; wrote for *Good Words* and *Sunday Magazine*; dean of Canterbury, 1857; published sermons, hymns, and classics translations; original member, Executive Committee, the College for Women.

Amos, Sarah McLardie (1833–1908). Born in Manchester; member, National Society for Women's Suffrage; married Sheldon Amos, 1870/71.

Amos, Sheldon (1835–86/87). Clare College, Cambridge; called to bar, 1862; wrote for *Westminster Review*; lecturer, Working Men's College, London; examiner in law and history, University of London; early member, Women's Suffrage Committee; opponent of C.D. Acts; wrote *Difference of Sex as a Topic of Jurisprudence and Legislation*.

Anderson, Elizabeth Garrett. See Garrett, Elizabeth.

Anderson, James George Skelton (?–1907). Raised in Scotland; worked in London for shipping firm that became Orient Line in 1878; married Elizabeth Garrett, 1871; helped direct her campaign for the London School Board; served on the College Committee; alderman and mayor of Aldeburgh.

Angus, Joseph (1816–?). Edinburgh University; minister, New Park Street Baptist Church, Southwark; secretary, Baptist Missionary Society; president, Stepney College; examiner in English, University of London and Indian Civil Service; member, first London School Board.

Argyll, Elizabeth Georgiana Campbell (?). Wife of George John Douglass Campbell, eighth duke of Argyll; married in 1844.

Arnold, Matthew (1822–88). Son of Thomas Arnold; educated at Rugby and Balliol College, Oxford; poet, literary and social critic, and religious and educational writer; published *Strayed Reveler*, 1849, *Poems*, 1853; elected professor of poetry at Oxford, 1857; published *Culture and Anarchy* (1869) and *Essays in Criticism* (1888); served as schools inspector; married Frances Lucy Wrightman.

Arthur, Jessie Mary Louisa (1855–89). Girton College, 1874–77; Moral Science Tripos, 1877; studied philosophy in Glasgow with Professor Caird; taught scripture, Devonport High School.

Austin, Annie Crow/Crowe (?). Sister of Jane Crow; attended Miss Brownings' School, Blackheath; with Davies began weekly reading meeting and classes for servants; member, House Committee preparing the house at Hitchin; Mistress, the College for Women, 1870–72.

Bagehot, Walter (1826–77). Economist and journalist; University College, London; wrote for *Inquirer* and *National Review*; edited and managed the *Economist*, established by James Wilson, whose eldest daughter, Eliza Wilson, he married; authority on banking and finance; literary critic.

Bain, Alexander (1818–?). Marischal College; wrote for *Westminster Review*; assistant secretary, Metropolitan Sanitary Commission; examiner in logic and moral philosophy, University of London; chair of Logic, Aberdeen; examiner, India Civil Service Examinations; published *The Minor Works of George Grote*; wrote biographies of James Mill and John Stuart Mill.

Baker, Eliza (1854–1924). North London Collegiate School for Girls; received the Certificate of Proficiency in political economy from the College for Women at Hitchin and Girton, 1876; Special Examination in History, 1877; Assistant Mistress, Highfield School; Senior Assistant Mistress, Bedford High School; married John Lewis.

Banks, Isabella Varley (1821–97). Wrote for *Manchester Guardian*; ran girls' school in Cheetham; member of Ladies' Committee of Anti-Corn Law League; published stories and novels, including *The Manchester Man*.

Barlee, Ellen (?). Wrote on labor and feminist issues, including *Friendless and Helpless*; *Sketches of Working-Women*; *Locked Out: A Tale for the Strike*; and *Life of Napoleon*.

Bastard, Thomas Horlock (1796–1898). Studied school systems in other countries and ran a middle-class school in Blandford; wrote *Scepticism and Social Justice*.

Beale, Anna Chrysogon (1835/36–1917). Sister of Dorothea Beale; taught at Cheltenham School; wrote on Froebel system of kindergarten teaching; member, Society for Promoting the Employment of Women; read paper at NAPSS.

Beale, Dorothea (1831–1906). Queen's College; principal, Cheltenham Ladies' College; leader in women's educational movement; testified before Schools Inquiry Commission; active in Headmistresses Association; vice president, Central Society for Women's Suffrage.

Becker, Lydia (1827–90). Secretary, Manchester Women's Suffrage Committee (later Manchester National Society for Women's Suffrage); wrote article on women's suffrage in *Contemporary Review*; elected to Manchester School Board.

Beesly, Edward Spencer (1831–?). Wadham College, Oxford; Assistant Master, Marlborough College; professor of history, University College, London; professor of Latin, Bedford College; wrote pamphlet on positivism; helped translate Comte.

Bennett, William Sterndale (1816–75). Composer and conductor; studied at Royal Academy of Music; taught at Royal Academy, London; conducted Philharmonic Society; professor of music, Cambridge; examiner in music, 1863 University Examinations.

Bernard, Marianne Frances (1839?–1926). Home and Colonial Training College; lived in India; Mistress, Girton College, 1875–84; member of College and Executive Committee; life governor, Girton College; married Dr. Peter Wallwork Latham.

Bernard, Montague (1820–82). Trinity College, Oxford, Scholar and Fellow; called to bar, 1844; Chichele Professor International Law and Diplomacy, Oxford, 1859; assesssor of Chancellor's Court, Oxford; cofounded and edited the *Guardian*; member, University of Oxford Commission, 1877.

Betham, Alice Barbara (Mrs. MacKenzie) (?). Girton College, 1873–76; Ordinary Degree standard in history, 1876; literary assistant to director-general of statistics for India.

Betham-Edwards, Matilda (1836–1919). Writer and poet; wrote about France for *Daily News*; published *A Winter with the Swallows* (1866); *Through Spain to the Sahara* (1867); and *Kitty* (1869), among others.

Bicknell, Herman (1830–75). University College, London; Royal College of Surgeons; served in India as army surgeon; lived in Middle East, including Algiers; made pilgrimage to Mecca; climbed mountains in Switzerland; translated Persian poet Hafiz.

Blackwell, Elizabeth (1821–1910). Born in Bristol, England; moved to New York, 1831; studied medicine in New York, Paris, and England; first English woman physician; opened clinic in New York with sister Emily, also a physician; returned to England, opened private practice, and lectured on medical philosophy.

Blackwell, Emily (1826–1910). Born in Bristol, England; received M.D. from Western Reserve University, Cleveland, 1854; cofounded with sister Elizabeth the first women's hospital in the United States; dean, Women's Medical College.

Blake, Barnett (1812?–66). Editor, *Exeter and Plymouth Gazette*; secretary, Exeter Literary and Scientific Institution; edited and managed *Liverpool Standard*; secretary, Yorkshire Union of Mechanics' Institutes; secretary, West Riding Educational Board.

Blake, Sophia. See Jex-Blake, Sophia.

Blumenthal, Leonie (?). Wife of Jacques Blumenthal (1829–1908); pianist to the queen; fashionable music teacher and composer.

Blythe, Isabella (?). Bedford College; lifelong companion to Nannie Leigh Smith; founding member, Portfolio Club; active in Langham Place; signed suffrage petition of 1866.

Bodichon, Barbara Leigh Smith (1827–91). Oldest daughter of Benjamin Smith and common-law wife, Anne Longden; wrote *A Brief Summary, in Plain Lan-*

guage, of the Most Important Laws Concerning Women; with Elizabeth Whitehead (Malleson) established Portman Hall School; with Bessie Rayner Parkes founded and published the *English Woman's Journal*; wrote on women's rights and suffrage, education, and slavery in *Macmillan's* and the *English Woman's Journal*; landscape painter with work shown at Royal Academy and French Gallery; one of the principal contributors to Girton College; married Eugene Bodichon from Algeria.

Bodichon, Eugene (1810–85). Born in Brittany; trained as physician in Paris; went to Algiers as an army surgeon, 1836; elected chamber of deputies for Algeria; helped abolish slavery there; wrote *Considérations sur l'Algérie* (1845), *De l'Humanité* (1851–52), and articles on Algiers; practiced medicine among the poor; married Barbara Leigh Smith, 1857.

Bodley, Thomas (1825–?). Queen's College, Cambridge; served as secretary of London Local Examinations.

Borchardt, Louis (1813–83). Born in Prussia; settled in Manchester; physician at Children's Hospital; founding member of Manchester National Suffrage Society.

Borchardt, Malvina Henrietta (?–1916). Daughter of Louis Borchardt; Girton College, 1873–77; College Scholar; Mathematical and Moral Science Tripos, 1877; taught at Hackney and Maida Vale High Schools; Headmistress, Devonport High School for Girls; studied girls' education in Germany; opened hostel for women students, Gower Street.

Bostock, Elizabeth Ann (1817–98). Helped Elizabeth Reid open Bedford College; served as Lady Visitor and Reid Trustee; involved in Cambridge Local Exams and Schools Inquiry Commission campaigns; oversaw Bedford College's move to York Place in 1874.[1]

Boucherett, Jessie (1825–1905). Worked for Society for Promoting the Employment of Women (SPEW); member, Kensington Society; supporter of women's suffrage movement; advocate for Married Women's Property Act; wrote *Hints on Self-Help for Young Women* and *The Condition of Women in France*; helped revive the *English Woman's Journal*, changing it to the *Englishwoman's Review*.

Bowling, Edward Woodley (1837–?). St. John's College, Cambridge, Scholar, Fellow; Assistant Master, Bromsgrove School; wrote light verse; contributed to *Punch* and the *Globe*; member, Alpine Club.

Bradley, Reverend George Granville (1821–1903). University College, Oxford; pupil of Dean Stanley; Assistant Master, Rugby; Headmaster, Marlborough College; educational reformer at Marlborough; Master, University College, Oxford; dean of Westminster; married Marian Jane Philpott.

Brassey, Baron Thomas (1836–1918). Son of prominent civil engineer and railway builder; University College, Oxford; called to bar; M.P. for Hastings; civil lord of admiralty, 1880; secretary to admiralty, 1884; took voyage around the world with his wife on their yacht; wrote on sea and naval issues; became peer in 1886; married (first) Anna Allnutt, (second) Sybil de Vere Capell.

Brodie, Sir Benjamin Collins (1817–80). Eldest son of Sir Benjamin C. Brodie; a surgeon; Balliol College, Oxford; Waynflete Professor of Chemistry, Oxford University; president of Chemical Society.

Brougham, Lord Henry (1778–1868). University of Edinburgh; wrote for *Edinburgh Review*; moved to England; called to bar, Lincoln's Inn; Whig M.P.; worked against slavery; attorney-general for Queen Caroline in divorce proceedings; introduced legislation for education for poor; wrote books and periodical articles; contributed to Mechanics' Institutes; cofounded the Society for the Diffusion of Useful Knowledge; supported London University and NAPSS.

Brown, Elizabeth Alba Grant (1856–1942). Girton College, 1874–77; College Scholar; Ordinary Degree standard in Chemistry, 1877; studied painting, Slade School; linguist skilled in French, German, Cingalese, and Russian; married Henry Leighton Crawford, 1885.

Bryce, James (1838–1922). Trinity College, Oxford; called to bar, Lincoln's Inn; assistant commissioner, Schools Inquiry Commission; Regius Professor of Civil Law, Oxford; elected to Parliament; worked on Ireland, university reform, and abolition of university tests; member, Girton College, 1872–1922; married Elizabeth Marion Ashton of Manchester.

Bulley, Agnes Amy (1852–1939). The College for Women at Hitchin and Girton, 1871–73; Newnham College, 1873–74; Moral Sciences Tripos, 1874; M.A. in 1928; Assistant Mistress, Manchester High School; secretary, Manchester and Salford College for Women; worked for women's suffrage and in women's labor movement.

Bullock, Reverend William Thomas (1818–79). Magdalen Hall, Oxford; secretary, Society for Propagation of the Gospel; chaplain, Kensington Palace; prebendary, St. Paul's; wrote and published sermons and theological articles; contributed to Smith's *Dictionary of the Bible*.

Burbury, Charlotte Kennedy (?–1895). Daughter of B. H. Kennedy; lived in London: member, executive committee, SPEW; secretary, Cambridge Local Exams and London National Society for Women's Suffrage; governor, London School of Medicine for Women and North London Collegiate School; ran unsuccessfully for London School Board, 1876; trustee, Camden School for Girls; member, NAPSS; married William Burbury, Master, Shrewsbury School.

Burgess, Elizabeth Lucy (1855–1918). Girton College, 1873–77; Ordinary Degree standard in theology, 1878; married Arthur Richardson, 1879.

Burgess, Mary Ann (1857–1947). Studied at North London Collegiate School; Girton College, 1877–79; Special Examination in theology, 1879; Ordinary Degree standard, 1880; did social and charitable work; married Arnold Joseph Wallis, c. 1880.

Burdett Coutts, Angela. See Coutts, Angela Burdett.

Buss, Frances Mary (1827–94). Queen's College; Headmistress, North London Collegiate School; active in movement to open University Local Exams to girls; gave evidence to the Schools Inquiry Commission; helped form Association of Headmistresses, Maria Grey Training College, and Teachers' Guild.

Butler, George (1819–90). Anglican priest and classicist; principal, Liverpool College; married Josephine Grey, 1852; active supporter of his wife's activities.

Butler, Henry Montague (1833–1918). Trinity College, Cambridge; Headmaster, Harrow School; dean of Gloucester; helped start college for working men at Cambridge; advocate of University Extension efforts and Workers' Educational Association; member, Council of Girton College; supporter of admitting women to university degrees, 1897; married (first) Georgina Isabella Elliot, (second) Agnata Ramsay (who scored First Class Honors in classics from Girton, 1887).

Butler, Josephine Grey (1828–1906). Worked among prostitutes in Liverpool; opened refuge for homeless women; signed first petition for women's suffrage, 1866; president, North of England Council for the Higher Education of Women; edited *Woman's Work and Woman's Culture*; active in Ladies' National Association for Repeal of C.D. Acts.

Buxton, Charles (1822–71). Trinity College, Cambridge; partner, Truman, Hanbury, Buxton, & Company; member of Parliament, 1857; worked with J. S. Mill to form the Jamaica Committee; wrote pamphlets on education in Ireland, slavery in West Indies, and temperance; published *The Ideas of the Day on Policy* and *Notes of Thought*.

Cairnes, John Elliott (1823/24–75). Trinity College, Dublin; called to Irish bar; Whately Professor of Political Economy, Trinity College, Dublin; published *Character and Logical Method of Political Economy* and *The Slave Power* and wrote for periodicals; professor of political economy, Queen's College, Galway.

Campion, William Magan (1820–96). Queen's College, Cambridge, Fellow, Mathematical Lecturer, dean, and president; member, first Council of Senate at Cambridge; honorary canon of Ely; edited book of prayer, 1866.

Carpenter, William Benjamin (1813–85). Brother of Mary Carpenter; Bristol School of Medicine; University College, London; member, College of Surgeons; president, Royal Medical Society; Fullerian Professor of Physiology, Royal Institution; examiner in physiology, University of London; Swiney Lecturer on Geology, British Museum; editor, *British and Foreign Medical Review*; registrar, University of London; secretary and administrator, Gilchrist Trust.

Cartmell, James William (1842–1918). Christ's College, Cambridge, Fellow, Tutor, and Senior Proctor; member, Modern Language Association, Oxford and Cambridge Examinations Board, and Local Examinations Syndicate.

Case, Esther Maria (1857–1939). Girton College, 1875–79; Classical Tripos in 1879; M.A., Trinity College, Dublin, 1907; Assistant Mistress, the School at St.

Andrews, Bedford Park School, Chiswick High School; Headmistress, Chiswick High School; Assistant Mistress, Streatham Hill; joint Headmistress, Chantry Mount School.

Chadwick, Edwin (1800–90). Called to bar in 1830; assistant commissioner, Commission of Inquiry into Poor Laws, 1832; secretary, Poor Law Board; wrote *The Sanitary Conditions of the Labouring Classes*; appointed, Metropolitan Sanitary Commission; member, General Board of Health; published reports on sanitation and poor law issues.

Chalker, Alfred Ball (1828?–88). Emmanuel College, Cambridge; deacon, priest in Ely; inspector of schools for Rochester; chaplain to bishop of Carlisle.

Challis, James (1803–82). Trinity College, Cambridge, Fellow until his marriage in 1831; Plumian Professor of Astronomy and Experimental Philosophy; director of Cambridge Observatory; wrote astronomical observations and scientific memoirs.

Chapman, Frederic (1823–95). Entered publishing house of Chapman and Hall in 1842, became partner, 1847, head of firm, 1864; began *Fortnightly Review*.

Charles, Albert Onesiphorus (1830–88). Clerk in church missionary society; secretary, Reformatory and Refuge Union; cofounder, Home for Little Boys at Tottenham, and secretary there until his death; wrote *The Female Mission to the Fallen* and *A Visit to the Irish Convict Prisons*.

Cheetham, Samuel (1827–1908). Christ's College, Cambridge; vice principal, Collegiate Institute in Liverpool; vice principal, Theological College, Chichester; professor of pastoral theology at King's College, London; chaplain, Dulwich College; Hulsean Lecturer at Cambridge; coedited *Dictionary of Christian Antiquities*.

Chessar, Jane Agnes (1835–80). Born in Edinburgh; educated at private schools in Scotland; trained and later taught at Home and Colonial Training College; taught for National Health Society; lectured at girls' schools; helped edit Mary Somerville's work on physical geography; member, London School Board, 1873.

Clark, Sir Andrew (1826–93). Member, Royal College of Surgeons and London College of Physicians; medical advisor to Gladstone; specialized in treatment of digestive and respiratory problems; married (first) Seton Mary Percy Foster, (second) Helen Doxat.

Clark, Edwin Charles (1835/36–1917). Trinity College, Cambridge, Scholar and Fellow; Professional Fellow, St. John's; early lecturer at the College for Women; called to bar, Lincoln's Inn; Regius Professor of Civil Law, Cambridge; examiner, University of London; wrote on law and classical history.

Clay, Walter Lowe (1833–75). Emmanuel College, Cambridge; minister in Lancaster; visited and wrote about prisons; minister at Holy Trinity, Coventry, and Christ Church, Marylebone, London; secretary, NAPSS conference at Manchester, 1866.

Clough, Anne Jemima (1820–92). Daughter of James Butler Clough; sister of Arthur Clough; attended first meeting of London Association of Schoolmistresses; helped start similar society in Liverpool; cofounder, secretary, and president, North of England Council; principal, Newnham College.

Cobbe, Frances Power (1822–1904). Anglo-Irish journalist, philanthropist, and advocate of women's rights; wrote about women's education, suffrage, employment, and domestic violence; activist in antivivisection movement; founded Victoria Street Society for Protection of Animals from Vivisection.

Cook, Harriet (?–1869). Daughter of Reverend John Cook of St. Andrews; sister of Rachel Cook; member, Kensington Society; signed 1866 women's suffrage petition; secretary for the suffrage petition activities with Louisa Garrett Smith; assistant to Emily Davies.

Cook, Rachel Susan (1848–1905). Daughter of Reverend John Cook of St. Andrews; sister of Harriet Cook; one of the pioneers at the College for Women, Hitchin, 1869–73; Classical Tripos, 1873; member, Girton College and Committee of Manchester High School for Girls; spoke on social, educational, and political issues; supported women's suffrage; wrote for the *Manchester Guardian*; published edition of Tacitus; married Charles Prestwich Scott of the *Manchester Guardian*.

Cookson, Henry Wilkinson (1810–76). St. Peter's College, Cambridge, Tutor, Fellow, and Master of St. Peter's and vice chancellor of the university; member of Council of Senate; president, Cambridge Philosophical Society.

Cotton, Sophia Anne Tomkinson (fl. 1845–70). Sister of Henry Tomkinson; married G. E. Lynch Cotton in 1845; wrote a memoir of him in 1871—including selections from his journal and letters—describing their life in India.

Courtauld, Samuel (1793–1881). Head of Courtauld & Co., crape manufacturers; married Ellen Taylor, who signed the 1866 suffrage petition; one of three founding male members of the *English Woman's Journal*; member, Manchester Society for Women's Suffrage, and Radical Club, London.

Courtney, Leonard Henry (1832–1918). St. John's College, Cambridge; called to bar, Lincoln's Inn; wrote for the *Times*, and pamphlets on statistics and finance; professor of political economy, University College, London; elected to Parliament; advocate for women's rights; member, Girton College.

Coutts, Angela Burdett (1814–1906). Heiress who devoted enormous wealth to philanthropy: churches, schools, working-class housing, and shelters and reform programs for prostitutes.

Craig, Isa (1831–1903). Wrote for the *Scotsman* in Edinburgh; secretary and literary assistant to NAPSS; member, Langham Place Circle; wrote poems and essays; joined the Ladies' Sanitary Association; began Telegraph School to instruct women in use of new technology; founding member, University Exams Committee; member, Kensington Society and 1866–67 Women's Suffrage Committee; married John Knox, her cousin.

Crockford, John (1823–65). Published numerous journals, including the *Law Times* and the *Critic*; manager, the *Field*; published the *Clerical Directory*, a biographical and statistical book of reference for Anglican clergy and church.

Crompton, Charles John (1797–1865). Father of Mary Crompton (Mrs. Llewelyn Davies); Trinity College, Dublin; Inner Temple, Court of Exchequer and Court of Passage at Liverpool; Justice of Court of Queen's Bench.

Crompton, Caroline. See Robertson, Caroline Croom.

Crosskey, Henry William (1826–93). Manchester College; Unitarian minister in Birmingham; member, Birmingham School Board and National Education League; wrote books on religion and science.

Crow/Crowe, Jane (1828/31–?). Miss Brownings' School, Blackheath (where she met Elizabeth Garrett); secretary, Society for Promoting the Employment of Women; member, Kensington Society.

Darwin, Charles (1809–82). Son of Robert Darwin; grandson of Erasmus Darwin; studied at Edinburgh University and Christ's College, Cambridge; left on voyage on the *Beagle*, 1831; published on geology and zoology, most notably *On the Origin of the Species*, 1859.

Davenport, Florence Hill. See Hill, Florence Davenport.

Davenport, Rosamond. See Hill, Rosamond Davenport.

Davey, Lord Horace (1833–?). University College, Oxford, Fellow, Senior Mathematical Scholar, and Eldon Law Scholar; called to bar, Lincoln's Inn; member of Parliament and solicitor general under Gladstone; married to Louisa Donkin.

Davies, Reverend J. Llewelyn (1826–1916). Brother of Emily Davies; Trinity College, Cambridge; rector, Christ Church, St. Marylebone; represented Marylebone on London School Board; principal, Queen's College, Harley Street; honorary chaplain to queen; ally of Frederick Maurice; actively supported his sister's work; contributed to periodicals; wrote volumes of sermons; copublished translation of Plato's *Republic*; married Mary Crompton, the eldest daughter of Charles John Crompton.[2]

Davies, Mary (Crompton) (?–1895). Eldest daughter of Justice Charles John Crompton and Lady Crompton; wife of Llewelyn Davies; involved in campaign to open University Local Exams; member, Kensington Society.

Davies, Mary (Hopkinson) (?). Daughter of John Hopkinson; wife of John Davies; mother of Emily and Llewelyn.

Day, George Edward (1815–72). Trinity College, Cambridge; studied medicine at Edinburgh; physician in London; lecturer at Middlesex Hospital; Chandos Professor of Anatomy and Medicine, St. Andrews, 1849–63.

De Grey, Thomas, Lord Walsingham (1804–70). St. John's College, Cambridge; barrister and author of *The Law of Settlement* and *Rating and the Relief of the Poor.*

Dicey, Albert Venn (1835–1922). Brother of Edward James Dicey; Balliol College, Oxford; Fellow, Trinity College, All Souls College, and Balliol College; called to bar, Inner Temple; public examiner for jurisprudence at Oxford; contributor to leading periodicals; married Elinor Bonham Carter.

Dicey, Edward James Stephen (1832–1911). Brother of Albert Venn Dicey; Trinity College, Cambridge; wrote for *Fortnightly Review, Nineteenth Century, Macmillan's,* and other periodicals; special correspondent to *Daily Telegraph*; edited the *Observer*; expert on Egypt.

Dixon, George (1820–98). Partner, head of Rabone Brothers & Co.; member, Birmingham and Edgbaston Debating Society; Birmingham Town Council, 1863; Birmingham Mayor, 1866; created Educational Aid Society; elected M.P., 1867; worked with W. E. Forster on Elementary Education Act; served on Birmingham School Board; married Mary Stansfield, 1855.

Dixon, Ella Hepworth (?). Edited *Englishwoman*; wrote fiction and articles for *Pall Mall, Sunday Times,* and *Woman,* among others; best known for *The Story of a Modern Woman*; studied art in Paris and traveled in the United States, Canada, Algeria, and the Mediterranean.

Doughty, Clementia. See Taylor, Clementia.

Dove, Jane Frances (1847–1942). Queen's College; the College for Women at Hitchin and Girton, 1871–74; Ordinary Degree standard in Natural Science; Assistant Mistress, Cheltenham Ladies' College; Mistress under Louisa Lumsden of the School at St. Andrews; cofounder, Headmistress, St. Leonard's.

Doyle, Richard (1826–83). Artist and cartoonist for *Punch*, resigned to protest the journal's anti-Catholic editorials; illustrated Christmas books, poetry, and novels; contributed drawings to *Cornhill*.

Drewry, Ellen and Louisa (1835–?). Sisters who signed suffrage petition, 1866, and Higher Education Memorial, 1867; supported Working Women's College in 1872; contributed to the *English Woman's Journal*; served on Committee for Medical Education of Women, 1872.

Durant, Susan (?–1873). Sculptor; studied with Baron Triquetri; commissioned by queen and others in royal family; did portraits of George Grote and Harriet Beecher Stowe.

Eastlake, Elizabeth Rigby (1809–93). Published travel book; contributed to *Quarterly Review*; writer, translator, and amateur painter; known for article in *Quarterly Review* condemning *Jane Eyre* as "anti-Christian"; married Sir Charles Lock Eastlake, director, National Gallery.

Edmunds, James (1833?–?). Son of a Dissenter minister; physician; district surgeon, Royal Maternity Charity; advocate of temperance reform and training and regulation of midwives; involved in founding London Temperance Hospital, British Medical Temperance Association, and Female Medical Society (1862), which became Ladies' Medical College, 1865.

Edwards, Amelia Blandford (1833?–92). Writer and Egyptologist; vice president, Bristol Women's Suffrage Society; signer, first suffrage petition, 1866; cofounder and honorary secretary, Egyptian Exploration Fund; wrote on Egyptology for *Encyclopedia Britannica*; member, Biblical Archaeological Society, and the Society for Promotion of Hellenic Studies.

Edwards, Matilda Betham. See Betham-Edwards, Matilda.

Eiloart, Elizabeth (1830–?). Novelist; author of children's books, including *Ernie Elton* (1865); *The Curate's Discipline* (1867); *Just a Woman* (1871); and *The Love that Lived* (1874).

Eliot, George. See Lewes, Marianne.

Ellis, Margaret, Eliza, Charlotte, and Isabella (?). Quakers; daughters of Edward Shipley Ellis in Leicester; signed suffrage petition, 1866; subscribed to repeal of C.D. Acts.

Elmy, Elizabeth Wolstenholme. See Wolstenholme, Elizabeth.

Ewart, Mary (?). Daughter of William Ewart, Liberal M.P. from Liverpool; traveled in Italy, Greece, and Egypt; studied French, German, Italian, and Latin; governor, North London Collegiate School; supported Bedford College and Somerville College, Oxford, and the lectures for ladies at Cambridge; member, Council at Newnham.

Faithfull, Emily (1835–95). Born in Surrey; educated in Kensington; secretary, Society for Promoting the Employment of Women (SPEW); founded Victoria Printing Press, began the *Victoria*, 1863; published a novel, *Change upon Change*; joined Women's Trade Union League; helped found Women's Printing Society; began weekly penny magazine, *Women and Work*.

Fawcett, Henry (1833–84). Trinity Hall, Cambridge; blinded in a shooting accident; gave up law career; returned to Cambridge; professor of political economy; published *Manual of Political Economy* and *Economic Position of the British Labourer*; Liberal M.P. from Brighton; opposed the war in Afghanistan; postmaster-general under Gladstone; married Millicent Garrett.

Fawcett, Millicent. See Garrett, Millicent.

Fearon, Daniel Robert (1835–?). Balliol College, Oxford; called to bar, Lincoln's Inn; inspector of schools; assistant commissioner, Schools Inquiry Commission; commissioner for Elementary Education Act of 1870; wrote "Girls' Grammar Schools" for *Contemporary Review*; assistant commissioner, Endowed Schools Commission; married Margaret Arnold Price, daughter of Bonamy Price.

Fitch, Sir Joshua Girling (1824–1903). University of London; inspector of schools; assistant commissioner, Schools Inquiry Commission and Endowed Schools Act; inspector of Training Colleges; wrote for *Nineteenth Century*, the *Quarterly*, and other periodicals; member, University of London Senate; early supporter of Girton; active in North of England Council, Girls' Public Day School Company, London School of Medicine for Women, and Maria Grey Training College; married Emma Wilks.

Forster, William Edward, (1818–86). Friends' School, Tottenham; manufacturer in Bradford; M.P. from Bradford; under secretary for the colonies; vice president, Committee of Council on Education; developed first national system of elementary education in England in Elementary Education Act of 1870; leading opponent of slavery; married Jane Martha Arnold.

Foster, Michael (1836–1907). University College, London; surgeon; professor of practical physiology at London; Lecturer at Trinity College; after repeal of Test Acts in 1871, elected Fellow at Cambridge; professor of physiology at Cambridge; wrote books on physiology; contributed to scientific journals.

Fox, Ellen Phillips. See Phillips, Ellen.

Froude, James Anthony (1818–94). Oriel College, Oxford; published *History of England from the Fall of Wolsey to the Defeat of the Spanish Armada*; wrote for *Westminster Review*; edited *Fraser's Magazine*; literary executor for Thomas Carlyle; published *Life of Carlyle*, 1882; married a daughter of Pascoe Grenfell, M.P., whose sister married Charles Kingsley.

Furnivall, Frederick James (1825–1910). University College, London, and Trinity Hall, Cambridge; philologist; founder of the Early English Text Society, Chaucer Society, and New Shakespeare Society; active in formation of Working Men's College.

Fyvie, Isabella (1843–?). Writer; published *The Occupations of a Retired Life* under the pseudonym Edward Garrett; contributed to periodicals, including *Good Words, Sunday Magazine, Young Woman,* and *Girl's Own*; wrote *Recollections of Fifty Years*; married John Mayo, 1870.

Galton, Francis (1822–1911). Trinity College, Cambridge; grandson of Erasmus Darwin; traveled in Africa, including trip to White Nile; won gold medal from Royal Geographical Society; did research in heredity, meteorology, fingerprinting, anthropology, and eugenics; elected to Royal Society; knighted, 1909.

Gamble, Isabella Harriette (1851–?). Attended the College for Women at Hitchin, then Girton through Lent term, 1874; apparently did not take examinations; married Robert Otter.

Garrett, Elizabeth (1836–1917). Daughter of Newson and Louisa Garrett; sister of Millicent Garrett Fawcett; Middlesex, St. Andrews, Edinburgh, and London Hospitals; received L.S.A. diploma, 1865; opened St. Mary's Dispensary for Women (later New Hospital for Women and Children); second woman on British medical register; M.D., Sorbonne University; visiting physician, East London Hospital; member, London School Board and the Kensington Society; supporter of women's suffrage; first woman member of British Medical Association; mayor of Aldeburgh, 1908; first woman mayor in England; married James Skelton Anderson.

Garrett, Louisa. See Garrett Smith, Louisa.

Garrett, Millicent (1847–1929). Daughter of Newson and Louisa Garrett; sister of Elizabeth Garrett Anderson; wife of Henry Fawcett; member, Committee of National Society of Women's Suffrage; active in suffrage and higher education for women movements; published *Political Economy for Beginners, Tales in Political Economy,* and *Janet Doncaster*; supported campaign against C.D. Acts; helped form Newnham College; president, National Union of Women's Suffrage Societies.

Garrett, Newson (1812–93). Father of Elizabeth and Millicent Garrett; owned corn and coal warehouse; developed fleet of small ships to transport malt; bought brickyard and invested in real estate; founded gas works; partner in brewery; agent for Lloyd's; Burgess in Aldeburgh; first mayor of Aldeburgh; first county councillor and alderman.

Gatty, Margaret (1803–73). Writer and editor of children's magazine, *Aunt Judy's Magazine*; married Alfred Gatty; they wrote *Life of Dr. Scott* (her father) and other books.

Gibson, Emily Caroline (1849–1934). Laleham School, Clapham; first applicant for admission to the College for Women; pioneer student at Hitchin, 1869–72, leaving without sitting for the Tripos; taught privately; active in women's suffrage movement; member, Fabian Society; organized Children's Care committees; married Chambrey Corker Townshend.

Gill, Jessie Simmonds (?–1909/10). Girton College, 1875–78; Mathematics Tripos, 1879; M.A., Trinity College, Dublin, 1904; Assistant Mistress, Hackney High School and Maria Grey Training College.

Gimingham, A. E. (?). Worked and wrote for the *English Woman's Journal*; published *Types and Antitypes of Our Lord Jesus Christ* (1884).

Gloyn, Elizabeth (?). Principal of school in Manchester; president, Manchester Board of Schoolmistresses; founding member, North of England Council for the Higher Education of Women; signed 1866 women's suffrage petition; attended founding meeting, Manchester National Society for Women's Suffrage.

Goff, Sarah. See Goff Heckford, Sarah.

Goldsmid, Sir Francis Henry (1808–78). Barrister; first Jew called to English bar; first Jewish queen's counsel; president of senate, University College, London; M.P. from Reading; founder of infant school for Jews and of Anglo-Jewish Association; early supporter of Girton College.

Goldsmid, Lady Louisa (1819–1909). Wife of Sir Francis Goldsmid; supporter, Women's Suffrage Committee; governor, London School of Medicine for Women; treasurer, University Local Exams Committee; one of first members of Girton College; founded Sir Francis Goldsmid Scholarship in her husband's name.

Goodenough, James Graham (1830/31–74). Naval officer appointed to the *Pearl*; as commodore of the Australian station, ordered to Fiji in 1873 to explore seizing it for British empire; shot and killed while cruising Polynesian Islands; married Victoria Hamilton, daughter of William Hamilton.

Goodwin, Harvey (1818–91). Caius College, Cambridge; Fellow and Mathematical Lecturer; dean of Ely; bishop of Carlisle; wrote religious commentaries, sermons, and mathematics books.

Gorst, Sir John Eldon (1835–1916). St. John's College, Cambridge; studied at Inner Temple; emigrated to New Zealand and married Mary Moore there; civil commissioner, setting up schools and newspaper for Maoris in indigenous language; returned to England, 1865; called to bar; Conservative M.P. from Cambridge; queen's counsel; member, Girton College.

Granville, Lord George William, Duke of Sutherland (1828–92). King's College, London; M.P. from Sutherlandshire; attached to special embassy for coronation of Tsar Alexander II; succeeded as third duke in 1861; entertained Garibaldi in London, 1864; accompanied Prince of Wales to India, 1875–76.

Graves, Charles Edward (?). St. John's College, Cambridge, Fellow, Lecturer; Lecturer, Sidney Sussex and Jesus College; chaplain, Magdalene College; edited two books of Thucydides, four plays of Aristophanes.

Gray, Charles (1832–1919). Trinity College, Cambridge, Fellow and Assistant Tutor; held various clerical positions.

Greenhill, William Alexander (1814–94). Trinity College, Oxford; physician in Oxford at Radcliffe Infirmary; member, Pusey's Theological Society; chairman, Gladstone's Committee; practiced medicine in Hastings; physician to Hastings Home for Invalid Gentlewomen; founder, Hastings Cottage Improvement Society; founder and secretary, London Labourers Dwellings Society; edited philosophical texts.

Grey, Maria Shirreff (1816–1906). Sister of Emily Shirreff; published, with her sister, *Passion and Principle* and *Thoughts on Self-Culture*; ran unsuccessfully for school board, 1870; worked with Committee of Society of Arts to promote women's education, leading to formation of Girls' Public Day School Company, Teachers' Training and Registration Society, and Maria Grey Training College; married William Thomas Grey.

Griffiths, John (1806–85). Wadham College, Oxford, Tutor, Divinity Lecturer, and Warden; one of the "Four Tutors" who signed protest against Newman's "Tract XC" in 1841; keeper of archives at Oxford; published work on Greek accents.

Grote, George (1794–1871). Businessman, historian, and reformer; early follower of James Mill; Radical M.P. from City of London; wrote history of Greece, *Plato and Other Companions of Socrates*; helped establish University of London; vice chancellor of university; trustee, British Museum; married Harriet Lewin.

Grote, Harriet Lewin (1792–1878). Writer; friend of J. S. Mill; signed 1866 women's suffrage petition; member, National Society for Women's Suffrage; wife of George Grote.

Grüner, Alice (?). Sister of Joan Frances Ottilie Grüner; Newnham College; donated £500 to the college to purchase Slavonic books for the library.

Grüner, Joan Frances Ottilie (1848–1936). Girton College, 1874–77; Ordinary Degree standard, 1877; M.A., Trinity College, Dublin, 1905; Assistant Mistress, Dulwich High School; principal, Hindhead School for Girls.

Gull, William Withey (1815–90). Fullerian Professor of Physiology, Royal Institution of Great Britain; Fellow, Royal College of Physicians; physician and lecturer, Guy's Hospital; medical superintendent, Guy's "lunatic asylum," where he instituted more humane treatments and procedures.

Gully, James Manby (1808–83). M.D., Edinburgh University; edited *Liverpool Medical Journal*; practiced hydropathy at Malvern; wrote drama and books on hydrotherapy and physiology.

Gurney, Emelia (1823–96). Daughter of Reverend S. E. Batten, Assistant Master of Harrow; friend of Julia Wedgwood and General Gordon; published *Letters from a Mystic of the Present Day* and *Dante's Pilgrim's Progress*; supported Local Exams campaign, women's suffrage, and College for Women; married Russell Gurney and with him established convalescent home for women.

Gurney, Russell (1804–78). Trinity College, Cambridge; called to bar, Inner Temple; queen's counsel; recorder of London; Conservative M.P. from Southampton; voted in favor of women's suffrage in Parliament, 1867; took charge of the Married Women's Property Bill in House of Commons, 1870; member, Jamaica Committee, January 1866; married Emelia Gurney.

Hales, John Wesley (1836–1914). Christ's College, Cambridge; called to bar, Lincoln's Inn, 1867; Assistant Master, Marlborough College; deputy inspector of schools; English Lecturer, Bedford College; active in University Extension movement; professor of English language and literature, King's College, London; wrote books on poetry; edited collection of ballads; wrote for *Cornhill, Quarterly Review, Macmillan's,* and *Fortnightly Review*.

Hare, Alice. See Hare Westlake, Alice.

Hare, Thomas (1806–91). Queen's College, Cambridge; called to bar, Inner Temple; inspector of charities; known for efforts to devise a system of proportional representation.

Harrison, Fanny (?–1917?). Bedford College, London; Girton College, 1874–78; Mathematics Tripos, 1879.

Hastings, George Woodyatt (1825–?). Attorney, called to bar, Middle Temple; cofounder and general secretary, NAPSS; wrote its history; secretary, Law Amendment Society; involved in the first efforts to reform married women's property laws; member, Girls' Local Exam Committee and the College Committee.

Hays, Matilda (Max) (1821–?). Writer, translator, and actress; signer of Married Women's Property petition; founding member, *English Woman's Journal*; lived for a time with Emily Faithfull and with Jane Crow; had relationships with

Charlotte Cushman, Adelaide Procter, and Lady Theodosia Monson; wrote *Helen Stanley*; translated Sand's *Mauprat* and *Fadette*.

Head, William Wilfred (?). Purchased part of Victoria Press from Emily Faithfull, January 1864, and additional share in Press, 1867; published *The Victoria Press: Its History and Vindication* (1869).

Heckford, Nathaniel (1842/43–71). Born in Calcutta; studied medicine at London Hospital and Edinburgh; married Sarah Goff and with her established East London Hospital for Children; surgeon there until his death.

Heckford, Sarah Goff (1839–1903). Irish heiress from Dublin; youngest of three daughters of William and Mary Goff; met Nathaniel Heckford at Wapping District Cholera Hospital during 1866 epidemic; with him founded East London Hospital for Children; visiting governor for the hospital; after her husband's death, she settled money on the hospital, went to India and Transvaal, wrote *A Lady Trader in the Transvaal* and two novels.[3]

Helps, Sir Arthur (1813–75). Trinity College, Cambridge; member, Apostles; private secretary to Lord Monteagle and Lord Morpeth; established a free lending library; published essays, plays, and history.

Herschel, Constance Anne (1855–1939). Youngest child of Sir John Herschel, astronomer, and Constance Brodie Stuart; Girton College, 1874–77; Natural Science Tripos, 1877; resident lecturer in natural science and mathematics, Girton; in charge of the chemistry lab presented by Lady Stanley; married Sir Nevile Lubbock, 1881, and they collaborated in work on the West Indies.

Heywood, James (1810–97). Trinity College, Cambridge, but as a Dissenter he couldn't take degree; called to bar, Inner Temple; M.P. from North Lancashire; active on academic and religious freedom issues; pioneer of Free Public Library movement; president, Royal Statistical Society; chairman, Royal Historical Society's Council; early supporter of Girton and member of the college; active supporter of women's suffrage.

Hicks, John Wale (1840–99). University of London and Sidney Sussex College, Cambridge; Lecturer in natural science, Sidney Sussex, Fellow, Dean; lectured in theology; wrote textbook on inorganic chemistry.

Hill, Florence Davenport (1829–1919). Daughter of Matthew Davenport Hill and Margaret Bucknall; sister of Rosamond and Joanna Hill, prominent reformers associated with Liberal politics, prison reform, and education; early supporter of women's suffrage; member, NAPSS; interested in reforming conditions for the poor; wrote *Children of the State* and other pamphlets; added Davenport to surname to avoid confusion with Octavia Hill.

Hill, Rosamond Davenport (1825–1902). Daughter of Matthew Davenport Hill and Margaret Bucknall; sister of Florence Davenport Hill; worked with Mary Carpenter in Ragged Schools and reforms for schools, prisons, and reformatories; candidate for London School Board; supporter of women's suffrage in 1866.

Hobart, Lord Vere Henry (1818–75). Trinity College, Oxford; clerk in Board of Trade, private secretary to Sir George Grey, Colonial Office and Home Office; special commissioner on Turkish finances, 1861; governor of Madras, 1872; married Mary Catherine Carr, daughter of bishop of Bombay.

Hodgkin, Thomas (1831–1913). University College, London; Quaker and businessman in banking firm at Newcastle; wrote for *Edinburgh Review* and other periodicals, and *Encyclopedia Britannica*; published book on Roman poets and lectures at Literary and Philosophical Society at Newcastle-on-Tyne; president, Friends' Historical Society; honorary secretary, Royal Geographical Society.

Hodgson, Shadworth (1832–1912). Corpus Christi College, Oxford; president, Aristotelian Society for Systematic Study of Philosophy; wrote *Principles of Reform in the Suffrage* and books on metaphysics, ethics, the supernatural, and the relationship between philosophy and science.

Hodgson, William Ballantyne (1815–80). Edinburgh University; secretary, then principal, Liverpool Institute; examiner in political economy, University of London; professor of economy, Edinburgh University; wrote lectures and books, including "On the Education of Girls and the Employment of Women of the Middle Classes"; member, Women's Suffrage Society, 1869; early member, Local Exams Committee.

Hoggan, Frances Morgan. See Morgan, Frances Elizabeth.

Holmes, Arthur (?–1875). St. John's College, Cambridge, Fellow and Lecturer; Lecturer at Clare College; Senior Fellow, dean of Clare; edited series in classics; published books on Demosthenes and Pindar.

Hort, Fenton John (1828–92). Rugby and Trinity College, Cambridge; rector, St. Ippolyts at Hitchin; early lecturer at the College for Women; Hulsean Lecturer, 1871; one of New Testament revisers; Hulsean Professor 1878–87; member, Alpine Club; friend of Llewelyn Davies and F. D. Maurice; married Fanny Holland.

Hoskins, Mary Georgina (1850–?). The College for Women at Hitchin and Girton, 1871–74; took Little-go but left, possibly to Paris to study medicine.

Hubbard, Louisa Maria (1836–1906). Born in Russia; family settled in Sussex; educated privately; interested in women's education; helped train women as teachers and nurses; lectured on work for ladies in elementary schools; helped edit *Woman's Gazette* and *Work and Leisure*.

Hullah, John (1812–84). Musician and composer; inspector of training schools; editor of vocal and educational works; professor of vocal music, King's College, London and Queen's College; member, Standing Committee of Professors at Bedford College.

Hutton, Richard (1826–97). University College, London; editor, *Inquirer*; joint editor with Walter Bagehot of the *National Review*; assistant editor, the *Econo-*

mist; joint editor and proprietor, with Meredith Townsend, of the *Spectator*; wrote essays on theological and literary issues and edited books.

Huxley, Thomas (1825–95). Studied medicine at Charing Cross Hospital; assistant surgeon in Royal Navy; Fellow of Royal Society; chair of natural history at Royal School of Mines; Fullerian Professor of Physiology at University of London; lectured to working men on Darwin's *On the Origin of the Species*; elected to London School Board; opposed denominational teaching in schools.

Jackson, Henry (1839–1921). Trinity College, Cambridge, Fellow, Assistant Tutor; Council of Senate of University; member, Girton College; Vice Master, Trinity College; published on Aristotle and Plato; daughter Gertrude Elizabeth Jackson attended Girton and founded University Women's Club.

Jameson, Francis James (1828–69). Caius College, Cambridge; Fellow, Tutor at St. Catherine's College; rector of Coton; author of academic and religious works.

Jekyll, Gertrude (1843–1932). Educated largely by travel; skilled artist, craftswoman, embroiderer, and—primarily—gardener; did planting for many of the houses designed by architect Edwin Lutyens.

Jex-Blake, Sophia Louisa (1840–1912). Daughter of Thomas Jex-Blake and Maria Cubitt; Queen's College; taught bookkeeping for Society for Promoting the Employment of Women; member, Kensington Society; attempted to study medicine at Edinburgh University; helped found London School of Medicine for Women, 1874; M.D., University of Berne; certified, Irish College of Physicians, 1877; practiced medicine in Edinburgh; founded Women's Hospital, 1885; opened School of Medicine for Women, 1886.

Kay Shuttleworth, Sir James (1804–77). Edinburgh University; secretary, Manchester Board of Health; assistant Poor Law commissioner; secretary, Committee of Privy Council on Education; helped develop new educational system; vice chairman, Central Relief Committee of Manchester during cotton famine; wrote on education, social class, and poverty, including *The Moral and Physical Condition of the Working Classes*.

Kennedy, Benjamin Hall (1804–89). St. John's College, Cambridge, Scholar, Fellow, and president of the union; member, Apostles; Assistant Master, Shrewsbury, then Harrow; Headmaster, Shrewsbury; chair in Latin at Cambridge founded in his honor; Regius Professor of Greek; wrote Latin grammar; edited Aristophanes; married Janet Caird; father of Charlotte Kennedy Burbury and Julia Kennedy.

Kennedy, Julia (?). Daughter of B. H. Kennedy and sister of Charlotte Kennedy Burbury; Tutor, Newnham College; suffragist.

Kilgour, Mary Stewart (1851–?). Attended and taught at Cheltenham Ladies College; took London University certificates; Girton College, 1874–78; Clothworkers' Exhibitioner Award; Mathematics Tripos, 1878; M.A., Trinity College,

Dublin, 1905, and Cambridge University, 1928; visiting mathematics teacher, Queen's College.

King, Gertrude (1834–?). Secretary, Society for Promoting the Employment of Women; member, Langham Place Circle and London Association of Schoolmistresses, 1866; signed women's suffrage petition, 1866.

Kinglake, Alexander William (1809–91). Trinity College, Cambridge; called to bar; visited the East; wrote book on his travels, *Eothen*; visited British troops during Crimean War and wrote articles describing conditions; published *The Invasion of the Crimea*; wrote for *Quarterly Review*; M.P.

Kingsland, Mary (1854–1937). The College for Women at Hitchin and Girton, 1871–74; first woman to take Natural Science Tripos, 1874; Gamble Prize, 1905; resident lecturer in natural science, Girton; staff of Bradford Girls' Grammar School; helped form National Association for Women's Lodging Houses; married Reverend Thomas Higgs, Congregational minister.

Kingsley, Charles (1819–75). Magdalene College, Cambridge; writer and clergyman; member, Broad Church movement; author of *The Water Babies*; influenced by Coleridge, Carlyle, and Maurice; preached socially conscious Christianity; wrote novels *Yeast* and *Alton Locke* and on scientific issues.

Kingsley, Frances Eliza (1814–91). Daughter of Pascoe Grenfell, M.P.; educated at home; attended women's suffrage meeting, 1869; married Charles Kingsley; wrote *Charles Kingsley: His Letters and Memoirs of His Life*.[4]

Knox, Isa Craig. See Craig, Isa.

Kyberd, Susan (?). Schoolmistress; signed petition to University of London to open examinations to women (1864); testified before Schools Inquiry Commission; ran Chantry School, a boarding school for girls, near Frome.

Lankester, Edwin (1814–74). University College, London; member, College of Surgeons and professor of natural history, New College, London; Lecturer on anatomy and physiology, Grosvenor Place School of Medicine; wrote on medical and natural history subjects; married Phebe Pope.

Lankester, Edwin Ray (1847/49–1929). Son of Edwin Lankester and Phebe Pope; Christ Church, Oxford; professor of zoology and comparative anatomy, University College, London; wrote on zoology and paleontology; deputy professor of human and comparative anatomy, Oxford; worked with father editing the *Quarterly Journal of Microscopical Science*.

Lankester, Phebe (1825–1900). Medical reformer, writer, and lecturer on science; wrote *Wild Flowers Worth Notice,* 1861; wrote weekly syndicated column in provincial newspapers on feminist subjects; married Edwin Lankester; mother of Edwin Ray and Phebe Lankester.[5]

Lankester, Phebe Fay (?–1924). Eldest child of Phebe Pope and Edwin Lankester; secretary, National Health Society (founded by Elizabeth Blackwell); lectured and wrote on hygiene and nursing; active in NAPSS.

Leigh-Smith, Barbara. See Bodichon, Barbara Leigh Smith.

Leigh-Smith, Isabella. See Ludlow, Isabella Leigh Smith.

Leigh-Smith, Nannie (1831?–?). Sister of Barbara Leigh Smith Bodichon; Bedford College; shareholder in and contributor to the *English Woman's Journal.*

Leighton, ? (?). Schoolmistress, Birklands School, Hornsey Road, London; original member of London Association of Schoolmistresses.

Leslie, Thomas Edward Cliffe (1827–82). Trinity College, Dublin; studied law, Lincoln's Inn; called to bar in Ireland and England; chair of political economy, Queen's College, Belfast; examiner in political economy, University of London; wrote for periodicals, and books on economics.

Lewes, George Henry (1817–78). Born in London; studied anatomy and physiology, language, and literature; wrote for *Edinburgh, Westminster, British and Foreign, Foreign Quarterly,* and *British Quarterly Reviews*; literary editor of *Leader*; wrote *A Biographical History of Philosophy* and *Comte's Philosophy of the Sciences*; founded *Fortnightly Review*, 1865.

Lewes, Marianne (1819–80). Born in Warwickshire; moved to Coventry, 1841, until father's death in 1849; traveled to Europe and settled in London; subeditor, *Westminster Review*; moved in with George Lewes; published *Scenes of Clerical Life* (1858), *Adam Bede* (1859), *Mill on the Floss* (1860), *Silas Marner* (1861), *Romola* (1863), *Felix Holt* (1866), *Middlemarch* (1871–72), and *Daniel Deronda* (1876).

Lewin, Sarah (1812–98). Secretary, Society for Promoting the Employment of Women; assistant, *English Woman's Journal*; when the *Englishwoman's Review* took over from the *English Woman's Journal*, Lewin became its bookkeeper.

Lightfoot, Joseph Barber (1828–89). Trinity College, Cambridge, tutor, Hulsean Professor of Divinity; examining chaplain to Dr. Tait, archbishop of Canterbury; canon, St. Paul's Cathedral; bishop of Durham; published editions of St. Paul's Epistles and sermons and articles in contemporary periodicals.

Lind, Jenny (1820/21–87). Born in Stockholm; star of Stockholm opera; toured Germany and sang before Queen Victoria there; toured London in 1847 and America in 1850; married Otto Goldschmidt of Boston; gave concerts for charitable purposes; retired in London.

Liveing, George Downing (1827–1924). St. John's College, Cambridge; professor of chemistry, Sandhurst and Cambridge; Fellow, Royal Society; early lecturer at the College for Women; wrote on chemistry and philosophy; founded first chemistry lab for undergraduates; active in establishing Local Exams at Cambridge, and the Oxford and Cambridge Schools Exam Board; member, Girton College, appointed by senate; married Katharine Ingram.

Longley, Frances Elizabeth (1840–1900). Daughter of bishop of Ripon, later archbishop of York and of Canterbury; early vice president, Women's Mission Association of Society for Propagation of Gospel.

Lloyd, Anna (1837–1925). Quaker; daughter of Samuel and Mary Lloyd; educated at home; traveled in Europe; pioneer student at the College for Women, Hitchin, 1869; left because of family pressures; later traveled, wrote poetry, maintained unpublished travel diaries; *Anna Lloyd: A Memoir, with Extracts from Her Letters* (1928) published posthumously.

Lloyd, Mary (?). Welsh sculptor; part of the circle of artists including Harriet Hosman, Emma Stebbins, Mary Somerville, and Charlotte Cushman; companion of Frances Power Cobbe.

Lubbock, Sir John (1834–1913). Trinity College, Cambridge; banker; member of Parliament; wrote scientific works, including *The Origin and Metamorphoses of Insects* (1874) and *British Wild Flowers* (1875); member, Public School Commission and Advancement of Science Commission.

Lucas, Margaret Bright (1818–90). Quaker; sister of John and Jacob Bright; married Samuel Lucas, editor of *Morning Star*; member, Anti-Corn Law League, London Ladies' Emancipation Society; signed 1866 suffrage petition; subscribed to 1866–67 Enfranchisement of Women Committee; member, London National Society for Women's Suffrage, 1867; involved in Temperance and Repeal of C.D. Acts.

Ludlow, Isabella Leigh Smith (?–1873). Younger sister of Barbara Leigh Smith Bodichon; member, Portfolio Club; friend of Matilda Hays; married John Ludlow; had three children.

Ludlow, John Malcolm Forbes (1821–1911). Born in India; raised in France; with Frederick Maurice founded night school, Little Ormand Yard; helped found Working Men's College; founded Working Association for Tailors and the Society for Promoting Working Men's Associations; called to bar, Lincoln's Inn; chief registrar, Friendly Societies; married Isabella Leigh Smith, Bodichon's sister.

Lumsden, Louisa (1840–1935). The College for Women at Hitchin, 1869–73, pioneer student; Classics Tripos, March 1873; Honorary LL.D., St. Andrews, 1911; Tutor in classics, Girton; teacher, Cheltenham Ladies' College; Headmistress, St. Leonards School, St. Andrews; member, Women's Suffrage Party; president, Aberdeen Suffrage Association; member, Scottish Society for Prevention of Vivisection.

Lushington, Godfrey (1832–?). Balliol College, Oxford; called to bar, Inner Temple; counsel to Home Office; assistant under-secretary of state for Home Department; permanent under-secretary at Home Office; married Beatrice Shore Smith, Barbara Bodichon's cousin.

Lyell, Sir Charles (1797–1875). Exeter College, Oxford; professor of geology, King's College, London; president, Geological Society. His books on geology—*Principles of Geology, Elements of Geology, Travels in North America, The Geological Evidences of the Antiquity of Man*—and journal articles pioneered and expanded the field.

Lyttelton, Lord George William (1817–76). Trinity College, Cambridge; principal, Queen's College, Birmingham; member, Royal Commission on Public Schools; royal commissioner on clerical subscription and on middle schools; chief commissioner, endowed schools; supporter of NAPSS; married (first) May Glynne, daughter of Sir Stephen Glynne, and (second) Sybella Harriet Mildmay, widow of H. F. Mildmay and daughter of George Clive, M.P.

MacDonald, George (1824–1905). University of Aberdeen; contributed to journals and periodicals; published over fifty books of poetry, fiction, children's stories, literary criticism, and sermons, including *Within and Without, Poems, The Hidden Life, The Disciple, The Vicar's Daughter,* and *The Wise Woman*.

McGregor, John (1825–92). Trinity College, Cambridge; called to bar; wrote and did drawings for *Punch*; member from Greenwich on London School Board; wrote books on travel and law, donating his profits to charities.

Macmillan, Alexander (1818–96). Bookseller and publisher, with brother, Daniel; publisher to Cambridge University (1860–80) and Oxford University (1863–80); helped start *Macmillan's* magazine (1859–1907).

Malleson, Frank (?). Related to Courtauld and Taylor families; partner in Fearon & Company, whiskey retailers and wholesalers; Unitarian; married Elizabeth Whitehead.

Manning, Charlotte Speir (1803–71). Unitarian; daughter of Isaac Solly; wrote *Life in Ancient India* and *Ancient and Medieval India*; president, London branch of National Indian Association; founding member, committees on women's suffrage and higher education; helped found Kensington Society; active in Ladies' London Emancipation Society; Mistress, the College for Women, Hitchin, Michaelmas term, 1869; married (first) William Speir, officer in India, (second) James (Serjeant) Manning.

Manning, Elizabeth Adelaide (1828–1905). Daughter of James Manning; stepdaughter of Charlotte Speir Manning; Bedford College; student at the College for Women, Hitchin, Michaelmas term, 1869; member, Girton College; active in educational work of Mary Carpenter; secretary, Froebel Society; active in Working Women's Colleges; member, London Association of Schoolmistresses; honorary secretary, National Indian Association; edited *Indian Magazine and Review*.

Manning, James (Serjeant) (1781–1866). Called to bar, Lincoln's Inn; wrote legal texts; serjeant-at-law, 1840; judge of Whitechapel county court, 1847; retired, 1863.

Mantle, Amy Annie (?–1913). Girton College, 1873–77; Special Examination in history, 1877; Ordinary Degree standard.

Markby, Reverend Thomas (1824–70). Trinity College, Cambridge; Headmaster, proprietary college school, St. John's Wood; private tutor, Cambridge; Classical Lecturer, Trinity Hall; secretary to Syndicate for Conducting Local Exams; edited Francis Bacon's books on learning; wrote on life and poetry of Chaucer.

Marks, Sarah Phoebe (Hertha) (1854–1923). Polish-Jewish immigrant; worked as governess while preparing for Girton Scholarship Exam; Girton College, 1876–81; Mathematics Tripos, 1881; nominated for Fellowship of Royal Society, 1902; active member, WSPU; vice president, Women's Hospital for Children; original member, NUSW; studied science with Professor W. E. Ayrton, Technical College, Finsbury; married Ayrton, had one daughter.

Martin, Adèle Emily (?–1930). Girton College, 1875–78; History Tripos, 1878, first Girton student to pass this Tripos; Assistant Mistress, Hackney High School.

Martin, Henry Newell (1848–96). Christ's College, Cambridge, Fellow; demonstrator to Michael Foster; professor of biology, Johns Hopkins, Baltimore; wrote biology texts, one with Professor T. H. Huxley.

Martineau, Harriet (1802–76). Sister of James; Unitarian writer on economics, abolition, education, and gender; wrote for *Monthly Repository, Daily News, Edinburgh Review, Household Words, Westminster Review,* and others, and books, including *Household Education* and *Autobiography.*

Martineau, Reverend James (1805–1900). Brother of Harriet; Unitarian minister; served in Dublin and Liverpool; professor of moral philosophy, later principal, Manchester New College; wrote on religion and philosophy, including *Study of Spinoza* (1882) and *Types of Ethical Theory* (1885); critic of materialism.

Masson, David (1822–1907). Edinburgh University; chair of English Language and Literature, University College, London; wrote for *Fraser's Magazine, Westminster, Leader,* and *Encyclopedia Britannica*; published *Critical and Biographical Essays*; wrote *Life and Times of Milton*; edited *Macmillan's*; edited and wrote for the *Reader*; formed Edinburgh Association for University Education of Women; subscribed to Edinburgh National Society for Women's Suffrage, and member of executive committee; married Emily Rosaline Orme, student at Bedford College.

Masson, George Joseph Gustave (1819–88). French Master and librarian, Harrow School; wrote French grammars and texts; contributed to the *Athenaeum* and *Saturday Review*; early lecturer at the College for Women.

Mathews, Charles Edward (1834–1905). Studied law under Arthur Ryland; called to bar, Gray's Inn, London; established Children's Hospital, Birmingham; elected to Birmingham Town Council; member, Water Committee; officer, Birmingham Education League; chairman, School Committee; founder of Alpine Club.

Maurice, Frederick Denison (1805–72). Trinity Hall, Cambridge; helped found Apostles; barred, as a Unitarian, from receiving his degree; edited the *Athenaeum*; joined Anglican Church; editor, *Educational Magazine*; professor of history and literature, King's College, London; leader, Christian Socialists; established Queen's College for Ladies; edited, with J. M. Ludlow, *Politics for the People*; cofounder and principal, Working Men's College; married (first) Anna Barton, and (second) Georgiana Hare.

Max-Müller, Friedrich (1823–1900). See Müller, Friedrich Max.

May, Sir Thomas Erskine (1815–86). Assistant librarian, House of Commons; called to bar, Inner Temple; examiner of petitions for private bills in the House; clerk-assistant, then chief clerk, at the House; wrote for *Law Magazine, Edinburgh,* and others.

Maynard, Constance Louisa (1849–1935). The College for Women at Hitchin and Girton, 1872–75; first Girton student to take Moral Science Tripos, 1875; Gamble Prize; with Louisa Lumsden, opened St. Leonards School, St. Andrews; studied at Slade School of Art; founder and Mistress, Westfield College; wrote books on religious subjects.

Mayor, John Eyton Bickersteth (1825–1910). St. John's College, Cambridge; Assistant Master, Marlborough College; College Lecturer, librarian, university professor of Latin, Cambridge; edited Juvenal and Cicero and journals on philology; biographer; historian of St. John's.

Mayor, Joseph Bickersteth (1828–1916). St. John's College, Cambridge, Fellow; Headmaster, Kensington School; professor of classics, King's College, London; wrote on classics and religion.

Metcalfe, Fanny (1829–97). Lived in Berlin with her sister, Anna Sophia Metcalfe, to study German; set up boarding school for girls, Hendon; in 1863, moved to Golders Green; helped found Westfield College, 1882; member, Executive Committee of Girton, London Association of Schoolmistresses, Council of Westfield College.[6]

Mill, Harriet Taylor (1807–58). Daughter of Unitarians Thomas Hardy and Harriet Hurst; married John Taylor and had three children; friend and influence on John Stuart Mill, whom she married after Taylor's death; wrote "The Enfranchisement of Women" for *Westminster Review,* 1851.

Mill, John Stuart (1806–73). Son of James Mill; educated as utilitarian; worked at India House; wrote *Principles of Political Economy* (1848), *On Liberty* (1859), *Utilitarianism* (1863), *The Subjection of Women* (1869), and *Autobiography* (1873); married Harriet Taylor.

Minturn, Eliza Theodora (?–1915). American; member of staff, Home and Colonial College; Girton College, 1875–79; excused from completing the ninth term due to illness; founded Jane Chessar Scholarship, Girton; M.A., Trinity College, Dublin, 1905.

Monson, Theodora (1803–91). Child of Latham Blacker of Ireland and Catherine Maddison; patron of the theater; intimate with Matilda Hays; helped set up reading rooms at 14A Princes Street and Langham Place; provided financial support to Society for Promoting the Employment of Women; married Frederick John, fifth Baron Monson of Burton, from whom she eventually separated.[7]

Morgan, Edmund Henry (1838–95). Jesus College, Cambridge, Fellow, Scholar, dean, Senior Tutor, Proctor; deacon in Chichester; priest at Ely.

Morgan, Frances Elizabeth (1843–1927). Studied medicine, Society of Apothecaries; completed studies, Zürich University; second woman to defend an M.D. thesis at Zürich, 1870; first British woman to obtain a European M.D. degree; appointed by Garrett Anderson as assistant physician, St. Mary's Dispensary; worked with Elizabeth Blackwell to found National Health Society; active in antivivisectionist campaign; married George Hoggan, obstetrician, with whom she published scientific papers.[8]

Morley, Samuel (1809–86). Businessman and Dissenter; M.P., Nottingham (1865–66), and Bristol (1868–85); treasurer of College, Homerton and of Home Missionary Society; member, London School Board (1870–76).

Moulton, John Fletcher (1844–1921). St. John's College, Cambridge; Fellow, Lecturer, Christ's College; Lecturer, Jesus College; called to bar, Middle Temple; Fellow, Royal Society; married Clara Thomson, of Edinburgh.

Müller, Friedrich Max (1823–1900). Born in Germany, educated at Leipzig and Berlin; worked in libraries of East India House and at Bodleian Library, Oxford; Deputy Taylorian professor of Modern European languages; curator, Bodleian Library; Life Fellow and professor in comparative philology, All Soul's College; published *History of Ancient Sanscrit Literature*; contributed to the *Edinburgh, Quarterly Review,* and *Times.*

Müller, Frances Henrietta (?–1906). Girton College, 1873; Moral Science Tripos, 1877; helped establish Women's Printing Society, Women's Trade Unions; ran for London School Board, 1879; secretary, Society for Return of Women as Poor Law Guardians; started newspaper for women; active feminist; traveled in Europe, America, and Asia.

Myers, Frederic William Henry (1843–1901). Son of Reverend Frederic Myers of St. John's Parsonage, Keswick; Trinity College, Cambridge, Fellow; president, Society for Psychical Research; inspector of schools; wrote essays and poems; married Evelen Tennant.

Neave, Sheffield (1799–1868). Merchant in London; director, Bank of England; deputy governor (1855–57); governor (1857–59).

Newman, Francis William (1805–97). Younger brother of John Henry Newman; Worcester College, Oxford; Fellow, Balliol College, resigned over Thirty-nine Articles; Classical Tutor, Bristol College; Latin professor, University College, London; honorary secretary, Bristol Women's Suffrage Committee; wrote on religion, mathematics, and logic; lectured on political economy, history, vivisection, temperance, and vegetarianism; contributed to *Westminster Review* and *Fraser's Magazine.*

Niven, William Davidson (1842–1917). Trinity College, Cambridge; Fellow, later director of studies, Royal Naval College, Greenwich.

Noel, Ernest (1831–1931). Trinity College, Cambridge; worked to promote working-class housing; wrote *Notes on the West Indies*; J.P., Sussex; chairman of

Artizans, Labourers, and General Dwellings Company; M.P; married (first) Louisa Hope Milne, (second) Lady Augusta Keppel, (third) Sidney Saunders.

Norris, John Pilkington (1823–91). Trinity College, Cambridge; inspector of schools, Staffordshire, Shropshire, Cheshire, Kent, and Surrey; canon of Bristol; vicar of St. George; wrote a variety of religious works.

Notley, Frances Eliza Millett Thomas (1820–?). Educated in England and France; wrote novels, some published under pseudonym "Francis Derrick," including *Mildred's Wedding, Simple as a Dove,* and *Love's Bitterness*.

Parkes, Bessie Rayner (1829–1925). Daughter of Joseph Parkes of Birmingham; granddaughter of Joseph Priestley; close friend of Barbara Leigh Smith Bodichon; published *Remarks on the Education of Girls*, 1854; worked on married women's property issue; began publishing and editing the *English Woman's Journal*, 1858; converted to Roman Catholicism, 1864; published *Essays on Woman's Work*; published poetry, essays, and memoirs; married Louis Belloc in France, returning to England after his death.

Parkes, Charles (1816–95). Clerk in Election Office of House of Commons; partner in Dyson and Company; director of railway in eastern counties; instituted improvements in rail line, increased rail traffic, and enlarged Liverpool train station.

Pattison, Mark (1813–84). Oriel College, Oxford; Fellow, Lincoln College; influenced by Newman; devoted to reforming university education; wrote *Oxford Essays* and for *Quarterly Review, Nineteenth Century,* and other periodicals; rector, Lincoln College; married Emilia Frances Strong—later Lady Dilke—who wrote *Renaissance of Art in France* and *Claude Lorriane*.

Pearson, Charles Henry (1830–94). Oriel College, Oxford; Scholar, Exeter College; Lecturer on English literature, then professor of modern history, King's College, London; edited *National Review*; lectured on modern history, Trinity College, Cambridge; emigrated to Australia, 1871; Headmaster, Ladies' Presbyterian College; member, legislative assembly for Castlemaine, then East Bourke, Australia; minister of education, Australia; returned to England, 1891.

Percival, Reverend John (1834–1918). Queen's College, Oxford; Master, Rugby School; Headmaster, Clifton College; president, Trinity College, Oxford; canon of Bristol; published collection of sermons; a founder of University College, Bristol; married (first) Louisa Holland, (second) Mary Georgina Symonds.

Phillips, Ellen (1846–90). Daughter of John and Mary Phillips, Quakers; helped reorganize London Hospital during cholera epidemic, 1866; with sister, Mary Elizabeth Phillips, founded and worked at North Eastern Hospital, Hackney Road (later Queen's Hospital for Children, then Queen Elizabeth Hospital for Children); member, Women's Temperance Association; married Alexander Fox; moved to New Zealand; returned to England after husband's death.

Pike, William Bennett (1831?–?). Trinity College, Cambridge; moved to Downing College; Fellow, Tutor, chaplain, Downing College.

Plumptre, Reverend Edward Hayes (1821–?). University College, Oxford; assistant preacher, Lincoln's Inn; chaplain, King's College, London; dean, Queen's College, London; prebendary of Portpool, St. Paul's Cathedral; professor of exegesis, King's College, London; principal, Queen's College, London; dean of Wells.

Ponsonby, Mary Elizabeth (?–1916). Maid of Honor to Queen Victoria; member, Girton College, 1872–1916; married Sir Henry Ponsonby.

Porter, James (1827–1900). Peterhouse College, Cambridge; Assistant Master, Collegiate Institution, Liverpool; Mathematical Lecturer, dean, bursar, Assistant Tutor, and Tutor, Peterhouse College; vice chancellor, Cambridge; chair of Syndics for Cambridge Press.

Porter, Mary Eliza (1836/7–1905). One of the early students at Queen's College, London; Assistant Mistress, later principal, Bolham School, Devon; testified before SIC; member, Kensington Society; involved in Cambridge Local Examinations for girls; ran school in Gateshead; Headmistress, Bradford Girls' Grammar School; Headmistress, Harpur Trust's Bedford Girls' Modern School; founding member, Association of Head Mistresses.[9]

Potts, Robert (1805–85). Trinity College, Cambridge; married after taking degree; tutored private pupils; wrote edition of Euclid; edited *Paley's Evidences* and *Liber Cantabrigiensis*; active in university reform; secretary of Cambridge Local Exam Committee, 1862.

Prest, Edward (1824–82). St. John's College, Cambridge; honorary canon, Durham Cathedral, 1860–63; rector, St. Mary's, Gateshead; resident canon and archdeacon, Durham, 1863–82.

Price, Bonamy (1807–88). Worcester College, Oxford; Assistant Master, Rugby School; wrote on political and economic issues; professor of political economy, Oxford.

Procter, Adelaide (1825–64). Daughter of Bryan Waller Procter and Anne Skepper; published poetry in *Household Words*; wrote for *English Woman's Journal*; active in sheltering homeless and in teaching; helped organize Society for Promoting the Employment of Women; edited *Victoria Regia*; active in Langham Place Circle.

Pusey, Edward Bouverie (1800–82). Christ Church, Oxford; Fellow, Oriel College; Regius Professor of Hebrew, Oxford; led Oxford Movement with Keble and Newman, issuing *Tracts for the Times* (1833–41); published sermons and theological works.

Quick, Robert Herbert (1831–91). Trinity College, Cambridge; curate to Llewelyn Davies, St. Mark's and Marylebone; Master, Lancaster Grammar School; Assistant Master, Harrow; head of a preparatory school in London; wrote on educational reform.

Raven, John James (1833–1906). St. Catharine's College, Cambridge; moved to Emmanuel College; Headmaster, Bungay Grammar School; Headmaster, Yarmouth Grammar School; published on mathematics and the history of Suffolk.

Reade, Charles (1814–84). Magdalen Hall, Oxford; called to bar, Lincoln's Inn; wrote for periodicals in London; wrote novels, including *Hard Cash*; published in *All the Year Round,* and plays, some with Tom Taylor.

Reyner, George Fearns (1817–92). St. John's College, Cambridge, Scholar, Fellow, junior dean, and senior bursar, 1857–76; Senior Lecturer in mathematics; married Emma Bishop, 1878.

Rich, Lady Julia (?–1874). Daughter of James Tomkinson, cousin of Henry Tomkinson; member, Girton College, 1872–74; married Sir Henry Rich, who died in 1869.

Richardson, Anna Deborah (1832–72). Eldest daughter of large Quaker family in Newcastle; formal education cut off by illness; continued to study actively, taking classes, attending lectures, and teaching herself Greek, Italian, and French; bought land, designed a home, Heugh Folds, in Grasmere; traveled to Scotland and Europe.

Ritchie, Anne. See Thackeray, Anne Elizabeth.

Richson, Reverend Charles (1806–74). St. Catherine's Hall, Cambridge; clerk in orders, Manchester Cathedral; senior residentiary canon, rector, St. Andrew's, Ancoats; active in education and sanitary reform; wrote on education, sanitary laws, and theology.

Robertson, Caroline Crompton Croom (1837–92). Sister of Mary Crompton Davies; daughter of Sir Charles Crompton and Lady Crompton; secretary to Girton College after Davies retired; bursar, Girton College, 1882–91; married George Croom Robertson, professor at University College, London.

Roby, Henry John (1830–1915). St. John's College, Cambridge; examiner in law, classics, and moral science; secretary, Cambridge Local Exam Committee; active in university reform movement; Undermaster, Dulwich College Upper School; professor of Jurisprudence, University College, London; secretary, Schools Inquiry Commission and Endowed Schools Commission; member, Girton College; wrote *Grammar of the Latin Language*; active in politics in Manchester; M.P. from Eccles; married Matilda Ermen.

Romer, Sir Robert (1840–1918). Trinity Hall, Cambridge; private secretary, Baron Rothschild; mathematical professor, Queen's College, Cork; called to bar, Lincoln's Inn; examiner in civil law, Cambridge; queen's counsel; married Betty Lemon, whose father was editor of *Punch*.

Rossetti, Christina (1830–94). Born in London; sister of Dante Gabriel and Maria; youngest child in family; suffered poor health; involved in Anglo-Catholic movement; lived retired life; published *Goblin Market* (1862) and other poetry.

Roth, Mathias, (?–1891). M.D., Vienna University; practiced in London;

moved to Brighton; founded Ladies' Sanitary Association and Society for Prevention of Blindness; wrote on chronic diseases, gymnastic exercises, scientific physical education, and hygiene.

Ruskin, John (1819–1900). Christ Church, Oxford; art and social critic; wrote *Modern Painters* (1843), *Stones of Venice* (1851–53), *Unto This Last* (1860), *Fors Clavigera* (1871–84), *Praeterita* (1885–89); taught art, Working Men's College; professor of fine arts, Oxford; advocate of pre-Raphaelites; critic of laissez-faire economics; married Effie Gray, 1848; marriage later annulled.

Rutson, Albert Osliff (1836–90). University College, Oxford; Fellow, Magdalen College; called to bar; private secretary to Home Secretary Bruce; member, Metropolitan Asylum Board; alderman, North Riding; member, London School Board.

Rye, Maria (1829–1903). Daughter of a solicitor; secretary, Married Women's Property Committee; active in Langham Place Circle; founded Female Middle-Class Emigration Society; wrote *Emigration for Educated Women*.

Sainton, Charlotte Dolby (1821–85). Born in London; entered Royal Academy of Music, 1832; contralto singing oratorio and English ballads; Mendelssohn wrote a part in the *Elijah* for her and dedicated his *Six Songs* to her; toured Leipzig, France, and Holland; married violinist Prosper Philippe Sainton, 1860; retired 1870; opened Vocal Academy, 1872.

Salt, Titus (1803–76). Founder of manufacturing plant, Yorkshire; owned factories in Bradford; built state-of-the-art factory near Shipley, covering almost twenty acres, including a Congregational church, baths, wash-houses, infirmary, and school; magistrate, then mayor, Bradford; president, Chamber of Commerce; M.P. from Bradford; married Caroline Whitlan, 1831.

Sanders, Samuel (1846?–1915). St. John's College, Cambridge; Headmaster, Northampton Grammar School; honorary canon of Peterborough; married (first) Roberta Henrietta Doüet, (second) Annie Elizabeth Pegg.

Scott, Charles Prestwich (1846–1932). Corpus Christi College, Oxford; magistrate for Manchester; member of governing bodies, Owens College and Victoria University; editor, *Manchester Guardian*; married Rachel Cook, 1874.

Scott, William Bell (1811–90). Painter; exhibited at Royal Academy; founder and Headmaster, Government School of Design, Newcastle; did pictures on history of Northumberland at Winter Exhibition of British Artists, 1865; wrote poetry, memoir of David Scott, his brother, and studies of Blake and Dürer.

Seebohm, Frederic (1833–1912). Friends' School, York; called to bar, Middle Temple; partner in banking firm, Sharples and Company, Hitchin; wrote on politics and economics for periodicals, and books: *The Oxford Reformers*; *Era of the Protestant Revolution*; *The English Village Community*.

Seeley, John Robert (1834–95). Christ's College, Cambridge, Fellow; professor of Latin, University College, London; Regius Professor, Cambridge; early lecturer at the College for Women; wrote *Ecce Homo* and other scholarly works; contributed to *Macmillan's* and other periodicals; edited *Student's Guide to the University of Cambridge.*

Selwyn, Edward John (1822–93). Trinity College, Cambridge; principal, Blackheath Proprietary School; rector, St. Paul's, Wokingham; married Maria Hughes.

Senior, Nassau William (1790–1864). Oxford; called to bar; Drummond Professor of Political Economy, Oxford; member, Poor Law Commission; wrote report on which the 1834 Poor Law was based; member, commissions on factories, handloom weavers, the Irish Poor Law, and education; wrote for *Edinburgh Review, Quarterly Review,* and *London Review.*

Shaen, William (1821–87). University College, London; called to bar, Lincoln's Inn Field and Bedford Row; clerk of convocation, member of senate, University of London; chairman of council, Bedford College; solicitor to Jamaica Committee; active reformer and feminist; solicitor to Girls' Public Day School Company and Girton College; cofounder, Bedford College for Women, London School of Medicine for Women.

Shaftesbury, Lord Anthony Ashley Cooper (1801–85). Christ Church, Oxford; elected to Parliament, 1826; worked to improve factory conditions and to reduce children's and women's working hours; sponsored Ten-Hours' Bill; president, Ragged School Union; worked for Reformatory and Refuge Union; early supporter, SPEW.

Shirreff, Emily (1814–97). Sister of Maria Grey; founder, National Union for the Education of Women (later Girls' Public Day School Company); with her sister, wrote *Thoughts on Self-Culture Addressed to Women,* and, independently, *Intellectual Education and Its Influence on the Character and Happiness of Women*; founder, president, Froebel Society; supported Maria Grey Training College; Mistress, the College for Women at Hitchin, 1870; member, College Committee; member, Girton College.

Shirreff, Maria. See Grey, Maria Shirreff.

Shorrock, Constance Mary (?–1905). Girton College, 1872–75.

Shuttleworth, Sir James Kay (1804–77). See Kay Shuttleworth, James.

Sidgwick, Henry (1838–1900). Trinity College, Cambridge, Fellow, Lecturer; member, Apostles; resigned fellowship for religious reasons; involved in Lectures for women, which led to formation of Newnham College; praelector of moral philosophy, Trinity; wrote about philosophy and political economy; member, Society for Psychical Research; married Eleanor Mildred Balfour.

Slade, Gertrude (?). The College for Women at Hitchin, 1870–71.

Smith, Charles (1844–?). Sidney Sussex College, Cambridge, Fellow, Lecturer, and Tutor; senior moderator, Mathematical Tripos; vice chancellor of university; wrote on mathematics; married Annie Hopkins.

Smith, Eleanor Elizabeth (1822–96). Born in Dublin; skilled linguist who taught herself Hebrew at seven; read Dante; and in old age resumed study of Greek; kept house at Oxford for her brother, mathematician Henry Smith; devoted to charitable and educational goals; member, Oxford School Board and councils of Somerville and Bedford Colleges.

Smith, Henry (1826–83). Brother of Eleanor Elizabeth Smith; Balliol College, Oxford, Scholar, Fellow, Senior Mathematical Scholar, Honorary Fellow; Savilian Professor of Geometry; keeper of University Museum; member, Hebdomadal Council, Royal Committee on Scientific Education, and University of Oxford Commission.

Smith, Julia (1799–1883). Sister of Benjamin Leigh Smith; aunt of Barbara Bodichon; befriended the Leigh Smith children; introduced nieces to Mary Howitt, Mrs. Somerville, and Harriet Martineau; active in foundation of Bedford College and in the abolitionist movement.

Smith, Louisa Garrett (?–1867). Sister of Elizabeth and Millicent Garrett; member, Kensington Society, Local Exams campaign; signed suffrage petition, 1866; secretary, Enfranchisement of Women Committee, 1866–67; married James Smith.

Smith, Nannie. See Leigh-Smith, Nannie.

Smith, William (1813/14–93). University of London; professor of Greek, Latin, and German languages, Highbury and Homerton Colleges; published *Dictionary of Greek and Roman Antiquities, Dictionary of Greek and Roman Biography and Mythology*, and *Dictionary of Greek and Roman Geography*; classical examiner, University of London; contributed notes to Gibbon's *Decline and Fall of the Roman Empire*; edited *Quarterly Review*; member of senate, University of London.

Soames, Laura (1840–95). Daughter of William Aldwin Soames, Brighton; active in educational work; member, Brighton School Board; author of book on English, French, and German phonetics.

Solly, Samuel (1805–71). Brother of Henry Solly, Lavinia Solly, and Charlotte Solly Manning; Guy's Hospital; member, Royal College of Surgeons, Council of College of Surgeons, and Court of Examiners; wrote on science; lectured on surgery and medicine; member, NAPSS.

Somerville, Mary Fairfax (1780–1872). Astronomer; wrote several scientific texts; honorary member, Royal Astronomical Society; presented mathematical library to Girton College; married (first) Captain Greig, (second). William Somerville.

Sparkes, John Charles Lewis (?). Artist and author; wrote *Hints to China and Tile Decorators* (1877), *Hand-Book to the Practice of Pottery Painting* (1878), and *Schools of Art: Origin, History, Work, and Influence* (1884).

Stanley, Lady Augusta Frederica (1822–76). Daughter of Thomas Bruce, seventh earl of Elgin; member, first Executive Committee of the College for Women; original member, Girton College; Westminster Training School for Nurses established in her memory; married Arthur Stanley, dean of Westminster.

Stanley of Alderley, Lady Henrietta Maria (1807–95). Daughter of Lord Dillon; raised in Florence; educated by radical French governess; active supporter of and contributor to Girton College, Girls' Public Day School Company, London School of Medicine for Women; member, Girton College; gave first chemical laboratory and Stanley Library to Girton; married second Lord Stanley of Alderley.

Steinthal, Samuel Alfred (1826–?). Born in Manchester; studied in Germany; engineer; interested in social and philanthropic work; Manchester New College; active in abolitionist movement; missionary to poor in Liverpool; worked with William Gaskell in Manchester; advocate of women's suffrage; active in Famine Relief for India.

Stephen, Sir James Fitzjames (1829–94). Brother of Leslie Stephen; Trinity College, Cambridge, Fellow; member, Apostles; called to bar, Inner Temple, 1854; secretary, Education Commission, 1858–61; Counsel, Jamaica Committee; published in *Saturday Review* and *Cornhill*; married Mary Cunningham, 1855.

Stephen, Leslie (1832–1904). Brother of James Fitzjames Stephen; Trinity Hall, Cambridge, Fellow; published *Essays on Freethinking and Plainspeaking, History of English Thought in the Eighteenth Century*, and *The Life of Henry Fawcett*; edited *Cornhill Magazine* and *Dictionary of National Biography*; wrote for *Macmillan's, Fortnightly, Saturday Review*, and others; married (first) Harriet Marion Thackeray, (second) Julia Prinsep Duckworth, mother of Vanessa and Virginia Stephen.

Stevenson, Flora Clift (1840–1905). Daughter of James Stevenson and Jane Steward; educated at private schools; attended classes at Edinburgh Association for University Education of Women; active in Edinburgh movements for women's suffrage and education; member, Medical Education for Women Committee; first woman elected to Edinburgh School Board; director, Edinburgh Philosophical Institution and Royal Blind Asylum School.

Stevenson, William Fleming (1832–86). Minister and writer; born in Ireland; University of Glasgow; missionary in Belfast; contributed to *Good Words*; published *Praying and Working*.

Storrar, John (1811–86). Physician; member of senate, University of London; chairman of convocation.

Stuart, James (1843–1913). St. Andrews University and Trinity College, Cambridge, Fellow; first professor of mechanism and applied mathematics, Cambridge; active in formation of Lectures for Women, University Extension programs; early lecturer at the College for Women; helped found Cambridge Higher Exam for Women; wrote on scientific, social, and educational issues; married Laura Colman, a Quaker active in philanthropy and reform movements.

Sutherland, Countess of, Harriet Elizabeth Georgiana (1806–68). Mistress of the robes to the queen; supported abolitionist movement, holding meetings at her town house in 1853; married George Granville, Earl of Gower.

Swanwick, Anna (1818–99). Born in Liverpool; studied German, Greek, and

Hebrew in Berlin; in London, studied higher mathematics under Professor Newman; member of council, Queen's College and Bedford College; assisted in founding Girton and Somerville colleges; taught at Working Men's College, London; published translations of Goethe, Schiller, and Aeschylus.

Taunton, Lord Henry Labouchere (1798–1869). Christ Church, Oxford; lord of admiralty (1832–34); vice president and president, Board of Trade; undersecretary and secretary of the colonies; chief secretary for Ireland during the famine; chair, Schools Inquiry Commission and Endowed Schools Commission.

Taylor, Clementia Doughty (1810–1908). Born in Norfolk; governess; member, Society of Friends of Italy; organized assistance for freed slaves during Civil War; member, Committee for Women's Suffrage, 1866; helped form Ladies' Educational Association to gain admission for women to University College; started Aubrey Evening Institute for working-class men and women; married Peter Alfred Taylor.

Taylor, Emily (1795–1872). Daughter of Samuel Taylor; sister of Edgar Taylor; wrote poetry, history, and fiction, including *Tales of the Saxons, England and Its People,* and *The Knewets.*

Taylor, Harriet. See Mill, Harriet Taylor.

Taylor, Helen (1831–1907). Daughter of Harriet Taylor Mill and John Taylor; member, Kensington Society; active in women's suffrage movement; member, London School Board, 1876.

Taylor, Peter Alfred (1819–91). Businessman, Samuel Cortauld & Co.; friend of Mazzini; chairman, Society of Friends of Italy; M.P. from Leicester; pioneer of international arbitration; advocate of women's suffrage; treasurer, London Emancipation Society and Jamaica Committee; proprietor, the *Examiner;* married Clementia Doughty.

Taylor, Sedley (1834–1920). Trinity College, Cambridge, Fellow; wrote on music, mathematics, and economics; member, College Committee and Girton College; established Organ Scholarship, 1910; donated orchestral scores to the college, 1911.

Temple, Frederick (1821–1902). Balliol College, Oxford, Scholar, Fellow, Mathematical Tutor; principal, Kneller Hall Training College; inspector of training schools; Headmaster, Rugby School; bishop of London.

Thackeray, Anne Isabella (1837–1919). Daughter of W. M. Thackeray; author of novels and stories, including *The Story of Elizabeth* and *The Village on the Cliff;* wrote biographies and literary articles on Tennyson, Ruskin, and Browning; married Richmond Thackeray Ritchie.

Thackeray, Harriet Marian (Minnie) (1840–75). Daughter of W. M. Thackeray; sister of Anne Thackeray; married Leslie Stephen, 1867.

Thomas, Frances Eliza Millett. See Notley, Frances Eliza Millett.

Thompson, William Hepworth (1810–86). Trinity College, Cambridge, Scholar,

Fellow, and Tutor; Headmaster, Collegiate School, Leicester 1836–37; Master, Trinity College 1866–86, Regius Professor of Greek, Cambridge, 1853–67; vice chancellor, 1867–68; published sermons, and translations of Plato.

Thornton, F. V. (?). Ran coeducational school, the Callington School; testified before Schools Inquiry Commission.

Tidman, Ellen Elizabeth (?). The College for Women at Hitchin, 1870–71, leaving because of poor health.

Tidman, Paul Frederick (1836–89). Uncle of Ellen Elizabeth Tidman; worked for East India merchants; developed new methods in aluminum industry; secretary, International Monetary Association; wrote on monetary issues, including *Gold and Silver Money* and *Money and Labour.*

Tomkinson, Henry Richard (1831–1906). Trinity College, Cambridge; Assistant Master and bursar, Marlborough College; managing director, Sun Fire Insurance Office; chairman, Associated Insurance Offices of London; staunch supporter of women's higher education, serving Girton in various positions for years.

Townsend, Meredith White (1831–1911). In India, editor and proprietor of *Friend of India*; returned to England, became co-editor and proprietor, with Richard Hutton, the *Spectator*; edited its political department.

Townshend, Isabella Frances Vere (1847–82). The College for Women at Hitchin, 1869–72, one of pioneers; scholarship for excellence in writing; Previous Exam in Classics, 1870; settled in Rome; studied painting; traveled with Anna Lloyd.

Trollope, Thomas Adolphus (1810–92). Brother of Anthony Trollope; Magdalen Hall, Oxford; novelist and historian; published *A Summer in Brittany* and *A Summer in Western France*; contributed to periodicals and journals in London; married (first) Theodosia Garrow, (second) Fanny Ternan, daughter of Thomas L. Ternan.

Tubbs, Fanny Cecilia (1831–1921). First woman member of School Board, Hastings; early subscriber to Girton.

Tuthill, Anna Elizabeth (?–1906). Girton College, 1876–79; Special Examination in Law; Ordinary Degree standard; married William Woodward, 1882.

Tyndall, John (1820–93). Born in Ireland; studied in Germany; gave lectures at Royal Institution; professor of natural philosophy; worked with Thomas Huxley studying glaciers in Switzerland; wrote on science; honorary degree from Oxford.

Venn, Reverend John (1834–1923). Caius College, Cambridge, Fellow, Lecturer in moral science; Hulsean Lecturer, Cambridge; examiner in logic and moral philosophy, University of London; Fellow, Royal Society; early lecturer at the College for Women; wrote on logic and chance, characteristics of belief, and symbolic logic.

Vernon, Matilda Julia (?). Secretary, Manchester Association for Promoting the Education of Women; managing secretary, Manchester High School for Girls.

Walker, Mary (1832–1919). M.D., Syracuse Medical College, 1855; assistant surgeon, U.S. Army during Civil War; Congressional Medal of Honor; wrote on political, medical, and social issues in works including *Hit* and *Unmasked: the Science of Immorality*; advocated comfortable clothing for women; founded Mutual Dress Reform and Equal Rights Association.

Wallis, Anne Selina (?–1922). Girton College, 1873–76; Examination in history, 1876; Assistant Mistress, Notting Hill School; Mistress, Park School in Glasgow; Assistant Mistress, Highfield School, Hendon; Headmistress, Richmond High School; and Assistant Mistress, Wycombe Abbey School.

Waterhouse, Alfred (1830–1905). Architect; designed Manchester Assize Courts, Owens College, and Manchester Town Hall; worked on Girton College; partially reconstructed Caius and Pembroke colleges, Cambridge and Balliol College, Oxford; designed Natural History Museum, South Kensington, and New University and National Liberal Clubs; member, Royal and Imperial Academy of Vienna; associate, *Academie Royale des Sciences, des Lettres, et des Beaux-Arts de Belgique*; Royal Gold Medallist, Royal Institute of British Architects.

Watney, Daniel (1825–93). Distiller and brewer; surveyor accountant of St. Paul's School, London; member of Mercers Company.

Watson, Robert Spence (1836/37–1911). Quaker; University College, London; practiced law; member, Newcastle School Board; supported University Extension movement; member and president, National Liberal Federation; founder, National Liberal Club; married Elizabeth Richardson.

Wedgwood, Hensleigh (1803–91). Grandson of Josiah Wedgwood; Christ College, Cambridge; original member, Philological Society; called to bar; wrote on geometry; edited dictionary of English etymology.

Welsh, Elizabeth (1843–1921). The College for Women at Hitchin and Girton, 1871–75; College Scholar; Classical Tripos, 1875; Classics Mistress, Manchester High School; resident classical lecturer, Girton College; Mistress, Girton College; member, Girton College and Girton Executive Committee.

Westlake, Alice Hare (?–1923). Daughter of Thomas Hare; member, Kensington Society; proponent of women's education and suffrage; honorary treasurer, Hospital for Women; member, London School Board; active in NAPSS; work exhibited at the Royal Academy; married John Westlake.

Westlake, John (1828–1913). Trinity College, Cambridge; called to bar, Lincoln's Inn; queen's counsel; professor of international law, Cambridge; foreign secretary, NAPSS; president, Institute of International Law, Cambridge; married Alice Hare.

Whewell, Reverend William (1794–1866). Trinity College, Cambridge, Fellow, Tutor, Master, professor of mineralogy and moral theology, vice chancellor of university; president, Geological Society; published on mathematics and science.

Wilson, James (1805–60). Quaker; founder and chief editor, the *Economist*; M.P. from Westbury; secretary, Board of Control for India; vice president, Board of Trade; daughter Eliza married Walter Bagehot and Zoe married Orby Shipley.

Winkworth, Susanna (1820–84). Daughter of Henry Winkworth, Manchester; studied under Reverend Gaskell and Dr. Martineau; did translations; wrote *Life and Letters of B. G. Niebuhr* and *Theologia Germanica*; translated Max Müller's *German Lore*; worked to improve housing for poor; governor, Red Maids' School, Bristol; member of council, Cheltenham Ladies' College.

Wolstenholme, Elizabeth (1834–1918). Helped establish girls' school in Manchester; member, Manchester Board of Schoolmistresses, North of England Council, Manchester Women's Suffrage Society, Married Women's Property Committee; after marrying Ben Elmy remained politically active; helped pass Infant Custody Act; founded Women's Freedom League and Women's Emancipation Union; wrote with husband on sex education for children; wrote poems and feminist essays using pen name "Ellis Ethelmer."

Wood, Janet (?–1905/6). Girton College, 1875–78; Special Examination in Law, 1878; Ordinary Degree standard; Assistant Mistress, The School, St. Andrews; married J. P. Clark, 1884.

Wood, Sir William Page (1801–81). Trinity College, Cambridge, Fellow; called to bar, Lincoln's Inn; Fellow, Royal Society; queen's counsel; M.P. from Oxford; married Charlotte Moor.

Woodhead, Sarah (1851–1908). The College for Women at Hitchin, 1869–73; one of pioneers; Previous Exams in Classics, 1870; Mathematics Tripos, 1873; taught mathematics, Manchester High School; Headmistress, Silverwell House, Bolton; wrote books on ethics and theosophy; married George Bentham Corbett.

Wratislaw, Albert Henry (1821/22–92). Christ Church, Cambridge, Scholar, Fellow, Tutor; Headmaster, Grammar School, Felstead; Headmaster, King Edward VI Grammar School; wrote books including translations of Czech poetry, sermons, and history.

Wrottesley, Lord John (1798–1867). Corpus Christi College, Oxford; original member, later president, Royal Astronomical Society; developed observatory at Blackheath.

Yonge, Charlotte Mary (1823–1901). Lived near Winchester; studied religion and history with John Keble; wrote over two hundred books, including *The Heir of Redclyffe*; edited *The Monthly Packet of Evening Readings for Members of the English Church*.

Young, Sir George (1837–?). Trinity College, Cambridge; called to bar, Lincoln's Inn, 1864; secretary, Factory and Workshops Acts Commission, 1875, and Irish Land Acts Commission, 1881; president of senate, University College, London.

Notes

1. Thanks to Sophie Badham, Royal Holloway University of London, Department of History, for providing information on Bostock from the *New DNB*.

2. Thanks to Professor Colin Matthew for providing information on Davies from the *New DNB*.

3. Thanks to Vivien Allen, contributor to the *New DNB*, for providing information on Heckford Goff from the *New DNB*.

4. Thanks to Norman Vance, University of Sussex at Brighton, School of English and American Studies, for providing information on Fanny Kingsley from the *New DNB*.

5. Thanks to Dr. Ann B. Shteir, professor, Humanities/School of Women's Studies, York University, Canada, for information on Phebe Lankester.

6. Thanks to Janet Sondheimer for providing information on Fanny Metcalfe from the *New DNB*.

7. Thanks to P. H. Waddington, professor emeritus, Victoria University of Wellington, for providing information on Lady Monson.

8. Thanks to Mary Ann Elston, senior lecturer in sociology, Department of Social Policy and Social Science, Royal Holloway, for providing information on Morgan from the *New DNB*.

9. Thanks to Dr. Mary Felicity Hunt for providing information on Mary Eliza Porter from the *New DNB*.

Sources

Adams, *A Dictionary of the Drama*; Adams, *Dictionary of English Literature*; Allibone, *A Critical Dictionary of English Literature*; Banfield, *Biographies of Celebrities*; Banks, *Biographical Dictionary of British Feminists*; Baptie, *Sketches of the English Glee Composers*; *Birmingham Faces and Places*; Boase, *Modern English Biography*; Bonner, *To the Ends of the Earth*; Bryan, *Dictionary of Painters and Engravers*; Cassell's *Biographical Dictionary*; Champlin, *Cyclopedia of Painters and Paintings*; Cooper, *Men of Mark*; Cox, *Norfolk, Suffolk, and Cambridgeshire*; Crawford, *The Women's Suffrage Movement: A Reference Guide 1866–1928*; *A Dictionary of Contemporary Biography*; *Dictionary of National Biography*; Dingsdale, "A Fine and Lofty Sympathy"; Donnison, *Midwives and Medical Men: A History of the Struggle for the Control of Childbirth*; Emden, *Jews of Britain*; *Eminent Persons: Biographies Reprinted from The Times*; *Englishwoman's Review*; Foster, *Men-at-the-Bar*; Gaskell, *Norfolk Leaders*; Gillow, *A Literary and Biographical History of the English Catholics*; *Girton College Register*; Grove, *Dictionary of Music and Musicians*; Gubar, "Blessings in Disguise," *Massachusetts Review* (1981); Hale, *A Cyclopaedia of Female Biography*; Hays,

Women of the Day; Herstein, *A Mid-Victorian Feminist: Barbara Leigh Smith Bodichon*; Hirsch, *Barbara Leigh Smith Bodichon*; Hollis, *Ladies Elect: Women in English Local Government*; Inglis, *The Dramatic Writers of Scotland*; Kirk, *Supplement to Allibone's Critical Dictionary*; Knight, *Biography*; Lacey, *Barbara Leigh Smith Bodichon and the Langham Place Group*; *Leading Men of London*; Leedham-Green, *Concise History of the University of Cambridge*; Leyland, *Contemporary Medical Men*; Low & Pulling, *Dictionary of English History*; MacLeod, *A Dictionary of Political Economy*; *Manchester Faces and Places*; Manton, *Elizabeth Garrett Anderson*; Martel, "British Women in the NAPSS"; Mellors, *Men of Nottingham and Nottinghamshire*; *Men and Women of the Time*; *Men of the Time: Biographical Sketches*; Mitchell, *Victorian Britain: An Encyclopedia*; *Norfolk and Suffolk in East Anglia*; Ottley, *A Biographical and Critical Dictionary of Painters and Engravers*; *Our Contemporaries*; Palgrave, *Dictionary of Political Economy*; Pilkington, *A General Dictionary of Painters*; Poss, *A Biographical Dictionary of the Judges of England*; Pratt, *People of the Period*; Sanders, *Celebrities of the Century*; Schaff and Jackson, *Encyclopedia of Living Divines*; Smith-Dampier, *East Anglian Worthies*; Stephen, *Emily Davies and Girton College*; Stephen, *Girton College 1869–1932*; Strickland, *A Dictionary of Irish Artists*; Tuke, *History of Bedford College for Women*; Venn, *Alumni Cantabrigienses*; *Victorian Britain: An Encyclopedia*; *Walford's County Families of the United Kingdom*; Waller, *The Imperial Dictionary of Universal Biography*; Ward, *Men of the Reign of Queen Victoria*; Wheeler, *A Biographical Dictionary of Freethinkers*; *Who Was Who 1897–1916*; *Who Was Who in America 1897–1942*; Worzala, "The Langham Place Circle."

Published Writings of Emily Davies

"The Application of Funds to the Education of Girls." Paper read at NAPSS, Sheffield. *Transactions of the National Association for the Promotion of Social Science.* London, 1865.

Are Women Suffragists Asking for Seats in Parliament? A Reply. Letter to the *Times,* 4 February 1907. Reprint, London, 1907, for the Society for Women's Suffrage.

"Cambridge Local Examinations: Report of an Examination of Girls, Held (by permission of the Syndicate) in Connexion with the Local Examinations of the University of Cambridge in 1863." London, 1864.

"Christian Teaching and the Lessons of Experience on Ideals of Womanhood." Letter to the *Spectator,* 28 July 1908.

"'Clericus Dunelmensis': Middle-Class Female Education." Letter to the *Record,* 1865.

"College Education for Women." Paper read at the Nottingham Literary and Philosophical Society, 8 February 1872.

"College for Women." *Birmingham Morning News.* 30 October 1871.

A Constitutional Sluice, or Steps in the Enfranchisement of Women. Including letter to the *Times,* 25 December 1907. Reprint, London, 1907, for the Society for Women's Suffrage.

"Discussion on the Education of Girls." Paper read at NAPSS, Leeds. *Transactions of the National Association for the Promotion of Social Science.* London, 1871, 369.

"Education of Girls." *Brighton Herald.* 12 November 1864.

"Employment of Women." Northumberland and Durham, 1861. Reprinted in *Thoughts on Some Questions Relating to Women, 1860–1908.* Cambridge, 1908.

"Female Education." *Queen.* 25 November 1865.

"Female Physicians." Letter to the *English Woman's Journal,* 1861. Reprinted in *Thoughts on Some Questions Relating to Women, 1860–1908.* Cambridge, 1908.

"Girton College." Letter to the *Spectator,* 7 September 1872.

"Girton College." Letter to the *Times,* 19 January 1877.

"Higher Education in Connexion with the Universities." *Journal of the Women's Education Union* 2, no. 14 (February 1874).

The Higher Education of Women. 1866. Reprint, London, 1988.

"Home and the Higher Education." Birmingham Higher Education Association. 21 February 1878. Reprinted in *Thoughts on Some Questions Relating to Women, 1860–1908.* Cambridge, 1908.

"The Influence of University Degrees on the Education of Women." *Victoria* (July 1863): 260–71. Reprinted in *Thoughts on Some Questions Relating to Women, 1860–1908.* Cambridge, 1908.

"Letters to a Daily Paper." Newcastle-on-Tyne, 1860. Reprinted in *Thoughts on Some Questions Relating to Women, 1860–1908*. Cambridge, 1908.

Letters to the *Times* and *Spectator* on women's suffrage, 1907–8. Reprinted in *Thoughts on Some Questions Relating to Women, 1860–1908*. Cambridge, 1908.

"Medicine as a Profession for Women." Paper read at NAPSS, London. *Transactions of the National Association for the Promotion of Social Science*. London, 1862, 810–11. Reprinted in *Thoughts on Some Questions Relating to Women, 1860–1908*. Cambridge, 1908.

"Needleworkers v. Society." *Victoria* (August 1863): 348–60.

"On Secondary Instruction, as Relating to Girls." Paper read at NAPSS, York. *Transactions of the National Association for the Promotion of Social Science*. London, 1864, 394–404.

"Parliamentary Franchise for Women." Letter to the *Times*, 31 March 1904.

"A Plea for Discrimination." London: Printed for the London Society for Women's Suffrage.

"Proposed Admission of Women to Cambridge Degrees." Letter to the *Times*, 24 January 1888.

"Proposed New College for Women." *Economist*. 18 July 1868.

"Proposed New College for Women." *Express*. 19 September 1868.

"Proposed New College for Women." *Jewish Chronicle*. 10 July 1868.

"Proposed New College for Women." *Literary Churchman*. 11 July 1868.

"Proposed New College for Women." *Queen*. 11 July 1868.

"Reasons for the Extension of the University Local Examinations to Girls." London, 1864.

"Report of a Discussion on the Proposed Admission of Girls to the University Local Examinations. Held at a Special Meeting of the National Association for the Promotion of Social Science." *Alexandra Magazine and English Woman's Journal* 1 (June 1864): 101–13.

"Social Science." *Victoria* (December 1863): 187–88.

"Some Account of a Proposed New College for Women." *Contemporary Review* 9 (December 1868).

"Some Account of a Proposed New College for Women." Paper read at NAPSS, Birmingham. *Transactions of the National Association for the Promotion of Social Science*. London, 1868, 400–403.

"Some Recollections of Work with Miss Buss." *Frances Mary Buss Schools Jubilee Magazine* (April 1900).

"Special Systems of Education for Women." *London Student*, no. 3 (June 1868) 131–42. Reprinted in *Thoughts on Some Questions Relating to Women, 1860–1908*. Cambridge, 1908.

"Speech at the Conference on University Degrees for Women, Convened by the Governors of the Royal Holloway College." London, 1897.

Thoughts on Some Questions Relating to Women. Pamphlet. London, n.d., Victoria Press.

Thoughts on Some Questions Relating to Women, 1860–1908. Cambridge, 1908.

"The Training of the Imagination." *Contemporary Review* 9 (September 1869). Reprint, London, 1869, for the London Association of Schoolmistresses.

"University Degrees and the Education of Women." *Victoria* (July 1863): 260–71. Reprinted in *Thoughts on Some Questions Relating to Women, 1860–1908.* Cambridge, 1908.

"University Local Examinations." Letter to the *Times,* 30 August 1872.

Women in the Universities of England and Scotland. Cambridge, 1896. Reprinted in *Thoughts on Some Questions Relating to Women, 1860–1908.* Cambridge, 1908.

"The Women's Suffrage Movement: Why Should We Care for It and How Can We Help to Further It?" Parts 1 and 2. *Girton Review,* no. 13 (Lent term 1905): 13–16; no. 14 (May term 1905): 10–15.

Appendix A

Letters Not Extant: Dated, Reproduced from
Barbara Stephen, *Emily Davies and Girton College* (1927)

These sixty excerpts of letters written between 1861 and 1875 do not necessarily comprise sixty separate letters. Many of the short, undated excerpts listed below in appendix B may be part of these dated letters. Furthermore, Stephen has sometimes quoted from the same letter at different times (see the 5 August 1868 letter to Tomkinson cited both on page 24 and on page 174). The letter to Adelaide Manning in October 1866 (page 113) might be part of the letter dated 29 October on page 210.

Approximately twenty of these dated letters are cited in appendix D.

24: ED to HT (5 August 1868)
111: ED to AM (22 April 1866)
111: ED to AM (28 April 1866)
112: ED to AM (26 June 1866)
113: ED to AM (October 1866)
118: ED to AM (14 June 1867)
124: ED to EG (7 December [1870])
149: ED to AR (25 October 1866)
149: ED to AR (29 December 1866)
157: ED to LB (March 1867)
174: ED to HT (5 August 1868)
195: ED to AR (1 February [1869?])
198: ED to AM (2 June 1869)
199: ED to AM (1 February 1869)
207: ED to AM (26 February 1869)
208: ED to HT (13 March 1869)
208: ED to HT (16 March 1869)
210: ED to AM (29 October 1868)
211: ED to CM (16 April 1869)
216: ED to BB (2 July 1869)
216: ED to AR (24 August 1869)
217: ED to AR (14 September 1869)
218: ED to CM (9 October 1869)
219: ED to AR (20 October 1869)
224: ED to AM (23 June 1870)
226: ED to HT (16 November 1870)
227: ED to AR (10 December 1869)
228: ED to AR (30 December 1869)
234: ED to CM (28 February 1870)
234: ED to CM (2 March 1870)

234: ED to CM (30 March 1870)
235: ED to AM (4 April 1870)
235: ED to AR (23 June 1870)
236: ED to CM (19 March 1870)
236: ED to AM (14 October 1870)
237: ED to AR (24 October 1870)
239: ED to AR (10 December 1870)
241: ED to HT (8 March 1871)
242: ED to HT (17 March 1871)
243: ED to AM (17 March 1871)
243: ED to HT (24 March 1871)
247: ED to AR (Twelfth Day, 1870)
249: ED to AR (1 August 1870)
251: ED to HS (31 December 1870)
254: ED to HT (22 December 1870)
255: ED to HS (19 May 1871)
256: ED to HT (4 May 1871)
258: ED to HT (15 May 1871)
258: ED to HT (17 May 1871)
260: ED to AR (27 September 1871)
262: ED to AR (15 January 1872?)
263: ED to WHC (November 1871)
269: ED to HT (25 March 1872)
270: ED to HT (10 June 1872)
271: ED to HT (17 July 1872)
271: ED to HT (19 July 1872)
271: ED to HT (25 July 1872)
279: ED to HT (25 February 1873)
295: ED to AM (3 January 1875)
296: ED to AM (8 May 1875)

Appendix B

Letters Not Extant: Undated, Reproduced from Barbara Stephen, *Emily Davies and Girton College* (1927)

In several cases the recipient of these forty-one letters assumed to be written between 1861 and 1875 is not known (see pages 163, 211, 213, 256, 262, and 295). As noted in appendix A, these snippets of letters may be part of letters cited elsewhere by Stephen with a date, since she did not cite the text of letters completely.

54: ED to AR	224: ED to AM
102: ED to AM	227: ED to AR
110: ED to AM	228: ED to AM
110: ED to AM	238: ED to AR
114: ED to AM	256: ED to ?
114: ED to AR	262: ED to ?
116: ED to AM	276: ED to AM
173: ED to HT	278: ED to HT
176: ED to AM	279: ED to HT
190: ED to AR	280: ED to HT
194: ED to AR	280: ED to HT
196: ED to AM	280: ED to ?
196: ED to HT	280: ED to HT
209: ED to AR	281: ED to HT
211: ED to ?	281: ED to AM
211: ED to AM	285: ED to HT
213: ED to MB	287: ED to AM
213: ED to AR	295: ED to ?
213: ED to ?	303: ED to AM
220: ED to CM	303: ED to AM

Appendix C

Extant Letters Cited, Reproduced from
Barbara Stephen, *Emily Davies and Girton College* (1927)

The approximately 138 letters listed below are cited by Barbara Stephen and fall within the period of this book (1861–75). Because extant copies of these letters exist, either in the Family Chronicle or in a draft or final version of the letter, we have included these letters in the body of our edition. In some cases, Stephen is clearly working with a different version—in most cases, it appears to be the original (no longer extant) from which Davies copied an excerpt into the Family Chronicle.

70: ED to JC (January 1864)
70: ED to JC (12 January 1864)
70: ED to JC (23 January 1864)
71: ED to JC (12 January 1864)
71: ED to AR (19 April 1864)
80: ED to BB (21 August 1869)
83: ED to AR (12 July 1862)
86: ED to HT (30 October 1863)
88: ED to AR (26 October 1863)
88: ED to HT (10 November 1863)
89: ED to HT (11 November 1863)
89: ED to AR (23 December 1863)
90: ED to HT (14 April 1864)
90: ED to HT (18 April 1864)
90: ED to HT (9 May 1864)
91: ED to AM (April 1864)
97: ED to CM (20 January 1864)
100: ED to HT (9 March 1865)
103: ED to RH (2 June 1866)
103: ED to RH (Spring 1866)
104: ED to RH (June 1866)
107: ED to AR (10 May 1865)
108: ED to BB (14 November 1865)
109: ED to HT (November 1865)
109: ED to HT (14 November 1865)
109: ED to BB (14 November 1865)
112: ED to H. Taylor (5 June 1866)
113: ED to H. Taylor (28 September 1866)
113: ED to BB (6 September 1866)
116: ED to BB (21 March 1867)

117: ED to BB (28 May 1867)
117: ED to BB (3 June 1867)
118: ED to AR (18 June 1867)
121: ED to HT (7 November 1870)
122: ED to HT (8 November 1870)
123: ED to HT (12 November 1870)
123: ED to HT (14 November 1870)
123: ED to HT (25 November 1870)
123: ED to AM? (21 November 1870)
130: ED to MA (23 December 1864)
131: ED to TA (28 December 1864)
131: ED to GG (30 December 1864)
132: ED to HR (17 November 1865)
135: ED to AR (25 October 1865)
135: ED to HR (18 November 1865)
136: ED to AR (12 December 1865)
138: ED to BB (undated: winter 1866)
140: ED to BB (19 February 1866)
146: ED to EP (September 1866)
150: ED to BB (29 January 1867)
151: ED to AR (4 February 1867)
153: ED to LB (11 March 1867)
157: ED to BB (6 April 1867)
158: ED to BB (26 May 1867)
158: ED to HT (21 June 1867)
159: ED to AR (18 July 1867)
161: ED to EG (30 March 1867)
162: ED to AR (24 August 1867)
164: ED to HT (9 November 1867)
164: ED to HT (15 November 1867)

166: ED to HT (7 December 1867)
166: ED to AR (13 December 1867)
166: ED to AR (17 December 1867)
167: ED to AR (28 December 1867)
168: ED to AR (6 March 1868)
169: ED to BB (15? March 1868)
170: ED to AR (27 November 1867)
171: ED to CM (25 November 1868)
171: ED to AR (21 February 1867)
172: ED to HT (April 1868)
174: ED to AR (15 August 1868)
174: ED to AR (1 August 1868)
178: ED to BB (September 1868)
182: ED to JC (21 August 1869)
188: ED to AR (30 December 1867)
189: ED to AR (4 February 1868)
190: ED to AR (28 February 1868)
191: ED to AR (17 March 1868)
191: ED to AR (23 March 1868)
192: ED to AR (27 March 1868)
193: ED to AR (23 May 1868)
193: ED to BB (18 March 1865)
195: ED to HT (6 January 1869)
196: ED to HT (5 February 1869)
196: ED to BB (September 1868)
202: ED to AR (31 January 1868)
203: ED to AR (4 February 1868)
204: ED to AR (27 March 1868)
204: ED to AR (23 April 1868)
205: ED to BB (23 November 1868)
207: ED to BB (March 1869)
208: ED to BB (2 March 1869)
208: ED to BB (March 1869)
209: ED to AR (25 June 1868)
   Note: This refers to two of the three sentences Stephen cites in that paragraph.
209: ED to AR (15 July 1868)
210: ED to BB (14 November 1868)
212: ED to MB (22 January 1869)
213: ED to MB (1 March 1869)

213: ED to AR (1 August 1868)
215: ED to BB (13 July 1869)
216: ED to BB (4 June 1869)
216: ED to BB (2 August 1869)
218: ED to BB (21 August 1869)
222: ED to BB (25 February 1870)
249: ED to BB (8 November 1870)
259: ED to BB (4 June 1871)
261: ED to BB (20 December 1871)
266: ED to BB (18 October 1870)
272: ED to BB (21 October 1872)
272: ED to BB (23 October 1872)
273: ED to EHM (21 November 1872)
274: ED to EHM (23 November 1872)
274: ED to EHM (25 November 1872)
275: ED to EHM (30 November 1872)
280: ED to BB (18 February 1873)
281: ED to BB (15 January 1872)
282: ED to BB (6 September 1873)
282: ED to BB (25 September 1873)
284: ED to BB (6 January 1874)
286: ED to BB (9? March 1874)
286: ED to BB (14 April 1874)
286: ED to BB (3 September 1873)
286: ED to BB (20 May 1874)
286: ED to BB (27 May 1874)
288: ED to BB (25 May 1873)
293: ED to BB (12 June 1874)
295: ED to BB (27 April 1875)
295: ED to BB (27 April 1875)
296: ED to BB (22 April 1875)
296: ED to BB (26? April 1875)
298: ED to BB (2 July 1875)
298: ED to BB (16 October 1875)
300: ED to BB (10 November 1874)
301: ED to BB (July 1875)
302: ED to BB (22 April 1875)
302: ED to BB (2 July 1875)
303: ED to BB (29 December 1875)

Appendix D

Letters Not Extant, Reproduced from Barbara Stephen,
Emily Davies and Girton College (1927)

This appendix comprises copies of a selection of nonextant letters that are quoted in the Stephen biography. These letters were included because they are of substantial length and may illuminate the reader's understanding of Davies. These letters are reproduced as per the Stephen text, including footnotes, but without the quotation marks Stephen sometimes used for letters. We have not edited these letters, except to indicate the recipient of each letter with angle brackets above the letter. No assurances can be made about the precision with which these letters were originally copied. A short introduction to this section has been added in order to provide clarity on some topics mentioned in these letters.

Stephen used letters that illustrate Davies's version of central policy and procedural disagreements, including those over the composition of the suffrage committee and those complicating the appointment of the first Mistress of the College for Women, Hitchin. Stephen also had access to a number of letters in which Davies teased out the content of the curriculum, and they illustrate how Davies ensured that most students entering the college would sit for the Tripos exams.

Stephen also used letters to describe the first entrance exam for the College for Women, held at the University of London in July 1869. Eighteen women sat for the exam, and thirteen passed. Three more were examined in October at Bodichon's house in Blandford Square. The debate over separate standards dominated the early years of the College for Women. Even Cambridge men tutoring students at Girton were divided over the approach to women's education, and many who were committed to educational reform felt that adhering to the same curriculum and methods being used at the University was a mistake (see introduction).

Several of the Girton pioneers have recorded their memories of the first year of the college. One letter used by Stephen offers a unique account of Davies's own impression of the first weeks of the new college. Stephen also had access to papers that show the College Committee's concern as the lease at Benslow House, Hitchin, approached expiration in 1872. The students were crowded in the building, with several in the so-called "Tin Tabernacle" and one in the gardener's cottage. The committee faced a difficult decision in deciding where to relocate and whether to move closer to Cambridge. Sidgwick proposed that the college merge with the fledgling lectures for women enterprise that he and the Fawcetts were founding. Davies, however, was reluctant on many grounds (see introduction).

The role of the Mistress was a highly contentious issue, especially when Davies took over the position and struggled with the committee over how much control the Mistress should have in shaping policy, and whether or not the students should have a voice in college matters. Some extracts from Stephen show the gravity with which Davies approached this issue.

The committee met in November 1870 and agreed to look for a site or building not less than three miles from Cambridge. Many on the Cambridge Committee were dissatisfied with this solution, however, and preferred to see the college move closer to town. Sidgwick apparently wrote to Davies, urging her to agree to locate in Cambridge (see introduction). The relationship between Davies and Sidgwick was a complicated one, but unfortunately no copies of her letters to him are available at Trinity or Newnham, so we have no reliable copies of what she said. Stephen cites two of the few available versions of a troubled correspondence and relationship.

The episode of the theatricals at the college has been much discussed and to a certain extent mythologized by historians of women's education. Unfortunately, we have no reliable, extant letters from Davies that discuss the issue. Stephen cites the only letter in which Davies indicated her opinion on the episode. She also had access to letters in which Davies expressed her deep interest in the fundraising campaign and the building of the new college at Girton. Davies was meticulous in examining not only architects' plans but also the regulations for the college. As many of the early college supporters were Dissenters, Girton College did not have a chapel until 1902. Clause 4 of the Memorandum of Association, incorporating the College, called for religious instruction according to the principles of the Church of England, but it also guaranteed that Dissenters would not be required to attend (see introduction).

As the college grew and Davies decided to resign as Mistress, the committee sought to formalize the role of Mistress and determine how much voice she would have in shaping policy, as opposed to daily management of the college. Nonextant letters used by Stephen indicate that Davies remained interested in all of these developments.

⟨To Adelaide Manning⟩

June 14 [1867].

Our meeting yesterday was pleasant in some respects but leaves one with a melancholy feeling behind it. Miss Taylor was perfectly unpersuadable, and I believe we might all have talked for a week without making the least impression upon her. It seems that Mr. Mill also is very strong in favour of excluding men from the Managing Committee, and Mrs. Knox went over to the enemy.... Mrs. Bodichon and I were obliged to give in.... I don't so much mind the having only women on the Managing Committee, as the sense I have that under the proposed management, the matter will get identified with the extreme section of the Liberal Party, and will be worked, as the Emancipation Society seemed to me to be, almost exclusively among the people who are convinced already. Conservatives and moderate Liberals will be treated, I am afraid, as hopelessly blind and stupid, and our chance of success will be very much injured, to say the least. But perhaps it may turn out better than I expect.

BS118

⟨To Henry Tomkinson⟩

August 5, 1868.

It is very good of you to suggest the heat of the weather as an apology for my hasty speaking, but everybody else was reasonable and polite, though it *was* hot. The real explanation, or excuse, is that the rest were pure English and therefore to be expected always to behave properly. If you have read Matthew Arnold, you will understand that the unfortunate people who are made up of an ill-assorted compound of Celtic and Anglo-Saxon blood, are by the nature of their constitution continually impelled to say and do what they are sorry for afterwards.

August 5, 1868.

I will try to be respectful to parents, but how is it possible to describe College life without showing how infinitely pleasanter it will be than home? It is the weak point which I am utterly at a loss to defend. I do not believe that our utmost efforts to poison the students' lives at College will make them half so miserable as they are at home. (The bad homes, I mean, of course. Please remember that the weather is still very hot.)

BS24, 174

⟨To Adelaide Manning⟩

October 29, 1868.

I feel impelled to write and beg you both not to harden and stiffen into a fixed decision about the College. I have seen Mrs. Gurney, and she is not going to let Mrs. Manning go. She says, Cannot we all besiege her? Mrs. Gurney pleads for *one* year. She thinks that of course one cannot judge for other people, but that the good done would be worth making a *great* sacrifice for, unless there is something which really *cannot* be sacrificed. I do not feel as if you had yet realized how much there is to be gained, and I want you to wait till you have, before influencing Mrs. Manning on the other side.

BS210

⟨To Adelaide Manning⟩

February 1, 1869.

I quite feel with you the importance of putting forward the Cambridge Examination as the distinctive feature and of not letting an alternative College Certificate appear as equal and parallel. But I think this has been avoided. . . . I do not see the same reason for keeping the *additional* subjects out of sight. Our position is this. Our students take the Cambridge Degree, as evidence that they reach *that* standard, at any rate. But the Ordinary Degree is obviously and notoriously adapted to ordinary men (or as some say, the refuse), and our students will not be ordinary women. Therefore there is no objection to their *adding* anything that it is desirable to learn. It is quite common for men to do this at Cambridge. I know one man who is going to take a Poll Degree and is learning Hebrew besides. . . . There is all the difference to my mind, between supplementing and substituting. I think perhaps you scarcely know what a strong feeling there is among the younger University men against the present University education. . . . Their idea is that women, who don't know what it is, are bent upon getting it because men have it, and it strikes them as ignorant and childish. Of course they are wrong, but I don't think we can afford to disregard their feeling, as we shall be in a great degree dependent on their support for getting what we want from Cambridge, and I think it can be met by the supplementary plan. . . .

It seems to me that we do want to charm people by an animating view of the studies and by the names of teachers. We want to attract the students, and for myself I feel decidedly more heartbroken at not being able to go, after realizing what the teaching will be. And also we want to enlist support by making people feel that what we are going to offer will be of a higher quality than women will have the least chance of getting anywhere else.

BS199

⟨To Adelaide Manning⟩

February 26, 1869.

I am glad you do not want us to start at Cambridge. Mrs. Bodichon has gone off upon that tack, and has been talking to Lady Goldsmid about it. She (Mrs. B.) seems to have made up her mind that we shall have no more students than we have promised now, and that we ought not to provide for, or look forward to, any more. . . . I fancy it is partly that Mrs. Bodichon has taken a dislike to Hitchin, and that being of a physical turn of mind, she cannot separate the essential idea of the College from the accident of the place in which it is located.... It is curious that you and I and Mr. Tomkinson, who in our *ultimate* ideas go the farthest, are the most decided against this Cambridge notion. Mrs. Gurney and Mr. Seeley however were very clear against it too, and their remarks were very practical. I was obliged to tell Lady Goldsmid that Mrs. Bodichon had had an attack of timidity, and she said she thought I had got an attack of audacity, but she seemed rather to admire it than otherwise.

BS207

⟨To Charlotte Manning⟩

April 16, 1869.

I enclose the motion passed at the meeting this afternoon. It is soberly expressed, as seemed to befit a solemn Resolution, but the Committee said a great deal which Adelaide would have liked to hear. They think it a great sacrifice for you to make, and a grand thing to do. We were quite unanimous.... Our number was small to-day, only Mrs. Gurney, Mr. Roby, Miss Metcalfe, Mrs. Bodichon, and Mr. Tomkinson. We were sure however that the absentees would agree with us.... I saw my brother this morning. He was of course much pleased but he greedily demands *more* sacrifice—a year, at least, not one term only. Miss Metcalfe spoke very nicely.... Mrs. Bodichon was very cordial too. It really is a delightful thing. It grows upon one. I do hope you will not find it too great a burden.

BS211

⟨To Barbara Bodichon⟩

July 2, 1869.

I have been seeing more of the students, and like them much. Those we are sure of are all past 20, and look like discreet young women. They seem, too, inclined to be good-natured about their accommodation, which is fortunate, as we shall certainly be cramped *inside* Benslow House, if we take it. It is offered now, and the House Committee go down to inspect next week. There are good grounds, and the right of walking over fifteen acres. The young people are beginning to plan games and bring their varied experience to bear.

BS216

⟨To Anna Richardson⟩

August 24, 1869.

Yesterday ... I had ... a staggering letter from Mr. Clark, our Classical lecturer. He had alarmed me when he was here a few weeks ago by remarking that Greek was of no use to ladies, and showing in other ways a narrow tone, and yesterday I had a letter to say that in his teaching he did not intend to make any reference to the Cambridge curriculum, having devised one of his own which he considered superior.... It is curious to see how possessed he must be with the female idea. He suggests the Cambridge Examination for women as the right thing for our students, having been devised expressly for their class. About the best thing that can be said of this Examination is that it is *probably* just a step above the Senior Local, i.e. about on the level of our *Entrance*. It was devised to suit struggling governesses, with no teaching, and no time for study except their evenings. But they and our students are alike females, and beyond this, Mr. Clark fails to discriminate....

As to what you say about Modern Languages, if questions are asked, the answer is that there will be classes as soon as there are enough students. Hitherto only Miss Woodhead asks for them, and we cannot have Lectures for only one pupil.... Our students have to pass in Latin and Greek grammar in a year, or rather more, and most of them are at the very beginning in Greek, besides having Mathematics, which to some will be very difficult.[1] I look forward to helping them with Greek during the first term. It is quite a waste of a University man's time to be hearing people say their declensions and verbs, and it will be a pleasure to me as a meeting-point with the students....

I hope the College students will find it possible to be in the highest spirits without trampling upon reverence. We are very happy in having a well-mannered group to start with, to set up good traditions.

BS216–17
  1. These were the Little-go subjects.

⟨To Anna Richardson⟩

September 14, 1869.

I am delighted to tell you that the difficulty with Mr. Clark is quite disposed of. My letter to him brought an answer by return of post which was almost a retraction, and a day or two later I had another, still more satisfactory.... I believe there is no doubt as to his being a first-rate teacher.... It is a little tiresome that they all dislike the Little-go subjects so much.... I think we are bound to do as *much* as the Poll requires, but if our students should prefer trying for Honours, it is open to us to prepare for the Triposes instead. Whichever they do, the Little-go must be passed, and the further question need not be decided for a year or more.

I want you to ... influence Miss Lloyd not to give up Classics.... For her own sake, it might *perhaps* (tho' I doubt it) be best to confine herself to Modern Languages.[1] But while the number of our students is so very small, it would be most inconvenient to have them divided into two Sections. Apart from any considerations of expense, it would be dispiriting to have such small classes as they must be, if divided. I will explain this to Miss Lloyd, but I want you to make her feel what a great loss it would be to herself to give up Classics, especially as she has done a little already at both Latin and Greek. It is not as if she had to begin the alphabet.

BS217-18
1. There was at this time no Honours Examination in Modern Languages.

⟨To Anna Richardson⟩

October 20, 1869 [*Wednesday*].

My Dear Anna,—

We are here. The little band arrived in due succession on Saturday, and we have now had three lectures. It is difficult to know what to say, except that you must come and see us. Adelaide has just been ejaculating ' It *is* so pleasant to be at the College,' and the students are saying it in their bright faces and in their tones all day. I scarcely expected that they could all have worked together with such entire cordiality and that so small a number could be so ' jolly.' Miss Lloyd is most valuable. Being a little older than the others, she makes a link between them and the authorities.... Miss Lloyd is a little behind the rest both in Latin and Mathematics, and incessantly proclaims her despair of doing anything. She sends you a message that she doubts whether she will live till Christmas, but whatever happens, she will stick to it till she dies. Mr. Clark's teaching of Latin is most interesting.... They say Mr. Stuart's explanations of Mathematics are exceedingly clear.... I find a great deal of time goes in talking with the students. They come here by ones and twos and we get into talks. Mrs. Manning is delighted with their faces, and wants to have photographs of them all. We are pretty civilized now and quite comfortable. We have good plain food, milk, bread, beef, and mutton, and it disappears very fast. The fresh pure air, and perhaps also being in good spirits, gives everybody an appetite. . . . Mrs. Austin undertook the worst of the furnishing and settling and did it admirably, but it is not quite finished yet.

BS219–20

⟨To Anna Richardson⟩

December 10 [1869].

How exhausting it must be to belong to a large family [a brother of Miss Richardson's had been ill]. . . . It is worse than the College, which I find an exciting thing to belong to. On the whole, our course this Term has run very smooth. It has been an exhilarating and encouraging time. We end to-morrow. . . .

Do you know anything of a Miss Emily Shirreff who wrote a book a long time ago on the *Intellectual Education of Women* ? She is to succeed Mrs. Manning, as a volunteer. In some respects, I like her better than anyone else that has been thought of. She has a Stoical way of talking which attracts me. Her view of coming here is simply that if she is wanted, and can do it, she ought. She takes a modest view of her duties, and undertakes them simply, without any grand air of self-sacrifice. It is a spirited thing to do, from mere interest in the idea, at her age. She is I believe about 55, ladylike and gentle in manner, and I fancy a good deal of a student.

BS227–28

⟨To Anna Richardson⟩

December 30 [1869].

The College reopens on February 5th and I shall go down a few days before. . . . I do not intend to be so much at Hitchin next Term as I was last, but I find it difficult to arrange my time. Besides wanting to be at *home*, I want to be in London, but then I also want to be at Hitchin for the sake of getting people to come down. We find that seeing is believing, and I am afraid saying to people, *Go* and see, will not be so effectual as saying *Come*. Evidently there is still a great deal to do in making the College known. . . . I am hoping that Miss Shirreff will bring in friends of a new set. She belongs to the Antrim family, and moves in such high circles that scarcely anybody I know has ever seen her. . . . We are to have Miss Wedgwood also next Term. The students think it would enable them to get on faster with Classics if they had some help from a resident Tutor, so Miss W. has kindly consented to come for a month, as an experiment. The difficulty in the way is her deafness. We can only find out by trying whether that is too great a drawback.... To have a person of her noble nature and keen interest in study is worth sacrificing a good deal for.

BS228

⟨To Anna Richardson⟩

Twelfth Day, 1870.

As to what you say about the College ... Getting our building at Cambridge seems to me so impossible that I might almost answer briefly—It cannot be done. But I would rather show you, if I can, why I am not inclined even to try. You say that if the Females set up at Cambridge, we, for the sake of equal vantage ground, ought to be there too. But in saying this you assume that we should gain by being there, whereas it is because (chiefly) there is reason to believe that we should lose in numbers and influence, that we do not try going there.... I think you do not give quite weight enough to the fact that we are pledged to the present plan. We have been asked, with hands held up in horror, were we going to Cambridge ? and have answered emphatically that nothing of the sort was proposed.... The question was brought forward at the last meeting of our Committee by Mrs. Bodichon, in connection with a letter from Mr. Sedley Taylor, about the Female Lectures. Mrs. B. wrote to him afterwards, and told him that she wished to go to Cambridge, but she thought no one else on the Committee did.... Young women are kept away now by parental fears. Their mothers would let them come if it was considered a creditable thing to do. Ladies of influence have to make other people think it creditable. It takes a good deal of zeal and courage to speak of the College as it is. If the more extreme course were adopted, a whole system of propaganda would be stopped. People like Mrs. Gurney and Lady Augusta would feel their mouths closed. As Mrs. Gurney said, they would be almost ashamed to speak of it....

Experience has not certainly made me think less of the real difficulties which would attend the location of the College in a University town. We had two visits from brothers, and tho' everybody concerned behaved with the utmost propriety, we felt thankful that brothers did not live within thirty miles. Without actually seeing something of College and University life, you can scarcely understand how disturbing it would be to have 2,000 undergraduates, most of them idle and pleasure loving, close to your doors.... I do not say that this will always be so. I am only speaking of English human nature as it has been made by social habits and by the system of separating boys and girls from childhood. We contemplate a removal to Cambridge as possible even so soon as in ten or twelve years. But what we have to do now is to meet present facts. And one fact is that we cannot wait ten or twelve years for our building. We shall want it next October....

You mention among the advantages that we lose at Hitchin, the wider choice of teachers. I do not think we lose anything in this way. There is not the least difficulty in getting eminent men to teach....

As to the ' associations,' surely the true bond is a spiritual one, and does not depend on locality.... As a *College*, we must create our associations. There is nothing to prevent our becoming part of the University, and taking our humble share in its traditions, in the fact of our being a few miles away from its local habitation. It seems to me that the excessive clinging to the visible locality is part of the superstitious and carnal habit of this age. I wish you could have heard a sermon of my brother's a few weeks ago, on the worship of relics....

One reason why I am not anxious to join hands with the ultras is that I do not care to have a set of lawless young Radicals, thinking it clever to disbelieve, and setting aside Christian teachers as narrow old fogies, not to be listened to.

BS247–48

⟨To Charlotte Manning⟩

March 2 [1870].

Miss Shirreff is certainly an amiable, affectionate person, and warmly interested in the College, and I feel inclined to persuade her to stay on, if she is willing, considering how difficult it is to find anyone exactly made for the post. ... She evidently thinks that the power of active helping depends much more than it does on being on the Committee.... It is quite true, I think, that the position of the Mistress will alter as the College grows. It will tend more and more to be governed by the resident body, when there *is* a body, over which the Mistress will preside. But this cannot be till there *is* a body grown up in College traditions and qualified by previous training to direct the studies, as well as the other departments. There are *no* women as yet fit to direct the studies, and to put such an important matter into the hands of a single, untried, and necessarily ignorant person (ignorant I mean of University arrangements of all sorts, to say nothing of the actual studies) would be manifestly unwise.... As to influencing the characters of those about her, that surely depends on the Mistress herself. It seems to me a position in which a powerful character might command great indirect influence without *doing* anything very definite. But *we* cannot confer the power.

BS234

⟨To Anna Richardson⟩

June 23 [1870].

The old students—they begin to grow venerable—separated in a pleasant state of mind ; I had a talk with them the evening I left on the results of one year, putting it in the form of the question whether it would be worth while to come for a year only. The thing Miss Lloyd feels to have gained is some appreciation of the scholarly, as distinguished from the man-of-business way of looking at things. Miss Lumsden said that before she came, she used to feel fearfully solitary. She was always having said to her, ' Oh, but you're so exceptional.' Now, she feels herself belonging to a body, and has lost the sense of loneliness. Miss Townshend has learnt that she does not know how to study. Before she came, she thought she did. Also, she feels it a relief to have taken a step, from which she could not go back even if she wished. She has got rid of the harass of the daily self-questioning about what she had better do with herself. Miss Gibson replied briefly that one year was much better than nothing. Miss Cook said she would rather not come at all than that, and being asked why, explained that it was because she would be so sorry to go away. Miss Gibson said she should feel that just as much at the end of the three years, to which there was a chorus of assent. Miss Woodhead answered my question with an emphatic ' Oh, I should think it *quite* worth while.' I asked what was the good of it and she replied with a still more emphatic *Oh* !—which remains unexplained, as my train would not wait. You will understand that we were not talking about the amount of *learning* to be gained. I do not wonder that they like being at the College for the sake of each other's company. They are delightful to live with. I only hope the new set may turn out as nice.

BS235–36

⟨To Elizabeth Garrett⟩

EXAMINATION ROOM,

December 7 ⟨1870⟩

The temporary Chair question does not seem to me very important. I was a little sorry that you should tell people, whether in jest or earnest, that you would very much like a position which, to my mind, would be incongruous even to the point of absurdity. I should feel it so in my own case, tho' as the Scotsman observed, I am ' of comparatively mature age,' and have had more experience of that sort. It is not being a woman (tho' that probably enhances it) but your youth[1] and inexperience that makes it strike me as almost indecorous to think of presiding over men like Lord Lawrence, etc. It may not strike others in the same way, and if there were a rule, it might be worth while to submit to it, but there can scarcely be precedents enough to constitute a custom, and unless necessary, I should be sorry for you to do anything which might give colour to the charge of being ' cheeky,' which has been brought against you lately. It is too true that your jokes are many and reckless. They do more harm than you know. . . .

I have had a nice note from Mr. Anderson. I like him the best of all your friends.

BS124

1. Miss Garrett was thirty-four and Miss Davies forty.

⟨To Henry Sidgwick⟩

December 31, 1870.

As you have been good enough to put the arguments in favour of having the College in writing, I should like to try to do the same on the other side, tho' it is a more difficult task. . . . The advantages are obvious and tangible ; the objections are more subtle, and difficult to put into words without making them look foolish.

I must speak first of some objections to which I do *not* attach much weight. These are : 1. The undergraduate difficulty, i.e. the supposed danger of annoyance to the students when out walking. 2. The mothers' fears, i.e. the supposition that mothers would be afraid to send their daughters to a University town. 3. The possible loss of supporters. No doubt there is some force in all these objections, but they do not seem to me to be formidable enough to keep us away from real advantages. I should choose to face them all, if I could see it to be for the real good of the College itself to be in Cambridge.

My difficulty is, the impossibility for women to carry on a free, healthy, undisturbed student-life in a town at all, and especially in a University town. It has come out pretty clearly in the course of the discussion that the promoters of the in-Cambridge scheme are divided into two parties. One party admit the difficulties, but would meet them by restrictive rules—the other, which is not represented at all I think on the Executive Committee, would trust to the strength of mind of the students and I suppose to the moral influence of the authorities. The first plan might possibly succeed, but it also might destroy the College altogether. We must not forget that the very existence of the College depends on its being very much liked by the students. They come because they like it and feel that it gives them what they want. And it is very questionable whether they want—or rather they emphatically assert that they do *not* want—anything like a grown-up boarding school. But supposing that we succeeded in getting a different kind of students—say girls fresh from school, to whom restrictions would not be galling—we should still feel that we were sacrificing one of our chief aims, that of giving to women an opportunity of laying out their own lives, in circumstances which may help them to lay them out wisely. Women have plenty of practice in submitting to little rules. We want to give them the discipline of deciding for themselves and acting upon their own responsibility. Then, it may be said, why not choose the other plan, which would give them such abundant opportunities of practising self-control? I think people who urge this so easily can scarcely have realized what young Englishwomen are from say 18 to 25. . . . I am quite sure that even our present students, who are as you would say the élite of mankind, are not all . . . superior to the attractions of society. I do not at all believe that they would feel the interest in their work that they do now, if they were constantly being diverted from it by interests of a different sort. . . . And then only consider the difference between the influences acting upon men and women in such a case. A man knows that his success in life depends to a great extent on the Degree that he takes, and everybody else knows it too, and the most worldly can see some sense in his sticking to his work and approve of him for it. But a woman would know that her success would not depend in at all the same way on her place in an examination, even supposing that we wished to encourage that kind of racing for places. On the contrary, the reasonable thing, from a worldly point of view, would be to take advantage of opportunities which she might not have at home, and make the most of them. This is what her friends and relations would urge upon her. . . . Then too, in the case of women, much visiting means much time and thought bestowed upon dress, especially by those who are not rich and have not maids to do things for them. And this would tell upon the tone of the College generally.

But supposing many should resist—and I do not mean to say that *all* the students would be severely tempted . . . it would, I believe, be at the cost of so much worry as would be likely to injure health. There is perhaps nothing more trying to the nerves than to be constantly called upon to make choices, where there is much to be said on both sides. Hitherto, the singularly good health of our students has been one of our strongest points. No doubt we owe it partly to the bracing air of Hitchin, and we shall lose in this respect by being even near Cambridge. But I trace it in great part to the quiet, regular, unperplexed life. And I cannot believe that we should sacrifice this to at all the same extent at two or three miles off as we should in the town itself. There would not be the morning calls and the dropping in and the servants coming with notes to wait for an answer, and the general victimization by idle ladies. It seems to me to make just the difference between the moderate amount of society which would be refreshing and cultivating, and the excess which would be injurious to mind and body. Then we would of course make a point of having a large garden (we hope also a swimming bath and gymnasium) so that the students could still, as they do now, go in and out without bonnets at all hours, getting air and exercise without fatigue whenever they want it. If we were to attempt this *in* Cambridge, the cost of the land would I suppose be more than we should make up by some saving in the expense of Lectures....

I believe the sum of what I have to say is this—that, supposing the superior convenience of Cambridge as regards Lectures and Museums to be all that it is said to be—and I cannot help thinking that this is somewhat exaggerated—this advantage would be counterbalanced by a decrease in the eager receptiveness of the students and possibly also a lower standard of health ; and that the loss would be decidedly greater than the gain. I say nothing to the argument about University recognition, tho' I think it also can be met, because tho' it has more weight with some of us than any of the others that you adduce, it is not, I know, a thing that you care about much.

I am quite prepared to hear that now the objections are stated, they seem to you to have less in them than you were willing to give them credit for, but I would rather risk this unfortunate result than say nothing....

I am sorry it is so long, but a *great deal more* might be said !

BS251-54

⟨To H. R. Tomkinson⟩

March 8 [1871].

A new kind of difficulty has arisen at Hitchin. The students have taken to acting, and last night they asked Mrs. Austin and me to see a rehearsal in the Library. It turned out to be, first, a passage from Swinburne's *Atalanta in Calydon*, then some scenes between Benedick and Beatrice, then Olivia and Malvolio, and the Page. We did not like any of it much, but what seemed to us seriously objectionable was the taking male parts and dressing accordingly.... Mrs. Austin intended to speak to some of the older ones in the morning, but they had seen that there was something we did not like, and began asking her before breakfast what it was. (They thought it might be their taking possession of the Library, which they had done without leave in rather a lawless way.) So she asked Miss Cook and Miss Lumsden to come to the drawing-room and explained to them what it was. They would not admit that there was anything to object to (Miss Lumsden said she had done the same thing at home).... Mrs. Austin was decided in refusing to allow it in any public room, and the discussion then shifted to the point whether they might have it in their own rooms, and generally to the question whether in their own rooms they might do exactly as they liked, without any cognisance on the part of the authorities. This, they felt, was a question of principle, which they were not prepared to yield. . . . I told them that Mrs. Austin and I had agreed that the question was one which we did not wish to decide alone, and that I should get two or three other opinions as to whether it should be referred to the Committee for decision. Mrs. Austin particularly begged me to consult you about it, partly because she was sure you would be inclined to give as much freedom as possible. . . . Mrs. Austin thinks . . . this trouble is partly due to much reading of *The Earthly Paradise*, which one sees constantly about, and other things of that sort. It is a kind of mixed notion of being artistic and worshipping Nature. Miss Wedgwood, who has been there lately, found them all (i.e. the elder ones) ' Pagan.'

BS241–42

⟨To Henry Sidgwick⟩

May 19 [1871].

I am sure it is generous inconsistency and not cruel mockery that makes you say you are willing to help us, when your scheme is the serpent which is gnawing at our vitals. It glides in everywhere. As soon as any interest is awakened, people are told there is something else, as good or better, and which does not ask for money. I daresay it does not end in their doing much for the Lectures, but it is enough to hold them back from doing anything for the College. We meet this hindrance at every step, and lately it has seemed to me that it bids fair to crush us. However, we are not going to give in yet.

BS255

⟨To Anna Richardson⟩

September 27, 1871.

I have been staying with Mrs. Bodichon at her cottage in Sussex, and greatly enjoying the change and the thorough quiet. Even the physical atmosphere is so still that it is an event when the wind blows. We had a great deal of talk about the College building and garden, etc. I hope you agree with us in liking an old-fashioned useful garden with autumn and spring hardy flowers all about. I think we ought to plant a belt of trees as soon as we can round our own domain, as we are sure to want that at any rate. Mrs. Bodichon recommends Austrian pines. . . . I have been learning from Mr. Waterhouse the cost of various items, so as to judge what will reduce expense at the least sacrifice. He is pleasantly ready to listen to non-professional suggestions. I was very glad of something you said in one of your letters about its being satisfactory to hear of building. Other people are so vexatious with their ' horror of brick and mortar ' that it is pleasant to find you rejoicing in it. I only wish we could get housed and begin to turn over the leaf and pay back to the Capital fund what has been borrowed for rent and furniture and maintenance. The amount advanced is small as compared with what it is common to risk at starting, and I am quite at ease about the temporary use of the money, as the contributions of the Executive Committee alone much more than cover the sum we have borrowed. But it would be delightful to be making money upon the students instead of spending it.

BS260–61

⟨To Reverend W. H. Crosskey⟩

November, 1871.

At the time this clause was under discussion, we made a special point of inserting the qualifying words ' as by law established ' distinctly on the ground that this would prevent the College from being connected with the Church merely as a religious sect.... It seems to me that the impossibility of saying what the principles of the Church of England were, when it was disestablished, would be a great hindrance to tying up the College on this point. Interpreters would probably be driven to ask what had been the practice of the College from the beginning. The answer would be that there was no chapel[1] and no chaplain, that the ' services ' consisted in the reading by the Mistress once a day of a portion of the Scripture and some prayers selected by her from the Common Prayer Book—that the ' instruction ' consisted in Lectures given from time to time as they are wanted, on the subjects prescribed for the University Previous Examination....

Many of those whose support we most value have a strong feeling that while those who do not want religion, in the form of instruction and observances, ought not to have it forced upon them, there ought to be some security that it will not be altogether excluded. They do not care much about the religious instruction, which practically comes to very little, but they care very much for the family prayers. A large proportion of our students come from homes in which it is usual to have prayers every morning, and to have a *resident* College, with no permanent provision for anything of the sort, would alienate many of our best friends. It is, however, carefully arranged that no one shall be obliged, even by moral compulsion, to be present, e.g. the marking, at which students are expected to appear, comes *after* Prayers, not before, so that any objector might be absent, without its being at all conspicuous. I mention what may seem a trifling detail, not merely as evidence of the liberality of the present management, but because I think you will feel that in a case like this, traditions are very important, perhaps more so than the letter of the Trust Deeds. Train up an institution in the way it should go, and when it is old it will not depart from it. From this point of view, the large proportion of Unitarians (two and one Jewess)[2] on the small governing body who will be the first Trustees, also seems to me important. There is no kind of religious qualification for Mistress or Lecturers or anything else. I do not at all suppose that this explanation can be entirely satisfactory to you. It is not possible, in the nature of things, that the College can be entirely satisfactory either to strong Churchmen on the one side or to Dissenters on the other. . . . My own feeling is that in a case like this, differences which one feels to be serious may be merged, in view of the pressing necessity of diffusing knowledge. None of us can achieve this object alone, but each of us may trust that in the light of real knowledge, the true opinions, whether one's own, or somebody else's, will ultimately prevail.

BS263–64
  1. The Chapel at Girton was not built till 1902.
  2. Madame Bodichon, Mr. Heywood, and Lady Goldsmid.

⟨To Anna Richardson⟩

January 15 [1872 ?].

I entirely sympathize in your repugnance to asking favours. I do not know anything that tires me so much, in carrying out the College, as the perpetual necessity of asking people to do something which they don't care for, and will only do, if at all, out of good-nature. Every meeting involves a series of appeals of this sort, and in most cases, I am not likely to have the opportunity of making any return for the good-nature. It is a pull upon one's pride, and it takes a great deal of care for a thing to wind one up to doing it. However, it must be done, and I go thro' a certain amount of hair shirt every day, as a matter of course, looking forward to the time when it will end. I hope this may be within a year or two.

BS262

⟨To Adelaide Manning⟩

May 8 [1875].

I had a little talk with one of our lecturers yesterday about what are sufficient reasons for giving leave of absence, etc., and I fancy that a Tutor has pretty much the same difficulties and perplexities that arise here. . . . I think you cannot realize what the position of the Mistress is, when you say in that easy way that she will probably hold her own. She *must* hold her own, or go. . . . I think you do not quite see how desirable it is that the Mistress should be strong *officially*.

BS296

Crompton, Mary, 243
Crosskey, Henry William, 360, 544
Crow (Crowe), Jane, 2, 12, 18, 42, 83, 87, 90, 94, 96, 99, 167, 222, 256, 287, 290, 328, 397, 475
Cushman, Charlotte, 10

Daily News, 64, 177, 291
Darwin, Charles, 195, 226, 375
Davenport, Florence Hill. *See* Hill, Florence Davenport
Davenport, Rosamond. *See* Hill, Rosamond Davenport
Davies, Emily: "Application of Funds to the Education of Girls, The," 163; *English Woman's Journal*, 7-18, 20-22, 24-28, 30-33, 40-46, 93; *Higher Education of Women, The,* 177-78, 203, 207; "Medicine as a Profession for Women," 93; "Reasons for the Admission of Women to University Examinations," 46, 135, 136, 137, 138, 141
Davies, J. Llewellyn, 8, 18, 19, 27, 83, 85, 86, 100, 101, 124, 159, 201, 243, 245, 251, 259, 260, 345, 347, 419, 434, 437, 533
Davies, Mary (Crompton), 1, 46, 83, 86, 100, 284
Davies, Mary (Hopkinson), 18, 21, 32, 84, 141, 191, 259, 272, 273, 333, 345, 415, 419, 435, 449
Day, George Edward, 9
Dicey, Albert Venn, 366
Dicey, Edward, 43, 44, 85, 179
dissenters, 30, 36, 165, 203, 210, 545
Dixon, Ella Hepworth, 295
Doughty, Clementia. *See* Taylor, Clementia Doughty
Dove, Jane Frances, 368, 389, 407, 409, 415, 435, 440, 442, 444, 451, 478
Drewry, Ellen, 3, 13, 15
Drewry, Louisa, 3, 13
Durant, Susan, 350

Eastlake, Elizabeth Rigby, 311
Economist, 181, 182
Edmonds, James, 28, 32
Edwards, Amelia Blandford, 362
Edwards, Matilda Betham. *See* Betham-Edwards, Matilda

Elementary Education Act (1870), 342, 345, 346
Eliot, George. *See* Lewes, Marianne
Elmy, Elizabeth Wolstenholme. *See* Wolstenholme, Elizabeth
Endowed Schools Commission, 331, 336, 341, 446, 451
Enfranchisement of Women Committee, 174, 213, 215
English Woman's Journal, 7, 8, 10, 11, 13, 14, 15, 16, 17, 18, 19, 20, 21, 23, 24, 26, 27, 28, 30, 31, 40, 42, 43, 44, 45, 93
Englishwoman's Review, 27
Ewart, Mary, 433

Faithful, Emily, 7, 12, 16, 21, 24, 25, 27, 32, 41, 42, 44, 55, 83, 85, 91, 92, 94, 97, 99, 100, 101, 106, 107
Fawcett, Henry, 59, 94, 215, 226, 331
Fawcett, Millicent Garrett. *See* Garrett, Millicent
Fearon, Daniel Robert, 165, 167, 168, 311
Female Middle Class Emigration Society, 193, 194
Fitch, Joshua, 106, 125, 145, 147, 155, 202, 212, 357, 402
Forster, William Edward, 107, 112, 138
Fortnightly Review, 157, 191, 193, 194, 195, 196, 199, 421, 431
Foster, Michael, 300, 425, 455, 479
Fox, Ellen Phillips. *See* Phillips, Ellen
Fraser's Magazine, 15, 21, 23, 24, 27, 44, 107, 194, 213
Furnivall, Frederick James, 3
Fyview, Isabella, 42

Galton, Francis, 414
Gamble, Isabella, 343, 390, 407, 424, 448, 478
Garrett, Elizabeth, 1, 2, 9, 10, 11, 13, 15, 17, 18, 19, 21, 23, 25, 28, 30, 31, 32, 83, 91, 93, 112, 118, 120, 140, 153, 155, 159, 177, 196, 199, 212, 213, 215, 221, 232, 235, 240, 243, 244, 273, 281, 285, 290, 300, 302, 303, 322, 326, 327, 333, 334, 335, 341, 342, 345, 347, 348, 349, 350, 352, 353, 355, 357, 426, 441, 539; medical education for women, 2-3, 112, 140, 158, 186, 187, 258, 320, 431
Garrett, Millicent, 1, 215, 216, 331

Garrett, Newson, 56, 197
Gaskell, Elizabeth, 139, 293
Gatty, Margaret, 255
Gibson, Emily, 285, 319, 320, 331, 356, 396, 400, 403, 539
Gilchrist Scholarship, 370, 424, 430-31, 433, 463, 477
Gill, Jessie, 479
Gimingham, A. E., 7, 12, 13, 16
Girton College, 361, 366, 369, 370, 371-479, 538-46. See also College for Women, Hitchin
Globe, The, 182
Goldsmid, Francis, 186, 188, 421, 471
Goldsmid, Louisa, 4, 6, 22, 79, 120, 169, 174, 186, 197, 207, 208, 212, 213, 214, 215, 221, 222, 224, 237, 240, 248, 252, 266, 300, 306, 309, 312, 339, 375, 421, 433, 474, 532, 533, 545
Goodenough, James Graham, 85
Gorst, John, 362
governesses, 68, 99, 126, 127, 139, 269, 275, 278, 411
Governesses' Benevolent Institution, 39
Granville, George, 140
Graves, Charles, 390, 392-93, 395-96, 450
Gray, Charles, 41, 50, 57, 65, 66, 67, 70, 71, 72, 81, 94, 108, 109, 142
Greatorex, Emily, 92, 425
Grey, Maria Shirreff, 348, 362, 412
Griffiths, John, 5, 50, 51, 71, 74, 75, 76, 78, 142, 144, 153, 246
Grote, George, 140, 141, 157, 175, 243
Grote, Harriet, 141
Grüner, Joan Frances, 436
Guardian, 69, 140, 141, 191, 203, 207, 291, 292, 329, 358
Gull, William, 260, 261
Gully, James, 10
Gurney, Emilia, 28, 63, 86, 97, 120, 206, 207, 208, 224, 225, 237, 248, 249, 252, 254, 261, 263, 266, 271, 280, 297, 306, 311, 322, 323, 330, 332, 349, 350, 353, 357, 358, 418, 444, 479, 531, 533, 537
Gurney, Russell, 4, 6, 22, 63, 97, 173, 195, 197, 206, 222, 224, 233, 234, 235, 236, 238, 239, 240

Hales, John, 270, 272
Hare, Thomas, 113, 155, 272
Harrison, Fanny, 431, 433
Hastings, George, 4, 6, 22, 43, 54, 70, 77, 83, 114, 121, 122, 124, 174, 180, 197, 208, 214, 215, 238, 239, 252, 300
Hays, Matilda 7, 8, 9, 10, 25, 42
Head, William Wilfred, 100
Helps, Arthur, 378
Herschel, Constance, 425, 451, 457, 475
Herschel, Constance Anne, 374, 419, 425, 427, 430, 442, 444, 448, 461
Heywood, James, 4, 6, 22, 33, 36, 37, 79, 97, 169, 174, 197, 215, 222, 236, 252, 258, 300, 306, 347, 418, 545
Hill, Florence Davenport, 186, 363, 461
Hill, Mathew Davenport, 70, 363
Hill, Rosamond Davenport, 363, 461
Hobart, Mary Catherine Carr, 244, 252, 434, 464
Hodgkin, Thomas, 157, 263, 307
Hodgson, Shadworth, 272
Hodgson, William Ballantyne, 97, 116, 167, 291, 292
Holmes, Arthur, 351, 377, 385
Home and Colonial School Society (Institution), 275, 276
Hort, John Fenton, 279, 300, 310, 327
Hoskins, Mary, 404, 424
Hubbard, Louisa Maria, 447, 451, 452
Hullah, John, 103, 108
Hutton, Richard, 43, 44, 83, 84, 85, 92, 97, 99, 101, 120, 170, 171, 175, 176, 182, 264, 320
Huxley, Thomas, 159, 188, 195, 243, 341

Illustrated News, 25
Illustrated Times, 85

Jackson, Henry, 464-65
Jameson, Francis James, 82
Jekyll, Gertrude, 467
Jex-Blake, Sophia Louisa, 12-13, 17, 50, 244

Kay Shuttleworth, Sir James, 113, 180, 195
Kensington Society, 155, 156, 157, 160, 174, 193, 214, 215, 257, 258, 321
Kilgour, Mary Stewart, 430, 438, 442-44, 457

King, Gertrude, 161, 163, 177, 416
Kingsland, Mary, 407, 439, 442-43, 448, 451, 456, 458, 459, 463, 472, 478
Kingsley, Charles, 43, 230, 235
Knox, Isa Craig. *See* Craig, Isa

Ladies' Emancipation Society, 112
Ladies' Institute, 27
Lancet, 186
Langham Place, 9, 18, 25, 27, 31, 42, 43, 44, 84, 85, 93, 100
Law Times, 180
Leigh-Smith, Barbara. *See* Bodichon, Barbara Leigh-Smith
Leigh-Smith, Isabella. *See* Ludlow, Isabella Leigh-Smith
Leigh-Smith, Nannie, 9, 11, 18, 20, 24, 26, 32, 90, 100, 167, 169, 221, 222, 224, 324, 325, 326, 358, 404
Leigh-Smith, William, 364
Lewes, George Henry, 157, 199, 247, 287, 316
Lewes, Marianne, 1, 10, 43, 157, 200, 246, 247, 248, 249, 250, 269, 287, 288, 316, 321, 322, 393
Lewin, Sarah, 7, 8, 9, 12, 17, 23, 24, 25, 28, 29, 33, 40, 42
Lightfoot, Joseph Barber, 347, 348
Literary Churchman, 279
Liveing, George Downing, 5, 41, 53, 54, 129, 264, 310, 327, 406, 408, 414, 418
Liveing, Katherine Ingram, 226
Liverpool Mercury, 131, 195
Lloyd, Anna, 284, 288, 320, 325, 342, 406, 535, 539
Lloyd, Mary, 327, 392, 393
London Association of Schoolmistresses, 204, 242, 310, 313, 334, 359, 372, 410, 416, 431, 470, 472
London School Board, 318, 342, 345, 346, 347, 348, 350, 354, 358, 373, 387, 406, 411, 415, 417, 419
London Student, 289, 290
London University. *See* University of London
Lubbock, John, 347
Ludlow, Isabella Leigh-Smith, 11, 18, 27, 169, 195, 398
Ludlow, John Malcolm Forbes, 26, 27

Lumsden, Louisa, 315, 317, 320, 324, 325, 326, 371, 377, 385, 386, 393, 394, 400, 418, 419, 427-28, 432, 434-35, 437-38, 442-44, 447, 455-58, 460, 461, 539, 542
Lyell, Charles, 84, 243, 290
Lyttleton, George, 54, 109, 110, 131, 138, 140, 221, 222, 224, 279, 331, 334, 336, 357

MacDonald, George, 9, 24, 44, 45, 112, 141
Macmillan, Alexander, 282
Macmillan's Magazine, 10, 13, 15, 19, 21, 24, 43, 44, 85, 116, 179, 181, 185, 187, 192, 194, 209, 282, 302, 308, 311
Malleson, Elizabeth Whitehead, 91
Malleson, Frank, 91
Manchester Guardian, 208, 212
Manchester High School, 392
Manchester Suffrage Society, 216, 217, 218, 219, 220, 226, 228, 229, 230, 234
Manning, Charlotte, 58, 62, 95, 97, 103, 105, 115, 120, 156, 157, 173, 190, 202, 214, 244, 245, 248, 252, 263, 271, 292, 306, 308, 314, 315, 319, 326, 327, 356, 388, 531, 535, 536, 538
Manning, E. Adelaide, 59, 62, 63, 96, 104, 115, 116, 119, 174, 176-77, 178, 190, 191, 192, 198, 201, 208, 211, 214, 215, 240, 244, 326, 350, 351, 387, 403, 409, 411, 412, 414, 416, 420, 432, 437, 441, 456-57, 464, 465, 474-75, 479, 530, 531-33, 545
Manning, James (Serjeant), 97, 98, 103, 188, 202, 314
Mantle, Amy, 373, 402, 427, 449, 457, 464, 479
Markby, Thomas, 76, 151, 152, 204, 256, 257, 264, 331
Marks, Sarah Phoebe (Hertha), 433, 436
married women's property, 180, 183, 184, 186, 187-88
Martin, Adele Emily, 468, 470
Martin, Henry, 479
Martineau, Harriet, 177, 317
Martineau, James, 243
Masson, David, 44, 86, 179, 192, 194, 315
Masson, George Joseph Gustave, 327
Maudsley, Henry, 421, 431
Maurice, Frederick Denison, 3, 27, 39, 62, 86, 101, 116, 155, 156, 157, 173, 260, 261, 315, 331

Max-Müller, Frederich. *See* Müller, Frederick Max
Maynard, Constance Louisa, 374, 404, 409, 427, 442, 461, 464
Mayor, Mr. (John Bickersteth or Joseph Bickersteth), 34, 37
McGregor, John, 387
Mechanics' Institutes, 1, 2, 26
medical education and women, 2, 3, 28, 91, 93, 112, 140, 158, 181, 186, 187, 197, 222, 258, 320
Metcalfe, Fanny, 251, 252, 306, 358, 359, 361, 378, 379-80, 396, 402, 432, 458, 459, 460, 477-78, 533
Metropolitan Education Board, 341
Mill, Harriet Taylor, 8, 11
Mill, John Suart, 16, 109, 110, 112, 113, 155, 157, 161, 170, 174, 182, 183, 184, 193, 195, 196, 203, 211, 219, 226, 227, 228, 229, 230, 231, 239, 349, 350, 371, 372, 401, 437, 530
Minturn, Eliza Theodora, 440, 442, 451, 469, 478, 479
Monson, Theodora, 12, 25, 27, 42
Morgan, Edmund Henry, 375, 380, 381, 382-84, 386-87
Morley, Samuel, 363, 424
Moulton, John Fletcher, 331, 332
Müller, Frances, 372, 373, 402, 432, 435-38, 448, 453-54, 469, 479
Müller, Frederick Max, 224, 410
Museum, The, 147
Myres, Frederic William Henry, 152, 234, 252, 254, 269, 272, 273, 274, 275, 278, 280, 290, 305

National Association for the Promotion of Social Sciences, 11, 21, 29, 93, 101, 109, 110, 115, 122, 124, 125, 142, 144, 155, 163, 180, 183, 185, 192, 193, 194, 195, 200, 201, 203, 213, 246, 266, 279, 282, 284, 289, 290, 318, 411, 465
National Review, 33, 85, 138
Newman, Francis William, 89
Newnham College (Merton Hall), 360, 392, 393, 425, 442, 447, 479, 530
Niven, William Davidson, 376, 380
Nonconformist, 203, 206, 207

Norris, John, 74, 80, 82, 89, 94, 113, 123, 124, 138, 158
North London Collegiate School, 162, 446, 451, 454
North of England Council for Promoting the Higher Education of Women, 202, 252, 270, 273, 274, 276, 278

Owens College, 257, 271
Oxford University, 145, 147, 148, 151, 197, 221, 224, 236; opening of examinations to women, 197; Oxford Local Examinations, 28, 38, 47, 48, 49, 50, 51, 52, 64, 71, 74, 75, 76, 78, 79, 88, 95, 112, 118, 142, 143, 144, 147, 153, 154, 248

Pall Mall Gazette, 177, 180, 192, 196, 203, 207, 231, 236, 286, 321, 333, 334
Parkes, Bessie Rayner, 7, 8, 10, 11, 13, 18, 20, 21, 23, 24, 25, 26, 27, 28, 29, 30, 31, 32, 40, 41, 42, 43, 44, 93, 100, 201, 213, 222, 232, 235, 238
Pattison, Mark, 159, 221, 224, 289
Pearson, Charles Henry, 33
Pen and Pencil Society, 92, 96, 104
Percival, John, 362
Phillips, Ellen, 186-87, 199, 222, 223
Pike, William, 76
Pipe, Hannah, 322, 391, 396, 397, 403
Plumptre, Edward, 62, 66, 95, 98, 101, 102, 103, 115, 116, 170, 204, 223, 232
Ponsonby, Mary, 300, 329, 339, 432
Porter, James, 385
Porter, Mary Eliza, 68, 163
Portfolio (club), 84, 87, 92, 93
Portman Hall School, 11
Post, The, 182, 208
Potts, Robert, 22, 23, 33, 36, 37, 39, 40, 41, 48, 49, 50, 51, 52, 53, 54, 55, 56, 57, 65, 66, 70, 71, 72, 73, 76, 79, 80, 81, 82, 87, 88, 90, 92, 94, 95, 96, 101, 102, 104, 105, 108, 109, 110, 111, 113, 114, 116, 117, 118, 119, 120, 122, 123, 125, 126, 127, 128, 129, 130, 131, 132, 133, 134, 135, 136, 137, 145, 146, 147, 148, 149, 150, 164, 235
Proctor, Adelaide, 3, 10, 11, 12, 42, 93, 98, 100
Pusey, Edward, 154, 254

Quakers (Religious Society of Friends), 2, 3, 55, 120, 165, 186, 224, 244, 253, 280, 300, 319, 326
Quarterly Review, 129, 183, 195, 196
Queen, The, 25, 31
Queen's College, London, 38, 39, 58, 62, 63, 65, 66, 68, 87, 89, 95, 98, 99, 101, 102, 103, 104, 108, 115, 117, 170, 203, 204, 210, 298, 381, 419, 447
Queen Victoria, 295, 300, 339
Quick, Robert, 364

Reader, The, 26, 27, 44, 46, 157
Record, The, 67, 99, 146, 243
Reid, Elizabeth Jesser, 20
Reyner, George, 356
Rich, Julia, 266, 393, 394-95, 412, 419, 431-32
Richardson, Anna, 2, 5, 18, 45, 51, 52, 53, 55, 59, 60, 83, 92, 93, 97, 102, 106, 112, 141, 146, 155, 156, 158, 164, 165, 204, 224, 238, 244, 245, 253, 254, 255, 259, 260, 261, 262, 265, 269, 270, 272, 273, 276, 279, 280, 282, 283, 285, 286, 288, 339, 422, 534-38, 539, 543, 545
Richson, Charles, 208
Ritchie, Anne. *See* Thackeray, Anne Isabella
Roby, Henry, 116, 149, 158, 162, 167, 221, 233, 241, 242, 252, 263, 271, 280, 285, 292, 296, 302, 304, 305, 306, 325, 332, 338, 350, 352, 358, 393, 432, 435, 479, 533
Roman Catholic Church, 23, 25, 348
Romer, Robert, 254
Rossetti, Christina, 9, 255
Roth, Mathias, 436
Ruskin, John, 317
Rutson, Albert, 244
Rye, Maria, 100, 194

Saturday Review, 308, 333, 358
Schools Inquiry Commission (Taunton), 121, 122, 138, 140, 149, 155, 159, 162, 163, 165, 166, 167, 221, 241, 242, 243
Science and Art Department, 275, 276
Scotsman, The, 59, 109, 133, 170, 177, 539
Scott, William Bell, 371
Seebohm, Frederic, 274, 279, 300

Seeley, John Robert, 244, 254, 255, 263, 264, 266, 267, 271, 285, 286, 289, 291, 300, 306, 310, 311, 327, 533
Selwyn, Edward, 96
Senior, Nassau, 43
Sewell, Elizabeth, 254
Shaen William, 4, 46, 120, 175, 195, 296, 297, 299, 307, 315
Shaftesbury, Anthony Ashley Cooper, 192, 194
Shirreff, Emily, 331, 333, 334, 336, 356, 389, 393, 396, 414, 417, 443, 536, 538
Shirreff, Maria. *See* Grey, Maria Shirreff
Shorrock, Constance, 373, 427, 453, 457-58
Sidgwick, Henry, 252, 281, 282, 283, 330, 331, 520, 540, 543
Slade, Gertrude, 342, 343, 406
slavery, 9, 42, 162
Smith, Eleanor, 163, 414
Smith, Julia, 12, 249, 251
Smith, Louisa Garrett, 174, 213, 215, 225, 226, 232
Smith, Nannie. *See* Leigh-Smith, Nannie
Smith, William, 10
Soames, Laura, 372, 468, 470
Social Science Review, 196
Society for Promoting the Employment of Women, 1, 2, 18, 87, 177; at Manchester, 209
Society of Arts, 19, 38, 336
Solly, Henry, 161
Solly, Samuel, 116, 120
Somerville, Mary Fairfax, 390-91
special examinations for women, 266, 269, 270, 271, 273, 274, 275, 278, 286, 330, 534
Spectator, 83, 84, 85, 86, 87, 99, 101, 120, 175, 177, 183, 184, 190, 206, 216, 220, 227, 264, 320, 373
Spencer, Herbert, 164
Standard, The, 177
St. Andrew's, 9, 11, 245, 279, 281
Stanley, Augusta Frederica, 251, 253, 255, 264, 268, 280, 295, 300, 330, 339, 537
Stanley of Alderly, Henrietta Maria, 117, 246, 251, 376, 398, 418, 422, 430, 443-44, 449, 453-56, 469, 471, 474-79
Stanley of Alderly, Lord, 271
Steinthal, Samuel Alfred, 226, 236

Stephen, Leslie, 177
Stephen, James Fitzjames, 107, 108
St. Leonard's, 475-76
Storrar, John, 159, 164, 166, 445, 446
Stuart, James, 245, 257, 327, 331, 332
suffrage (extension of parliamentary franchise to women), 60, 160, 161, 162, 170, 173, 174, 178, 179, 182, 183, 184, 185, 186, 187, 188, 189, 190, 191, 192, 193, 194, 195, 196, 198, 200, 201, 202, 203, 205, 206, 207, 208, 209, 211, 212, 213, 214, 215, 216, 217, 218, 219, 220, 222, 225-31, 232, 233, 234, 235, 236, 237, 238, 240, 241, 242, 243, 257, 336, 345, 407, 479
Swanwick, Anna, 243

Taylor, Clementia Doughty, 42, 92, 96, 174, 178, 189, 191, 192, 194, 195, 198, 202, 206, 209, 213, 215, 231, 240, 243, 393
Taylor, Emily, 9
Taylor, Harriet. *See* Mill, Harriet Taylor
Taylor, Helen, 160, 170, 173, 176, 177, 178, 182, 185, 187, 190, 191, 192, 193, 194, 195, 196, 199, 202, 204, 207, 208, 210, 213, 215, 223, 226, 229, 230, 231, 240, 242, 257, 320, 372
Taylor, Mary, 255, 266, 267, 283, 288, 317
Taylor, Peter Alfred, 195, 206
Taylor, Sedley, 246, 250, 252, 253, 258, 260, 265, 278, 281, 284, 285, 296, 304, 305, 306, 327, 329, 330, 361, 394, 398, 537
Telegraph, The, 99, 206
Temple, Frederick, 48, 49, 144, 233, 236
Thackeray, Anne Isabella, 18, 19, 26, 100, 184
Thackeray, Harriet Marian (Minnie), 100
Thackeray, William Makepeace, 1
Thorold, Anthony Wilson, 445, 446
Tidman, Ellen, 343
Tidman, Paul Frederick, 345
Times, 67, 177, 193, 291, 293, 336
Tomkinson, Henry Richard, 6, 19, 32, 33, 36, 39, 47, 48, 49, 50, 51, 53, 54, 56, 57, 60, 61, 65, 66, 67, 69, 72, 73, 74, 77, 79, 80, 98, 110, 111, 112, 113, 114, 118, 120, 124, 133, 137, 151, 153, 159, 161, 163, 238, 240, 241, 245, 246, 251, 252, 257, 272, 285, 296, 297, 300, 305, 307, 312, 343, 347, 349, 351, 353, 357, 358, 367, 368, 379, 394, 406, 412, 432, 433, 443, 465, 471, 531, 533, 542

Townshend, Isabella, 319, 320, 356, 396, 400, 428, 539
Trollope, Anthony, 43, 83, 99, 139
Tubbs, Fanny, 433, 467, 475
Tuthill, Anna, 474

Unitarians, 404, 545
University Local Examinations, 3-4, 5-6, 11, 19-20, 22, 28, 32-39; 41, 47-82, 84, 87-90, 93, 94-99, 101-37, 139-40, 142-44, 148, 151-60, 162, 164, 166-72, 180-81, 184, 189, 197, 202, 204, 210, 212, 235, 236, 245, 248, 256, 257, 260, 265, 268, 272, 275, 277, 292, 293, 313, 318, 332, 336, 339, 340, 342, 351, 353, 369, 387, 391, 410, 431, 433, 447
University of Cambridge. *See* Cambridge University
University of Durham, 168, 175
University of Edinburgh, 109, 110, 171, 175
University of London, 159, 167, 168, 170, 175, 180, 181, 196, 197, 204, 210, 214, 271, 303, 351, 419, 424; examinations for women, 2-3, 4, 49, 84, 91, 104, 141, 155, 159, 167, 168, 170, 171, 175, 210, 214, 215, 270, 275, 286, 298, 370, 419; medical degrees for women, 2, 30, 181

Venn, John, 310, 327, 372, 404, 464
Vernon, Matilda, 317, 333, 407, 415
Victoria Magazine, 27, 41, 42, 43, 44, 46, 52, 60, 83, 84, 85, 91, 92, 93, 97, 106, 107, 108
Victoria Printing Press, 41, 66, 93

Wallace, Annie, 402
Wallis, Annie, 407, 427, 455, 479
Waterhouse, Alfred, 222, 224, 279, 282, 302, 340, 360, 364, 366, 367, 368, 371, 375, 379, 388, 404, 405-6, 408, 413, 414, 420, 439, 448, 450, 462, 469, 476, 543
Watson, R. Spence, 259, 263
Wedgwood, Hensleigh, 238, 331
Wedgwood, Julia, 333, 334, 401, 536, 543
Welsh, Elizabeth, 440, 442-43, 453, 455, 459
Westlake, Alice Hare, 63, 186, 188, 200, 218, 220, 222, 462
Westlake, John, 63, 94, 113, 186, 214, 222, 226, 368, 462

Westminster Review, 11, 46, 194, 199, 230
Whewell, William, 131
Wilson, James, 84, 107
Wolstenholme, Elizabeth, 153, 163, 195, 199, 201, 209, 216, 224, 226, 229, 238, 244, 252, 255, 269, 270, 279, 290
Wood, Janet, 479
Woodhead, Sarah, 319, 320, 331, 345, 371, 376, 378, 388-91, 399, 401, 407, 415, 419, 436, 443-44, 534

Working Man, The, 180
Working Men's Club, 161; committee, 115, 161, 350
Working Men's Colleges, 194
Wratislaw, Albert, 133
Wrottesley, John, 159

Yonge, Charlotte Mary, 139, 254, 255, 279, 280
Young, George, 231

Victorian Literature and Culture Series

Daniel Albright
Tennyson: The Muses' Tug-of-War

David G. Riede
Matthew Arnold and the Betrayal of Language

Anthony Winner
Culture and Irony: Studies in Joseph Conrad's Major Novels

James Richardson
Vanishing Lives: Style and Self in Tennyson, D. G. Rossetti, Swinburne, and Yeats

Jerome J. McGann, Editor
Victorian Connections

Antony H. Harrison
Victorian Poets and Romantic Poems: Intertextuality and Ideology

E. Warwick Slinn
The Discourse of Self in Victorian Poetry

Linda K. Hughes and Michael Lund
The Victorian Serial

Anna Leonowens
The Romance of the Harem
Edited by Susan Morgan

Alan Fischler
Modified Rapture: Comedy in W. S. Gilbert's Savoy Operas

Emily Shore
Journal of Emily Shore
Edited by Barbara Timm Gates

Richard Maxwell
The Mysteries of Paris and London

Felicia Bonaparte
The Gypsy-Bachelor of Manchester: The Life of Mrs. Gaskell's Demon

Peter L. Shillingsburg
Pegasus in Harness: Victorian Publishing and W. M. Thackeray

Angela Leighton
Victorian Women Poets: Writing against the Heart

Allan C. Dooley
Author and Printer in Victorian England

Simon Gatrell
Thomas Hardy and the Proper Study of Mankind

Jeffrey Skoblow
Paradise Dislocated: Morris, Politics, Art

Matthew Rowlinson
Tennyson's Fixations: Psychoanalysis and the Topics of the Early Poetry

Beverly Seaton
The Language of Flowers: A History

Barry Milligan
Pleasures and Pains: Opium and the Orient in Nineteenth-Century British Culture

Ginger S. Frost
Promises Broken: Courtship, Class, and Gender in Victorian England

Linda Dowling
The Vulgarization of Art: The Victorians and Aesthetic Democracy

Tricia Lootens
Lost Saints: Silence, Gender, and Victorian Literary Canonization

Matthew Arnold
The Letters of Matthew Arnold, vols. 1–6
Edited by Cecil Y. Lang

Edward FitzGerald
Edward FitzGerald, Rubáiyát of Omar Khayyám: *A Critical Edition*
Edited by Christopher Decker

Christina Rossetti
The Letters of Christina Rossetti, vols. 1–3
Edited by Antony H. Harrison

Barbara Leah Harman
The Feminine Political Novel in Victorian England

John Ruskin
The Genius of John Ruskin: Selections from His Writings
Edited by John D. Rosenberg

Antony H. Harrison
Victorian Poets and the Politics of Culture: Discourse and Ideology

Judith Stoddart
Ruskin's Culture Wars: Fors Clavigera *and the Crisis of Victorian Liberalism*

Linda K. Hughes and Michael Lund
Victorian Publishing and Mrs. Gaskell's Work

Linda H. Peterson
*Traditions of Victorian Women's Autobiography:
The Poetics and Politics of Life Writing*

Gail Turley Houston
Royalties: The Queen and Victorian Writers

Laura C. Berry
The Child, the State, and the Victorian Novel

Barbara J. Black
On Exhibit: Victorians and Their Museums

Annette R. Federico
Idol of Suburbia: Marie Corelli and Late-Victorian Literary Culture

Talia Schaffer
The Forgotten Female Aesthetes: Literary Culture in Late-Victorian England

Julia F. Saville
A Queer Chivalry: The Homoerotic Asceticism of Gerard Manley Hopkins

Victor Shea and William Whitla, Editors
Essays and Reviews: The 1860 Text and Its Reading

Marlene Tromp
The Private Rod: Marital Violence, Sensation, and the Law in Victorian Britain

Dorice Williams Elliott
*The Angel out of the House: Philanthropy and Gender in
Nineteenth-Century England*

Richard Maxwell, Editor
The Victorian Illustrated Book

Vineta Colby
Vernon Lee: A Literary Biography

E. Warwick Slinn
Victorian Poetry as Cultural Critique: The Politics of Performative Language

Simon Joyce
Capital Offenses: Geographies of Class and Crime in Victorian London

Caroline Levine
The Serious Pleasures of Suspense: Victorian Realism and Narrative Doubts

Emily Davies
Emily Davies: Collected Letters, 1861–1875
Edited by Ann B. Murphy and Deirdre Raftery